John Muir Publications, P.O. Box 613, Santa Fe, NM 87504

© 1975, 1974, 1969 by John Muir
© 1997, 1994, 1992, 1990, 1988, 1985, 1981 by Eve Muir
All rights reserved.
Printed in the United States of America

Seventeenth edition. Second printing June 1997

Library of Congress Cataloging-in-Publication Data

Muir, John, 1918-1977
    How to keep your Volkswagen alive : a manual of step
by step procedures for the compleat idiot / by John Muir
& Tosh Gregg : illustrated by Peter Aschwanden. —
16th ed.
    p.   cm.
    At head of title: 1200, 1300, 1500, 1600, 1700, 1800 & 2000.
    Includes index.
    ISBN 1-56261-343-X
    1. Volkswagen automobile—Maintenance and repair—
Handbooks, manuals, etc. I. Gregg, Tosh. II. Aschwanden,
Peter. III. Title.
TL215.V6M8   1992
629.28'722—dc20   92-25984
                                          CIP

Typeface: Times Roman
Printer: Banta Company

Distributed to the book trade by
Publishers Group West
Emeryville, California

	INTRODUCTION	3
CHAPTER I	HOW TO USE THIS BOOK	5
CHAPTER II	HOW WORKS A VOLKSWAGEN	10
CHAPTER III	HOW TO BUY A VOLKSWAGEN	21
CHAPTER IV	TOOLS AND SPARE PARTS	29
CHAPTER V	HOW TO DRIVE A VOLKSWAGEN	36
CHAPTER VI	FLAT TIRE!	38
CHAPTER VII	ENGINE STOPS OR WON'T START (AND ORIENTATION)	42
CHAPTER VIII	RED LIGHT ON! (GENERATOR OR ALTERNATOR)	62
CHAPTER IX	GREEN LIGHT ON! (OIL RED LIGHT)	83
CHAPTER X	MAINTENANCE (3,000-MILE): Valve Adjustment, Timing, Tune-up, Lubrication, Distributor, Carburetor, Fuel Injection	92
	Tune-Up Checklist	96
	Ignition Timing Chart	110-111
CHAPTER XI	VOLKSWAGEN DOESN'T STOP	167
CHAPTER XII	SHIMMIES AND SHAKES (FRONT END)	189
CHAPTER XIII	SLIPS AND JERKS (CLUTCH)	207
CHAPTER XIV	GRINDS AND GROWLS (TRANSAXLE)	213
CHAPTER XV	ENGINE OVERHAUL	235
CHAPTER XVI	KNOW-HOW: Mechanic's Information and Data	325
	Table of Torque	341
CHAPTER XVII	WITHIN THE LAW (LIGHTS AND SOUNDS)	347
	Wiring Diagram (Typical)	348
CHAPTER XVIII	HI-PERFORMANCE MODIFICATIONS by Colin Messer	357
CHAPTER XIX	VW MANIA by John Hilgerdt and Peter Aschwanden	403
CHAPTER XX	HOW TO KEEP YOUR VOLKSWAGEN ALIVE FOREVER by John Hilgerdt and Peter Aschwanden	427
CHAPTER XXI	THE GRAB BAG, or Things We Always Thought Should Be in the Book But Didn't Know Where to Put	437
CHAPTER XXII	ELECTRICAL IMPULSES	445
	CHANGES AND NEW IDEAS	453
	INDEX	461

Acknowledgements

This book is dedicated to those beautiful people who have greasied their hands and noses to check out these Procedures and to those who have helped prepare the book:Peter Aschwanden, Debbie Benson, Phil Cooke, John Counter, Walter Dawley, Ken and Barbara Luboff, Tosh and Julie Gregg, Evalynne Rippel, Chan Laughlin, Bob Nugent, Sam Perea and Judy, Dick Showalter, Stafford Smith, Mike Walker, Elizabeth West, Joan Parker, Sam and Sandy Bertram, Dick Hughes, Lee Faubert, Eddie Peinado, Elaine Gilmartin, Poor Richard, Hal, Cree, and Johnny Stick. Weaver, Artist, Writer, Toymaker, Photographer, Dancer, you were wonderful in your understanding and tears as you struggled with translating words into actions—actions that took skin, guts and time. I love and admire you. To Eve, my wife and main prop, there must be special words to thank, to praise you, to describe what you have done, but they are all inherent in our living, together with love.

The photographs on pages 93 and 324 are by Ed Buryn, wonderful photographer, writer, friend. Photograph page 233 by Eve Muir.

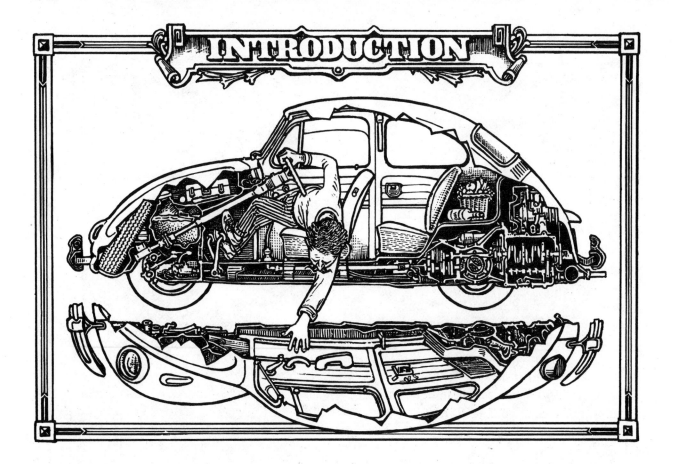

"Come to kindly terms with your Ass for it bears you."

Your Volkswagen is not a donkey but the communication considerations are similar. Your car is constantly telling your senses where it's at: what it's doing and what it needs. I don't speak "donkey," but am fairly conversant in "Volkswagen" and will help you learn the basic vocabulary of this language so your Bus, Bug, Ghia, Fast/Squareback, Safari (The Thing), 411 or 412 can become an extension of your own sensory equipment. Perhaps the idea of feeling about your car is a little strange but herein lies a type of rapport which will bridge the communication gap between you and your transportation.

I am a man, engineer, mechanic, lover-feeler who has worked and felt with cars of all descriptions for many years. This book contains the product of these years: clear and accurate Procedures to heal and keep well your Volkswagen. I don't expect you to become a mechanic—I have done that! My understanding and knowledge will be yours as you work. You supply the labor, the book will supply the direction, so we work as a team, you and I.

While the levels of logic of the human entity are many and varied, your car operates on one simple level and it's up to you to understand its trip. Talk to the car, then shut up and listen. Feel with your car; use all of your receptive senses and when you find out what it needs, seek the operation out and perform it with love. The type of life your car contains differs from yours by time scale, logic level and conceptual anomalies but is "Life" nonetheless. Its Karma depends on your desire to make and keep it—ALIVE!

CHAPTER I

HOW TO USE THIS BOOK

Now that you've spent your bread for this book—read it! Read it all the way through like a novel, skipping the detailed steps in the procedures, but scan all the comments and notes. This will give you a feel for the operational viewpoint I took when I wrote it. The intent is to give you some sort of answer for every situation you'll run into in the life of your car.

In these days of gaps—credulity, intelligence, information and many others—it's tough to locate the exact gap one can fill. This book has been designed, in addition to making me some bread, to fill the gap between *What to* and *How to*. The books and manuals that have been written satisfy the *what to do* thing with elan, but you have to have some preliminary knowledge, understanding and ability to carry out the instructions they give you. I'm trying to close this gap and have assumed you know nothing, i.e., that you are an idiot mechanically. Most of the published material has used photographs as a visual aid but this book has line sketches which show only the detail you are being asked to understand.

As I've said, the main idea of this book is to give you a way to handle every situation you will come across, with **any** air-cooled Volkswagen. It will show you how to maintain your VW to keep the emergencies down to a bare minimum and will cover the emergency situations so you'll know what you can do to get back on the road yourself or when you'll need help.

Nobody knows it all! There has been a problem, an idiosyncrasy, in every vehicle I've ever owned, a natural part of its character which I live with, occasionally making an attempt to fix it. But as it doesn't really affect the ability of the car to carry me from place to place, it sometimes goes on as long as I own the car. The '58 bus had an air blower switch which would sometimes go on when on a bumpy road; the '63 bus had a red light that glowed at night, the '71 bus generator light sometimes stays on after the key is shut off, like that. I put a piece of tape on the blower switch, painted the glowing light with fingernail polish and learned to restart and reshut off the engine or find the battery dead. By asking around, you might find definite answers for these things and be able to fix them but I figure that they are part of the car's personality and tend to keep my head straight about where it is with the car.

There are three types of procedures: Diagnostic, Maintenance and Repair. **See Changes and New Ideas.**

Diagnostic Procedures will determine what is wrong with your car; for instance, *Volkswagen Stops or Won't Start*, Chapter VII, will tell you what to do when this happens. It will also tell you how to repair minor troubles like a wire that is broken or fallen off and like that and finally refer you to the proper Repair Procedure when you have determined what needs to be repaired.

Maintenance Procedures tell you what to do to keep your VW in proper working order by doing periodic tasks. The chapter on how to drive belongs in this category.

Repair Procedures tell you how to do actual repair jobs and are classified into three Phases according to tool and skill requirements.

The idea is to never let you get hung up about what to do in any situation.

Here is a Procedure on how to run Procedures to get you on the way. **See Chapter XX**, How to Keep Your VW Book Alive Forever.

PROCEDURE ON HOW TO RUN PROCEDURES

Condition: You are going to run a Procedure.

Tools and Materials: ability to read basic English, ability to follow directions without adding embellishments or deleting parts of the steps. *Short cuts, whether your or a friend's idea must be avoided—same with long cuts.*

Remarks: A procedure is designed to give step-by-step instruction for the performance of an operation with a minimum of thought, proficiency and ingenuity on the part of the personnel. The writer assumes nothing and tries to include every contingency.

Step 1. Analysis

Read the procedure all the way through before you start. This will familiarize you with the problems and prepare your head for the operations that will be required.

Step 2. Preparation

Get all the tools and materials needed for the procedure together, prepare the location by maybe sweeping the area before putting the car there. Have the blocks and safety equipment ready. Make sure there is hand soap and rags, things like that. If the procedure calls for help, make arrangements with a friend. Arrange for any needed transportation.

Step 3. Safety

Cars can be dangerous and deadly weapons. They kill more people by accident than are shot on purpose. Keep your eye on your cute little bug and your wits together when working in and around its machinery. Especially when it's running; spinning and sparkling, be super aware. A reader wrote us that it took his Bug, with a half a tank of gas, a few seconds less than 10 minutes to be consumed to nothing (zilch) by fire.

No matter how tired, cold, miserable or pissed off you are, don't make "border line" decisions **against** safety and **for** convenience.

As we couldn't possibly think up every bizarre situation you might run into, we're listing a few "regulars."

Carbon monoxide kills, so never run the engine in an enclosed garage or other building without plenty of ventilation. (This is suicide!)

Gasoline burns fast and well; that's why it's such good fuel for internal combustion engines. Make sure to wipe up all drips, spills, puddles, etc., right when they happen, especially when working around the engine compartment. And don't light matches. Beware of the combination of spark and gas. By the way, use a professional drop light with a wire or plastic cage or shield around the bulb when lighting up the engine compartment, and don't hang it where it will drop. The hot filament of a broken bulb can cause gasoline to ignite.

Take off all jewelry, including rings (finger, nose or ear). Also remove scarves, neckties or any loose clothing and tuck long hair into a stocking cap when working on a car. A friend of ours had just finished doing a valve job, the engine was in and she started it with one turn of the key, when she went to the back to admire her engine and her prowess. She spaced out about her long, loose hair and leaned in to get a better look. A piece of that beautiful black hair got caught in the pulley and was yanked off her scalp. Fortunately, John was there with the instant reaction to turn off the key. She looked at that hank of hair, about ½" in diameter with some scalp on it, and tied it to the handle of her engine compartment as a reminder. For months we saw that little red bug, with the pony tail flying behind it, zipping around Taos.

When you need to support the car to work under it, support it well on **level** ground. Use good firm wooden blocks or good quality jack stands to block it. We definitely don't recommend using cinder (cement) blocks, but if you're caught in an emergency and there's nothing else, make sure the holes in them go up and down, and not sideways. None of us would ever get under a car held up by cinder blocks.

Use safety goggles if there's any chance a piece of flying metal (maybe even dirt) could land in your eye.

If while you're working you have loose and dangly wires hanging around, disconnect the battery ground strap.

Having a fire extinguisher around may be handy, but we hope you'd never have to use it.
Most important—**KEEP ALERT AND AWARE! See Changes and New Ideas** at the back of the book.

Step 4. Miscellaneous Instructions

Get someone to read the steps to you the first time you do a procedure and even the second. There's nothing worse than trying to turn pages with greasy hands or trying to read while lying under the car with dirt falling in your eyes. Besides, two heads are better than one but you must know that.

Double check everything! In other words, do the step and then have it read again so you can see if you did everything right.

Equip the reader with a pencil so notes can be taken while you are down there looking at the thing.

Take your time! Just do the job once and well. You have an eternity! DON'T IMPROVISE!
Just do it the way it says.

Wear the right clothes. There's no way better to keep peace in the family than to wear car clothes to work on the car.

Step 5. Goof-ups

When you strip a thread, twist off a stud, drop a bolt into the engine and like that, don't freak out—turn to Chapter XVI, written for these contingencies. Smile!

Step 6. Cleanliness

Keep everything clean as you go along. Clean parts so they shine, or get someone to do it. When you are through, clean your tools and put them away before you take your coveralls off, then clean yourself and change your clothes before you drive the car or at least cover the seat with something so you don't get the inside greasy.

Step 7. Love

This is a tough one and will make or break you. You must do this work with love or you fail. You don't have to think, but you must love. This is one of the reasons I have nice tools. If I get hung up with maybe a busted knuckle or a busted stud, I feel my tools, like art objects or lovely feelies until the rage subsides and sense and love return. Try it, it works.

GOOD LUCK!

P.S. The Procedures may read like gibberish in the living room in front of the fire but will come clear as you work directly with the hardware, the tools in your hand.

P.P.S.   There are four types of Volkswagens with air cooled engines: I, II, III and IV. See **Chapter XVI** for a complete description of each Type and the various models made in each Type, but for now I want you to learn to call a Type a Type, like:

Type I is what is known in the world as a Bug, a Kafer, a Sedan, a Convertible, a Safari (the Thing), a Karmann Ghia, even a Beetle, Super Beetle, or Luv-bug and finally, a Pulguita.

Type II is called a Van, a Kombi, Station Wagon, a Pickup, Bus, Camper, Double-cab Pickup, Campmobile, Transporter, plus certain blue words.

Type III is called a Fastback, Squareback, Notchback (Sedan) and Variant.

Type IV is called a 411-2 door, 4 door or wagon and the 412-2 door, 4 door or wagon.

The reason you should know the Type designation for your own particular Volkswagen is: this is the only way we have of separating out the operations to be performed on each Type so if the book says:

Type I, 1965 and on, and you have a 1970 Pulguita, the message is for you. Or:

Type II, 1973, and you have a 1973 Campmobile, latch on.

I know it sounds complicated, but unless you are loaded with Volkswagens, there's just one type number that applies to you and your car. If there is no Type number mentioned, the usual case, then the directions apply to all air-cooled Volkswagens. They are not really too different one from another. **See Changes & New Ideas in the back of the book.**

P.P.P.S. John died in November of 1977, at home, surrounded by friends...family...having decided the day before that it was time. He went as a Warrior.

Half an hour after he died, a friend happened to look up towards the mountains behind Santa Fe and saw John on a roller coaster dipping over the foothills, laughing his head off.

In 1989 we added Colin Messer's Chapter, "High-Performance Modifications," in 1990 came John Hilgerdt and Peter Aschwanden's "VW Mania" and in the 1992 edition John and Peter's "How to Keep Your Volkswagen Alive Forever" was added along with a Chapter we've wanted for a long time: "The Grab Bag" or "Things We've Always Thought Should Be In The Book, But Didn't Know Where To Put." 1994 saw the 25th anniversary edition, and this year, Mr. Stick (John Hilgerdt) has added "Electrical Impulses." "Changes and New Ideas" is still at the end before the Index. The idea is that if you see "See Changes" or "See Changes and New Ideas" in the text, go to the back of the book and read the information on the page number you've been referred from, OK?

T-shirts are still available from Der Wagonwerks, P.O. Box 1347, Elyria, OH 44036, 216-322-9459. But *The Velvet Monkeywrench* by John is out of print. Good Road!

—Eve Muir, 1997

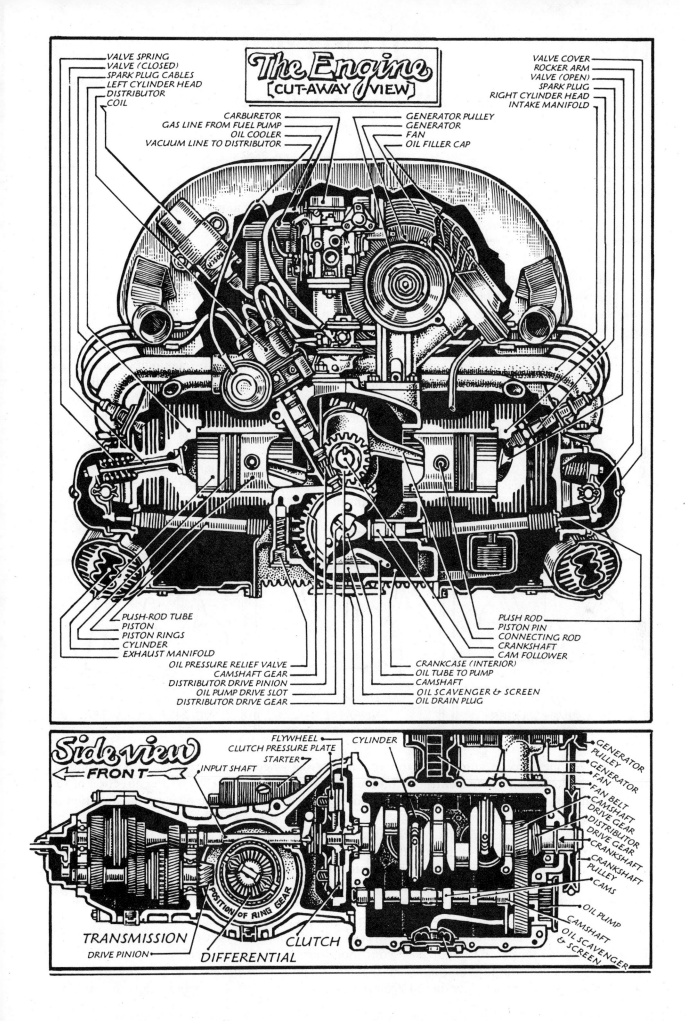

The Engine
CUT-AWAY VIEW

VALVE SPRING
VALVE (CLOSED)
SPARK PLUG CABLES
LEFT CYLINDER HEAD
DISTRIBUTOR
COIL

VALVE COVER
ROCKER ARM
VALVE (OPEN)
RIGHT CYLINDER HEAD
SPARK PLUG
INTAKE MANIFOLD

CARBURETOR
GAS LINE FROM FUEL PUMP
OIL COOLER
VACUUM LINE TO DISTRIBUTOR

GENERATOR PULLEY
GENERATOR
FAN
OIL FILLER CAP

PUSH-ROD TUBE
PISTON
PISTON RINGS
CYLINDER
EXHAUST MANIFOLD

PUSH ROD
PISTON PIN
CONNECTING ROD
CRANKSHAFT
CAM FOLLOWER

OIL PRESSURE RELIEF VALVE
CAMSHAFT GEAR
DISTRIBUTOR DRIVE PINION
OIL PUMP DRIVE SLOT
DISTRIBUTOR DRIVE GEAR

CRANKCASE (INTERIOR)
OIL TUBE TO PUMP
CAMSHAFT
OIL SCAVENGER & SCREEN
OIL DRAIN PLUG

Side view
FRONT

FLYWHEEL
CLUTCH PRESSURE PLATE
STARTER
INPUT SHAFT

CYLINDER

GENERATOR PULLEY
GENERATOR
FAN
FAN BELT
CAMSHAFT DRIVE GEAR
DISTRIBUTOR DRIVE GEAR
CRANKSHAFT
CRANKSHAFT PULLEY
CAMS
OIL PUMP
CAMSHAFT
OIL SCAVENGER & SCREEN

POSITION OF RING GEAR

TRANSMISSION
DRIVE PINION

DIFFERENTIAL

CLUTCH

CHAPTER II

HOW WORKS A VOLKSWAGEN

Along with word problems in Math and Zen Principals, the operation of a motor car seems to be a first water mystery. One definition of a mechanic is someone who looks at an automobile as a system. In this frame of reference an idiot would be one who looks at a car as a series of problems. Here is a generalized story to help you put a little light on how a car runs so you can dig it.

Note that **front** always means the *front of the car.*

The **wheels** are important, all four of them, plus a spare in case one of the tires goes flat. In the Volkswagen, all four are free to bounce up and down with the vagaries of the road—individually suspended. The front two are mounted on hinged axles, or king pins, so they can turn to give the car direction. The geometry is complicated but the principle is easy. There is caster, camber, and toe-in but they combine to give the best angle between the wheels and the road for maximum control, ease of handling and comfort with minimum of tire wear. The rear wheels apply the force to the road that makes the car go. All four wheels are attached to the **frame** (body) through **torsion bars**—those tubes which run across the front and back of the car—which return the car to its proper level after each road irregularity. The **shock absorbers** (vertical round tubes) merely dampen the up and down movement for rider comfort and safety.

The rear wheels of the Volkswagen have an attitude which is peculiar to cars with individually suspended driven wheels. The torsion bars are set for a normal position with a normal load so the attitude of the wheels is dependent on the amount of weight in the car:

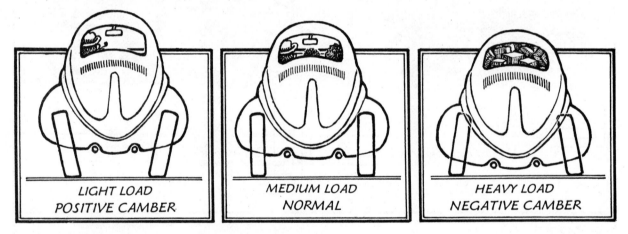

LIGHT LOAD
POSITIVE CAMBER

MEDIUM LOAD
NORMAL

HEAVY LOAD
NEGATIVE CAMBER

The steering force is applied by you to the **steering wheel** inside the car and is transmitted through a hollow rod to the **steering box** mounted on the frame which changes the direction of the force to an arm which pushes and pulls the **tie rods** and **tie rod ends** and so changes the direction of the wheels.

The **horn** is an electro-magnetic device designed to make noise and act as a warning signal. The hot wire from the battery goes through the fuse box to the horn. The ground wire, to complete the circuit, runs up through the hollow steering rod to the horn button.

The **brakes** apply negative acceleration to stop the car. The **brake drums** are part of the wheels and the stopping force is friction applied to these drums by **brake linings** on **brake shoes** which are hinged at one point and pushed apart at the opposite point by a hydraulic **wheel cylinder**. These wheel cylinders are slave cylinders and are operated by the **master cylinder** which is moved by the **brake pedal** inside the car. When you push your foot down on the brake pedal, you move the master cylinder which pushes on the brake fluid and that movement is transmitted, evenly, to the four wheel cylinders and the brake lining is shoved against the drums to stop the wheel and thus the car. OK?

Disc brakes are found on the front wheels of late model Types II, III and IV. These have a disc which is part of the wheel and a caliper which is bolted to the car. A double (dual) master cylinder is used to transfer your foot force to the hydraulic fluid. One section operates the rear drum brakes and the other pushes the brake pads out of the caliper to apply friction to the discs.

The emergency brake is a pair of cables which pull the front shoes of the rear brakes into contact with the drums. The handle in the car has notches and a release to hold and let go the tension in the cable and therefore the braking action. Don't drive with it on.

The two rear wheels are powered by swing drive-shafts which extend to each wheel from the differential, a device used to allow one wheel to travel at a different speed from the other. This is needed to go around curves as the inside wheel on a curve travels a shorter path than the outside. It is well known in human endeavor that we try to make the outside like the inside for sanity but here the inside is obviously not possibly the same as the outside, ergo the internal adjustment—in a car, the differential. The railroad people ingeniously use a flanged, tapered wheel and centrifugal force to enable them to use a solid axle between the wheels, so:

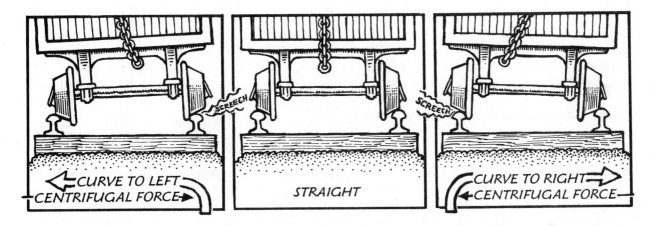

The automobile engineers use the differential, so:

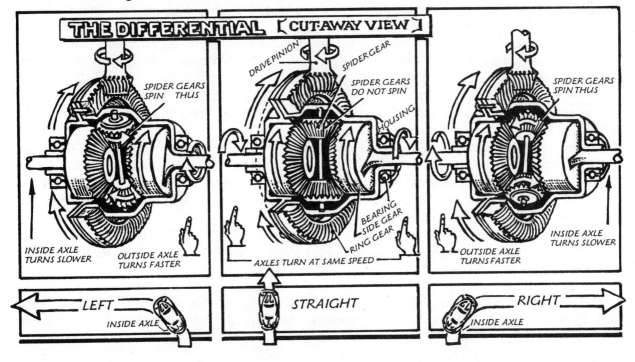

The differential also changes the direction of the twist from the round and round of the motor to the round and round of the wheels. For this it uses the **ring and pinion gears** as shown. Actually, in the Volkswagen, the axles also move up and down with the road and they are spade-ended shafts that fit into sockets which let them operate in separate planes. Late models have shafts that bolt to the differential and use two **universal joints** to transfer the power to the wheels.

The **transmission** is a box containing many gears, shafts, retainers, shifting mechanisms and is complicated in the extreme, but operates on the simple principle that a larger gear will make less revolutions when driven by a smaller gear (with the same size teeth), so:

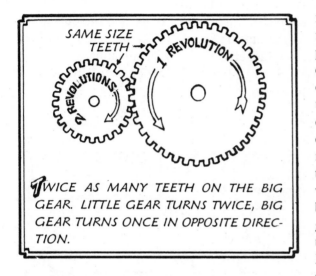

SAME SIZE TEETH → 1 REVOLUTION 2 REVOLUTIONS

TWICE AS MANY TEETH ON THE BIG GEAR. LITTLE GEAR TURNS TWICE, BIG GEAR TURNS ONCE IN OPPOSITE DIRECTION.

In the VW, high gear is arranged so the twist from the engine makes almost the same number of revolutions going out as when it came in. The pinion gear shaft comes out of the transmission and drives the ring gear and these two gears have a ratio of about four to one, so the wheels are actually turning about one fourth the revolutions of the engine when the transmission is in high. This isn't exactly correct but I'm telling you a story, not making an engineering analysis. If engines put out the same twist at all revolutions, the problem wouldn't exist but the Volkswagen engine works best between 2,000 and 3,500 revs per minute. The gears in the transmission increase the ratio between the engine and the turning of the rear wheels in the lower or first gear and about the same in reverse. In second the engine turns about eight times as fast as the wheels and in third about six times and, as we have said, about four times the wheel revolutions in high. With the engine turning a constant 3500 rpm, the car will be going about 10 miles per hour in first, about twenty in second, about thirty-five in third and about fifty-five in high or fourth. The transmission is then a gearing device to match the speed of the engine (relatively constant) with the speed and power requirements of the rear wheels. The old Bus has an extra set of straight gears out by the wheels which adds ground clearance and increases the ratio of the engine speed by one and a quarter to one, which slows the Bus a little, but also adds power at the wheels for extra load-carrying capacity.

Late model Buses no longer have these extra gear boxes at the rear wheels but use **double jointed swing axles**, thus gaining higher highway speed and losing a lot of noise and some power. Reverse twist to move the car backwards is obtained by using an **idler gear** to change the direction of the twist.

The transmission is connected to the engine through the **clutch**, a spring-loaded friction device which connects and disconnects the engine from the car for starting, idling and shifting. The **flywheel** provides one face and the **clutch assembly** provides the other with the two-surfaced **clutch plate** between. The clutch assembly is spring loaded and presses the clutch plate between its surface and the surface of the flywheel to make the connection and you know how important that can be. When you push on the **clutch pedal** in the car, you are actually compressing the springs in the clutch assembly through a lever and the clutch release bearing and letting the clutch plate run free, effectively disconnecting the engine from the transmission.

The **flywheel**, a heavy machined chunk of steel, serves a triple purpose. The machined face acts as part of the clutch. There are teeth all around the outer circumference which the starter assembly engages to turn the engine over for starting. It also serves as a heavy rotating body bolted to the end of the crankshaft to maintain the revolving inertia of the engine through its cycles.

The crankshaft (a heavy steel forging) is fastened to the flywheel with four pins and a gland nut. It runs in four bearings, called **main bearings**, which are massive and pressure-lubricated. The crankshaft has four cranks, or throws, which serve to translate the back and forth movement of the **pistons**, through the **connecting rods**, into the round and round motion of the crankshaft and flywheel assembly. The connecting rod bearings are also pressure-lubricated. Both the main and connecting rod bearings are thin shells which can be replaced as they wear. The crankshaft assembly looks so:

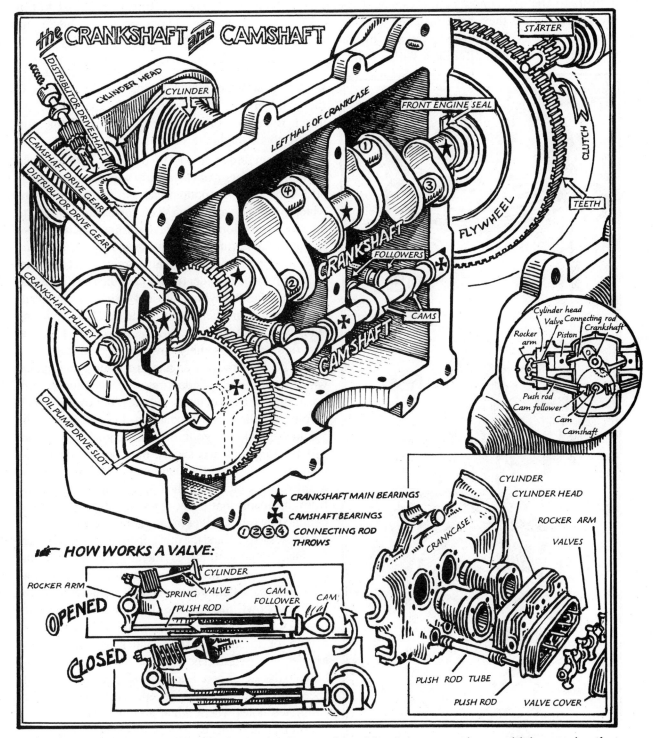

the CRANKSHAFT and CAMSHAFT

STARTER

DISTRIBUTOR DRIVESHAFT

CYLINDER HEAD

CYLINDER

LEFT HALF OF CRANKCASE

FRONT ENGINE SEAL

CAMSHAFT DRIVE GEAR

DISTRIBUTOR DRIVE GEAR

CRANKSHAFT

FLYWHEEL

CLUTCH

TEETH

FOLLOWERS

CRANKSHAFT PULLEY

CAMS

CAMSHAFT

OIL PUMP DRIVE SLOT

Cylinder head
Valve
Connecting rod
Rocker arm
Piston
Crankshaft
Push rod
Cam follower
Cam
Camshaft

★ CRANKSHAFT MAIN BEARINGS

✠ CAMSHAFT BEARINGS

①②③④ CONNECTING ROD THROWS

☞ **HOW WORKS A VALVE:**

ROCKER ARM
CYLINDER
SPRING VALVE
CAM FOLLOWER
CAM
PUSH ROD

OPENED

CLOSED

CYLINDER
CYLINDER HEAD
ROCKER ARM
VALVES
CRANKCASE
PUSH ROD TUBE
PUSH ROD
VALVE COVER

The **crankcase** is a split aluminum casting machined in the proper places, which contains that portion of the engine known as the **bottom end**. The main bearings and the **cam shaft** bearings run through the case so that one half of the bearing is on each part of the case. The **cam shaft** is geared to the crankshaft and has **cams** or **lobes** which operate the **cam followers** which in turn push the **push rods** which operate the valves:

The crankcase also acts as an oil sump to collect, store and help cool the oil that is pumped through the bearings by the oil pump. The crankshaft has a funny sideways gear, called a worm gear, pressed on the shaft next to the cam shaft drive gear. This worm gear turns the distributor drive gear which has a slot on top that turns the distributor and an off-center bump which operates the fuel pump through a push rod. The **oil pump** fits into a slot in the end of the cam shaft and turns with it. In the older models, the cam shaft bearings are merely machined into the crankcase but in the later models, they have installed bearing shells to take the wear. On the opposite end of the crankshaft from the flywheel, outside of the crankcase, is attached the **crankshaft pulley** which drives the **generator or alternator** with a belt.

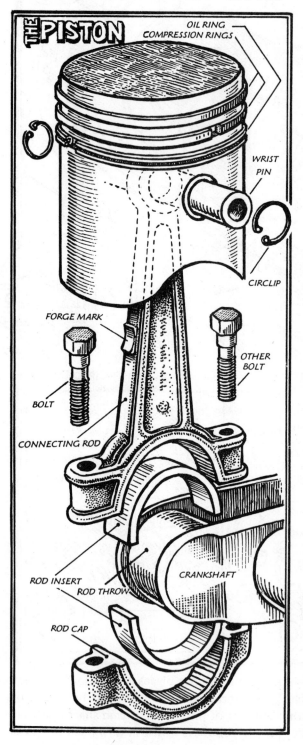

THE PISTON

OIL RING
COMPRESSION RINGS
WRIST PIN
CIRCLIP
FORGE MARK
OTHER BOLT
BOLT
CONNECTING ROD
ROD INSERT
ROD THROW
CRANKSHAFT
ROD CAP

The **pistons** move back and forth in the cylinders and are sealed to the machined sides of the cylinders by the **piston rings.** The pistons are attached to the connecting rods by the **piston pins** which go through the pistons, so:

The **cylinder heads** fit over the cylinders and contain the **valves** and **valve train** which consists of the push rods from the bottom end and the **rocker arms** which push the valve open. The valves are returned to the closed position by the valve springs. There are two valves to each cylinder, one intake and one exhaust, and they are operated by the valve train to let the fuel mixture into the cylinder (intake) and then let the burned gases out after the cylinder is fired (exhaust). The heads and cylinders are held tight to the crankcase by long studs which are screwed into the crankcase. The head nuts tighten this assembly down to the crankcase.

The Volkswagen engine is a four cycle engine which means each cylinder fires once every two revolutions, that is, each cylinder requires four cycles or half revolutions for power production. Let's start with the gas in the tank and go through the complete schmuts. The liquid gasoline is sucked into the fuel pump and then pushed into the carburetor by a neoprene **diaphragm** which is pushed up and down by the rod from the cam shaft. The sucking-pushing action is obtained by wafer valves in the pump: one opens to suck and closes to push and the other opens to push and closes to suck. The gasoline is thereby pushed into the carburetor bowl. There is a float in the carburetor bowl which closes a float valve when the carburetor is full. From the bowl, the gasoline flows into the accelerator pump which is used to pump liquid gas into the carburetor throat in a spray and is operated by the **accelerator pedal.** The gasoline also flows from the bowl to the jets. There is a jet for idling, one for middle speed and one for high speed. These jets are just calibrated holes where liquid gasoline exists, ready to be sucked into the engine as demanded. There is a **butterfly valve** at each end of the carburetor. The top butterfly is the choke and when closed it limits the air intake to the carburetor throat, thereby making the gas-to-air mixture richer in gasoline. The butterfly valve at the bottom of the carburetor opens the throat to the engine and is attached to the accelerator pedal which controls the speed of the engine. The **accelerator pump** is used to add the necessary extra liquid gasoline when the pedal is pushed hard for extra power. Now we have the gasoline available at the throat of the carburetor and a method of controlling its flow.

1975 and later Types I and II and some Types III and IV have no carburetors. The fuel is supplied directly to the area behind the intake valves, atomized and ready to mix with the incoming air by a system called **Electronic Fuel Injection** (Types III and IV) or **AFC Fuel Injection** (Air Flow Control, Types I and II). These systems use an **electronic fuel pump** to suck the gasoline through a **filter** and pump it into a circular system at about 28 pounds per square inch (psi). The unused gasoline is returned to the tank. The pressure is regulated by a **pressure regulator** to keep a constant supply of 28 psi fuel ready to be injected. The **injectors** are atomizing valves operated by solenoids which open and close at the direction of the **Electronic Control Unit** (brain). This control unit gets messages from various sensors, digests them, then opens the injectors for a specific amount of time, thus injecting atomized fuel right in back of the intake valves ready to be sucked into the cylinders. Although this brain has about 300 (electronic) or about 80 (AFC) diodes, transistors, resistors and condensers, it does a simple task: it determines the amount of time each injector is open, thus making the amount of fuel fit the existing conditions exactly. In order to do its job, the control unit needs to know the temperature and pressure conditions it is going to inject fuel into, OK? It is connected to the **crankcase** or **manifold temperature sensor,** the **head temperature sensor,** the **pressure switch** (electronic only) and **pressure sensor** (electronic only) and finally to the **timer** on the distributor. There are other components for cold starts and rapid acceleration and electric relays to supply a constant voltage to the fuel pump and control unit. However, under steady-state conditions, the factors are: temperature, pressure and timing.

As soon as the engine is warmed up and running at a fairly steady rate, the temperature sensors, which tend to put in extra fuel for a richer mixture, get out of the action. Then what's left is the timing and the pressure. The timing is provided by a double contact switch under the distributor which merely tells the control unit which two injectors (electronic) or which injector (AFC) to open. This trigger contact is a simple cam and contact system which tells the control unit which cylinders are ready for fuel.

Here, the electronic and AFC systems differ, so we'll start with the **electronic** and explain the **pressure switch** and **pressure sensor.** The accelerator is connected by a cable to the **throttle valve** which is a butterfly valve in the **intake air distributor.** When you push on the accelerator, the butterfly valve opens allowing air from the air cleaner to enter the intake manifold. The pistons are moving up and down in the cylinders sucking air into the intake system and pushing it out through the exhaust system, so the pressure in the manifold is usually less (negative pressure) than outside in the world. The amount the butterfly valve is open (foot pressure on the accelerator) determines the air pressure in the manifold—all right so far?—and the pressure sensor connected to the manifold measures this air pressure and sends the dope along to the control unit which then applies the juice to open the injectors which spray the fuel in back of the intake valves to mix with the air and the mixture is sucked into the cylinder when the valve opens.

When the engine is at idle, the throttle valve (the butterfly valve in the intake air distributor) is closed and air for idle is provided by the **auxiliary air regulator.** The **pressure switch** was used on early models to provide extra fuel at full throttle. This job was next given to an extra circuit in the pressure sensor and now is done by a new throttle valve switch (1972-'74).

With **AFC** fuel injection when you push on the accelerator, the air flap opens which sends a message directly to the control unit which regulates the amount of fuel sent to the cylinders by the injectors. This system is a lot simpler than the older electronic one.

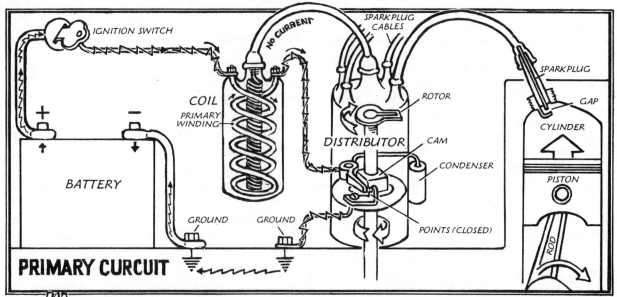

PRIMARY CURCUIT

When the points are open, the condenser stops the primary circuit, preventing the electricity from jumping the points gap and going to ground. The coil responds to this circuit break by producing a high voltage (secondary) current that goes through the distributor to the appropriate spark plug and hence to ground.

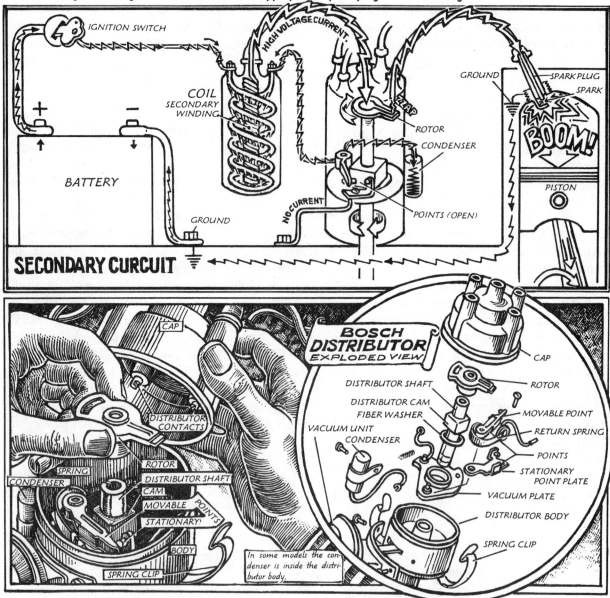

SECONDARY CURCUIT

In some models the condenser is inside the distributor body.

Whether fuel injected or carbureted, we need a method of setting this gasoline-air mixture on fire in the cylinder and that's where the ignition system comes in. Let's start with the wire that comes from the battery and goes to the key. When the key is turned all the way, part of the current is used to go to the ignition system and part to the **solenoid** on the starter. The solenoid is an electromagnet which, when energized, pushes the starter gear into engagement with the teeth on the flywheel and also closes a contact which draws current from the battery through a much heavier wire to turn the starter motor and thus the engine. As soon as the motor starts the key is relaxed and the solenoid drops the starter gear back away from the flywheel.

The other portion of the current from the key goes to the **ignition coil** which is a cylinder hanging on the fan housing. It has three connections, two small ones and one big one in the center. The current from the key goes to one of the small bolts and then out through the other bolt connection to the distributor. This circuit is called the primary and puts six (or twelve) volt current in a coil in the ignition coil. Inside this primary coil are thousands of turns of wire making up the secondary coil which increases the voltage to something around ten thousand volts, which is now available at the center large outlet and connects to the center large connection at the distributor cap. It takes a lot of voltage to make a spark jump and this is the way we get it.

You are starting to see that we are going to burn our gasoline-air mixture with a spark and for that we need **spark plugs**, one for each cylinder and a heavy wire from each plug to its corresponding hole around the distributor cap.

The **distributor** is a device to time the spark impulses to the spark plugs so they fire at the proper time, to burn the mixture, to give the power. The **distributor shaft** is driven round and round by a funny gear on the crankshaft. As it goes round and round inside the distributor it opens and closes a set of points. The distributor shaft is almost square and at each point of the square it opens the **ignition points** and in between the high places allows the ignition points to close.

When the points are closed, the 6 (or 12) volt current from the battery to the key (ignition switch) goes through the primary winding in the **coil** through the closed points, to ground. Electricity, like water, will follow the path of least resistance and if one path is closed, it will follow another. A small cylinder, called the **condenser**, located either outside or inside the bottom of the distributor, is part of this path while the points are open (not touching). The condenser stops the 6 (or 12) low voltage current and keeps it from jumping the point gap and going to ground. This stopping of the current also prevents the points from burning and pitting too rapidly.

When the primary circuit is broken by the condenser, the secondary winding in the coil builds up voltage (pressure) and this high voltage electricity flows from the coil to the center of the distributor cap to the rotor and jumps the post in the cap to the proper wire to the proper spark plug.

So you see that when the points are closed, the 6 (or 12) volt current goes directly to ground. It is only when the points are open and there's a break in this primary circuit that the coil produces the high voltage (like 30,000 volts) necessary to make the spark jump and be distributed to the spark plug whose turn it is. And this happens over 7,000 times a minute!

Now we have provided the three things necessary to the operation of the engine—fuel-air mixture, spark and compression (the rings and valves)—so let's go through the cycles which make it work.

The **power stroke** takes place when the gas in the combustion chamber (the top of the cylinder and bottom of the head) is burned and forces the piston toward the crankshaft through the connecting rod to the crankshaft throw which translates the sideways motion and power of the moving piston in the cylinder to the round and round motion of the crankshaft. The valves are both closed until the burning is complete at the bottom of the stroke, then the exhaust valve opens and the piston on its way up shoves all of the burned gases out through the exhaust manifold to the muffler and so to the atmosphere. This is the **exhaust stroke**. As the piston comes again to the top of its movement,

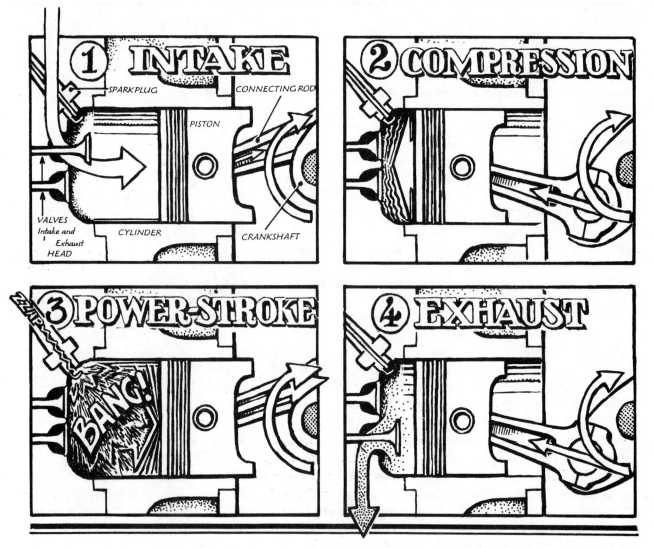

the exhaust valve closes, the intake valve opens, and the **intake stroke** begins. The piston sweeps downward again and sucks the mixture from the intake manifold into the cylinder. As the piston reaches the bottom and the cylinder is full of the gasoline and air mixture, both the intake and exhaust valves close and the piston starts up on the **compression stroke** which jambs the mixture up into itself at a ratio of about seven to one as the piston comes to the top again. Just a mite before the piston gets to the top of this stroke, the points open and the plug fires and the mixture burns as, valves closed, the piston is shoved down in the power stroke. There, that's not too hard. Note that I

said **burns** (oxidizes rapidly). When the air-fuel mixture explodes, it causes a pinging noise which indicates that the mixture is being ignited before it is completely compressed and that a change in the timing of the engine is needed. If your engine pings due to a change in altitude or fuel octane, the spark timing should be retarded (slowed down).

The Volkswagen engine is air-cooled, which means that the heat of combustion in the cylinders and heads is carried away by the flow of air. These parts are cast with fins to aid in the removal of heat. A **blower** is provided to force air down through the spaces between the fins to carry the heat to the atmosphere. The entire engine is shrouded by sheet metal to hold the flowing air to the most efficient path. The blower in Type I and Type II (up to 1971) engines is attached to the back of the generator and is thus driven with the generator by a belt from the crankshaft pulley. The blower is encased in a **fan housing** which is attached to the shrouding to make an air-tight assembly. The cooling air is sucked from the front of the fan housing and blown down through the cylinders. Also in this fan housing, bolted to the top of the crankcase, is an oil cooler which stands up in the stream of air like a radiator and cools the oil which is pumped through it.

In the Types II (1972 and on), III and IV engines, the fan is attached to the rear of the crankshaft and thus is driven directly. The generator, to the left on Type III's and to the right on Type IV's is driven by a belt. The oil cooler is laid on its side and the resulting flat profile has resulted in the name **pancake** engine for these types.

The **generator or alternator** is an electrical device which makes six or twelve volt current to charge the battery, and to supply directly the lights when running at night.

The **starter motor** is a simple 6 or 12 volt electric motor used to turn the engine over for starting.

The **voltage regulator** is a box with a lot of wires coming out of it, either on top of the generator or bolted to the side of the engine compartment, which controls the current and voltage to the battery and acts as a relay to operate the lights directly at night.

Structurally the VW Bug uses a bottom pan which is part of the body itself as a frame to bolt the running gear onto the bottom and the seats and things on the top. The Bus is much the same idea but does have a frame to give added strength, as do the other types.

This is very simple but will give you some answers to how the Volkswagen does what it does.

HOW TO BUY A VOLKSWAGEN

This chapter can also be used to check your own car to determine whether you should keep it or if it is, in fact, time to start looking around for another.

The Volkswagen has proven itself over the years to be the best transportation buy available. The upkeep has been expensive due to the high cost of parts and service. By scrambling around for lower parts prices and doing your own service and maintenance, you can keep your transportation costs down to the bare minimum. It is a matter of balance but the scale is heavily in favor of the Volkswagen if you can beat this maintenance nut.

I have no advice for you about buying a new VW. This chapter is intended for those who are buying a used one. The authorized VW dealers have a program through which they put every used car before it goes onto the lot. This allows them to give it a guarantee. They won't bargain much, these dealers, and they have a price computed to allow them to spend time and parts fixing up the car so they can stand behind it. Some dealers will have older cars that they sell as is and these must be checked carefully, as they are suspect in front.

There are cheaper ways to get a good Volksie: from a friend, from a secondhand dealer, from an ad in the paper or just finding one that some cat has given up on and will drop out of for pimples. It is over these that we will spend some time.

First, look at it. Does it sag and look beat? Walk all around it looking for rough spots, wrinkles and bumps. Has it rusted out under the doors? Do the doors open and close well? Does it look like it has been hit? Do the compartment doors open and close? Do the windows work? Check all the lights—brake, signal, head and interior.

Put your foot on the brake and see how much pedal you have. It should stop three inches from the floor or more. Stand outside the car with the front door open on the driver's side and push the clutch pedal down with your hand to where it gets hard to push. Let it up again and see how much free play there is. It should be about one-half to one inch. If it is more than two inches, the clutch is immediately suspect. Look at the wear on the rubber clutch and brake pedal covers. If they are badly worn, so is the car. New ones are just as suspicious.

Look at the upholstery. Is it original and a little beat up? That is a better sign than new seat covers. Is the driver's seat in approximately the same shape as the passenger's? Or is it squashed flat and out of shape? These are all signs and signals of use and should give you an idea of what kind of life the car has had and also allow you to estimate what kind of life it will give you.

Open the engine compartment. Is it clean? Remember that this is an air-cooled car and the cooling air comes through the engine compartment. If the engine and its compartment are filthy, the loss in cooling efficiency will soon cause repairs. Look under the car where it has been sitting. Are there oil spots under the transmission or under the engine? Look at the bottom of the engine. Is it oily and dirty? Be cold! Be objective! You are macroscopically examining a possible new member of your family and the choice is really yours.

Now go to the left front wheel, get down on your knees and put both hands at twelve o'clock on the tire and push and pull to check for play. Put one hand at nine o'clock and one hand at three o'clock, push with the left and pull with the right and then the opposite. If either of these motions produces a lot of looseness, mark it in your mind.

Now stand back and look at it again. Does it stand up with pride? Does it feel good to you? Would you like to be its friend? Use your other senses. Sit in the driver's seat and scrunch your butt around. Hold the wheel and close your eyes and FEEL!

You've spent ten minutes and gotten your knees dirty and your hands so now go wash your hands and let the data you have obtained soak through from your conscious to your subconscious and grok the car. If it is a Bus, crawl around in the back and feel how it is to be back there. Look at the head lining. How long will it last? Have happy people been back here balling and talking and laughing and living?

If you were lucky you were able to do all this without the owner or salesperson fast-talking you; if not, tell them you want a little time with the car alone, then do it.

Get away from the car and the owner or salesman to let your mind and feelings go over the car and the idea of the car. What has its Karma been? Can you live with the car? Walk around or find a quiet place, assume the good old Lotus and let the car be the thing. At this point some revelation will come to you and you will either be gently guided away from that scene and can start looking again or you will still be attracted toward the car and can continue with your inspection. It is important that you neither run the motor or ride in the car until this preliminary scene has run its course. It also puts owner-salespeople up the wall because they have no idea of what you are doing and will be more pliable when the hard dealing time comes.

You have decided to allow the car to get a little closer to you to see if it fits your life so get together a few tools and a friend, if possible, and lay out an hour for the pre-purchase procedure that follows. If the car has belonged to a friend and you have ridden and driven and thought and felt about the car, then the preliminary inspection will have already permeated your consciousness and you can start out with the final check-out.

The whole idea of the second phase is to decide what, if anything, the car is worth so the first thing is to find out what a guaranteed one is worth. Go to the Volkswagen dealer and find a similar car, look it over a little to get a comparison and find out what they want for it. If you have the bread, you might just think about buying it so find out about the guarantee and all that jazz—but no, the other one is more attractive and you know that you can save some needed bread so write down what the dealer wants for the car and get ready to run the Pre-purchase Procedure. The whole idea of the procedure is to determine exactly what you will pay for the car plus or minus. You have already decided that you can live with it and after you pay for it, you will.

If you decided that the Volkswagen is your meat you might turn to the tool section and get the Phase I Basic Owner's and Operator's tool kit, as it contains everything you will need to check out the car.

If you are checking out your own car, the following procedure will determine what it is worth to you, monetarily.

PRE-PURCHASE PROCEDURE

Tools: Phase I tool kit or the following equipment: compression tester, 1 lb. hammer, spark plug wrench, screwdrivers, large and small, pliers, vise grip, 10" or 12" crescent wrench, jack (if the car doesn't have one), flashlight, oil can, old clothes, ground cloth, rags, stocking cap for your long hair.

Note: If this is your first procedure, have your friend read the steps to you as you do them and make a small pencil check as you finish them. He or she can also make any notes you care to jot down. 1969 and later models have two red lights, one marked "oil," the other "gen." Newer models have three red warning lights: "oil," "gen" and EGR." The "EGR" light need not concern you here. Let's start: Check for rust. If it's very bad around the door jambs and pedal assembly, the car is probably not worth buying. See **Chapter XX**, The Real Enemy.

Step 1. Check Red (Gen) and Green (Oil) Lights, Engine Off (since 1969 Both are Red)

Get the key and put it in the lock. Turn the key to the first notch and see if the red and green lights go on. If they do, proceed to Step 2, but if they don't, turn to the appropriate chapter on the red and green lights and find out how to fix the problem. If it is a simple connection to make, fix it. If you can't fix it readily, stop right here and have the owner-salesperson get it fixed, for NO VOLKS-WAGEN ENGINE SHOULD BE RUN WITHOUT THE RED AND GREEN LIGHTS WORKING!

Step 2. Red and Green Lights, Engine Running

Turn the key back to "off" and then turn it to start. The engine should start easily and the red and green lights should go out as the engine is revved. The red light may blink a little at idle but the green light should go off and stay off. If it flickers and doesn't go completely out until the engine is revved, make a note of it. If either light stays on when the engine is revved, shut off the engine and fix the trouble before driving the car.

Step 3. Check Muffler and Exhaust

Let the engine idle and go to the rear of the car to check the muffler. Get down on the ground and look for holes and leaks. Pass your hand around it feeling for leaks. Then put your hand(s) over the tail pipe(s), quickly because they'll soon be hot and feel the pressure. Feel the pulses; they should be even. Just for a second—don't get burned. Then hold your hand(s) about four to five inches away, letting the exhaust pass over them. The pulses should be even and about the same temperature. If they are not, the engine needs or will soon need a valve job. Make a note.

Step 4. Check Brakes and Driving Qualities

Put the emergency brake on, put the car in first and let out the clutch. A good emergency brake will kill the engine. Release the emergency brake and restart the car, if necessary. Drive down the street and try the brakes. If they don't stop the car well, get them fixed before you go on. If the brakes are OK, continue testing. The car should shift and accelerate smoothly and move on the road like you dreamed it would. Take it on the freeway and get it up to speed. Move the wheel back and forth, letting it return to center by itself. If it doesn't, the front end will need work. Make a note.

Step 5. Check Transmission

The two things that indicate a worn transmission are hanging up putting it into gear and popping out of gear. The driving check has told you if it goes into any gear hard so now check for popping out. Find a deserted street and get the car moving in reverse. Take your foot off the accelerator and your hand off the gear shift. Does it pop out of reverse? Try it again. Now try low gear (first). Put the car in gear and accelerate to ten MPH, take your foot off the gas and see if the car pops out of gear. Try it twice. If it pops out once try it several times—easy. Then get the car up to twenty in second and take your foot off the accelerator and see if it pops out of second, then up to thirty-five in third and let your foot off again and see if it pops out of third. Then back to the freeway and try letting your foot off at fifty-five in fourth (high). If it pops out of any gear, your tests are over and the car is rejected unless the price is so right that you can afford a new transmission. Get a firm price from a garage that specializes in Volkswagen transmissions and make a note of that.

Step 6. Check Differential

Your ears have been checking out the differential throughout the previous steps. It will have told you its troubles by howling and growling and rumbling. A worn differential in a Volksie is seldom found but when it is, you know it. So if there have been no untoward noises from the rear and it hasn't jumped out of gear, you may assume that the transmission and differential are OK.

Step 7. Excess Engine Noise and Clutch

The engine too has been delivering its message to your ears. An air-cooled engine is a noisy beast at best but there are limits and if your ears have not been put out of joint by engine noises, it is probably OK. With the car in third, put your foot down on the pedal and slip the clutch a little. Feel for chattering. The clutch should be smooth and sure.

Step 8. Check Engine for Heating

Pick a level spot where you won't mind crawling around. Shut off the engine, go around to the back and prop open the engine compartment so it won't bust you one, then feel if the engine is hot. You can smell it. Pull out the dipstick and check the oil level right away. It will be higher in a minute or two but you are looking for evidence of heat. If you can't get the dipstick out with your fingers, use the pliers. Take the cap off the oil filler. If you see a little smoke, the oil is too hot. Check the tension of the fan belt. It should deflect about one-half inch. Is it shiny where it goes over the pulleys? That means it's been slipping and could explain the heating. A hot engine is a dirty engine and the only way to fix that is to take it out of the car and clean it and if you have to do that you might as well overhaul it. That's why we did all that checking. The dipstick is really the best index. A cool engine will have a dipstick that is just barely too hot to hold in your fingers but by passing it from hand to hand you can manage to keep it from burning them. If you can't hold it at all or even get it out and the engine smells hot, then it is. If the engine is really too hot, then you have to decide whether the car is worth an engine overhaul soon or not. If the engine is very hot and you are not into doing the extra work, reject the car.

Step 9. Check Compression

Now get the spark plugs out so you can make a compression check. Grab the spark plug connector (plastic), not the wire, and pull it off the plug. Use the pliers (gently) if it is too hot for your fingers. Pull all four of them off. Put the ones from the back cylinders to the rear and the front ones to the front so you can put them back into the same places they came from. Remember, "front" is always the front of the car. Put the spark plug wrench over the plug and pull on the handle (counterclockwise) until the plug is loose, then take the handle off and use your fingers on the extension to unscrew the plug and lift it out. Repeat with the other three plugs. Put the plugs in a known order like 1, 2, 3, 4, with the sparking end toward you. They will be too hot to handle so just let them slip out of the socket where you can see them. If they are all uniformly tan to brown, they are fine. Even if they are light grey, they'll do but if any are black and foul, take note, for the rings or valves in that one are probably bad.   Your friend or the owner-salesperson is now seated in the driver's seat and has just made the note that the plugs are OK, or something. Make sure the car is out of gear. Insert the compression tester in number 1 cylinder, the front one on the right, make sure the tester is seated well and holler to your friend to turn the engine over. Let it turn over at least six times.   The dial on the tester will record the compression so tell your friend what it is for writing down. Then click the release on the tester and do number 2, which is the back one closest to you on the right, then number 3, the front one on the left, then number 4, the last one. If the readings have all been 100 or over and within five pounds of each other, pass on to Step 10. If the readings are under 100, squirt a few squirts of oil into each cylinder through the spark plug holes and do the tester thing again on all four cylinders and write the second set of figures down. Put the plugs back in. They are cool by now, so slip the plug into the socket and tip the plug into the hole, use your fingers to get them hand-tight, then slip on the ratchet handle and tighten them good and firm and then just a hair more to set the plug down on the gasket. Repeat with the others. Don't forget the gasket. Put the plug wires back on the plugs in their proper order and have your friend start the engine for a minute to see if you did right. If the plugs are too loose, you will hear them leaking and if the wires are in the wrong places the engine won't run. If that happens turn to the tune-up section, Chapter X, and find out how to get them right.

Step 10. Compression Test Analysis

Now you have tested the compression and after a last look around the engine compartment, you can close it up. What does the compression test mean? Well, it is the best gauge to engine wear available without tearing the engine down. If the readings were 120 pounds on all four cylinders, the engine has been lately overhauled. From 120 down to 100 pounds, with all the cylinders within five pounds of each other, the engine is in good shape. The first 15,000 miles will probably wear the engine down to the 100 pound reading but it will stay at about 100 for many thousands of miles, depending on treatment. One weak cylinder indicates an imbalance in wear, improper installation of the rings or a burnt valve.

If, however, the compression readings were under 100 pounds, the engine is on its way down and out, especially with one weak cylinder. When the compression is less than 80 pounds, an overhaul is necessary. If squirting the oil in the engine raised the compression materially, say 10 pounds, the rings are badly worn. If the readings were low, or one or two were low and were not raised by the addition of the oil, then the valves are leaking and will soon need work. This is not vital information in the Volksie, as you would do the rings and the valves together as long as the engine was out of the car, but it will show where the engine is and that's important.

Step 11. Jack Up One Side

Check the jacking points on the car. The Bug has two and the Bus, four. It is a real bug if they are mashed up or twisted around and new ones should be welded on if the old ones aren't serviceable. Never use a regular or hydraulic jack on these jack points. They are for the VW jack and the others foul them up. There's a good place for a regular jack right in back of them. Find four impeccable blocks, bricks or rocks and block (for the Bug) the right hand side wheels fore and aft so the car can't get away from you. Put the jack in the left hand side jack socket and jack up the car until the rear wheel is two inches off the ground. In the Bug, the whole left side of the car will rise. If you're looking at a Bus, block the left side so the car can't move, put your jack in the rear socket and jack up the right rear wheel so that it has two inches clearance.

Step 12. Check Differential

Now you have the rear wheel raised off the ground and the car blocked so it cannot move. With the car in gear, check the play in the differential by gently rotating the rear wheel with your hands. It will have about one to two inches of play at the tire when it is adjusted correctly. If it has as much as three inches, you should have heard it when you were driving the car and you should start considering a rebuilt unit. Have your friend start the car and run it through all the gears while you listen for the ballsy rumble that indicates bad bearings. I can't describe the sound better, but if the bearings are bad, you'll know it. The wheel will rotate quite rapidly in high and if it bounces around badly, the wheel is out of balance. Have your friend put on the brakes and watch the wheel. It should come smoothly to a stop. If not, the brake lining is suspect. This test is to check the smooth running of the gear train and to check for excessive bearing wear. Just use your ears and eyes and be careful. After you've shut off the engine, check for a bad axle bearing by placing your hands on the tire at six and nine o'clock and give it the push-pull routine. If there's play, the rear bearing is going out.

Step 13. Check Front End

If you are checking a Bus, let the rear wheel down, move the jack to the front point and jack up the front wheel. In the Bug the front wheel is already off the ground. Grasp the tire with both hands at nine and three o'clock and give it the push-pull to try for play. Try again at six and twelve o'clock. If there is none, let the car down and go to Step 14. If there is play you should try to find out where it is. The front wheel bearings could be out of adjustment. If you suspect that, go to the section on front wheel bearings and check the adjustment—Chapter XII. Have your friend wiggle the front wheel while you use the flashlight to check the tie rod ends and the king pins for wear. I knock the front wheel bearing cap off with the hammer and the screwdriver, tap the lock ear away from the outer unit, remove the outer nut with the crescent wrench, then tighten the inner nut until there is no possibility of movement in the front wheel bearings, then check for play. If there's still play after you tighten the inner nut down on the bearings, you will need front end work and that's what you want to know. In the transporter the weak spot is the bushings on the big pin in the center of the front end, called the swing lever pin and if it is bad it's a big job, so check it well. Adjust the bearing and replace the cap per Chapter XII. Now unjack the car. I feel that one side tells me enough but both sides can be done for thoroughness. You either need front end work or not.

Step 14. Check Brake Lining

Take the hub cap off the wheel and check the brake lining in each wheel. You can see it through the adjustment hole with the flashlight. You may have to roll the car back and forth a little to get the lining in view and if the outside light is strong, a jacket or cloth over the fender and your shoulders will cut the daylight so the lining can be seen. If the lining is about one-eighth of an inch thick, you have plenty, but if it is less than a sixteenth, you will soon have to reline the brakes and you should know that.

If you are looking at a late model Ghia, Bus, Type III or IV, it will have disc brakes in the front so check the discs for grooving and unevenness by feeling the discs with your fingers, then check the pads with a flashlight to see if they still have their all-important grooves. If the pads are flat they'll need replacing and if the discs are not flat (like grooved or scored), they'll have to be refaced or replaced.

Step 15. Check the Tires and Wheel Wells

Take the small screwdriver in your hand with your thumbnail held near the point and check the depth of the tread. If this is about one-eighth of an inch thick, you have plenty but if it is less than a sixteenth, you will need tires soon and you should know that. Look under the wheel wells for rust, a demerit.

Step 16. Clean Up

Now remove all evidences of your visit. Return the bricks and rocks, pick up your tools, wipe the steering wheel and door handles with the rag and in general clean things up. Return the key to the owner-salesman and gently ask him what he wants for the car. Write that down without comment and retire to the closest quiet place to evaluate what you know. Don't let the car trap you now! It is assumed that you haven't rejected the car.

Step 17. Fuel Injection

If your examination of the engine didn't turn up any carburetors and the prospective purchase is a 1975 or newer Type I or II, a Type III after 1967 or a Type IV, then you are facing a fuel injected engine. You have already tested its ability to run, found out whether it gets hot or not and by now know if it drives to suit you. If you feel while driving the car that it isn't running well and it has fuel injection, it might be a very serious reason to stop looking its way. Anyway, turn to the Fuel Injection section of the Tune-up Procedure in Chapter X, read what you have to do to keep the system alive, then add that consideration to the others.

Step 18. Evaluation

You need a sheet of paper and a pencil. Write down on top of the paper the two prices, the one you got from Volkswagen and the one the owner-salesperson gave you. Subtract $200.00 from the VW price for the guarantee. That's what it's worth. Talk over the whole scene with your friend. Has anything occurred that would eliminate the car? No? Well, then, start with Step 1 and go through the procedure subtracting what you think it will cost to fix the car up to the standard set by the VW dealer. We have eliminated cost estimates in the following list as they change so rapidly. Phone your nearest VW dealer for that day's prices. Dealers, in general, are very helpful. The one in Santa Fe has been terrific to us.

Page 22:

Step 1 — OK.

Step 2 — If the green light flickers, the oil pressure system is weak but the other wear data will probably show the engine needs overhaul. Read the chapter on the Green Light.

Step 3 — Needs a new muffler—subtract the price of parts and vexatious work. See Chapter XVII.

Step 4 — OK. Will show up in Step 13.

Step 5 — OK.

Step 6 — OK. If Steps 5 and 6 are not OK, Step 12 will show it.

Step 7 — OK. If clutch is bad, subtract the price of a new one plus labor.

Step 8 — See Step 10.

Step 9 — See Step 10.

Step 10 — This is the engine evaluation step and should include the data from Steps 8 and 9. If the compression is low and the car heats up, the motor will need immediate work. If the green (oil red) light also flickers, I would figure a rebuilt motor so subtract that, but if the green (oil red) light goes right out and stays out ask the price of a valve and ring job and include a new clutch.

Step 11 — Subtract the cost of new jack points.

Step 12 — Usually a new transmission-differential will eliminate the car, but find out the price of a rebuilt one installed.

Step 13 — If the car needs front end work, get a guesstimate.

Step 14 — Subtract the cost of new brake linings and/or disc pads.

Step 15 — The tires are your baby. I can't advise you but subtract what you think they're not worth.

Step 16 — Clean up!

You now have three figures of note, the VW price for a similar car, the owner-salesperson's price and your final figure which is the cost of repairs subtracted from the VW dealer's figure. Upholstery and appearance are only important when they're unacceptable. For example, if the car needs body work, you could take it to a body shop for an estimate and subtract that from the VW price. The same with window glass. The windshield wipers should work and rust should be minimal.

Step 19. Negotiation

Now you go and talk to the owner-salesperson and make an offer, probably $200.00 less than your top figure and then dicker, really dicker, but try not to pay too much more than your calculated figure. It depends on how bad you want that particular car. But buy or no, feel good!

Now, of course, you would like an example of an actual deal, how it worked out and all that. The '63 Bus I used to drive will serve so let's see how I bought it and how it served me. On the first of August, 1968, my old '58 bus made the fatal error of breaking down in the mountains causing untold travail so we patched it up and made it to Albuquerque looking and seeking. We went to the two Volkswagen dealers first and found out that an early '64 bus would cost $1095 and it was, we decided, about what we wanted but we didn't have that much bread. We bought a paper and found an ad that said: "Volkswagen Station Wagon for sale—1963, gas eater—good condition—(the address)."

We found out that the gas eater was gas heater and that the Bus was sitting out in the parking lot of a bowling alley. We looked it over; it was dusty but it looked good. It had a cracked back window but it sat and felt good and we all liked the green and white color. We spent our thinking time checking on the final price of the '64 at the Volkswagen dealer's. I got him down to $995.00 with a three month or three thousand mile guarantee. That was on a no trade-in basis, as several people wanted my old '58.

Back in the bowling alley, we got the key and the cat was busy so no B.S. We drove the car and found that the motor and trans seemed OK but the front end was loose and the engine needed tuning. We took it back to the lot and ran it through the other steps. The compression was a mite over 100 lbs. all around. The motor didn't heat and the engine compartment was dusty, but clean. The bottom of the engine and trans were both oily and there was a little oil drip. The swing lever bushings were badly worn and the front end was really loose. The red light stayed on very dim when the headlights were on so I checked the belt and generator but could find nothing wrong so I figured there was a bad ground and made a note to fix. I went to European Motors with my motor number and found out that the motor was an early 1500 engine and that parts were available but that I had better ask for them by motor number, not just by the 1500 designation.

With my final figure reading about $750.00, I walked into the bowling alley to talk to the guy and the thing I talked about was the loose front end. He said that he had gotten an estimate of $100 to get it fixed (about right) and that because of the front end and the window, he would let the car go for $700 so I offered him $650 and we settled on $675 and the deed was done. We went to the bank where it cost (there and at Motor Vehicle) about $16.00 to get the Bus transferred. We put our new tires from the old '58 on the car and installed the new swing lever kit in the front end the next day.

By June of 1969 we'd put 17,000 miles on the car (we travel a lot) and outside of the regular maintenance, I had to install a new voltage regulator to stop the red light from glowing—which didn't fix it—and get a new battery, adjust the clutch and put in new spark plugs and points; the tune-up that I mentioned. But that is all. The compression was still at 100 pounds. I had to put a new rear axle grease boot on at Villa Hermosa. The rear seal in the engine still leaked oil, about a quart in 300 miles but I gladly fed its habit since it ran so well. I fixed that oil seal when I overhauled it. That's the story and I hope that yours are all so happy.

TOOLS AND SPARE PARTS

People who philosophize about tools say, "the best are none too good," but the semantics of "best" are beyond anything. Every Volksie has some tools kicking around. Some come with the car from the factory and are supposed to handle the simplest things but if you've ever tried to get the lug nuts off a flat tire with that—that thing—they call a wrench, then and only then do you realize how impractical they are.

The Volkswagen uses the metric system so you must provide yourself with tools to match (except for the feeler gauges). On the following pages you'll find three lists of tools and miscellanea you'll need to keep your Volkswagen alive. There's a basic set that every VW owner should carry in the car (yes, even if you never intend to do anything) so the shining knight in the Mustang will have the right tools (and these directions, of course) when he stops to help you. His tools won't fit. There are two general methods of obtaining your tools. If you have the bread, just go buy them. At current labor rates for mechanics, the tool investment is soon back in your pocket. If you're beat for bread, read the procedure, make a list of what you actually need, then buy or borrow just that much. In time your stock of tools will get built up. You might get hung up with a road emergency or two but that will just speed your accumulation of a tool stash. I've found some of my tools in pawn shops, surplus stores, used furniture places and like that. When the VW bug hit me, I was equipped to keep a '51 Ford thirty-three passenger Army bus afloat and had lots of U.S. tools, some of which are directly useable. The wrench substitutions that can be made are: 11mm (7/16''), 13mm (1/2''), 14mm (9/16''), 16mm (5/8''), 17mm (11/16''), 19mm (3/4''), 21mm (13/16'', spark plug size), 22mm (7/8'') and if you file a 3/8'' open end just a little in the jaw, it will nicely fit a 10mm nut.

As VW's become more and more complicated, so does the tooling required to keep them alive. You can do a valve adjustment on any of them with a 13mm (1/2") box end, a screwdriver, a feeler gauge, and a 21mm (13/16") box end or even a crescent wrench to turn over the engine. The same 21mm will take out the oil drain plug to change the oil; the same screwdriver will adjust the carburetor and a 10mm box-open end will allow you to adjust the timing. There's usually one of those pressed metal spark plug wrenches in a Volksie as they come with the car and they do work for the spark plugs, but not very well as a lug wrench. What I'm saying is that the regular maintenance tasks do not require a lot of expensive tools. A new car probably wouldn't need much more than the above handful for the first year or more. The older, the more tools required.

The basic set of tools is called **Phase I** and will perform the Procedures so marked. The next degree of difficulty or proficiency, whichever, calls for **Phase II** tools and **Phase III** tools include just about everything you would ever need for a VW. Mostly the tool scene depends on just how independent you wish to become from the service organizations and garages. With the tool lists are basic spares kits which you should have with you in the car at all times, a different bunch for each Phase. To save bread you can buy tools from one of those discount stores that are everywhere these days and are not excellent, but are probably good enough if you only work on one car.

There are rental tool places where you can rent pullers, ridge reamers, drills and even large socket sets—things you may need to use but not buy. If you can afford it, buy professional tools which cost so much more you won't believe but they are beautiful, last forever and feel good. The feeling well made tools brings makes the work easier to do with love. And you don't mind cleaning tools which cost a lot.

PHASE I, TOOLS

Bilstein jack   The kind that turns with your lug wrench. It should come with
                         the car from Germany.

PHASE I, TOOLS (Cont'd.)

Lug wrench	The kind that looks like a crank. They are hard to find but excel. The cross type is second choice
Flashlight	Get a good one with magnet holder-oner
Big screwdriver	18" or 24" with a plastic handle.
Screwdriver set	The kind with a handle and several different blades
3/8" drive metric socket set	They come in a flat metal box with sizes from 8mm to maybe 19mm. Buy a spark plug socket, 21mm (13/16") and a universal drive. The set will have a couple of extensions.
Box open end wrenches	7mm, 8mm, 9mm, 10mm, 11mm, 13mm (1 short, 1 long), 14mm, 17mm, 21mm
Boy Scout or Swiss army knife.	You know the kinds.
Hammer	Light ball peen.
Static timing light (test light)	You can buy a nice one or make one like the sketch. Keep it in a Bull Durham bag. **See Changes and New Ideas.**

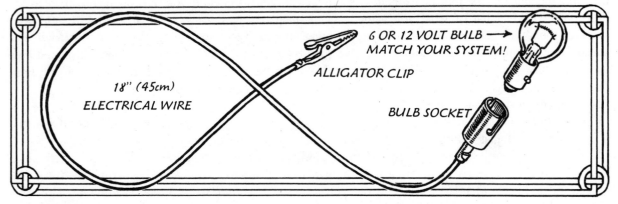

18" (45cm) ELECTRICAL WIRE

ALLIGATOR CLIP

6 OR 12 VOLT BULB → MATCH YOUR SYSTEM!

BULB SOCKET

Safety equipment	Such as fire extinguisher, safety goggles, etc.
Tach Dwell meter	To set points and idle RPM.
Allen head, metric set	In a plastic envelope, all sizes. Plus a big one, 17mm for checking the transmission oil level.
Chisels, punches and drifts	Various sizes of each.
Files	Point file, flat file, half round and a rat tail
Vice grip	6" or 8" with a narrow jaw.
Crescent wrench 10"	Handy to have, even if you don't use it much.
Feeler gauges, blades or set	If you just buy the blades, get the .004"-.006" (.15mm) and .006"-.008" go-no-go blades for the valves, a .016" (.4mm) for the points and one of those round wire type gauges for the spark plugs .028" (.7mm).
Compression tester	
Wire brush	A small one like a tooth brush
Pliers	Two pairs, a regular type and a thin nose
Tire gauge	To check air pressure in the tires
Miscellanea	Two feet of 2" fine emery cloth, rolled up with a rubber band. Never use it on generator or starter. Use sandpaper. A roll of soft tie wire (haywire). (Bus) A small piece of mirror.
For hot wiring	3 foot piece of No. 14 wire with an alligator clip at each end.
Conveniences	Pair of coveralls, stocking cap for long hair, rag, cleaning pan, low stool to sit on while you work, drop light.

Type III Only:
Generator pulley
wrench

I consider this as much of a necessity as a spark plug wrench. There is no easy way to change the fan belt without one and you can imagine what this might mean some cold dark night when your fan belt snaps. You can try to buy one from the Belzer tool person if there's one in your area but it's an easy item to make or have made. Chapter VIII, Step 1, Procedure for the generator pulley, has a description of how to make one and a drawing of what it looks like. Believe me, take whatever trouble necessary to get or make this tool and keep it handy.

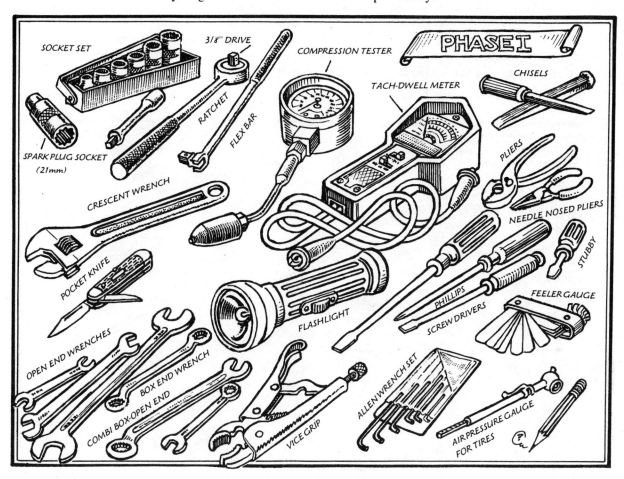

PHASE I, SPARE PARTS

These are the things I wouldn't even go to the drive-in without:

Spark plugs

When you do the 3,000 mile maintenance gig get your plugs, points and condenser for the next job or get your second set of plugs cleaned right away. You should have this stuff in the car. I use Bosch plugs and points

Ignition points
  and condenser

go together like bread and butter.

Fan belt

Never be without this spare. VW will not run without one. Buy it from VW dealer; they fit better.

Overhaul gasket set
or valve cover
gaskets only

Really handy and you can replace the ones you use. A set of valve cover gaskets will handle 90% of emergency leaks.

PHASE I, SPARE PARTS (Cont'd.)

Rubber spark plug covers	You'll need them to keep your engine cool.
Oil	Carry one or two quarts of the kind you use.
Fuses and bulbs	Buy a package of fuses and a couple of tail light and turn signal bulbs. I carry a small bulb for the warning lights.

Before you throw up your hands in the face of an impossible outlay of money, I would like to point out that tools arrive as needed. You buy only what you need to do the job you're doing. It actually takes very little to get started and for a few bucks you can set up to do the maintenance work. Then, as time goes on, you can build up the full Phase I set as you do the Phase I Procedures. If you equip yourself for Phase I right away, you'll spend a lot for tools, less for spare parts, and the price of this book, and you're ready. When that fan belt breaks in the middle of a snowy night, raise your face and smile.

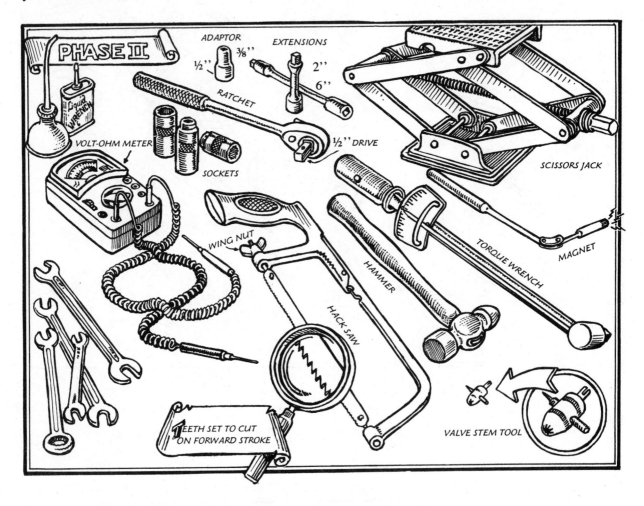

PHASE II, TOOLS

If the first Phase has worked well for you, you'll want to equip for the more involved Procedures.

Torque wrench	1/2" drive, 0 to 150 ft. lb. capacity
Ratchet	1/2" drive, a good one.
Adapter	1/2" to 3/8" so you can use the sockets you have.

PHASE II, TOOLS (Cont'd.)

Extensions	1/2" x 2" x 6"
Sockets	1/2" drive, 30mm, 36mm and others as you might need them.
Box open end	You'll need the rest of these, 9mm, 12mm, 15mm, 17mm, 19mm.
Magnet	Inspector's type with about a 1/2" round magnet on an extendable handle.
Ratchet screwdriver	It's a little ratchet with a flat blade on one side and a phillips on the others.
Valve stem tool	
Engine air pump	
Hack saw and blade	
Bar	18'' bar with a point on one end and a chisel on the other.
Hammer	1-1/2 lb. or 2 lb., ball peen or single jack.
Scissor jacks	Two No. 1049 Auto Specialties Mfg. Co. They use little space and raise from 3" to 14".

Double jointed axles only:

Allen head wrench	3/8" drive 6mm
Special wrench for Type IV only	3/8" drive 10mm 12 pt.

Type III only:

Harmonic balancer— puller	With two 8mm bolts about 2" long with nuts and washers. The type used on Chevy's. It's for pulling the crankshaft pulley.

Dual Carbs Only:

Multiple carburetor synchronizer like Syn-scope or Uni-Syn, Orequay, with a metal tube 2" inside diameter 4" long (2" pipe or tin can)	This is a must for balancing the carburetors on all dual carb engines like the 1500S, the Type III's with dual carbs and the Bus, 1972, 1973 and on.

Fuel Injection Only:

Fuel pressure gauge 0-35 pounds (psi)	Fuel injected engines like the Type III from '68 to '73 and the Type IV's require both these tools to do the fuel injection checks in Chapter X.
Volt, Ohm, Ammeter (VOM) with either 50,000 or 100,000 Ohms	This VOM must have a scale reading for 0-10 Ohms to check out the injectors. The VOM is a handy tool in any case to make battery, continuity and other electrical checks. See operation directions in Chapters X and XVI.

PHASE II, SPARE PARTS

Generator brushes
Starter rebuild kit
Carburetor rebuild kit, extra float valve, too
Can of front wheel bearing grease
Push-on connectors
Can of brake fluid, heavy duty
Tube repair kit
Fuel injection spares to your taste and pocketbook

PHASE III, TOOLS AND SPARES

This is the all-out, do-anything-anywhere kit of tools and I carry them everywhere I go. They all fit into a metal aircraft camera box which we use as an extra seat in camp. With this set, I can even overhaul a transmission, but I'd never do this unless a dire emergency struck and then I'd have to go for parts.

Large puller	Combination type
Torch set	Butane type with extra tank
8" C clamp	
1/4" socket set	Handy for small work
Metric tap and die set	
Bars	2' wrecking bar, 1' trans bar
Clip pliers	
Ridge reamer	
Ring compressor	VW special tool
Electric drill and high speed bits	
Set of easy-outs	
Files	Several
Rubber hammer	

Don't worry about all this crap. You won't need it often and I carry it around because it's pretty and I hate to put it down.

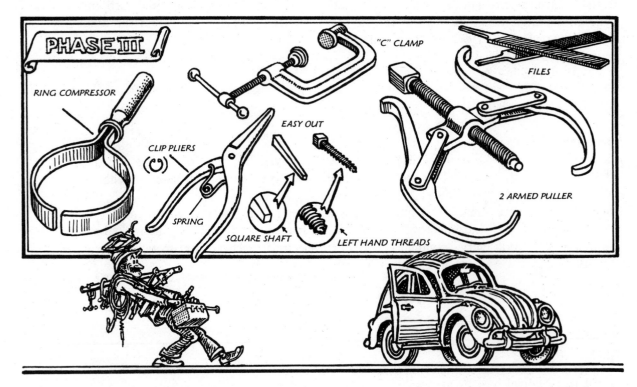

I carry a lot of spares, too: a set of rings, four new sodium-cooled valves, spare coil, spare carburetor, spare Porsche type distributor, spare wire and tubing, a spare swing lever kit. That damned box is heavy! Also, I have a spare clutch plate and discs for the front brakes. Most of the time I feel foolish loading that heavy box into the car, but when you're a million miles from nowhere and happen to have just what you need to make it back to the highway, it sure pays off. Maybe this is my kind of security?

Something that only time will bring you is a nice round candy box full of lock washers, metric bolts, spare studs (that maybe you left out of the engine), miscellaneous bits and pieces like starter bushings and, as they say, etc.

The point here, I think, is that you don't need tools for Phase III jobs, just Phase II ones, plus the extra items for special jobs you're doing. As time goes on, your tool kit builds itself up anyway.

OTHER SOURCES OF INFORMATION

There are many fine books written for and about the Volkswagen, each with its value and place. This one, for example, has no photographs, but there are many on the market loaded with pictures. I feel that a quick sketch of the particular operation you're performing is clearer for the amateur than a photo which may have too many extraneous elements.

I recommend the Volkswagen publications wholeheartedly. They're well done with excellent illustrations. The Volkswagen *Owner's Booklet* is an absolute must for every glove compartment. It will tell you, for instance, which fuses are which, what oils and greases to use, when to service what and the like. The Volkswagen *Owner's Service Manual* is great and if you can get one that fits your car, do.

Libraries are wonderful sources of information. (You may even have borrowed this book from one.) You may be able to find specific wiring or hose diagrams, etc., for your model.

Volkswagen dealers can be very helpful with information. They also have a "Shop Manual" and a "Parts Manual" which can show you blow-ups of various parts of your model. By the way, if you can score either one of these at a flea market or somewhere, jump on it. They are not usually for sale and the artist loves the Parts Manual. See "VW Mania," **Chapter XIX**, for further publications.

There are other books and magazines on "hopping up your bug," on making a sand buggy or a street job and all these have their place. My goal for my VW is simple dependable transportation anywhere in the world I might choose to go. One of my ideas for a sequel to this book is "How To Make Your Volkswagen Last Forever." That's where it's at for me. **See Chapter XX.**

CHAPTER V

HOW TO DRIVE A VOLKSWAGEN

With love, of course—probably the best advice I can give you—but there are certain differences from American Iron that might help you understand what this particular type of Love means.

First, in the Volkswagen, you have to shift—and that requires a degree of coordination between your left foot (clutch) and your right foot (accelerator) that only practice will develop. There are four gears forward and you have to use them all, all the time. No short cuts like starting in second and skipping third. You must use all four gears.

Second, you must get used to shifting on hills and the gradual progress that a Volksie bus makes in the mountains means just one thing—start earlier!

Third, **don't over-rev the engine.** Later models have governors that prevent over-revving on the high side but don't help when going down a steep hill in third. To make the engine run too fast (over-rev) at any time means stretching the engine past its ability to return to the same shape—real trouble. There are speeds you shall not exceed in each gear. Learn them and stick to them and love it.

Fourth, **never lug the engine**—you must shift down on that hill or in town to keep the engine rpm about 2,000 or you will soon pay for your perfidy with a new engine.

Fifth, and perhaps most important, warm up the engine before moving—ninety percent of engine wear happens in the first fifteen minutes of operation. Warming up the engine is a sacred rite, just like checking the oil before you start.

So—here's a procedure for driving with mind and love together:

PROCEDURE FOR DRIVING A VOLKSWAGEN   See Chapter XX, The Obvious.

Step 1. Check Oil and Generator Belt

Lift the engine compartment and prop it up so it won't bust you one. Check the quantity of the oil. Under the mark? Add ½-1 quart (see Chapter IX). Check the quality of the oil: look for water (condensation), feel for grit and smell for gas. If there's water or grit, change the oil. If there's gas, check the fuel pump (Chapter VII, Procedure for Checking Fuel and Ignition Systems, Steps 5 and 6).

Feel the generator belt. If it deflects more than ½'' to ¾'', tighten it (Chapter VIII) or make a note to do it later. Put the hood down.

Step 2. Check Gas and Warning Lights

Get in the car, put the key in the switch and turn it to the first notch and check the gas gauge. Now check to see if the red and green lights or the two red lights or all three red lights are on. If they're not, you don't have a car to run until they're fixed, so turn to Chapter VIII or IX for the GEN or OIL light and have at it.

If your dash has a red light with EGR on it, it means Exhaust Gas Recirculation. If it stays on after the car has started, which it will do every 15,000 miles, push the reset button on the other side of it (under the dash) and make a note to check the EGR valve. (See Chapter VII.)

Step 3. Warm it Up

With the warning lights OK, now turn the switch back to off and then over to the start position. The engine should start easily and rapidly unless it's really cold. If it drags and hesitates, make a note to do a tune-up. Check the mileage since the last one. When it starts, don't rev it up nervously. There's nothing worse to do! Just let it idle slowly a minute, then a little faster to warm it quicker but like a lamb, not a lion sort of thing. Figure ½ to 3 minutes to do the whole job right and you can contemplate your navel for the nonce, or you can get out and look around at the tires or even read. But this is bread, brothers and sisters. Do this warm-up thing and it will make your VW last a third longer, minimum.

Step 4.   Through the Gears

With the engine warm, check the handbrake and make sure it's off. Now you are ready to go so put it in reverse, if need be, to get yourself straight with the road. Shift to low, push with right and let up with left and smoothly accelerate to 10 mph, then shift to second and take a second to check your brakes, especially in San Francisco. At 20 mph, shift to third. If you are in town, that's as far as you need go. The VW sedan will go to 15 mph in first, 25 in second and to 40 in third. The Bus will go to thirty-five in third. This means that for ordinary driving in town, i.e., 35 to 40, you will never get your Volkswagen into fourth (high) until you get on the freeway or out of town on the highway. Remember that! The worst thing, next to not warming up the engine and over-reving, is to lug the VW. "Lug" means to under-rev the engine with a load on it. So if we can't over-rev the engine and we can't under-rev it, what can we do? Learn to feel with your car and treat it right with the correct revolutions and coordinations and warmitup. Shifting down has similar parameters. The Bus should be shifted from fourth to third when the speedo says 35, and down to second when the speedo says 20 and into first at 10 mph, just like the other way: 10—20—35—60. Memorize 10, 20, 35, 60; that's for the Bus. For the Bug it's 15—25—40—70 and 40—25—15 the other way.

As the above was written in 1969, there have naturally been some changes in the speeds you can drive in each gear since then. OK, for the newer Beetles, Ghias, Type III's (most Type IV's have automatic) you can use: 20—30—50—80. But you still drive in third in town in all Volksies. For the Bus you can use 15—30—45—65 and you can go up to 50 in third as you accelerate, then shift to fourth. If you can't do this, please go buy a Ford with an automatic transmission as you'll be unhappy in a Volks.

Step 5.   Driving Tips

The Volkswagen, Bus or Bug, was not designed to be driven fast. I have made 120 mph in a souped-up buggy but didn't feel as safe as at 155 in my old Porsche. They need something else to be driven fast and I don't quite know what it is. I drive my '71 bus at a steady 65 mph and the Bug at 75 mph and that's about it for safety, for me. You can go to hell in your own way. In a high wind, I cut 5 mph off those figures as both types have a tendency to skitter in a cross wind. Near Socorro, New Mexico, I have been literally blown off the road by a cross wind. Try to remember that you're driving a big box with a little engine and you can't crab like you do in a plane. Shift down going downhill, especially with a load. Brake before the turn, not in it. Sometimes, in the mountains, you can back up a steeper hill than the bus will climb in low.

If you have to take a driver's test in the Bus, please practice backing into a parking space before, not during, the test. The front wheel is under your butt, remember?

Step 6.   Safety

The semantics of driving safety become more confusing every day as safety equipment gets more complicated and sophisticated. If safety equipment like seat belts, rubber baby bumpers, folding steering wheels had lowered the accident rate, I'd be for it but I feel it has increased accidents. If your car is properly maintained, with good brakes and steering, clean windshield, lights and wipers that work and all that, then your safety is a direct function of what you are—what you are being as you whistle down the road. If we all constantly drive as if we were strapped to the front of the car like Aztec sacrifices so we'd be the first thing hit, there would be a helluva lot less accidents. One safety thing I do is to mount my spare in the front of my Bus which I feel is as good as having an engine in front of me if I ever hit a cow or something. Good Road...

CHAPTER VI

FLAT TIRE!

It may seem redundant to most of you to have a chapter on the lowly tire but perhaps there are some who would like specific direction in this most common of road emergencies.

I really hate to disagree with the Volkswagen people, but the way they show to change a wheel in their driver's instruction booklet just won't make it. I twisted one of the pressed lug wrenches into scrap trying to get one of the lugs off after an overenthusiastic tire man with an impact wrench had put them on. I now carry a lug wrench made like a crank that you can kick down with your foot to loosen the lugs and I also kick them tight. It's really more a stomping motion than a kick. Outside of that, their procedure of: block the car on the other side, remove the hubcap with a big screwdriver, loosen the lugs before jacking, jack up so wheel is barely off the ground, remove the lugs and the wheel, then roll the spare wheel into place, find a lug that will start with the tire still on the ground and get one started, then jack just a bit more so the wheel can be rotated to get another lug started, tighten the lugs all around, let the jack down and kick the lugs really tight—will do the job.

If you can't find a lug wrench made like a crank, and they are hard to find, then one of the cross-type lug wrenches like they use in tire shops is a necessity. Get a long one and it will make you happy you have it some dark night.

Now all you town and city people who drive your Volksies on the freeway and the highway all the time, close your ears for I am going to talk about tubeless tires. Much of our driving in either the Bus or the Bug is done off the highway, on the desert, in the mountains, in Mexico on little-travelled roads and I want tubes in my tires. One of the first things I do in a new car (to me) is to put tubes in all around. The reason for this is twofold: with the tubes, I can fix my own tires if I happen to have two flats—or even three, I remember, on one spine-covered desert trip—also, on rough and rocky roads the wheel rims tend to get beat up and the tubeless tires depend on these rims to hold air. If you do a lot of off-the-highway driving, I recommend tubes in your tires.

Backing off may either be a function of my getting older or of tires getting better, but I have driven a set of Michelin tubeless steel radials on my 1971 Bus for over 40,000 miles with a perfect record—no flat tires, and the kind of driving I am doing gets rougher. So I can say that I am happy with the new tubeless tires but I bought a little rubber band shooter repair kit just in case I pick up a nail, which I've never used. There is no Procedure herein for fixing tubeless tires mostly because I don't know how, but the directions on the repair kit seem clear. The big problem is getting air into a tubeless after it has been put back onto the rim. A friend writes that a piece of nylon cord can be used like a tourniquet by wrapping it around the outside of the tire and twisting it with a big screwdriver to force the beads of the tire out against the rim so the air will start to fill the tire as the bead seals. He says to take the cord off as soon as the tire starts to accept air—when the bead seals to the rim. The same procedure for removing and replacing a tube type casing can be used for the tubeless type.

I carry a type of air pump which screws into a spark plug hole and uses the impulse of the car piston to drive a small piston in the pump. It does not take air from the inside of the engine but just uses the engine as power. It is called the Engineair, costs about five bucks and has a gauge built in to tell you the pressure in the tire. It is slow but does a good job. With tubed tires, a requirement is to carry a patch kit with patches and cement. Get the expensive type which are all cut, ready to use. There is also a small vulcanizer on the market which uses heat to make the patch but I have never tried it. Here is a short procedure which might be handy to break and repair a flat if you have the materials available and tubes in your tires.

PROCEDURE FOR REPAIRING A TUBE-TYPE TIRE. Phase II

Condition: You have just had your second flat and having the above available, you are about to fix your first tire.

Tools and Materials: Phase II Tool Kit

Step 1. Breaking the Bead

Fix the first flat if possible but if the second flat is in better shape, then you have to change the wheel before you start. The reason for this is that you need the jack free and all four wheels on the ground, as you will see. Lay the tire you're going to fix under the jack point of the car, run the jack up until it fits in the jack point and on top of the tire. Get the bottom of the jack as close to the rim as you can and jack the tire down off the rim. If you break the bead on one place, usually it will come loose all around by jumping on it close to the rim. Turn the tire over and break the bead on the back side with the jack in the same way.

Step 2. Pry Off Tire Bead

The wheel rim has a depression in the center and the bead must be worked into that before the tire will come off, so stand the tire up and make sure the bead slides into the low point on the wheel. Now lay the wheel down outside up in the smoothest place available, take the big screwdriver and insert it between the tire bead and the rim near the valve stem. Don't pinch the tube. Pry the tire bead out and over the wheel rim. Insert the bar or a small screwdriver to hold the bead from returning to the rim and move the big screwdriver a few inches around and pry the tire bead out and over the rim again. Keep repeating this motion until the tire bead is entirely free of the rim. If the tire resists being pried off the rim, you have to lift the lower bead of the tire into the center depression of the wheel.

See **Changes and New Ideas.**

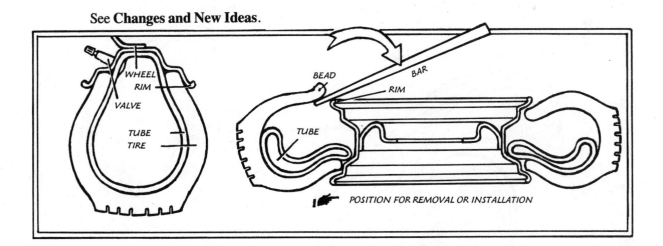

Step 3. Remove Tube

Now the tire bead is entirely free of the rim and you can pull out the tube. Start at the valve stem by pushing the stem inward from its hole in the wheel, then you can pull the tube out of the tire. Don't move the valve stem hole in the wheel in relation to the tire. When you get the tube out, lay the tire and wheel down.

Step 4. Locate Hole

If you have the Engineair pump, open and prop up the engine compartment, take out No. 2 plug with the spark plug wrench, insert the pump and tighten it into the spark plug hole with the pliers. Use the valve stem tool to remove the valve stem core from the tube. It unscrews when you insert the part of the tool with the little ears into the valve stem and twist counterclockwise. Screw the fitting on the Engineair onto the valve stem. Start the engine and the tube will fill with air. When the tube is about the size of the tire or a little bigger, shut off the engine. Find the hole. It may be obvious and it may take a little time. If you have a little water or spit, you can use that to find the leak, as it will bubble where the air is leaking. Mark the hole in the tube with the pencil or pen or whatever, then lay the tube on top of the tire so the valve stem is about the same position as it was when it was inside. Make a mark on the tire at the point where the hole is in the tube with the pencil. Let the air out of the tube.

Step 5. Repair the Tube

Lay the tube with the hole up on a flat place where you can work. Using the scratcher in the tube repair kit, or emery cloth or a file, scratch the tube around the hole for a distance that will let the patch fit completely into the scratched or roughened area. The tube surface will be made unshiny and blacker by the roughening process. Coat the roughened place with cement, rub it in with the big blade on the Scout knife, and let it dry while you are peeling the cloth off the patch. Try not to touch the edges of the patch with your fingers. Place the patch on center of the hole and press it down firmly, roll it down with the patch kit box, and use a knife or file to press it down all around the edge. Use some pressure as well. Lay the tube down carefully with the patch up to dry.

Step 6. Find the Nail or Whatever in the Tire

Lift the tire up a little so you can get your hand in and feel the object, carefully so you don't cut your fingers. It should be where you made the mark or about there. Pull it out with the pliers and check the rest of the inside of the tire—carefully—to see that there was only one.

See **Changes and New Ideas**.

Step 7. Check the Tube

Start the engine and fill the tube again until it is about the size of the tire and check again for leaks. Spit on the area around the patch to make sure. If there are other leaks, patch them, but if the tube is OK and you have removed what caused the hole, you are ready to reassemble.

Step 8. Reassembly

Lay the tire in a smooth place with no stones that might get caught between the tire and the rim. Remove the tire pump connection from the tube and when the tube is not quite flat, replace the valve core and screw it tight with the tool, clockwise. Start putting the tube back into the tire with the valve stem leading. As soon as the valve stem is in the hole, screw the pump connection back onto the stem so you don't lose it. Then pack the tube carefully and smoothly into the tire. Feel it all around to make sure it is not folded or pinched. Make sure the bottom bead is in the wheel depression and start the top bead into the rim with the big screwdriver—don't pinch the tube. Now put your foot on the place where the bead is started into the rim and start around with the hammer, beating the bead onto the rim, moving your feet to hold what you gain. It is rather easy so if it is going hard, check the bottom bead again. It should be in the depression in the wheel. But that's the idea, just hammer the bead into the rim. It will come. After the bead is in the rim, make sure the valve stem is sticking straight out of the hole in the wheel and make the adjustment by sliding the tire around until it is straight, then start the engine and pump the tire up to the required pressure. Make sure that you didn't pick up any rocks or brush on the back of the wheel while you were pounding on it. When the tire is up, check the valve stem for leaks with spit.

Replace wheel and get moving.

Fixing your own tires is purely an emergency measure, but if the price of fixing flats keeps going up, it might again be economically feasible. I used to fix a couple a year, but when I did, it was a flat out emergency or I was broke.

TUBELESS TIRES

If your tires don't use tubes, the majority now-a-days, and one of them develops a leak, you can buy a rubber band shooter repair kit in an auto parts store and fill the leak. One of the brand names of this stuff is "Flat Tire." If shooting rubber bands into the leak doesn't work, do the procedure for the tube-type tire to remove the tire from the wheel and take it to your nearest gas station to have it repaired. It's a good idea to take it **immediately**—not space it—so as to have a repaired tire in case of another flat.

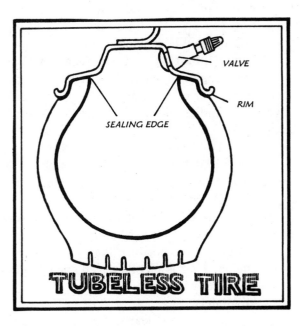

CHAPTER VII

ENGINE STOPS OR WON'T START AND ORIENTATION

ENGINE COMPARTMENT ORIENTATION

Before we try to fix anything or get into detail, let's take a guided tour inside the engine compartment of the various models and assign titles to the complicated hunks of equipment that do things to make the car go. A program, if you will, so you can tell the players by their position on the team.

If you know the names and can recognize the distributor or carburetor by sight, you can skip all this orientation and pass on up through the Chapter to where the work starts, where it says: "Engine Stops or Won't Start." Note there is deliberately no picture to guide you as it is the semantics of the engine that we are dealing with. The picture you want is your very own engine.

I know you have only one engine in front of you and you don't care about the other models, but this book is written so that operations on all models (which usually differ only slightly) can be described in the same place, so maybe you're being indoctrinated as well as learning the semantics of your engine - peace!

Type I, like Bug, Ghia, Safari (The Thing), Super-Beetle

The engine compartment is covered with a hinged lid with a hood latch. The back of the car, the rear lid! In all but the Ghia the latch is a push button and lifter—push or strike the button with the heel of your hand, then lift the lid. If it won't stay up, prop it up with a stick. In the Ghia the lid latch is on the left side back of the driver's seat; pull the knob, then go to the rear and lift the lid.

Type II, Bus

The engine compartment is reached by opening a door in the rear. Push or strike the latch to release, then lift the door. If it doesn't stand up by itself, prop it with a stick. The 1973 and on Bus has an additional access lid in the car over the engine compartment. Move the bed, roll back the mat and there you are—the finest idea any VW access engineer has had. Turn the two handles a quarter turn, lift and you're looking down at your engine—Hooray! I want one like that.

Type III, Fast/Squareback, Sedan and Variant

Your engine is under a lid at the rear of the car—in the trunk in the sedan and under all that crap in the rear of the wagon. Open the trunk or the rear access door, roll back the mat, turn the two wire handles and lift. Put the lid forward out of the way and you are face to face with your engine.

Type IV, Two and Four Door Sedans

The lid latch is above the door latch on the driver's side rear door; pull the lever toward you to release the catch, then go to the rear and lift the lid. Voila!

Type IV, Station Wagon

Move the crap out of the rear of the wagon, roll the mat out of the way, turn the two wire handles, lift the lid forward and there you are.

I'm taking the position that you've never opened your engine compartment before, so look at your engine. That is a Volkswagen engine...yours. Imagine it is a picture in the newspaper and we're matching faces with names.

All Models

First find the air cleaner. Through 1972 it is a large round metal black thing with metal clips on it and thin and fat hoses going to it. It can be on top of the engine or to either side of it; it has oil in it and it provides your engine with clean air. You've found it—OK, remember it. In 1973 and later models, even the late Bug, the air cleaner is a flat or roundy black plastic thing with clips on it and hoses to it. These plastic air cleaners have a paper filter in them which can be changed. When you first look at the 1973 and '74 Bus engine, the thing which strikes your eye is the Smog Pump, that metal thing with a pulley and belt to turn it and a control valve sitting right next to it to tell it when to pump. Now, in back of the smog pump is your flat black plastic replaceable-paper-filter air cleaner, OK? Have you found your air cleaner? If you have, let's go on with the tour.

IGNITION SYSTEM

The ignition system is basically the same for **all models**, indeed for all internal combustion engines. This system is designed to get spark to the cylinders to burn the fuel to make the power to turn the engine, the transmission, the differential and, finally, the wheels. Look to a little left of the center of the engine and find a brown or black round plastic thing with five heavy wires sticking out of it. That's the **distributor cap.** By the way, **Front means the Front** of the car and the driver's side (except in England, etc.) is the left side, OK? Under the distributor cap is the **distributor** and inside the distributor are the **rotor,** the **points** and sometimes the **condenser** but usually the condenser, which is a 1/2" x 1" cylinder, is attached outside of the distributor. There is a bright metal, about 3", biscuit on the side of the distributor with a metal tube or hoses leading out of it; this is the **vacuum advance.** If you don't have this biscuit, your distributor is a centrifugal advance type, like mine.

Back to the heavy wires coming out of the distributor cap. These are the **spark plug wires** which carry high voltage current to the **spark plugs.** Two go to the left to cylinders 3 (front) and 4 (rear) and the other two go to the right to cylinder 1 (front) and 2 (rear). On the spark plug end of the heavy wire is a plastic **spark plug connector** which screws on the end of the wire. You must never pull on the wire; always pull on the plastic connector to get the connector off the spark plug—they just push on. Around the plastic spark plug connector is a **rubber seal** which keeps air from coming out of the shrouding (all that tin). These seals must always be in good condition and pushed into place so as to seal the air in or the engine will get hot. If they are beat, make a note to get new ones and put them on.

Now go back to the distributor cap again and find the heavy wire that comes out of the center. Follow it to a 2" x 5" cylinder which is the ignition coil or **coil.** The coil is mounted on the **fan housing** in all models, but the fan housing changes around some and we'll get to that when we talk about cooling. Anyway, find the coil. It has a center high voltage connection out of which comes the heavy wire to the distributor cap. It also has two side connections where smaller wires are either bolted or push-on connected. You will find on one side the **thin wire that goes from the coil to the distributor,** then on the other side are: the wire that brings the juice from the ignition switch, the wire that goes to the automatic choke and maybe a wire to the carburetor cut-off jet (if you have carburetors). In all engines but the Type IV, the spark plugs are way down on the sides of the engine; in the Type IV's ('72 and on Bus, too), the spark plugs are right on top of the engine. That's the entire ignition system for all models.

FUEL SYSTEM—Carbureted Models only (Fuel Injection see Chapter X and procedures further on in this chapter.) See Chapter XX, Gasoline.

Relocate your air cleaner. It is either sitting right on top of your carburetor or to one side of the engine with a big fat hose going over to the **carburetor,** which is that complicated gizmo with levers and springs in the center of your engine. If you have a screwdriver handy, loosen the little clamp on top of the carburetor and lift off the air cleaner or air cleaner connection. In the top of the carb (short for carburetor) there is a butterfly valve, the **choke,** which is either: operated manually by a stiff wire coming from the front of the car to a lever on the side of the carb (you have a real oldie), or operated by a round thing on the side—see the electric wire going over to the coil—which is called the automatic choke. I don't like the automatic choke on account of it wastes gas and said wasted gas has a tendency to wear the engine out quicker by washing the oil off the cylinder walls, but I digress.

Inside the bottom of the carburetor is another butterfly valve (you can't see it, but trust me) which opens to supply air and fuel to the engine. It is operated by that complicated lever, called the **throttle lever** which attaches to the accelerator cable which comes from the FRONT of the car where it is attached to the accelerator pedal. On the throttle lever there is a **return spring.** From 1967 on (carbureted models only) there's been a complicated smog control device, a vacuum operated throttle positioner, mounted on the BACK (toward you) of the carb. This positioner effectively takes the control of the throttle lever away from your foot—oh, you push OK but the vacuum really decides when the action will take place. This complication was added to lower your engine's emissions. The key is that little rod from the vacuum device to the throttle lever. There is another fancy thing on most carbs since 1967; that cylinder that screws into the side of your carb with an electric wire leading over to the coil. That is the cut-off jet to cut off fuel to your carb when the key is turned off. Note two more things about your carburetor. See the hose that comes into the top of what is obviously a bowl? That is the **fuel supply line** and the fuel goes into the **bowl** through a **float needle valve.** At the bottom of the bowl is a nut and either behind that nut or screwed to it is your **main jet** which controls the amount of fuel your carb has to spend.

Follow the fuel supply line down and around to right next to the distributor where the line is connected to a tube coming out of a round metal device bolted to the engine. This is the **fuel pump.** There is another connection with a short hose to a metal tube which, if you follow it far enough, goes to the gas tank. This is called the **gas line.** There are three types of fuel pumps; one has a little bolt to remove the cap to get at the screen, one has a screw, and one has four screws (no screen).

The carburetor is bolted to the top of the **intake manifold,** the metal tube with legs on it, which carries the air-fuel mixture down to the sides of the engine to where the valves are. Under the intake manifold is welded a smaller tube, the **heat riser tube,** which brings up exhaust gas to heat the air-fuel before it goes to the valves. In 1971 and on, the intake manifold comes in three sections; the double tube dual intake section on each side which is clamped to the single tube section on which sits the carburetor.

Depending on the year your engine was built, there are **hoses**—simple early, complicated late. I will discuss them in the order they were added so you can find them on your engine. You might not believe it but there used to be none. Then smog struck and VW put a hose from the oil filler pipe to the air cleaner to take the oil fumes to the carburetor for burning. A lot of complaints were received from cold country people about their carburetors icing up and that it took too long to get the fuel warmed up for burning, which caused the next hose to be installed. It is called the Pre-heater hose and runs from a heater box to the air cleaner again. The pre-heater hose is the larger of the two hoses to the air cleaner. Starting in 1963, VW introduced the "clean-air" engine which has two fat hoses that come down from the fan housing to the heater boxes to supply air to heat the interior of the car.

Type III and Type IV

You really look down on these engines—I mean they are below you. Find the air cleaner. If there are two tubes that curve up from the sides of the engine and end in a metal box and the air cleaner is also attached to the metal box, you have electronic fuel injection and the system is described under Fuel Injection in Chapter X. However, the metal box is of interest. It is called the **intake air distributor** and supplies air to be mixed with fuel at the **injectors** and burned in the engine. Either on the side or the top of the intake air distributor is a lever, the **throttle lever,** which is attached to the accelerator cable which comes from the front of the car. To the throttle lever there is attached a return spring. If your engine has fuel injection, please move on to the Cooling System.

Type III with one carburetor

Looking down, find the air cleaner. If your air cleaner or air cleaner connection sits on top of one complicated gizmo in the center of the engine, you have a single down draft carburetor and if the air cleaner connection is fastened to the side of the carb, you have a single side draft carburetor. In either case, the carb is bolted on top of the intake manifold and the thinner tube welded to the intake manifold is the heat riser tube which brings warm exhaust to the manifold to heat the fuel before it goes down to the valves to be burned. At the air cleaner end of the carburetor there is a butterfly, either manually operated by a stiff wire coming from the front of the engine, or by that round thing, the automatic choke, on the side of the carb which has an electric wire running over to the coil. The bottom of the carb has another butterfly valve which is operated by a lever, the **throttle lever**, which is attached to the accelerator cable from the accelerator pedal in the front of the car. Attached to the throttle lever is the return spring.

Type III, Type IV and Type II, 1972 to 1974 with Dual Carburetors

If your air cleaner is attached to two complicated gizmos, one on each side of the engine, you have dual carbs. Between the two carbs is a rod or tube which makes both throttle butterfly valves operate at the same time. This is called the **throttle linkage** and the lever in the center (approximate) which is attached to the accelerator cable is called the **throttle lever** which has a return spring. There are two intake manifolds and no heat riser. From the bowl of the carbs there are fuel supply lines which join into one then go to the fuel pump.

Type III

Your **fuel pump**, a roundy thing, is just to the right of the distributor. The fuel supply line is attached to one of the tubes on the side of the fuel pump and the other connection goes to a tube which goes to the gas tank and is called the gas line. The fuel pump has a cover which can be removed to clean the screen.

Type IV and 1972 to '74 Bus

Your **fuel pump** is out of sight—and almost out of mind. It is on the right side of the FRONT of the engine next to the flywheel. If you crawl under the car you can see it. If you need a new fuel pump, the engine has to come out to remove the old and install the new

COOLING　See **Chapters XVIII and XXI**, No Need to Freeze...

The Volkswagen engine is air cooled and the principle is the same in all models. A fan sucks air and pushes it into the fan housing through the shrouding to cool the engine. The location of the fan and the fan housing is different in different types.

Type I, all years, Type II (through 1971)

Find the **fan housing**, that large black semi-circle dominating the background of the picture. The air is sucked into the fan from the front of the fan housing and is blown down through the shrouding. Inside the fan housing (you can't see it) is a stand-up oil cooler through which the cooling air passes to cool the oil.

The circular fan is on the right side and you can feel it—*engine shut off*—by reaching around in FRONT of the fan housing. Sometimes you have to do this to clean crap out of the fan. The **fan** is attached to and turns with the inside part of the **generator** (that big shiny cylinder) and both are driven by the **generator pulley**. The **fan belt** runs from the generator pulley (the top pulley) down to the **crankshaft pulley**, which is fastened to the rear of the crankshaft. The coil is bolted to the left side of the fan housing.

Just to the right of the generator is the **oil filler** and **oil filler cap** which you twist off so you can put oil in your engine. Directly below is the **dipstick** to check the oil level. On the very early models, there is a tube which goes through the shrouding to vent the crankcase to the atmosphere but since about '65 there is a hose which is attached to the oil filler which goes to the air cleaner so the crankcase fumes are burnt by the engine.

Type III

You are looking down on your engine and at the rear there is a large black rubber accordion pleated boot, the air intake to the cooling system. It just guides the air to the fan. It is fastened to the rear of the fan housing which is aluminum and stretches clear across the rear of the engine to guide the air from the fan into the shrouding to cool the engine. From left to right, mounted on the fan housing, are the coil, then the generator, then down and center is the fan. There is an access cover to the rear of the generator. Pry up the clips which hold it on and you can see the generator pulley, the fan belt and the crankshaft-fan-pulley. The fan belt goes around this pulley and the fan is just in front of where the belt rides.

Find the distributor again and look to the right of it. There is a tube coming up out of the engine with a flat cover on it. This is your crankcase breather and there is a hose to carry the crankcase fumes to your air cleaner so they are burned with the fuel. To the right rear, outside of the engine compartment, there is a round cap. This is the **oil filler cap** and if you unscrew it and pull, you find that the **dipstick** is a part of this cap.

Type IV Sedans

When you open your rear lid, the first thing you see is a big air funnel covered by a screen. At the bottom of this funnel you can see the fan, the **crankshaft-fan-pulley**. Bolted to this funnel is an electric blower with two fat hoses which go to the heater boxes. This is a heater blower to blow air through the heater box, then up into the car to keep you warm—nothing to do with the operation of the engine.

Type IV Station Wagons

As you look down at the rear of the engine you see a boot which is the air tunnel leading air to the fan. To the side is an electric blower which blows air through two fat hoses to the heater boxes to warm the inside of the car.

Type IV, All Models

To the right of the distributor is a tube which leads down into the engine with a lid on top. This is the crankcase breather and **oil filler**. There is a tube which takes the crankcase fumes to the air cleaner. Just to the right of the oil filler is the **dipstick**.

Type II, 1972 and later Buses

The fan is the circular thing at the rear of the engine. (In the '73 and '74 models, the Smog Pump belt is in back—toward you—of it). The fan sucks air directly from the engine compartment and blows it into the fan housing. Around the left side of the screen on the fan housing, which goes around the crankshaft-fan-pulley, are some numbers that are used to time the car. Hanging from the top of the engine compartment is an electric blower which forces air through those two fat hoses to the heater boxes to warm the inside of the bus.

Just to the right of the distributor is a short tube with a flat box on top of it which goes down into the engine. This is the crankcase breather and there is a hose that takes crankcase fumes to the air cleaner. The **oil filler** is a tube with a cap and is located to the right rear in back of the alternator. The **dipstick** comes out of the fan housing inside the oval line made by the fan belt.

Type IV, All Models and 1972 and later Buses.

Once you have located the crankshaft-fan-pulley which lives in the fan housing, you have the fan housing located. The coil is bolted on the left side of the fan housing and to the right is the alternator. The fan belt makes a sideways oval from the crankshaft-fan-pulley to the alternator pulley.

ELECTRICAL SYSTEM

This is different from the ignition system and we will only locate the three major parts: battery, voltage regulator, and generator or alternator. The electrical accessories like lights, horn, etc., are discussed in Chapter XVII. The **battery** is a big box with two posts sticking out of the top and either three (6 volt) or six (12 volt) little filler caps on top so you can put water in. Most new batteries are sealed; you cannot add water. The **voltage regulator** is a metal box about 3'' on a side, with places to attach wires around the bottom edge. The **generator** is a large round silver cylinder with a pulley on the rear end to drive it and a belt from the crankshaft pulley. It has a slot close to the rear through which you can see a brush and, deeper, a commutator. The **alternator** is also a round silver cylinder with a pulley to drive it but there are no brushes nor slots to see them through. Inside the alternator are several diodes to convert the alternating current to direct current. Your model has either a generator or an alternator. They both do the same thing—make electricity.

Type I and II through 1971

The generator is directly above the crankshaft pulley, driven by the fan belt, and until 1963 (Bus) and 1969 (Type I) the voltage regulator sat right on top of the generator. In 1963, the voltage regulator in the Bus was moved to the right front of the engine compartment and mounted to the side. In 1969, the Type I voltage regulator was moved to under the rear seat where also lives the

Type I battery. The Bus battery is in the engine compartment to the right of the engine.

Type III

The generator is to the left of the crankshaft-fan-pulley, driven by the fan belt with access through that little cover. The battery and voltage regulator are under the rear seat.

Type I, 1974 and on, Type II, 1972 and later and Type IV

The alternator is above and to the right of the crankshaft-fan-pulley driven by the fan belt. Types I and IV have their battery and voltage regulator under the rear seat. The Bus has the voltage regulator mounted on the front right of the engine compartment and the battery is to the right of the engine.

Things Done to the Volkswagen Engine in the Name of Smog Control

There is a little tank which lives in various places but all models have them. It takes the fumes off the top of the gas tank and puts them into the air cleaner through a hose so that these fumes, too, can be burned. In the Bus this little tank lives right over the battery. In the Type I's and III's, it sits right next to the gas tank up in the front compartment. In the Type IV's, it is stuck in the back of the engine, behind the alternator. This tank is called the Activated Charcoal Filter.

In carburetor models, the **throttle positioner**, a vacuum device designed to take control of the throttle away from the driver has several forms. Look on the back (FRONT is front) of the carburetor and down. Is there a round flat place framed by three ears with a screw in each and with two hoses coming out of it? OK, that's it. There may also be two hoses going over to the side of the compartment from it which would only mean that there are two parts to it. This throttle positioner is not on the newest models.

If you have a '73 or '74 bus and are wondering what all those shiny tubes do that wander around your engine compartment, they're the smog pump tubing and are part of the **smog pump** assembly. The first thing you see when you open the lid of a '73 or '74 bus is the smog pump with the belt and pulley on it. The belt is driven by a pulley snouted out from the cooling fan. The smog pump pumps air with oxygen in it to the exhaust valves to add extra oxygen to burn the leftover fuel and CO as they come out of the engine. Would you believe "afterburner"—just like a jet? VW doesn't say if it needs service or when so I guess you just have to keep the belt tight.

Starting in 1972 Volkswagen put an **EGR (Exhaust Valve Recirculation) valve** on some models sold in California. Through the years, this EGR valve has been added to all models. This system takes exhaust gasses and separates and filters them into inert (non-explosive) gasses and introduces them into the combustion chambers through the intake manifold. These gasses take up space in the combustion chambers (like 10% of the space) but do not explode, which lowers the temperature in the chambers, which lowers the amount of emissions. Models after 1975 have a third red light on the dash with "EGR" on it which goes on every 15,000 miles as a reminder to check the valve. See the end of the Procedure for Checking the Fuel and Ignition systems in this chapter for what to do.

This brings us to the end of our tour. **See Changes and New Ideas A.**

ENGINE STOPS OR WON'T START

This Chapter covers the Battery, Starter, Solenoid, Starter Pinion and Fuel Supply, with some about Ignition and Carburetion. **"Front" means the front of the car, with "left" the driver's side; counterclockwise, to loosen, clockwise to tighten, facing the screw or nut. See Changes and New Ideas B.**

Suppose the engine quits in mid-flight, you have read this, and your wits are present. Glance down at the red and green light area. (In the new models, both lights are red but we'll continue to refer to the oil warning light as the green light.) The car's still coasting so leave it in gear and look at the lights. There are none? Good, this is the Chapter you want. Stop by the side of the road but leave the key on. If the engine is still running at idle and just won't accelerate when you push on the gas pedal, your accelerator has come loose from the throttle lever. In any case, turn the key off and open the engine compartment. Then look at the place where the cable coming from the front connects to the throttle lever. If the cable is hanging free, it has just come out of the little cylindrical clamp that attaches it. If the little clamp has fallen out, find it. It will be in the engine compartment somewhere, usually under the crankshaft pulley or under the throttle lever. Put it back in the throttle lever, push the cable forward and then back into the hole in the cylindrical clamp and let it come through the hole a little, then tighten the screw with the small screwdriver or wrench and you are on your way. If this happens and the cable is still attached to the clamp, check for a broken cable or perhaps the front end of cable is off. See **Chapter X**. See **Chapter XXI**, Other Cold Weather Tips.

If the engine quits altogether, first check if it's hot—you can tell—for instance, you wouldn't be able to touch the dipstick. Also, it would smell very hot. Turn to Chapter VIII on the Red Light, even if it didn't go on. Overheating as a cause for your engine quitting is covered in that chapter for Type I and Type II (through 1971).

If you have a Type III or IV "pancake" engine or a '71 and later Bus and your engine is very hot, first check to see that your fan doesn't have a rag or something stuck in it. If not, go to Chapter X in the Tune-Up Procedure and retime your engine.

This Chapter covers the instances when your car won't start—in the morning, after it has run a while, just any time. First I'll cover the starting system itself: the battery, starter, solenoid, ignition switch and miscellaneous connections. Then fuel and ignition. Sometimes a hunch is the first place to look but lacking that, the order given here is how I would go about finding the main trouble, while fixing the minor things on the way. The idea is to find out what the hell is wrong with the car.

There are three requirements for the operation of the internal combustion engine: fuel, gasoline and air mixed in a ratio of about seventeen to one, compression provided by the tightness of the rings and valves and spark at the proper time. Compression is usually lost over a long period of time as the rings and valves wear and lose their ability to seal, so if your trouble happens suddenly and without expensive-sounding noises, the compression is probably not at fault. At any rate, the compression check can be found in the Tune-Up Procedure, Chapter X.

If your engine won't start, there are two sets of conditions extant: the battery won't turn the engine over at all or turns too slowly. For this condition use the battery, starter, solenoid, switch procedure. The other condition is that the red and green lights come on when you turn the key to the first notch and when you try to start it, the engine merrily turns over but won't start—then you use the fuel and ignition procedure, dig?

PROCEDURE FOR CHECKING THE BATTERY, STARTER, SOLENOID AND SWITCH. Phase I

Condition: Engine will not turn over or will not turn over fast enough to start.

Tools and Materials: Phase I tool kit and maybe distilled water.

Step 1. Starter Stuck?

Turn the key to the first notch and see if the red and green lights go on. If they don't, turn to Chapter VIII or IX and get them working. If they do go on, turn the key to the starting notch. If you hear a click or cluck, or nothing, the starter gear may be hung up in the flywheel, which happens from time to time. Turn off the key, put the car in third gear and push it **backwards** to unlock the starter assembly from the flywheel gear. If the fan belt is turning around, the starter can no longer be stuck, so try it again. If it starts, be happy, there are worse things. If it happens often, turn to the Starter Overhaul Procedure in this chapter and tighten the starter bolts—they may be loose.

Step 2. Battery Troubles   **See Changes & New Ideas.**

Turn your headlights on and if they are nice and bright your battery's okay, so turn them off and turn the switch to Start. If nothing happens except a little dimming of the red and green lights, go on to Step 5. If the headlights are dim and nothing (or just a click) happens, then this is the next step. You have either a dead or dying battery or your connections are bad. If it's either one the car will run on the generator, so get a push to start the engine and make it on down to your regular service station. On those batteries where you can add water, check and fill the battery with distilled water and if it was low on water, run it half an hour to see if it comes back up to charge, then try the starter again. (You need a piece of mirror and a flashlight to check the water in the bus battery.) If the red light goes out and the battery doesn't charge up, have the person in the station check the battery. You may have a bum cell. Watch the testing procedure to keep the attendant honest.

Note: If a Volt-Ohmmeter has become part of your tool kit, please turn to Chapter XVI where you will find directions for checking out your battery with this tool.

If your battery is shot, buy a new one and have the place where you buy it put it in, but watch to make sure they clean the terminals more or less like in the next step as they do the installation. Give a thought to new battery cables at this time. Don't forget to check the date on your battery—you may have enough credit time on the guarantee to save you some bread on the new one.

Step 3. Battery Connections

If the battery checks out OK and you're still having starting troubles, clean the battery connections. The corrosion on your battery is acid and if it gets on anything it will eat it up, so be very careful to clean up as you go. Get out the Phase I tool kit. The only difference in models is the location of the battery but you should be able to find it.

Fuel Injection and Batteries

If you have a fuel injected engine there are a few special things you must know about your battery and how to deal with it or really, how not to deal. To do any type of battery charge, the battery must be disconnected from the posts—especially true of quick charging. If your battery is not up to snuff; that is, does not have more than 9.6 volts under the starter load, the car will not start because the injection system requires more voltage. If you have a stick shift, you will be able to start it by pushing if the battery has enough charge to give the injection system what it needs. If that doesn't work, you have to take the battery out and have it charged or install a new battery. When installing a battery in a fuel injected car, take special care to attach the ground cable to the negative post of the battery and the positive hot lead to the positive post.

Another practice that might damage your tender fuel injection system is that of using jumper cables from one battery to another when your battery is dead. 1974 and on Type I, 1972 and later Buses and Type IV had better heed the same advice about no jumper cables to start the car. It could blow your alternator sky high. Fuel injection car owners had better prepare to have a well-charged battery in their cars at all times, or have a dual-battery set-up.

All Models

With the 13 or 14mm wrench take off the ground strap, the webbed metal strap where it bolts to the frame. Now unclip the battery hold-down and take the cover off. Push the hold-down assembly out of the way. Take the 13 or 14mm and loosen the clamp bolt on the positive battery connection (+), the one that heads for the starter. This battery connector or clamp may be very corroded, so clean it enough to get at the bolt but clean up the smutch right away; acid, remember. The idea is to get the positive cable off without breaking the pole of the battery. It's a clamp, as you can see, and the clamp must be spread a little to come off. Loosen the nut with your wrench first—you may have to hold the bolt head with your vice grip if it turns. After the nut is loose, take the screwdriver and try to pry the clamp apart—not off. Get one screwdriver between the two sections of the clamp and another under it and work it off. If it's really stuck, take the clamp bolt out completely and tap one side of the clamp using a chisel and the small hammer. Tap carefully! Don't break that pole. Here's what you have:

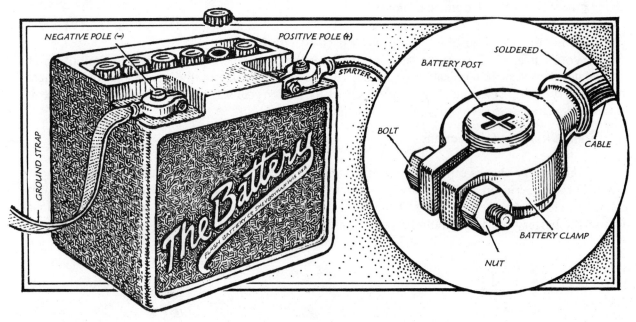

When you get this positive clamp off, remove the battery from the car. Keep it upright! Acid. Don't bang it around. Set it down and remove the ground clamp the same way you did the positive clamp. Take your Scout knife and wire brush and clean the terminals, the one in the car, too, until they shine. Clean the battery poles with the knife and then scrape the place where the ground cable bolts to the frame until it also shines from your labors. Make sure there is distilled water up to the proper level in the water filler holes. Put the ground strap clamp on the smaller post (-) and tighten the clamp while it is easy. Hold the battery posts against the force of your wrench as you tighten so you don't break the posts off. Then put the battery back in the car and reconnect the positive clamp. Position the battery so the cover and hold-down strap go on and install them. Make sure the battery cover is not touching the positive cable. The final step is the ground strap to the frame, but go on to the next step.

Step 4. Shorts

You are about to install the ground strap to the frame and you may as well take this opportunity to check for shorts. Go around to make sure that everything electrical is turned off, then touch the ground strap to the shiny place on the frame where it bolts. If a small spark comes, you have a short. Some wire is bare and touching the frame or in some way the current from your battery is being used when it shouldn't be. If your battery has been running down every day or two, you've found the difficulty. Now to find the short. Go to the fuse box, usually located under the dash and pull the first fuse on the left, then try the ground clamp again. Still sparks? Well, put the fuse back in and try the next one. Try each fuse like that until you find the system wherein lies the short, then get out your Owner's manual to find out which system the short is in and trace down the wires until you come to the bare place. Tape it with plastic tape and try the ground strap again. After you get no more sparks, bolt the ground clamp on securely and you are through; through, that is, after you've cleaned up your mess and made sure there's no corrosive material left around.

Step 5. Check the Solenoid, Starter and Switch

If the headlights are bright but the starter doesn't turn, you have to check the solenoid, the starter and/or the switch. Get out a screwdriver, the small hammer, flashlight and the ground cloth. If you have a Type I, III and IV, you may want to block the left side of the car so it can't move and jack up the right side a little, not so the wheels are off the ground but enough so you can get under the car. Make sure the key is off and the car is out of gear!

Slide under the right side of the car so your head is just forward of the axle (approx.) Coming out of the engine will be a round thing that looks like an electric motor and it is, in fact, the starter and the smaller round thing attached to it is the solenoid. When you turn the ignition key to the start position, the current comes from the switch to that small connection on the top of the solenoid and activates the solenoid which pushes the starting gear (pinion gear) into the flywheel teeth. At the end of the solenoid travel there's a contact that connects the battery directly to the starter motor and turns the motor, which turns the gear, which turns the flywheel, which turns the engine to start it. Now locate yourself with the flashlight. Check all three connections on the solenoid and tighten them if they're loose. Take the screwdriver and hold it across the two big connections.

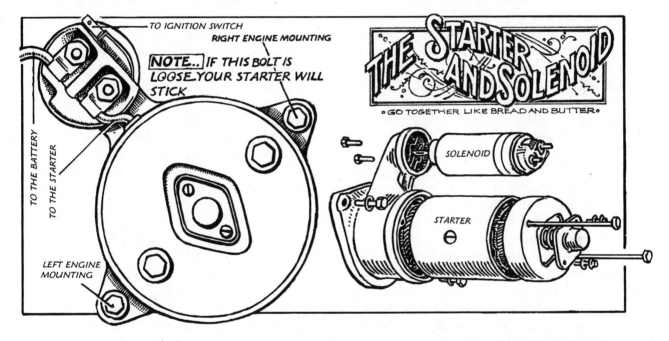

When you put your screwdriver across the two large bolts on the solenoid, you are connecting the battery to the starter motor directly without the solenoid operation, so the motor should whirr into action but not turn over the engine. If it doesn't and you know that your battery is good (headlights) and you have done Step 1, then your starter is shot and you should turn to the Procedure on overhauling the starter in this chapter. If the starter whirrs satisfactorily, without untoward noises, then you can assume the starter motor is OK, so check the solenoid.

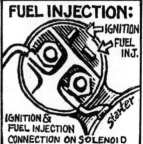

One of the big terminals is connected to the battery with a cable and the wire from the other plunges into the starter motor. The third wire, the one on the smallest terminal, comes from the ignition switch. Make sure: car out of gear, key off.

Connect your screwdriver across from the battery terminal to the small terminal and see what happens. If this ploy makes the starter operate as it should, i.e., the engine gaily starts to turn over, then you have either a dirty solenoid or trouble with the ignition switch in the car. Try it again with the screwdriver. Works fine? OK, take the small hammer and tap the solenoid with it wherever you can reach, except where the wire connections are, then crawl out and try the switch. If this has done the job and the car starts right off, you have a dirty, rusty solenoid that doesn't want to operate all the time. I had one in the old Bus and it's a drag but when it didn't want to work, I just rolled under the Bus with the screwdriver and hammer, made it work a few times and bounced it around a little. It'll work for a long time before you need to do it again. Are you a purist? You may want to overhaul your starter and install a new solenoid right away.

The solenoid may not be getting enough voltage from the ignition switch to operate. This is a peculiarity of older Buses. There are three ways to cure this problem. One is to run a heavier wire from the ignition switch to the solenoid (a tough job). The second (my way) is to splice a wire into the wire that comes from the switch to the small connection on the solenoid close to the solenoid, run the other end into the engine compartment with the bare end taped. When the solenoid acts up, or when I want to turn the engine for any reason, I remove the tape and touch the bare end of the wire to the "B" terminal on the voltage regulator and the engine merrily whirls—then I remember to tape it back up after. A permanent cure can be made by installing a horn relay to match your car's voltage in the circuit. There are three connections to make. Connect the wire from the ignition switch to the input side of the relay, then a new wire from the output of the relay to the small connection on the solenoid and finally, a new wire from the "B" terminal on the voltage regulator to the "B" terminal on the relay. Test the set-up by operating the starter switch, then mount the relay to the firewall with self-tapping screws. It'll save a lot of rolls under the Bus. **See Changes and New Ideas.**

If, however, when you try the switch, it doesn't turn the engine over, you have switch troubles. **In the Bus**, reach around in front of the key and wiggle the terminals on the back of the switch and try again. You may just have a loose wire. **In the Types I**, you can get at the switch from the front. Lift the hood, take out that piece of cardboard up against the dash on the outside and you can see and wiggle the connections. You can jump the switch with your screwdriver from the hot wire to the wire to the solenoid. This connection should make the engine turn over if the switch is shot. If the switch still doesn't work, go back down under the car and make the connection with your screwdriver from the battery terminal to the small terminal. Now if the starter works well, go and buy a new switch. The switch is easy to change. It is held by a single screw to the dash. Just put the terminals on the switch the same way you took them off. Try the switch before you secure it, but it should work well. Throw the old switch away, clean up and you're on the way.

Models 1968 and on

The foregoing paragraph works very well for all models until about 1968 when Volkswagen started putting locking steering column switches on. They started out to make a VW hard to steal and succeeded. The switch itself is much more expensive and you have to have the key turned on to replace it. Disconnect the battery before you start any shenanigans with your switch. The tumbler section is held in by a tiny allen head but that doesn't help getting at the electrical part of the switch. For models up to 1971, you can buy just the switch which has pig tails that connect the same way they came off up under the dash, except that there are two red wires that look alike, so some experimentation is necessary. It is essentially the same task but made a lot harder and will strain your patience. My 1971 Bus sits outside with a bum switch right now because of my own hardnosedness. When they told me I couldn't buy just the switch, that the whole clamp which holds the steering column to the dash which has the switch in it, came as a unit for thirty seven dollars, I walked out and have been nursing a bum switch ever since and I get real pissed every time I start the Bus because after it starts, I have to wiggle the key around until I find a contact where the bus will run.

P.S. Wriggling the key around finally didn't do the trick, so John (still pissed at not being able to buy only the parts he needed) bypassed the ignition switch entirely and put in a simple off/on toggle switch under the dash. This bus still starts by flicking a light switch first, then turning the key to start.

There are two possibilities that we left hanging when we were testing the solenoid connections: one is that the solenoid didn't operate at all when we connected across from the battery cable to the small wire to the solenoid (from the switch). In this case, turn to the Procedure in this chapter and install a new solenoid. Two: the starter turned over real great when we connected across the two big terminals, but when we connected to the solenoid (same as above), the starter turned over like

Step 5. (Cont'd.)

molasses in winter or just tried to turn and didn't make it—then the problem is in the pinion drive gear, so go on to the Starter Procedure. By the way, a loose right hand engine mount bolt can cause the starter to bind.

Unfortunately, most motor rebuilders don't overhaul the starter at the time when they have the engine out. This is the logical time to do the job but I guess they are trying to keep the bill down. The starter is much harder to get out of the car when the engine is in, so I try to make both my starter and generator do until overhaul time, then I do them both to match the like-new engine.

Now that you have bought a new battery and overhauled the starter and the damn thing still won't start, you might like to turn to the next procedure, the Fuel and Ignition Systems and have at it. Smile!

PROCEDURE FOR CHECKING THE FUEL AND IGNITION SYSTEMS: ALSO THE EGR VALVE, Phase I

Condition: Car won't start.

Tools and Materials: Phase I Tool Kit

Note: Fuel injection engine owners: I strongly advise that you go through as many of the Steps that follow as are applicable to your system, then if your car still won't start, turn to Fuel Injection in Chapter X.

Step 1. Check Fuel

Sounds silly, but how about gasoline? Go to the front of the Type I, III and IV or to the side of the Bus, take off the gas cap, and rock the car. If you hear the sound of silence, go get some gasoline to pour in the tank. If you hear a swishing noise and have no fuel gauge, check the reserve valve to make sure it's open and if it is go on to the next step.

Step 2. Check Coil and Choke Connections

Open the engine compartment and prop it, if necessary, so it doesn't bust you one. Look at the three wires that attach to the coil, that cylindrical thing hanging on the fan housing. Push on the center big wire and make sure it's in its socket. Push the other end down into the distributor cap, too. See if the other two wires are well connected. If they are loose, get a pair of pliers and tighten them. If they are push connections and one of them has fallen off, Eureka! Push it back on. Check the thin wire that goes from the coil to the distributor to see that it is connected. On the right hand side of the carburetor(s) is a wire that should be attached to the automatic choke but sometimes it comes loose and grounds, robbing the current from the coil. If any of these were loose, you have found the trouble, so go try the engine again. Don't run the battery down if it doesn't start right away. No luck? Turn the key off.

Step 3. Check Fuse and Ignition Switch

Check fuse #15 in the fuse box. If it's blown, replace it. Car still won't start? Take that jumper wire out of your tool kit and attach the tail clip to the hot wire (the big red one) on the voltage regulator and the other clip on the connection for the wire on the coil that comes from the switch, not the one that goes to the distributor. Try the starter again. If the car runs with the jumper wire attached and won't run without it and the switch connections are tight, then you need a new switch or a new wire from the switch to the coil. It's usually a bad switch. You can check the wire by running a substitute about twelve feet long from the connection to the switch to the connection on the coil. If

Step 3. (Cont'd.)

the switch is bad, buy a new one and replace it. It's held by one screw through the dash so take it out and put the terminals on just the way they came off. If your new switch has push-on terminals and the old one had screw-ons, buy the push-ons and put them on the wires. They simply squeeze on the bare wire with the pliers. See rap about switch changing in the previous procedure.

Step 4. Check Spark at Spark Plug

First check the spark at the coil by doing Step 9, then check the spark at the plugs: turn the key to ON, pull a spark plug connector off the spark plug and unscrew the connector. Hold the end of the wire about 1/8'' away from the engine (not the carb or fuel pump) while your other hand turns the engine over. **Types I, II and IV** turn the engine with the 21mm wrench on the generator or alternator nut. **Type III** turn the engine with a large screwdriver through the hole in the center of the fan housing as in Chapter X, Valve Adjustment Procedure. **All Models:** You should get a spark, in which case go to Step 5, but if you don't, skip to Step 8. Screw the connector back on and put it back on the plug. Turn the key off.

FIRE WARNING!!! Please make sure there is no loose gas around when you make like sparks in the engine compartment (or light matches, either). If you have spilt a little gas, wipe it up and wait for the engine to dry before you proceed. You might carry a fire extinguisher in your car. See Changes and New Ideas.

Once in a while you will find an annoying, seemingly untraceable miss and I advise you (a friend told me) to check out the spark plug connectors. Some of them have resistors to reduce radio static in them. If you find one bad, replace them all. While we are on the subject of radios, that round thing mounted on your late model generator is a condenser to eliminate static from the radio.

Step 5. Check Fuel Pump

Note: Not for Fuel Injection

The spark plug wire gave you a spark so let's move on to the fuel system. Pull the hose from the fuel pump to the carburetor off and turn the engine over with the 21mm wrench. You should get gasoline being pumped out the hose by the fuel pump. Try it again. If there is a goodly stream of gas coming out the hose, reconnect the hose to the carburetor, take off the 21mm wrench, make sure everything is connected, let the gasoline dry, then go try the engine again. You have spark and gasoline so it should go. If it doesn't start, you have deeper trouble like compression, the carburetor, or the timing is way off so go to the tune-up procedure in Chapter X. However, if there is very little or no gasoline being pumped out of the hose by the fuel pump, then you have found a trouble and can proceed to isolate. **See Changes and New Ideas for Fire Warning.**

Step 6. Clean Fuel Pump Screen
Note: Not for Fuel Injection or for Type I 1975 and later, Type II 1972 and later or Type IV. These have electric fuel pumps. **See Changes and New Ideas.**

If your fuel pump is to the right of the distributor (in 40 hp and on), use the 8mm wrench to take the little bolt out of the top of the fuel pump and carefully pry the little cap off the top of the pump. There is a screen under the cap and it may be plugged up with crap. Blow out the screen and replace it. Be sure to get the gasket in, whole. Replace the cap and screw and tighten the bolt with care. Tighten the two bolts that hold the fuel pump down. Try the fuel pump again by turning the engine over with the wrench. If you get a good stream of gas, this time from the pump, put the gas line back on, remove the 21mm wrench and try the engine again.

If your fuel pump is below the distributor (36 hp), try to wiggle it. If it is loose, it won't pump

Step 6. (Cont'd.)

and the nuts must be tightened using a 14mm wrench. You will find it tough to tighten the inside nut with a wrench but by tapping it around with the screwdriver and the small hammer, you can get it fairly tight.

If you still don't have a good stream of gas, take the 12 or 13mm wrench and disconnect the fuel line that comes from the tank to the fuel pump. Put the line in your mouth and blow. When the line is clear, you can hear the bubbling in the tank. If your tank is over half full, the gasoline will run out this gas line by gravity but if your tank is low you will have to suck on this line to get the gas out. If blowing and sucking do no good and the gas will not come easily when you suck on the line, get a long piece of thin wire and work the wire through the line until the gasoline will come. When you're sure that this line is clear and gasoline is coming to the fuel pump, replace the fuel line in the pump and tighten the nut. Now suck on the fuel line from the pump to the carb to fill up the pump. Wash your mouth out with beer and try the pump again.

Step 7. Replace Fuel Pump

Note: Not for Fuel Injection or for Type I 1975 and later, Type II 1972 and later, or Type IV.

If the pump is tight and fuel is coming freely from the tank and the pump still doesn't do its thing, then you will need a rebuilt fuel pump. As it is a simple job, I'll tell you how to do it right here.

Take the two nuts off with a 13 or 14mm wrench. Use a 12mm open-end to take the gas line off. Then truck on down to the parts store and trade it in. Pack the part of the fuel pump that fits onto the two bolts with wheel bearing grease or Bosch grease to seal it, then install the new pump with the same shims and the new gasket. Connect the gas line and try the pump. If it doesn't put out a husky stream, take one of the shims out. Most of them don't have any shims, so don't worry if yours doesn't. A word to the 36 hp people: if you can't get a wrench on the back nut that holds your pump, take the medium screwdriver and the small hammer and point the screwdriver at one of the points of the nut and bang it in a direction to turn the nut, counterclockwise for off, clockwise for on.

Step 7A. Replace Fuel Pump, 1972-'74 Bus with Dual Carbs.

Unfortunately, the engine will first have to be removed as in Chapter XV. These busses have mechanical fuel pumps located on the right front of the engine next to the flywheel. Pull off the hose to the carburetors and remove the seven sheet metal screws that hold the top and bottom deflector plates (tin pieces) on the engine. Remove the connection for the carburetor pre-heater hose, then remove the two 13mm bolts that hold the pump on.

Whenever the fuel pump is off, you should check the stroke of the push rod on the fuel pump, like this: install two gaskets, then the plastic intermediate flange and the fuel pump push rod, then another gasket. Have a friend turn the engine over by hand until the push rod is at its highest point. Now, with a ruler, measure the distance between the tip of the rod and the gasket. It should be 0.2''. Remove or install a gasket until the measurement is correct. The total push rod length should be 5.492''.

To replace the fuel pump, do this step in reverse. But, while you're here (that is, with the engine out) this would be a good time to check the clutch and throw-out bearing (p. 265, steps 1, 2 and 3), and grease the pilot shaft (p. 299, step 17).

Step 7B. Replace Electric Fuel Pump, for Fuel Injected Type I 1975 and later, Type II 1975 and later, Type III and Type IV.

See Procedure to Replace Fuel Pump in Fuel Injection section of Chapter X.

Step 8. Check Distributor, Points and Condenser

Get out the timing light and test the bulb by clipping the tail wire to the hot wire on the voltage regulator and grounding the base. The bulb should light. If not, replace the bulb. Turn the key on, attach the tail clip of the timing light to the wire that comes to the coil from the ignition switch, ground the base of the timing light to the engine. If the bulb lights, we have juice at the coil. If not, go back to Step 3, Ignition Switch. Now clip the timing light to the wire (on a bare place, dig) that goes from the coil to the distributor, pull the center wire out of the coil, put the spark plug wrench on the generator pulley nut and turn the engine over.

Type III: Stick your large screwdriver in the hole on top of the fan housing (rear of engine) and turn the engine.

The light should go on every time the points open. Try it all the way around so it lights four times. If the light stays on all the time, there's crap in the points or something is not allowing them to close. Remove the distributor cap, clean between the points with a rag and watch them open and close as you turn the engine over with the spark plug wrench. If the light doesn't go on as the points open, the condenser is faulty or there's a short in the distributor. Look at the points and if they have a big tit on one side, they may be your trouble. Now check the condenser, as you never put in new points without a new condenser and vice versa. Your distributor cap is off, the key is still on. Look at the points and rotate the engine with the spark plug wrench until the points are fully open. Put a piece of thin cardboard between the points. Disconnect the wire from the distributor to the coil at the coil end. Connect the tested timing light tail clip to the coil terminal and hold the wire that goes to the distributor on the base clip. In other words, you now have a bulb between the coil and the distributor. If the light goes on, your condenser is caput, so turn to Chapter X to replace the points and condenser (Distributor Overhaul).

Step 9. **Check Coil (Remember Fire Warning!)**

If the car still won't start after you put in new points and condenser, your coil may be too weak. Connect the tail clip on the tested timing light to the terminal from the switch to the coil, ground the bulb base on any exposed metal. If it lights, you have juice to the coil. If it doesn't light, go back to Step 3. Given juice to the coil, let's check the coil. Pull the wire out of the center of the distributor cap. Put the 21mm wrench on the generator nut and turn the key to "on." Pick up the coil wire with a rag or something for insulation and hold the wire 1/8'' away from the engine (not the carb or fuel pump). With your other hand turn the engine over as in Step 4. If you get bitten, find something better for insulation and try again. If the spark is bright blue-white or white, you have a good coil. If the spark is yellow and strong, you'll eventually need a new coil, but it's OK for now. But if the spark was a weak orange or there was no spark at all, replace your coil (Chapter X).

Step 10. Check Carburetor(s)

Note: Not for Fuel Injection

One of the things that happens in a carburetor that will make your engine quit in traffic, start hard and generally screw up is the float needle valve sticking but when that happens, it is obvious, for you will see gasoline running out of the carburetor. The cure is a few well-placed knocks with the plastic handle of a screwdriver or hammer handle on the bowl of the carburetor. If the car makes a habit of letting the float stick, then you may have to get a rebuilt carburetor or rebuild it to stop this annoyance. See **Changes and New Ideas**.

In the VW carburetor the bowl acts as a sediment bowl and sometimes water and crud will collect in the bottom of the bowl. On the side of the bowl there is a plug-nut-main jet assembly that can be removed with a 14mm wrench. Take it out and let the gasoline and any crud run out, blow the little holes in the jet out with your mouth and put it back in—don't forget the gasket. In later models, the main jet is behind this plug and it takes a stream of air to blow it out.

If your car still won't start, try the accelerator pump by taking off the air cleaner connection on top of the carburetor and operate the accelerator back and forth. There should be a spray of gasoline into the throat of the carburetor as you release the accelerator lever. If there isn't, then the carburetor must be removed and cleaned or rebuilt. Usually if the carburetor is getting gas from the fuel pump and the accelerator pump is working, the car will start, no matter how badly the carburetor needs rework. The procedure for the carburetor work is in Chapter X. For dual carbs, you may have to do some of this step twice.

Step 11. Remarks

You have checked the systems that your car depends on or needs to start and run and should have found the difficulty by now but if you haven't, you should turn to Chapter X and run the whole tune-up procedure, which should bring the trouble out into the light. The compression check may indicate a serious loss of compression in the engine.

Once, a sad day ago, a real enemy put sugar in my gas tank and nothing I did helped to get the engine started but I mention it because it happens in these violent days. If it happens to you, you have to do a complete overhaul with everything apart to get the burnt sugar off the moving parts. Also, sometimes a gas tank will get crudded up; the only thing you can do is to take it off and steam-clean it with all the openings open. I haven't covered extreme things like this because they make me ill.

Step 12. Check EGR (Exhaust Gas Recirculation) Valve.

This valve is found on the following models:
    1972 Types I and III with automatic transmission, sold in California only.
    1973 Types I and III with automatic transmission, sold nationwide.
    1973 to the present Type II
    1974 Type IV with automatic transmission
    1974 to present Type I
    1975 to present, All Models

If the red light marked "EGR" on the dash stays on after the engine is started, reach around in front of the light (Front is FRONT of the car) and push the reset button. This light will go on every 15,000 miles as a reminder to check the valve. Models before 1975 do not have this reminder on the dash, so you'll have to keep your own 15,000 mile tally. On the '79 Bus you'll have to remove the phillips head screw that holds the cardboard panel under the dashboard (driver's side). Pull the panel back and you'll see a plastic box with a speedometer cable and wires on it. Push the white plastic button on the front of the box and the light will go out. Replace the panel and the screw.

Condition: If the engine wants to quit at idle and you've been through the other checks in this procedure, check the valve.

1972-'74 Type I (except 1974 California model)
The engine should be idling at operating temperature. Pull the vacuum hose off the top of the EGR valve (located to the rear of the carburetor) and put the black hose from the intake air pre-heating thermostat in its place. The idle speed should fall or stall if everything is OK. If the idle speed doesn't change, first check if any of the hoses are blocked or cracked. If not, the valve needs to be replaced.
    1974 Type I (California model) and **1974 Type II** California model with manual transmission
On these California models there is a visible pin on the EGR valve (still to the rear of the carb) which should move in and out as the engine rpm goes up and down. If the pin doesn't move, check the hoses for blockage; if they're OK, replace the EGR valve.

Step 12. (Cont'd.)

1975 and on Types I and II (all transmissions) and **1974 Type IV** (with automatic trans.)
The engine should be running at operating temperature. Pull the vacuum hose for the EGR valve (located to the left rear side of the intake air distributor) at the "T" fitting and replace it with the hose from the flow valve of the air pump (the only one that fits). The idle should drop off or stall. If it doesn't, check the hoses; if they're not blocked, replace the EGR valve.

1972-'73 Type III
Remove the vacuum hose and then remove the bolts holding the EGR valve to its base (right of the intake air distributor). Put the vacuum hose back on the EGR valve and put the valve back on its base and have someone start the engine. Remember SAFETY! The engine should stall. If it doesn't, the vacuum line between the valve base and the intake manifold is clogged and should be cleaned.

To test the valve, run the engine at 2,000 to 3,000 rpm. The closing pin on the EGR valve (next to the base) should pull in 0.15'' (.4mm) and return immediately to its original position at idle. If it doesn't, replace the EGR valve using new seals.

Step 13. Change EGR Filter

Condition: The EGR filter should be changed every 30,000 miles or whenever the symptom (engine won't idle) occurs and you've done a tune-up and EGR valve check.

1972 Types I and III have a cyclone filter that can be cleaned with solvent. Unscrew the connections between the carburetor and the filter and the exhaust flange (muffler side). Take the filter off and run solvent through it several times. These cyclone filters can be replaced with the later type disposable filters.
1973 and on Types I, II and III and 1974 Type IV with automatic trans have a throw-away filter. Unscrew the connection(s) from the carburetor (intake air distributor on fuel injection) to the filter and from the filter to the exhaust flange on the muffler. Replace the old filter with a new one.

Step 14. Change EGR Valve

Condition: You found in Step 12 that the EGR valve needs replacement. You'll need a new EGR valve for your model.

1972-74 Type I, all transmissions.
Pull off the vacuum hose(s) and unscrew the fitting on the metal pipe going to the EGR filter. Remove the two bolts holding the EGR valve to the intake manifold and remove the valve. Put the new valve on and put everything back in its place.
1975 and on Type I and II, all transmissions
Unscrew the two bolts holding the metal pipe going to the EGR filter. Pry off the clip holding the throttle lever to the EGR valve and then remove the two allen head bolts holding the valve to the intake air distributor. Replace the valve with the new one and put it all back together.
1972-73 Type III
Remove the two bolts holding the metal pipe between the EGR valve and the intake air distributor. Now remove the two bolts holding the EGR valve to the metal pipe going to the EGR filter. It's now ready to remove and replace.
1973 Type II
has two EGR valves, one on each side of the engine. Disconnect the vacuum hose going to each EGR valve. Unscrew the metal pipe from the one EGR filter to each EGR valve. Remove the bolts holding the EGR valves to the intake manifolds and the valves can be removed, replaced and everything put back together.

Step 14. (Cont'd.)

1974 Type II
There are two vacuum hoses to pull off of the EGR valve; one from the brake vacuum unit and the other from the intake manifolds. Unscrew the connection on the metal pipe from the valve to the filter. The valve can now be pulled off and replaced.

PROCEDURE FOR STARTER, SOLENOID AND PINION GEAR REPAIR, Phase II

Condition: One of these things is not working.

Tools and Materials: Phase II tool kit, liquid wrench, Permatex No. 2, solenoid, if needed, pinion gear if needed. If you have an old type (pre '61) or lots of guts and a new-type starter, you could use a propane torch, resin core solder (Hi-temp is preferred), sandpaper, new brushes and a new bushing.

Remarks: I recommend that you leave the starter work to the experts at the shop. I don't do mine, unless I'm broke and real tired of pushing the car and parking on hills. I'm going to tell you how to get the starter out of the car and put it back in because that is something that anyone can do. I will also tell you how to change the solenoid and the pinion gear, as these are straight replacements and do not require that you get into the electrical part of the starter. If your starter needs an overhaul, just take the whole thing to the shop. In the big cities you can trade it for a rebuilt one and install that. If you do decide to take the starter apart and change the brushes and clean the commutator— just about all you can do at home, anyway—I wish you luck. In the new starters, the brushes are soldered in place and the brush plate just floats in the space between the case and the cap.

Step 1. Remove Starter, Engine in Car

First off, disconnect the battery ground strap. On the Type I and III, the battery is under the rear seat and in the Type II, it's on the right side of the engine compartment. The ground strap is the webbed one going to the body.

If you have a Type I, III or IV, you may wish to, or need to, jack up the right side of the car so you can get under it. Block the left side so it can't roll in either direction, install the jack on the right side and turn it up so you can get under the car, but leave the wheels touching the ground. Put a couple of blocks under the body near the jack to act as a safety. If you have a bus, you don't need to jack it up. Open up the engine hood and prop it up. The top bolt on the starter is a dual-purpose bolt and holds the engine to the transmission as well as holding the starter in place. The first move is to get this bolt out, so take your 17mm box open-end wrench and reach in front of the fan housing in the engine compartment and find the nut which is the upper right hand one of the four that hold the engine to the transmission. Put the box end of the 17mm on the nut and loosen the nut until the bolt starts to turn, but usually the bolt will turn. Take the vice grip and get it clamped good and tight onto this nut so when you turn the bolt from down under the car, the nut will be held against turning. Put down the ground cloth, put on your stocking cap and crawl under the car with your tools handy. Locate the starter and solenoid over the right rear axle with your flashlight. Take the three external wires off the solenoid: one from the switch, the little one's a push-on, the big one that comes from the battery and the hot wire from the engine. Put the cable from the battery where it won't short against metal or tape it. Put the 17mm socket on the long extension on the ratchet and work it around so you can get it on the top bolt that holds the starter. This is the one you have your vice grip hung up on on the other side. Put the socket on it and turn it counterclockwise until you hear the vice grip drop. Reach up and pull the bolt out. Use the 17mm to take off the nut that holds the bottom of the starter. **Note:** If you don't feel a bolt head on the bolt, you have self locking bolts (1968 and later models). In this case, what you do is turn the nut loose from the top with a 17mm wrench, then use your fingers, pulling out as you turn.

Step 1. (Cont'd.)

All Models: Now you have the starter loose and it takes both hands to get that mother out, so get flat on your back and reach up with both hands. Pull it straight back until it is free of the transmission, find a path for it through the heater hose and controls and gently lower it down on your chest. It's heavy, so be prepared and don't drop it.

Step 2.   Remove Solenoid

Condition: Solenoid or Pinion Assembly needs replacing.

Locate the two screws that hold the solenoid to the starter. Put a few drops of "Liquid Wrench" on these screws and let it soak in. While you're waiting, use a 13 or 14mm wrench to remove the nut and lock washer holding the wire that comes out of the starter body. Take the wire off the bolt, then replace the washer and nut for safe storage. Clamp the vice grip on the screwdriver blade near the handle, find someone to hold the starter while you put the screwdriver blade in the screw slot and turn the screwdriver with the vice grip counterclockwise to remove the two screws holding the solenoid. When they are out, the solenoid can be unhooked from the operating lever and removed. Don't try to repair the solenoid, buy a new one if it's bad.

Step 3.   Remove Pinion and Replace

Condition: Pinion needs replacing.

The operating lever from which you just lifted the solenoid has a pivot pin. Take out this pin with two 13mm wrenches and the lever will be loose in that funny round neck that the solenoid bolts to. Look at that round thing on the end of the starter shaft. It's a retainer for a ring clip that fits in a groove on the shaft. Drive this retainer down the shaft toward the starter body with a hammer and a dull chisel. You will eventually reveal the ring. The ring can be removed with a small screwdriver and a pair of pliers. When it's off, the retainer will also slip off the shaft. Now lift the operating lever and the pinion assembly can be pulled off the shaft. Clean the spiral threads on the shaft and slip the new pinion onto it, making sure the pinion slides back and forth easily. Replace the little retainer, then the ring. Drive the retainer back over the ring with the chisel so the ring cannot escape. Wiggle the operating lever until its ears are on the pinion in the obvious place. Put in the pivot bolt, replace the nut, tighten it and the pinion is in.

Step 4.   Install Solenoid

Take a good look at the back end of the solenoid at the opposite end from where all the wires are attached. There's a slot in the end of the rod and this slot needs to have a definite relationship with the body of the solenoid to operate correctly. The back of the slot should be 3/4" from the back of the solenoid body and if it isn't you should let off on the adjusting nut and change it to that and tighten the lock nut.

Step 4. (Cont'd.)

With this adjusted, you can hook the slot over the operating lever and put the solenoid in place. But before you do this last, rub a fingertip full of Permatex No. 2 around where the solenoid fits to the starter—not too much, now. Replace the screws and tighten them and again. Use the big screwdriver and the vice grip and someone to hold the starter for you. The solenoid is in.

Step 5. Test Starter

With your starter overhauled, or even with a new or rebuilt one, you should test the starter before you put it back in. When the engine is out of the car, I just install the starter in place and test it with a screwdriver, but when the engine is in the car, that's too much trouble just for a test, so crawl under the Bug or Bus and find the battery cable—it bolts to the terminal on the solenoid. You will have to hook the ground strap back up for this step. Take a screwdriver in one hand and hold the starter firmly against the axle or something so it has a ground. Test the motor first by placing the screwdriver across the two big terminals to see if it whirrs well, then from the battery cable to the solenoid connection. The gear should jump out and the starter should turn. Then you can go on to the next step and install it. Remove the battery cable from the solenoid terminal before you start. If it doesn't work, recheck all your connections, then if it still doesn't work—back to the auto electric shop you go.

Step 6. Install Starter in the Car, Engine in Car
(Turn to Procedure in Chapter XV if Engine is Out)

Get under the car. Work the starter up between the hoses and wires until you get it in the hole, push it in with the solenoid on the upper right hand side (passenger side) until the bottom ear fits over the bottom stud. It is a moot point whether it is easier to put the upper, long, bolt into the hole in the starter before you put it up there or to put it in later. It hit me on the nose once, so I put it in later. Put the 17mm nut on the lower stud and screw it up hand tight. Now work the upper bolt around the starter and get it shoved through until it goes all the way in. Then with the 17mm socket tighten the bottom nut until it is just fairly tight. Crawl out and holding a long screwdriver against the threads of the bolt to keep it from turning, start the nut on the bolt. You can't see it, but it's good feeling practice. When the nut is started on the bolt, clamp the vice grip on it, but not so far forward that the nut cannot go flush. Crawl down below again, put the 17mm socket on the long extension on the ratchet, find the bolt head, put the socket on it and tighten it as tight as you can. Then tighten the bottom one tight. **Note:** If you have self locking bolts, push the bolt in all the way and turn it until you can feel it lock (it won't turn), then put the nuts on from on top. Pull back as you thread the nut on to keep the bolt from unlocking.

All Models: Now put the battery cable and the hot wire from the engine on the big bolt on the solenoid, put on the nut and tighten. Push or screw the small wire from the switch onto its connection. Crawl back out, reach in and take the vice grip off, put the 17mm box end on and give the nut a final tightening. You're through. Don't forget to hook up the battery ground strap. **Note:** Fuel Injection models have an extra small wire to the solenoid.

CHAPTER VIII

RED LIGHT ON!

(GENERATOR OR ALTERNATOR)

This chapter is about the electrical system, the generator (or alternator) and the voltage regulator; the equipment which is in question when the generator red light goes on.

Type I through the years, Type II through 1971.

The crankshaft pulley on the back end of the crankshaft drives a "V" belt which drives the pulley on the generator (or alternator) which drives the generator (or alternator) itself, making juice for the battery and lights. On the same shaft that goes through the generator (or alternator) is bolted a fan which rotates in the fan housing and pushes the air through the engine and the oil cooler to carry away the heat made by the operation of the engine.

You have also been referred to this chapter if the engine stops running and is hot as hell when you open the back compartment.

Type II 1972 and later, Type III and Type IV

The cooling air for the engine is supplied by a fan attached directly to the end of the crankshaft. Around the diameter of the crankshaft pulley there is a belt running to the generator (or alternator). This means that the belt which drives the generator (or alternator) has nothing whatever to do with the cooling; it has only to do with making electricity for the car. So if you're the proud owner of one of these models, please temper all the following remarks with this knowledge. Your generator or alternator has nothing to do with the cooling.

All Models

A generator produces direct current (DC). An alternator produces alternating current (AC) and changes it to DC. Alternators were put on Type I's in 1973, on Type II's in 1973, never on Type III's and Type IV's have always had them. If your car has an alternator, some of the following procedures apply to you and some don't. They are marked to guide you.

When the generator light goes on while you're driving, something is wrong in the electrical system. This dash light may be green, may say "GEN" or may have a picture of a battery.

In order to have this warning system in operation, the red light itself must be operating, so the first procedure has to do with the circuit repairs necessary to get the red light to go on when the key is turned to the first notch.

Note: If the red light should ever stay on when the ignition key has been shut off, then action is indicated right now! Your regulator is shot and is trying to make the generator (or alternator) run like a motor. This will ruin your battery charge. Get a screwdriver, run to the rear of the car, open the compartment and find the regulator (in the Type I since 1969 and all Types III and IV it's under the rear seat). Take the hot wire (B+) off the voltage regulator with the screwdriver or pull it off if it's a push-on. If you have to drive the car, you can usually reconnect, start the motor and make it to VW for a new regulator. Work fast.

This little panicky thing can happen on new models without the voltage regulator being shot. With nothing wrong with anything, the generator red light stays on after the key is turned off. If this happens, turn the engine over with the key, then turn it off again—no red light? OK, but if the red light is still on with the key off, you must disconnect the regulator from the battery as it says. The new models all have push-on connectors, so it's easy.

If you are the owner of an older model Type II (bus) that suffers from a dimly glowing red light at night when the lights are on, it's nothing more than high resistance in the wire running from front to back. Don't worry about it. It has been suggested to paint the glass above the light with red fingernail polish.

PROCEDURE TO CHECK AND REPAIR THE RED LIGHT (GENERATOR OR ALTERNATOR) CIRCUIT, Phase I

FRONT means the front of the car with LEFT the driver's side.

Condition: The red (GEN) light does not go on when the ignition key is turned to the ON position, the first notch.

Tools and Materials: A screwdriver and a new bulb, if needed.

Step 1. Check Connections and Bulb

If neither the red nor the green (oil) light goes on when you turn the key ON, try to start the car. If it won't start, check the water level in the battery. If it's low, top it up. Still won't start? Your switch is probably defunct, so turn to Chapter VII, Fuel and Ignition System Procedure, Step 3, to check the switch. If the green light goes on but the red light doesn't, check fuse #15. Fuse OK? Find the voltage regulator. In the older models it's on top of the generator. In the Bus since 1963 it's bolted to the engine compartment to the right of the engine. In the 12 volt Types I, III and IV, it's under the rear seat next to the battery. There are four connections to the regulator: two that go to the generator, one big one (the hot wire) and the one we seek, marked 61, a thin wire that heads for the front of the car. This is the red light wire and is usually a push-on. When the regulator is on the generator, it is the rear connection on the right side. If it has fallen off or is loose, you have found the trouble so put it on tight. Leave the key ON and if the red light is still not on, pull the red light wire (61) off the regulator and ground it. If it goes on this time you have bad news; your regulator is shot or is not grounded. Tighten the screws that hold the regulator to the generator or to the car body, replace the wire on its terminal and try again. Still no red light? There's one more thing to try before we replace the regulator. Your generator brushes may not be touching the commutator.

Type I(All) and Type II(through 1971). Models with alternators, skip to **All Models.**

Find the generator; it is the big silver cylinder with a pulley and a belt which turns the pulley. In front of the pulley there are two slots, one to left of center and one 180 degrees to the right. In the Type III's the generator is to the left of center and you can only get to the upper slot. Leave the key on and the wire in place. In these slots there are some carbon things with springs holding them down. They have pigtails screwed to the holder. These are the brushes and if they aren't touching the thing they ride on, the red light won't go on. Look at the brushes and springs. Is one of the springs broken? Are the springs touching the metal holder and not holding the brushes down? If they are worn and beat up, you should turn to the Generator Procedure and do something. But for now, push them down and see if the red light goes on when you do. You can only do one brush in the Type III. If you suspect the bottom brush, turn to the Generator Procedure. If they have contact with the commutator and the other things are all like they were, your regulator is shot, so turn to the Regulator Procedure and do the thing. Sometimes this poor contact with the commutator will happen in a rebuilt generator before the brushes have had a chance to seat. Now go back and make sure by pulling the red light wire off the regulator and grounding it. It lights up? New regulator!

All Models
Let's get back to less expensive ideas, like a burned out bulb. If the light does not go on when

you ground the red light wire with the key ON, then the bulb is burned out or the wire is faulty, probably near the ends, so look at the wire and the connector. It's probably a bad bulb, so buy one to fit your car and install it. The bulb socket pushes into the front of the speedometer. Pull the bulb socket out, hold it in one hand, push the old bulb in, twist it counterclockwise and pull it out. Insert the new bulb, push it in and twist clockwise, then push the bulb socket into its place in front of the speedometer.

A loose battery connection can keep the lights on. Tighten or remove and clean the connections. Turn to Chapter VII, Step 3, Battery Connections, if you're not sure what to do.

PROCEDURE FOR CHECKING COOLING, FAN AND GENERATOR (OR ALT) SYSTEM

Condition: You've been blowing and going down the highway when, of a sudden, the red (GEN) light flashes on.

Step 1. Check Belt and Pulleys, Type I (All) and Type II (through 1971)

If it flashes off, then on, then off and like that, you can hunt a good place to get off the road but if it goes on and stays on, shut the engine off and coast to the first stopping place. Read this: if it's dark, get your flashlight, go to the back, open the engine compartment and prop it up. If you hadn't immediately noticed the red light, the engine will be very hot, but check the fan belt, probably the trouble. A slipping fan belt is shiny. If the belt is broken, turn to the Procedure for Replacing and/or Tightening the Fan Belt in this chapter and have at. If, however, the belt isn't broken but is just very loose, check the crankshaft pulley. Once in a blue moon, this mother will break and give you a piece of trouble. It is two pieces of pressed steel and breaks in the weld area. You'll find the procedure for removing and installing this pulley further on in this chapter. If it is broken, you CAN NOT run the car. Push it to a safe place, lock it up and go get a puller and a new pulley. You don't need a tow truck, it's something *you* can do. The pulley on the generator also breaks very occasionally. This, again, is a simple replacement you can do. Get a new pulley and put it on per the Procedure for Replacing and/or Tightening the Fan Belt. If the belt is tight (1/2" to 3/4" deflection) and the engine is not hot, go on to Step 2. If the engine is hot, go to Step 3.

Check Belt, Types III and IV and 1972 and later Bus

If the red light (Gen) flickers or goes on and stays on, please remain cool and pull off at the next place to stop. If it's dark, get your flashlight, go to the rear and open the engine compartment. If you don't know how, turn to Chapter VII, Orientation. When the compartment is open, check the generator or alternator belt. In the Type III's, you have to pry the access lid clips off and open the generator access lid to get at the belt. If the belt is broken, turn to Procedure for Replacing or Tightening the Fan Belt in this Chapter and have at. If the belt is loose—deflects more than 3/4", then do the same. (A slipping belt is shiny.) If the belt is good and tight, then go on to Step 2, you have generator (alternator) or regulator problems. However, in these models this belt has nothing to do with cooling your engine, so you can drive without this belt. For instance, if you don't have a spare belt (Impossible, you say), you can clean all the parts of the old belt out of the pulleys so they don't get into the cooling system and drive to a parts house for a new belt, or even drive home and wait until morning as long as your battery is strong, then go get one.

Step 2. Check Generator (Not for Alternators)

Note: **Dual Carburetors and Fuel Injection:** Have a friend step on the accelerator pedal to raise the rpm as it's easier than messing with the idle adjustment. All the rest of the procedure for checking the generator is the same.

If you have long hair, please get out your stocking cap and tuck your hair into it. Start the engine to reaffirm that the red light is still on, first, before you start it. Then after it is running, tighten

Step 2. (Cont'd.)

the idle screw on the carburetor with a screwdriver so the engine will run fairly fast, about 1,000 rpm. (It's a screw on the accelerator of the carburetor.) You're going to be working around a rapidly turning pulley and belt, so put your cautious head on. Look at the generator for a minute and you'll see two long slits at the end nearest the pulley. In those slits, one on each side, are the generator brushes which run on the commutator. Carefully put your finger in the slit, locate the brush and push on it, repeat on the other side. On the Type III, you can only get to one brush for this test. If this starts the brushes sparking on the commutator, which they are supposed to do, check the red light again as it will probably now be out. If this simple thing starts the generator working, you can go on your way knowing that your generator needs an overhaul. If nothing changes when you push on the brushes, get out your little piece of sandpaper—*sandpaper*, not emery cloth—cut a narrow strip and fit it over the end of a slender piece of wood. Don't use a pencil as the graphite will really foul up the commutator. An orange stick is perfect. Now stick this assembly into the slot on the left side and clean the commutator with the sandpaper. It'll take a little practice to get the sandpaper in the right place. If you are in doubt at all, shut off the engine, find the right place to put the sand-paper with the flashlight, then start it again and clean the commutator as shiny as you can. Now push on the brushes again, with the stick if you prefer, to see if the generator starts sparking. Rev up the engine a few times and check the red light. If it goes out after this treatment, you can go your way contemplating the generator job. If this hasn't helped, turn to the Generator Procedure in this chapter and run as much of Step 1 as you can. In daylight, your battery will carry you most all day but at night, three or four hours is about all a good battery will run you. I have made a thousand-mile trip with my generator caput by driving in the day and getting quick charges at service stations. These last are real hard on the battery, by the way. The red light will be on all the time so check your fan belt and pulleys occasionally if you run the car this way.

Note: The regulator checking methods are in Step 1 of the Procedure for Checking Regulator and Generator in this chapter.

Step 3. Check Cause of Heating

Condition: A very hot engine without the red light going on. When you open the engine compartment, the engine smells and feels hot.

Type III and Type IV and 1972 and later Bus
As the fan belt doesn't run the cooling fan on the Types III and IV, overheating is probably caused by the engine being out of tune so turn to Chapter X and run a tune-up which includes a compression check. Also look for anything clogging up the fan area like a piece of paper or rag. If it's heating badly, you're probably due for an overhaul, Chapter XV.

Type I (All) and Type II (through 1971)
First, check the generator belt tension. If the belt deflects more than 1/2" to 3/4", turn to the fan belt procedure and tighten the belt. Look at the surface where it runs on the pulley. If it's shiny and has obviously been slipping, tighten it. Now with the belt tight, if the engine still overheats, you have a dirty engine. So, with key off, reach around in front of the fan housing where the fan is attached to the generator to see if there's paper or other crap in the fan. I once found a whole piece of newspaper in a guy's fan. Another time, the insulation they used to put around the gas tank fell into my fan. I had to pull the engine to get it all out. One other reason for overheating is that the engine's not running properly—it's missing or is out of time. Turn to Chapter X and run a tune-up which includes a compression check, from which you can decide when to overhaul the engine. If it's heating badly, I'd do it soonest, Chapter XV.

PROCEDURE FOR CHECKING REGULATOR AND GENERATOR (OR ALTERNATOR) PLUS A MINOR GENERATOR REPAIR, Phase I

Condition: You suspect that your generator or regulator is not working properly because the red light is acting up or from other indications, such as dim lights at night, battery goes dead often, you have a high whine or the car won't start.

Tools and Materials: Phase I tool kit, sandpaper, wooden stick, new brushes, ice pick.

Step 1. Diagnostic Things

(A) If you have been picking up a high whine from your engine that was never there before and it's getting louder and louder.
Type I (All) and Type II (through 1971)
Get out the spark plug wrench and the medium screwdriver. Loosen the fan belt (see the Procedure in this chapter if you don't know how), reach around in front of the generator where the fan is and find that big nut with your right hand while you grab the generator pulley with the other and wiggle. If there is any movement at all, you are losing one of the two bearings that the fan and generator run in and will need a major generator overhaul, specifying a new bearing, right away. Tighten the fan belt.
Type III and Type IV and 1972 and later Bus
Take the fan belt off the generator or alternator and crankshaft pulley and run the engine. If the noise stops with this, one or both of your generator or alternator bearings are caput and you'll need a major generator overhaul.
All Models
(B) If your red light doesn't go out until a high rpm is reached, try Step 2.

(C) You can check the generator no-load voltage with the timing light. Disconnect the hot wire from the voltage regulator (B+, 51). It's the big one. Start the engine, ground the light to the generator, then rev the engine. The light should be dim at idle and quite bright at high rpm (7.5 to 8 volts, if you want to connect a voltmeter). If you don't get any light at all, either the regulator or the generator is shot and the next item will separate the goat from the sheep. If you get a very dim light, run Step 2.

If there are two wires attached to the battery connection of the voltage regulator (terminal B+, 51) as many Type I's have, take them both off but you will have to hold them together with tape or a clothespin in order to start the engine.

(D) **Condition:** Red light (Gen) is on when the car is running. Get the timing light, disconnect the two wires to the generator from the regulator. Clip the timing light onto the heavier of these two (D+, Armature), start the engine, ground both the base of the light and the thinner wire (DF, Field) to the generator. The engine should be just a little above normal idle as at high rpm you will burn out the bulb. If the light does its thing nice and bright, your regulator is gone, so replace it. If the light doesn't go on, check the whole connection scene over, run the engine up to a higher rpm with the screw on the accelerator lever and try it again. Still no light? Your generator is bad and will need a major overhaul but try Step 2 anyway—you might just fix it.

(E) Here's another test to check your regulator. It involves an old car ammeter, 6 volt or 12 volt to match your car and maybe a spare bulb for your timing light. With the engine off, disconnect the hot wire from the regulator and clip the jumper wire from the terminal (B+) to one post on the ammeter. Clip the wire from the timing light to the other post of the ammeter. Now start the engine. Touch the wire you took off the terminal on the regulator (B+) to the base of your light. If the ammeter is right, it should read zero at idle. Turn on the headlights, the radio, the windshield wipers and like that, then go back to the engine and hold the base of the timing light to the wire with one hand and rev the engine with the other. The ammeter should go to the plus side and read some amps— it's not important what. Now let the engine drop back slowly and watch the ammeter. It should go

Step 1. (Cont'd.)

down past zero to minus as the battery tries to pick up the load through the generator, then the cut-out switch in the regulator should act and the ammeter should return to zero. If the ammeter does not show any charge rate at all, the regulator is defective, so replace it. If the cut-out isn't working right as shown by the above test, I would replace the regulator even if the other circuits are working.

Note: If you have a VOM, a Volt Ohmmeter, turn to Chapter XVI, "How to Use a Volt Ohmmeter," for Generator Alternator checks.

Step 2. Minor Generator Overhaul, Generator in Car (Not for Alternator)

The brushes in the Volkswagen can be changed with the generator in the car. It's a real bear in the Bus. But this is what you need to do to get going again.

Get out the thin-nosed pliers, the small screwdriver, the new brushes, the flashlight, the wooden stick (a doctor's tongue depressor, a popsicle stick, whatever your habits acquire), the sandpaper and let's go.

Get the old brushes (which consist of a piece of graphite and a pigtail) out by unscrewing the screw on the pigtail and working them past the brush spring. Don't hurt these brush springs as the **damn** generator might have to come out to change them. Just push them out of the way so they **hang up**, then pull the old brushes out with the thin-nosed pliers. It's a real tight fit in the old gen-**erators**. Anyway, get the old brushes out. Tear or cut a strip from your sandpaper the width of the **brush**. Start the engine. If you have long hair, put your stocking cap on as you will be working next to some rapidly rotating machinery and it can yank you hankless if you don't look out. Now start the engine. Shove the sandpaper into the groove you just took the brush out of; use the hole you can get at easiest. Clean the commutator with the sandpaper until it shines. Clean all the area under the brushes and as much to the side as you can. Use several strips of sandpaper. Now shut the engine off. Use the ice pick to clean those little slots in the commutator, a job calculated to make you mean but

Step 2. (Cont'd.)

get it done all the way around or even twice around if you're not married. Put in the new brushes with the pigtails pointing toward the place where they screw on. Get the brush spring worked around so it holds the brush, then put the screws in which hold the pigtails and you're done. If this doesn't fix the trouble, you'll need a major overhaul.

Note: A lady states that she has changed the brush springs with the generator in the car by compressing (wrapping) the springs with a thin copper wire, inserting the springs with needle nose pliers, then removing the wire. I haven't tried it, but it sounds possible.

Type III
Since you can only get to one brush, you'll have to loosen the two nuts on the generator hold-down strap and rotate the generator to where you can get to the other slot. Rotate the generator back to its original place where the dot on the strap lines up with the line on the generator and tighten the two 13mm nuts.

PROCEDURE FOR REPLACING AND/OR TIGHTENING THE GENERATOR (OR ALTERNATOR) DRIVE BELT (FAN BELT) AND THE GENERATOR (ALTERNATOR) PULLEY, Phase I

Condition: Red light on. Fan belt is broken or is slipping (shiny) or the generator (alternator) pulley is broken. If the red light flickers, it could mean that the fan belt is slipping.

Tools and Materials: Phase I tool kit, fan belt (if needed). (I always buy mine at VW because they seem to fit better. The American made belts are just a shade larger and don't give as much adjustment.) New generator pulley (if needed).

FRONT means the front of the car, with LEFT the driver's side.

Step 1. Remove Crankshaft Pulley Collar, Loosen Generator Pulley Nut

Type I (All) and Type II (through 1971)
The newer engines have a thin shield that fits over the crankshaft pulley. If your engine has one, remove the three screws with the big screwdriver, then remove the tin shield. Look at the generator pulley. It's made of two pieces and in the piece closest to the generator there are two square-cut notches. Put the medium screwdriver in one notch and push it down toward the shaft. The idea is to hang up the pulley so you can turn the nut. Now fit the spark plug wrench onto the generator pulley nut and turn it counterclockwise—the screwdriver slipped?—OK, relax and try to hang the screwdriver up on the generator while the pulley notch catches the screwdriver shank and turn the nut again. Fine, it comes loose. See the sketch on following page to show you what you're doing. It also illustrates the new type of generator pulley.

Type III
Find the generator belt cover (on top of the rearmost piece of tin) and pry the two spring clips loose with a big screwdriver. Take the cover off and take a good look at the generator pulley and nut. See the collar with a flat place on each side in front of the nut? Well, this is what you grab onto to hold the pulley when loosening the nut. If you don't have the wrench or have to change the fan belt right now, try this. Put your strongest hand around the fan belt and a crescent or 21mm wrench on the pulley nut, mightily squeeze the belt and turn the wrench counterclockwise. Here's how to make the tool so you don't have to scrape up your hand squeezing the belt in that little hole.

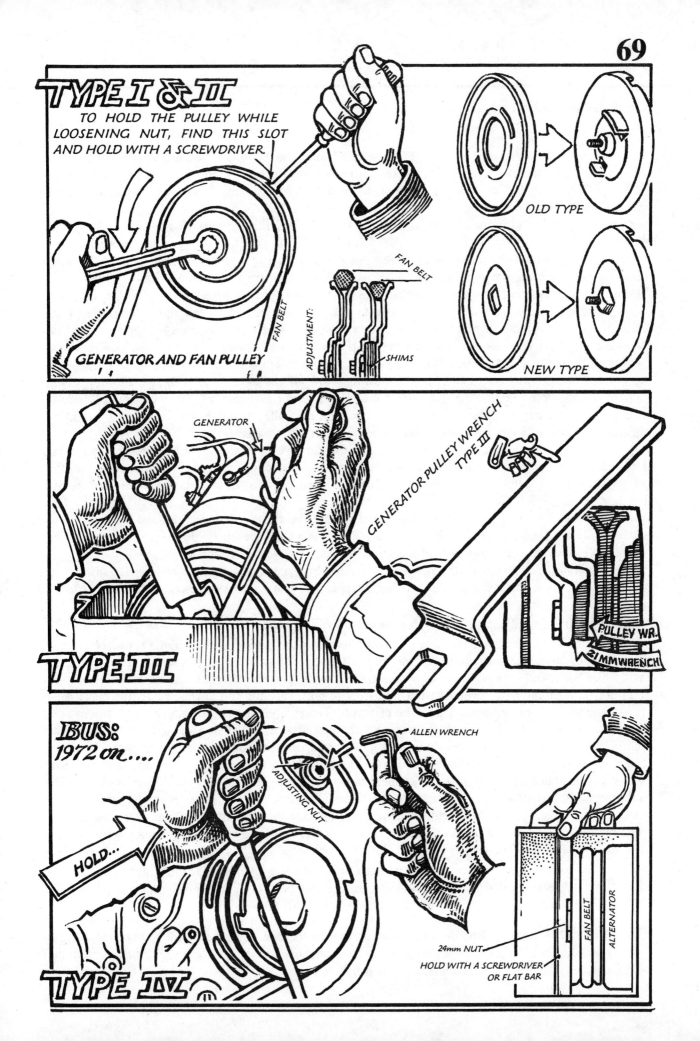

TYPE I & II

TO HOLD THE PULLEY WHILE LOOSENING NUT, FIND THIS SLOT AND HOLD WITH A SCREWDRIVER.

GENERATOR AND FAN PULLEY

FAN BELT

ADJUSTMENT:

FAN BELT

SHIMS

OLD TYPE

NEW TYPE

TYPE III

GENERATOR

GENERATOR PULLEY WRENCH TYPE III

PULLEY WR.

21 MM WRENCH

BUS: 1972 on.....

HOLD...

ADJUSTING NUT

ALLEN WRENCH

TYPE IV

24mm NUT

HOLD WITH A SCREWDRIVER OR FLAT BAR

FAN BELT

ALTERNATOR

Step 1. (Cont'd.)

Buy a piece of flat stock metal, 2'' wide, 10'' long and ⅛'' thick. Measure to find the center (widthwise) and mark it on one end. (The following measurements are for one particular collar size. Measure yours before you start to cut the wrench out.) Measure out 11mm (widthwise) from each side of center and make a mark with a knife or end of a file. Now measure 30mm from the end running through one 4mm mark. Measure 30mm from the end running through the other 4mm mark. This is the area you want to cut out. If you don't have or have the use of an oxyacetylene torch or other means of heating the metal, you'll have to take it to a welding or machine shop to have the work done, if you have the means. Here we go. Cut the lines from the end with a hacksaw until you're 30mm down. Now heat the piece of metal until it's red hot, almost white, and quick cut along the bottom line with a sharp chisel. You may have to heat the piece of metal a few times before the chisel falls through but anyway there's the opening minus an edge, which you can file off later. Now for the two bends necessary for clearing the edge on the pulley. Measure 45mm down from the open end and heat it up on this line and make a 90° bend. Now measure another 15mm from this bend and make a 90° bend the other way so it looks like the drawing. Now all you have to do is file the 22mm opening until it fits the collar behind the generator nut and you've got a wrench of your very own. 24mm is what it should wind up being. Put your new wrench on the collar and a crescent wrench or 21mm on the nut and turn it counterclockwise. See sketch on preceding page.

If making your own tool is too much hassle, the old type VW wheel bearing wrench works fine for holding this collar. It's available through the Snap-On or Mac tool person. Get the wrench with the bent head so your other wrench will fit in. There are two collar sizes so measure yours first before buying.

Here's how to do it with no tool at all: First remove the electrical connections and the two 13mm nuts on the hold-down bracket. Now tilt the pulley end of the generator down so the belt can be slipped off. Use the vice grip to hold the collar as you remove the 21mm nut.

Installation is, of course, the reverse procedure. Put in the approximate number of shims you think it will take to make the belt tension right. Hopefully, you will have guessed right the first time.

Replacing or Adjusting Alternator Belt on Type IV and 1972 & later Bus

Note that Volkswagen up until the Type IV has used the principle of changing the effective generator pulley diameter with shims, so the belt is tightened by taking out the shims. The Type IV is made like American cars with the alternator pulley solid and the alternator hinged at the bottom. The belt is tightened by loosening the adjustment bolt, pushing the alternator to the right, then tightening the adjustment bolt. That's the principle. To replace the belt, loosen the adjustment bolt, push the alternator to the left all the way, put the belt around the alternator pulley first, then start the belt at the bottom of the crankshaft-fan-pulley and work it around until it is in place. Now you can push the alternator to the right to tighten the belt. Hold it in place with a large screwdriver in the left hand while you tighten the adjustment bolt with the right, OK? See sketch on page 69. The adjustment bolt is under that plastic cap above the alternator, so pry it off with the small screwdriver, get out your set of allen head wrenches, find the one that fits into the head of the adjustment bolt, put it in the head of the bolt and turn it counterclockwise to loosen and clockwise to tighten. The belt tension must be so the belt will deflect a hair over 1/2'' when pressed in the center. (See belt note below.) Again—loosen the adjustment bolt with the allen head wrench, get the big screwdriver under the alternator, push to the right until the tension is right, then tighten the adjustment bolt—got it? It has to be right. Too loose, no juice, too tight, no bearing.

Note to '73 and '74 Bus owners: You can tighten the belt as above but if you are replacing a belt, you will have to loosen the smog pump bolt, remove the smog pump belt, then install the alternator belt and then replace the smog pump belt.

Note to all models: Look at the numbers on your fan belt. If it says DA or XDA, you have to tighten the belt tighter until you get a hair more than 1/4" deflection because nylon stretches.

Step 2. Adjusting Washers

Type I, Type II through 1971 and Type III

Now it makes a difference which you're doing: if you're putting on a new belt, don't take the pulley off, just loosen the nut as much as you can without its coming off. If you're just tightening the belt, you'll have to take the pulley off to transfer one or two of the washer-type shims from between the two parts of the pulley to the outside of the pulley where there are others, then fit the outside pulley half back on. Make sure the two halves of the pulley are fitted correctly. There are two male plugs on the outside half, one larger than the other; they fit into corresponding holes on the inner pulley half.

If you're installing a new pulley, pry the inner section of the pulley off with the big screwdriver on one side while tapping towards you with the hammer on the other side. Slip the new front half of the pulley over the half-moon key on the generator shaft (that square bump on the shaft), tap it on and put on the new rear pulley half. Replace all the shims, the bell-like thing, and the nut—just barely, so it won't fall off—and we're ready to put the belt on.

Type III

I know it's not easy working in that little space but you can do it. Hold one hand under the pulley assembly while you put the parts on so if something does drop, you can catch it. If anything drops, please fish it out with a long extension magnet.

Step 3. Install Belt

The idea is to put the belt into the generator pulley (the top one), then pull, push with the screwdriver, use both hands or do just anything to get the belt around the crankshaft pulley (the bottom one). It has to fit well down into the generator pulley to fit around the lower one. If it will not go, loosen the generator pulley nut a little more, spread the two halves of the pulley apart and try again. It'll go, I guarantee it, if you've bought the right belt—but of course you did. (Another reason why I buy my belts at VW.) When you get the belt around the lower pulley, start tightening the generator nut. Make sure the spare washers are on the shaft before you tighten too much. Hang up your screwdriver in the notch, for a turn in the other direction this time, and tighten the nut clockwise. Now relax your screwdriver, but keep turning the nut to let the belt come up in the pulley, hang up the pulley with the screwdriver to tighten the nut, relax the screwdriver but turn the nut. Keep repeating until the nut is really tight. Try the belt tension: note the line the belt makes, then push it in with your finger. It should only deflect 1/2" to 3/4". If it's too loose, take out more shims from the middle; if too tight, put a shim or two back into the middle. Remember to put the crankshaft collar back on if yours is a newer model engine.

Type III

Put the belt around the big crankshaft pulley and then up against the front half of the generator pulley. Use the same number of shims unless you're using a new belt in which case use one or two less. Fit the rear half of the pulley onto the front half so the two tabs (one is larger than the other) fit into the two slots all the way. Put the collar on the shaft and start the nut with your fingers. Run the nut up as tight as you can, then tighten it with a crescent wrench until the engine turns or the belt just slips. Now put your wrench on the collar (or your hand around the belt if you didn't make or buy the wrench) and tighten the nut firmly. Check the belt tension. It shouldn't deflect more than 1/2" to 3/4". If it's too loose, take out more shims from the middle; if it's too tight, put a shim or two back into the middle.

PROCEDURE FOR CHANGING THE VOLTAGE REGULATOR, Phase I

Condition: Voltage regulator needs replacing.

Tools and Materials: Phase I tool kit, new regulator, push-ons, masking tape, a ratchet screwdriver is handy for the Bus.

Word of Advice: Never fool with the inside of the Bosch regulator, just buy a new one. I fixed one once and fixed it so well, in my infinite knowledge, that not only did the red light go off but I sizzled a cell in the battery in about 300 miles and had to buy a new battery, a new regulator and overhaul the generator. Buy a new one! They last long and the only time they need to be adjusted for more output is when you have a CB transceiver or a big tape rig. If so, take it to VW to have the output set with their myriad of dials and testers.

Step 1. For Regulators on Top of the Generator

Hold the new regulator up to the old one. Are they the same? Did you have screw-on connectors and your new one has push-ons? Relax, you should have some in your kit, else go buy some and install them on the wire ends. They just squeeze on with the pliers. The touchy leads are the two going down into the generator. They're held to the rear of the voltage regulator with screws. The thinner one is the Field (F or DF); the thick one is the Armature (+ or D+). On the Bosch regulator, the + terminal is on the right, the Field terminal on the left. On the right side of the regulator there are two connections; one small and one large with perhaps more than one wire coming to it. The small one is the connection to the red light and the other is the battery connection. It's hot, so don't let it touch metal. Mark the small one "L" and the big one "B" (tape is handy for this). Take the "B" wire off first, then take off the other wires using the screwdriver. There are two screws holding the regulator to the generator. Take the screwdriver and remove them. In the Bus there is very little head room, so use the ratchet screwdriver (see tool section) to remove the screws. Take the old regulator off, put the new one on, replace the screws and tighten them well. Replace the wires exactly where you took them from. Connect the "B" wire last. See Step 4, Polarize, in Generator Procedure for Type III's before you connect the "B" wire.

Step 1. For Regulators on Side of Compartment or Under Rear Seat

If your regulator is on the side of the engine compartment, you have to make sure that you have the right regulator. They make four types and each type has its own connections. It is almost worth while, if you can, to have the VW people do the job but I have changed a lot of them and it's just a matter of being careful. They are all push connected and the ground is through the attaching sheet metal screws, a lousy arrangement. Make sure that you have the right voltage, also as they now make both six and twelve volts. When I buy the spare for mine, I go right out and check to see if they sold me the right one by comparing all the terminals and the appearance of the regulator. The voltage is stamped on the regulator. If the connections are the same the regulator will be OK. Using the screwdriver, remove the screws that hold the regulator to the car body but don't take any of the connections off. Now put the new regulator right alongside of the old one facing the same way. Change the connections from one to the other, one by one, it's easy this way. Do the heavy one from the battery last. (See Step 4, Polarize, in Generator Procedure for Type III's before you connect the "B" wire.) Then take your knife and scrape the area around where the regulator screws on and put the new regulator back the same way as the old one came out, replace the screws and tighten them well. 1965 Bus and newer (with the air cleaner on the right)—remove the air cleaner so you can get to the regulator. That's it.

Now start the engine to make sure the red light goes off. If it does, throw the old regulator away and make a note to buy another spare when you have the bread. If the red light still stays on, put the old regulator in the box and start running the generator procedure in this chapter. Keep your cool! You always wanted a spare regulator anyway.

PROCEDURE FOR REMOVING AND INSTALLING GENERATOR FOR A MAJOR OVER-HAUL, Phase I (NOT FOR ALTERNATORS, except 1973 and on Type I)

Note: Type I, 1973 and later: You have an alternator but follow this procedure and write "alternator" wherever it says "generator." See **Changes and New Ideas**.

Condition: The generator needs more than new brushes and a commutator scrubbing.

Tools and Materials: Phase I tool kit, bolt can

I recommend that you always overhaul the starter and generator at engine overhaul time. The Overhaul Procedure has steps for the removal and installation of these electric motor items. If the generator fouls up between engine overhauls and needs shop treatment, it's a big saving in bread if you can take the generator out yourself, buy the bearings, brush springs and brushes (if you haven't just put new ones on) and take it to the Auto-Electric shop of your choice—call them first and see if they will do a VW generator. There isn't that much difference in the work between the American and VW generators. Slow as you are, you'll tie up your car less time if you do the removal and installation yourself. They will put you on the schedule. Also you are hung with the VW dealer to do the job unless you are near a big city where small foreign car shops abound.

PROCEDURE FOR REMOVAL AND INSTALLATION OF GENERATOR FOR:

1950 to 1961 Bug and Ghia, 36 hp with Manual Choke

Note: Watch how they get more complicated as the years go by.

Step 1. Disconnect Generator

Remove hot wires and red light wire from voltage regulator. Tape the hot wires.

Step 2. Remove Fan Belt

See Procedure, this chapter.

Step 3. Remove Air Cleaner

It's the large round thing on top of the carburetor. Use the large screwdriver to loosen the clamp. Lift it off carefully—it should have oil in it.

Step 4. Disconnect Accelerator and Choke Cables

Use the small screwdriver to loosen the screw on the accelerator clamp (that little cylindrical thing in the accelerator lever on the carburetor), pull the cable forward out of the hole. Remove that

Step 4. (Cont'd.)

little cylindrical clamp and put it in the safe. Use a small wrench or the pliers to loosen the clamp that holds the wire to the choke arm and pull the wire out. Back to the accelerator cable and push the cone thing forward and pull the cable end back, remove the little split washer that holds this assembly together and put it in the safe. Now the choke and accelerator cables are free, right? Put all the bolts, nuts and small parts in the bolt can.

Step 5. Remove Generator Strap

Use the 13mm socket on the long extension on the ratchet and the 13mm box end to remove the generator strap bolt, then pull the strap out and put the bolt in a hole and screw the nut on. Put it in a safe place.

Step 6. Lift Fan Housing

Find two pieces of wood about 1-1/2" thick and have them ready. In front (front, remember) of the fan housing there's an air control ring, held by two bolts. You may not have an air control ring—someone may have removed it and not put it back. See discussion on this in the beginning of Chapter XV. Loosen these two bolts with the 10mm box and you can slide this short cylinder up and out of the fan housing. Remove the two screws that hold the fan housing, one on each side, and lift the housing up (carefully, please—the oil cooler is under it) and slip the two blocks of wood under the housing.

Step 7. Remove the Generator and Fan

Use the 10mm box end to remove the four bolts holding the generator plate to the fan housing and pull the generator and fan out of the housing. Take off the fan belt pulley by tapping it with the small hammer and maybe a little prying with a screwdriver. Don't lose that little half-moon key. Put the pulley, shims and key in a safe place.

Step 8. Remove the Fan and Generator Plate

Now you need a table or block of wood that can stand a little pounding and a friend with the same characteristics. Put the generator on the table with the plate and fan hanging over the edge. You are facing that great big nut that holds the fan to the generator shaft and you're going to loosen it. Clamp the vice grip on the shaft on the back of the generator (back, remember) as close to the generator as possible. Put the 1-7/16" (36mm) socket on the breaker bar and loosen the nut counterclockwise until the vice grip rests on the table. The vice grip will hold the shaft from turning while you continue to turn the nut. Take the nut and washer off, pull off the fan, then the shims and collar. Remember to put these same shims on when you put it together or you'll have a howling screamer. Collect all the parts, the little key, too, and store safely. Remove the generator plate. There are two 10mm nuts and a ring.

Step 9. Shop Work

Take the generator and the parts to the shop to have them do the work. You may have a bum armature, in which case a new or rebuilt generator will be better. Leave the regulator on and ask the shop to check it if they will. So work it out and come back to the reassembly table with a good generator. If you do get a different generator, stop by Volkswagen and get a few extra fan shims so you can shim the fan in the housing.

Step 10. Reassemble Fan

Put the generator plate down onto the bolts, put the little backing ring on, then the four nuts and tighten them with the 10mm. Put the key in the slot and slide the collar over it. Put the shims you took off on the collar, then the fan with the washer and the nut. If you have a new generator, try it in the housing and see that it has plenty of clearance. If not, change the shims. Don't tighten the big nut all the way for these tests but tight enough to tell. Get your friend to hold the generator on the table while you tighten the big nut with the 1-7/16'' or 36mm socket on the breaker bar. Put the vice grip on the shaft and turn clockwise until the nut doesn't move. It only needs 45 foot pounds so don't get too tough with it. With a file, remove any marks your vice grip made on the shaft. If you don't have a 1-7/16'' or 36mm socket, see Chapter XVI, Removing and Installing Large High Torque Nuts With a Hammer and Chisel.

Step 11. Install Generator and Fan in Housing

Put the fan in the housing and put in the four bolts that hold the generator plate and tighten them with the 10mm box.

Step 12. Install Fan Housing

Pull out the two blocks of wood and let the fan housing down into place. It should go inside the shrouding all the way around. Put the two side screws in that hold the fan housing but don't tighten them yet. If you've decided to keep the air control ring slip it into the slots for the bolts, then tighten the bolts. You should check this later. When the engine is cold, the ring should just barely touch the housing and when the engine is warm, you should be able to get your thumb in crosswise (3/4'') between the horn and the housing, with the engine shut off, please.

Step 13. Install Generator Strap

Hold the generator strap up in front of the generator to see how it came off. The old bent places should fit where they were so the bolt on the right side is in the open space where you can tighten it easily. Now take the bolt out and slip the strap around the generator and pedestal, replace the bolt and tighten with the two 13mm wrenches. Tighten the two side screws that hold the fan housing.

Step 14. Reconnect the Carburetor

Pull the choke wire through the clamp so it's tight in the housing and tighten the clamp with a small wrench or the pliers, then get the wire through the hole in the choke lever and tighten the little clamp, holding the wire with the pliers and using the vice grip or small wrench to tighten the little nut.

Pull the accelerator cable through and straighten the tube it fits in until it slides all the way into the housing to the hilt, so to speak, put the spring on, then the cone thing with the biggest end forward. Pull the cable end back while you push the cone and spring forward, then slip that little split washer-key over the cable between the cable and the cone thing. This will hold the assembly together. Put the little cylindrical clamp in its place on the accelerator arm, push the cable end forward and work it into the hole in the clamp. When it is through the hole a little, tighten the screw in the clamp to hold the cable end firmly. Try the accelerator to see that it's working properly.

Step 15. Install Fan Belt

Turn to the Procedure in this chapter for this.

Step 16. Replace Air Cleaner

Wipe the inside out with a rag and refill with oil to cover the red line. Put it on the carburetor and tighten the screw with the large screwdriver.

Step 17. Reconnect Generator

If you have a new generator, you'll have to install the voltage regulator on the generator. See the procedure for changing the voltage regulator in this chapter. Then you are ready to start the engine, warmitup and if there are any problems, do the checks you did before. Polarize...see Step 4, Generator Procedure for Type III's.

PROCEDURE FOR REMOVING AND INSTALLING GENERATOR FOR A MAJOR OVERHAUL, ENGINE IN CAR, FOR:

1961 to 1964 Bug and Ghia, with Automatic Choke

The difference in the automatic choke models is that you have to remove and install the carburetor, so after the preceding Step 4, do:

Step 4A. Remove Carburetor

See Chapter X, Carburetor Procedure, for this jewel, then go back to Step 5.

Step 13A. Install Carburetor

See Chapter X, Carburetor Procedure.

The other steps will all be the same, except you don't have the choke wire to contend with in Steps 4 and 13. In the late 64's, you may have two air hoses to disconnect from the housing with a phillips screwdriver to be able to lift the housing but that connection is easy.

1965 to 1967 Bug and Ghia, with the new Air Control System

Now here is another complication. In order to lift the fan housing, you have to remove the thermostat from under the right side of the engine and the air hoses as mentioned above, so we have two additional steps plus the steps 4A and 13A above:

Step 6A. Hose and Thermostat Removal

With a phillips screwdriver, loosen the clamps that hold the big air hoses to the fan housing and slip them off. You may have to twist them a little to get them free. Now go down under the right side of the engine and remove the screws that hold the bottom plate under the cylinders. Or take two out and bend that bottom plate so you can get at the thermostat. It is a round brass accordion-pleated thing. Take out the bottom screw from the thermostat, slide it out of the bracket and unscrew it from the rod. Put it in a safe place.

Step 10A. Install Thermostat and Hoses

Go under the right side of the engine, screw the thermostat back onto the rod, replace it in the bracket, replace the bolt and tighten. Bend the plate back up, install the screws and tighten.

Now for the Transporter Series (Bus), and here we have real trouble. I ran into it early in the game and bought a 1-7/16" (36mm) socket and got a piece of 1" pipe about 18" long. The socket was expensive, the pipe was free. You must have this tool to get the Bus generator out while the engine is in the car, all the way from 1950 until 1963-64 when the change in the shape of the fan housing gave enough head room to get both the generator and fan out together. So I'll formalize it with some extra steps.

PROCEDURE FOR REMOVAL AND INSTALLATION OF GENERATOR FOR:

1950 to 1963 Bus without Phase III Tooling
—to be exact, a 1-7/16" 1/2" drive socket and an 18" by 1" pipe cheater.

Step 1A. Remove Engine from Car

See Chapter XV for this Procedure. Just follow it until the generator can be removed.

Step 14A. Replace Engine in Car

See Chapter XV for this Procedure

1950 to 1964 Bus with Phase III tools, the 1-7/16" (36mm) socket and pipe cheater

Steps 2A and 8A. Remove Fan from Generator Shaft

Do this before you disconnect the fan belt, as it will help you hold things together. Reach around in front (FRONT, remember) to loosen the two bolts holding the air control ring, if any, and slide the ring up and out of the fan housing. Get the 1-7/16" socket on the short extension (if you need the extension—depends on the clearance) on the 1/2" drive ratchet—this is just the spark plug wrench with a different socket. Slip the pipe cheater over the end of the ratchet handle. Put the medium screwdriver in the notch on the front of the generator pulley (front is front, remember). Reach your big socket around the front of the generator and get it firmly on the big nut, which you can't see, but can feel. Find a spot for the ratchet handle and cheater combination that is as high as it will go, like about two o'clock with the pipe out on the handle. Now firm up with the screwdriver on the generator pulley hold and pull down with the cheater and ratchet handle combination. This is turning the big nut counterclockwise if you're facing it. It may take a few trials but it will come. When the nut is loose, take it and the washers out. You can put them down there in the engine compartment, but safely!
In Step 8, remember to be careful of the shims, that little key and the collar.

Step 10A. Install Fan

Put the half-moon key in the generator shaft, slide the collar and the shims into the hole in the fan, reach around in front and get the fan firmly on the collar, put on the washer and nut and tighten them as tight as you can by hand. That will hold it together until you have finished Step 14, then go on to Step 15 and put the fan belt on.

Step 15A. Tighten the Big Fan Nut

Now you do the reverse of Step 2A and you will hold the generator pulley against turning with the medium screwdriver and get the socket, ratchet and cheater, with the ratchet reversed at about four o'clock and push it up to tighten the nut. You can get it as tight as you can hold the generator pulley. It takes 45 foot pounds but there is no way to measure, so put some beef into it.

1959 to 1963 Bus with Automatic Choke, Phase III

Now you have to take off and replace the carburetor in addition to running Steps 2A-8A, 10A and 15A. So run Steps 4A and 13A also.

1963 to 1967 Bus, Phase II

Back to the Bug Procedure without all that hassle with the big socket. Now there's enough head room to get the generator out. You have to run Steps 4A, 6A, 10A and 13A but **not** Steps 2A-8A or 15A.

1967 and later Type I and Bus (through 1971), 12 volt system

Note: Type I, 1973 and later, follow this procedure even though you have an alternator.

When they changed the voltage to 12 volts, they had to put in a pressure cooling system and so the placement of the generator plate that bolts to the fan housing became critical to provide the proper cooling. They've also moved the voltage regulator on the Bug to under the back seat. The Bus regulator has been screwed to the side of the engine compartment since about 1963 but the wires to the generator haven't changed. The thin one, the Field, goes to the F or DF connection on the generator, and the heavier wire is the Armature and goes to the D+ or + connection. Physically the heavier wire goes closest to the center of the engine. Now let's see what changes the generator cooling system makes. Step 10 is a little different.

Step 10B. Install Fan and Generator Plate

In the 12 volt models, the generator plate must be positioned just so before installing and has no little round ring for the bolts to go through, as mentioned in Step 10. That little notch in the generator plate must go down as it is installed in the engine so hold the generator in your hand with the brush end toward your belly and then the generator so the connections are to your right—you know, the place where those wires attach. Now this is the way it sits in the car, so position the notch on the generator plate down. Polarize—see Step 4 in the next Procedure for Type III's.

PROCEDURE FOR REMOVAL AND INSTALLATION OF GENERATOR FOR TYPE III VW'S
Phase I

Step 1. Remove Generator

Lift the back seat up and disconnect the battery ground strap (the webbed one). Go to the back and open up the engine compartment lid and locate the generator. With an 8mm wrench and a screwdriver, remove the three wires going to the generator. Only one of the nuts has to be loosened a bit for the wire to slip off. Replace the nut and screw as they are easy to lose. Pop off the two spring clips on the generator belt cover and pull the cover off. Remove the fan belt as in Step 1, Procedure on the Fan Belt, earlier in this chapter. With a 13mm socket, long extension and ratchet, remove the two nuts on the generator hold-down strap. Now you can remove the generator by pulling it forward and up just like that.

Step 2. Shop Work

Take the generator to the shop to have them do the work. You may have a bum armature, in which case a new or rebuilt generator will be better. So work it out and come back to the reassembly table with a good generator.

Step 3. Install Generator

Put the generator back on the engine so that the two terminals are to the left of an imaginary vertical line and replace the strap washers and nuts, but don't tighten the nuts yet. The generator must be aligned for proper cooling. Look on the top of the generator and the strap. There should either be a painted line or a dot on the strap and a line on the generator. These marks should line up. If you don't have any of these marks, the D+ terminal on the generator should be 36° left (counter-clockwise) from an imaginary vertical line. This is so the slot in the generator (the one the brushes are in) is lined up with the hole in the fan housing for generator cooling. Now you can tighten the nuts. Put the fan belt back on as in Step 3 in the fan belt procedure. Connect the three wires: the one with a slot in the end connection goes on the terminal the nut doesn't come off of. The other heavy wire goes to the other terminal and the thin wire goes to the ground screw. Like that.

Note: Step 4 is for all models with generator

Step 4. Polarize—All Generator Models—Not for Alternators

Before you connect the regulator to the generator any time they have been apart, but especially whenever you've installed a new regulator or a rebuilt generator, the generator must be polarized to the battery. Take your long lead with the two clips on it and connect it from the negative pole, or the ground clamp from the battery, to the ground screw on the generator. Then take another piece of wire with bare ends and hold it to the positive (hot) side of the battery and touch it to the hot wire coming out of the generator. It is always the larger lead out of the battery (usually, but not always, red). This will assure that the generator and the battery are in loving harmony.

PROCEDURE FOR REMOVING AND INSTALLING THE ALTERNATOR FOR TYPE II, 1972 AND LATER AND TYPE IV, Phase I

Note: Type I, 1973 and on, use Generator Procedure

Condition: You are removing your alternator to replace or repair it. See **Changes and New Ideas.**

Remarks: There should be an easier way.

Step 1. Remove Belt

Locate the alternator to the right of the crankshaft-fan-pulley. Above the alternator is a plastic cap which you can pry out with a screwdriver to get at the adjusting bolt, an allen head. So get your set of allen head wrenches, find the one that fits and remove this adjusting bolt. Put it in a bolt can or other safe place. In the Type IV's, remove the air tunnel. Now push the alternator all the way to the left. Work the fan belt off the alternator pulley. In the 1973 and 1974 Bus you will have to loosen and remove the smog pump belt.

Step 2. Remove Alternator Hinge Bolt

Put your stocking cap on and get under the car; you may want to jack up the Type IV sedan or station wagon a little so you can get under it. Above the junction of the right-hand heater box (heat exchanger) there is a nut and it is a bear but you can get a 13mm box end on it; turn it a little at a time until it comes off. You may want to think about what you are going to do about getting it back on. Anyway, get it off and put it in the bolt can. Push the hinge bolt with the screwdriver so you can get a hold of it from the rear. Someone may have to lift the alternator a little while you do this.

Step 2. (Cont'd.)

Go to the rear, fasten your vice grip on the alternator hinge bolt, get something under the alternator to hold it up, then pull out the hinge bolt.

Step 3. Disconnect Alternator

Use the screwdriver and vice grip to remove the shrouding bolts and screws and take off all the shrouding in your way, then lower the alternator a little. Remember how the shrouding came off so you can get it back on. Disconnect the wires from the front of the alternator—they may just push in and pull out but be careful. Disconnect the air supply line to the alternator. It either screws or pushes on. There is a gasket to care for.

Step 4. Remove Alternator

Here's where the cheese gets binding. Volkswagen and others state that you have to take off the muffler, Chapter XVII and/or the heat exchanger, Chapter XV, to get the alternator out of the 1972 and later Bus while the engine is still in the car and you may well have to. I would loosen and remove the right-hand motor mount bolts and put a block of wood and a scissors jack under the engine and jack it just enough to get the alternator out—upwards and rearwards. In the Type IV's there is plenty of room to pull the alternator out to the rear and up. I have never taken one out of the new Bus and am in no position to tell anyone how to do it. I hope you don't have to do all that extra work of removing the muffler and/or the heat exchanger.

Step 5. Shop Work

Take the alternator to Volkswagen or to a Bosch or Motorola agency—depends on which alternator you have—and let them work it over, feeling that you've saved yourself the removal and installation money, anyway. When you get it back, make sure they give you a new air intake gasket.

INSTALLATION

Step 6. Replace Alternator and Reconnect

Push the alternator up close to where it goes and block or hold it into approximate position, then connect the leads the way you took them off.

Put the new air intake gasket on the cover and install the screws, making sure there is a good seal at both ends of the rubber air intake.

Step 7. Replace Hinge Bolt

Hold the alternator in position and push the hinge bolt through the hole. Try the action and check underneath to make sure the hinge bolt is in the place you took it from.

Step 8. Install the Shrouding

Step 9. Put Nut on Hinge Bolt

Have a friend hold the hinge bolt nut in place while you turn it from the front—under the car, remember. You may have to use a thin nosed pliers or vice grip to hold it.

Step 10. Replace and Tighten Belt

Replace the belt with the alternator held to the left, then pry the alternator to the right and install the adjustment bolt—allen head—and hold the belt tension until the belt deflects a hair more than 1/2". Tighten the adjustment bolt, then the hinge bolt. Make sure the shrouding is tight and you are through—after you clean up. Remember to install and tighten the smog pump belt in the 1973 and '74 Bus.

PROCEDURE FOR REPLACING THE CRANKSHAFT PULLEY, ENGINE IN CAR, TYPE I, TYPE II THROUGH 1971, Phase I

Types III, IV and Bus '72 and later: You have a different type of pulley that doesn't suffer from this problem so this Procedure is not for you.

Condition: Broken crankshaft pulley

Tools and Materials: Phase I tool kit, plus a borrowed or rented puller. As this puller is a little special and can be made rather easily, I'll describe it. It is the kind that uses two bolts, one on each side of the central pulling bolt. See sketch:

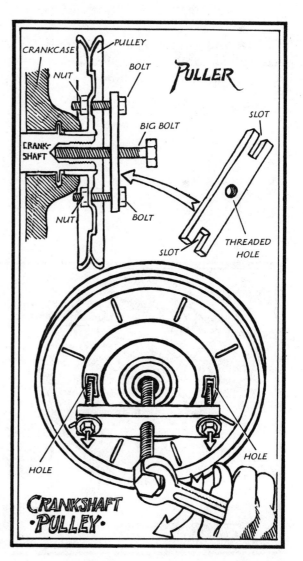

You will need a new pulley, of course.

Step 1. Remove Rear Piece of Shrouding

In the pre-Clean-air models, this is a simple four-screw operation with the large screwdriver. In the Clean-air engines, start with the piece of shroud over the crankshaft pulley—three screws. Then remove the two big air hoses with the phillips screwdriver. Loosen the clamps and work the hoses off the bottom connections, twist and push the hoses up and off. Remove the two plates, three screws each, around the heat riser pipe, part of the intake manifold. Pull the hot air hose off from the air cleaner. Now you can take the four screws out of the rear piece of shrouding and lift it out over the heater connection pipes. Leave the hot air hose through the hole, just work the tin up the hose and get it out of the way.

Step 2. Remove Crankshaft Pulley Nut

With a 27mm socket on the breaker bar loosen the crankshaft pulley nut. As soon as it's loose, you can unscrew it with your fingers.

Step 3. Remove Pulley

First try prying and banging the pulley off. This may be the best way to do it if the pulley is

Step 3. Remove Pulley

badly beat up. Put the big screwdriver in front of the pulley on one side and beat it off with the hammer. Too tight? OK, get out the puller and assemble it. Put a washer on one puller bolt. Work the bolt into one of the slots on the pulley from around in front so the bolt sticks out toward you, then do the same thing with the other bolt. Put the puller over the bolts and put the nuts on. Make sure the main puller bolt is not touching the threads inside the crankshaft. Don't mess up these threads! Now you can tighten up on the main puller bolt and pull the pulley off.

Step 4. Install Pulley

Slide the pulley onto the crankshaft with the neck going into the engine. This neck has threads on it to keep oil in the engine, not to attach to anything. There is a half-moon key on the shaft that the notch in the pulley must go over. Slide it in until you are sure the key has started into the notch, then tap it the rest of the way with the hammer. Put the nut and spring washer into the crankshaft and turn it as far as it will go by hand. You can use a pliers or crescent wrench to get it fairly tight. Then use the breaker bar and the 27mm socket to tighten the nut so the spring washer is completely flat.

Step 5. Replace Belt, Hoses and Tin

Turn to the Fan Belt Procedure in this chapter and install the fan belt. Install the rear shroud and with an early model you're done but with the Clean-air engines you need to connect the hoses to the crankshaft pulley shroud and install the two small pieces of tin in the reverse order used in Step 1.

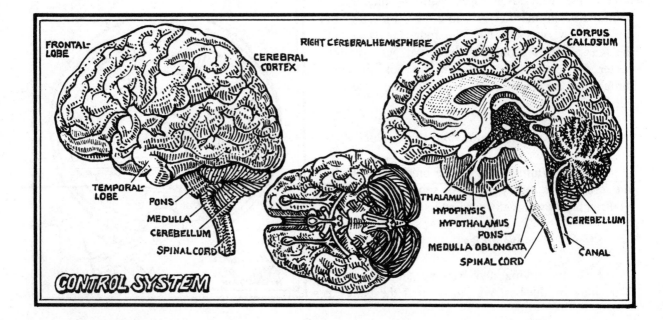

GREEN LIGHT ON!

(OIL RED LIGHT)

When the green light goes on, or even flickers at speed, STOP! It's the least you can do for the beating heart of your Volkswagen. You may be in for an overhaul or you may just need a quart of oil. Stop and check.

Note: The warning light for the oil system of the 1969 and later models is red and says "Oil" but I will continue to use "green" light and you can translate.

Lubricating oils are discussed in Chapter X; it's the oil system that's discussed here.

The Volkswagen oil system operates without a great volume factor of safety. It contains comparatively little oil which is spread out in a comparatively large area. If you're a quart low, your engine can be from 25 percent to 50 percent low in oil. One of the suggestions I make is that you put in an oil filter, which increases the capacity by one quart. Never put too much oil in the crankcase. This is a sure way to blow out the front seal (around the flywheel), which can only be replaced by pulling the engine. When the oil is above the add-oil mark, the lowest mark on the dipstick, never add oil. When it is below the add-oil mark, you can add a quart. The top line on the dipstick is the full mark. Remember to let some time elapse after the engine stops before you check the oil. Also make sure the car is on level ground. As a rule, I check my oil in the morning before starting the car but if I'm in a filling station I don't check the oil until the gas is in and the cap on. Don't let the attendant check the oil while the gas tank is filling. This time-saving gimmick will cost you oil money and blow your seal. One thing at a time, in life as well as in your Volkswagen.

A one pint, leakproof, plastic bottle will allow you to add one pint of oil at a time to the engine. Open the quart can, fill the pint bottle, tighten the cap, wipe it off and store it with your spare oil in the car. Pour the rest into the engine. That first mark on the dipstick down from the full mark means just one pint low, so by adding a pint at a time, you can better modulate the amount of oil in your engine.

You put the oil in the filler tube and it goes down to the sump where the oil pump sucks it through a screen, not a filter, and pushes it through drilled holes in the crankcase and crankshaft to the main bearings and connecting rod bearings. The oil also flows to the camshaft bearings and to the cam followers. From the cam followers it goes up the hollow push rods to the valve train in the heads. After it oils each item it flows down to the sump and the whole process is repeated. The cylinder walls are oiled by the splashing of the rods in the sump. When the oil gets too low, it is the cylinder walls that suffer first.

There are three items in the oil system which must be kept in good working order for the system to operate properly; the oil cooler, the oil pump and the oil pressure relief system. The oil cooler develops leaks. The oil pump wears and doesn't pump right. The pressure relief valve gets crudded up and sticks.

The main problem in the oil system is keeping the oil cool and both the oil cooler and the pressure relief valve are installed for this purpose. If the oil gets hot for any reason, it stops lubricating properly and then the rods burn out, the main complaint.

The warning light for the oil system tells when the oil pressure is too low—the green light goes on. The green light on the dash has a hot wire coming to it from the ignition switch and the other connection (ground) goes to the engine, where the wire (usually green) attaches to the oil pressure sensor. When the engine is stopped, the sensor contacts are closed and the light goes on. The proper oil pressure separates the contacts in the sensor so there is no ground, ergo no light. This means that if the wire is not attached to the sensor, there will be no green light, so always test the green light by trying the ignition switch in the first notch before you start the car. It is a habit that must be developed. Just turn the key to the first notch and check both the red and green lights, then back to zero, then start the engine.

There is another reason for the green light to go on that's not at all related to the oiling system. However, it can heat the engine up and thus the oil and on goes the oil light. This has to do with the air system.

Get down on your hands and knees and look under the right side of the engine. See the curved piece of sheet metal between the engine case and the cylinder head? OK, above this sheet metal you'll see a little brass accordion like gizmo attached to the engine case. That's the engine air thermostat—or bellows. If it's fully expanded and warped that's the problem. When stuck in this position, the thermostat closes off the air flaps in the fan housing cutting off the supply of cooling air to the engine.

To remedy this problem, slide under the car with a large screwdriver and a 13mm wrench. Locate the four sheet metal screws that hold the sheet metal onto the heater box and engine case, and remove the screws with the large screwdriver. Pull the sheet metal out of the way and remove the bolt holding the thermostat to the bracket with a 13mm wrench. Push the thermostat up enough so it can be screwed off the rod. Screw the new thermostat back on the rod and bolt it back on the bracket. Make sure the square protrusion on the bottom of the thermostat seats in the bracket. Replace the sheet metal and screws.

The Green Light Procedure is designed to check out the whole oil system for each condition so when you have to use it, run down the steps until you find the condition that matches your problem, fix that and follow through until you get it working again.

FRONT MEANS THE FRONT OF THE CAR, with LEFT the driver's side!

PROCEDURE FOR CHECKING GREEN LIGHT, Phase I

Condition: When you turn the ignition switch to the first notch before starting the engine, the green (oil) light does *not* go on. If the red light doesn't go on either, go to Chapter VII and check the ignition switch.

Step 1. Check Wire Connection

Go to the rear of the car, lift the engine hood and find the oil pressure sensor. It looks like this:

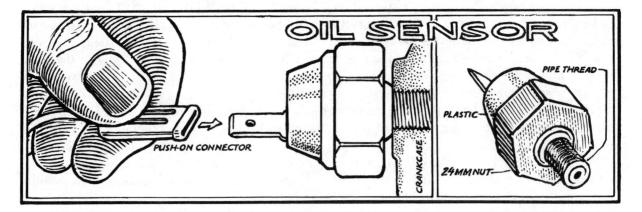

Type III
It will be on top of the oil cooler, which is the metal box that disappears under the tin in front of the distributor (left side).
Type I (All) and Type II (through 1971)
It will be screwed into the crankcase under the distributor and should have a wire (usually green) leading to it.
Type IV and 1972 & later Bus
The oil pressure sensor is under a little cap in front of the distributor. Pry the little cap up and out with your screwdriver.

All Models

If the wire is missing from the back of the sensor, find the loose wire and connect it. It will either be a simple push-on connector or a small screw clamp. If the wire has broken loose from the push-on, get a new push-on connector from your kit, clean the insulation from the end of the wire and use the pliers to squeeze the connector on, then install it on the back of the sensor. This is usually the problem, so if the wire has come loose, just fix it and the light will come on when you test it again. TEST IT AT THE SWITCH EVERY TIME BEFORE YOU START THE ENGINE!

Step 2. Check Light Bulb

If, when you find the sensor, the wire is well attached, wiggle it to make sure it has a good connection and test it again (if it lights, go on your way), but if it still refuses to go on, pull the connector loose from the back of the sensor and wedge it where it makes a good ground contact with the engine, then try it again, or if you have someone with you, turn the key on and have them watch the green light while you ground the end of the wire on the engine. The idea is to find out if the bulb in back of the green light on the dash is OK. If the light goes on now with a good ground, go on to Step 3. If the light does not go on when the key is on and the wire to the sensor is grounded, either the wiring or the bulb is at fault. Check the connections in front of the switch and if they are OK, get a new bulb. Pull the socket out of the front of the speedometer, hold the socket and push the old bulb in and twist counterclockwise. Take out the bulb, put the new one in, push and twist clockwise. Now you can replace the socket in the speedometer and push it in.

Step 3. Check Sensor

The bulb goes on when the wire has a good ground so the sensor is at fault. Go to Volkswagen and buy a new sensor (be sure and get a six volt sensor if your car is 6 volt and a twelve volt sensor for a 12 volt system), then use the crescent wrench to carefully unscrew the sensor from the crankcase (oil cooler, Type III) and especially carefully screw the new one in. It has taper threads for sealing so don't turn it too tightly. Connect the wire and test the light again. If the light goes on now, throw the old sensor away and go your way. If the light still doesn't go on, take the sensor back to VW and get another. Once in a blue moon, they sell you a bad one. You have checked everything else.

PROCEDURE FOR CHECKING OIL SYSTEM, Phase I

Condition: You are blissfully driving along and the green light goes on or you just notice it. STOP THE CAR—RIGHT NOW! Get over to the side of the road wherever you are. SHUT OFF THE ENGINE! More VW engines have blown when this green light is on than in any other condition but then, most people die in hospitals, too. Relax. Whatever is going on has already happened, so pull yourself together. You may just need a quart of oil.

Step 1. Check Engine and Oil

Go to the rear of the car and look into the engine compartment. If the engine is obviously hot—you can smell it—and you can't hold the dipstick handle (if you can hold the handle try touching the dipstick itself), check the fan belt tension. Push the left-hand side of the belt toward the right. It shouldn't deflect more than 1/2" to 3/4". If it is looser than that and there are shiny places on the belt, turn to Chapter VIII to tighten the fan belt when the engine is cool enough to work on it.

If the fan belt tension is right and the engine is still too hot to touch the dipstick, you must wait. Do nothing more until the engine cools! Read, enjoy the scenery, take a little walk. If you have a bus, and a friend, it might be a good time to go in the back and ball. Eat your lunch. Give the engine at least a half hour or more to cool before you take any further action. Ya hear?

Type III, IV and 1972-on Bus owners please do all these things, but as your fan belt has nothing to do with the cooling system, you have to look elsewhere for the cause of heating. Turn to the Tune-up Procedure in Chapter X.

All Models

If the engine is cool when you open the compartment, check the oil. If it's really low, add a quart and try the engine. Let it idle a few minutes to get the oil circulating again and listen for expensive noises (Step 3) but if low oil was the trouble, the green light should go out and you are on your way—with a watchful eye on the green light and a bent ear for unusual noises.

If the engine is cool and the oil level is above the add-oil line, start the engine and let it idle while you listen for expensive noises (Step 3), rev it a little with the lever on the carb and listen. If it sounds good and there's no obvious reason for the green light to be on, go on to Step 2, and check the oil sensor. If this has happened before and you have checked the sensor, I would suspect the Pressure Relief Valve so run the procedure on it in this chapter, but the engine would probably be hot if it is sticking.

Now back to the hot engine people: your engine is hot, but you can finally grasp the dipstick with your bare fingers, so check the oil. If the oil is low, add a quart, start the engine and listen for expensive noises (Step 3), let the engine idle a few minutes to get the oil circulating again. Look under the engine for oil leaks. Rev the engine a little and see if the new oil has cured the green light problem—give it a minute or so before you give up. If the light goes out, you are on your way with thoughts and carefulness and a new attentiveness toward that green light. If the green light is still on with the addition of the oil, you're in trouble, but I suggest that you run through Step 2 and even the procedure on the pressure relief valve before you give up and go for help.

If your engine is hot and when you check the oil there is plenty, you have trouble. Let the engine cool a while before you start it. Your engine got so hot that the oil got thin and refused to lubricate; that's serious. When the engine is cool, start it and listen for expensive noises (Step 3). If the green light goes out after the car has idled a few minutes, rev up the engine and listen for engine damage. If the noise level is about like it was, go your way, but with the knowledge that something is wrong. Is it a hot day? Have you been bucking a headwind? What reasons did your engine have for getting hot? Is the engine dirty? (See Chapter VIII.) When you get home read the introduction in Chapter XV about the reasons for overhauling your engine. The foregoing is pertinent whether you added oil or not. If your engine gets hot enough to turn on the green light, there's a reason for it.

If the green light stays on no matter what you do, try Step 2, then the Pressure Relief Valve Procedure. If nothing helps you to get that green light off and you aren't familiar enough with engine noises to judge whether your car is hurt or not, I would go for help and have the car towed in or at least get some good advice. The same thing is true if you have those expensive noises whether the green light is on or off!

Step 2. Clean and Check the Oil Sensor

If your green light went on and the engine is hot, the sensor is probably all right. Find the sensor: it is below and in front of the distributor.

Type III
It's in front of the distributor on top of the oil cooler.

Type IV
It's in front of the distributor under a little cap.

Pull or disconnect the wire from the sensor. Put the crescent wrench on the metal part and carefully unscrew it counterclockwise. It has taper threads and no gasket. When it's out, take a small piece of wire and clean out the hole in the crankcase you opened when you removed the sensor. If you have company, pull the center wire out of the coil so the engine won't start, then have your friend turn the engine over with the starter while you watch the hole the sensor was in. Let a little oil run out to flush the hole, then hold your finger tightly in the hole to feel for pressure, a slight pushing against your fingertip. It's only six pounds or less at idle, so don't expect too much but there should be some. If you're alone, pull out the center coil wire and lay a rag or piece of paper out under the hole, then go up front and turn the engine over a few times with the key. With pressure, the oil should have spurted out onto the rag or paper. With no pressure, the oil just dribbled out and maybe didn't even reach the paper so go to VW to have them run a pressure check on your pump— see the end of the Procedure on the Pressure Relief Valve in this chapter.

If it seemed as if there was pressure, with or without friend, mop up the mess, then clean out the sensor with the piece of wire. Pull the hose off the carburetor to let a little gasoline drip into the hole in the sensor. Get it clean, then put it back into the cleaned hole and screw it back *carefully* with the crescent wrench—not too tight, now. Replace the wire on the back of the sensor and the wire to the coil. Check to see if the green light goes on when you turn the key to the first notch, then try the engine. Let it run while you go back to listen for those expensive noises we all fear. If the light goes out and the engine sounds OK, go your merry way.

If the green light stays on after the sensor has been cleaned, listen to the engine for a minute or two and if it sounds the same as usual, no expensive noises, shut it off and think. Like: Is there a VW place close by where I can get another sensor? Did I really feel pressure with my finger in the hole? Did the oil squirt out of the hole with verve onto the paper or rag? This is a matter of judgement and you must decide. If it's daytime and there's a VW place in a few miles and there are no expensive noises, drive there very sedately to buy and install a new sensor. If you're close to home you could drive there and buy the sensor in the morning. There are an infinity of choices. If there are no unusual noises in the engine, a new sensor is the next step. If your green light is acting strangely, do the procedure on the pressure relief valve in this chapter.

Step 3. Listen for Expensive Noises

A few words about expensive noises may be useful to you. It takes a real expert to *know* but with a little imagination, you can *guess* and often that'll be close enough for your purposes. If you spend some time listening to your engine when you know it's right, you'll have a basis for the interpretation of the unusual sounds that can make your life miserable. A connecting rod about to burn out its bearing will make a tick-tick-tickety-tick sound changing to a tock-tock-tockety-tock sound, usually associated with a loss of the oil pressure causing the green light to come on but not until the rod is really gone.

A broken ring will make almost the same tickety sound but higher in pitch. As the main bearings in the VW are very massive the sound they make when they are worn is almost impossible to detect, so the green light flickering at low rpm is the best indication. But the camshaft bearings, when worn, will give the same flickering of the green light. At any rate, when the green light flickers, it is the signal of a worn engine and an impending overhaul. A tight valve makes no sound whatsoever but is fraught with danger for your engine. A valve adjusted too loosely makes a steady tinny click-click-click sound and is not very important. **See Chapter XX, Tune-Ups.**

Step 4. Unusual Noise Decisions

You've added the oil and when you listen to the engine, you find it's making an unusual noise. Shut off the engine. Take the things you don't want to leave out of the car and go for help. Don't try to drive the car with that ticking or tocking noise. It may make the difference between a minor overhaul to replace the rod bearing and a major overhaul calling for a new crankshaft. If the rod breaks and goes through the case, you will need a new engine. Save your bread! You might make a few miles but they could cost you a lot so get the car pulled—either home or to a garage. Make sure the garage you pick does VW work as a usual thing. Neither you nor I have enough time or money to let some mechanic learn about Volkswagen engines on our cars. If you are going to do the work yourself, see Chapter XV.

PROCEDURE ON THE PRESSURE RELIEF VALVE(S)

Condition: The green (oil) light goes on while you're driving, the oil level is OK, the engine is, perhaps, a little too warm but is making no unusual noise. When you run the engine again, the green light goes out so you drive down the highway but in another few miles, comes the green light again—you curse, but replace the sensor as it says in the Procedure for Checking Oil System, Step 2, and drive on. The next thing you know that damn green light is on. The oil level is OK and the engine still sounds good. Your pressure relief valve is stuck. If you're close enough, nurse it home. Drive until the light goes on, stop to let the oil cool while you fume. Drive it a little way, let it cool and so on. Do not drive with the green light on! If you're on a trip, you might as well pull over and fix it right now. The pressure relief system looks like the sketch below. Starting in 1970 there is also a Pressure Control Valve. See worm's eye view on next page.

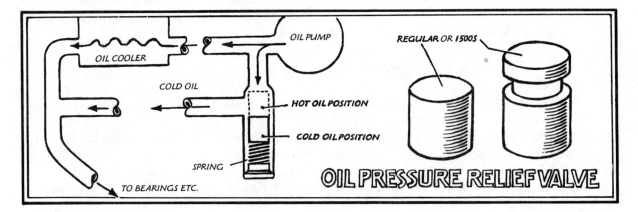

Step 1. Disassemble the Pressure Relief Valve

Spread the ground cloth out under the engine a little to the right of center. Lie down on your back so you can look up at the engine and scrooch yourself under, taking the medium and large screwdrivers, the vice grip and a can to catch the oil drippings with you. Look up at the engine to locate the pressure relief valve. It's to the left of center toward the rear of the engine and is a large, flat-headed screw about 3/4" in diameter. (If the engine's out of the car, look on the bottom of the engine but above the fin area.) You will have to clean some crud off and clean the screw slot with the large screwdriver. It's the only thing resembling a screw head under the engine so you can't miss. Clamp the vice grip tight onto the blade of the large screwdriver right next to the handle and put the point of the blade into the slot. Push up (engine in car) or down (engine out of car) with the handle of the screwdriver and use the vice grip like a socket wrench handle to turn the screw counterclockwise. As soon as it's loose, you can take the vice grip off and unscrew the bolt out of the crankcase. Save the washer-gasket. (Overhaul People: find your new one.) Hold the can up to catch the oil, then place it under the hole on the ground to catch the drops. The bolt may fall out of the hole in the engine or it may have to be pried out with the medium screwdriver but get it out. The valve plunger and spring may also fall out, but with the trouble you've experienced, it's not likely. If the plunger is stuck fast as we suspect, the spring will come out anyway. Try to work the plunger loose by push-

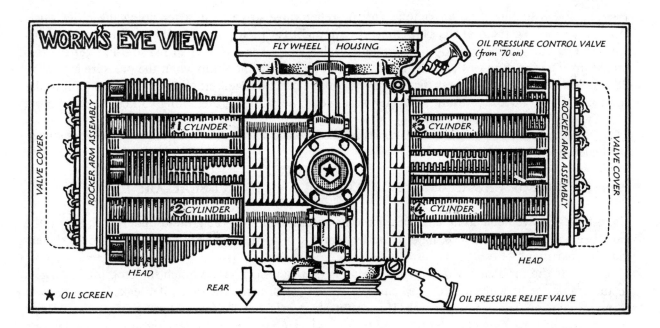

WORM'S EYE VIEW

FLY WHEEL   HOUSING

OIL PRESSURE CONTROL VALVE
(from '70 on)

VALVE COVER

ROCKER ARM ASSEMBLY

1 CYLINDER

2 CYLINDER

3 CYLINDER

4 CYLINDER

ROCKER ARM ASSEMBLY

VALVE COVER

HEAD

HEAD

★ OIL SCREEN

REAR

OIL PRESSURE RELIEF VALVE

Step 1. (Cont'd.)

ing it up into the hole with the medium screwdriver. If your large screwdriver will wedge into the hole in the plunger, you may be able to hang it up there and work the plunger out. If so, go to Step 2 but if it's tough, then so must you be. Get out your magnet, if you have one, and try pulling with it. The inside of the plunger can be tapped with a 10mm tap and pulled out—good news?—where the hell can I get a 10mm tap out here on this road?

Try wedging the screwdriver or something else that fits into the hole again and pulling on it. If the plunger will push up and just sticks at the bottom of the hole, often the case, push the plunger up and clean the bottom of the hole with your Scout knife. Work with it until that plunger is out. There's a grooved plunger available for the 40 hp and newer that helps keep the oil cooler. Ask for the 1500S plunger.

Step 2. Clean and Reinstall

Use the Scout knife to scrape the hole in the crankcase; remember it's aluminum so don't change the shape of the hole or damage the threads, just get all the crud out of it. When the hole is clean and shiny, open the engine compartment, pull the center wire out of the coil so the engine won't start and turn the engine over a little to run oil through the hole to flush it out. Let this oil run onto the ground. Now clean the plunger itself. As it's steel, use a little sandpaper or emery cloth to get it smooth and shiny. Clean the spring and the bolt with solvent or get a little gas from the gas line to the carburetor. With everything clean, slide back under the car and try the plunger by pushing it into the hole. If it falls right back out and is free and easy in the hole (remember that the hole in the plunger points down) then you can put in the spring, then the bolt with the washer-gasket on it and screw it up tight. (Overhaul people: to test the plunger in the hole, put a magnet on it and push it in and out to see if it's free and easy.) Put the vice grip on the screwdriver for the last bit of tightening. You don't want it to fall out. Replace the wire on the coil. Start up the engine. With a clean pressure relief valve and a new sensor, your troubles should be over but if the green light still acts up when the engine is warmed up and the engine sounds and runs OK, your oil pump may have worn past the allowable tolerances so go to VW and have them do a pressure check on your oil pump. If it's shot, have them install a new oil pump as they have the right tools.

All Volkswagens from 1970 on have an oil pressure control valve in addition to the relief valve. It's located on the same side of the case on the front (FRONT is front). The procedure for removing, cleaning and installing it is the same as for the relief valve so go to it, after doing the relief valve. Don't try handling them at the same time as you might get their parts mixed up. Note that the control valve is not grooved on top like the relief valve and takes a shorter spring so don't get the two mixed up. The function of the control valve is to return oil to the sump when the pressure gets over 28 psi. What this means to me is that if it ever, for some reason, gets stuck open (returning oil to the sump), oh boy, no oil pressure, rod city here we come. Just another thing to keep your eye on.

Type IV and 1972 and later Bus

The extra pressure relief (control) valve is on the crankcase between the two push rod tubes for number 1 cylinder. **See Changes and New Ideas**.

PROCEDURE FOR CHECKING THE OIL COOLER AND FRONT SEAL—OIL LEAKS

Condition: You've been using a lot of oil and have found a lot on the ground underneath where the car's been parked or oil is leaking out the left-hand side of the engine or there's oil all over the engine compartment.

One of the problems with the VW engine is that too much is too much so if too much oil gets in the crankcase, it will tend to blow out the front seal or make the oil cooler leak. If you've been using a lot of oil, try to find the leak. If it definitely drips from the front of the engine-center (look on the ground), that's where the front oil seal is and you have seal trouble, so you may keep adding oil until you get somewhere you can pull the engine to replace the seal and maybe do a valve job at the same time. At any rate, turn to Chapter XV. If, however, the oil is leaking down the left-hand side of the engine, out of the shrouding to the left of the oil pan, then you have a leaky oil cooler. By the way, careless pouring of oil into the filler will make the right side look the same way. (This is not true on the Type III.) The oil cooler will only leak after the engine is warm and running at speed, but your oil consumption will be way up and you can see where it's been leaking on the left side.

In the Type I's, you can get at the oil cooler without pulling the engine by doing the generator procedure in Chapter VIII to loosen the fan housing, then pull the fan housing completely off. In the Ghia, it'll just come up but in the others, you'll have to remove the engine compartment lid, then remove one screw from each of the lid hinges and spread the hinges out so they resemble horns on a cow to get the fan housing off. I usually just pull the engine to change the oil cooler. It doesn't take long. In the Bus, you have to pull the engine. See Chapter XV.

The oil cooler in the Type III can be replaced with the engine in the car. It lays on its side and if you take the tin off over it on the left side of the engine, you can get at the 10mm nuts and work the oil cooler out.

You cannot get the oil cooler out of the Type IV with the engine in the car. So far nobody seems to have had any trouble with this system. One source of oil leak to check would be around the new "screw-in" oil filter—that round thing under the left side of the engine.

If you find oil all over the back of the engine, you're pumping oil out of somewhere. Wipe all that messy oil up to see if you can tell where it's coming from. Check for evidence of a leaky oil cooler on the top left side of the engine. The fuel pump could be loose; tighten the two 13mm nuts with the box end. Or it could be coming from underneath the distributor, in which case see Chapter XV, Dismantling Procedure, Step 15, and Engine Assembly Procedure, Step 10. Tighten the four 13 or 14mm nuts holding down the generator pedestal. Check the anti-smog hose (the one from the oil filler pipe to the air cleaner) to make sure it's attached securely at both ends. Check the valve covers for leaks.

If none of the above-mentioned tightenings stop your oil leak, it looks like you're in for an engine pulling job (See Chapter XV), but meanwhile check the oil often to make sure you don't run out.

Conclusions: The green (oil) light is the only gauge of your engine's oil system and must be checked every time you start the car to see if it lights. Then develop the habit of checking it once in a while as you drive. If it lights while driving, you must stop and locate the trouble or you can cost yourself much bread unnecessarily. The sooner you catch the green light, the less the repairs will cost you. Use your ears and nose and those other senses to minimize your repair bills.

MAINTENANCE

(3,000 MILE): VALVE ADJUSTMENT, TIMING, TUNE-UP, LUBRICATION, DISTRIBUTOR, CARBURETOR, FUEL INJECTION

This chapter is the heart of this book, as the engine is the heart of your Volkswagen—an understatement, really, because Maintenance is the liver, kidneys, as well as the soul of the program to keep your Bus, Bug, Ghia, Square/Fastback, etc., ALIVE; that's what I promised you in front.

Chapter X is also where you get your bread back: the cash you laid out for the book as well as for the tools you need to perform the tasks outlined herein. We figure that five tune-ups made yourself will pay for your tools and the book, plus paying for the Tach-Dwell meter you now need. Less, if you scramble a little and make some substitutions.

It says here that this is the 3,000 mile maintenance but this figure is just a guide. The work should be done, completely, every 3,000 miles or every time the car doesn't start easily or starts to miss after it is warm (sign of a tight valve) or before you start a long trip or every four or five months no matter what the mileage says. If you drive on dusty roads, and bumpy, no doubt, do it every 1,500 miles.

Freeway driving is hard driving, so if you're on the freeway much of the time, do your maintenance things every 1500 miles for a longer lasting engine. **See Chapter XX** . . . Change The Oil . . . 1976 and on Vanagon owners, see **Changes and New Ideas**.

The valve adjustment is the most important item going for your Volkswagen. Let me tell you a "for lack of a nail" story. Suppose No. 3 cylinder has a slightly tight exhaust valve—No. 3 is usually the one that burns because it sits behind the oil cooler and gets less cooling air than the others. A valve can burn in about 500 miles and you only feel a loss of power. The next step is that the oil gets hot because only three cylinders are doing the work. When the oil gets hot it stops lubricating and the connecting rods start to go or a piston will freeze up and break from lack of lubrication or the whole engine will sieze up tight as a drum—all from an improperly adjusted valve.

The major reason I feel that each Volkswagen owner should do his or her own valve adjustments is because they should be adjusted dead cold. Volkswagen books say they can be adjusted at less than 50 degrees centigrade, so the dealer puts a blower on the valves and cools them until they are at this temperature. I've found too many tight valves in engines adjusted to this specification to believe a word of it; 50°C (122°F) isn't cold.

One bit of investigative work you must do is to find the valve setting for your particular engine. You cannot depend on even your owner's booklet that came with the car to tell you. I'll tell you all that I know about it. If there is a decal on the fan housing, you can trust and use that. Write it somewhere else so if the decal comes off you will have the data.

The 36 hp engine from 1954 until 1961 (with the fuel pump under the distributor) has always used .004" for all the valve clearances. We use .006" for the exhaust valve on No. 3 cylinder as it gets the hottest and is the most likely to burn. The 40 hp and 1500 Type I, II and III engine from 1959 to 1965 (with the fuel pump to the right of the distributor) uses different valve settings because, strangely enough, of the difference in the length of the studs holding down the rocker arm assemblies in the heads. The way to tell whether you have the long or short studs in your heads is by looking and feeling under the No. 2 cylinder between the push rod tubes for the long steel bolt coming down from the center to the bottom of the head. If you can feel this bolt, your engine has the long studs. Step 5 in the Valve Adjustment Procedure shows you how to find out.

If you have long studs, I recommend that you hie yourself off to Volkswagen or some foreign car garage and have the short studs put in—it's called a "stud kit" and they know about it. It takes a special tap so you can't do it. With the stud kit in, you, too, can set your valves at .006". Since 1965 your engine comes with short studs from the factory.

RAP ON OIL

If you rub two pieces of metal together, the friction of the contact between the surfaces creates a lot of heat and if there is pressure, too, you soon have a galled, burned mess. Two things are required to allow these two metallic surfaces to operate together mechanically: one is tolerance and the other is lubrication. You always thought that oil was all you needed but it also takes space for the oil. Human situations are quite analogous—grease and space. Riots! Who needs them?

Volksie engineers have provided a very solid basis for excellent lubrication in their main bearings, also the rod and camshaft bearings seldom fail when they are kept supplied with oil that's lubricating. The problem is determining just what kind of oil to use. As there's been lots of mail about oil, I'll try to calm the troubled waters with some. The whole idea is to get a tough, thin, protective slippery coating between the two rapidly moving pieces of metal. If the two pieces ever touch—off to rod city. If we admit that all engine failures are due to lack of lubrication, which is at least approximately correct, then what is the usual cause of lack of lubrication? HEAT! Oil also breaks down not only with use but also with the time it's exposed to the air, but the usual failure of an engine, even remotely maintained, is caused by some part of the engine getting overheated. Over means "past the temperature where oil retains its ability to lubricate." The whole idea of "wear limits" has to do with the distance between two rapidly moving pieces of metal so that the oil film can be maintained—too far apart usually means too close together on the other side. And if the pressure gets too great to maintain the film, heat is the natural result. OK?

An air-cooled engine has a higher operating temperature than a water cooled ditto but for whom are most lubricating oils compounded? Viscosity is measured by the ability of an oil to flow and has nothing to do with the ability to lubricate. The ability of an oil to lubricate is determined by various industry and military determined standards. Oil, like most everything else, is made up of molecules but in oil's case where it came from makes a difference in the molecules—where it was deposited, if you want to bring in Geology. Each location produces, in general, a different type of oil with different lubricating characteristics. Like "Pure Pennsylvania" used to be a byword; "Mid Continent" usually means Texas and Oklahoma, then there's "Western." The difference is in the ability of the molecules making up the oil to form and continue to form a lubricating film under pressure and heat. In engines and in geology pressure and heat do almost the same thing.

With modern transportation and new techniques of molecule building, lubricating oils are now "compounded" out of many types of basic oils from different places. The molecules that continue to lubricate the longest are the most expensive. They also put detergents (cleaning agents) in oil which dissolve burned molecules of oil, carbon and other crap that forms in the engine and carry these particles in the body of the oil. For Volkswagens we used to think that the non-detergent oils were best because there was no filter to filter out the crud. But experience has shown that the detergent kind is best as long as you change oil fairly often. Believe me, oils are better today than ever before. However, when in the process of compounding a motor oil, the companies try to use as few of the expensive molecules as the standards they try to meet will allow—that's the name of the game. When an oil is made to have the same or similar flow characteristics over a broad temperature range, a certain amount of ability to lubricate in the higher temperature ranges is sacrificed. A "10-40" oil will do its thing from the temperature where you would ordinarily use a 10 weight oil (zero degrees Fahrenheit in a VW) all the way up to where you would use a 40 weight oil (120°F) but experience has shown that the multi-grade oil's ability to lubricate is not as good as the mono-grade oil's ability at the high temperatures at which an air-cooled engine runs. Therefore, in this book we recommend that you use the best monograde, heavy duty (HD), API Service SE-CC, MS (Military Standard) oil that you can buy. This is a detergent oil. The HD is an industry standard which implies that more of those expensive goodies are put in than in regular oil. MS means that the oil has passed a standard for lubricating quality and has a certain amount of detergent that the military wanted to use in the service they wanted to use it for, which is also the service we want to use it for.

As I have developed, with time, a certain ability to keep myself out of temperature extremes, my Bus has never had anything in it but 30 weight, S.A.E. And now we come to name—brand name, that is. Certain companies make oils that are used for racing and tough use and have a dollop more of the kind of ingredient that keeps the oil operating and lubricating at higher temperatures so that owners of racing cars will actually use their oil. There are several of these but I use Castrol. This lays a load on my back to carry my own oil wherever I go because this oil is found only in racing and hot-rod stores. So I usually carry six quarts.

We've had a lot of mail over the past few years asking our opinion on synthetic oils, so here goes. There is little doubt that the synthetic oils do have excellent lubricating properties and don't break down as easily as petroleum products. One of the things that holds me back from synthetics is their cost. They are much more expensive and even a light leak can drain your bread. Also, the fact that most VW's don't use an oil filter means you should change oil often, right? Well, this sort of defeats the purpose of long lasting synthetics.

To sum it up, if your engine is like new, without leaks and has an oil filter and you like the idea, use synthetic oil. If all these conditions aren't happening, it's probably a waste of money.

A quick way to ruin a VW is to put detergent oil in after non-detergent oil has been used for a while. The particles picked up by the detergent oil usually are nicely stored in the oil cooler and everywhere else oil can stand and settle. One question you have to ask when you buy a car is what kind of oil has been used. If the seller doesn't know, it probably was detergent unless the seller was a cheap oil freak. The guy I bought my '63 Bus from was a confirmed non-detergent oil man and I had to follow suit until I tore the engine down and put in a new Porsche oil cooler and an oil filter to go with it. You can change from detergent to non-detergent without ill effect but there's no use. Use the viscosity that fits your conditions. Look it up in your Owner's Manual. Install a magnetic oil drain plug. Use a Porsche-size oil cooler in the Bus—plus a filter, if you drive it hard. Install a 1500S type oil pressure relief valve plunger for cooler oil, if your car doesn't already have one. (Not for engines with a pressure relief valve and a pressure control valve.)

I usually get my grease jobs at the VW dealers if they can fit their work into my schedule. They charge more but they have all the right grease and stuff and do the doors and latches real nice, too.

VOLKSWAGEN ENGINES USE NO WATER FOR COOLING—OIL AND AIR DO IT ALL!

Now about **WARMITUP**, another heavy mail subject. In the VW engine, the connecting rods splash about in the oil sump and this oils the cylinder walls. While a car sits all night the oil film between the pistons and cylinder walls comes loose due to the action of gravity. In addition to this you always start the engine with a shot of raw gas, either by pumping the accelerator pedal or by choke action and raw gas has a tendency to wash the oil off the cylinder walls. OK? All the super warm-up equipment that VW hangs on their engines doesn't change this one whit. I warm my engine up for the two or three minutes it takes me to roll a cigarette, light it and get it drawing well. I have disconnected my automatic choke so I don't have that worry, but I do pump the accelerator a little to get some gas down there to start the cold engine. In those one-half to three minutes, depending on the weather (the colder, the longer), the rods are doing their thing in getting the oil on the cylinder walls, all the way around; the raw gas that I pumped in has been used, and there is enough of a film of oil protecting my cylinder walls from being excessively worn by the passage of the rings. Now when I put a load on the engine, it is the oil that carries that load, not the metal.

The morning warm-up is the nicest thing you can possibly do for your engine. Another nice thing is to start out gently—put a minimum load on the engine until it reaches operating temperature. You'll feel it. When we get to the carburetor, I will tell you what I think about chokes as the major item of built-in obsolescence that has been perpetrated on us as car owners.

Now I should put some words of love and confidence to enjoin you to dig doing the Valve Adjustment and Tune-up Procedures that follow. When you get interested in doing for your car as much as you would for a horse or mule, then some of the proper spirit will spring forth.

Translating words into actions is easy when you do it one step at a time. You are not going to intellectualize on these mechanical things, you are going to **do** them and that's different. The idea to grasp well here is one of Return. You are going to return the car to a position of well-being by adjusting certain things that have worn, been used up or been bounced out of alignment. As the I Ching says, "Perseverance Furthers," and that is your thing. Take your time and do each step completely before you even think about the next.

From the mail, I have garnered the feeling that a lot of you who would like to do your own valves don't because you feel you don't know anything about cars, engines, like that. So hear this! No one has enough money anywhere—Banker, Indian Chief, Gestalt Therapist, no kind of person—to not set their own valves on their own Volkswagen! It's a personal thing between you and your transportation. Due to the guarantee provisions on new cars, I have had my valves set by dealers in the United States, Mexico, Germany, Italy, Switzerland and England and the next morning I get out the tools and check them out. With no exceptions, the valves have been too tight—NO exceptions! Set your own valves, in the morning, COLD, and your engine will last you many more miles. If one of your valves is constantly loose or tight for some period of time, keep it in mind as it indicates you're probably in for a valve job.

Another subject is thinking,* improvisational thinking, that is. Don't do it! Do what the book says. Don't take short cuts or long cuts. Do no more nor no less than it says. The Procedures work

---

*See *Son of Ye Olde Maile Baggie*

just the way they are. They are designed so people who know nothing, who have never had a tool in their hands before, can do this work. DOING THE VALVES, TIMING AND MINOR MAINTEN-ANCE ON YOUR OWN CAR WILL NOT ONLY CHANGE YOUR RELATIONSHIP WITH YOUR TRANSPORTATION BUT WILL ALSO CHANGE YOUR RELATIONSHIP WITH YOURSELF!

Good Luck!

There are several allied things that I do on "tune-up" day: "Clean the oil screen every second time" is in the tune-up procedure but there are other things from other chapters that I try to do while I am already dirty, greasy, and irate, anyway. ("Tighten the Torsion Arm Link Pins," Chapter XII, at 6,000 miles; "Tighten Transmission Front Support Nuts," Chapter XIV, at 6,000 miles; "Clean the Pressure Relief Valve," Chapter IX, at 6,000 miles.) There are other periodic trips I like to take on the car's day. You will find your own way.

CHECK LIST

Here is a condensed check list for those of you who have done a valve adjustment and tune-up several times and no longer want to wade through all the wordage. But please read through and follow the entire procedure unless you feel you qualify as an expert who just needs reminders.

I.   **Valve Adjustment**
    A. Remove distributor cap, rotate engine to No. 1.
    B. Remove the right valve cover making note of any leaks.
    C. Rotate engine to Top Dead Center (TDC).
    D. Adjust right front valves.
    E. Rotate engine 180°, counterclockwise.
    F. Adjust right rear valves, clean and replace valve cover and gasket, if necessary.
    G. Rotate engine 180° counterclockwise, remove left valve cover, note leaks.
    H. Adjust left front valves.
    I. Rotate engine 180° counterclockwise.
    J. Adjust rear valves, clean and replace valve cover. Gasket?

II. **Adjust Points**
    A. Remove rotor.
    B. Make sure the nylon rider is on top of the distributor lobe.
    C. Check with feeler gauge for proper gap.
    D. Check condition of points and other connections in the distributor.
    E. Loosen hold down screw, put feeler gauge between the contacts and adjust until the proper clearance is reached.
    F. Tighten hold down screw.
    G. Connect Tach-Dwell meter.
        1. Red (+) lead to No. 1 terminal of coil.
        2. Black lead to a good ground.
        3. Switch meter to 4 cylinder position, (or 8 cylinder if there's no 4 cylinder position on your meter.)
        4. Start engine (Safety!), note dwell: 4 cylinder position/scale $50^\circ \pm 2^\circ$
                                      8 cylinder position/scale $25^\circ \pm 2^\circ$
        5. If the reading is too high, the points are too far closed and vice versa.

III. **Timing**
    A. Check timing with static or strobe light.
    B. To change timing, loosen 10mm nut under distributor and...
    C. Hook up static or strobe light. Set timing to proper mark.

IV. Check Vacuum Advance
    A. Take off distributor cap, pull rotor.
    B. Pull hose from distributor to carburetor.
    C. Suck on the hose and watch the points plate—the whole plate should move.

V. Change Oil
    A. Remove 21mm drain plug or entire sump plate on newer models.
    B. Remove and clean screen and replace. Remember oil filter.
    C. Put in oil.

VI. Compression Check
    A. Have engine at operating temperature.
    B. Remove spark plug connections, then the spark plugs. Check spark plug color (tan to brown OK; black, no good).
    C. Place tester in each hole while a friend turns the engine over six times with the key. Remember your stocking cap! Safety!
    D. They should all be over 100 and within 5 lbs. of each other.

VII. Spark Plugs
    A. Gap .025'' (.6 mm)
    B. Replace

VIII. Coil
    A. Pull center wire from distributor cap and hold it ⅛'' to ¼'' from a ground: bright blue to white, good. Yellow, OK. Orange, bad.

PROCEDURE FOR VALVE ADJUSTMENT, Phase I

Condition: 3000 mile maintenance. **Please note:** 1978 and on buses have non-adjustable hydraulic valves, so '78 and on bus owners skip this Procedure, and see **Chapter XX**, Tune-ups. Also see **Changes and New Ideas.**

Tools and Materials: Phase I tool kit, valve cover gaskets, quick-drying glue, wheel bearing grease.

Step 1. Get Ready

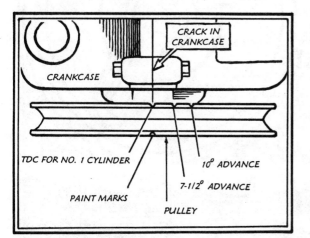

Throughout this book we use directional conventions to make pointing to things easier. Front is always the front of the car, making left the driver's side. When you are doing this work, remember, Front is front. Read "Engine Compartment Orientation" in Chapter VII.

The night before you are going to adjust your valves and do a tune-up, park your car in a nice place to work, as you cannot start the engine before setting the valves. Block the car so it won't roll when it's out of gear. Open the engine compartment and put your stool down in back of the car, tools at hand and friend ready to read you these words: the ideal way to run Procedures.

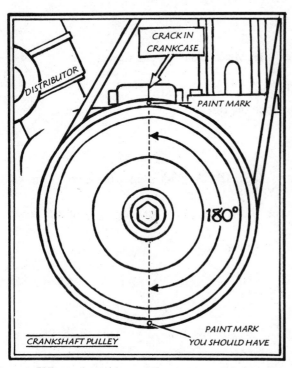

CRACK IN CRANKCASE

DISTRIBUTOR

PAINT MARK

180°

CRANKSHAFT PULLEY

PAINT MARK YOU SHOULD HAVE

Step 2. Mark Crankshaft Pulley or Crankshaft-Fan-Pulley

First thing is to get the 21mm or crescent wrench on the nut that holds the generator pulley on, so you can rotate the engine at will. If turning this pulley doesn't turn the engine, your belt is too loose, so turn right now to Chapter VIII and tighten the fan belt per the procedure. Turn the engine over clockwise a couple of twists just to get the feel of it.

Now find the crankshaft pulley at the other end of the belt. The crankshaft pulley has some filed notches on the front of the pulley (front, remember). There may be one, two or three notches and I'll clue you about them later as they are the timing notches. There should be a paint mark on the back side of the pulley (the side closest to you) and one opposite it (180°). If these aren't there, you have to paint them on, so send somebody for a paint stick or equal—white is best. If your paint marks are there, go on to Step 3.

When the paint stick comes, make a white mark on the crankshaft pulley where you can easily see it by the notches, then get a ruler and carefully make a mark just opposite or 180° around the pulley. See sketches on this and preceding page.

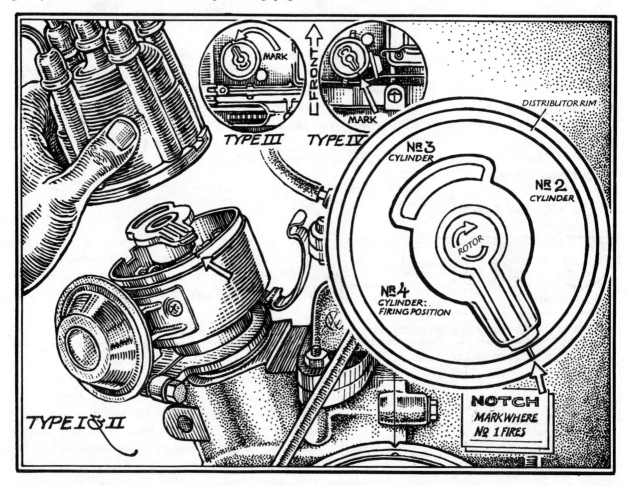

TYPE III   TYPE IV

TYPE I & II

DISTRIBUTOR RIM

Nº 3 CYLINDER Nº 2 CYLINDER

ROTOR

Nº 4 CYLINDER: FIRING POSITION

NOTCH MARK WHERE Nº 1 FIRES

Type III, IV and 1972-77 Bus

Your pulley is different but the action you take is the same. You need a mark 180° from the 0 mark on your kind of pulley so you can tell when the valves in the next cylinder are at top dead center—ready to set.

Step 3.   Get Cylinder No. 1 into Firing Position

All Models

Find the distributor. The cap is held on by two spring clips, so take the medium screwdriver and pry them off the cap. Lift the cap and push it out of the way. Find the filed line on the distributor rim (where you just took off the cap). See sketch on preceding page.

Type I (All) and Type II (through 1971)

Rotate the engine clockwise (forward, the way it runs) until the distributor rotor points to the line on the rim. Now line up your TDC mark with the notch or crack in the crankcase. This is Top Dead Center (TDC) for Cylinder No. 1. See sketch on preceding page.

Type III

Find the generator belt cover (rear of generator), pry the two spring clips off with a large screwdriver and remove the cover plate. Now you can see the generator belt and the crankshaft pulley. Above the center of the pulley is a hole with a rubber plug in it. Pull the plug out, stick your large screwdriver in the hole and catch the point of the screwdriver in between the teeth of the pulley. Pull or push the handle of the screwdriver to either side so the engine turns. Turn the engine until the distributor rotor lines up with the line on the rim of the distributor. Take the screwdriver out and look down the hole at the pulley. There will be two, three or four lines on the edge of the pulley. Stick your screwdriver back into position and turn the engine until the line furthest to the LEFT lines up with the pointer (the pointer is a protrusion on the aluminum fan housing). This is top dead center (TDC) for cylinder No. 1, where you adjust the valves for cylinder No. 1. Here's what you're seeing:

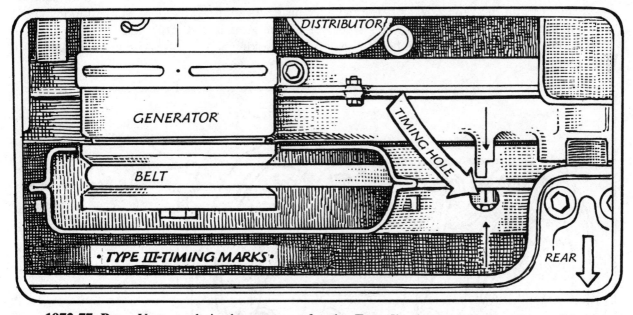

1972-77 Bus—Your work is the same as for the Type I's, but you have to use a 24mm or crescent wrench on the alternator nut to turn your engine. The timing notch on your pulley must line up with the "0" mark on the scale (those numbers going half way round the circle). This is top dead center (TDC) for cylinder No. 1, where you adjust the valves for this cylinder.

Type IV—Turn your engine the same as 1972-77 Bus. You have two notches on the crankshaft-fan-pulley which you can see by removing the large plug in the top of the fan housing above the pulley.

Step 3. (Cont'd.)

The black notch in the pulley is the timing mark for 5° before top dead center. For top dead center (TDC) this black notch should be 5° (1/8" is close enough) to the right of the 0 mark. The red notch has nothing to do with setting your valves.

Step 4. Expose the Valves

All Models

DO NOT JACK UP THE CAR! Make sure it's blocked and out of gear. Spread out the ground cloth under the right side of the engine and extending out to the rear, put on your stocking cap, take the 13 and 14mm, box open end wrenches, the medium screwdriver, the feeler gauge, and the flashlight and slide easily under the right side of the car, kind of on your right side so you are facing the right side of the engine.

Before you touch anything lie quietly and consider the scene in front of you. The engine is pretty well shrouded with sheet metal but you can see the oil sump portion of the crankcase. It has the plug for draining the oil and the round place where the oil screen is. As you look up there is an oval piece of pressed steel held to the engine with a loopy, thick, springy wire, like a bail on a bucket. This is the valve cover and under it is the valve assembly. Before you take the valve cover off, look at its lower edge. It may be cruddy but it should be dry. If the lower edge of the valve cover looks like it has been leaking, you should install new valve cover gaskets. The gaskets will look good when you get them off, so you must make your decision based on what you see now and the only criterion is: Has it been leaking? If one looks oil wet, replace them both, always. Now reach up with the 13mm and hook the ear of the open end under the wire and pry it out of its groove and down, then hook the 14mm ear under the other end of the wire and with the two wrenches walk the wire clip off the valve cover. When you get it started you can put the wrench behind the wire and pry. The clip will fall down when it has been pried loose. Put it out of the way, drop the wrenches and use two hands to pull the valve cover off the cylinder head. As soon as it's loose, start thinking about catching a possible oil drip. I put the valve cover on the ground under the place it came from to catch any oil that might be in the head. Now you are looking at the valves, rocker arms and push rods, like so:

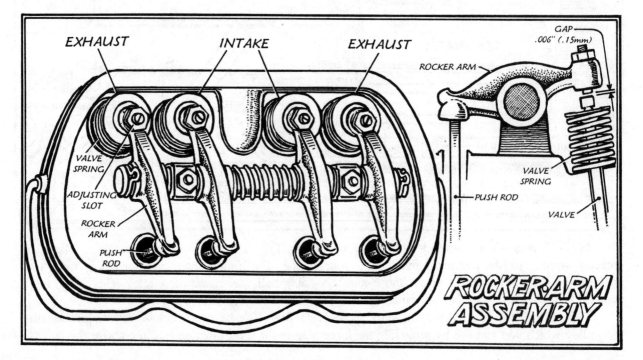

Step 5. Determine Valve Clearance

Models Older than 1965 (40 hp only.)

If you have divined from the introduction what your valve setting should be or if you have a decal to go by, skip this step.

You have exposed your valves and looked at them and the sketch. If you have a bolt head on the rocker arm hold-down, you probably have short studs, but check them anyway. If you have a nut (and washer) holding down the rocker arm assembly, there has to be a stud coming out of the head for this nut to screw onto to hold the assembly in place. How long is it? Reach around to the rear of the engine, up between the two push rod tubes that come up to the No. 2 cylinder (see sketch below) and feel if the rocker arm bolt goes clear down to the bottom of the head or if it stops just past the rocker arm block that you can see in front of you. If it goes clear down, you have long studs. Check both heads. I've found several engines with a stud kit in one head and long studs on the other. If you have short studs in any engine, you can use .006'' (.15mm) for the intake and .006'' for the exhaust. I set mine at .006'' and .006'' in all cylinders and let them click a little. Now VW also says .006'' for all valves.

If you have a 40 hp engine and long studs, set your valves at .008'' for the intake and .008'' for the exhaust. If you have an early 1500 engine and long studs, set them at .008'' for both intake and exhaust.

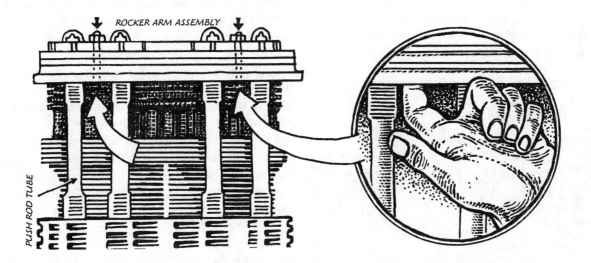

If you have long studs, think about getting the stud kit installed as soon as the bread is available.

From 1965 on, the valve clearance for all air-cooled Volkswagens is .006'' for the intake valves and .006'' for the exhaust valves. All you people with fuel injected engines have to be very careful to get the intakes as close to .006'' as you possibly can. It's important because the injectors are timed for exactly this valve setting, OK? The engine will idle rough if the valves are not right on.

A lot of people have written us asking why we recommend setting valves at .006'' when the little tag on the fan housing clearly says .004''. We found several years ago, along with other independent mechanics and even VW, that the looser setting of .006'', even though it cuts down the power (hardly enough to notice), helps prevent burned valves which was always a big VW problem. Your valves may clatter a little more but do it, OK? Put a piece of tape on the .004'' tag if it bothers you seeing it there.

Step 6. Valve Clearance Adjustment

All Models

Number one cylinder, which is in firing position, is the front one (front of car) on the right side. Take a little time to adjust to your body position. You are lying on your right side with both hands in position to work on the valve assembly. Take the 13mm (14mm) wrench and make sure the rocker arm hold-down nuts (or bolts) are tight. Don't twist them off. It takes a steady hard pull with the six-inch wrench (14 foot pounds) to get them tight. To keep the scene simple, I am going to use .006" for the intake and .006" for the exhaust, so if you have long studs and a different clearance, substitute the settings you need.

Get out the feeler gauge with the .006" blade ready for action. Start with the front valve (this is the exhaust valve in No. 1 cylinder). Push down with your left thumb on the bump on the lower end of the No. 1 exhaust rocker arm to tighten up the valve train. Hold the .006" blade like a straight razor between your thumb and forefinger so you can push with the finger and slip it into the gap between the valve and the upper end of the rocker arm where the adjusting bolt lives. If the .006" blade won't go into the gap, try the .004" blade. If it won't go, you have a tight valve. If the .006" blade just falls through the gap, you have a loose valve. If the blade slides through the gap with a slight resistance to easy sliding, the valve is right. If you want to make sure, try the .008" blade and if it won't go and the .006" does, you know you're right. Take your time. You can build up speed later but right now you have an eternity. Close your eyes and feel, slide the blade back and forth so you know the sensation. If you have a friend you trust who knows how to work a feeler gauge, this friend can check your first valve. Listen to what s/he tells you. You can actually feel the blade slipping between the two metal surfaces.

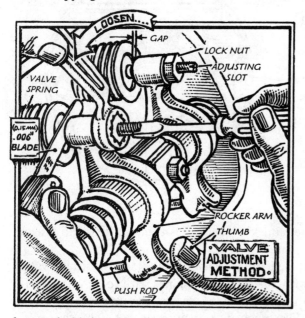

Whether the valve is too tight or too loose, the procedure for changing the setting is the same. The idea is to change the position of the adjusting bolt back or forth in the top of the rocker arm. It screws clockwise to make the distance between it and the valve less and counterclockwise to increase this clearance. This bolt has a locking nut to hold it in position after it's been adjusted. This locking nut must be loosened before you can adjust the bolt to change the gap. Take the 13mm (14mm) box end wrench and get the box end firmly on the lock nut. Make sure the wrench is secure on the nut as this is a place where skinned knuckles abound. If the nut doesn't come loose with one hand, use two. When this nut is loose, you can put a screwdriver in the slot in the end of the adjusting bolt and screw it in or out to make the clearance what you want it to be, but it isn't quite that simple. After the lock nut is loose, hold it with the wrench and work the adjusting bolt back and forth in the nut with the screwdriver to get the threads in a little better adjusting shape.

I have two methods for adjusting valve clearances and it depends on how easily the lock nut moves on the adjusting screw. If the nut moves easily, I use the "Imprisoned Feeler Blade" method and if the nut turns hard on the screw, I use the "Memorized Slot Location" method and sometimes a combination of both.

For the Imprisoned Blade, you put the wrench on the lock nut, the screwdriver blade in the bolt slot. Let the wrench go and get the proper feeler blade between the bolt and the valve, screw the adjusting bolt until it imprisons the blade by squeezing it between the valve and the bolt. Then let go of the feeler and tighten the lock nut on the bolt. Now try the feeler blade to see if you did it right.

The Memorized Slot is useful when turning the lock nut tends to turn the bolt also. Put the screwdriver in the bolt slot and the feeler blade in place and tighten the bolt until the clearance seems right. Memorize this position of the slot. Now get the wrench and turn the lock nut down on the bolt. Turn the bolt a little loose so the nut will twist it to the memorized place when you tighten.

In both methods, tighten the adjusting nut down tight and check the clearance again. If it is correct, go on to the next valve. If it isn't you're back where you started, so begin again. Remember that a little looser is better than a little tighter. It will take time and patience to get them right, especially the first time. Stay cool. Get the gaps right as they are important. If the nut sticks onto the adjusting stud, don't fight it, replace the stud with a new one.

When the exhaust valve is right, do the intake valve in No. 1 cylinder with the .006'' blade, then crawl out for a rest. After you've been setting your own valves for a while and are familiar with them there will only be one or two in the whole engine that need to be changed.

Step 7. Move the Engine

All Models except Type III

Turn the engine backwards (counterclockwise) 180° (1/2 circle) or until the paint mark on the crankshaft pulley (where the timing mark or notch isn't) is lined up with the crack in the crankcase or the 0 mark. Now cylinder number two is in firing position and you may crawl back under the right side of the car and proceed to do Step 6 for cylinder No. 2. Remember you've now moved the valves, so you can no longer check the adjustment in No. 1.

Type III

Crawl out from under the car, grab the large screwdriver and turn the engine backwards (counterclockwise) 180° or until you see the section of the pulley with three bridged teeth. Line up the center of the bridged section with the pointer above and there you are, No. 2 cylinder is in firing position and its valves are ready to adjust. Crawl under the right side of the car again and do Step 6 for Cylinder No. 2. Remember, you've moved the engine so you can't check the valves on cylinder No. 1 again.

Step 8. Replace Valve Covers

All Models

If the valve covers were leaking oil you should put in new gaskets. So you take the Scout knife and scrape and cut the old gasket out and clean the valve cover. **Make sure there is no grease where the gasket goes.** When it's clean you coat one side of the gasket and the place where the gasket fits in the valve cover with quick-drying glue and put the two coated surfaces together. NEVER PUT GLUE ON THE SIDE OF THE GASKET WHICH FITS ON THE HEAD! In fact, when you have stuck the gasket into the valve cover, scrape off any glue that might get on the outside of the gasket and clean it with a rag. If you glue the gasket to the head, you will have to put on new gaskets every time, besides cleaning a mess. Let the glue dry a little before you put the valve cover back on, which you can do when both No. 1 and No. 2 are adjusted. If the old gaskets were OK or if you have the new ones ready to go, clean out the inside of the valve cover, wipe the sealing face on the head with a rag, and make sure the gasket in the valve cover is free of crud. I put a thin coating of wheel bearing grease on the face of the gasket that fits to the head. Put the valve cover up to the head with both hands, make sure it is on the head, catch the wire clip with your thumb and hold the wire and cover with one hand while you get the screwdriver under the wire with the other hand to pry the wire up into its slot.

Step 9. Move the Engine

All Models except Type III

Get out from under the car, crank the engine with the wrench counterclockwise another 180°

Step 9. (Cont'd.)

until the timing mark or notch is again lined up with the crack in the crankcase or the 0 mark. This is where cylinder No. 3 fires, the front one on the left side. Move your ground cloth and run Step 4, then Step 6 on cylinder No. 3. The two center valves are Intake and the two outside valves are Exhaust.

Type III

Crawl out from under the car. Turn the engine counterclockwise 180° with the screwdriver until the LEFT mark on the pulley lines up with the pointer on the fan housing above. This is where cylinder No. 3 fires, the front one on the left side. Move your ground cloth and run Step 4, then Step 6 on cylinder No. 3. The two center valves are intake and the two outside valves are exhaust.

Step 10. Move the Engine

All Models except Type III

Crank the engine counterclockwise another 180° until the paint mark, not the timing mark or notch, is lined up with the crack in the crankcase or the 0 mark. This is where cylinder No. 4 fires, the rear cylinder on the left side, the only one you have left. Run Step 6 on cylinder No. 4 and then do Step 8 on the valve cover. There, you've adjusted the valves. OLE!

Type III

Crawl out from under the car and turn the engine counterclockwise another 180° until the center of the bridged part of the pulley lines up with the pointer. This is where cylinder No. 4 fires, the rear cylinder on the left side. Run Step 6 on cylinder No. 4 and then do Step 8 on the valve cover. There, you're done. OLE!

RAP ON DISTRIBUTORS

Just what kind of distributor do you have? Volkswagen has used three main types through the years: mechanical (centrifugal) advance, semi-mechanical advance and vacuum advance. The first two types have been the same all the way but the vacuum advance distributor has gone through several modifications and has been standard equipment on all models for many years. I hate them! They are another sop to American buyers who refuse to learn to shift a car with a little coordination. This is just a personal beef, so forgive me. I use a straight mechanical advance distributor, called the Porsche Type, which advances the distributor on rpm as the engine speeds up. Most VW race cars and beach buggies use the same. It gives a very good power curve on the VW engine.

The vacuum distributor advances the spark based on the vacuum in the carburetor (as opposed to rpm) and they will never make good since the principle is wrong. That, however, is what they give you with the car. I saw a demonstration 1969 accessory car on a VW showroom floor with a speed set-up on the engine and guess what? Right. It had a mechanical advance distributor on it and at only $30.00 extra, so when you get bread ahead, buy one for your jewel. You have to block up the hole (or holes) in the carburetor so it doesn't leak vacuum. Vacuum leaks burn valves, if you didn't know. Now that's out of my system. **See Changes and New Ideas.**

Type III and IV with Fuel Injection can't use any other distributor than the one that comes with the car because of the extra set of trigger contacts in the bottom.

TUNE-UP

To put you in the mood, I will tell you how I work it. I have two distributors and two sets of spark plugs. When it starts getting toward tune-up time, I remember to do an overhaul and check of my spare distributor and have the plugs cleaned and tested at the gas station. This cuts my "down time" by quite a lot on tune-up day as it becomes a straight replacement job. I make sure to have new rubber air seals available in the spares kit so if they're getting beat I can replace them. I use Bosch plugs, points and condensers as they seem to work well with the German blood in the car.

Now I have to tell you how to tune up your car because I can't expect you to do it the same way I do. So, in the following procedure, I start you with tuning the distributor by just setting the points and assuming that the condenser is OK since the car is running well. Then I do a separate thing on changing points and condenser. By the way, I never install new points without also installing a new condenser and vice versa and I advise you to do the same. Something happens when you break up the old team. I don't understand it but I have observed it and pass it on to you. It will save you trouble some mountainous day.

TUNE-UP PROCEDURE: ADJUSTING POINTS, TIMING, SPARK PLUGS, COMPRESSION CHECK, COIL, CLEAN OIL SCREEN, ADJUST IDLE, LUBRICATION, Phase I

Tools and Materials: Phase I tool kit and, if needed: two oil screen gaskets, new spark plugs, new rubber seals for the spark plug holes, new ignition points and condenser, wheel bearing grease. You'll need solvent to clean the screen and things, heavy duty brake fluid for the reservoir and diesel to run through the carb...all three things can be bought at a gas station. Note: People with newly overhauled or new engines should not run diesel through their carbs. Use diesel only for older engines with like 40,000 or more miles on them. Get four quarts HD-MS oil—usually 30 weight. Don't change brands between oil changes. A Tach-Dwell meter is a necessity for all models, 1968 on. As you save the cost of one with the first tune-up, why not? If you have dual carbs, you'll need to buy or borrow a vacuum measuring device called a Uni-Syn or equal to set them. A piece of .016'' (.4mm) wire makes a handy gauge to check your point gap.

Step 1. Adjusting Points

All Models
Get out the stool and sit down. Pry the two spring clips off the distributor cap with the screwdriver, pull the cap off, and store it out of the way. Look at what you're seeing. Pull the rotor off for a better view.

Type IV: Pull the rotor off and then the plastic dust cover.

All Models
Put the 21mm (24mm) or crescent wrench on the generator (alternator) nut and rotate the engine clockwise, the way it runs, and watch the points open and close as you turn the engine. See how that nylon rider on the moving point spreads the points open as the nearly square distributor shaft rotates its corners, called lobes, under the rider. At each point of the lobe the points are separated the maximum amount. This amount, in the Volkswagen, all years and models, is set to .016''.

Filing Points—Old Fashioned—Emergency Only
Note: I guess filing points is gone like the nickel cigar. With the new tungsten points, filing just doesn't hack it. Put in new points and use a Tach-Dwell meter to set the gap.

The part about filing points I'll leave in for field emergencies—I still carry a point file but I set my points with a dwell meter.

Get the point file between the two points, put a finger on the moving point to hold tension on the file and move the file back and forth until that tit is gone off one point and they both are fairly smooth. The idea is to get an accurate adjustment with the feeler gauge so get them smooth enough so the feeler gauge will slide through. After you have them filed to your satisfaction, clean the point faces and the area with a clean, dry, oil-free rag. If the points are too far gone to file, go to the next procedure and install new points and condenser.

Adjusting Points
There are several point set-ups in the various distributors but they all have a similar scheme. The

Step 1. (Cont'd.)

moving point has to be at its widest point, which occurs when the rider is at the peak of one of the lobes on the distributor shaft. So move the engine with the wrench until the rider is exactly on a lobe. Get out the feeler gauge and find the .016" blade. I use a flashlight to make sure I'm seeing what's what. Try the blade between the points, you just might be lucky. The adjustment is made by moving the stationary point. It has a hold-down screw which now must be loosened—unless you were lucky. Get the screwdriver blade with the best point as these hold-down screws are notoriously tight and beat up as well. Clamp the vice grip on the screwdriver blade to help you turn the screw if necessary. Get the screw loose, then just a little tight, so the point will move when you change its position, then stay there. Locate the adjustment device. It might be a screw in the tail of the stationary point plate or it might be a notch in the plate with two little bumps on the distributor plate, or whatever, but there's always a way to move this point tiny amounts so you can make the adjustment in something under an hour. Put the screwdriver in the adjustment device and the feeler blade between the points and the other screwdriver on the hold-down screw and the other hand holds the flashlight and your tail is swishing the flies off and there you have it. Anyway, get the points so they are .016" apart when the nylon rider is on a lobe, then tighten the hold-down screw. Put a whole sharp pencil-point full of wheel bearing grease between the shaft and the nylon rider. I always give the points a last cleaning with a super-kleen rag after I finish. Take a knife and brighten up the sparking end of the rotor and put it back on the shaft. Type IV—put the dust cover back on and then the rotor. It can only fit one way.

Check the Point Setting with a Tach-Dwell Meter

Connect the positive (red) lead of the dwell meter to terminal No. 1 on the coil (wire from coil to the distributor). Connect the negative (black) lead of the dwell meter to a good ground (bare metal). Switch the meter to the four cylinder position (eight cylinder position if yours doesn't have a four cylinder position). Make sure the other switch is on the dwell position and not tach. Start the engine and note the dwell. On a 4 cylinder scale, it should read 50° plus or minus 2°. On an 8 cylinder scale it should read 25° plus or minus 2°. If the dwell is too high, the points are too far closed. If the dwell reads too low, the points are too far open so adjust the points accordingly.

RAP ON TIMING

Why is timing? To make the spark jump across the spark plug at the proper intensity, duration and at the strategic time to properly *burn* all the fuel so the burning will be: complete, for no smog emission; powerful, to get the most power to the rear wheels; efficient, for economy; and cool, so you don't burn up your engine. If the best timing for power were the same time for minimum emission or if the engine were going to run at some constant rpm, the timing problem would be simple, but the timing device (the distributor, so called because it distributes the spark to the spark plugs) must be able to apply the spark at the right time and for the right duration throughout the entire rpm range.

The fuel and air are compressed by the piston being pushed through the cylinder toward the head. This compression makes a hot, explosive mixture which must *burn*, not explode (detonate, ping). With detonation comes excessive heat, a hard hammer thrust to the piston top and damage to the head and the whole rest of the engine. Detonation happens when the spark plug fires too soon (the timing is too advanced). There is one best time to strike the match (timing) and one best length of time for the match to burn.

Think of the crankshaft turning 360° each revolution. *Dwell* is 1/2 the number of degrees the crankshaft turns while the ignition points are closed. VW dwell (all models) should be $50^\circ \pm 2^\circ$ and that's what you set when you gap your points at .016" with the nylon rider on the high point of the cam lobe. In other words, the length of time the match is lit is constant throughout the rpm range.

Remember this: Top Dead Center (TDC or DC, 0°) is the point where the piston stops dead still, changing its direction from toward the head to toward the crankshaft.

Now back to the exciting, explosive timing story. At idle, the one best time for the spark plug to fire (the match to be lit) is somewhere around TDC or a little before but as the rpm's increase, the timing must be advanced, the match lit sooner, so all the mixture can be burned in the relatively less time allowed. This means that the burning starts before the piston reaches TDC and continues on past. Imagine this burning process at 3600 rpm happening 1800 times a minute in No. 1 cylinder alone. If we don't light the match faster—sooner, the mixture has no time to burn properly. Let's use the 1970 engine as an example as its timing is set both statically and at idle at TDC or at 0°. If the spark plug fires too soon, the mixture detonates; too late, the mixture doesn't all burn. At idle, the spark fires the mixture at TDC and it burns efficiently. As the rpm's increase, the spark is advanced degree by degree to about 20° somewhere around 2500 rpm. The relationship between the degrees of timing advance and rpm can be put on a graph and the resulting curve is called an Advance Curve. The way your car drives from standstill, through the gears and finally on the highway in fourth is determined by this curve.

The Mechanical advance type distributor uses the centrifugal force of rotating weights to advance the point plate around so the points open sooner. The Vacuum type uses vacuum from the carburetor to suck the points around. The third type is a combination of the above two and was used on the old 36 hp and now again on most models since 1971. Each type has its own driving characteristics; with the Mechanical type, you must keep your foot on the accelerator with verve, elan and confidence as it won't forgive inattention. The Vacuum type allows a great deal more carelessness but power and efficiency suffer. The combination type is just that but is evidently what is needed to get a decent advance curve and still pass the emission standards. Most of these distributors are returned to the retard position by springs except for models which have a vacuum retard for idle.

History is usually somewhat of a drag but I gotta make a point, so let's go back to the Model T Ford. The distributor was attached to a rod which ended on the left side of the steering wheel in a lever. The throttle lever was on the right and you didn't forget which was which, either. To start the Model T you gave it about a quarter throttle and retarded the spark all the way by moving the lever up (if I remember correctly), then you went out and cranked the engine over. The choke wire came out of the radiator where it was handy and a vitriolic vocabulary was almost a necessary stock in trade. If you forgot to retard the spark the engine would fire backwards and the crank would either break your arm, tear off a thumb, throw you over into the ditch or all three. After the engine started, the spark could be advanced as was required by the speed you were driving. At anything over a few miles an hour, it was all the way advanced. OK, that was then. Now the spark is retarded by the springs in your distributor so the engine will start and idle. Then a vacuum or centrifugal advance moves the points around to advance the spark for higher speeds.

Thus, timing the engine becomes the simple task of setting the distributor so the engine starts and idles well, then advances as the rpm increases to some efficient point, OK? The Volkswagen is an air cooled car and the Model T and all its descendents are water cooled but that doesn't explain the real difference—remember we are talking about timing. The Volkswagen and most air-cooled cars have very tight valve trains and water-cooled engines have notoriously sloppy ones. And that, in a nutshell, is why water-cooled engines are timed in an rpm range wherein the spark timing is advanced and air-cooled cars are timed either statically or at idle when the timing is retarded. If a water-cooled car, at speed, is timed too slow, it will run hot. If an air-cooled engine is timed too fast, it will run hot. A water-cooled engine should be brought up to speed under load and timed to where it just doesn't ping or detonate. If an air-cooled engine is timed that way, it will burn itself up in a very few miles.

Now I told you all this to make one point: a water-cooled engine needs a strobe light so the timing can be set at a high rpm and an air-cooled engine can be much more accurately timed when it is standing still, statically. Volkswagen engines should be timed standing still, not at idle when there are too many operator errors possible. You, maybe a mechanical idiot, can do a better job timing your VW engine in your own back yard than all the mechanics in the world can with all that electronic equipment. I fear that when the strobe light way of timing started for VW's it was just a device to get your Volksie in the hands of people who have tachometers and expensive stroboscopic timing lights and all that jazz—who needs 'em?

Volkswagen has done a pretty good job of brainwashing most people into believing that their engines need to be timed with a strobe light. In fact, for the last few years, they have given their timing data based on using one, a practice which I decry. Those engineers know better. OK, so what I am doing is to reduce the timing and timing marks and timing specifications so all of you can time your own engines, statically, with a static timing light you can make. Then, for those who are brainwashed, Tosh has written up the way to time your late model, maybe fuel injected, jewel the way VW says to do it. So take your choice. **See Changes and New Ideas.**

Note: There is a relation between timing and the octane rating of the gas you use. Here is the rule to remember: the lower the octane the slower the timing should be set (more retarded). For example: you have a 68 Type I which is designed to be timed at 0° TDC using 91 RON (octane) gas, right? Well, let's say the cheap gas you're using is rated at say 82 octane. To compensate for the lower octane, you'll want to move the timing to the left—after TDC one or two degrees.

The best indication that the timing is set too fast for the octane you're using is if your engine pings when a load is put on it (i.e., when you're pulling up a grade in high gear) or if it "runs on" when you turn the key off. This situation is harmful to the engine and should be remedied quickly by either retarding the timing enough to stop the pinging or "running on" or changing to a higher octane gas. **See Chapter XXI for High Altitude Timing.**

The operation of timing is simple: you just loosen the 10mm nut on the clamp bolt at the base of the distributor and rotate the distributor until the timing is set right, then tighten the nut—this you do whether you time it statically or with the strobe light.

Step 2. Timing

The first step in timing your engine is setting the point gap which you did in Step 1. If at any time this point gap changes, through a bump in the road or the wearing of the nylon rider, then the timing has to be changed for the new point gap. First point gap, then timing-OK?

Now look in the timing chart for whichever type of Volkswagen you are going to time. Volkswagen, from the beginning to today has only four static positions for sea level: 10° Before Top Dead Center (10 BTDC), $7\frac{1}{2}^O$ Before Top Dead Center (where the piston is at the top of its compression stroke—7½ BTDC), 5° Before Top Dead Center (5 BTDC) and 0° or TDC. Now what's yours?

Now I'll tell you where that little clamp nut is for all Types and we can proceed to time your engine—statically. They all turn counterclockwise to loosen and clockwise to tighten.

Type I (All) and Type II (through 1971)

The clamp bolt and nut to adjust the timing are at the base of the distributor right next to the fuel pump. The nut is facing you—10mm socket and extension on the ratchet.

Type III

The clamp nut sticks out of the clamp at the base of the distributor. The bolt is longer than in Type I's so you can reach it with a 10mm open end wrench. Stick your wrench to the rear of the distributor, between it and the fan housing and you will be right on.

Step 2. (Cont'd.)

Type IV and 1972-on Bus

The nut is a 2'' long one so you can find it without benefit of your eye—you can't see it but you can feel it. It is in FRONT of the distributor, sticking out to the right. Reach in and feel with your fingers, then get your 10mm open end wrench on it.

There are three ways to rotate engines:

Type I (All) and Type II (through 1971), use your spark plug or 21mm wrench on the generator nut.

Type III use a screwdriver down through the access hole to pry the engine around.

Type IV and 1972-on Bus, use a 24mm or crescent wrench on the generator pulley nut.

Are we ready?

All Models

Unfasten the clips that hold down the distributor cap—a Scout knife screwdriver blade is handy for the back clip on the Type III's and IV's. Lift off the cap, find the notch on the rim of the distributor either by sight or run your fingernail—if you still have any—around the rim under Number 1 spark plug wire. Take the rotor out and be sure you know which part of it the spark jumps across from. They come in the center and go out the side—the rotor is pointing that way or there's a brass thing on roundy rotors. Put it back. Rotate the engine until that part of the rotor is approaching the notch in the distributor rim, then put the cap back on and clip it down. See Timing Chart.

Get out your static timing light, test the bulb, then clip the clip to the connection on the coil where the thin wire from the coil to the distributor is connected. (See Orientation, Chapter VII to find the coil.) Make sure the thing the bulb is screwed into is touching a piece of metal as a ground. Turn on the ignition key. Rotate the engine clockwise watching your timing notch and the light at the same time, so when the light comes on you are ready to stop turning. If your engine is timed correctly, the light will go on when the notch in the pulley has the proper relationship with the crack in the crankcase (Type I and II through 1971) or the pointer (Type III), or the line on the fan housing (Type IV) or the correct number on the scale (1972-on Bus). See Static Timing Data. If the light comes on and stays on no matter how you turn the engine there's crap in your points or for some reason your points won't close, so take off the cap, clean off the points and start over. If the light doesn't go on at all, check all your connections and the bulb.

It wasn't perfect? OK, so move the engine backwards a little to take the slack out of the distributor, then clockwise again until the notch is exactly at the place it should be—or at least where I say it should be. Now you can loosen the distributor clamp nut and rotate the distributor until the light just flashes on, tighten the clamp nut and try it. If it's right, you're through but if it isn't right, loosen the nut, move the distributor, tighten the clamp nut, try it—until it's right.

Timing with the Stroboscopic Timing Light

The strobe light emits an extremely bright light which is flashed from a pistol-like instrument. The clip with the heavy wire is attached to a spring which is inserted between the distributor cap and the spark plug wire that goes to No. 1 cylinder. Follow the instructions that come with your light. You pull out No. 1 plug wire, put the spring in the hole in the cap, attach the wire to the top of the spring, then fasten the clip with the heavy wire to the spring. The other two leads go to plus and minus 12 (or 6) volts from the battery. When you pull the trigger on the strobe light, with the engine running, it produces a very bright light which you use to see what the relationship is between the

TYPE I

Year	Engine Code	MT		AT	
1950-65	1200-G1500	10ºBTDC[1]		———	
1966-67	FI, HI, HO	7.5ºBTDC[1]		———	
1968-70	HI, BI, H5000001	0ºTDC[1]		0ºTDC[1]	
1971-73	AE, AH	5ºATDC[2.5]		5ºATDC[2.5]	
1974	AK	7.5ºBTDC[3]		7.5ºBTDC[3]	
1974	AH	5ºATDC[2]		5ºATDC[2]	
1975	AJ	5ºATDC[6]		5ºATDC[6]	
1976 on	AJ	5ºATDC[6]		0ºATDC[6]	

TYPE II

Year	Engine Code	MT		AT	
1954-65	1200-G1500	10ºBTDC[1]		———	
1966-67	FI, HI, HO	7.5ºBTDC[1]		———	
1968-70	HI, BI, H5000001	0ºTDC[1]		———	
1971	CA	5ºATDC[2]		———	
1972	CB	5ºATDC[2]		———	

If you're not sure how to time your '71 on engine statically and can't put the bread out for the strobe light, I suggest you borrow or rent a strobe light or take it to VW and let them set it to the proper strobe mark. When you get home, attach your static timing light just like you were going to time the engine, rotate the engine until the rotor is almost to where No. 1 fires, then **carefully** a little more until the timing light goes on. Try it a coupla times to make sure. Take a file and make a mark opposite the crack in the crankcase or the zero mark and you can time your engine to that mark forever after. Please look at the sketches.

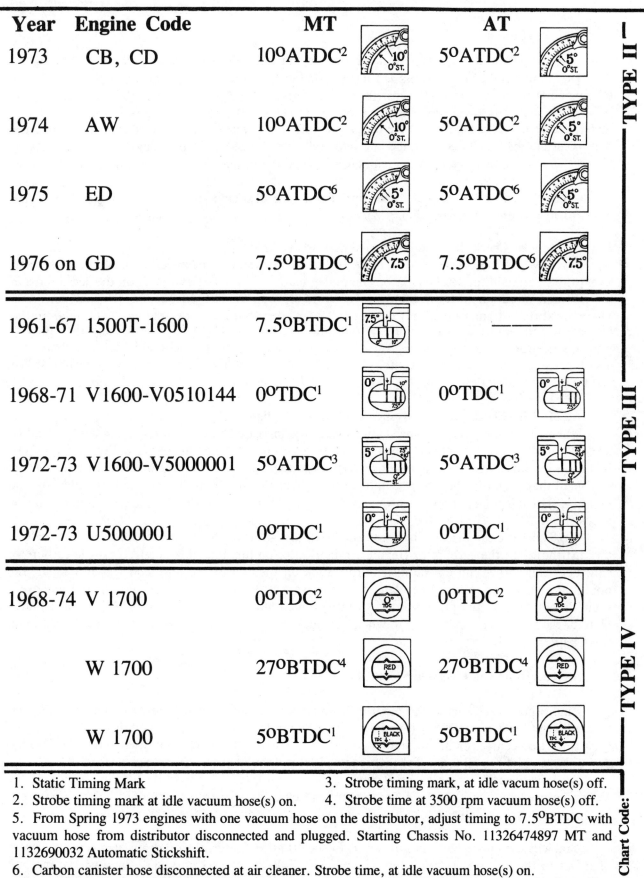

Year	Engine Code	MT	AT	
1973	CB, CD	10°ATDC[2]	5°ATDC[2]	**TYPE II**
1974	AW	10°ATDC[2]	5°ATDC[2]	
1975	ED	5°ATDC[6]	5°ATDC[6]	
1976 on	GD	7.5°BTDC[6]	7.5°BTDC[6]	
1961-67	1500T-1600	7.5°BTDC[1]	———	**TYPE III**
1968-71	V1600-V0510144	0°TDC[1]	0°TDC[1]	
1972-73	V1600-V5000001	5°ATDC[3]	5°ATDC[3]	
1972-73	U5000001	0°TDC[1]	0°TDC[1]	
1968-74	V 1700	0°TDC[2]	0°TDC[2]	**TYPE IV**
	W 1700	27°BTDC[4]	27°BTDC[4]	
	W 1700	5°BTDC[1]	5°BTDC[1]	

1. Static Timing Mark
2. Strobe timing mark at idle vacuum hose(s) on.
3. Strobe timing mark, at idle vacum hose(s) off.
4. Strobe time at 3500 rpm vacuum hose(s) off.
5. From Spring 1973 engines with one vacuum hose on the distributor, adjust timing to 7.5°BTDC with vacuum hose from distributor disconnected and plugged. Starting Chassis No. 11326474897 MT and 1132690032 Automatic Stickshift.
6. Carbon canister hose disconnected at air cleaner. Strobe time, at idle vacuum hose(s) on.

MT — Manual transmission   TDC — Top dead center   ATDC — After top dead center
AT — Automatic transmission   St. — Static timing mark   BTDC — Before top dead center.

Timing Chart Code:

Step 2. (Cont'd.)

notch in the pulley and the timing mark on the fan housing or crankcase. OK on strobe lights?

This timing is the same process as for static timing. The difference is that the work is done while the engine is running. Loosen the distributor clamp nut enough so the distributor requires a strong twist to be moved but will stay where it is moved to. Then with the strobe light and the Tach-Dwell meter, connected as in Step 1 start the engine. Set the rpm to match the specification rpm on the Tach, then point the light at the crack in the crankcase (all Type I's and Type II through 1971) or the pointer (Type III) or the timing mark on the fan housing (Type IV) or the scale (1972-on Bus). The idea is to line up the notch in the pulley with the indicated place, then move the distributor until the relationship is per specification, then shut off the engine, tighten the distributor clamp nut, then start the engine again to make sure the relationship is per spec. When it is, the timing is done.

All Models—Check distributor advance with strobe light

Here is where the strobe light is handy. If it is still hooked up, engine idling, push on the throttle lever while you hold the strobe light on the pulley mark—or have a friend push on the accelerator in the car—and watch the notch in the light. It should move to the left (advance) as the rpm's increase. There are different amounts of advance for different distributors, but if the notch advances to the left as the rpm is increased to about 2500, 3000 rpm (maybe 15 to 24 degrees) and then returns, your distributor advance is working and you can put away the timing light and Tach-Dwell meter in a safe place and go on to the next step. If the advance unit isn't working, go to the Distributor Procedure in this Chapter.

All Models—Check vacuum advance without strobe light

When the engine picks up speed, the vacuum is increased in the combustion chambers and intake manifold(s). This vacuum increase is transferred through the vacuum hose (from the carburetor or intake air distributor on the fuel injection engine) to the biscuit on the side of the distributor. There is a small diaphragm in the advance unit on the side of the distributor, connected to a rod. The rod pulls the plate the points sit on and advances the timing as the engine speed increases. Here's how you check it out.

First take the cap off the distributor and pull the rotor off. Now pull the hose from the side of the distributor to the carburetor (intake air distributor on fuel injection engines) off the carburetor end. Leave the other end on the distributor. Suck on the end of the hose and watch the plate the points are sitting on. The whole plate should move a little bit. Some types of distributors have a small diaphragm and the plate won't move very much but it should move some. If your distributor plate doesn't move, doesn't advance when you suck on the tube, go to the Distributor Procedure in this Chapter.

Step 3. Drain Oil, Clean Oil Screen, Put in Oil

Find a pan that's sort of flat (so it'll fit under the car) and that will hold two and a half quarts (three quarts for Type IV). Put it under the oil drain hole in the center of the bottom of the engine (just to left of center for 36 hp and Type IV's on). Use the 21mm or 19mm wrench to remove the drain plug and let the oil drain. Take a break and let it drain about 15 minutes.

Do you have oil screen gaskets? Since the little oil screen is the only filtering device on the Volkswagen except for Type IV's, we recommend cleaning it every other time you change the oil. Find your 10mm wrench and take it with you while you slide under the center of the engine.

Type I, Type II through 1971 and Type III

You will see a plate with six nuts on it. In the 40 hp and later, the oil drain plug is in the center of it but in the 36 hp the drain plug is to the left. Take off the six nuts, save the washers, and pull the plate off. It won't be too bad as the oil has been draining for a while. If you do this first, as logic might dictate, you get oily. Pull the screen out and clean it in solvent. Clean the plate, too. Get the

Step 3. (Cont'd.)

gasket off the sump. Put a gasket on each side of the oil screen and work it up on the studs with the clean plate right after. Replace and tighten the washers and nuts, around and around the circle — not too hard, they're tender; just get them tight. Put the new gasket on the drain plug, put the drain plug in and tighten it with the 21mm wrench. Types I and II, 73 and on have no drain plug.

Type IV and 1972-on Bus

The oil screen is to the right of the oil drain. The oil screen is bolted with a single 17mm bolt in the center, so use a box end or socket to loosen the bolt, then pry off the oil screen, gently, with a small screwdriver. Clean the screen and plate with solvent, put on the two gaskets and replace the oil screen in the oil sump. Start the bolt and put it up hand tight.

THIS BOLT MUST NOT BE TORQUED OVER NINE FOOT POUNDS OR THE CAMSHAFT WILL BE HARMED!

OK, if you have or can borrow a torque wrench, no sweat, just torque the bolt to 9 ft. lbs. If you don't have a torque wrench, try this: It's kinda like bunting in baseball when you choke the bat. Choke the wrench by holding it and applying the turning force 6'' (half a foot) from the center of the bolt. Now you can guess how much force is 18 pounds. Apply just that much at the 6'' point and the torque will be right—at least as right as you guess about the 18 pounds. Set a bathroom scale up on its side and practice pushing 18 pounds. If it's too loose, it will leak a little oil and you can tighten it a little more but if you get it too tight...The Type IV and 1972-on Bus engine (they're the same) has another little surprise for you. It has a full flow oil filter; that round thing under the left side of the engine. Change it every other oil change. It just screws out of its hole and the new one screws in. BY HAND! You may have to use a filter wrench or a jar top remover to get the filter off. After you clean the sealing area put some oil on the neoprene seal so it will slide around, then just screw it up by hand; you can use both hands if you want. Buy your filters from Volkswagen as they have the ones with the correct flow factors. The other change that this filter brings is that it takes a full three quarts to bring the oil almost to the full mark. See **Chapter XX**, Change Oil.

All Models

Get out from under the car and put two and a half quarts of oil in the filler hole (three quarts for Type IV) and replace the cap. Check for leaks. **Here's a quick dipstick trick:** If you suspect that your dipstick might be the wrong one for your engine, fill the engine with 5.3 pints, wait 15 minutes for all the oil to reach the sump, then check your dipstick. If it reads anything but full, buy the right dipstick from VW.

Step 4. Warm Up the Engine

All Models

Take the distributor cap in your left hand and the scout knife in the other to clean the four posts in the distributor cap where the sparks have been jumping. The rotor is in, right? So put on the distributor cap and install the two clips. Snap the back clip on first, then the front clip with your fingers. The distributor cap fits into a notch so make sure it's right. Oil in? OK, you can start the engine and warm it up. If not, go back to Step 3, then make sure the engine runs about ten minutes to warm it for the compression check. In the new Type IV's and 1972-on Bus, there is a plastic dust cap over the points in the distributor. If you forgot it, put it in now.

Step 5. Check the Compression

Type IV and 1972-on Bus—Note for Removing Spark Plugs

The spark plugs sit right on top of the engine at an angle that will seem crazy to you until you get the hang of it. All the plugs are set in so their bottoms are closer to the center of the engine than their tops are. It isn't a big angle (10 to 15 degrees) but just enough to drive you crazy getting them in

Step 5. (Cont'd.)

and out. To get at Number 1 in almost all of the Type IV engines, you will have to take off the crap that's interfering with a clear shot at the plug. In the 1973-74 Bus, the pre-heater hose is in the way so pull it off and stash it out of the way. In the 1972 Bus the bottom of the air cleaner is in the way so unclip the clips and move it and so it goes—don't forget to put these goodies back when you are through.

Another handy thing is to have different length extensions handy. For example, nine inches of extension works for number 1 (you can make this up with a 3" and a 6"). While the 6" is fine for number 2, use a 3" on number 3 and back to the 6" for number 4. Once you get the idea it will go easy. The bottoms of the plugs all point toward the center of the engine, remember.

ALL MODELS: If a plug feels as though it's tightening up as you remove it, it's probably stripping the threads out of the cylinder head, or seized up, as they say. The only remedy is to pull the engine out. See rap in Step 6.

Pull the spark plug connectors off all four plugs, put the front wires to the front and the rear wires to the rear so you can get them back on where they came off. Take the spark plug wrench and loosen all four plugs until they're like hand-tight, pull the ratchet off the wrench and use the extension and socket to screw them out of the last few threads. They will be too hot to handle so lay them out in a row with the socket. If the car has been idling to warm up, there's not much use in examining them for color but if you've been on the road, you can tell by the color how your engine is running. The porcelain around the center electrode should be tan to brown if your engine is in good shape. If the porcelain is black, the rings are probably worn. I go more by the compression check and the sound of the engine. With all the plugs out you are ready to make the compression check, so find your tester. The idea is to hold the rubber end of the tester down into the spark plug hole, tightly (REMEMBER SAFETY!), while a friend turns the engine over six times with the key and writes the results down. This is a record of how your engine is running and you should keep the data.

It'll take a little practice: you should feel the pressure, but hear very little sound. If you don't get any reading, try it again. The test results should be over 100 pounds and within about five pounds of each other. Number three will usually be the lowest as it runs the hottest. If your tests show less than 90 pounds, squirt some oil into each spark plug hole, then test again to see if that raises the compression. If you have over 100 lbs. compression and it's approximately equal in each cylinder, your engine is good, so save the readings and go on to Step 6.

If your readings are low or if you get one low reading or if the addition of oil raises the compression, turn to the Introduction in Chapter XV, the overhaul chapter, and read what it says about compression checks and what they mean. Go on to Step 6 anyway unless you are going to do an overhaul right away. You can read Chapter XV later.

Step 6. Adjust and Install Spark Plugs

All Models: Never tighten spark plugs when the engine is hot.

You either have a new set of plugs or a set of cleaned and tested plugs. They have to be adjusted to VW specifications. The gap between the bottom bent electrode and the center straight electrode has to be an exact dimension for the pressure and heat conditions in the cylinder. This gap has to be between .025" (0.6mm) and .028" (0.7mm) for the VW. I have a spark plug gapper, one of those round things with wires all around it to set mine, but you can do it close enough with any feeler

Step 6. (Cont'd.)

gauge. The bent electrode can be carefully bent in and out to make the adjustment. Try the gap with the .025'' (0.6mm) blade or wire, then bend the electrode and if it needs adjusting try it again. Keep at it until the wire or blade just fits. That's all there is to it.

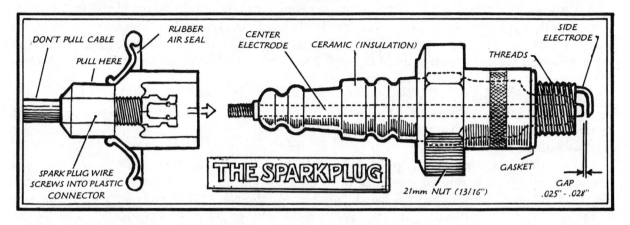

Make sure there is a gasket on each plug, then put the plug in the socket of the spark plug wrench. Use your fingers on the extension to tighten them as far as they will go by hand. Do this to all four, then put on the ratchet and tighten them all. They have to be fairly tight to seal but not like a big nut, so just tight and a little more to set the gasket, OK?

Put the plug wires on the way you took them off. They got mixed up? Well, it's easy to get them right. Look at the wires coming out of the distributor cap. No. 1 is the closest to the rear of the engine. Around the circle counterclockwise, the wires are 1-2-3-4 so just trace the wires down to the cylinders. No. 1 is the front one on the right, No. 2 the rear cylinder next to it. No. 3 is the front one on the left with No. 4 the rear one next to it. Pull the wires a little to make sure you have the right ones. Put the new rubber seals on, if needed, then push on the connectors. If your engine misses and you've looked everywhere—check these spark plug connectors. Sometimes they have radio spark suppressors in them that screw up. **See Changes and New Ideas.**

Here is a spark plug problem that can stop you cold on tune-up day. If a plug seems to be coming out very hard and comes out with strips of metal hanging around the threads, you have a **stripped spark plug** hole in the cylinder head.

Unfortunately, the only remedy for this is to pull the engine out (chapter XV), take the sheet metal off over the offending cylinder head and take the head down to a machinist who will shoot a heli-coil in the stripped hole. We recommend going to the trouble of taking the cylinder head off so metal shavings don't get into the combustion chamber, thus causing more troubles than you'd want to believe. When the engine is together again and in, leave the plug out of the newly threaded hole and spin the engine over a few times with the starter in an attempt to blow out any shavings in the works. Then put in the plug. OK.

A word of advice here. I find that Bosch, Beru and NGK tend not to strip spark plug holes nearly as often as the other brands. There are also several anti-seize compounds on the market you can apply on the threads to prevent this from happening.

Step 7. Check Coil—Replacement

All Models

Every time you do a tune-up, take a moment to check your coil. Pull the center wire out of the distributor, get something really insulated to hold it, like a pair of pliers with plastic handles or use two plastic-handled screwdrivers like chop sticks. Hold the end of the wire about 1/8'' to 1/4'' from a bare metal surface and have someone turn the engine over with the key. If you get a bright, hot blue-white spark, your coil is like new. If you get a good strong yellow spark, your coil is getting

Step 7. (Cont'd.)

old but is still serviceable. If you get a weak, orange spark that will hardly jump the 1/4" gap, you need a new coil.

Coil Replacement—All Models except Type III

If you buy your coil at VW, it will have the right connection marks on it and will fit the installation location but you can use any six (twelve) volt coil. I get mine at VW. The removal and installation consists of removing the two 10mm bolts that hold the old coil to the fan housing, putting the new coil in place and replacing and tightening the bolts. The socket wrench makes the job easier but it can be done with the box end or open end.

Type III

With a 10mm wrench, remove the nut on the bolt holding the coil bracket to the fan housing, then remove the bolt through the fan housing.

All Models

On the VW coil, the terminals are push-ons, and if you have the old type you will need to change the wire terminals. The thin wire coming up to the coil from the distributor connects to terminal No. 1 (-), the one from the ignition switch connects to terminal No. 15 (+), and the center big wire to the center of the distributor. Try the check on the new coil to see what a good spark looks like.

Step 8. Adjust Idle

All Carburetor Models

If you have fuel injection, go ahead to Procedure for Adjusting the Fuel Injection System in this step.

On the Volkswagen, the closest thing to a sediment bowl is the carburetor bowl and there's a plug on the left side of the bowl to drain it. Use the 13mm (14mm) to remove that plug on the left side. Let the gas run out—it will soon dry. If you suspect crud in the gasoline (engine sputtering, running erratically) get a shot glass or equal to catch this gas as it runs out to see if it has cruddy balls of water and dirt in the bottom of the glass. You may have to clean your gas tank, in which case it has to be removed and taken to a shop with cleaning facilities for this operation. In the older models there is a jet in the plug you took out, so blow it out before you reinstall it in the carburetor. Screw the plug or plug with jet back in—don't forget the gasket. Just tight, not a dying strain. Wait a few minutes for the gasoline to dry, then start the engine. See **Changes and New Ideas**.

Note: If you have dual carbs, the following is not how you set your idle so just read on until you come to **All Carburetor Models**, then **Procedure for Synchronizing Dual Carburetors**. It isn't that dual carbs are all that different, just that there are two that have to work together.

Single Carbs Only

Right in back of the big plug you just put back in there's a screw with a spring on it. This is the **idle air screw**. Put your stocking cap on so your long hair won't get caught in the machinery, make sure your necktie is well secured. This adjustment must be made when the engine is warm. Reach in with a long-bladed screwdriver and turn this little screw in the engine clockwise until the engine starts to slow down, then turn it back out until the engine runs faster and then starts to slow down again. You are changing the amount of air that mixes with the gasoline at idle. Now screw it back in until it slows the engine again, then back out (counterclockwise) until the engine is running its fastest, then a half turn more. That's a good place for the idle air screw.

The **idle screw** faces to the rear and mechanically adjusts the throttle lever for a proper idle. Adjust this after the idle air screw has been set. Make sure it is on the lowest point of that fast-idle cam on the carb. Set it so the engine runs just fast enough to make the red light on the dash go out. Or you can set it to 850 rpm with a Tach-Dwell meter.

On the 1970 and on carburetors, the idle is set with a fuel screw on the left side of the carb. The

Step 8. (Cont'd.)

idle air screw is set at the factory to match the total air volume of each engine so all you do after the engine is timed and warm is turn that big screw (the fuel screw) until the idle is the way you want it. As the engine now idles with the butterfly closed, the set screw, formerly the idle screw, on the throttle arm should not touch anything unless the choke is in operation. It should be close but not touching as you adjust the idle. OK?

All Carburetor Models

There comes a time when the idle air screw(s) has no effect on the speed of the engine—screw it in, no change, screw it out, no change. This means that the place it screws into is crudded up so much that the crud is making the adjustment for you. The carburetor(s) needs cleaning. You can remove it. There's a step in the next procedure for this to clean it or have it cleaned and reinstall it but I'll tell you what I do. I buy two cans of STP Gas Conditioner and put one in my gas tank. The next time I fill up, I put the other one in. When that tank has run out, I try the idle adjustment again and then if it won't adjust, I pull the carburetor and clean it. You've probably been wondering what the hell the diesel fuel is for, so now we're going to use it.

Note that this diesel stunt is to help an engine that is older and starting to ail. I don't think you should run diesel through your engine until it has about 40,000 miles and is starting to burn some oil. If you have two carbs, run the diesel through both.

Take the air cleaner off the carb(s) and have one of your many assistants open it up and clean it out per Step 10 while you get one hand on the throttle lever, the quart of diesel in the other and slowly pour the diesel into the top of the carburetor while the engine is running. Keep the engine running as you pour. Don't let it die. If you're loaded with bread, you can use Bardahl but the diesel is as good. What we are doing is burning out some of the carbon in the engine—cleaning it, in other words. Run the whole quart through. You will be surrounded by choking smoke by the time you're through but don't quit. Hang in there and get all the diesel through the engine. Don't shut off the engine before the big clouds of smoke stop coming or your plugs might foul.

If you have a single carb, go forward to Step 9.

PROCEDURE FOR SYNCHRONIZING DUAL CARBURETORS
(This Procedure is part of Step 8)

Condition: You have dual carbs and it's tune-up time or your engine has been running rough, missing or is burning more gas than you (and our resources) can afford.

Tools and Materials: Medium screwdriver, a Uni-Syn or equal, Tach-Dwell meter, humility and for Type III's a small frozen orange juice can and rubber ring seals, if needed.

Using the Uni-Syn

The Uni-Syn is a vacuum flow meter and it uses a bouncing ball in a tube to visually indicate the vacuum an engine is sucking down through the carb throat. It makes no indication as to the amount of vacuum but is only interested in comparing the vacuum in two carbs so you can balance the adjustment...this is called synchronization. If the two carbs are not balanced, you find the conditions in the Condition.

You put the Uni-Syn directly on top of each carburetor—one at a time. (Or for Type III on top of a small frozen orange juice can which fits into a rubber ring seal on top of the carbs. If your rubber ring seals are gone from the carbs, get some now and put them on; they also seal the air cleaner.) Look at your Uni-Syn and note that the tube with the ball in it has marks on it. These marks are a comparator gauge. With the Uni-Syn on top of the carb (or O.J. can) and with the engine running, the ball should rise to somewhere in the center of its tube. It may go clear to the top or stay at the bottom. Don't freak, there's a dial in the center of the Uni-Syn which you turn one way or the other to adjust the height of the ball.

Step 8. (Cont'd.)

If the ball rides steadily in the tube of the Uni-Syn you have a good seal but if it bounces around the seal between the Uni-Syn and the top of the carb it is questionable, so make sure the device is well sealed to the top of the carb. Then if the ball bounces around making it difficult, if not impossible to do your balancing act, you have to fix some vacuum leaks either in the carb mounting or in the carb itself. The 1972 Bus has had a little trouble with the seal at the base of the carburetors where the butterfly valve shaft comes through the body. This is the throttle and if this shaft has worn the body of the carb, just about all you can do is get new carbs, a very expensive process, or have your carbs bushed in a machine shop. Take your carbs around and get a firm bid. It should cost less than 20 bucks a carb.

When we say throughout this Procedure to "see if the carbs are balanced," it means to do the following:

Get your hair well tucked up into your stocking cap. Warm up the engine so it is running smoothly. Put the Uni-Syn on top of the carb (or the O.J. can) and watch the little ball. It will rise in the tube. Adjust the dial so the ball is about in the center, then move the Uni-Syn to the other carb and see where the ball is. If the ball rises to about the same height on both carbs, your carbs are balanced but if the ball is at a different height on one carb than on the other, you have to make the adjustments indicated in this Procedure, so let's get to Step A.

Your valves have been adjusted—COLD—to exactly .006'' Intake and .006'' Exhaust. The timing is right on the money, too. In all dual carburetor and fuel injected engines, the valve setting is fairly critical so if you haven't adjusted them, have at.

Step A. Remove Air Cleaner—Clear the Decks

Type III
The air cleaner is held down by three wing nuts, so unscrew them (you will have to pull off the hoses watching where they come from and maybe marking them for when you replace them) and lift the air cleaner up and out. Be careful, it has oil in it.

Type II, 1972 and Type IV
The air cleaner is mounted in the engine compartment with connections to both carbs. Free the clips that hold the air cleaner connection on top of the carbs, remove the bolts that hold the air cleaner and haul it out. There are hoses to remove and remember how to replace.

Type II, 1973-74
Your air cleaner sits in the center of the engine with connections to the tops of both sides. It is a paper filter type with no oil in it. Remove the connections and lift the whole thing up out of the way. The paper filter should be replaced every 18,000 miles so check your speedometer. Remember how the hoses come off so you can replace them.

Step B. Check Engine Idle and Carb Balance

All Models
Hook up the Tach-Dwell meter. The positive (usually red) lead attached to the coil at the same place as the thin wire coming from the distributor is attached. The other wire can go to any convenient engine ground. Put the switch on Tach, start the engine and get it warm and running well. Read the tach. If it indicates an rpm of about 900 for Types II and IV or 600 for Type III, don't touch anything. Use the Uni-Syn to see if the carbs are perchance balanced. If the idle is OK and the carbs balance, go to Step D. If your idle is not OK or if the carbs don't balance, follow along with Step C.

Step C. Setting the Idle and Balancing the Carbs for Type III and Type 411

Check your automatic choke butterfly valves at the top of the carbs to make sure they are all

Step 8. (Cont'd.)

the way open. There are two screws we will be fiddling with so get them straight in your head. There is a lever with a screw in it on the side of the carb. This screw regulates the amount the throttle butterfly valve (inside the carb) stays open during idle and is called the **idle screw**. The screw that screws into the carb, either on the side or under the bowl, is called the **idle air screw** or **volume control screw**. Find both the idle screw and the idle air screw and be prepared to manipulate them as required.

If your engine has been running well and you're just doing a tune-up but the idle is a little fast or slow, you can adjust the idle screws on both carbs the same amount until the idle is 900 (Type IV) or 600 (Type III), then see if your carbs balance. If the balance is close, don't mess with anything else and go to Step D. The rest of the Step is for engines that are not running well.

Type III

Adjust the idle so the engine is running at about 600 rpm, then find the place where the linkage to the two carbs and the throttle lever are attached. Pull off the linkage to the **right** carb; the linkage rod ends are spring loaded to fit over the balls on the linkage lever. Just pull on the end to compress that little spring inside, then lift the linkage rod off the ball.

With the right carb linkage free, you can proceed to adjust each carburetor separately.

Use the medium screwdriver to turn the idle air screw all the way in—not too tight—then turn it out 1-1/2 turns. Do the same for the left carb. Now turn the idle screws so the tach reads 600 rpm, then start moving the idle air screws (both) just little tiny amounts, while watching the tach. If the rpm's increase, OK but if they don't, turn the idle air screw the other way. When the engine is running at the highest rpm allowed by these little adjustments to the idle air screw, put the Uni-Syn on top of the carbs and adjust the idle screws so the two carbs balance (the ball rises the same height on both) and the Tach is reading 600. I try to stay away from the idle air screws at this point but they can be adjusted slightly to make the engine smooth out. OK, the engine is idling at 600 and the carbs are balanced, so now adjust the length of the right hand linkage rod with the pliers so you can reconnect it. It should slip over the ball with no strain or rpm change. With the linkage connected, tie a piece of soft wire to the throttle lever and pull on the wire until the tach is reading about 2500 rpm's. Then fasten the wire to the handiest thing and put the Uni-Syn on both carbs to see if they balance at 2500 rpm. If they do you are through and go to Step D. If they don't, shut off the engine and adjust the right-hand linkage rod a little, start the engine, and try the balance and repeat until the carbs balance at about 2500 rpm. OK? Now try it at idle again by removing the wire. If they balance, you are through and go to Step D but if they are a little out of balance make the adjustment with the idle screws so the carbs balance out at 600 rpm. If you are doing this on carbs that have been in imbalance for a long time, you might have to do the above two or three times the first time but once you get them set, you will find that just a touch-up at tune-up time will keep them up to snuff.

Type 411, 1968-70

Adjust the idle to 900 rpm and shut the engine off. Find where the linkage to the two carbs and the throttle lever are attached to the linkage shaft. Remove the linkage rod to the left carb—just pull it off. Take the left linkage rod out of the car, and with a ruler, measure the distance from center to center of the ball sockets...should be a hair less than 4-1/8". If it's not, loosen the lock nut and set it to 4.114" (4-1/8" = 4.125").

Look inside the engine where you took the rod from. The top of this rod connects to the ball in the linkage arm. The linkage arm is clamped to the linkage shaft. Loosen the clamp bolt so the linkage arm turns freely on the linkage shaft, then replace the rod and return spring where they came from. Turn the idle screws counterclockwise on both carbs until the throttle butterflies are fully closed, then turn the idle screws clockwise until the screws just contact the stops—then clockwise again 1-1/4 turns. Turn the volume control screws on both carbs in...softly...until they contact their seats—you can feel this contact—then counterclockwise one turn. Start your engine (Tach-Dwell meter still connected) and turn the idle screws equally until the tach reads about 900 rpm. OK? Turn the volume control screws clockwise on both carbs equally until the rpm drops off a bit, then clock-

Step 8. (Cont'd.)

wise until the engine smooths out (you'll hear it), then 1/4 turn more—counterclockwise still. Now turn the idle screws equally until you get 900 rpm again. See if the carbs are balanced with the Uni-Syn. If not, make the adjustment with the left carb idle screw. When the carbs are balanced at 900 rpm, tighten the linkage arm clamp on the linkage shaft. Recheck the balance at idle. Get it right, then fasten a wire to the throttle lever on the linkage shaft, pull the wire back and fasten it to something when the engine speed is 2500 rpm (watch the tach). See if your carbs are balanced at 2500 rpm using the Uni-Syn. If they're out of balance, you have to shorten or lengthen the left-hand linkage rod (the one you took out and measured before). When the carbs balance at 2500, loosen the wire and check with the Uni-Syn at 900 rpm again. If they balance, go to Step D. If not, remember, we said humility and keep trying.

Type II, 1972-74

Check the automatic choke butterfly valves at the top of the carbs to make sure they are all the way open. Locate the adjusting screws which are on top of the left carb. The big one is the idle speed screw and the little one is the volume control screw. If your engine has been running well and you're just doing a tune-up, hook up the Tach-Dwell meter, set it to Tach and adjust the idle speed to about 900 with a medium screwdriver in the idle speed screw.

Put the Uni-Syn on first one and then the other carb and see if the carbs are balanced. Tie a wire on the throttle lever on the throttle linkage bar, pull the wire until the tach says 2500 give or take a little, tie it off to some handy projection, and try the Uni-Syn on the carbs for balance again. If the carbs are in balance, at 900 and at 2500 rpm, you can go to Step D.

If your engine has been running rough or you've had the carburetors off or the gas mileage has been bad, you can start by setting the carburetor linkage. Shut off the engine. Make sure that the lever on the lower part of the carb is not being held open. In these carburetors, the idle circuit bypasses the throttle butterfly valve in the base of the carburetor so the butterfly must be allowed to close completely. See that the wires to the automatic choke and the cut-off jets are connected.

Now pull the ball socket off the linkage to the **right** carb. Make sure that both throttle butterfly valves are closed. Check the relationship between the socket and the ball you just removed the socket from. Are they at the same elevation? Or is the rod too short or too long?

If you find a misalignment of the rod and socket, go along the linkage tube, the thing that moves both carburetor throttles at the same time, until you get to the left end of it. Right there is a bolt with a long thread and an adjusting nut. If you adjust this nut, the ball and socket on the right carb can be made to align. Don't change the length of the rod except as a last resort. When this adjustment nut has been moved so the ball will fit into the socket with both throttle butterflies closed, push the socket on the ball. Start the engine.

Adjust the idle to about 900 rpm and balance the carbs with the Uni-Syn. If the carbs do not balance, shut off the engine, pull off the left-hand carburetor ball and socket and change the length of the rod just a little. Connect the ball and socket, start the engine and try the balance again. OK? If not, do it again. When the carbs are balanced at idle, fasten a soft piece of wire to the throttle lever on the linkage, pull on the wire until the Tach says 2500 or a little more, then tie off the piece of wire so the rpm stays steady. Now balance the carbs with the Uni-Syn. If they are not in balance, adjust the nut on the left-hand end of the linkage tube—the same nut you adjusted before—until the carbs are balanced. OK? Turn loose of the wire so the engine idles. Set the idle with the idle screw to 900 rpm and balance the carbs at idle, OK? Fine, but if not go back to setting the left-hand ball and socket, then try the balance at 2500 rpm again. The first time you do this, you will probably have to fool around more than you want to to get it right, but after you get them right once, they don't get out of synchronization often so it will be just a matter of checking the balance at tune-up time. Don't get discouraged.

When the carbs are balanced at both idle and 2500 rpm, you can adjust the volume control screw. Use a small screwdriver to turn the volume control screw clockwise until the engine speed slows down a little—watch the Tach—then turn the screw counterclockwise until the Tach reaches a

Step 8. (Cont'd.)

high point. You will have to do this a coupla times to be sure. Now turn the volume control clockwise until the rpm drops 20 to 30 rpm, then counterclockwise 1/4 turn. Voila! Now adjust the idle speed screw until the Tach says 900 rpm. Remove the wire from the throttle lever and disconnect the Tach. You're through.

Step D. All Models

Replace the cleaned (per Step 10) air cleaner so all the hoses are connected the way you took them off, fasten the clips or wing nuts, bolt the air cleaner down, clean up the engine and that's it.

PROCEDURE FOR ADJUSTING THE ELECTRONIC FUEL INJECTION SYSTEM, 3000 MILE TUNE-UP, Phase I

Part of Step 8 for those with electronic fuel injected engines. Note: Please read the Rap on Fuel Injection further on in this Chapter before doing this part of your tune-up.

Tools and Materials: Phase I tool kit including a Tach-Dwell meter, a fuel pressure gauge which reads up to 30 psi and a fuel filter.

Step A. Adjust Idle

The engine should be warm and running. Get out the Tach-Dwell meter, hook the positive (usually red) lead to the No. 1 terminal on the coil and the negative (usually black) lead to a good ground.

The throttle must be fully closed to adjust the idle, so open the throttle lever a bit, then close it. It makes a slight click when it's closed. If you don't know where the throttle lever is, have a friend push the accelerator pedal up and down while you watch to see what moves. That's the throttle lever. Locate the idle screw on the left side of the intake air distributor (the aluminum or black metal box that the throttle lever is on). The idle screw is either a screw with a lock nut on it or a screw with a spring under it. If it has a lock nut on it, loosen the lock nut with a 15mm wrench. Turn the idle screw clockwise to increase the rpm and counterclockwise to decrease the rpm. It takes a few seconds for the engine to respond to the adjustment, so just hang loose. If you have a Tach-Dwell meter, 850 rpm is where you want it. If you don't have a Tach-Dwell meter, adjust the idle until the red light on the dash goes out and then maybe a 1/4 turn more. If you have a lock nut, hold the screw with a screwdriver and tighten the lock nut.

Note: If your engine refuses to idle and you've done this step, check the EGR valve, Chapter VII.

Step B. Adjust Throttle Valve Switch

The throttle valve switch is the black plastic gizmo on the right side of the intake air distributor. Pull off both the electrical connection and the rubber elbow from the air cleaner. Look in the mouth of the intake air distributor with a flashlight and make sure the brass butterfly valve is fully closed. Now look at the switch. There are two screws that hold it to the intake air distributor. Above the top screw on the intake air distributor, there is a single notch and on the switch plate below the notch there are graduated lines. Find them. Loosen the two mounting screws and rotate the switch body clockwise facing it. Now slowly rotate the switch body counterclockwise until you hear a slight click. Note which line on the switch body lines up with the notch on the intake air distributor when you hear the click. Rotate the switch in the same direction (counterclockwise) one further gradua-

Step 8. (Cont'd.)

tion. That's it. Tighten the two screws and put the electrical connection back on remembering the bevel on the electrical connection has to line up with the electrical connection on the switch.

Step C. Adjust the Fuel Pressure Regulator

Get out your fuel pressure gauge and a screwdriver. Look between injectors No. 1 and 2 and you'll see a T connection with a screw on top. OK? (If you don't know where the injectors are, they are next to the spark plugs.) Hold the T firmly with one hand and remove the screw on top with the screwdriver in the other hand. Now put the fuel gauge hose over the T connection you just opened and tighten the clamp. Start the engine and go back and see what the gauge reads. If it's 28 to 30 psi it's OK. If not, find the fuel pressure regulator (on the frontmost piece of tin on the right side of the engine). Use your 13mm wrench to loosen the lock nut on the regulator and the 10mm wrench to adjust it. Turn the 10mm bolt until the gauge reads 28 psi, then tighten the lock nut and check it again. You'll have to wait about two or three minutes for the fuel pressure to go down before you can pull the hose off the T fitting. Remember to replace the screw on the T. That's it. If you had to change the pressure, go back to Step A and check the idle.

Step D.   Replace the Fuel Filter (every other tune-up)—For AFC also.

The fuel filter is the plastic box next to, or from 1969 on, on top of the fuel pump. It should be changed every 6,000 miles. It can't be cleaned so you'll have to buy a new one from VW. To remove the filter, pull the line off of it that goes to the gas tank above and shove a pencil in the hose to prevent gas from gushing out. Please—light no matches. If it's mounted on top of the fuel pump, you will have to take the pin out of the bottom of the mounting bracket and bring the filter down to where you can get to it. Pull off the other hose.
Look at the new filter on the seam where the part number is. See the arrow. Put the filter on so the arrow points toward the fuel pump. If the filter is mounted on top of the pump, the arrow should point toward the hose going into the pump. In other words, it should point in the direction of the flow of fuel (from tank to pump).
Once you have determined the proper direction of flow, reconnect the hoses and install the new filter just like you took the old one out.

PROCEDURE FOR ADJUSTING THE AFC FUEL INJECTION SYSTEM, 3000 MILE TUNE-UP, Phase I
Part of Step 8 for those with AFC Fuel Injected Engines. Note: Please see the end of this chapter to adjust idle and Step D. (above) to replace the Fuel Filter.

Step 9. Clean Fuel Pump Screen (not for Fuel Injection). See Changes and New Ideas.

There are three types of fuel pumps used on Volkswagens and they all need the screens taken out every other tune-up, or every—in a dusty land. You just take out the screen, clean it in solvent and put the screen back in, making sure the gasket is tightly sealed. There is the old type with a little bolt on the top of the dome—loosen the bolt, take off the dome, clean the screen and put it back. The second type has a screw instead of a bolt so repeat the above substituting "screw" for "bolt." The third type has four screws in the top, which don't come out unless you are overhauling the pump. There's a bolt in the rear of this type and the screen lives in front of the bolt, so clean the screen and put it back...mind the gasket.

Step 10. Clean the Air Cleaner (or Replace the Paper Filter)

All Models

My friend Dick says the two main causes of Volkswagen engine failure are tight valves and dirty oil bath air cleaners. The air cleaner should be cleaned at every oil change in a dusty clime and every other in clean air and where can you find that these days? All you have to do is unscrew, unbolt or unclip the air cleaner, take it off and wash it clean with solvent and rags, then add oil up to the red line (from the half quart you have left—Type IV open new quart). Put the air cleaner back on and tighten or snap the clamp around the carburetor. I let the filter part, all full of copper wool, soak in solvent or even gasoline all the time it takes me to do a tune-up and then let it dry out before I put it back. It's just another dirty chore that will add many miles to the life of your engine.

All (most?) 1973 and on models have paper replacement type filters and they say they will last 18,000 miles and I have no reason to doubt them so that's every sixth tune-up. Will you remember?

Fuel Injection Note: Never allow the oil over the red line—a little under is better.

Step 11. Lubrication

That extra quart of oil you bought is to store in the car for later, as you shouldn't change brands between oil changes, but now you can use the rest of that one half quart you have left to fill your oil can.

Type I, II and III pre 1965

Turn to Chapter XII, Procedure for Tightening the Torsion Arm Link Pins. This should be done every 6,000 miles and before the grease job. All Models:

Ride on down to the place where you get your grease jobs to have them grease the car. If you take it to VW, they won't let you watch but in the regular gas stations they will and in Mexico you have to. With the car on the rack, you can check everything under it for dangerous loosenesses. Tighten the front support bolts on the transmission with a 17mm wrench, for instance. The trans support nuts or bolts are the two 17mm ones that bolt the trans to the frame at the front of the trans. They won't be loose in the new models, but in the older Busses they occasionally need tightening. The best time? While the car is on the grease rack.

You can also make sure they check the transmission level and in the Bus the transfer cases. On trips you should carry the long nut or the 17mm allen head that takes out the plugs as lots of places can't get the fill plugs out. The most important thing to watch is the transmission oil level—not low but too much. The average service station attendant will fill it up with the gizmo, then jam the plug in to hold the extra oil in the case. DON'T LET THEM DO THIS TO YOU!! Extra oil in the transmission will blow your seals! When they add oil to the trans, you make sure either by instructions or better, by watching, that all the extra transmission oil is drained out of the fill plug before they put the plug in. Listen to me—this is like $$$.$$ important. In the spring I have them drain the old transmission oil and put in new.

With the number of things a grease job giver has to do becoming fewer and the price of grease jobs skyrocketing, it's probably time you set up to do your own. Here's how:

LUBRICATION PROCEDURE, Phase I—All Models

Condition: 3,000 mile maintenance plus miscellaneous items. Pack front wheel bearings at 30,000 miles, see Chapter XI. Drain and fill transmission and pack rear wheels at 30,000 miles. Pack the CV joints every 15,000 miles, see Chapter XIV.

Tools and Materials: Phase I tool kit, grease gun with flex hose. Be sure to buy one that takes cartridges of grease, then you just shove the old cartridge out, pull the ends off a full one, shove it in, screw the end on and you're in business. Have the person in the store show you how to change the cartridge if you have questions. You will have to buy the flex hose separately and put it on. Cartridge of grease, heavy duty brake fluid, bottle of window cleaner (VW), oil can with 30 wt. oil, tube of graphite, rags, grease stick or petroleum jelly, 17mm allen wrench (transmission check).

Step 1. Lubricate Front End

Jack up one side of the front end either with regular or scissors jack. The grease won't go in unless the weight is off.

NOTE: How to use a grease gun of the hand pump type: See Changes & New Ideas.

On the end of the flex hose there's a female alemite fitting. There are males screwed into all the places on the front end that need grease. Clean the male fitting until the ball is shiny, using a rag or paper towel. Push the female over the male at an angle, then pull the female back straight; that makes the connection. Grab the barrel of the gun with one hand and the handle with the other and pump a little. If grease starts to come out of the connection, stop right away and make the connection over. If grease does not come out of the connection, you're in business, so you can pump until you see grease coming out of the thing you are greasing indicating that it is full. If you get a big glob of grease on the whateveritis, wipe it off with a rag. If the connection between fitting and hose refuses to seal, the fitting has been damaged and will have to be replaced—they just screw in—I find the small vice grip a worthy tool. If you cannot force grease through any of your fittings, you will have to take it to the service station and get the power grease gun on it but make sure grease goes through all the fittings and then you will be able to do it after that.

All Models 1964 and earlier without ball joints

You have six places to grease on each side, two for the king pins, two for the torsion arm link pins and two places for the torsion tubes. If there are grease fittings on your tie rod ends, grease them too. Check the tie rod ends for play and the whole front end while you're at it.

All Models 1965 and later with ball joints

You have two fittings to grease, one on each torsion tube—those big tubes that run all the way across the front end.

Bus, all models

In addition to the above, you have one fitting in the center, the swing lever arm, to grease. Try it when you have the first side jacked up but if it won't take grease, relax and try it again when you have the other side up. Sometimes you have to get both wheels off the ground before the grease will go into the fitting.

All Models

Jack the first side down and repeat for the other side. When you have finished both sides, jack the car down, clean the grease gun and put it away. That's all you use it for.

Step 2. Fill the Brake Fluid Reservoir

This is located in various places according to type and model—like under the spare in the Type I, III and IV, under the floor mat under your right foot in the old Bus, in front of the steering column in the new Bus; anyway, find it and fill it, but not full. Leave about 1/2" clear space to allow for expansion. Replace the cap.

Step 3. Fill the Windshield Washer Tank

If you don't have one, skip this step. The tank is under the spare in the Type I and III and under the dash on the right side in the Bus. Use about 1/2 cup of the VW window washing fluid (more if it gets real cold where you live), then fill it up to the top with water. Put the top back on and pressurize it to 40 psi at the gas station.

Step 4. Miscellaneous

All Models

Put a drop of oil on everything that moves on the carburetor.

Use the grease stick or petroleum jelly on all the door catches. Don't forget the back catch on the new Bus sliding door. It doesn't hurt if you use too much but wipe the excess off with a rag. Squirt a little powdered graphite in each key slot and work the key and the lock a few times. If you have loose graphite, dip the key in the powder.

Fill the battery with distilled water.

Fill the tires to your selected pressure—the spare, too.

See your Owner's Manual for any further maintenance and lubrication tasks for your particular model, like Type I with swing axles should take their cars to VW for a front and rear wheel bearing cleaning, adjusting and packing every 30,000 miles.

1968 and on

Fill the reservoirs on the door hinges with oil.

If you have one, check the little rubber valve on the lower end (under the car) of the oil breather pipe, If it's beat up, replace it.

Step 5. Transmission

If you have a Type I, III or IV, you will probably want someone in the service station to check and fill your trans but the more adventurous of you may want to join the Bus owners in checking your own oil level. Take out the top fill plug with a 17mm allen wrench and stick a finger in the resulting hole. The oil level is correct when the oil is even with the bottom of the hole. Then off to the station to get it filled. If you wish to equip to add your own trans oil, you will need a suction pump about 2" in diameter with a long flex nozzle and, of course, some 90 wt. Hypoid gear oil. It's a spilly job so bring some rags. The same admonitions about overfilling apply to you as to the service station.

That's all there is to it. You're through for another 3,000 miles, so smile.

DISTRIBUTOR PROCEDURE: REMOVAL, OVERHAUL AND INSTALLATION

Condition: Distributor needs new points and condenser, oil is leaking around the distributor base.

Tools and Materials: Phase I tools, new points and condenser to fit your distributor; use the number on the side of the distributor to order them. Wheel bearing grease, new rotor, if needed; new rubber "0" ring, if needed (it's in the gasket set).

Step 1. Distributor Removal

All Models

Note: Bug and Ghia (pre 1967) owners don't have to take the distributor out to change the points and condenser but all others should. It's hard to work if you can't see, which you can't in the Bus engine room.

Take the medium screwdriver and snap off the two clips that hold the distributor cap, pull the cap off and store it out of the way. Pull off the vacuum line, if you have one (it goes to the carburetor). Turn the engine until No. 1 cylinder is in firing position. See the Valve Adjustment Procedure in this Chapter, if you don't know how. Note where the notch in the distributor rim is in relation to the engine. It points to the rear. FRONT is front, remember. Pull the thin wire to the coil off at the coil.

There are two ways of removing the distributor in a VW and you can take your choice. One is

Step 1. (Cont'd.)

to loosen the clamp nut at the base of the distributor with a 10mm wrench and pry the ears of the clamp apart then pull the distributor out. The other is to take the nut off the distributor clamp stud to the right of the distributor and lift the distributor out complete with clamp. A friend says this way is much easier on the distributor "0" ring than the first way. It may also be easier to do on some models.

Once the distributor is out, take off the rotor and you're ready to install new points and condenser. Don't move the engine while the distributor is out and it will still be where No. 1 fires when you're ready to replace the distributor.

Step 2. Replace Points and Condenser

When you install new points, it's a good idea to clean them in alcohol before installing them to remove the manufacturer's oil. Use the drug store kind, beer won't work.

There are so many types of distributors it's impossible to cover them all, so I will give you a method that should cover your needs. The first thing to do is to check the advance mechanism. In the vacuum type, just suck on the place you pulled the vacuum line off of and watch the plate in the distributor. It should rotate when you suck, stay as long as you suck, then return when you stop. If it doesn't, the diaphragm is ruptured. Another way of testing the vacuum diaphragm is to move the point plate around, hold your wetted finger to the vacuum tube and see if the points go back. If they do, the diaphragm is ruptured. With the combination vacuum and mechanical types, you have to do something different. The older ones have a smaller diaphragm assembly than the purely vacuum advance ones and you test them the same way you do the mechanical. They are found on the 36 hp engines and can, by the way, be converted to mechanical advance distributors by stripping the vacuum stuff out of them. The new combination types (1971 and on) with two vacuum hoses have both a vacuum advance and a vacuum retard plus a mechanical advance. The same method applies: suck where the vacuum hoses came off and see if the points move. You'll have to do it twice. Also check it like a mechanical advance. The way you test the mechanical and the semi-mechanical is to hold them up to your ear and twirl them—twirl the shaft, that is, and listen for crashing and thrashing noises that would indicate that the weights are out of their springs or that the springs are broken.

If **either** the vacuum type or mechanical type fail their test, take them to the shop or get a rebuilt distributor. You already know how I feel about the vacuum type, so you might want to replace it with the cheaper and better mechanical type if the diaphragm is broken. Not true for fuel injection—you have to keep the type of distributor that came with the car.

The next task is to find out *how* the points change. Put the top of the distributor in a good light and study the point arrangement. Compare with the new points. There are two points, one that moves as the shaft rotates and another that stands still. Look at how the condenser is fastened. I unscrew the condenser outside the distributor or inside and let it hang by the wire while I bolt the new one in or on. Then I find out how the moving point slides down on its shaft and what holds it there before I turn it loose and take it out. Lastly, I remove the stationary point and real quick put the new stationary point where the old one came from and start the screw into it. I figure that the condenser wire and the wire or spring to the moving point will fasten on the same screw so now I change that over to the new set-up and the points are in. (With some distributors you have to take the whole assembly out together because the point and condenser wires are pressed into a plastic gizmo in the bottom of the distributor. The point set-up is fairly straightforward so you won't forget how to put it back together again.) On all distributors the stationary point fastens to the distributor plate and is grounded. The moving point and condenser must always be separated from ground by fibre things or other insulation. If they touch a ground, the distributor won't work. I use a small screwdriver and a long-nosed pliers to change the points. Get out the feeler gauge and find the .016" blade—make sure the moving point is insulated and free to move—then turn the shaft until it's on a corner (lobe) and then move the stationary point until the .016" blade will just go through the gap between the

Step 2. (Cont'd.)

point faces, then tighten the hold-down screw on the stationary point. Put a sharp pencil-tip full of wheel bearing grease on the back of the nylon rider, where it will lubricate the shaft and the rider but not the points. Take a small piece of super clean rag and clean the point faces.

Many people have written in and asked how best to install the type of condenser which has the plastic plug that goes into the bottom of the distributor. What I do is to take out my scout knife and carve just a little bit around the plug, up toward the little shoulder, but just a little. Try it and see if it fits. It should push in with some resistance. If it doesn't, carve a little more and like that until it goes.

Step 3. Installation

Here is where the rubber "0" ring comes in. I always put one in every 200,000 miles whether it needs it or not unless there comes some oil up the hole, when I change it right away. If you are going to change yours, just pry the only rubber ring there is off the distributor where it goes down into the hole and roll the new one up until it's in the groove you pried the old one out of. If you have not moved your engine you can point the slot in the distributor shaft toward the notch in the distributor rim and start the distributor in the hole. The notch should be approximately pointed to the rear of the engine, like I told you to remember when you took it out. Now shove the distributor down into the case, twist the shaft until the bottom slips into the slot and you're home. If you have installed a new "0" ring, it might not be just that easy. In the Types I, III and IV you can get above it to put all your weight on the palms of your hands, one on each side of the distributor and that will usually push it in. If you've taken the distributor clamp out with the distributor, put the clamp over the stud, install the lock washer and 10mm nut and tighten.

Installation Note: There is a spring in the center of the top of the distributor drive shaft, so look down the hole the distributor goes into with the flashlight before you put the distributor in and be sure this spring is there. If it isn't, find it and put it in the hole—just slip it in the hole. **See Changes and New Ideas.**

Take the file and touch up the brass on the rotor; slip it on. Now go to Step 1 of the Tune-up Procedure and set the points with a Tach-Dwell meter, then time the engine according to Step 2.

Note: In the new distributors, the complicated rotor contains a speed limiter which prevents your over-revving the engine. It cuts off the juice to your spark plugs at, say about 55, in second and is maybe a good thing but doesn't stop over-revving when down braking with the gears on a steep hill, where over-revving usually occurs. When it fouls up, it makes an intermittent missing in the engine that is damn hard to find unless you know about it, which you now do.

In answer to many questions: In my 1971 Bus, I was using a Bosch mechanical advance distributor which cost about $23, timed at 7½°...note that the vacuum lines must be plugged to the carb. Our '78 and '79 buses have the distributor that came from the factory.

CARBURETOR PROCEDURE: REMOVAL, OVERHAUL AND INSTALLATION

Condition: The carburetor has to come off for some reason—for overhaul, for cleaning, to get the generator out, like that.

Tools and Materials: Phase I tool kit, wheel bearing grease, new gaskets.

Step 1. Removal

There are many kinds of carburetors used on VW's, getting complicateder and complicateder as the years pass. They are still a device to mix fuel with air to make a combustible mixture for the engine to burn. This Procedure will tell you how to take it out so you can take it to an expert for repair, then how to put it back in.

Step 1. (Cont'd.)

Type I (All) and Type II (through 1971)

Remove the air cleaner with the large screwdriver (careful of the oil) or remove the connection to the air cleaner. Take the medium screwdriver and pry the two clips off the distributor cap; remove the cap and store it out of the way. Pull off the rotor (this is just to give you wrench clearance) and cover the open distributor with a rag. Pull off the gas line. If the tank is plumb full, stuff a pencil in the end of the tubing or it'll leak gas. Beware of fire. Pull off the vacuum connection to the carburetor. If you have an automatic (ugh) choke, take the wire off it, or if you have an electromagnetic cut-off jet (I'm speechless), take the wire off'n it. If you have a manual choke, use a small 6mm $\pm$ wrench to loosen the clamp, then the vice grip and the pliers to loosen the little wire clamp on the choke lever. Use a small screwdriver to loosen the screw in the end of the little cylindrical clamp on the end of the accelerator cable. Push the cable end forward out of the little cylinder. Work the little cylinder off and put it in a safe place—the car won't go without it.

Take the 13mm (14mm) box end and loosen the nuts that hold the carburetor on. If you can't get a wrench on the front (front, remember) one use a screwdriver and a small hammer to drive it around counterclockwise until you can take it off with your fingers. Remove the rear nut and lift off the carburetor. Don't be afraid to just take the carb off or of the throttle positioner on the back of it, if you have one. The throttle positioner just makes it a little more complicated. I won't tell you what to do with this positioner as it would undoubtedly be against the law—at least in California— and just nobody is ever banned in California. Remember to put a rag in the hole left by the carburetor's absence.

Type III Single Carburetor

Remove the wing bolt on top of the air cleaner, pull the hose off between the crankcase breather and the air cleaner and loosen the screw on the rubber elbow on the rear of the carburetor. Lift the air cleaner off and put it somewhere. Be careful of the oil. There are two wires on the carburetor: one on the automatic choke (the round ceramic thing on the right side of the carb) and the other on the electric cut-off jet (the round cylinder on the left side of the carburetor). Pull both wires off. With a small screwdriver loosen the screw in the small cylinder clamp on the throttle lever. If you can't find it, have a friend push up and down on the accelerator pedal while you watch to see what moves. That's it. Loosen the screw and slide the cable out. Pull off the two hoses on the left side of the carburetor. The big one is the fuel line and the smaller one is the vacuum line. Put a pencil in the fuel line so it doesn't leak and light no matches. Now remove the two 13mm nuts that hold the carburetor to the intake manifold. Pull the carb off and stuff a rag in the hole in the manifold.

Type III Dual Carburetors

Loosen the wing nuts on top of both carburetors, pull the hose off the main body of the air cleaner and pull the rubber accordion tube off the front side. Remove the wing nut on the center front of the engine—the one holding the air cleaner down. Lift the air cleaner off. Pull the woven hose off each carb and the thinner one off the left carb. There are two wires going to each carburetor, one goes to the round ceramic thing (automatic choke) and the other goes to the round cylinder sticking out of the side of the carbs (electric cut-off jet). Pull both wires off both carbs. On the rear of each carb is a lever to which long rods are attached that go to a lever on the center of the engine. Remove these carburetor linkage rods from each carb by pulling and sort of twisting them a bit at the carburetor end. Remove the return springs (one on each carb) below the levers going to the tin below. Now with a 13mm open end wrench, remove the two nuts holding the carburetor to the intake manifolds below. Pull the carbs off the intake manifolds and stuff some clean rags in the manifold holes.

Type II, 1972-74 Dual Carburetors

Remove air cleaner by unclipping the clips that hold the connections to the carbs, unbolt the air cleaner body and lift the whole assembly out. You can leave the air cleaner in but it is really in your way so I think it is better to take it all the way out.

Disconnect the electric wires from the automatic chokes and the cut-off jets on both carbs and

Step 1. (Cont'd.)

the idle mixture cut-off valve on the left carb.

Disconnect the fuel lines and vacuum lines. They just pull off. Put pencils in the fuel lines and make no sparks. Remove the throttle return springs—disconnect the idle mixture line and the idle air intake line. They run between the two carbs. It's one connection on the right carb and two on the left.

Right under the ends of the linkage tube there is one bolt on each carb that holds the linkage assembly so unscrew the bolts and put them into the bolt can. Pull off the two linkage arms to the carbs and lay the assembly down out of the way.

Now you can loosen and remove the nuts and washers that hold the carbs to the manifold. Remove nuts and washers before trying to lift the carb. Use the magnet if necessary. With the nuts and washers out of the way, check to see if there is anything else loose that could fall into the intake manifold; if not, pull the carbs up off the studs and out. Fill the manifold holes with rags so nothing can get down in the holes.

Step 2. Overhaul

All Models

Take off the old gaskets and take the carb(s) to an expert. I'm real good with the old PCI's and even the PICT's, but I feel that you have to overhaul two or three carburetors a week to stay in practice. The main bug is the cleaning, which should be done in a special tank and if you don't really clean it you shouldn't start to overhaul it. There are rebuild kits available and it is just a matter of taking it apart, cleaning it, then assembling it with the new jets, accelerator pump and like that. If you're into this thing, get the VW publication *Owner's Service Manual* for your model. They do a real nice job, with plenty of photographs showing you what to do to overhaul your carburetor. However, once upon a trip, I started smelling gas. Gas tank overfull? Coleman stove leaking? I pulled over to check but everything looked all right. A few miles further with many complaints from the passengers I stopped again, this time leaving the engine running and sure enough, there was gas running out of the carburetor. We looked in the book and found that it said to bang on the float chamber with a plastic handle to unstick the float. OK, I did that, but the gas flowed unabated. The book gave no further help so I had to use my native ability. I took off the carburetor per the Procedure and blew through the gas entrance hole. I could blow through the valve even when the carb was upside down which meant the float needle was not holding. I took off the four screws that hold the float chamber and being very careful of the gasket, lifted the cover off. Inside I found that vibration had loosened the needle valve assembly and it was about to fall into the float chamber. I tightened it up (14mm box), put the carb back together and went my way thinking—this had never happened to me before.

My point is: you are not to be afraid to take the carburetor apart on the road when it is obviously screwing up. You may be able to find the trouble and fix it. Be careful, check all the jets for plugging, tighten the screws that hold the accelerator pump, blow through the holes, clean out any crud and like that, then put it back together the way you took it apart. Tighten the fuel pump a little while you are there. I did.

Step 3. Installation

Type I and II (through 1971)

You have picked up your rebuilt carburetor at the shop or you have traded it in on a rebuilt one and are ready to install. First the gasket, the new gasket, coat it with a little wheel bearing grease on both sides to seal well, then put it on the carburetor studs and slip the studs down into the manifold. Take the rag out first. Put the washers and nuts on the studs and turn them up finger tight. If you can get the 13mm box on the front nut, (front is front) get it down pretty tight while the rear nut is still hand tight, then when you tighten the rear nut the carburetor will be tight on the gasket

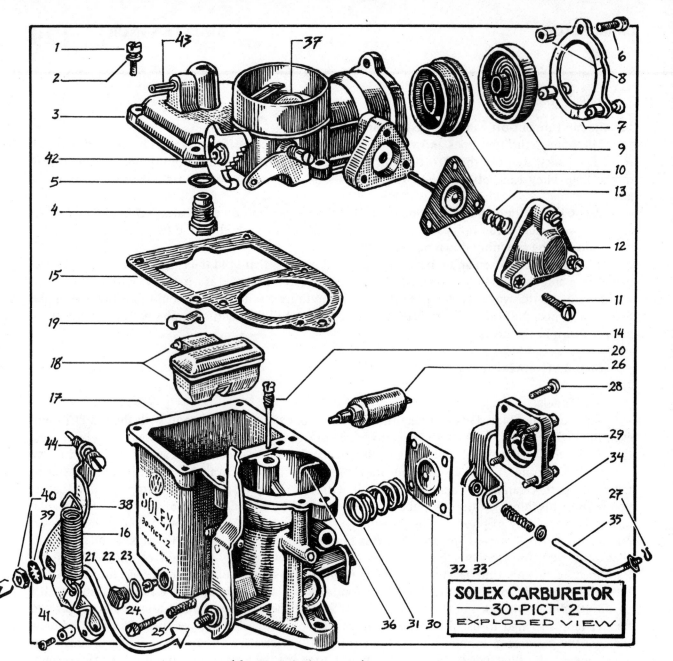

1. Screw
2. Spring washer
3. Carburetor—upper part
4. Float needle valve
5. Float needle valve washer
6. Retaining ring screw
7. Cover retaining ring
8. Cover spacer
9. Automatic choke
10. Cup (plastic)
11. Screw
12. Vacuum diaphragm cover
13. Vacuum diaphragm spring
14. Vacuum diaphragm
15. Gasket
16. Throttle lever spring
17. Carburetor—lower part
18. Float and pin
19. Float pin retainer
20. Air correction jet
21. Plug
22. Plug seal
23. Main jet
24. Idle air screw
25. Spring
26. Bypass mixture cut-off valve
27. Clip
28. Screw
29. Pump cover
30. Pump diaphragm
31. Pump diaphragm spring
32. Pump diaphragm arm
33. Washer
34. Vacuum diaphragm spring
35. Connecting rod
36. Accelerator pump injector tube
37. Choke butterfly valve
38. Throttle lever
39. Lock washer
40. Nut
41. Barrel clamp
42. Idle cam lever
43. Fuel line connection (from fuel pump)
44. Idle adjusting screw

—A typical carburetor. Yours probably won't be exactly like this.

Step 3. (Cont'd.)

and sealed. If you can't get the wrench on the front nut, use the screwdriver and the small hammer to tap it around until it is tight, then do the rear nut.

Find that little cylindrical clamp and put it in the accelerator arm, push the accelerator cable forward and then back into the hole in the cylinder clamp and when it has come through the hole a little, tighten the little screw with the small screwdriver. If you have a manual choke, pull the heavy wire through the fan housing and put it in the clamp, then tighten the clamp (on the side of the carburetor) with a 6mm $^{+}_{-}$ wrench. Use the pliers and vice grip to tighten the wire clamp on the end of the choke lever onto the end of the wire. Try the choke to see that it works correctly, a full swing, that is.

If you have an electromagnetic cut-off jet, push the wire onto it and make sure it is tight; if you have an automatic choke, push the wire onto it. Push the rotor back into the distributor, push the cap on and snap the rear clip, then the front clip to hold it on. Be sure it is in the right place by twisting it just a bit. Push the fuel line from the fuel pump onto its connection. Push the vacuum line from the distributor onto its tube on the side of the carburetor. Install the air cleaner (level), and tighten the screw. Hook up the anti-smog hose if you had it off. If you have a Bus, hook up the neck connection from the air cleaner to the carburetor and tighten it with the big screwdriver. Go to the tune-up procedure to set the idle air screw and the idle screw. Remember that the engine must be warm to set these right. It may take a minute to start the engine as the bowl has to be pumped full. That's all.

Type III

You have picked up your carburetor(s) at the shop or you have traded it (them) in on rebuild(s). Take the rag or rags out of the hole(s).

Single Carburetor

Get the new carburetor gasket, put it over the studs and slip the studs into the manifold. Put the two washers and nuts on the studs and turn them tight with your fingers. With a 13mm box wrench, tighten the nuts firmly. Find the little cylindrical clamp and put it in the accelerator arm, push the accelerator cable forward and then back in the hole in the cylindrical clamp. Pull it tight and tighten the set screw on the clamp. Push the wires back on the automatic choke and on the electric cut-off jet. Push the two hoses back on the tubes on the carburetor: they fit only the right tube so you can't make a mistake. Put the air cleaner back in place and connect the hoses and rubber elbow. Keep the air cleaner level so you don't spill any oil out of it. Go to the Tune-Up Procedure to set the idle mixture screw and the idle speed screw. Remember the engine has to be warm and running to make these adjustments. It might take a minute to start the engine as the float bowl has to be pumped full. **That's all. See Changes and New Ideas.**

Dual Carburetors

Get the new carburetor gaskets and put them over the studs on the manifolds. The carburetors go on so the throttle lever faces the rear (FRONT is front). Put the washers and nuts on the studs on both carbs and tighten them with your fingers. Now with a 13mm open end wrench, tighten them firmly. Push the fuel lines back on both carburetors, then the vacuum line (the thin one) which goes on the left carburetor. Put the two wires on each side on the automatic chokes and the electric cut-off jets, one on each carb. Snap the throttle rods back on the levers on the rear of the carbs, and connect the throttle return springs to the hole in the levers. Go to the Tune-Up Procedure to set the idle and balance the two carburetors. The engine should be warm and running for this adjustment. It might take a minute to start the engine as the float bowls have to be pumped full. After you've done the adjustments, put the air cleaner back on and you're done.

Type II, 1972-74 Bus, Dual Carburetors

When the carbs come back from the shop, put some wheel bearing grease on both sides of the new gaskets—not a lot, just a coating, and put the gaskets down over the studs. Pull out the rags.

Put the carbs on the studs, then the washers, then the nuts. Tighten the nuts a little at a time. You know, the back one a while and then the front one a while. When they are tight, you can start

Step 3. (Cont'd.)

with all the other stuff, the order doesn't really matter.

Install: the fuel lines, the vacuum lines, the wires to the automatic chokes, the wires to the cut-off jets, the wire to the idle mixture cut-off valve on left carb. Connect the idle mixture line and the idle air intake line.

Lift the throttle linkage into place and put in the bolts that hold it to the carbs and tighten them. Push on the linkage connectors and go to Step 8 of the Tune-Up Procedure and balance your overhauled or repaired carbs and set the idle. It tells you to put the air cleaner back on over there but remember to connect all those little hoses the way you took them off.

There are a few items to clear up about the fuel supply and control system that I don't know where to put so here they are:

Sticky Accelerator Pedal: The accelerator mechanism on the carburetor needs a few drops of oil from time to time to make it work smoothly. Twist the tube the cable runs through in the fan housing. The cable may be binding up in the tube or where it runs through the front shrouding.

Broken Accelerator Cable: Buy a new cable from VW, block the car and jack it up (not the Type II). In the bus you have to remove that pan between the front wheels, about ten 10mm bolts. Pull the broken cable out of the tube, push the new one through, greasing it with Bosch grease or wheel bearing grease all the way. Disconnect the rod the old cable is fastened to and replace the new front hook on the rod the same way it came off. This is all in the car or in the front of the Bus. Go to the back and disconnect the old cable from the carburetor and housing assembly: that spring, tube-cone washer assembly. (Chapter XV, Engine Removal, Mechanical Disconnection.) Now go under the car and the cable will be all tangled up where it came out from the front of the tube. Run it from there through the highest place you can to where the clutch adjustment lever is. The cable goes into the hole in the shrouding right there. Reach around in front (FRONT) of the fan housing and guide the cable in through the tube holes in the fan housing. You have to work it through the fan housing until it comes out the hole right in front of the carburetor. Push that long tube through the fan housing to guide the cable. When you get it through, work it a little to make sure it's free, then put the tube on the cable and work the tube through the housing. Pull the cable through the tube again, then connect it to the carburetor. The official way to hook up the cable to the lever on the carb should be used the first time you do it: have a friend hold the accelerator pedal all the way down while you put the cylindrical clamp as far forward as it will go. It's damned hard to get a screwdriver down in there, so I just see where the clamp goes on the cable end in this position (wide open), then tell my friend to let up on the pedal and make the connection with the system relaxed: the easy way.

If your cable breaks at either end where you can get at it and you're out in the boonies, here's what to do: With your needle nose pliers bend the broken end of the cable over and tie a piece of mechanic's wire through the eye you made. Attach the other end to the throttle lever or the accelerator foot pedal and off you go. In 1973 I got through Guatemala and Mexico (where they don't sell Type III parts) with this setup.

ABOUT CHOKES

The amount you pay for your choke, especially the automatic choke, would astound you. I tore the whole choke assembly out of my carburetor before I put it on the car. No chokes for me. I pump a little raw gas in the manifold to get it started, then let it idle until it's warm. That richer mixture in the morning or any time allows you to take off quicker—and smoother—but you pay, brothers and sisters. You pay in wear in your engine and if the damn automatic electric choke fails, it fails right in your lap and can ruin an engine sooner than quicker. OK, I'll stop, but I really feel you've been sold the biggest item of built-in obsolescence possible: the automatic choke. As I roll my own cigarettes, so the warmup time gives me leisure to roll one with no rush and hurry. By the time the cigarette is drawing good, the engine is warm.

Automatic Choke Disarmament: Because of my reactionary position on the automatic choke, I refuse to tell you how to adjust it, but I will tell you how to make it *not* work. Do you suppose this is being an activistic reactionary? Find the automatic choke. It's the round thing on the upper right-hand of the carburetor. There is a wire coming to it; disconnect the wire and tape it so it won't ground on the engine. Look at the choke. It's a ceramic thing with a heat element in it held in position by a ring clamp and three screws (so it can be adjusted, which it has to be four times a year or it tends to over-rich your fuel and further ruin your engine's lubrication—they didn't tell you that?). Loosen these three screws and you hold its life in your hands. Turn the ceramic element so that it opens the butterfly valve in the top of the carburetor, turn it the other way and you'll see the valve start to close, just to get your direction right. Turn this ceramic so it opens the butterfly and then all the way in the same direction, as far as it will go—now clamp it down with the three screws and you have disarmed the mother. However—you can disarm and arm the auto-choke at your will. In winter, if the car starts hard, rearm! Check to make sure the wire from the ignition switch is connected to the choke, then remove the air cleaner (or air cleaner hose), push the throttle lever down to free the little step arm on the left side, loosen the three screws that hold the ceramic element and turn the ceramic until the choke butterfly closes, barely. Start the engine and see if the butterfly opens after the engine warms; if it doesn't, readjust. Come spring—Disarm! By the way, the choke can appear on either side of the carb.

On the opposite side of the carburetor there is a swinging arm with teeth in it that presents various faces to the idle screw to make for a fast idle. In fact, it's called the fast idle cam. Now that you've disarmed the choke, you must tie this down so you can get a steady idle. A heavy rubber band around the fuel line slipped over the top of the fast idle cam will hold it back or a piece of wire, whatever. You don't want it engaged at all.

Electromagnetic Cut-Off Jet, 30 PICT Carburetor and all carbs since: This is another one of those engineering dreams that went wrong. They changed the carburetor to provide a little more fuel at the jets and found that with the high temperature in the engine, the damn thing would run without ignition until the gas in this jet was run out—after the ignition was shut off. This embarrassed them so much that instead of going back to the old carburetor (a better one), they stuck in this electromagnetic cut-off jet right under the choke, which shuts off the fuel to the jet and saves the engineer's embarrassment. You can check it real easy by turning on the key and pulling the wire to it off and touching it right back again. You should hear a slight click, that's all. If it fouls up, put a new one on if you like but VW sells a screw-in jet to take its place. It just screws in the hole (tape the wire) and remember that your engine might run a second or two after you shut off the key. Stop it by putting it in gear and you will have a nice little pile of gas ready to go in the jet when you get back from the store.

A little about carbs and jets: The 36 hp had the 28PCI with manual choke. The 40 hp used the 28PICT and the 28PICT-1 with the automatic choke, the 1300 and 1500 went to the 30PICT, the 30PICT-1 and 30PICT-2 ('69). The 1970's (1600) have a 30PICT-3 and the 1971's have the 34PICT-3 and so on to the pair of PDSIT-2 and -3 used on the 1973 Buses.

In my 1963 Bus I used a 28PCI with two big jets and many questions have been asked about the jet sizes. Well, I don't remember, but working back and talking with friends indicate I probably had a 24mm venturi and a 170 or 180 air correction jet. If these mean anything to you, OK, but the all out condition for the 28PCI, as old Case says, is 145 main, 180 air correction and take out the replaceable venturi altogether making the venturi diameter about 28mm (the inside should be smoothed).

Now let's get back to the carburetors that will do your job, dependable transportation. The standard carbs with standard jetting furnished on your car are usually the most economical and dependable. The usual change from standard VW carburetion is an increase in the main jet size which also helps your engine run cooler. Main jet sizes run through a range of from 110 to 150, so how do you tell which to use? OK, wipe out the end of your exhaust tail pipe, or pipes, with a rag, run about 100 miles (timed correctly) and look at the tail pipe. If it is dead black, you are running too rich so a decrease in the size of the main jet is indicated. If the color of the deposit is tan or brown, you are running too lean and an increase in jet size is indicated. If the color is a rich grey, you're about right.

The color of the ceramic part of the spark plug will tell you the same story (the ceramic that's been in the engine!), white for lean, brown for right and black for rich. The main jet is located inside the big bolt on the left side of the PICT carb, screwed into the flat chamber. Unscrew this bolt and look at it—if there is a jet screwed into the bolt (older models), you can deal with it in hand, so to speak, but if you find a solid brass bolt, the main jet is further in the float chamber (later models) but still right in back of it. In the later models, if you take the carb off, you can change the jet with a medium screwdriver but if you want to change jets with the carb on, you will need a jet wrench which grips the jet so you can get it out. Magnets don't work on that brass.

Your jetting problem is an experimental one depending on the combustion conditions in your engine. I put a 132 main jet on my '71 Bus and will probably increase it to a 135 when I install the tuned exhaust system I am contemplating.

After a month in San Francisco, I guess it is time for me to back off a little on my Smog Control position. In the cities, which I avoid like the plague, the standard Volkswagen Emission Control System does materially reduce the smog your ass is putting out, so to keep from being conscience stricken, I suggest you use it. You can still tune the engine yourself. However, out in the boondocks or on a trip, etc., you *can* use the larger jet, tune it better, disconnect the throttle positioner and not have to put up with overheating, burned valves, spark plugs that last 5,000 miles and like that.

Don't use a 28PICT carb on the 36 hp unless you also use a mechanical advance distributor. Don't trade your 30PICT-1 for a 30PICT-2 in the rebuild shop. The 30PICT-2 takes three seconds to come down to idle from running speed.

There are air cleaners that let more air pass than the oil bath type but please use the regular oil bath air cleaner on the PICT's. They are designed to work together.

The best anti-smog devices for the Volkswagen are neither gimmicks nor laws; they are humans who keep their cars in good shape, the compression around one hundred, in good tune and who drive so they never accelerate or decelerate rapidly, which brings us to:

Smog Control Devices used on air-cooled Volkswagens: The first of these is the tube that takes the crankcase fumes to the air cleaner from the crankcase breather. It is a hose and works as long as you remember to connect it if you have had the air cleaner off.

In 1970 or 1971, they installed a little tank which is filled with charcoal to absorb the fumes which rise from the gasoline tank. These fumes are blown through a tube to the air cleaner to be burned. **See Changes and New Ideas.**

Type I (all) and Type II (through 1971) and Type III Carburetor Models

Starting in about 1966 VW installed a Throttle Positioner and in 1970 neatly split it into two parts, one of which, the vacuum control, is bolted to the side of the engine compartment. All models of throttle positioners have a vacuum cylinder that operates a rod which is attached to the throttle lever. This rod pulls the throttle lever open a little when you are coasting down a steep hill or up to a stop sign and can cause embarrassment if not in good working order. Effectively, it causes the engine to keep on running after you have taken your foot off the accelerator. There are two adjustments you can make: 1) the length of the rod; you can loosen the nut and turn the rod to shorten or lengthen it and 2) the left screw on the back of the vacuum control unit—you can turn this screw to adjust the time it takes for the throttle positioner to return the throttle. Technically, the vacuum control is adjusted so the rpm will drop from 3000 to 1000 in three to four seconds or while you count 1 and 2 and 3 and...**Please note that it affects not one whit the way you tune your engine.** The throttle positioner disconnects quite easily from the throttle lever. If it fouls up by letting your engine roar for several seconds before it calms down when you pull up to a stop sign, you can use your native ability and cunning to adjust it or...

1973's and 74's and automatic shift models have another device which is used to slow the throttle lever in its mad dash toward shut which I guess can be considered in the direction of smog control. It is a small hydraulic snubber, almost like a shock absorber in action. It is mounted on the throttle lever stop and when you take your foot off the gas it acts to slow the throttle lever, kinda like a door stop.

FUEL INJECTION

Introduction: If you have a fuel injected engine, you will not need any introduction to it. It'll have introduced itself to you through the repair bills, unless your car is new. Let us introduce you to it anyway. Owner meet system.

Fuel injection is nothing new. It's the most efficient way to introduce fuel into an internal combustion engine. Diesel engines use fuel injection and when you see a big truck with black smoke coming out the exhaust, it's the injectors that need to be cleaned or replaced. However, the injection system in that truck often costs more than an entire Volkswagen. Some airplane engines are fuel injected as well. However, they're mechanical systems, not electronic **or AFC (Air Flow Control).**

Bosch came up with a low (relatively) pressure system of fuel injection which is timed by an electronic device which automobile manufactures can almost afford to put on their engines. Volkswagen put it on their 1968 Type III and it has proven, to me at least, that it is an efficient, least smog producing way of fueling our engines. It is still out of sight expensive and the parts are almost prohibitive but Tosh's 1968 Type III gets 37 miles to a gallon of gas and puts out less harmful emissions than any engine we've been around. So while we're discouraged about the costs, we're pleased with the results. Efficiency doesn't always have to do with money.

The **Bosch Electronic Fuel Injection system** is on the Types III and IV. The Volvo has it, too, and I predict that many others will join the parade. It does solve the emissions problems, you see.

1975 and later Types I and II and the 1974 Type IV with automatic transmission have the **AFC (Air Flow Control) Fuel Injection** system. **See the last few pages of this chapter if this is yours.**

Now for a tour. As we take you to see the various elements of the system, we have to talk about the system and the system we talk about is Electronic Fuel Injection. (AFC works on the same principles, but is a lot simpler with fewer parts.) We'll reinvent it as we go. That way you can be assured there is nothing you cannot understand—and most assuredly there is nothing to be afraid of. OK? (Front of the car is front.)

The first thing we need is fuel under pressure to inject into the cylinders to mix with the air to form an efficiently burning mixture. And for that we need a pump, in this case an **electric fuel pump.** In order that our pump has a constant source of electricity with enough voltage, we must provide a

pump relay. So the electricity comes from the battery through a relay which assures the pump a sufficient supply of voltage. Let's figure that our system needs 28 pounds per square inch (psi) pressure to properly atomize (like spray cologne) the fuel. We'll need a **fuel dampner** to smooth out the surges from the pump. Then—we assure that we always have 28 psi at the injectors by putting a **fuel pressure regulator** in the system which we can adjust whenever we feel like it to keep the pressure constant. Because the engine is always needing different quantities of fuel, we also have to provide a **fuel by-pass** which allows the unused fuel pumped by the pump to return to the fuel tank.

The fuel pump, fuel filter and fuel dampner all live up front on the right side behind the front axle. The fuel pump relay is under the dash (Type III) or in the engine compartment (Type IV). The fuel comes out of the gas tank through the filter into the pump where it's pumped out through the damper into the fuel loop. Fuel pumped but not used is by-passed at the pump and goes back into the tank. The fuel loop goes from the pump, through the tunnel along the length of the car into the engine compartment and back to the gas tank. It loops around past No. 3 and 4 cylinders connected to No. 3 and 4 injectors, then goes across the top of the rear of the engine to No. 2 injector. Between No. 2 and No. 1 injectors, there is a T connection with a screw on top. This is where you plug your pressure gauge to measure the pressure. The loop then continues to No. 1 injector and on to the fuel pressure regulator which is where you adjust the pressure to 28 psi. The fuel pressure regulator is mounted on the front shrouding on the right side. The tube from the front of the pressure regulator returns unused fuel to the gas tank. That's all there is to the fuel system until the 1970 models when they added a fuel connection to the cold start jet.

The air to mix with the fuel is sucked through an air cleaner (oil bath or paper filter) into the **intake air distributor** which is the metal box (sometimes aluminum) at the front of the engine. The throttle butterfly valve is inside this box. The four tubes coming out of the box are the intake manifold tubes and carry the air to the cylinders. The **throttle butterfly valve** is opened by the **throttle lever** which is connected to the accelerator cable which in turn is connected to the accelerator pedal. This means that when you push on the pedal, you are allowing more air to be drawn into the intake manifold tubes and thus to the cylinders. At idle, the throttle valve is closed and the air for idle is supplied by the **auxiliary air regulator** and adjusted by the **idle air screw** on the left of the intake air distributor. This screw allows air to by-pass the throttle valve and thus controls the idle speed.

Starting with the 1970 models the cold start system injects fuel into the intake air distributor through a jet. The fuel is then sucked into all four intake manifold tubes while the engine is warming up. There is a thermostat under the intake air distributor which operates the cold start jet through a relay until the engine is just a little warm. This system isn't really needed except in very cold weather.

If you have automatic transmission, there is a vacuum line going to the trans from the intake air distributor and the throttle valve assembly is complicated by the "kick-down" switch which shifts gears when you push real hard on the accelerator pedal. Don't be confused or confounded, it all means something—does something.

The four intake manifold tubes go down to the cylinder heads and in the bottom of each tube is the **injector** for that cylinder, which brings us to the electrical system.

Find the distributor, the thing with the five heavy wires coming out the top. Down under the cap is the distributor body. In the lower part of the distributor body is a plug with three prongs and this plug is pushed into a curved plate which is held in by two screws. The two **trigger contacts** on this device are opened by a cam lobe on the distributor shaft and are closed by a spring after the lobe goes by. Every time the trigger contacts open on one side, a signal is sent to the **Electronic Control Unit,** a small computer, to open the injectors for cylinders No. 1 and No. 4. Then the lobe goes around and opens the other set of trigger contacts sending a signal to the Control Unit to open the injectors for cylinders No. 2 and No. 3. The signal comes back from the Control Unit to operate the solenoids in the injectors thus pulling the injectors open and allowing fuel from the fuel system to spray into the intake manifold a little to the side and over the intake valves where the fuel mixes with the air from the intake manifold, is sucked into the cylinder and is fired by the spark plug in the usual manner. Whew! The trick of this system is the length of time the injectors are open. The length of time the trigger contacts in the base of the distributor are open is not the length of time the injectors are open, so the Control Unit actually changes the amount of time the injectors are open. OK?

The Control Unit is part of the next system we'll discuss, the Electronic System. It's known variously as the **Electronic Control Unit**, The Control Unit, the Black Box (it isn't always black, however), the computer box or other names unprintable. It lives in different places on different models so consult your Owner's Manual to locate yours. It's a flat metal square box and may not even be in the engine compartment. It's connected to its various sensors and to the injectors by a thick cable full of wires that runs down into the engine compartment where the wires separate to go to all the various sensors we're going to talk about. Also, one wire goes to each injector (four in all) and carries the electricity to its injector in properly timed impulses so the injector will open at the correct second and make your engine run well under different power, load, speed, temperature and pressure conditions.

The Control Unit receives and processes data from several sensors and uses the result to change the time duration of the signal it receives from the trigger contacts so the injectors are open the exact amount of time needed for the engine to operate efficiently and smoothly under different speed, load and temperature conditions.

There are about 200 transistors, diodes, condensers, etc., in the Control Unit and it is certainly not our task to tell you how to repair it but we will try to tell you a little about what data it gathers from various places and how it uses that data to control the length of the actual pulse to the injectors. The Control Unit has a direct source of electricity from the battery. A relay called the **main relay** is used to make sure the voltage is maximized.

The **manifold pressure sensor** is mounted under the left side of the engine compartment and is connected to the intake air distributor by a hose. The aneroid barometer senses the pressure in the manifold (usually negative) by moving an iron rod in two magnetic fields, one inside the other. The variations in induction set up in the fields are transmitted to the Control Unit. The pressure sensor senses load data and gives the Control Unit the data it needs to supply fuel for load from heavy to no load conditions. The 1972-74 models have a new type of pressure sensor which has been made practically frictionless by carrying the armature on leaf springs.

When the throttle valve is opened suddenly or completely the **pressure switch** closes its contacts and signals to the Control Unit for immediate enrichment of fuel. The pressure switch is a spring loaded diaphragm connected to the intake manifold by a tube. It is located under the right side manifold in the 68 and 69 models. When the pressure in the manifold approaches zero or atmospheric, which happens with the throttle all the way open, the contacts close and the signal for more fuel is sent.

The **throttle valve switch** does almost the opposite from the pressure switch. When the throttle is all the way closed (when your foot is all the way off the pedal), a micro-switch is closed and the signal is sent to shut off the fuel completely. It is actually an over-ride switch, overriding the signal from the Control Unit. When the rpm gets down to 1250, the switch opens to allow the engine to operate smoothly. In the 1972 and later models, the pressure switch and throttle valve switch are combined into the throttle valve switch—in foreign models the fuel cut-off feature is not used. The throttle valve switch in the Type III's is on the right side of the intake air distributor opposite the throttle lever and in the Type IV's it's under the intake air distributor next to the throttle lever.

The crankcase temperature sensor, called **Temperature Sensor I**, sends a signal to lean out the fuel mixture—shorter time duration of the injector impulse—when the crankcase or intake air reaches a certain temperature. In the '68 and '69 models, it's in the crankcase to the right of the distributor and in later models is mounted in the left side of the intake air distributor. **Temperature Sensor II**, the cylinder head temperature sensor, sends a signal to lean out the fuel mixture as the heads get hot. It's mounted to the rear of cylinder No. 4 ('68 and '69) and between cylinder No. 3 and No. 4 ('70 and on).

The **auxiliary air regulator** supplies the air to the by-pass circuit for engine idle. It has a bimetal spring set in the top of the crankcase which operates a valve in the air passage from the air cleaner to the intake air distributor. When the crankcase is cold, less air, and vice versa. The idle air screw in the intake air distributor adjust the air for idle.

There are a few items of smog control equipment that you might confuse with fuel injection equipment and we will describe them so you can tell the sheep from the goats. The gas tank fume equipment consists of a tank full of charcoal which is connected to the gas tank and absorbs the fumes that rise from the gas while the car is sitting in the hot sun. This tank is located in various places, like under the front hood in the Type III's, right in back of the engine in some of the Type IV's and under the car in front of the engine in others. There are, of course, hoses: a hose that runs to the gas tank from the charcoal filter; a hose that runs from the fan housing to the charcoal filter; a hose that runs from the charcoal filter to the air cleaner so the absorbed gas fumes can be burned; and a hose from the crankcase breather that goes to the air cleaner so the fumes from the crankcase can be burned. In the 1971's and on there is an exhaust recycling system, mostly on automatic transmission models. This system consists of a connection to the muffler, a filter, and a solenoid which controls the amount of exhaust that is sent to the intake air distributor to be reburned. The crankcase ventilation system in the 72's and later is more complicated and adds a hose from each valve cover to a junction box where these holes join and go into the air cleaner.

That's the full tour so please read the warning and if you are doing your maintenance at 3,000 miles, you can return to Step 8, Fuel Injection, in the Tune-Up Procedure. If you are here because your car won't start or run, go on to the Fuel Injection Checkout Procedure that follows.

WARNING!

The usual tactics employed by service stations and helpful people to start your fuel injected car can be very harmful and expensive. DO NOT USE JUMPER CABLES TO START YOUR FUEL INJECTED ENGINE! DO NOT QUICK (OR SLOW) CHARGE YOUR BATTERY WITHOUT DISCONNECTING THE GROUND STRAP AND THE BATTERY POSITIVE CLAMP! In other words, take the battery out of the car for charging.

NEVER RUN THE ENGINE WITH THE BATTERY DISCONNECTED!

All these warnings are to protect the fuel injection control unit which will burn out if subjected to an excess of voltage.

PROCEDURE FOR CHECKING OUT THE ELECTRONIC FUEL INJECTION SYSTEM, Phase I—ENGINE WON'T START

Condition: You have been referred here from Chapter VII because your engine won't start, won't run or is missing.

Tools and Materials: Phase I tool kit, including the Tach-Dwell meter. You'll also need to buy or borrow a Volt-Ohmmeter (VOM) 50,000 ohms per volt or 100,000 ohms per volt with a scale that will measure 0-10 ohms (for checking the injectors) and a fuel pressure gauge 0-30 psi, with a 2 foot hose. See **Chapter XVI** on How to Use a VOM.

Remarks: Before you start this Procedure, it is expected that you've eliminated any other cause for the trouble your engine is demonstrating. You've made sure there's gasoline in the tank. You've set your valves to the correct setting. You've set the points and timed the ignition system so you know the spark is getting to the cylinders at the proper time. You've run a compression check so you know you have at least fair compression in all four cylinders. Your starter, solenoid and switch are all in working order. If possible, you've set the idle, adjusted the throttle valve switch and the fuel pressure regulator. OK, we're not going to think about these things because by reading this you're assuring us you've done everything you can to find the trouble before starting to fool around with your fuel injection system. In other words, you've run the Tune-Up Procedure for your car but it still has troubles.

Please allow us one further favor. Through the Procedures we run into one Multiple Prong Connection after another, so to save our ecology and our fingers, we're going to use MPC to designate this type of connection which the fuel injection system has a multiplicity of. I feel as long as you don't confuse MPC with MCP which (I hear) means Male Chauvinist Pig we won't forget, either of us. Also, when you remove or separate one of these MPC's you must pull on the connection, the plug, not the wires. OK, let's get on with it.

Step 1. Check Electrical Ground Connections

One of the troubles found most often in the fuel injection system is the absence of a good connection between all of the components and the Control Unit and a good connection between the component and ground. Thousands of towing miles have been spent getting a fuel injected car to the dealer only to find out that one little wire has fallen off. That shall not happen to you!

There's no wiring diagram included in this material, but if you can read and understand one, there are many available which show you, schematically, how things are connected, one to another—but they have no basis in reality as a wiring diagram is not a blue print. We're going to deal with the actual location of things and connections, using semantics. With your fuel injected car (the actuality, instead of a picture) in front of you, you can locate each item to be checked, then check it. You will, however, have to deal with some numbers as each connection in the system has a number. Most connections from the components terminate in the Control Unit but some go to other places like the relays, the voltage regulator, the grounds and like that. A relay looks like a small voltage regulator, which it is. See the System Diagram.

In order for any electrical system to work, the path for the electricity must be completed. In automobile applications, there is usually a hot wire to bring the juice, plus a **ground** to provide continuity. In the Volkswagen the ground is the negative side and ultimately connects to the negative (-) pole on the battery. This makes the positive side and pole the "hot" side. As the ground strap of the battery is connected to the body of the car, the whole car, engine and chassis is therefore the ground. In England, ground is called the **earth**.

In the fuel injection system the ground is extremely important because of the critical voltage requirements of the system. In other words, you can have juice to a component but if the juice does not have sufficient voltage, the damn thing won't work. So while everyone else is concerned with the hot wires in the fuel injection system, we are going to start off with getting the ground connections right. The first ground we'll inspect is good old number 11—what might be called the **principle ground.** It is a wire that comes out of the large cable (loom) in the center of the engine and goes down to a push-on connector to the crankcase. It has to be well connected and when we get to the Control Unit, you'll find that number 11 is indeed the Control Unit ground. However, that isn't always the extent of ground number 11 as it also runs over to the ground connection on the fuel pump relay, making a ground loop but that's only in the Type IV's. Your task, no matter which Type you have, is to make sure that ground No. 11 is well attached at the crankcase. **See Changes and New Ideas.**

The next ground, the main fuel injection relay **(main relay)** ground comes out of the main relay and is screwed to the side of the car under the back seat in the Type III's and to the left side of the engine compartment in the Type IV's. The relay itself is over the battery, next to the car's voltage regulator under the rear seat on the Type III's and on the left side of the engine compartment in the Type IV's. There's a wire connected to terminal 85 of the main relay which is screwed to the car; make sure it's tight. Now find the **fuel pump ground.** In the Type III's, it attaches to a screw under the dash on a bracket over the steering column. In the Type IV's, the fuel pump ground is usually connected close to the fuel pump relay in the engine compartment. Get the fuel pump ground solidly attached to the car.

Fuel Pump Relay Ground: In the Type III, there's no ground to the fuel pump relay as this function is done by the Control Unit. In the Type IV, it is grounded by that loop I mentioned before to number 11.

The next pair of grounds are for the fuel injectors and there's one **ground for each pair of injectors.** These are push-on connectors just forward of the injectors under the intake manifold. These injector grounds have numbers. Like 28 and 29 (on one connector) ground the injectors for number

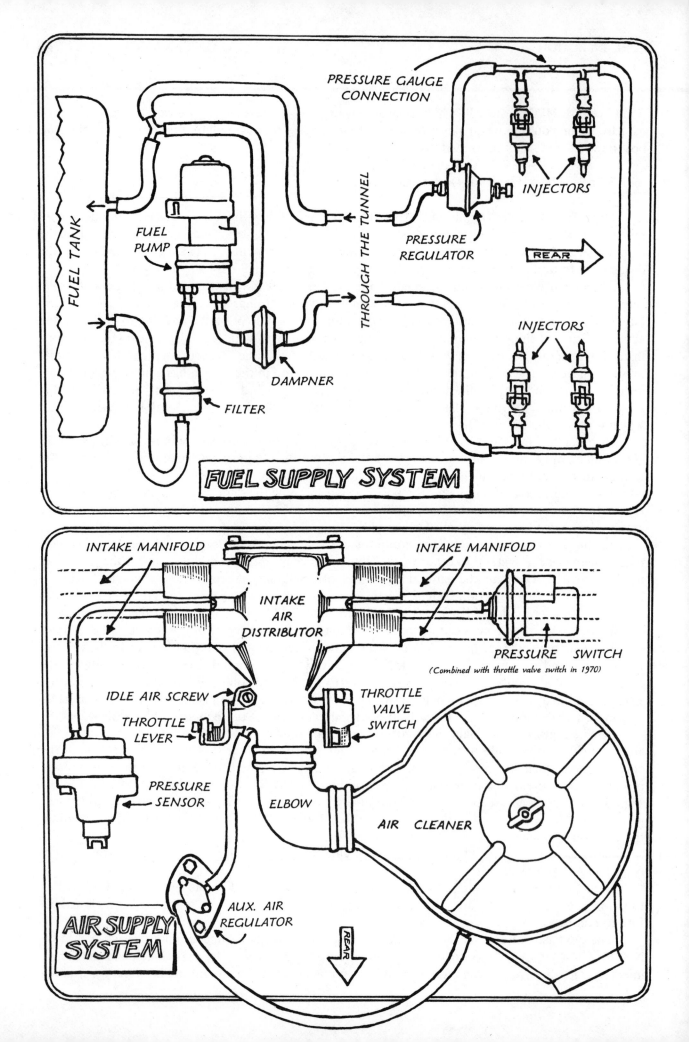

PRESSURE GAUGE
CONNECTION

INJECTORS

FUEL TANK

FUEL
PUMP

THROUGH THE TUNNEL

PRESSURE
REGULATOR

REAR

INJECTORS

DAMPNER

FILTER

FUEL SUPPLY SYSTEM

INTAKE MANIFOLD

INTAKE MANIFOLD

INTAKE
AIR
DISTRIBUTOR

PRESSURE   SWITCH

(Combined with throttle valve switch in 1970)

IDLE AIR SCREW

THROTTLE
LEVER

THROTTLE
VALVE
SWITCH

PRESSURE
SENSOR

ELBOW

AIR   CLEANER

**AIR SUPPLY
SYSTEM**

AUX. AIR
REGULATOR

REAR

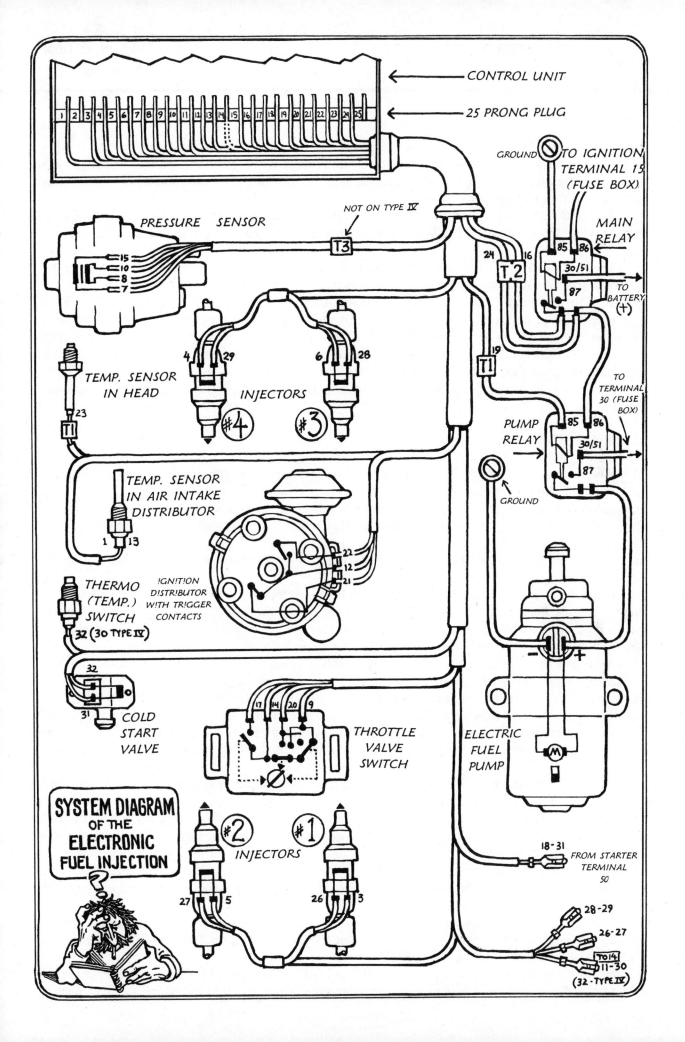

CONTROL UNIT

25 PRONG PLUG

1 2 3 4 5 6 7 8 9 10 11 12 13 14 15 16 17 18 19 20 21 22 23 24 25

GROUND

TO IGNITION TERMINAL 15 (FUSE BOX)

MAIN RELAY

85 86
30/51
87

TO BATTERY (+)

NOT ON TYPE IV

T3

PRESSURE SENSOR

15
10
8
7

24

T2

16

19

T1

TO TERMINAL 30 (FUSE BOX)

PUMP RELAY

85 86
30/51
87

GROUND

TEMP. SENSOR IN HEAD

23

TI

4   29   6   28

INJECTORS

#4   #3

TEMP. SENSOR IN AIR INTAKE DISTRIBUTOR

1   13

IGNITION DISTRIBUTOR WITH TRIGGER CONTACTS

22
12
21

THERMO (TEMP.) SWITCH

32 (30 TYPE IV)

32

31

COLD START VALVE

17 14 20 9

THROTTLE VALVE SWITCH

ELECTRIC FUEL PUMP

−   +

M

SYSTEM DIAGRAM OF THE ELECTRONIC FUEL INJECTION

#2   #1

INJECTORS

27   5   26   3

18 - 31

FROM STARTER TERMINAL 50

28 - 29

26 - 27

TO 14
11 - 30

(32 - TYPE IV)

Step 1. (Cont'd.)

3 and 4 cylinders, and 26 and 27 likewise for cylinders 1 and 2. Some people who've had trouble with these injector grounds, have spliced and soldered longer wires to the connections and then have found a handy bolt on the engine to attach the wire to, to make the grounds more secure—like do you drive on rough roads a lot?

The **cold start system** on the 1972 on models has a separate **ground** wire which is attached with number 11 to the crankcase. The 1972 on **pressure sensor** also has a separate **ground** wire connection.

Your plan of action to secure these grounds is simple: take your screwdriver and tighten all the screws that fasten anything that remotely resembles a voltage regulator, a ground wire or a relay to the car. With these tight, you've assured a good ground to the relays and the fuel pump, OK? Check ground number 11 on top of the crankcase and if it's loose, pinch the push-on connector a little with the pliers and push it back on. Then there's the two ground connections for the injectors. They are just forward of the injectors. If they are loose, pull them off, pinch them slightly and push them back on. That's the grounding system for your fuel injection.

Now try your engine to see if it starts and runs. If it doesn't, continue with Step 2 to find the trouble.

Step 2. Check Voltage Supply Connections

When the ignition switch is turned on, juice is supplied to the fuse box to make voltage available to all the things that work only when the key is on. A wire comes from Terminal 15 in the fuse box and goes to the coil. (In previous Procedures, called the wire that goes from the switch to the coil.) In the Type III's, it stops off on the way to go to the main relay and in the Type IV the connection to the main relay is made after the wire gets to the coil. This wire is connected to Terminal 86 of the main relay and is, therefore, the connection that operates the relay when the key is turned on.

From Terminal 30 in the fuse box comes a hot wire to the 30/51 terminal on the fuel pump relay to supply juice to it. Directly from the battery comes the hot wire to Terminal 30/51 on the main relay. You can see all this on the   System Diagram but sometimes words make it clearer. OK, Terminal 85 on the main relay is the ground you've already heard about. Terminal 87 of the main relay has three connections: number 24, which is one hot wire to the Control Unit, number 16 which is another hot wire to the Control Unit and a third which goes to Terminal 86 on the fuel pump relay to operate it. Terminal 85 of the fuel pump relay (the ground) goes into the Control Unit through a T1 single connector so the Control Unit can decide when the fuel pump is to pump. Terminal 87, the hot wire from the fuel pump relay goes to the fuel pump and the actual fuel pump ground is separately grounded to a screw near the fuel pump relay. That's the hairy story of how juice is supplied to the fuel pump and Control Unit as you turn on the ignition switch to start the car.

The 1972 on auxiliary air regulator gets its juice to heat the idle air from the hot lead on the fuel pump relay and the cold start system (72 and on) gets electricity from the number 30 connection. The Control Unit does not supply electricity to the fuel pump, the auxiliary air regulator or the cold start system. It, however, does tell the fuel pump when to run. When you turn the key to start, there is another connection from the Control Unit to the fuel pump which runs the pump for about 1-1/2 seconds. You will find this extra wire attached to the starter solenoid. The voltage for the Control Unit comes from the battery through the main relay. When the key is turned on, theconnection from the fuse box activates the relay to send the voltage on to the Control Unit. The action part of this Step is to check the terminals and fuses at the fuse box—all of them—and if you find a loose wire or blown fuse, you can replace the wire or fuse, then try the engine again. See the VOM Procedure in Chapter XVI for a way to check the fuses.

Now look at the connections on the positive pole of the battery. There's the big heavy one that goes to the starter and two smaller ones: one goes to the hot connection on the car's voltage regula-

Step 2. (Cont'd.)

tor and the other goes to Terminal 30/51 on the main relay. If any of the connections are loose or corroded, they deserve immediate attention.

Car still won't start or run? Continue, please.

Step 3. Check Fuel System

If you've run the fuel pressure check in the Tune-Up Procedure, Step 8, and you have 28 psi in the fuel loop, skip this Step. However, if you don't have 28 psi, you need to check out the fuel system. The items in the system are: pump, pump relay, filter, damper, fuel pressure regulator and a bunch of hoses. Let's start with the pump and pump relay which you gotta locate before you can check them. In both the Type III and Type IV the fuel pump is just to the rear of the front axle; on the Type III it's on the right side and on the Type IV it's on the left near the steering box. Now for the relays. In the Type IV's, both the main relay and pump relay are attached to the left side of the engine compartment. In the Type III, the pump relay is under the dash. The relays are practically identical but the wire from terminal 85 on the pump relay goes into the loom and the wire from terminal 85 on the main relay is the ground we were talking about in Step 1. The fuel pump only runs a second and a half when you turn the key on so we need a way to keep it running for testing. Volkswagen has provided a way to do this. Turn the key off.

In the **Type III**, the T1 connector to operate the fuel pump for testing is in the engine compartment to the front of the left manifold. The wire the connector is on comes out of a small loom and goes right back into the big one that goes to the Control Unit. This connector has two push-ons put together in a plastic holder. Pull out the one that comes out of the small loom and if you ground it to the manifold with the key switched on, the pump will run as long as you want.

In the **Type IV's**, find the wire that comes out of the pump relay and goes into the loom. This is wire 19 and on it is a single wire connector (T1) which you may pull apart so the wire that comes out of the pump relay can be grounded. With this wire grounded, when you turn on the key the pump will run at your will.

Is your fuel pressure gauge still hooked up? If not, hook it up like it says in the Tune-Up Procedure, then get out your jumper wire with the two clips on it. Clip one clip to the wire coming out of the pump relay (terminal 85) and the other clip to ground. Turn on the key and go and listen for the sound of your fuel pump running. If it is, check the pressure it is pumping. If the pump isn't running, reach in and check the pump connections at the pump, wriggle the plug around. Check the ground again. Once you've checked all these connections two or three times and the pump still will not run, you can begin to suspect a bum pump or pump relay. The third, rather remote possibility is a broken or grounded wire, so let's try all three.

If you think we're being overly cautious about the fuel pump, wait until you find out what one costs. Key on. Leave terminal 85 grounded (i.e., your clips attached) and try terminal 87, the pump hot wire on the relay. To do this find a short piece of wire with bare ends, hold one end on terminal 87 of the fuel pump relay and see if you get a spark when you just touch it to ground—just a touch now. If you get a spark, your fuel pump is probably shot and if you don't, your relay is in need of replacement. To check the pump wire, take the short piece of wire and find the fuel pump. Pull off one of the connections, push the wire into the connector slot and touch the other end of your test wire into the connector slot and touch the other end of your test wire against ground. Try both connections and if you don't get a spark out of either one, go get a new relay. If you do get a spark and the pump won't run, you better start thinking about a new fuel pump. (This is a field check—use the VOM if you have one.)

When using a VOM, the hot wire to the pump should give you a 12 volt reading if the relay is OK. If you have to replace either a relay or a pump, turn to the Procedures for Replacing Components, Fuel Pump or Relay later on in this chapter. Turn off the key, take off the jumper wire and connect T1.

Step 3. (Cont'd.)

Now what about if the pump runs but the pressure on the gauge is less than 28 psi and adjusting the fuel pressure regulator doesn't change anything? Key off, leave the pump relay connection, Number 85, grounded, unclamp your pressure gauge—this is why our test gauge has such a long hose on it—pull the gauge off. Find a small container like a beer can or equal. Hold the open end of the hose in the beer can and turn the key on. You should get a good stream of gas from the hose. Count slowly to ten and the beer can should be full. If you're having fuel pump troubles, you may just get a dribble of fuel. Take the gas cap off and if gas starts coming then, your gas tank vent is plugged. So unplug it. In the older models, the gas tank vent is in the gas tank cap, so clean the cap. In the later models, it's in the fuel evaporating system in the filler neck which goes from where you put gas into the gas tank. In the filler neck is a hose—look in the front compartment. Blow out the hose. If taking off the gas cap doesn't help, put it back on and shut off the key. Find the fuel pump and remove the hose from the fuel filter to the pump. The fuel filter is either on top of or beside the pump. The gas from the tank goes through the filter into the pump. Take the beer can with you to catch the gas. If you have a good flow here, your damper or pump is in trouble but if the gas just dribbles out of the filter, take the filter off and if you suddenly get a good flow, your filter is the culprit so replace it. You should have a spare. If the flow from the gas tank is a dribble, you have a plugged gas line or a dirty tank. So run a wire through the line, blow it out with air and if it really is a dirty gas tank, you will have to take it out and clean it or have it cleaned, then put it back in.

However, if your pump won't pump about a pint of gas in 10 seconds, you'll have to replace it so go to the Procedures for Replacing Components and have at.

If your pump does put out a pint in ten seconds, shut off the key, put the fuel pressure gauge back on its hose, tighten the clamp, turn the key on again. If the pressure is still low, try adjusting the fuel pressure regulator again and if it won't adjust up to 28 psi, you need a new fuel pressure regulator, so proceed to the Procedures for Replacing Components and put on a new one.

You can check the damper by disconnecting the hose from it and see if you get good fuel flow through it. If not, replace it. It's a metal biscuit after the fuel pump. Replacing it is similar to replacing the filter so just buy one and put the hoses on the new one.

Don't forget to remove your jumper wire and reconnect connection T1.

Remember that this Procedure is based on the premise that your engine will not start or will not run. Your valves are adjusted, your points are set, your engine is timed and now the fuel system has 28 psi in the fuel loop. You have checked all the grounds and all the input leads and the engine still won't start or run.

You'll need a Volt-Ohmmeter (VOM) and if you are not familiar with one, go to Chapter XVI to read the Procedure for Using a Volt-Ohmmeter. We will call this instrument a VOM from now on. We assume that when we indicate a certain scale and reading, you know whereof we speak. If not, to Chapter XVI you must go to find out before you make a bad guess and screw up the VOM.

Right after poor grounds and poor connections, the next most frequent reason a fuel injected engine won't start or run is low voltage to the Control Unit and/or other components, so:

Step 4. Check the Starting Voltage

Locate the battery. It's under the rear seat. Set your VOM to either the 0-15 DCV scale or 0-50 DCV scale, whichever you have. Put the leads in the COM (-) hole and the volt ohm (+) hole and put the probes on the battery—Ooops, the needle took a dive—change the probes around. Now check the battery voltage. With the key off, the meter will read between 12 and 12.5 volts in a good battery. Have a friend turn the starter over with the ignition key while you watch the needle on the VOM. It must read over 9.5 volts to operate the fuel injection system. Find the main relay, (you might have to disconnect it from its mounting to see the numbers), put the probe you had on the negative pole of the battery to a good ground and the other probe to the 30/51 terminal on the main relay. Without the key on, you should read 12 to 12.5 volts. Now have your friend try the starter

Step 4. (Cont'd.)

again and you should have 9.5 volts or better. Leave the key on and try the other terminals of the relay. If you have 12 volts at the 30/51 terminal and the same at No. 86 and zero at 87, you need a new main relay so turn to the Procedures for Replacing Components and do it. If you don't get the minimum of 9.5 volts while the starter is turning over either at the battery or at terminal 30/51, go back to Chapter VII and check out the battery and starter system. Either your battery is insufficient or your starter is sucking too much juice from the battery to allow the fuel injection system to operate. If there is no voltage at terminal 86, check the wiring, the fuse box and the ignition switch. If the above tests were all OK and your engine still won't start or run, go on to the next Step.

Step 5. Miscellaneous Electrical Checks

Look at the system as though it were an old fashioned string of Christmas tree lights: when one bulb is burned out, they all go out. There are some things like that so let's check them. Find the distributor. At the base of it is an electrical (MPC) plug which you can carefully remove, exposing three pins. Set your VOM to the Rx1 scale, pull out the heavy wire from the center of the coil so you don't get bit, then put one probe of the VOM on the center pin (this is connection 12 for future reference) and the other probe on either of the outside pins (connections 21 or 22) and rotate the engine with the wrench—clockwise. Be patient and when the trigger contacts open and close the needle on the VOM will fluctuate between zero and infinity. Move the probe to the other outside pin and rotate the engine some more. If both trigger contacts are OK, they will do that zero to infinity thing indicating they are opening and closing. If they don't go on to the Procedures for Replacing Components and put a new set of trigger contacts on.

There are two temperature sensors in the system and if either of them are caput the engine will not start. Of course, the same thing is true if the Control Unit is not putting out. Let's start with the head temperature sensor which is to the rear of the No. 3 cylinder (Type III before 1970) or between cylinders No. 3 and 4 (all other models). It sticks down in a hole in the shrouding and has one wire coming from it. This wire has a T1 pull-apart single connector which is right next to where the wires come out of the cable in front of the distributor. The idea is to get a contact with the circuit without pulling the connector apart—you know, find a bare spot. Set the VOM to the 0-15 or 0-50 DCV scale, turn the ignition switch on and check the voltage between this connector and ground which is any good place on the engine. If the VOM reads 12 volts, you've found the reason why your engine won't start. It should read 7 to 8 volts cold, 2 to 3 volts hot. Get a new head temperature gauge for your engine number and install it per the Procedures for Replacing Components. The head temperature sensor can also be checked with the Rx10K scale, but turn the ignition switch off and pull the connector loose. If the connection is now made between the wire to the sensor and ground, it should read 2,500 ohms. This is assuming a cold engine which yours must be if you're still here. In a hot engine the reading would be on the Rx1 scale and read only 60 ohms. We'll check the sensor out in the next Procedure again.

Turn off key. Next let's check the crankcase temperature sensor (Type III, 1968-69) or the intake air distributor temperature sensor (all other models). The early Type III's had this sensor mounted into the crankcase just to the right of the distributor and since 1970 it's mounted in the intake air distributor on the left side. Pull off the MPC and set your VOM to Rx10, touch the probes together and set the dial to zero, then put a probe on each pin (where you took the MPC off the sensor). The needle should read about 300 ohms, cold. If the reading is either zero or infinity, you need a new sensor so off you go to the Procedures for Replacing Components.

Now for the Black Box, the Control Unit. We left it 'til last because the cost is more than we can bear to contemplate and it's the most dependable member of the team (we hope). So let's make a quick check to see if it's putting out. Pull the thick wire out of the coil (so the engine won't start—ha ha). Pull one of the plugs (MPC) off any injector, set the VOM to 25mA (25 milliamps). Place the probes into the connector so they have a good contact and have your friend turn the engine over

Step 5. (Cont'd.)

with the key while you watch the dial on the VOM. If you get no reading, you may have to switch probes so one is where the other was. If your Control Unit is putting out a signal to the injectors (its main job), the needle will swing over to some value (what is not important—about 5 or so) and it will stay about there and jiggle, because even at the starter speed the pulses are too fast for the VOM needle to ever get back to zero. If you get no action here, try another injector MPC and if the needle doesn't move, you've found the reason your engine won't start, so go on to the next Procedure for checking out all the connections to the Control Unit and at the end of that, we will help you decide whether you need a new Control Unit or not. If the needle does move at all four injector plugs and you are still having trouble then you can either go to the Electrical Procedure or go to the Procedures for Replacing Components, your choice. Put the heavy wire back into the coil.

There is one more story and that is wet—WET—if your engine ever really gets wet and then quits; you know, like when you run it through a river or something, you gotta dry it. Pull each MPC off one at a time and blow the moisture out of it, remove the trigger contacts, dry them and if you can (without getting the MPC's mixed up), leave all the MPC's off the connectors to speed the drying time.

PROCEDURE FOR CHECKING THE FUEL INJECTION ELECTRICAL SYSTEM, Phase I

Condition: You want to make a complete check of the electrical system at the Control Unit because the car runs poorly, doesn't accelerate, is burning too much gas, starts hard or still doesn't start after doing the preceding Procedure.

Tools and Materials: Screwdrivers, contact cleaner, pencil and paper and a VOM (Volt-Ohmmeter) that has an Rx1 scale which usually means a 50,000 Ohms per volt or 100,000 Ohms per volt capacity.

Remarks: Please read the Procedure for Operating a VOM in Chapter XVI, making sure you understand how to hook up the VOM and how to read the scales. It is assumed you've run a complete Tune-Up per the Procedures in this chapter: valves, timing, the whole schmutz—before you even start this Procedure. Also, it would be a good idea to read the Procedures for Replacing Components that follow this procedure, especially the remarks, before continuing here.

And before you go any further, check all the fuel injection related wires with the engine running by pushing down on the MPC's and wiggling them around one by one. SAFETY! You might just have a bad connection in which case the engine will run better when you wiggle the right wire. Pinch the connecting end of the offending MPC as in Sketch A. Then push it back on to see if it works OK.

Step 1. Disconnect the Control Unit

First, you have to find the Control Unit. In the Type III Fastback, it's under a piece of upholstered trim on the left side rear of the rear luggage compartment. In the Squareback it's under the interior panel at the left rear; just pry the panel completely off with a screwdriver to get at it. In the Type IV Sedans, the Control Unit is on the left side of the engine compartment under an insulating flap right over the two relays (main and fuel pump). In the Type IV station wagon, it's on the right side next to the rear passenger seat; you have to push the arm rest forward and remove the interior panel. In the Porsche 914, it's under the battery.

In the Type IV wagon, loosen the mounting screws but do not remove them. Lift the unit up and out. In the other models, remove the two top screws and lift the unit up and out.

Lay the Control Unit in a comfortable place and look at the end where the cable comes out.

Step 1. (Cont'd.)

Here, you'll see a plastic cover. Use your phillips head screwdriver to unscrew the screw in the cable clamp on the cable and push the top half of the clamp around out of the way. Slide the plastic cover toward the cable, then over it and off. Now put your thumb and forefinger in the handy dandy square holes and slowly and very straightly pull the connector plug (a super MPC) off the Control Unit. See sketch:

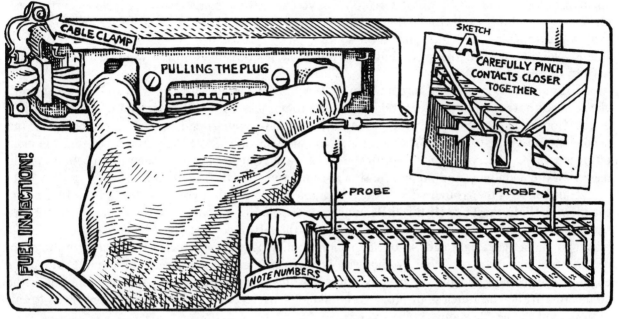

    Put the Control Unit proper in a paper or plastic bag to protect it from the elements. That's all we idiots can do with the "Electronic" part of our fuel injection system.

    Now examine your find. This is the terminal end of the electrical circuitry of the fuel injection system. See all the numbers set in the plastic. Turn the connector over and see where all the metal (brass) strips come out through the plastic. That's where you make contact with your VOM probes to check out the system in the following steps. On our unit, we've repeated the numbers with a felt tip red pen so we don't have to keep turning the Unit over to see the numbers. If you do the same, make no mistakes, you are dealing with a kind of heart operation so pretend it is your very own heart. Practice with the probes a little to see how to make contact between the brass strips and the points of the probes. Each of the numbers means that the brass strip is directly connected to some point in the system. Try to suss it out a little so you can find out from it what you need to know—don't be overawed, just be surehanded. OK? Plug the VOM ends of the probes into the plus and minus (or com and v ohm holes).

    Note: You'll need a really good friend to help with this Procedure: to hold probes, write down the actual values you read, check off tests done and smile a lot. Please refer to System Diagram, pages 140 and 141, throughout.

Step 2. Check Grounds and Measure Voltage to the Control Unit

    The ignition switch is off. Turn the switch on the VOM to Rx1 (this means resistance times one), touch the probes together and adjust the needle to read zero on the ohm scale with the dial or knob provided for this purpose. After every reading or change in scale, you must do this adjusting act to get accurate results. We'll remind you by saying "adjust to zero," but you have to remember, too. Put one probe on the metal strip in the Control Unit super-MPC where it says number 11, the ground for the Control Unit. Have your friend touch the other probe to the engine. The needle will swing from infinity (which means infinite resistance or no contact at all) to zero (which means no resistance

Step 2. (Cont'd.)

or direct contact). If the needle doesn't move, make sure the probes are in direct contact with the metal. If the needle moves but doesn't go all the way to zero, there's some resistance in the ground connection. So find where number 11 is attached to the crankcase—it's a wire that comes out of the wiring loom(harness, thick cable, whatever you call it) with a push-on connector on its end, pushed onto a connector in about the center of the engine below where the manifold tubes join to the intake air distributor. If the needle doesn't go to zero, you are getting some resistance, so wiggle the push-on, make sure the ground connection is tight at the crankcase, reset the VOM to zero when the two probes are touching, and like that. You should have no resistance at number 11, i.e., the needle should swing to zero. If the ground at 11 is not good, it's possible that the whole wiring loom may have to be replaced.

Examine the super MPC where number 14 is and see if there's a wire to it. If there is none, don't check it but note it on your paper. Like, "no wire to number 14." If there is a wire connected to 14 in the Control Unit MPC, put your probe on it and have your friend touch the engine again; the needle should swing to zero. If it doesn't and you have an early Type IV, you have to find the main relay and then, while you touch your probe to 14, have your friend touch the other probe to terminal 85 on the main relay and the needle should swing to zero. OK on number 14?

Number 19 is the ground wire to the fuel pump and to check it you have to find the T1 connector in wire 19. In the Type III this little connector (two push-ons connected together in a little plastic box) is in front of the intake manifold a little to the left of center. The wire comes out of the big plastic loom and goes right back into the smaller loom. This is the connector that allows you to check out the fuel pump. In the Type IV this wire is between the fuel pump relay on the left side of the engine compartment and the big plastic loom. Pull the wire that goes into the big loom out of the connector. While you touch your probe to number 19, have your friend hold the other probe to this push-on and the needle should swing to zero.

Now, measure the supply voltage connections so TURN THE IGNITION SWITCH ON AND LEAVE IT ON FOR THE REMAINING TESTS, unless otherwise noted.

Turn the dial on the VOM to the 0-15, 0-30 or the 0-50 DCV scale (whichever you have) and find the scale you are supposed to be reading when the needle moves. DCV means direct current voltage. Put one probe on the brass strip at number 11 and the other probe on number 16. If the needle tries to go below zero, switch probes so the one that was on 16 is on 11 and vice versa. With the negative probe on number 11 and the positive probe on 16, the needle should swing to 11-12.5 volts. Write down the reading so you don't forget what you've checked and how it checked. Have your friend turn the ignition key to the start position and run the starter about five seconds (probes still at 11 and 16), the needle should read above 9.5 volts. Now move the probe from 16 to 18 and have your friend operate the starter again. The voltage shouldn't drop below 9.5 volts. This checks the voltage at terminal 50 at the starter. Move the probe from 18 to 24 and without your friend's services at the starter, the needle should swing to between 11-12.5 volts. Key still on, OK?

If the readings are less than the above values, turn to Chapter VII to check your battery and starter systems and fix them until your tests indicate sufficient voltage at these connections.

Step 3. Check Pressure Sensor. See Changes and New Ideas.

Leave the dial on the VOM at Rx1, adjust to zero. Now, let's check the windings in the pressure sensor. Put the negative probe (the same one) on good old number 11 again. Then put the positive probe on 7—the needle doesn't move? Good, that's what we want. If it does move, you're going to be out some bread for a new pressure sensor so check it again, OK? Now try number 8, then 10 and finally 15 with the other probe at number 11. The needle stood still, didn't move, on any of these contacts? That's what you want. If the needle moved, it showed a shorted pressure sensor or a short in the wiring to the pressure sensor, so check the wires in Step 9, then if necessary go to the Procedures for Replacing Components to replace the sensor. But you might as well finish this checkout

Step 3. (Cont'd.)

before you do.

The switch on the VOM is at Rx1, adjust to zero. Put one probe on number 7, the other on 15 and the needle should swing to about 90 ohms. This is the primary winding.

Change the switch on the VOM to the Rx10 scale, adjust to zero, then put one probe on number 8 and the other on 10. The needle should swing to about 350 ohms (it may be a little less).

If there are no shorts and the resistances measured are about as shown, the basic requirements for a good pressure sensor are met. There may be mechanical considerations, however, which we'll get to later in the Procedures for Replacing Components.

Step 4. Check Trigger Contacts in the Distributor

Switch the VOM to Rx1 and adjust to zero. Put one probe on number 12 and the other on 21. Have your friend operate the starter a second or so while you watch the needle. It should move to about the center of the dial and wiggle as the trigger contacts open and close. Now move the probe from 21 to 22 while your friend turns the starter again. The result should be the same. If the needle doesn't move and you're sure your probes are making a good contact, your trigger contacts are not working or there's a short in the wiring, so go to Step 9, then to the Procedures for Replacing Components, if necessary. To get a full needle swing from zero to infinity to zero to infinity and so on, you have to hold the probes as above and have your friend turn the engine with a wrench, because the needle doesn't have time to make this full swing when using the starter.

Step 5. Check Throttle Valve Switch

VOM on Rx1, adjust to zero. If you have a '68 or '69 model, only the second part of this test applies to you.

First part (mixture enrichment 1970 and on): Put one probe on number 9, the other on 14 and have your friend push the accelerator slowly all the way down. Key still on. The needle should swing from infinity to zero about ten times as the pedal is depressed—try it again—the needle swings back and forth? OK. If the needle doesn't swing, move the probe from 14 to 11 and try again. If the needle goes to zero and stays there, you may need a new throttle valve switch or the wiring may be shorted, so test the wire, Step 9, then go to Procedures for Replacing Components, if necessary.

Second part (throttle valve switch, all models): Put one probe on number 17, the other on 20 and have your friend do the above accelerator stunt. With the pedal up (throttle closed), the needle should swing over to zero or almost zero and with the pedal down (throttle open), the needle should stay at infinity. If it doesn't, it's usually only a matter of adjustment, so adjust the throttle valve switch (Tune-Up Procedure, Step 8, for Fuel Injection). If that doesn't fix it, check the wire in Step 9, this procedure. If the wire checks OK, replace the switch per Procedures for Replacing Components.

Step 6. Check Pressure Switch, 1968-69 Models Only

VOM on Rx1, adjust to zero. This is the fuel enrichment method of the old models. You have to open the engine compartment to do this check. Have your friend disconnect the vacuum hose to the pressure switch. It lives under the right-hand pair of manifold tubes. Pull the vacuum hose in position to be sucked on—with your friend's mouth. Now put one probe on number 9, the other on 14 and watch the needle move from infinity to zero as your friend sucks on the hose. If the needle does not, check the wiring in Step 9, then if necessary go to the Procedures for Replacing Components. Put the vacuum hose back on. Note: if number 14 didn't check out right, try number 11. See Step 10 for explanation.

Step 7. Check Temperature Sensors

Temperature Sensor I, Crankcase or Intake Air Distributor: Switch VOM to Rx10, adjust to zero. Put one probe on number 1 and the other on 13. The needle should swing to about 300 ohms (assuming a cold engine; the warmer the engine, the less the reading). If the needle doesn't move or swings to zero, check the wiring per Step 9, then go to Procedures for Replacing Components, if necessary.

Temperature Sensor II, Head Temperature: Switch VOM to Rx100, adjust to zero. Put one probe to number 11 and the other on 23. In a cold engine, the needle should swing to about 2,500 ohms but in a hot engine this could be as low as 60 ohms. If the needle swings to zero—check it again—or does not move at all (unlikely, unless the wiring is bad), you'll need a new sensor. Go to the Procedures for Replacing Components.

Step 8. Check Injectors

Switch VOM to Rx1, adjust to zero (carefully). Put the negative probe on number 11 and the other on 3; the needle should swing to 2-3 ohms. This is the resistance in the injector for No. 1 cylinder. Leave the negative probe on 11, put the other one on 4; the needle should swing to 2 to 3 ohms (cylinder 4). Now move the probe to number 5 (cylinder 2) and finally to 6 (cylinder 3)—the readings should all be 2 to 3 ohms. If they aren't, you have a suspect injector or wiring, so go to Step 9, then to the Procedures for Replacing Components, if necessary. The readings can be out of whack a little but usually with a bum injector or bum wiring, the resistance will go up.

Step 9. Check Wiring and Plugs (MPC's)—Continuity Checks

Throughout the previous eight steps you've been checking the voltage and resistance to various electrical devices. If the tests came out the way it says, the wiring has to be OK but if you get a no voltage reading where there should be voltage or the needle doesn't move when there should be some resistance, the wiring could be defective or the connection to the component could be loose or otherwise at fault. So before you rush off to VW to buy some component or other, let's check the continuity of all the wiring in the loom: those bunches of wires that run all over the car. For this we don't need juice so shut off the ignition switch. Look at the System Diagram, page 125. It shows the numbers of the connections at the Control Unit MPC. Each component has its very own numbers to match. Just for fun, let's check the whole system systematically. Make a list of numbers like: 1-2-3-4-5-6-7-8-9-10-11-12-13-14-15-16-17-18-19-20-21-22-23-24-25. These are the numbers in the Control Unit. Make a second list:

> Injector grounds: 26-27-28-29
> Cold start or ground: 30-31-32
> Main relay: 30/51-85-86-87
> Fuel pump relay: 30/51-85-86-87 and
> Starter: 50

We're going to check the wiring and MPC's on every one of these numbers but you don't need to follow it all. If you have a certain system that didn't check out, merely check continuity in that system. But please read how to check Number 1 and 13 first. The basic idea is the same for all the tests and we don't repeat. We're not going to repeat locations and will start with number 1 on the Control Unit MPC and go right through. On a component, we'll start with the first number, then include the others involved in that component or system. Check the number off your list as you go. If, after completing this Step, you find no continuity in one or only a few wires, you probably can wire around the loom but if you experience a lot of bum wires, you'd be better off to buy a new wiring loom for your model and install it. It's a tough job but with the following continuity checks to help, you can do it by carefully replacing the old with the new.

When pulling an MPC off, pull carefully on the plug, not on the wires. The ignition switch is

Step 9. (Cont'd.)

OFF, the VOM is set to Rx1—remember to adjust to zero before each check.

Numbers 1 and 13, Temperature Sensor I: Pull the MPC at the sensor and put your probe on number 1 at the Control Unit MPC and have your friend put the other probe in one hole in the sensor MPC so it makes contact with the metal—not shove the probe in the hole, just make contact. Did the needle swing to zero? If this hole makes the needle swing to zero, it's the connection between 1 and the sensor MPC. Your friend should try the probe in the other hole of the sensor MPC. If this also makes the needle swing to zero, the wires are shorted. If the needle swings to zero only in one of the holes, fine. You have continuity from the connection in the Control Unit to the connection in the component and the wiring and the plug are OK. If the needle didn't swing either time, you have a broken wire or a poor connection in the plug. Repeat the performance with your probe in the Control Unit MPC at number 13. Put the sensor MPC back on.

Number 2 is blank: Don't do anything.

Numbers 3, 4, 5 and 6, Fuel Injectors and Numbers 26, 27, 28 and 29 Grounds: Leave VOM at Rx1, adjust to zero. Put your probe on number 3 at the Control Unit MPC while your friend carefully pulls the MPC off the injector for No. 1 cylinder and puts the probe in one hole of the MPC touching the metal. Did the needle swing to zero? Friend should try other hole. If the needle swings to zero both times, the wire is shorted. Needle didn't swing either time? Broken wire or poor connection. Try it again. If the needle swings in one hole, have your friend move probe to the other hole and if the needle doesn't swing again, move your probe so it touches the engine. If the needle swings to zero now, ground connection number 26 and the wiring are OK. If the needle doesn't swing to zero, check the push-on connector in front of No. 1 cylinder and try again. If the needle still does not swing to zero, the ground wire is broken.

Repeat with your probe in Control Unit MPC Number 4, friend's probe in MPC for injector for No. 4 cylinder, then with your probe on the engine (ground 29) and so on until all four injector MPC's are checked. Put the injector MPC's back on. The front plugs (1 and 3) are black; the rear plugs (2 and 4) are grey.

Numbers 7, 8, 10 and 15, Pressure Sensor: Put your probe on number 7; friend pulls the MPC from the pressure sensor and puts the other probe in the holes one at a time. Continue with 8, 10 and 15, checking them off the list as you get continuity. In the 1972 pressure sensor, there'll be five holes in the MPC and the fifth one is ground so check it by touching your probe to the engine and/or to numbers 11 at the Control Unit MPC. Remember to put the pressure sensor MPC back on.

Numbers 9 and 14, Pressure Switch, 1968-69 Type III
Numbers 17 and 20, Throttle Valve Switch, 1968-69 Type III
Numbers 9, 14, 17 and 20, Combination Throttle Valve Switch, 1970 and on:

Type III before 1970 has two MPC's to check: one on the pressure switch and the other on the throttle valve switch. Models 1970 and later have just one. Put your probe on number 9 on the Control Unit MPC while your friend pulls the MPC on the pressure switch or combination switch and finds the contact. On the 1970 and on switch, there are four holes (sometimes five) so while your probe is on 9, your friend must try all the holes until the needle swings to zero but if the needle swings to zero on more than one hole—short! Number 9 will always connect with one of the holes on the component MPC, however, number 14 on the super MPC may not even have a wire to it or may be the main relay ground (early Type IV). If this is your case, while your friend holds the probe on a hole of the component MPC, you touch yours to the engine to test 14. If you have an older Type III, your friend now pulls the MPC off the throttle valve switch but in any case, test 17 and 20 and put the MPC(s) back. If the needle won't swing to zero for 17, see step 10.

Numbers 12, 21 and 22, Trigger Contacts: Same action. Put your probe on MPC 12; your friend pulls the MPC at the trigger contacts on the distributor and puts the other probe in the center hole. Number 21 is one side and number 22 is the other. Put the MPC back on.

Numbers 16 and 24 and voltage supply from terminal 87 on main relay: Now comes the idea of an extension wire to your friend's probe, as the distance may be too great for the VOM probe to

Step 9. (Cont'd.)

reach unaided. For instance, in this check, put your probe on 16 at the Control Unit MPC and hold the other one to a bare end of a longish wire while your friend connects the other end of said wire to terminal 87 of the main relay which in the Type III is under the seat. After checking from 16 to 87, move your probe to 24. The needle should swing to zero for both checks.

Number 18 and Starter Terminal 50. This is an obvious place for an extension. Hold your probe on 18 at the Control Unit MCP and hold the other probe on the extension wire while your friend crawls under the right rear of the car and reaches up to where the small wires come into the solenoid which is the small cylinder on top of the big cylinder (starter) and holds the other end of the extension wire to the place where the small wires attach. If there are two places, then one or the other is where number 18 comes to the solenoid. The push-on connector may have to be pulled off to make the connection. If the needle swings to zero, the wire from 18 to 50 is continuous but if it doesn't swing, the wire is bad.

Please tell your friend not to move from under the car or there might be strong words exchanged when the following is revealed:

If your car is a **1968-69 Type III**, you have either no cold start system (in which case your friend can crawl out after pushing the connector back on the starter) or a **modified** cold start system. All models, 1970 and on have a **regular** cold start system. To check (in a 1968-69 Type III) if you have a modified cold start system, look for the relay. It is a little box with wires coming out of it, one to a temperature switch in the intake air distributor and another to a jet mounted into the intake air distributor but the clincher is a T connection mounted into the fuel line making a mess of the fuel lines between number 1 and number 2 fuel injectors. If you have this extra fuel connection to the cold start jet, find the relay. It has to be around there somewhere. When you locate it, put your probe on the terminal marked 85 and the other probe on the extension while your friend holds the other end of the extension on the connector to terminal 50 on the starter. It is the wire we are checking, not the solenoid. If this wire is continuous, the needle will swing to zero. Your friend can push the connector back on the starter and come up.

Numbers 31 and 30 (Type IV) or 32 (Type III) and Starter Terminal 50. In the 1970 and later models, find the cold start valve on the right side of the intake air distributor. There will be an MPC on the valve and it will be one you never checked before. Pull off the MPC and touch one probe to one of the holes and the other probe to the extension wire while your friend continues to hold the other end of the extension to the same wire connector (which attaches to terminal 50). If the needle swings, that hole is number 31 (the voltage supply to the cold start system). If it doesn't swing, try the other hole. Is this 31? One of the holes is. Tell your friend to push the connector back on the starter and come up. Put one probe in the other hole (the one that wasn't 31) and the other on the connector on top of the temperature switch. This is connection number 32 (Type III) or 30 (Type IV) and if the needle swings, the cold start system is at least continuous. Don't worry about it; it doesn't keep your car from running.

Number 30 (Type III) or 32 (Type IV) is an engine ground which goes to terminal 14 on the throttle valve switch. You check it by putting one probe on number 14 (throttle valve switch MCP) and the other on the engine, which you've probably already done.

Number 19 and Fuel Pump Relay Number 85. Connect your probe to 19 on the Control Unit MPC while your friend's probe or extension is held to terminal 85 of the fuel pump relay. The needle should go to zero.

Number 23, Head Temperature Sensor. Hold your probe on number 23 on the Control Unit MPC and have your friend hold the other probe on the single connection (T1) which comes out of the head temperature sensor. If the needle swings to zero, the wire is OK.

Number 25 is blank. Do nothing.

Number 30/51 on the Main Relay is always hot and you'll damage your VOM if you check it using the resistance scale (Rx1). You must use the DCV scale and it should read 12 to 12.5 volts. You've already checked this connection earlier.

Step 9. (Cont'd.)

Number 30/51 on the Pump Relay and Number 30, Fuse Box. There should be continuity (needle swings to zero) between these two terminals when you touch one probe to each—Rx1 scale, don't forget to adjust to zero.

Number 85 Main Relay is a ground connection screwed into the car, so touch one probe to it and the other to the engine. Not true for old Type IV—See Step 10.

Number 86, Main Relay and Number 15, Fuse Box should be continuous. Touch a probe to each using the extension.

Number 87, Fuel Pump Relay is the hot wire to the fuel pump. You can check it with the key off and the extension. One probe on 87, fuel pump relay and the other attached to the extension which then goes to the hot lead on the fuel pump MPC. The other hole in the fuel pump MPC is ground.

There, that checks the continuity of the fuel injection system.

Step 10. Changes to the Control Unit

There's been, through time, some fiddling with the Control Unit and we'll try to advise you of it in this Step. Take number 14: in the early model Type IV, it acted as the ground for the main relay, probably as some sort of protective device for the Control Unit—we don't really know. Anyway, be advised so if you have an old Type IV, your main relay terminal 85 might go up into the loom and come out at number 14 on the Control Unit MPC. In all other models, number 14 is the ground for either the pressure switch or the combination pressure-throttle valve switch. Which brings us to Terminal 17 in the Control Unit. It is an inactive terminal if your model does not have the fuel cut-off feature, mostly on cars built to sell in other countries. We here in the U.S. like to cut the fuel off as we coast, so 17 is usually active.

For the Type III, the basic Control Unit part number is 311-906-021. Then they started adding change letters like -021A (which, by the way, they don't rebuild) and -021B in 1968, then -021C when they changed Temperature Sensor I and installed it in the intake air distributor. Then they changed the part number to -021D and they now have an -021D with a black sticker (which, you should be warned, should not be used with Temperature Sensor I, with part number -181B). VW will substitute Control Unit -021D for -021C and when they do, you must also buy a new temperature switch for the cold start system, the -161C. If you don't have a black sticker on your -021D Control Unit, you can install an -081B intake air distributor Temperature Sensor and save some fuel. The 1972 Type III started a new Control Unit number -021E with a black color code and it cannot be fitted to the older models. This new Control Unit can be adjusted for CO emissions and we'll get to how after we talk about the Type IV Control Units.

The Type IV uses a different part number for some of its fuel injection equipment but also has a lot of parts that are exchangeable with Type III. Parts numbers with 311 as the first three digits are Type III parts and parts with 022 as the first three digits are Type IV parts. The 906 indicates the fuel injection system and the last three digits are the actual part number. The letter indicates the change. So the Type IV Control Units started with 022-906-021 and changed to -021A along with pressure sensor 022-906-051A. In 1970, they added a blue sticker to some of the -021A Units and these cannot be combined with Temperature Sensor II, Part number 022-906-041A. The next change was to Unit number 022-906-021B along with a new pressure sensor, 022-906-051B (which can be substituted for the 051A sensor). Then on to the -021C which has a blue color code and should be used the Temperature Sensor I, part number 311-906-161C. Then, with a burst of un-German enthusiasm, they *skipped* letter D and brought out Control Unit 022-906-021E which can be substituted for the 021C Unit as long as you remember the Temperature Sensor I change after the 161C (probably "D" but who knows). Anyway, we are now up to the new Control Units with the Carbon Monoxide (CO) adjustment. The Type III Control Unit (CO adjustable) part number is 311-906-021E,

Step 10. (Cont'd.)

color code black and is teamed with pressure sensor 311-906-051D, color code green which cannot be substituted for older models. The Type IV Control Unit (CO adjustable) is number 022-906-021E and the pressure sensor teamed with it is 022-906-051C which can be substituted for the "B" sensors.

OK, how about adjusting the new CO adjustable Control Units? Start with a complete tune-up including setting the throttle valve switch in the Tune-Up Procedure, set the idle, you know—everything is hunky-dooley except the good old CO adjustment. Connect the exhaust gas analyzer according to the manufacturer's instructions. When the engine is warmed up and running well at 850 to 900 rpm's, turn the adjustment screw on the upper left corner of the Control Unit until the CO is about 0.7% volume content. And, of course, each of you has an exhaust gas analyzer stuffed in the tool box? No? OK, then we'll just have to do it the idiot way. I forgot to tell you to take the Control Unit out but as this is just a continuance of the Control Unit check what you really have to do is to put it together first which is in Step 11. With your Control Unit back together but still out and your valves set, the engine timed, etc., turn the adjustment screw in the Control Unit counterclockwise until it stops, then turn it clockwise until you hear twelve little clicks. Don't put the Control Unit away yet. Take the car out on the road. Get it up to speed, then lift your foot, if the engine pops and backfires, turn the adjustment screw three to four more clicks. It'll be right just about there and please remember that this is only a rough adjustment which, if you want fine, you gotta go to VW or somebody who has laid out a lotta bread for a gas analyzer, part of which will be subtracted from you. You do this adjustment when you have your Control Unit out for some reason, especially if your car is popping when you lift your foot off the gas.

Step 11. Replace Control Unit

If your car isn't running even yet, you may need to buy a new or rebuilt Control Unit but there are several things to do before you finally jam it together for the last time and spend all that bread. Whether your car is running or not, do this Step to put your Control Unit together. If your car is running well, you might skip the ice pick bit.

Make sure the ignition switch is off. Look at the Control Unit MPC where you've been putting your probe for the testing operation. Look at the slot where the connections are made. Now get the Control Unit out of its sack and look where all the metal strips fit over the plastic tongue. Those are the connections in the Unit where the slot in the MPC fits. More units have been replaced for poor connections here than for any other reason. What can you do to assure a good contact between the male member in the Control Unit and the female connection on the MPC? Put the Control Unit aside and concentrate on the contacts in the MPC. You'll need two pointed tools, maybe like an ice pick and a knife or a thin fingernail file; something that will fit into the little slots so you can bend the "U" shaped contacts together a little, so when they are pushed over the strips in the Unit, they will make a good contact with all the strips. The ice pick or equal is to hold the bottom of the "U" so it will bend—just a little—when you push on the top part. As too strong will be a disaster, you have to go slow and feel your way. Practice with number 2 as it isn't connected to anything. Put the pointed thing under the "U" and your knife on the top of the "U". It's like pushing a horseshoe together. You don't want to go too far, so get a steady grip on both and just push down until the top piece bends down a little. If you push it together too far it won't fit over the part in the Control Unit—so just easy. OK, now do it to the other 24 "U's", then coat all the connections with contact cleaner. Get the Control Unit out again and coat all the little brass strips with contact cleaner. Don't get any cleaner down in the Unit. OK, count to ten and push the plug straight into the Control Unit until it is all the way in. There are two little tracks it must slide on, so you cannot make a mistake. When the plug is all the way in, set the Control Unit aside and go start the engine. If it runs and idles well, you are through with the Control Unit so slide the plastic cover over the open end. Swing the cable clamp over the cable and tighten the screw; put the Unit into place, then put in and tighten the screws. Put back the upholstering or side panel and you are through.

Step 11. (Cont'd.)

But what if your car doesn't start? Well, that would ordinarily mean you need a new Control Unit but first get out the VOM, set the dial to 25mA and make the check on the injector plugs to see if there was any juice coming out of the Unit to the injectors.

If not, pull out the Control Unit MPC again and check all the brass strips for signs that all the contacts or the MPC were making a mark on the strips in the Unit. If you see these marks, we would finally believe that the Control Unit is shot. If, for instance, there has been no good contact on number 12, work over the number 12 contact in the MPC until you know it grabs the strip in the unit and like that. But if there is good contact on all the strips and still no juice at the injectors—you might check them all and even pull a pair before giving up on the Unit and maybe even check the trigger contacts again—but when the evidence is all in and the engine won't go, the only thing left is a new Unit. It will install just like the old one. Read the dope in Step 10 on Control Units, so you get the right one for your engine and sensor number.

PROCEDURES FOR REPLACING COMPONENTS. Phase I

Condition: From foregoing tests, you feel that a component needs replacing. The choice at the end of the Procedure for Checking the Fuel Injection System—Car Won't Start, stated that if you were getting juice from the Control Unit to the injector MPC's, it's probable the Control Unit is OK and you came here to make further checks on the injectors, the pressure sensor, the throttle valve switch or other components before checking the Control Unit and the wiring loom. On the other hand, you may arrive at this Procedure having checked the Control Unit and the wiring loom.

Tools: Phase I tool kit and a Volt Ohmmeter (VOM).

Remarks: Each member of the fuel injection team has to be able to do its particular job or be replaced by a part that will. You've done some tests that lead you to believe that a component needs replacing. Here, we'll give you some further tests to do on the component itself to help you decide if it has to be replaced, then tell you how to replace it. However, none of the parts can be checked properly out of its context as a part of the fuel injection team so you cannot blithely remove parts and expect to be able to judge by SEEING if they are OK. Taking a part to the dealer and asking if it is satisfactory may work with ones that have tolerances that can be measured but all the parts in the fuel injection system must be able to perform individually and together. You have to decide for yourself about fuel injection parts; there is no higher authority.

In these Procedures, we assume you've run the Procedure for Checking Out the Fuel Injection System—Car Won't Start and have at least read the Procedure for Checking the Electrical System so you know, for example, that "adjust to zero" means to set the VOM to some scale, like Rx1 and touch the probes together and adjust the ohms to zero with the dial or knob provided for this purpose. OK? You should also know where the components are located on your model and that when removing an MPC, you should pull gently on the plug and not on the wires. If you've done the preceding Procedure, you checked the holes (female) on the MPC's—here, you will check the pins (male) on the components. Be clean, clean, super clean throughout these Procedures.

Procedure for Replacing the Pressure Sensor

Step 1. Check it. See Changes and New Ideas.

Pull the MPC off the pressure sensor, set the VOM to Rx1 and adjust to zero. If your sensor has four pins, put one probe on the engine and the other on the pins one at a time. None of them should make the needle on the VOM move. If it has five pins, one of them is ground so put the negative probe on the ground pin and test the other four for shorts by touching each with the positive

Step 1. (Cont'd.)

probe and watching the needle. It shouldn't move. If it does—new pressure sensor.

VOM at Rx1, put one probe on each of the two outside pins (of the four). These are pins number 7 and 15, the primary coil and the needle should read about 90 ohms. Change your VOM to Rx10, remember to adjust to zero and try the two inner pins, 8 and 10, the secondary coil. The resistance here should be about 350 ohms, maybe a little less. Any substantial difference indicates an out of spec sensor even if the coils aren't shorted.

Another thing that fouls up in pressure sensors is that little rod that moves between the coils. It could be sticking and not moving freely. When this happens, the power of the engine is erratic like when you take off in first gear, there's no power at all, then all of a sudden the power comes on and falls off again. Try it like this: Put the MPC back on and start the engine. Pull off the vacuum hose that goes to the sensor at the intake air distributor end and get it into position so you can suck on it. The vacuum inlet you opened allows more air to the engine, so suck on the vacuum hose and if you can make the engine run faster by sucking on the hose and the action seems smooth, the sensor is OK mechanically. But if the sucking either doesn't make the engine run faster or the action is erratic, suspect the pressure sensor.

Materials: Pressure Sensor. Take both the engine number and the Control Unit part number to VW as different sensors team with certain Control Units. You might see if the vacuum hose needs replacement as well or even instead of.

Step 2. Remove Pressure Sensor

Gently pull the MPC off the sensor, pull the hose off and put the end up and out of the way. Look on top of the sensor where it's mounted to the body. There are three screws. Loosen the two front screws with a phillips head screwdriver but don't take them all the way out. Now remove the rear screw and slide the sensor toward the rear of the car and out. There it is.

Step 3. Install Pressure Sensor

You've got a new pressure sensor in hand and you're ready to go. First, you'll have to take the rubber mount off your old sensor and put it on the new one. To do this, take out the two 10mm nuts and washers and lift the mount off and place it on the new sensor the same way it came off. Slip the mount (with the sensor on it) under the two screws you loosened when you took the sensor off and replace the rear screw. Tighten them all firmly. Now pick up the MPC and look at the end of it. See how one side has a bevel on it. Look at the connection on the sensor and note the side the bevel is on. Put your thumb and forefinger on the MPC and slip it in the sensor with the bevels matched—all the way in. Pull the plastic shipping dust cap off the sensor and put the hose back on.

Procedure for Replacing the Pressure Switch on 1968-69 Type III Only.

The pressure switch is located directly under the right intake manifold pipes, just to the rear of the pressure regulator.

Condition: The pressure switch is the fuel enrichment device for the above models so if you have been experiencing no pick up when you push the accelerator pedal all the way down—and if the pressure sensor is OK—pressure switch. Here's an electrical check to help you decide: Set VOM to Rx1, adjust to zero. Pull the MPC at the pressure switch and put one probe on one pin and the other on the other, remove the vacuum hose at the switch and have your friend suck on it while you hold the probes and watch the needle. If it does not swing to zero and back to infinity as your friend sucks and lets off, the switch has to be replaced.

Materials: A pressure switch for your engine number.

Step 1. Remove it

Very gently pull the MPC off the switch, if it's still on; same for the hose at the switch end. The mounting bolt (10mm) is between the two intake pipes. It takes a really slim 10mm socket to get it out, but if you don't have one, just put the end of your open end 10mm wrench on it and turn the wrench with a pair of pliers. Remove the bolt and washer and pull the switch out from under the manifold.

Step 2. Install Pressure Switch

Slip the switch under the manifold pipes with the end the hose goes on facing the center of the engine. Start the 10mm bolt with washer in the mounting hole and tighten it using the end of your wrench and a pair of pliers. Now pick up the MPC and look at its end. See how it's beveled, so is the receptacle on the switch. Put it back on so the bevels match, then slip the hose back on.

Procedure for Replacing the Throttle Valve Switch

Condition: You suspect your switch is bad but please make sure it's not just out of adjustment before you replace it. It's a sturdy component with a simple operation. Let's adjust it again to make sure. In the Type III, it is on the right side of the intake air distributor and in the Type IV, it is under it. The principle is the same in both Types. The Throttle Valve Switch is mounted on a graduated plate and is held in position by two screws. Inside the Switch there are two contacts which must be closed (touching) when the throttle is closed (foot off). They close with a "click" you can actually hear. You can also make an electrical check at the exact moment of their closing: set the VOM to Rx1, adjust to zero, put one probe on pin number 17 and the other on 20 (1968-69 Type III) or one probe on 17 and the other on ground 70 or 71 (other models with fuel cut-off) or one on 9 and the other on 20 (1972-73 without fuel cut-off). When the points close, the needle will swing to zero. OK, whether you're using sound or electricity, the idea is the same. Loosen the screws, rotate the switch toward open, then rotate the other way until the VOM needle swings to zero or that little click is heard—stop right there. Try it again. Stop right where the points close. Then look at the graduated scale and turn the switch one more graduation on the scale (that's two degrees), tighten the screws and the switch is adjusted. Now, if it flunks the electrical tests, you have to replace it. To make sure the throttle is moving smoothly, you can take off the return spring and move the throttle back and forth. Replace the spring and try this electrical test (not for 1968-69 Type III): With the VOM set at Rx1 and adjusted to zero, find the number 9 pin on the throttle valve switch. (See Systems Diagram, page 141). Put one probe on it and the other on number 14 (or just to the engine—this is a ground). Note: 1972-73 models without fuel cut-off, use pins 9 and 20. OK, have your friend push on the accelerator pedal while you watch the needle on the VOM. It should swing from infinity to zero about ten times. Now move the probes to pins 17 and 20. When the accelerator is up, throttle closed, the needle should swing to zero. When your friend pushes on the pedal, the needle should go to infinity. If any of the results are not as above, decide on a new throttle valve switch.

Materials: New throttle valve switch for your engine number.

Step 1. Remove it

Pull off the MPC. **On the Type III,** remove the two screws (one on top and one on the bottom) that hold the switch on the body of the intake air distributor and remove the switch. **On the Type IV,** loosen the 8mm bolt on the throttle cable and slide the cable out and pull the return spring off. Now remove the two screws holding the air horn (aluminum end of the intake air distributor) on

Step 1. (Cont'd.)

and take it off the intake air distributor. Remove the two screws holding the throttle valve switch onto the air horn and gently remove it.

Step 2. Install it

Put the switch in place and replace the two screws. Adjust as in the Condition. **Type IV,** you and your friend can adjust the switch while one of you holds the air horn and rotates the throttle. then put the air horn back on, tighten the two screws and replace the return spring and throttle cable and you're done.

Procedure for Replacing the Fuel Pump-for AFC also.

Condition: Your car won't start or run with a bad pump. You have deduced from the electrical or capacity checks that the pump is bad.

Materials: New pump for your engine number, new type hose clamps and three pencils.

Step 1. Remove Fuel Pump

Slide under the front of the car and look to the rear of the front axle on the right side or left side. The fuel pump is the round cylinder with all the hoses attached to it. It's electrically operated by the Control Unit. To remove the pump, first pull off the line that comes from the gas tank to the pump. It's the one that has the plastic box between the gas tank and the pump. Stick a pencil in the hose to stop the flow of gas. Where the hose fits on the pump there will either be a screw type clamp or a band of metal with a hump on it. If it's the screw type clamp, just loosen the screw with a screwdriver but if it's the other type of clamp, squeeze it with a pair of pliers first, on the hump first, then on the side until the clamp expands enough to come off. If this is the type of clamp yours has, throw it away and replace with new type—screw type hose clamps. This applies to all the connections. Remove the other two hoses in the same manner, put pencils in them. See the wire going into the side of the pump. Pull back the rubber cover and put your thumb and forefinger on the white plastic plug (MPC) and pull it out. Now remove the two mounting nuts with a 10mm wrench.

If you buy a new pump, it may look different than your old one. The new type pump has the hose outlets all in a line but it'll work on the older models just fine.

Step 2. Install Fuel Pump

First, place the pump over the rubber mounts and put the two 10mm nuts on and tighten them. Look at the plastic plug with two wires on it. On one side there is a half circular cavity. Now look at the socket where the plug fits into the pump and see the half circular hump inside it. Put the plug in the socket so that the two half circles fit together. Push it all the way in. If you have the old type pump with two pipes on one end and the other on top of the same end, this is how it goes: The hose with the plastic box on it goes to the bottom pipe on the end. The hose with a round metal disc (damper) on it goes on the top pipe on the end. The hose with a Y connection on it goes to the top pipe. If you have the newer type pump with three pipes in a line, it goes like this: The hose with the plastic box on it goes on the pipe furthest away from the electrical plug. The hose with the round metal disc (damper) on it goes to the center pipe. The hose with a Y connection on it goes to the pipe closest to the electrical connection. Tighten all the hose clamps with your screwdriver.

Procedure for Replacing Trigger Contacts

Condition: Your trigger contacts are suspect. To check the trigger contacts, set the VOM to Rx1 and adjust to zero. Pull off the MPC on the distributor. Put one probe on the center pin (number 12) of the connection on the distributor (not on the MPC) and the other probe on one of the outside pins (number 21 or 22) and have your friend turn the engine over with the wrench or screwdriver. As the points open the needle will swing to infinity and as they close, the needle will swing to zero. Try the other pin and if the needle doesn't swing all the way to zero when the points are closed or if the needle doesn't move (you have to be patient), your trigger contacts are not doing their thing.

Materials: New trigger contacts for your distributor number.

Step 1. Remove Trigger Contacts

The trigger contacts are located in the bottom of the distributor. You'll have to pull the distributor (as in Tune-Up Procedure) to get at them, so do it. Remove the two screws on the curved metal plate on the bottom of the distributor and pull the contact plate out. That's it.

Step 2. Install Trigger Contacts

Slip your new set of contacts back in the slot in the distributor and replace and tighten the two screws. Put the distributor back in and retime the engine as in the Tune-Up Procedure. Remember to put the MPC back in making sure the bevels on the two ends match up.

Procedure for Replacing the Pressure Regulator

Condition: You can't adjust the pressure by turning the screw on the regulator. Your car won't start or run without 28 psi.

Materials: New pressure regulator for your engine number, two new screw type hose clamps and two pencils.

Step 1. Remove the Pressure Regulator

The pressure regulator is located on the very front piece of tin on the right side (Type III or left side of Type IV) of the engine. It's the one with a screw and lock nut facing the rear of the car. Loosen the connection on the fuel line on the regulator and pull the line off and quick, stick a pencil in the hose. Now crawl under the car and look up above the starter motor (Type III) or high up on the left side (Type IV) and find the other end of the regulator. There's another fuel hose coming in from this end so loosen the clamp and pull the hose off and stick a pencil in it. Right in back of where the hose was there is a 17mm lock nut so use your box end wrench to remove it. Now go around to the back of the car and pull the regulator off.

Step 2. Install Pressure Regulator

Put the regulator in place on the front piece of tin on the right-hand side (Type III, left side of Type IV) of the engine and crawl under the car while a friend holds the regulator in place. Start the 17mm lock nut and tighten it with an open end wrench. Put the hose back in place and tighten the clamp. Go to the back of the car to replace the hose there and tighten the clamp. Check for gasoline leaks. Now turn to Step 8 in the Tune-Up Procedure and adjust the regulator to 28 psi.

Procedure for Replacing the Fuel Injectors

Condition: You have checked the wiring and know that the problem is in the injectors themselves, not in the wiring. You would also be here if you were going to pull the injectors for any reason, like to see if they are opening and closing properly and like that.

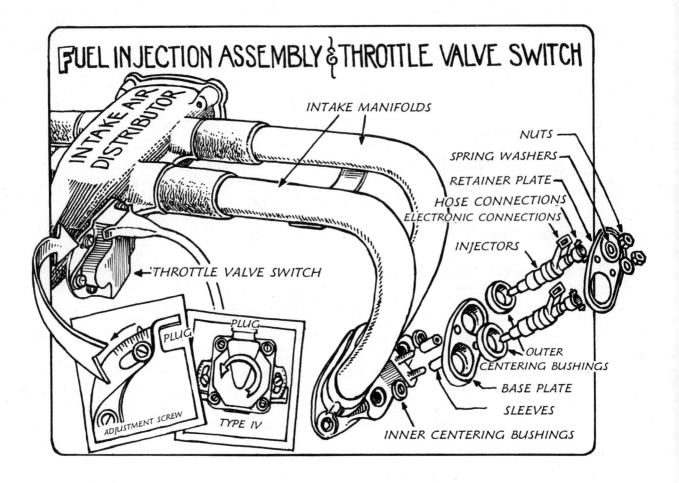

Materials: New inner seals. New injectors and outer seals, if needed. New screw type hose clamps to replace the crimped type. Get enough of these to do your whole fuel system while you're at it. The crimped type are for one time use. Pinch them off and throw them away, then replace with the screw type on all your fuel system hose connections. Can to catch gas.

Step 1. Remove Injectors

In the Type III, the injectors are mounted into the intake manifold in pairs. Each injector has its own MPC and fuel line connection, but one injector clamp holds a pair of injectors into the manifold on two studs. In the Type IV, each injector has its own injector clamp and you can remove one injector at a time. The injectors are the same and the tests are the same, you just have to remember that in the Type III you pull two injectors at a time and in the Type IV you pull only one.

Take off the 10mm nuts that hold the injectors to the manifold, leaving the MPC's and fuel lines connected, and get both the nuts and the lock washers into the bolt can. Pull the injector free of the manifold to where you can see the nozzle. See if the seals came off with the injectors, they are little rubber or plastic (?) rings that fit around the end of the injector to seal it to the manifold. If the ring is not on the injector, take a small screwdriver and gently pull it out of the hole the injector came out of. Put the seals out of the way. You should replace these seals whether you need to replace injectors or not.

Step 2. Test Injectors

Get something to catch the gas that is going to come shooting out of the injectors and have it in position. Run the pump to get the pressure up to 28 psi in the fuel system. If everything is connected and you are doing this out on the road, just turn the key on—you can hear the pump running (if it is). Run it for about 1-1/2 seconds, then turn the key off and turn it on again, the pump will do it's short time thing again. This should get the pressure up to 28 psi. Turn the key off and go look at the injectors. However, if you are doing this at home and have your pressure gauge hooked up and the jumper wire is hooked into the pump ground side of the T1 connector, you can run the pump by grounding the other end of the jumper wire and turning the key on. Anyway, when the pressure is at 28 psi, look at the injectors. There should be a drop of gas forming at the end of the injector. If more than two or three drops a minute come out of the injectors (when they are supposed to be closed), the seat on the injector is getting worn, so think about new injectors as this drip will make your car run rich as hell.

Reach down and push the shiny rod coming out of the end of the injector with your thumbnail. The injector will open and spray gas all over your hand. Let a little run out to clean the seat, then let go of it.

Run the pump a couple of hits to build up the pressure again and go to the next injector. The seats are clean and should close when you let up on the nozzle pin. Pull the thick wire out of the coil so the engine won't start and have your friend turn the engine over so you can watch the injectors firing. They will spray gas for about 2 to 10 milliseconds, then close promptly and well and so on if they are working properly. If an injector doesn't fire (spray gas), check the connection at the MPC to see if it's on tight. Wiggle it a little while the engine is turning over. You may have a loose MPC. Do this to all four injectors. If you find one that leaks excessively or isn't firing or doesn't close promptly, you should think about replacing that injector.

The electrical check for the injectors requires the VOM and you don't have to have the injectors out to make this check. Set the VOM on Rx1 and adjust to zero. Pull the MPC off the injector and put one probe on one pin and the other on the other on the injector connection. The needle should swing to between 2 and 3 ohms (2.4 to be exact). If the needle doesn't move or swings to zero, the injector is shot. Be sure you have a VOM that will read two or three ohms. The small VOM's won't read this close. If the resistance is much higher than the correct value, the injector will fire but will be sloppy, firing erratically and like that. You will need a new injector anyway but you might like to know why your engine was doing what it was doing. Take the assembly apart and the injector out.

Step 3. Install Injectors

Now as we install the injectors, we are concerned with sealing. There is the little ring that fits over the nozzle (called the inner ring) and a bigger ring that fits up higher on the injector, called the outer ring. In the Type III these fit into a hard plastic two holer gizmo which should not be cracked or damaged; the plate fits over all this and holds the assembly onto the intake manifold. Put the little inner seal rings on the injector just before you slip the injectors into the holes. The Type IV is about the same without the duality of the plastic gizmo and double plate. The one nut and lock washer holds the plate which holds the outer seal and when the bolts are tightened, the seal is also secured. That's about it. The black plastic MPC covers go to the front of the car (1 and 3) and the grey to the rear (2 and 4) so you can't get them mixed up. You must be clean around the injectors as they are very sensitive to tiny pieces of crud. The nuts should be tightened with an easy swing of the ratchet, not too tight. If you use a torque wrench, the value is 4.5 foot lbs.

Procedure for Replacing Temperature Sensor I, crankcase or intake air manifold temperature sensor.

In the 1968-69 Type III, this sensor is just to the right of the distributor and in the other models it's installed in the left side of the intake air distributor.

Condition: Your sensor failed its electrical tests or you're going to check it now. Pull off the MPC exposing the pins. Set the VOM to Rx10 and adjust to zero. Put one probe on each pin and the needle should swing to 300 ohms. The hotter the engine, the smaller the resistance reading will be. If the reading is a lot higher or infinity, the circuit is open and the sensor is caput. The same is true if the needle swings to zero.

Materials: New Temperature Sensor I for your engine and Control Unit number.

Removal and Replacement: Use a 13mm wrench to loosen the retaining nut, take out the old sensor and put the new one in. Tighten the retaining nut, but not too tight, just an easy push on the wrench. Reconnect the MPC.

Procedure for Replacing Temperature Sensor II, head temperature sensor

In the Type III, 1968 and 69 models, this sensor is in the top on No. 4 cylinder head, in the other models, it's down a hole in between cylinders 3 and 4.

Condition: It has failed its examination or you're going to examine it now. Find the wire that comes up out of the sensor. It has a T1 connector on it. Pull the sensor side connector free. If your engine is cold, set the VOM at Rx100 and adjust to zero. Put one probe to the connector and the other to ground. The needle should swing to about 1500 ohms. If the engine is hot (you can't touch it with your hand), set the VOM to Rx1 and the needle should swing to 60 or so. If the needle swings to either infinity or zero, the sensor has had it so put in a new one.
Materials: Temperature Sensor II for your engine and Control Unit numbers.

Removal and Installation: In the 1968-69 Type III, you can use a 13mm open end to unscrew the retaining nut but in the other models you will need a deep 13mm socket which you may have to borrow. We don't have one either. If you have one of those old VW socket wrenches that came with the car, one end of that is 13mm and will work. Unscrew the sensor and remove it. Screw the new one in. Make sure the threads don't get crossed, you can tell, it should turn easy. It doesn't have to be very tight, just so it won't fall out. Connect the T1 and you are done.

Procedure for Replacing the Auxiliary Air Regulator

This is the source of air for your engine when it is idling. It is located at the left front edge of the intake air distributor on the Type IV and to the right of the distributor in the Type III. If your engine dies at idle and the idle adjusting screw doesn't help, suspect the auxiliary air regulator. In the 1970 and on models there is a hot wire to heat the air before it goes to the intake air distributor. The air system, however, has nothing electrical. It is a bi-metal spring that closes the regulator as the engine gets warm. They sometimes leak. This you can test by getting the engine warm so the regulator closes completely, then pull the hose at the air cleaner or intake air distributor and put your hand over the end of the hose. If the engine speed drops noticeably, you need a new auxiliary air regulator.

Condition: You cannot adjust the idle or the regulator leaks as above.

Materials: New auxiliary air regulator for your engine number.

Removal and Installation: Make sure key is off. Pull electrical (if any) and hose connections. Remove two bolts, lift out regulator, install new regulator, push on hoses and electrical connection (if any).

Procedure for Replacing Relays, Main and Fuel Pump

Condition: The relay has been checked and found defective during the tests in either of the two previous procedures or you are checking it now. If either relay is shot, your car won't start.

In the Type III, the main relay is under the seat and the pump relay is on a bracket under the dash over the steering column. In the Type IV, both relays are on the left side of the engine compartment. The main relay is the one that has a wire going to ground.

Step 1. Check Main Relay

You may have to unscrew the mounting screw to read the numbers on the relay. Tighten the ground screw. Set your VOM to 0-15, 0-30 or 0-50 DCV. Put the negative probe to ground and check the voltage at number 30/51. With the key off or on, the needle should swing to about 12 volts. Turn the key on, with the negative probe to ground, connection 86 should read about 12 volts, now move the positive probe to number 87 and if you have no voltage at 87, the relay is shot.

Step 2. Check Fuel Pump Relay

You may have to demount it to see the numbers but leave all the connections on. Turn the key on and check the voltage with the VOM as above, between ground and pin 30/51. It should read about 12 volts, then try pin 86 and it should read the same; now try between ground and pin 87 and if you don't get 12 volts, the relay is gone.

Materials: New relay—specify which and take your engine number.

Step 3. Removal and Installation

These are done at the same time and are the same for both relays. Unfasten the bracket. It's held by a screw. Hold the new relay up to the old and take the terminals off the old and put them on the new at the same places, one at a time. Mount the relay on the car or on the bracket (put the bracket back where it came from, making sure you get the grounds under the screws) and you are through.

In 1972 VW added a simple piping change and a deceleration mixture control valve on the models sold in California. This piping change and addition of one valve in the engine compartment allows the smog control experts to control the slowing down of the engine, another step toward making the throttle butterfly less a function of your foot. However, it does operate to control emissions and can be found and handled the same way as the other emissions control components.

To remove and install the intake air distributor and manifolds, see Chapter XV.

What to Take Along on a Trip to Mexico for Electronic Fuel Injection:

We know that someone is going to ask us this question so here is one answer—what we take for our Type III when we go to Mexico (where no fuel injection parts are available). First of all, we run the component checks and take any component that looks as though it might be starting to fail. For instance, if the fuel pump is having a little trouble filling a beer can in ten seconds—fuel pump. It all depends on your pocketbook but a pressure sensor would be nice (we take one) and, for sure, one spare injector, gaskets and seal rings for the injectors and a long piece of fuel hose—extra fuel hose clamps for sure. Take a relay; one will do for either main or fuel pump. How about a little extra wire for wiring around stuff and like that. You can get plugs soldered in little radio shops. For more information see "The People's Guide To Mexico," by Carl Franz.

The last subject on electronic fuel injection is the cold start system and we're going to cop out. Our Type III starts at 20 below without it and if we had one, we'd neatly pull the wire off the temperature switch and tape it up on account of our belief that dumping a lot of raw gas into the engine is bad for it.

AFC (AIR FLOW CONTROL) FUEL INJECTION

This new AFC system is on 1975 and later Types I and II and the 1974 Type IV with automatic transmission. It operates the same as the old fuel injection system with a couple of important changes. For example, instead of two injectors firing at once, now all four fire every time the points open. The points send RPM signals to the control unit and thus no separate trigger contacts are used.

The throttle valve switch, which in the old system provided enrichment through the RPM range, is not adjustable in the new system and only furnishes enrichment at the full load position of the throttle. The temperature sensor No. 1 which, as always, tells us the intake temperature, has been relocated in the new intake air sensor, that pot metal and plastic contraption that the air filter snaps onto.

Temperature sensor No. 2 which tells us how hot the cylinder heads are is in the same place as in the old system.

The control unit which used to have a mighty 300 components and was located on various places around the chassis (see old system) now only has 80 components and is located next to the battery on the Type I and on the right side of the engine compartment in the Type II.

The fuel pressure regulator is connected by a vacuum hose to the aforementioned all important intake air sensor, and we cannot adjust it. It always puts out 35 psi. If the pressure needs any adjusting, the intake air sensor takes care of it. If there is any malfunction of the pressure regulator, it has to be replaced.

The auxiliary air regulator, also found in the old system, provides extra air during warmups in cold weather.

The work of the intake air sensor is to measure the air volume and the air temperature, sending appropriate signals to the control unit. It also controls the fuel pressure through the fuel pressure regulator mounted in front (FRONT) of the engine on the firewall.

The injectors are checked out, removed and installed the same as in the old system, remembering that they all four fire at once when the points are open.

The cold start valve, now located in the end of the air distribution box, is the same as in the old system. The air distribution box is the metal box on top of the engine with pipes going to each cylinder.

Now we are going to refer you back to the original instructions for fuel injection in this chapter for the cause of the engine not starting. You'll find that all the electrical and ground checks are similar. Some differences are: In the new system, the ground on the Type I is on top of the alternator and on the Type II, it's under the left side of the intake air distributor.

You can be assured there is power in the system if the light goes on by connecting your test light to terminals 88y and 85 on the double relay.

To check the intake air sensor, pull the connector off the intake air sensor and connect your VOM to pins 6 and 9 on the intake air sensor and the VOM should read 200 to 400 ohms. Connect the VOM to pins 7 and 8 and it should read 120 to 200 ohms. Put the connector back on the intake air sensor.

To check the whole system, put your VOM on pins 85 and 86a on the double relay and you should get a reading of 0 to infinity when the starter is operated.

If the choke does not stop operating it is possible you have a fuel leak in the system which could come from temperature sensor No. 2, the cold start valve or the thermo-time switch or some other place that would allow a fuel leak.

To check the auxiliary air regulator pull the hose off between the auxiliary air regulator and the intake air distributor but leave it attached to the regulator. Blow through the hose and if you can blow through it, the auxiliary air regulator is OK, but if the hose is clogged up, you'll have to replace the aux air regulator.

To check the intake air sensor, put the hose back on and connect your VOM to contacts 36 and 39 on the intake air sensor and operate the starter for a few seconds. The needle should swing between 0 and infinity.

If the idle speed stays the same, turn in the idle adjustment screw located on the intake air distributor. If the RPM doesn't drop until the screw is turned in all the way, the auxiliary air regulator isn't closing, so block the hose between the aux air regulator and the rubber elbow on the intake air sensor. If the speed doesn't drop, your aux air regulator is defective. Replace all the hoses. Now pull the electrical connector off the aux air regulator and connect your test light to both pins on the connector. If the light goes on, the electrical system to the regulator is OK.

If your top speed is too low and the general output of the engine is weak and you've already checked all those tune-up things, pull the multi-pin connector off the control unit and connect the VOM to pins 3 and 18. Open the throttle fully and the needle should swing from 0 to infinity. If the needle swings to 0 and stays there, there is an electrical fault in the intake air sensor so go back to the procedure for checking the intake sensor and check the resistance on pins 6 and 9 and 7 and 8. If the resistance isn't OK, the intake air sensor is defective. If it checks out OK, it's a mechanical fault with the flap inside the air sensor, so take it apart and check out the flap. To take it apart, unscrew the hose clamp on the rubber elbow attached to the intake air sensor and pull the elbow loose. Pull the two hoses off the plastic vacuum unit and unsnap the air filter element. Now you can take the whole intake air sensor out and remove the four 10 mm bolts that hold the plastic air filter receptacle onto the sensor unit. Right there where it bolts on is the little metal air flap. It should move back and forth smoothly. If it doesn't, try cleaning it out with a dry rag as just a little crud in the right place can make it stick. Put the whole business back together when you're through.

If the resistance reading on pins 3 and 18 remain at infinity, there is a break in the wiring to the throttle valve switch or the switch is defective. Replace the multi-pin connector on the control unit when you're finished.

If you've run all the checks and the engine is still not running right, check the fuel pressure by pulling off the hose between the intake air distributor and the pressure regulator. Connect the pressure gauge and start the engine. The pressure should be 35 psi both at idle and full throttle. If the pressure drops at full throttle, the fuel supply is restricted somewhere, like a kinked fuel line, a clogged fuel filter or tank strainer, or the pump just isn't putting gas out like it should. To replace the fuel pump, see procedure under Electronic Fuel Injection earlier in this chapter.

If the pressure is low at idle and full throttle, the pressure regulator is defective in which case you'll have to replace it. Put the fuel line back in place.

If all these procedures check out OK and engine power is still low, the control unit is probably defective.

If you're experiencing high fuel consumption, the first check should be fuel pressure. If the pressure is too high, that's the problem, in which case it's either a defective pressure regulator or a blocked or pinched fuel line between the tank and the pressure regulator, so check it out.

If all this is OK, check the resistance of the cylinder head temperature sensor (sensor No. 2). Disconnect the wire on the sensor and connect one end of the VOM to the wire and the other end to ground. The resistance should be less than 300 ohms. If it's above 300 ohms, the sensor is faulty or not seated properly in the head.

If the resistance is below 300 ohms, check the cold start valve for leaks. If it's OK, one of the injectors might be leaking, so pull the injectors (procedure is the same as the old system). Pull the injectors, but leave them connected to the fuel ring. Pull No. 1 wire off the ignition coil and turn the engine over a few times by hand. Each injector should not leak more than two drops in one minute. If one leaks more than this, you'll have to replace it. If none of the injectors leak and you've run through all the procedures, the control unit may be at fault. Put the injectors back in with new seals, if necessary. Put No. 1 wire back on the coil.

In the control box, pin No. 1 is the ground connection. We have already referred to pins 3 and 18 and you'll find that the control box itself checks out the same as the old one did. In our experience we have had no control box troubles other than bad connections where the main plug plugs in.

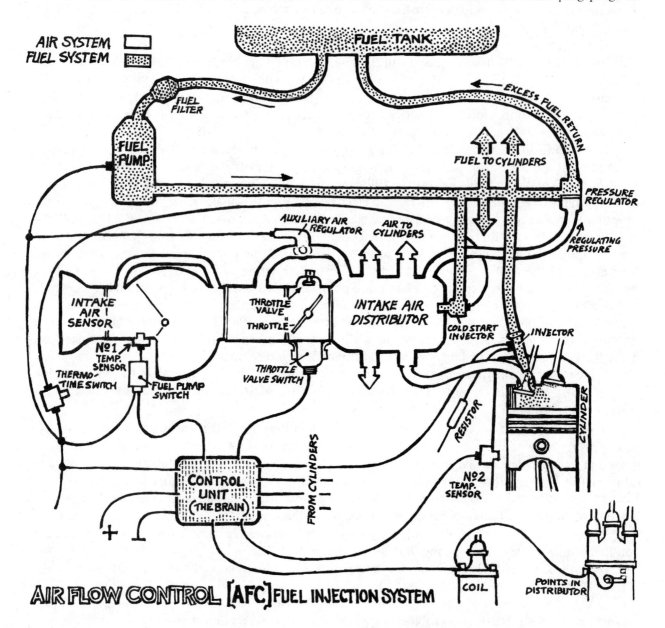

AIR FLOW CONTROL [AFC] FUEL INJECTION SYSTEM

If your engine refuses to idle and you've been through all of this, check the EGR valve as in Chapter VII.

WARNING!

DO NOT USE JUMPER CABLES TO START YOUR FUEL INJECTED ENGINE! DO NOT QUICK (OR SLOW) CHARGE YOUR BATTERY WITHOUT DISCONNECTING THE GROUND STRAP AND THE BATTERY POSITIVE CLAMP! In other words, take the battery out of the car to charge it.

NEVER RUN THE ENGINE WITH THE BATTERY DISCONNECTED!

These warnings are to guard the Control Unit (brain) which will burn out if subjected to an excess of voltage.

CHAPTER XI

VOLKSWAGEN DOESN'T STOP (BRAKES)

The VW brakes are similar to their American cousins. There is a **Master Cylinder** directly attached to the **brake pedal** and four slave cylinders, called **wheel cylinders,** one in each wheel. In the Bus there are two slave cylinders in each front wheel but they act the same—just like the two halves of a single wheel cylinder. When you push on the brake pedal you move the hydraulic fluid in the master cylinder and, as Archimedes says, the pressure in an interconnected fluid system is the same in all parts of the system, so the pressure you put on the pedal is transmitted equally to the four wheel cylinders which move the **brake shoes** into contact with the **brake drums.** The brake shoes and wheel cylinders are fastened to the **brake plate** which is stationary.

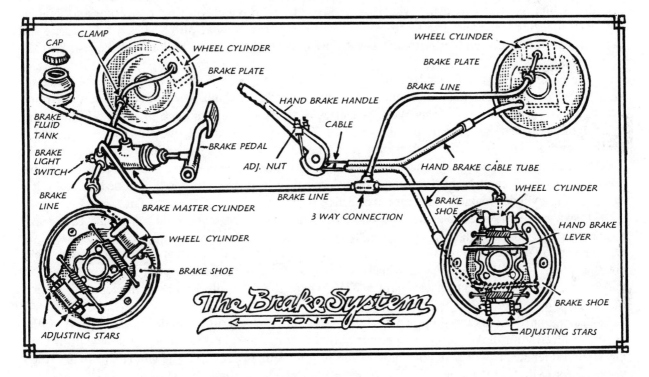

The idea of **adjusting the brakes** is simply to move the brake shoes as near the brake drums as they will go without undue rubbing so when you push on the pedal, the shoes have the shortest possible distance to travel. The idea of **bleeding the brakes** is to remove the collected air in the system because air is a compressible gas, brake fluid is relatively incompressible and you want your fluid as incompressible as possible.

You need a brake adjustment when the brake pedal goes half way to the floor before the brakes take hold. When you have to pump, an adjustment is overdue. You need to bleed the brakes when the pedal feels spongy under your foot or any time the system has been open. The pedal should be firm and unyielding when you press on it.

The **stop light switch** is a simple pressure switch that turns on the stop lights when the pedal is pushed. It screws into the front end of the master cylinder.

Since 1967, all models have a Dual Circuit Tandem Master Cylinder which means that your brake foot is connected to two master cylinders (in one long piece), one for the front brakes and one for the rear. If either of them fails, the other will do the job for both, except for disc brakes. You can adjust and bleed these brakes as usual. The Super Beetle has slightly larger front brakes than other Type I's but otherwise are the same.

Brake Warning Light

If this red light on your dash goes on when you apply the brakes, it means that one of your dual master cylinders is not up to snuff but, even without the light, your foot would be aware because with a master cylinder not working, it takes more foot pressure and more time to stop the car.

If this light comes on while braking hard it can also mean excessively worn shoes or pads or badly adjusted brakes. Check these things out first before you tear into the master cylinder, OK?

The following procedures include the operations necessary to repair your brake system, except the overhaul of the master cylinder, which should be done by an expert. We do tell you how to remove it and put it back on, however.

Because your front brakes are the leading brakes, the front shoes wear out much faster than the rear shoes. I have averaged three sets of front shoes to one set of rear shoes and two-to-one is probably the national average.

Many of the new models have disc brakes in front and they are operated by the same hydraulic principles as the drum brakes with the pressure forcing a pair of pads out of a caliper to apply friction to a disc which is attached to the wheel. Just put your thumb and forefinger together and imagine you are squeezing a turning disc to stop it from turning, that's what disc brakes do. There are still two parts to a master cylinder with the front part operating the front brakes and the rear part the rear brakes.

The criterion for wheel cylinder repair is usually leakage: you will see a wet spot on the inside of your wheel or tire where fluid is running down out of the brake drum. If the wet spot is on a front wheel, it can mean only one thing: your wheel cylinder is leaking fluid and must be rebuilt. If one front cylinder is leaking, prepare to rebuild all the front cylinders in the two front wheels. Likewise for the rear cylinders. If the wet spot is on a rear wheel, you have to decide whether the leak is brake fluid or transmission oil. Leaky wheel cylinders are not the only criterion for repair. If your brakes are low or mushy and can't be bled or adjusted out, you may have a piston that's corroded so badly it's stuck in the cylinder making that brake ineffective.

Leakage is always trouble, but you can tell. Get your can of brake fluid out of the car—leave the cap on—get some of the leakage off the rear tire onto your forefinger and raise it gently to your nose or a friend's nose if you have a cold. Then open the can of brake fluid and smell it. If the smells are the same, you have a leaky rear wheel cylinder. If they are different, your rear bearing seal is leaking. In the latter case, turn to Chapter XIV, where the rear wheel work is procedured, to find out what to do.

Leakage in the brake system can be both ways: air can leak in or fluid can leak out. If you're having to bleed your brakes often, you either have a leaking connection at one of the wheels or your master cylinder needs work. If your brake fluid is going somewhere, and the wheels are all dry, then your master cylinder is leaking.

To check leaks in the master cylinder, first find it. It's attached to the brake pedal. In the Bus, it's hidden above that pan between the front wheels. You'd probably find evidence of leakage around the pan if it's leaking. In the Types I and III, you can see the master cylinder by looking back of the left front wheel. It's that thing with the tubes coming out the side of it, with two wires attached to the front of it. The Type III may have a cover protecting the master cylinder. In the Type IV, it's under the dash to the right of the steering column or as in the Type III.

The ability to stop is often more important than any other capability—humans, cars, whathaveyous. Do a good slow solid job on your brakes.

See **Chapter XX**, Stopping Is Important, Too.

BRAKE ADJUSTMENT AND BLEEDING PROCEDURE, Phase I

Condition: The brake pedal goes halfway to the floor before the brakes take hold (adjustment) or the pedal feels soft and mushy (bleeding). You should also both adjust and bleed the brakes any time you've had the system open for any reason.

Tools and Materials: Phase I tool kit, can of heavy-duty brake fluid, flashlight.

Remarks: The Ghia and Type III from 1966 on, the Bus from 1971 on and all Type IV's have disc brakes up front. Disc brakes adjust themselves. Hooray! You still have to adjust the rear brakes, however, and bleed all four. If your car has disc brakes, check the pads for wear (Procedure for Changing Disc Wear Pads in this chapter) and if they need to be changed, change them before doing the rear brakes.

Step 1. Block and Jack

All Models

I have developed the habit of starting with the wheel the furthest away from the master cylinder and I do the adjustment and bleeding operations at the same time, first adjust, then bleed. This means the rear right wheel comes first, so block the left side of the car so it cannot move, then jack up the right rear wheel. When it's adjusted and bled let it down, then move your blocks to the right side, jack up the left rear wheel, then follow the same pattern for the right front and finally the left front, the closest to the master cylinder.

Step 2. Locate the Adjusting Stars and Check the Lining

Use the large screwdriver to pry the hub cap off the right rear wheel and right under the hub cap near the wheel rim, you'll find a hole. Except if you have a **Type I or II from 1968 on, a Type III from 1966 on or a Type IV**: the hole for adjusting the brakes is on the inside of the wheel, so you'll have to slide under the car to find it. There's a rubber plug in the hole which you'll have to pull or pry off.

All Models

Do you see the hole? OK, put both your eye and the light from the flashlight into this hole at the same time. Anyhow, try. If the daylight is too bright, try a jacket over your head. What you want to see is the brake lining, which is a fibrous material attached to a metal rim (the shoe). You want to find out how thick the brake lining is! 1/16" or less, you need new lining. A fat 1/8", your lining is in good shape. Each wheel has two shoes so rotate the wheel and check both linings. If you've been riding around with the hand brake on, the front shoe in the rear wheel may be totally shot. It's the shoe used by the hand brake. Anyway, now you know where your brake linings are for future reference. You are here to adjust your brakes, not to admire them, so while you are scanning the inside of the wheel through that silly hole—remember that scene in "The Journeyman"?—look for some brass stars, (wheels with notches on the outside of them). These are the adjusting stars and if you don't see them, don't worry. I'll tell you how to find them—in the dark, if necessary. These stars don't face you but present their sides or notches to you as you look through the hole.

Location of Adjusting Stars, rear wheels:

Type I, III and IV, they are just to the left and right of 6 o'clock.

Type II, they're on each side of 12 o'clock.

Location of Adjusting stars, front wheels:

Models with disc brakes have none.

Type II with drum brakes: As the Bus has two front wheel cylinders in each wheel, each has its own adjusting star. These are at almost 6 and almost 12 o'clock.

Type III with drum brakes: Has front brakes like the bus except the stars are at 9 and 3 o'clock.

Type I from about 1968 on: are reached from around the inside of the brake plate through two holes in the plate instead of from an outside hole in the drum. The holes are in the bottom of the brake plate and so are the stars.

Rest of Type I: Get under the car to look at the inside of the brake plate. The stars will be centered on a line 180° (half circle) around from the hole in the back of the backing plate. They'll be about 3" apart, so figure 1-½" on each side of this imaginary line. Look in your owner's manual as it usually has a good picture.

Step 3. Adjust the shoes

The idea is to move these little stars so the brake shoes are moved as close as possible to the drum without binding. Here is a sketch:

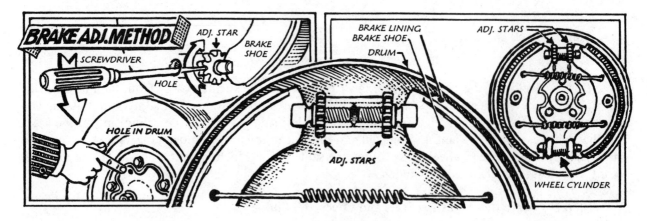

Use a medium screwdriver through the hole to pry the stars around, as it shows, until the shoe tightens up on the drum (until you can't turn the wheel), then pry the star the other way one or two pries to release the shoe so the drum can turn freely. You may hear scrapings, but the drum must not bind anywhere. With both shoes adjusted, you can go to Step 4, bleed a little, then jack the car down and go to the next wheel. It's not that easy, you say? OK, I'll try to tell you which way to turn the stars but first look in your owner's manual at the picture.

The second concept you can use is the "cut and try." Just turn the star until you have turned it ten to fifteen notches—that's the wrong way, so turn it the other way back the 10 to 15, then on until the shoe tightens to the drum. You say you want to know how to figure it out? OK, pay attention. Bus owners first. In your rear wheels, the stars are to the left and right of 12 o'clock. I can't get my little finger in the hole so I use the screwdriver to find the star. If you are coming up from the left, pry the star so the handle of the screwdriver moves toward the closest part of the tire to tighten the shoe to the drum. If you are coming up from the right, pry the star so the handle moves away from the tire to tighten the shoe to the drum. In a Bus with front drum brakes, you always pry the star so the handle of the screwdriver moves away from the tire to move the shoe toward the drum.

Now for the Types I, III and IV. In the rear wheels, the adjusting stars are centered on each side of 6 o'clock, so insert the blade of the screwdriver in the hole and move the wheel and thus the screwdriver blade into the star, gently. If you are coming down from the left, pry the star so the handle of the screwdriver moves away from the closest part of the tire to tighten the shoe to the drum and if you come down from the right, the handle should move toward the tire to tighten the shoe. The same thing is true for the front wheels with drum brakes when the adjusting stars are at the bottom. If the adjusting stars are located at 9 o'clock, usual from about 1960 to 66 or so and if you and your screwdriver blade come down into the adjusting star, you pry the star so the screwdriver handle moves away from the tire; coming up to the star, toward the tire. Before 1960 or so, the adjusting stars are at about 1 o'clock so pry the left-hand star so the handle moves toward the tire to tighten and the right-hand star the opposite way. That's enough of that.

As you gain experience the work goes faster and faster. The first adjustment may take you 30 minutes or so (Perseverance Furthers) but the last one may take less than five minutes.

Remember to put back the rubber plug in the adjusting hole if your model is supposed to have one.

Step 4. Bleeding Brakes

A bleeder bolt is a bolt screwed into the back of the wheel cylinder through the brake plate

Step 4. (Cont'd.)

and the brake plate is toward the inside of the car (behind) the brake drum or disc. Lie down under the car beside the wheel and look for the bleeder bolt next to where the brake hose (the flexible line) is attached. On the front wheels of the Bus the bleeder bolt is on the bottom of the brake plate. Some models with disc brakes up front have two bleeder bolts on each side so be sure to bleed them both. This bolt should be identifiable by the rubber cap on it but sometimes they get knocked off. One thing that will identify it is a hole in the top of it but under the rubber cap. The idea is to have your friend pump the brakes up with the pedal until you holler "hold," whereupon your friend holds the pedal down steady while you momentarily open this little bolt with the hole in it with the vice grip so the air can escape.

Start with the right rear as it's furthest from the master cylinder. Find the bleeder bolt, remove the rubber dust cap, get the vice grip clamped (or the 7mm wrench) onto the bolt so it will open and close — try it before signaling your friend. If the bolt breaks off in the cylinder, try removing it with the vice grip. If this fails, you'll have to remove the cylinder and have the offending bolt removed at the machine shop. OK? Close the bleeder bolt and have your friend pump the brakes about six or seven pumps, then holler "hold" and do the thing: a quick open and shut. If nothing comes out but clear fluid, tighten the bleeder bolt, put the rubber dust cap back on, then go on to the next wheel but if it spluttered and fizzed, bleed it again.

You'd better add some fluid before letting too much out. The fill place is a little plastic tank with a plastic cap that pries off with your fingernail. In older buses it's under the driver's right foot or on the front wall above the brake pedal (where it's handy) or behind the driver's seat (where it's a bug, using the best storage space for canopy poles, slide screens and other long thin things). In buses from '78 on it's under the rubber flap under the right corner of the driver's seat. In the Type I, this little tank sits in the front compartment under the spare tire (make sure it's the brake fluid tank and not the windshield washer tank before filling). In the Types III and IV, the brake fluid tank is in the front compartment just in front of the dash.

Bleed the brakes in all four wheels, then fill the little tank up again and you're through.

MASTER CYLINDER PUSH ROD ADJUSTMENT

Whenever you've adjusted and bled the brakes and there is still too much free play in the brake pedal, the problem is more than likely the adjusting of the master cylinder push rod. The push rod is located in front of the brake pedal inside the car. Loosen the 13mm lock nut on the push rod with a 13mm open end wrench and turn the rod until it feels like it's flush up against the piston in the master cylinder (no free play). Turn the rod back about half a turn and tighten the lock nut on the rod. That's it. If this master cylinder push rod needs adjustment, it indicates the master cylinder and/or wheel cylinders need attention.

WHEEL PROCEDURE: REMOVAL AND INSTALLATION. RELINING BRAKES, OVERHAULING WHEEL CYLINDERS AND REASSEMBLY FOR FRONT AND REAR DRUM BRAKES. REPACKING AND ADJUSTING FRONT WHEEL BEARINGS, REPLACING FRONT WHEEL SEALS AND FRONT WHEEL BALANCING FOR DRUM OR DISC BRAKES.

Condition: VW says that the front wheels need packing every 30,000 miles. If your drum brake cylinders (front or rear) have been leaking, you have to remove the drums to fix them or if your disc brake calipers have been leaking, ditto. Whether or not they're leaking, you should do the packing of the front wheels with grease (30,000 miles). If your car has been pulling to the left or right, there may be grease or fluid on the linings (drum brakes) or on the pads (disc brakes) or a wheel bearing could be out of adjustment. To cure this, you have to take off the front wheels. If your brake linings (drum brakes) or brake pads (disc brakes) are worn, you'll be replacing them and will want to inspect and repack the front wheel bearings. Your hand brake cable may have broken and if so, you're at the right procedure. If a front wheel has been making funny noises, run the procedure to check the front wheel bearings. If you are following this procedure to get deeper into the front end, like for king pins or torsion arm bolt bushings (Chapter XII), do as many steps as you possibly can so you won't have to get into the wheels again for a long time. Grease and time are cheap.

The step for balancing the front wheels at the close of the procedure may seem silly to you in the face of all the fancy equipment they use for this in the shops, electronic flashing guns, etc., but it works and has the advantage that *you* can do it. The first time you hit a curb, skid to a stop or just run 300 miles, your wheels are out of balance anyway.

Tools and Materials: Phase I tool kit, wheel bearing grease, brake fluid, cleaning solvent and pan, rubber bands, alcohol, Brillo pads, 6mm allen wrench for new-type wheel adjusting nuts, piece of broomstick about one foot long, rags and transportation to the parts store.

Parts: New wheel bearing lock plates (different sizes for different models) and, if needed, new bearings and new seals for drum brakes, new wheel cylinder rebuild kits and relined brake shoes, if needed. A bag of wheel weights for balancing.

Remarks: Start with front wheels. If you have disc brakes, read the two procedures at the end of the chapter so you'll know what to expect.

There's a little problem in nomenclature that we'll clear up. The **wheel** is the rim with the tire on it so when we say "remove the wheel," we mean to remove the lugs (either nuts or bolts) and take the wheel off. . .like changing a flat. The wheel bearings are in the hub which goes on the axle and many people also call this the wheel. We're going to call it the **hub** while everything together is generically termed the **wheel assembly** but from now on, the "wheel" is the rim with the tire on it, OK?

At this point the names for things depend on what kind of brakes you have. If you have **one piece drum brakes**, drums that are not "composite," the drum and hub are made of the same piece of steel. . .in other words, the hub is the central piece of the brake drum. If you have **composite** drums (found only on the rear of Type III '66 and on, Type II '71 and on and on all Type IV's), the hub and the drum are two separate pieces of metal. The drum is held to the hub by two 6mm Allen head cap screws. If you have **disc brakes** (found on the fronts of the Ghia and Type III '66 and on, Type II '71 and on and on all Type IV's), there's a hub and a disc which are one piece.

No matter what type of brakes your car has, there's a stationary round plate behind (toward the inside of the car of) the drum or disc. This plate is slightly larger than the drum or disc and is called the **brake plate**. Mounted on the brake plate are the **wheel cylinders** (drum brakes) or **calipers** (disc brakes). Inside the front hub are two bearings, the **front wheel bearings**, outboard and inboard, and lots of grease. The **axle** runs through the bearings, then changes shape so there's a flat place with three or four holes in it. The brake plate is bolted to these holes.

Step 1. Jack Car and Release Brakes

All Models

Block both rear wheels, front and back, so the car cannot roll. Or block both front wheels if you're removing a rear wheel. Jack up the wheel you're removing. Use a scissors jack, if you have one, so only the one wheel and not the whole side is up. It's safer. Set your stool facing the jacked up wheel and pry the hub cap off with the large screwdriver. **Drum brakes**: turn back to the Brake

Adjustment Procedure to move the adjusting stars until the brake shoes are as far away from the drums as possible. **Disc brakes**: remove the wheel, then the calipers per Procedure on Discs and Calipers. Don't remove the calipers, just hang them up and out of the way. **All models**: Now that your brakes are released, you can roll the wheel (drum brakes) or hub (disc brakes) around and listen for the ballsy rumble that means rough and worn wheel bearings. You'll examine them later, but listen now for the sounds of wear. If you're working on the left front wheel, look at the hub of the wheel. There's a little square thing coming out of the cap (if your speedometer's been working). Take off the cotter key or the little spring clip holding the square thing. It's the speedometer cable shaft and you can reach around to pull it out of the axle and out of your way, if you like. Just remember which hole it came out of.

Step 2. Remove Hubs

FRONT
Use the big screwdriver and the small hammer to tap and pry the hub cover off the round thing in the center of the hub. Put some Liquid Wrench on it. If it is absolutely hung, go borrow a big pipe wrench and twist on it until the hub cover comes off. In the new-type hub, there's a nice lip to pry on, so put the hammer in back of the screwdriver to pry against.

With this cover off, you are facing: in the **older type**, the two adjusting nuts with the lock plate between them; in the **new type**, a clamp nut on the wheel shaft with an Allen head bolt clamping it on the shaft. We'll do the old type, then the new type.

Old Type Hubs With Two Lock Nuts. If you're on the left wheel, the spindle has left hand threads, clockwise—off, and counter clockwise—on. Bend down the ear of the lock plate so you can remove the outside nut with the crescent, pull off the lock plate, then take off the second nut. Take off that big washer and throw everything into the cleaning pan. Bracing yourself for a pull, grab the tire at 3 and 9 o'clock and pull. No luck? I didn't think so, so push it in a little way and get your screwdriver under the outboard bearing and pry it out. Take it off the axle. Now the wheel will come. Put a rag under the inner hub to catch the inboard bearing when you knock it out. Prop the wheel up on something, take the piece of broom handle, put it through the hub from the outboard end until it hooks on the inboard bearing, then bang it, move it around, bang it, and so on, until the inboard bearing falls out on the rag, you hope.

What you are actually pounding out of the hub is the seal. The seal is that metal and rubber round thing that holds the bearing into the hub. OK?

New Type Hubs With Clamping Adjusting Nut. (includes all disc brakes). Use the 6mm Allen wrench to loosen the clamping bolt, then remove the nut with the crescent and your fingers (left side has left hand threads), pull the washer off the axle and throw nut and washer into the cleaning can. Pull the wheel out as far as it will go, then push it back in and pry the outboard bearing out and into the cleaning pan. Now the wheel will come off. Put a rag under the hub to catch the inboard bearing and seal. Use the piece of broomstick and the hammer to bang the bearing and seal out onto the rag. Move the broomstick around the circle a little as you hit it. The bearing and seal will finally fall out, then you can clean them.

All Models: Wipe the brake drum or disc with a rag, then examine it with your fingernail for grooves. Roll the wheel under the car, hubside up and back of the jack so it is out of the way and acts as a safety besides. Pick up the bearing off the rag, sit right down and clean both front wheel bearings in the solvent. Clean them until they shine, then inspect them for rough spots and wear in the race, then either pass them or reject them. If you know nothing about bearings, ask an expert. If you pass them wrap them in a rag and put them in the car on the LEFT side. Never get these wheel bearings mixed from wheel to wheel as there are *two* races to each bearing and the other race is either on the axle or in the drum and you can't mix races—at least bearing races. I mean at least, wheel bearing races. Now you can go around and disassemble the other wheel, unless you are just packing the bearings with grease, in which case inspect the brakes very carefully: linings (or pads) for oil and wear; wheel cylinders (or calipers) for leaks; check the seals—if there is grease inside the drum or disc around the hub, buy new seals. If everything meets your approval, go on to Step 7, pack the wheel with grease and put it back together.

Remove Drums—Rear

If your car has composite rear drums, your rear brakes are a lot easier to service than one piece drum brakes. If you have one piece drum brakes, go to Chapter XIV, Rear Wheel Procedure, to remove your rear drums, then return to this Procedure, Step 3, for the brake work. If your car has composite rear drums, remove the rear wheel and take out the two allen head cap screws that hold the brake drum to the hub, pull off the drum and your brakes are exposed.

Step 3. Brake Job—Remove Shoes.

Disc brakes: skip this Step for the front brakes, go straight to Step 6. If you're just replacing the hand brake cable (emergency brake), go to the Mini Procedure in Step 5 and do it, as the shoes needn't be off. If you're just taking off the brake plate to do front end work in Chapter XII, skip this Step, do your front end work and come back to this Procedure, Step 7, unless you want to do the brakes and bearings while everything's apart anyway.

There are certain basic decisions you must make about a brake job. Do you need new drums? Are the linings so thin that you need to trade the shoes in? Feel the grooves in your drums. If they are really deep, plan on two new ones. Never turn VW brake drums on a lathe or let anybody turn yours. There isn't enough metal to carry the heat away and on a mountain road, someday, you may find yourself going faster the harder you push. This is brake fade, which is caused by heat. If the drums are grooved, but not too deeply and you don't have the bread, just remove the shoes for new linings and when replaced, the linings will wear up into the grooves. You'll have to adjust the brakes a couple of times while they're wearing in, but anything is better than cutting metal off the brake drums.

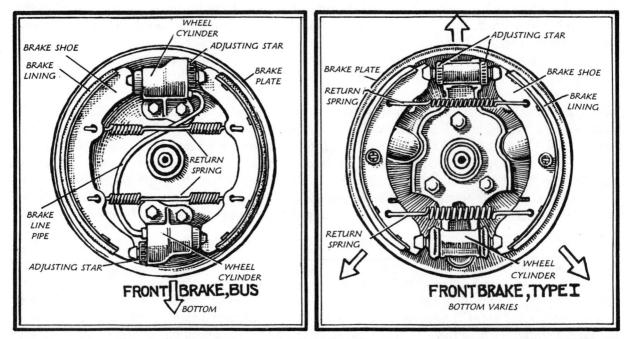

FRONT BRAKE, BUS   BOTTOM

FRONT BRAKE, TYPE I   BOTTOM VARIES

If you're too beat for bread to trade your old shoes for relined ones and the old ones are loaded with oil and fluid, there's a trip you can take: after the shoes are off per this step, soak them in white gas or Coleman fuel for an hour, then lay them out on the ground and light them. You might want your fire extinguisher

Step 3. (Cont'd.)

handy. After the shoes have burned out and are cool, check if the linings are still solid to the shoes. If they are, put them back in, thinking all the time about new shoes for baby. If they're not, don't drive until the bread for new shoes comes your way. If the car has been pulling to the right or left, look the linings over very carefully. If the side that's been grabbing is greasy, that's your answer, but there's another. Occasionally some schmuck has replaced the shoes on one wheel only, which causes a different friction factor on one side, so compare the linings for sameness. If they're not the same, trade in for a whole new set. If the linings are well over 1/16'' thick, they're cool for awhile, but 1/8'' is right. If your brakes have been chattering and the ends of the brake linings are square, take a file and put a champfer (angle) on the leading edge of the lining. The front drum brakes on the Bus and Type III are different from the Type I and all rear brakes.

Type II and Type III Front Brake Shoe Removal

Look at the shoes. See how the springs are attached through the holes under the webs of the shoes. There is nothing holding the shoes on the brake plate except the slots in the adjusting bolt and the wheel cylinders—two of them. There are two springs and they hook from down under, so you have to pry the front shoe out of the lower slot and toward you to get the spring unhooked, then you can pry the top tongue of the shoe web out of the upper cylinder. Unhook the top spring, then the rear shoe will pull out of its slot and the shoes are off. Repeat for the other wheel.

All Models Rear Brake Shoe Removal

Before doing the rear brakes, loosen the two 10mm adjusting nuts on the handbrake lever, as they are probably cranked all the way down. Look at the following sketch and see where the hand brake cable is connected to the lever. This cable connects on the bottom in all models except the Type II where it appears at the top. Take out the little springs, spring clips and pins. Just push and twist. Put them in a bolt can. Remove brake shoe return spring closest to the hand brake cable. It would be the upper in Type II models and lower in all others. Now unhook the hand brake cable. Grab both shoes and twist the ends out of the adjusting device, then pull the shoes out gently until they can carefully be removed from the wheel cylinder ends. Take off the other spring and operating link. Take off the lever before you trade your shoes in.

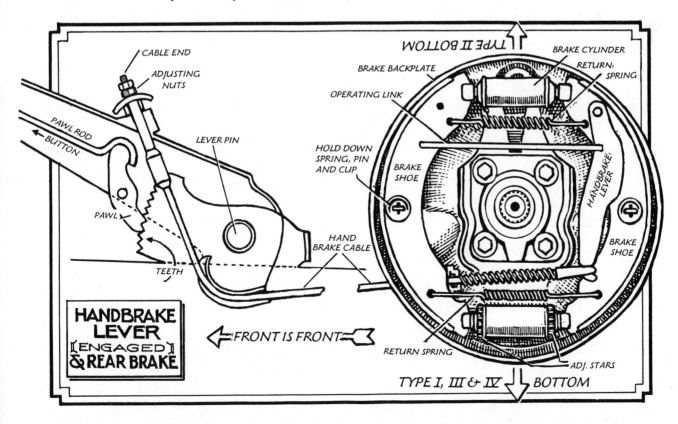

Type I—Front Brake Shoe Removal: Look at the brake assembly; you'll find there are return springs holding both ends of the shoes toward each other. Look at how they're fastened—see how they're anchored. You'll have to replace them the same way. If you have new brakes, there are only two springs, the older brakes have three and ancient models have four. Clamp the vice grip on the closest spring to you then pry it out of its hole with the screwdriver. Remove the other springs the same. Take out the two round springs with caps over them in the center of the brake shoe webs, holding the shoes to the brake plate. They'll come off with your fingers, so hold the pin in the back of one with your forefinger and push and twist on the little cap with the thumb and forefinger of the other hand. When that little cap is 90° around on the pin, it will come off and the whole thing will come apart. Take a close look, you have to put them back on. The pin comes thru the brake plate and thru the shoe web. The spring comes next then that little cap. Remove the other spring-cap-pin assembly from the other side. Now you can work them out of their slots. Snap a rubber band tight around the wheel cylinder slots so the wheel cylinders won't come apart. Now run Steps 1, 2, then this one on the brake shoes on the other wheel.

If there's been no leakage at any of your brake cylinders, this is as deep as you need go. Take the old shoes and any bearings or seals that need replacing to the store for parts. If you can't decide whether the bearings and seals are bad, take them with you and ask. If you buy new bearings, check their numbers to make sure they're the same as the old ones. Don't forget wheel bearing grease and brake fluid if you don't already have them.

If your wheel cylinders have been leaking, first do the next Step, then take the old parts with you when you shop. You need to get exactly what you take out. If you're going to overhaul your old wheel cylinders, buy some rubbing alcohol at the drugstore, as it's better than solvent for cleaning cylinders. Remember the Brillo pads.

Step 4. Wheel Cylinders: Remove, Clean, Overhaul, and Replace.

Type II and Type III Front Drum Brakes

There are two cylinders on the brake plate. Clamp the vice grip on the bleeder bolt on the inside bottom of the brake plate and turn it open. Pull off the **boots** and the **pistons** will pull out. Put them into the box to go shopping, then do the other wheel, as you always replace all the cylinders in both wheels at the same time.

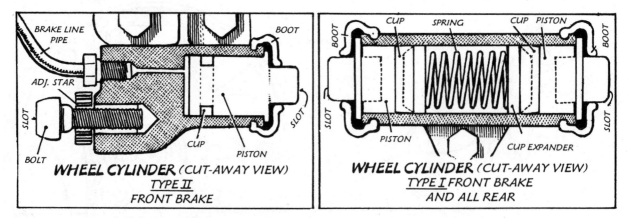

WHEEL CYLINDER (CUT-AWAY VIEW)
TYPE II
FRONT BRAKE

WHEEL CYLINDER (CUT-AWAY VIEW)
TYPE I FRONT BRAKE
AND ALL REAR

Type I Front Drum Brakes and Rear Brakes All Models

Open the bleeder bolt, pull one boot off, then the other. Push the assembly out into one hand with a finger and note the order: boot, piston (two parts in the older ones), cup, cup expander, spring, cup expander, cup, piston, boot. That's the order they have to go back in, so try to remember.

All Drum Models

Put everything you took out into the box and get ready to go shopping. Not so fast! You're not quite through. Get a clean rag to wipe out the cylinders and look for grooves. If one of the cylinders is grooved or badly scratched, you will have to remove the brake line and the bolts that hold the cylinders to the brake plate and take them down to the shop for honing. I buy new ones because new ones last 50,000 miles while the honed ones I don't know about. If the person you take them to for honing says they're past the pale, buy new ones. I'll whistle whilst you're gone.

You're back! First thing, bolt the wheel cylinders back in, then get real cautious while you put the brake line back in, making sure the threads are started straight, but don't tighten them like a nut. They seal with a double flare, so just get them good and firm. It's better to have to crawl under to tighten up a leak than to split or break one of these connections—you know what I mean. If you put in new or honed cylinders, skip the following part.

Dip a Brillo pad in alcohol and put it in the cylinder, then twist it round and round, not back and forth, with a screwdriver to clean the cylinder until it shines. Use two screwdrivers, one on each end of the Brillo pad and twist (round and round); use another pad, more alcohol, more twisting until they are clean—but like CLEAN.

Pull the adjusting stars out of their holders and clean them thoroughly and then brush them with a wire brush until the part that goes into the holder shines. This will make future brake adjustments easier.

A very common mistake when assembling drum type brakes is neglecting to turn the adjusting screw slots the correct way. The adjusting screw is the slotted head on a threaded shaft that screws into the brass adjusting star. The slots should be positioned so the shoes go on in the most retracted (smallest) position. If they are the wrong way, you'll never get the drum back on.

Assembly of the Wheel Cylinders, Bus Front Drum Type

The Bus rebuild kit is just a boot and a cup. The cup fits over the piston with the biggest diameter facing the cylinder—got that? Put the piston-cup in some brake fluid for a minute. Dip a clean rag into brake fluid and swab the inside of the cylinder. Make sure the bleeder bolt is open and push the piston-cup into the cylinder. You might do the other one. Hold them both in with your fingers while you close the bleeder bolt, then slip the boots over the pistons. Do the other wheel, and cylinders are done.

Type I, Front Drums and All Models, Rear.

You can get out the rebuild kits and soak them, the whole schmutz except the boots, in brake fluid. It makes them slippery to handle, but they work better and last longer. Swab the cylinder with brake fluid on a clean rag. Start with either end and put the piston in, then slip the boot over it. Slide the cup for that piston in from the other end, so the flat side will bump against the piston face. Then put a cup expander on each end of the spring. Shove this assembly in so it will expand the cup you have just put in. Now the next cup goes in so the cap part fits over the expander, then the piston and the last boot. It helps to reach around and open the bleeder bolt with the vice grip when you are putting the second cup in. Close the bleeder bolt after the piston is in and the boot is on. Put the outer piston parts on (if you have them); wrap a rubber band around the piston slots so they won't come apart and go around to the other wheel and reassemble it while you're in practice.

Type III Front, Drum

Soak the new piston, cup and expander in brake fluid. Swab the cylinder out with brake fluid on a CLEAN rag. Put the spring in first, then the expander (cup end towards the spring). Now put the cup on the cup expander with the cupped end on the expander, then the piston and boot. It helps if you open the bleeder bolt when assembling the parts, then close it when it's together. Wrap a rubber band around the cylinder while you do the other one if the piston wants to pop out. Now go around and do the other wheel.

Step 5. Install Brake Shoes, Front

I know you compared the new shoes with the old ones at the store, so you have the right shoes

Step 5. (Cont'd.)

for your car, right? You have cleaned the brake plate almost shiny, right? Remember I told you to take a good long look at your spring setup so you could get them back the way they came off. The method for installing Bus front shoes is different, so I'll start with it.

The Bus has two cylinders, so look at your brake shoes to see that the part of the shoe web with the tongue fits into the cylinder—really into the piston. You have two springs and they must hook underneath. Pick up one shoe with the tongue down and the lining toward the rear of the car. Install the two springs so the spring parts will be inside the web. This is the back shoe. Put this shoe in the piston slot and adjusting slot. Let the springs hang. Now pick up the other shoe with the tongue end up, the front shoe. Hold it with one hand while you hook the two springs from underneath. Pull and pry the upper tongue end into the piston of the upper cylinder. Pry the lower end into the adjustment slot with the screwdriver. Center the shoes so the lining is the same distance from the edge of the brake plate all around. Check to see the spring isn't rubbing against the brake line running 'twixt the two cylinders. Now check it over. The linings are centralized, the springs are inside the webs of the shoes and the webs are well in the slots. Do the other side the same way.

Type III Front

Pick up one of the brake shoes and put it on the top so the slot in the web of the shoe fits closest to the rear cylinder. Put the two springs on the shoe (remember they fit from underneath) and let them hang there. They should be underneath the brake hose that goes from one cylinder to to the other. Now take the other shoe and put the end with the slot toward the front. Hold the shoe with one hand and with the other hand put the two springs on from the back of the shoes. Pull and pry the front end of the shoe into the cylinder—really the piston, with a screwdriver, then put the other end into the adjusting slot of the rear cylinder. Make sure the springs are not rubbing up against the brake hose going between the cylinders. Center the shoes so the lining is the same distance from the edge of the brake plate all the way around. Now check the whole scene over once more. The linings are centered, the springs are inside the webs of the shoes and the webs are inside the slots of the cylinders. Do the other wheel the same way.

The Bug, through the years, has had one very helpful orientation feature: that slot in the web of the shoe has always been close to the wheel cylinder. How many springs do you have? *Four,* **wow!** you have an oldie. OK, hook the two small springs into the brake plate, then into the holes in the shoes. With one shoe in each hand, bring the shoes in at the top and start the webs into the slots, then spread the shoes so they will go into the other set of slots. These slots could be either cylinder or adjustment slots; you should remember which, but you can tell by the place where the return springs fit. This double-handed operation also works with the *three* **spring set up.** Hook the small spring across the holes opposite the two spring ends and start the two shoe webs into the slots. Spread the shoe out so the other ends will fit into their slots, then install the return springs. Use a screwdriver to pry the spring onto the knob or into the hole. The *two* **spring set** up starts the same as the three spring with the smaller spring hooked first, then close the shoes at the other end, put the webs in the adjustment slots, and spread out the webs into the cylinder slots. Note: In the later models, the adjustment slots are at an angle, so set the slots to point toward the axle, approximately.

Now you can put in those round springs that hold the webs of the shoes to the brake plate. Get the pin through the hole in the brake plate and through the web, then hold the pin on the inside with a finger, put the spring and cap (cap part in) on the pin, then get the slot in the cap over the pinched part of the pin. Push and twist the cap with your thumb and forefinger. Use a pliers if you have to, and when you have twisted the cap 90°, the cap will be hung up on the pin. Do the other shoe.

Now you can hook the other spring or springs. If you have two left, hook the funny end in the shoe, then pry it over the button or into the hole with the screwdriver. You may have to clamp the vice grip on the spring and pry it on. If you only have one spring left, it just goes across from one shoe to the other. Use the vice grip clamped on the spring and pry it over and into the hole.

Now check the whole thing over. Make sure those slots in the brake shoe web are close to the wheel cylinder. See that the springs are well hooked into their holes. Check those little pins to make sure they are seated in their places in the caps and like that. If it all looks good to you in both wheels, the brake shoes are on.

HAND BRAKE CABLE MINI PROCEDURE

Condition: Broken hand brake cable and that rear wheel is off.

Parts and Materials: New hand brake cable and wheel bearing grease.

Unhook the old hand brake cable from the lever, then take the bolt or bolts out of the retainer clip on the back of the brake plate. (If the shoes are on, you may have to take off the little round spring thing to work the cable out of the brake plate underneath the shoe). Go up into the front of the car to remove the rubber hand brake cover, use two 10mm wrenches to unlock the two nuts on the other end of the cable, and remove the nuts with the 10mm open end wrench and the screwdriver. Pull the old cable out from underneath. In the Bus, you have to take the pan between the front wheels off—ten 10mm bolts. Lay the new cable out alongside of the old one, holding the broken ends together to check the new cable for length. If they're not the same length, back you go to VW for another, the right length. Same length? OK, push the new cable thread ends into the tube forward of the rear wheel, liberally apply wheel bearing grease to the cable as you shove. Go up front and pull the cable out the front end of the tube and start it into the adjustment hole on the handle, but just start a nut on it for now. Go back to the wheel and work the cable end into the brake plate, hook the cable end over the lever and fasten the retaining clip to the brake plate with the bolt or bolts and the cable is in. (Replace the little spring and pin in the brake shoe web, if the shoes are on and the cable is in). You cannot adjust the hand brake until the brakes have been adjusted, so reassemble the wheel (if you've taken it apart), adjust the brakes, then adjust the hand brake according to the words further on in this chapter.

Install Brake Shoes Rear, All Models.

Install the hand brake lever on the rear shoe. See the sketch earlier for the way it hangs. Put the operating link between the two shoes. Now install the spring next to the link. This is all done before you approach the brake plate. If the brake cylinder is on top of the brake plate, (all models except the Bus), you are holding the bottoms of the shoes, one in each hand—in the Bus you are holding the tops—and you're ready to put them in. Twist the shoes a little to get the ends started into the wheel cylinder end slots. When they slide in, you can push both shoes into place. Hold them in and get a pin, spring and cup ready to go. The pin comes in from the back of the plate and the spring and cup go over the pin which you hold in place while you twist the cup 90 degrees and then it will hold the brake shoe to the plate. Do the other one. Hook the hand brake cable onto the lever. Hook the other return spring, put the pin assembly in and your shoes are on. Now you push the shoes so they are in the center of action or the drum won't go on.

One piece drum people return to Chapter XIV to replace your drums, then return here to Step 10. Composite drum people, slide the drums on and put the two cap screws in, tighten them well with the allen head wrench, put the wheels on, tighten the lugs and go to Step 10.

Step 6. Install New Bearings, Front Wheels

All Models—including Disc Brakes

If you've bought new bearings to install in the hubs, you've made sure you bought the right ones, eh? You have to knock out the old races then put the new ones in before you can start to put the wheel back on.

Old Type Hubs

Take your good chisel and the hammer and knock out the outer race of the outboard bearing the same way you did for the outer races and seal of the inboard bearing in Step 2. Put the chisel in the hub and find the ridge with the point of the chisel and tap it (or rather hit it), move the chisel around, hit it and like that until the outer race comes out. Safety goggles! You'll need a picture:

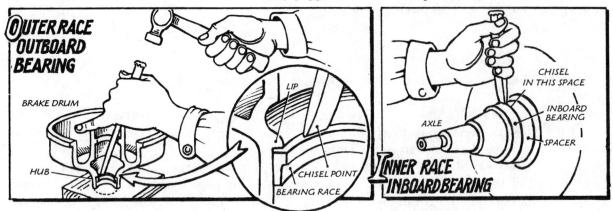

You see there are two races to each bearing—that's why you keep the left wheel bearings separate from the right wheel bearings. When you put in a new bearing you have to replace both races. So knock the outer race of the outboard bearing out of the hub and the inner race of the inboard bearing off the axle. It helps to clean inside the hub so you can see what you're going to be hitting. Be careful of the spacer back of the inboard bearing race on the axle; the seal rides on it. We've had to heat this inner race to get it off, but if you have a new bearing, heating the old one won't hurt.

New Type Hubs. In the new type wheels, the inboard inner race does not stay on the axle like it does for the old type wheels. Take the hub to the VW dealer and ask to have the old new-type races pressed out and new new-type races pressed in. They have fixed it (we think, so far) so that it takes a special press tool to do this job. Pay them and thank them nicely, then go home and start below where it says, "All Models".

Install Bearing Races—Old Type Hubs, Only. The only difference in the different models is the size of the bearings, except in the old Bug, which has ball bearings instead of roller bearings. Clean everything. Pick out the inboard bearing, the larger one, and hold it up the way the race has to go on the axle with the heavy part in. Slip the inner race onto the axle. The spacer is still there, right? And not beat up, either, as the seal rides on it. Never heat this race as you put it on. Tap it on the axle until it is started evenly all around, then use a punch and move the punch (or dull chisel) around the circle of the race as you knock the race on, little by little, around and around. It should seat good and tight on the spacer.

All Models: Now comes the outer race of the outboard bearing. It goes into the CLEAN wheel hub. Hold the whole bearing up to the hub to make sure you know how it goes, with the heavy part in, then get the outer race started in the hole evenly all around. We use two hammers, one on the race and one to tap it with. Tap this race into the hub until it is inside the hub, then the dull chisel routine as above until the race is seated on the shoulder in the hub. You can tell by the solid sound when it's seated. Now you can go on to the next Step and install the packed bearings.

Step 7. Pack Wheel Bearings—Install Front Hub.

All Models Including Disc Brakes.

The bearings are absolutely clean and absolutely dry. If they still have solvent on them, you cannot pack them until they have dried completely so put them in the sun and wait. The VW people,

Step 7. (Cont'd.)

have an odd idea about packing wheel bearings and it is their car, so we go with them. They pack the hub full, as you probably discovered when you cleaned it. In the American cars the bearings are packed, not the hub. The Types I and III take 50 grams of wheel bearing grease, a small handful, while the Bus and Type IV take 80 grams, a big handful, then, they say, it'll last 30,000 miles.

Old Type Hubs Only: Start with the inboard bearing and dip a slug of wheel bearing grease into the palm of your hand, then work the bearing into the grease (press it hard). You want to get grease all through that bearing and around the rollers or balls, and throughout the cage. Take some time to do it right. When you have worked grease all through it, put the bearing in the inboard race, clean your hands, start the seal in all around evenly, then tap the seal in using the small hammer on the seal and the big hammer to tap the little hammer. Move the little hammer around as you tap it. Get the seal into the shoulder of the hub flush with the hub or a little in. The difference between the new type and the old type is just in the race that the seal holds in, so that's easy.

All Models: Start jamming grease (wheel bearing) into the outboard end of the drum hub, fill the whole hub with your other hand covering the inboard hole. Push the grease in really well; think of the 30,000 miles and smile. Untangle yourself from this situation long enough to pack the outboard bearing the same way, then put it in an unsullied place, ready to hand. Wipe your greasy hands clean again, grab the wheel and push it onto the axle. Help is nice at this point as you are trying to put the wheel on the axle while keeping grease in the hub with your third and fourth hands. As soon as the axle appears out the hub, pick up the outboard bearing and push it on, as it helps to hold the grease in. Don't be so enthusiastic about shoving grease back that you push it out the back hole. Just use all it will hold. When the axle is out as far as it will come, tap the outboard bearing into its race with the hammer and dull chisel. Lift the wheel straight up with your foot so you can tap the bearing in. Clean up around the place a little with a rag or rags, then on to Step 8.

Disc Brakes: Reinstall the calipers (disc and caliper Procedure, this Chapter), check your pads for wear (pad Procedure, this Chapter), put the wheels on and tighten the lugs.

Step 8. Adjust the Bearings

All Models

The main difference between adjusting the old type wheel bearings and the new type wheel bearings is that the washer won't move as far in the new type bearings. The acceptable end play (axial movement) is the same: .001" to .005". The way the adjustment is held is much better in the new style than in the old, so the wheel bearing should last longer. VW measures the hub end play with a dial gauge which we ain't got. We'll start with the **old type.**

Put the washer on the axle, then the first nut. (left axle has left-hand threads). Use the crescent to run this first nut up pretty tight (15 foot pounds) on the axle, turning the wheel as you tighten the nut. This turning will take the slack out of the bearings. Now loosen the nut with the crescent a little at a time until you can just move the washer under the nut with the big screwdriver. Tighten it again, then loosen it until you can just move the washer. When that washer first moves upon prying it, this is the point that gives the wheel about .001" of end play. Now slip the new lock plate on the axle end, hold it down on the first nut and take a look. Is there a nice flat place to beat the washer ear down on or is it on a point where it will make a bent mess? If it's on a flat place, screw the second nut down on the lock plate to hold the plate while you beat the ear down to hold the first nut in place. If the first nut will present a nice flat spot by loosening it just a bit, do so, then screw the second nut down and bang the ear down on the first nut. You are now at about .003" end play.

The next step is the toughest: turning the second or locking nut down tight without changing your end play setting or breaking the little tit on the lock plate that fits down into the slot on the axle. A very flat wrench the right size for the inside nut would be perfect to hold the inside nut still while you tighten the locking nut with the crescent. Well, there's one way you can tighten the lock nut without a thin wrench. Make a scratch mark on the washer at one of the inner points of the inner

Step 8. (Cont'd.)

nut where you know the adjustment is correct (where you can barely move the washer), then turn the outer nut down on the plate until the inner nut starts to move. Knock the inner nut back into position with the hammer and dull chisel while you hold the outer nut in position with the crescent wrench. Remember: left hand threads on the left side of the car. Repeat the above process until the adjustment is correct and lock nut is tight.

Now you can beat the other ear out onto the outer nut to hold the assembly together. Don't put any grease into the hub cover—they figure enough is enough, I guess. Too much grease in the left hub will gum up your speedometer!

When you're through adjusting the left wheel, push or pull the square speedometer shaft through the little square hole in the hub cover, put the cotter key on it and tap the hub cover into the hub.

The new type, including disc brakes, adjust the same way as above with the idea of the moving washer, but when the washer first moves (do it three times to make certain it's right) loosen the nut just a hair more, tighten the clamp bolt in the nut and try the washer again. If it's really loose, adjust it over again, but if it moves just a bit, it's right. Left hand threads on the left side, remember. You can tighten the clamp bolt fairly tight (7 ft. lbs.) with the Allen head wrench. If you're working on the left side, do the speedometer thing (see above) and tap in the hub cover.

Step 9. Balance the Front Wheels

All Models

You can buy little bags of wheel weights at an accessory store or you can buy a few of each size at a gas station. Now, you're balancing the wheels right after a wheel pack but you can balance them at any time you think they need it by jacking the wheel up and releasing the brake shoes so they don't scrape on the brake drums or bind. Disc brakes are self adjusting. . .ready to balance any-time.

Give the wheel a good spin to get the grease spread out on the bearings, then spin the other way and let it come to rest. Grab the bottom of the tire and gently rotate it up 90 degrees and let go. If it doesn't return to the same place, turn the wheel another 90 degrees. If it still doesn't move, the wheel is in good balance. This is what you seek, a wheel that doesn't tend to roll no matter where you put it. If the wheel returned to its same resting place, put a two-inch-or-so weight on the rim at the top of the wheel directly opposite the heavy spot, which is always the bottom.

These weights just clamp to the rim. If a weight is too loose, tap the little clamp a little closer together so it grabs the rim when you hit it with the small hammer. If you have to take off a weight, use the screwdriver in the hole in the little clamp to pry the weight off the rim. All you do is let the wheel settle, jog it a little to make sure the heavy spot is on the bottom, then put a weight on top of the rim to balance the heavy spot on the bottom. Move the wheel around, then let go. If it doesn't move from any position, you have the wheel in good balance. If a wheel is really badly out of balance in one spot, put your second weight on the inside of the rim. That's all there is to it. This method for balancing works only for the front wheels, as the rear wheels have too much drag on them from the differential.

Step 10. Adjust and Bleed the Brakes

All Models, Front and Rear
Disc Brakes: Adjust the rear brakes (first procedure in this Chapter), then bleed.
Drum Brakes: Adjust the shoes in the drums per the first Procedure in this Chapter, then bleed.
All Models: Before you bleed the brakes, pump the brakes with the brake pedal about 50 to 60 times. Pumping works the air out of the system. Don't begrudge the brake fluid you seem to waste as you bleed the brakes out onto the ground—it helps to flush out the brake system.

Step 10. (Cont'd.)

Let the car down off the jacks, put on the hub caps, clean up your mess and your tools and yourself. Change your clothes and take the short out for a test ride.

EMERGENCY OR HAND BRAKE

The hand brake consists of a lever which you pull; a notched locking arrangement (pawl teeth fall into ratchet teeth), which holds the lever in place; and two cables which go back into the back wheels and pull, through a lever, the front brake shoes in the rear wheels against the drum. When the handle won't stay back, it's because the pawl teeth have fallen down causing a wire to fall off the pawl and without the wire the button on the lever pops up. You don't need a procedure to fix anything here. A little explanation of how to adjust it and what to do about its falling apart should suffice.

The main idea with the emergency brake is maintenance: keep it adjusted and it won't come apart. Adjust the rear brakes, then adjust at the handle. If it's loose either at the handle or the rear wheels, the handle will pull back too far on the notches and the little nob will pop out and not hold anymore. When this happens, you have a lot of work to do for your carelessness in letting the adjustment get too far out of whack.

This is how the emergency brake releases: when you push the button down on the handle, it moves a wire downward which lifts the pawl teeth out of the ratchet teeth and releases the brake. When it's out of adjustment so much that you can pull the brake handle back too far, the pawl teeth fall off the ratchet teeth, the wire comes loose from the pawl and the brake no longer holds. See sketch page **175**.

Fixing The Hand Brake. To fix it, you have to take the whole thing apart, put the pawl teeth back into the ratchet teeth, replace the hooked wire on the pawl and hold this assembly together while you put the emergency brake back into its place.

You can replace the pawl rod end over the pawl without taking the whole thing apart by loosening the cable nuts, relaxing the brake handle, pushing the release button for maximum slack; now, if you are a bit of a contortionist, you can work the pawl rod end over the pawl with a small screwdriver.

Here's a more detailed description: Rear brakes adjusted? OK, in the Type I, III, and IV take out the front seats and in the Bus take off the large metal cover between the front wheels (10mm bolts, ten of them). Remove the rubber boot from the brake handle, take the two 10mm nuts off each cable, take the little locks off the shaft with the screwdriver (in the car for Type I, III, IV, under the Bus), pull the cables out of the holes, pull the shaft out, and you can take the mother out. The ratchet gizmo will come out, then you can start putting it back together. Get the wire from the bottom hooked onto the rounded end of the pawl (the thing with teeth on the other end that fit into the ratchet). Put some wheel bearing grease on the ratchet piece and hold it up into place while you reinstall the handle in the car. In the Bus, the accelerator assembly has to come loose so you can hook that slot on the ratchet over it to hold the assembly solid; in the Types I, III, and IV, this little slot fits over the edge of the frame. In all models you now have a real rat's nest and it's nice to have four hands to unscramble it. As you put the whole thing together: the wire on the pawl; the pawl caught in the teeth of the ratchet; the slot in the frame (Types I, III and IV) or the accelerator bar (Bus); put the handle into the clevis and put the pin back in; put the little snap clips back on the pin and pull the cables through; put the holes in the side of the handle and put the two little nuts on each cable; then adjust the cables. Think about keeping the hand brake adjusted so it doesn't happen again. Put the car back together.

Adjusting the Hand Brake. Get both rear wheels off the ground and make sure the rear brakes are adjusted. Leave the wheels up. Go to the front of the car and remove the rubber boot from the brake handle, use two 10mm wrenches to loosen the top nut on top of the cable, and loosen both sides. Hold the cable from turning with the screwdriver in the slot. Turn the bottom nuts down on the cables until they stop the rear wheels, then relax the nuts, pull the handle back and forth to make sure the cables are returning, and leave the nuts where the wheels are just free to roll. Pull the lever two notches. This much should slow down the turning wheels. When you are four notches on the handle, the wheels should be stopped so well that you cannot turn the rear wheels by hand. Release the brake again. Does this free up the wheels so they turn easily? If not, balance them out with the bottom nuts. You may have one side tighter than the other. When the brakes are tight at four notches on the lever and free when the lever is released, you have them right. If they are sticking, pull the cables under the car back and forth to loosen them. When they are right, you can run the top nuts down on the bottom nuts. Hold the bottom one with one wrench while you tighten the top one—this locks the adjustment. Put the rubber boot back on.

STOP LIGHT SWITCH

To find the stop light switch, you first have to find the master cylinder (see below under MASTER CYLINDER). In the Bus, you have to take down that pan between the front wheels, but once you take it down, the work is easy. Take the 10 or so bolts out of the pan, which will then fall on your head if you're not holding it. It's light and doesn't hurt much. Get the pan out of the way and look at what you've uncovered. All models: the stop light switch is screwed in the front of the master cylinder and is a plug-looking thing with two wires pushed onto terminals in the front of it. If you're checking the brake light (stop light), have your friend turn on the key and go to the rear of the car. You take the medium screwdriver and short across the two terminals on the front of the brake light switch. If this makes the stop lights go on, and pushing on the brake pedal doesn't, you need a new stop light switch. You don't have to put the pan on the Bus to drive down to VW and buy a new one. When you replace the switch, don't be too heavy on the tightening—these are pipe threads and a good twist with the crescent wrench is tight enough to seal the connection. Push the wires on, try the switch, then put the pan back on. If there are two switches on your master cylinder, you have a dual circuit master cylinder, so check both switches.

MASTER CYLINDER

The master cylinder is attached to the brake pedal and is that cylinder with tubes coming out of the side of it like a spray, and a lever with a clevis (a Y thing with a pin through it) around it at the rear. The brake lever comes down from the foot pedal. In the Bus, the master cylinder is under the pan between the front wheels. In the Types I and III, it's available behind the left front tire. In the Type IV, it's in the car over the brake pedal.

Did we agree that you would take your master cylinder to an expert to have it overhauled? If fluid is leaking out or air in (you find you have to bleed the brakes a lot) or the brakes just don't work even though the wheel cylinders aren't leaking, you need a master cylinder overhaul. The dual master cylinder in cars since 1966, has two hoses and three sets of wires to disconnect. Outside of the extra work and extra memory required, you can still remove it and install it, but it should go to the expert to be overhauled.

To Remove The Master Cylinder:

Bus. Take the pan down from between the front wheels, pull the pin on the clevis, carefully remove the three brake lines, and when you remove the two bolts holding the cylinder to the frame, the cylinder is free.

Types I and III. You can turn the wheel enough to get at the switch to test it or replace it (see above), but take the wheel off to remove the master cylinder. The heads of the two bolts and the clevis are in the car under the accelerator pedal.

Type IV. If your master cylinder is above the brake pedal, put some rags on the floor to protect it and take the bolts out of the cylinder. Types I, III, and IV: The clevis is quite a trip. You have to unscrew the connection on the tube on top of the master cylinder that comes from the filler jar in the front. The master cylinder pushes forward and out when you get it loose.

To Reinstall the Master Cylinder:

Bus: Put the cylinder in the frame, put the bolts in hand-tight (loose), then get the brake lines started. These are double flared, so be gentle with them; tighten them until you can feel they are well seated, then just a hair more, that's all. Now you can tighten the bolts to the frame and put the clevis back together. Reconnect the stop light switch and put the pan back up and bolt it on.

Types I, III, and IV. Read the foregoing on the Bus and make sure to just start (by hand) the bolts that hold the cylinder when you put it back in, then do the brake lines—four of them this time—and tighten them before you tighten the bolts. Put the pin in the clevis, then reconnect the stop light switch.

All Models:

WHENEVER YOU HAVE THE BRAKE SYSTEM OPEN, YOU MUST BLEED THE WHEEL CYLINDERS.

After one of these operations, you can try to catch the fluid that you bleed out of the bleeder bolts in a clean jar, but I let it run out and keep filling the cylinder with fluid with the idea that I'm flushing the system and that a can of brake fluid is a good investment. Clean it up when you are through. (Off the driveway, that is.)

FRONT WHEELS WITH DISC BRAKES

In 1966, disc type brakes were installed on the Karmann Ghia (Type I) and on the Type III. Type IV's have had disc front brakes since their beginning and in 1971 the Bus was, to our delight, added to the list of fine motor cars with disc brakes. They do the thing of stopping your car, especially the front portion, quicker and smoother than the drum type brakes. All models of Volkswagen use approximately the same configuration of caliper, the "C" clamp that grabs the disc applying the friction and negative acceleration necessary to stop your mad dash.

The Type II, in order to qualify as a one ton vehicle, has added a vacuum assist to the brake system, so when your car is heavily loaded, you can stop it with a light pressure on the brake pedal. After 45,000 miles and one pad change, our 1971 Bus has the best non-sports car brakes I've pushed on.

There's a device called a pressure regulator which divides the foot pressure on the cylinder between front and rear brakes so your rear end is stopping as fast as your front. The master cylinder and warning light system is the same as for drum brakes, except you have to figure that the front half of the master cylinder is for the front brakes with the rear brakes being pushed by the rear half, while the pressure regulator acts as an umpire to make sure neither gets too much.

The pressure regulator in the brake system is a very well mannered device and unless unequal front and rear braking becomes very evident, don't fool with it. If the rear wheels skid when you made an emergency stop, take it to the dealer or someone with some experience to have the pressure regulator repaired and/or adjusted. It requires special gauges with bleeders to set the regulator up for service.

There are two things you can do for your disc brakes on the front wheels: change the pads and remove the calipers and discs. Like:

PROCEDURE FOR CHANGING DISC WEAR PADS, Phase I

Check for Wear

Every 6 to 10,000 miles, at your regular Maintenance time, you should check the disc pads for wear. The disc brakes are self adjusting, but the pads wear. The work on the rear drum brakes hasn't changed but start with the disc brakes. Block the car, loosen the lugs on the left front wheel, jack it up, remove the wheel and put the wheel under the disc as a safety. Look in the open space in the caliper with a flashlight—see sketch—where the disc passes through the pads and look at the pads. The grooves in the pads should be more than 1/16" deep or the pads need replacement immediately.

When there is no groove (no way to live) there is no place for the wear particles to go, and trouble from lack of elimination is what is going to do us all in, not just your brakes. Your pads need replacing? Run this procedure, but if you see a brake fluid leak when you examine your pad, look at the following procedure and see if you're up to it or take your baby to have the calipers removed for overhaul.

Condition: The brake pads are worn.

Tools and Materials: Phase I tool kit, small punch, 4 new pads, Heavy Duty Brake Fluid (VW or Lockheed best), small hammer.

Step 1. Block, Jack and Remove Wheel.

Again? Right!

Step 2. Remove the Old Pads.

With the small punch and hammer, drive the pin that holds the disc pads in the calipers out toward the center of the car. In the Bus, Type III and IV there are two pins. Pry out the flat retainer spring, put the pin or pins and spring in a safe handy place. Use the medium screwdriver to hook into the hole in the ear of one pad and remove the pad—now remove the other one. With a clean rag, either dry or dipped in alcohol, clean out the place where the pads were. Loosen the bleeder bolt a little and push on the boot (piston) with your finger so you can clean. It's OK if a little fluid runs out of the bleeder bolt, but don't get any on you.

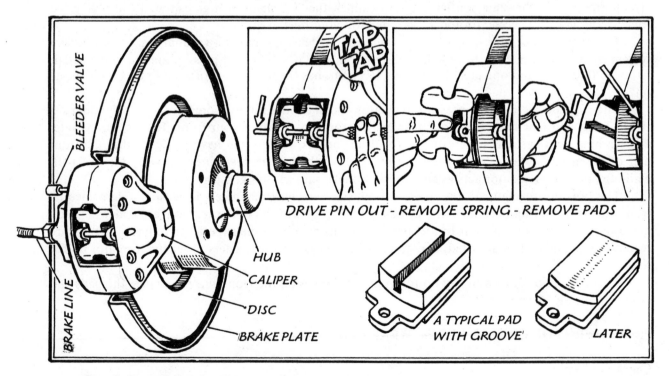

DRIVE PIN OUT - REMOVE SPRING - REMOVE PADS

BLEEDER VALVE

BRAKE LINE

HUB

CALIPER

DISC

BRAKE PLATE

A TYPICAL PAD WITH GROOVE

LATER

TAP TAP

Step 3. Install the New Pads. See Changes and New Ideas.

The bleeder valve is still just barely open, right, so push on the boot back of that rubber thing you just cleaned and shove one new pad in one side and the other pad in the other side, grooved sides toward the disc. Close the bleeder bolt. By the way, if you have two bleeder bolts, open them both, just a tiny, then close them both when the pads are in. On the Ghia, if the groove is not in the

Step 3. (Cont'd.)

middle, the wider side goes down. Put the punch away. Install the flat retainer spring and drive the pin in from the inside with just the small hammer until the split washer is flush and the pin or pins is in so the pads can't get out. Repeat for the other wheel. You must always change all four pads at one time. Replace wheel, tighten the lugs and down jack. Now go to Step 4 of the Brake Adjustment and Bleeding Procedure to adjust and bleed the rear brakes—that's all.

BRAKE PADS HAVE 2 EARS AND ARE HELD ON BY 2 PINS

PROCEDURE FOR REMOVAL AND INSTALLATION OF FRONT DISC AND CALIPERS, Phase II.

Condition: You are packing the front wheels, or you found a brake fluid leak and are going to remove the calipers to take them for overhaul. And/or to replace the discs if they are gouged and worn.

Tools and Materials: Phase II tool kit, torque wrench, 6mm Allen wrench, new caliper bolts and lock plates.

Step 1. Block and Jack

Put some safety blocks under the car so it doesn't fall on you. Take the wheels off at the lug nuts or bolts.

Step 2. Remove Calipers

See sketch on preceding page so you can see what you are taking off. The caliper is held to the steering knuckle with four special steel bolts that must not be reused. Find the socket that fits your model, 17mm or so, use the flex handle and loosen these bolts. It will take a heave. If you are taking the calipers or the disc to the shop for overhaul, remove the brake hose from the caliper, lift the caliper off the disc and put it safely down. If you are doing a wheel pack only, leave the brake hose on the caliper, take the bolts out, hang the caliper on the tie rod with some handy dandy hay wire (or other) and you're ready to go back to the wheel procedure.

Step 3. Remove Discs To Take To VW If They Are Gouged Or Worn.

To replace the disc on the other models, you have to replace the whole hub and disc assembly, so take the whole thing to VW. With the 6mm Allen head wrench, remove the two bolts that hold the disc and its hub to the wheel hub. The disc can now be pulled off the studs and removed.

Step 4. Replace Discs, Bus.

Work the disc hub over the studs, install the two Allen head bolts and tighten to about 14 foot pounds, then go back to the Wheel Procedure, Step 1.

Step 5. Install Calipers.

Your calipers should come back from overhauling ready to install with the piston rotated to the proper position and the boots installed, ready to go, so check them before you leave the shop. Install the brake hose now and tighten carefully, or unwire your calipers. Place the calipers around the disc, install the NEW lock plate and NEW bolts. Check to be sure the discs run free in the calipers, then tighten the bolts to 43 ft. lbs. with the torque wrench (see note below). Bend the locks up so the bolts cannot turn. Refer to the foregoing procedure to install new pads (or put back the old ones, if they came out). Go back to the Wheel Procedure, Step 10. Bleed the front brakes first with a dual master cylinder. By the way, do the procedure to both front wheels.

Note: The 1973 and on disc brakes for the **Type II and Type IV** have been made stronger and tougher with 14mm thick brake pads and new heavier discs. The steering knuckle has been changed and strengthened. The only action item in this for you is that they have increased the size of the caliper mounting bolts from 12mm to 14mm and the tightening torque (1973 and on Type II and Type IV only) has been increased from 43 ft. lbs. to 102 to 126 ft. lbs.

* * * * * * * * * * * *

Brakes perform a negative function. They apply negative acceleration to stop the car. They remain inert when not being used. Think of them negatively as you drive, use them sparingly, shift down on steep grades, save them for the rare emergency. Develop driving habits that minimize their use and so, maximize your safety.

From the German Edition

SHIMMIES AND SHAKES (FRONT END)

When the Volksie front end needs your tender attention, it'll let you know by feeling insecure, a not-unknown trip in any relationship. This insecurity can be evidenced in many ways: wandering mindlessly across the road, impulsively darting here and there, wearing tires out in funny patterns or making nerve-wracking noises on dirt roads. These are the symptoms and you are the doctor, at least almost a doctor. I've told you so many things to do, it's a real pleasure to tell you something not to do. **Don't rotate your tires!** It takes about 500 miles for a tire to get used to its position on a car, and changing it around just messes up its head. It will last as long or longer right where it is. The **reason I tell you this now is that changing the tires around will sometimes make your front end feel insecure when there's nothing wrong with it. 1980 and on Vanagon, see Changes and New Ideas.**

Before telling you even one thing to do, I must orient you around your front end; name names, define things and like that. Just take the book out to the car with your overalls on for a guided tour.

Front End Orientation and Things Diagnostic

Stand alongside the car where you can move the steering wheel through the open window while you watch the left front wheel. Turn the steering wheel to see how much it moves before the front tire starts to move. Make sure your wheels are pointing straight ahead and try it again. This steering wheel play should be about one inch in most well adjusted Volkswagens—it's 1/2 to 5/8" in Type IV and Super Beetle. Don't rush for the tools yet as there are several places this play could be, so you cannot be sure the steering is at fault until you've checked everything. Visualize the path of the steering column (the column under the steering wheel that the signal light switch is on) through the bottom of the car to find the **steering box** at the lower end. It's practically the frontest thing in the car so you can't miss it. It's a steel box with gears in it at the bottom end of the steering column. If you can't see it right away, put your head under the front of the car while someone blows the horn, the steering box is right next. The wire coming out of the horn goes into the steering column and up to the button on the steering wheel. If your horn ever sticks blaringly in the middle of town, this wire has probably shorted out against the steering box. Don't pull it out in your excitement, as it's hell to replace. Just tape the bare place in the wire.

The steering box has a steering arm coming out of the bottom of it. Have someone move the steering wheel while you get down on your back under the car to watch the way the steering arm works. At the end of the steering arm are attached two tubes that go over to the wheels to move them. These tubes, **tie rods**, are attached to the steering arm with **tie rod ends**, those bolts through the arm with ball joints to let them twist as you steer.

Type I (except Super Beetle) and Type III, you don't have the following assembly because your tie rod ends are attached directly to the steering arm on the bottom of the steering box.

The Bus needs an extra assembly because the steering wheel is in front of the front wheels. The **steering arm** comes out the side of the steering box and has a tie rod end bolted into it which is attached to a **drag link** that disappears into the pan between the two front wheels and comes out the other end—crawl in a little further to see. The drag link goes to another arm with another tie rod end.

A tie rod end is a bolt with a ball joint on top of it. The bolt has a tapered shank and is pressed into a tapered hole. The arm the drag link is attached to is called the **swing lever arm**, which swings on the **swing lever shaft** (pin), which rotates in the swing lever assembly welded to the lower torsion **arm tube**. There are two tie rod ends in the other end of the swing lever. These are attached to **tie rods** which go out to the wheels to turn them. While you're here with someone to turn the steering wheel, watch the rear of the swing lever as it goes back and forth. It should *not* move up and down as it goes back and forth. If it does, it makes your Bus wander all over the road and needs work.

Type IV and Super Beetle, you also have a swing lever arm assembly called an **idler arm,** but it's mounted on the other side of the frame from the steering box, not on the torsion arm tube (which you don't have). The two tie rod ends that turn the wheels are bolted into a center tie rod which runs between the steering arm from the steering box and the idler arm. The idler arm should not move up and down, only sideways. If it does move up and down, it makes your car wander all over the road and you'll have to take it to VW as fixing this is not covered herein.

All Models

The tie rods are attached to an arm on the wheel assembly with another tie rod end. Look under the car, back at the steering arm in the Type I and III, the swing lever arm in the Bus or the idler arm in the Type IV and Super Beetle and you'll see a tube that either goes over to the frame or over to a torsion tube. This is an hydraulic thing like a shock absorber called the **steering dampener** and it stops the road shocks from coming up through the steering wheel to your hands. The steering dampener is a horizontal shock absorber; as such it's treated in the shock absorber procedure at the end of this chapter. If your car shimmies on rough roads, potholes, etc., or at about 45 mph, 9 times out of 10, it's caused by a worn out steering dampener.

That's the steering system of the VW and it terminates in an arm on the steering knuckle with a tie rod end. Go back to the steering box and find the exterior adjustment. It's a screw with a lock nut around it and is on top of, to the left of or on the bottom of the steering box. Don't touch it now, just recognize it when you see it again in the procedure for adjusting the steering box. There is an interior adjustment as well, but you'd better leave that one to the experts.

Now check the kind of front suspension you have. Look at the arm where the tie rod is attached to the wheel itself. If it's a spidery thing with two ball joints attaching the wheel assembly to the torsion arms, your car has **ball joint front suspension,** which was put on all VW's starting about 1965-66. If your wheels are attached to the torsion arms by two cylinders with horizontal **torsion arm link pins** with a vertical cylinder between them, a **king pin,** you have **king pin front suspension.** We don't cover the repair and alignment of the ball joint front suspension as the work requires special tools and methods needing experts. You'll probably have less trouble with **ball joints** than king pins, but when they go, they need to be replaced at Volkswagen. **See Chapter XXI.** The front wheel brakes, bearings and adjustments are covered in Chapter XI for both types of front suspension.

Models older than 1965 have **king pin front suspension** and the Super Beetle and Type IV have something called **McPherson strut suspension,** which was put in largely to gain more storage space in the front luggage compartment. Instead of torsion arms, it consists of two large struts (shock absorbers) that come up from the track control arm through the steering knuckle to the body mounting bracket on the inside of the wheel wells (fenders). The two track control arms are hinged from the front axle carrier (a large T—the two top bars of the T go between the front wheels and the stem goes toward the back of the car). The axle carrier is mounted to the frame in three places. There's a stabilizer bar that goes across in front of the front axle carrier. If you have McPherson strut suspension, you can check for play and adjust the front wheel bearings. You can also do the Procedure in this chapter for changing tie rods and tie rod ends, checking and adjusting toe-in and adjusting the steering box, but the rest of the front end you'll have to leave to the experts.

Now that you know what kind of front suspension your car has, we'll help you diagnose the problem that brought you here in the first place, then tell you what to do to fix it. Remember with king pin front suspension, you can fix almost anything; with ball joint or McPherson front suspension, the number of things you can do is limited. Find your jack and lug wrench, block the right side of the car so it can't roll and jack the left front wheel slightly off the ground. You're going to test for play in the front end. If, when you've finished these tests and have found no play anywhere, but your car drives funny and the tires are wearing out unevenly, check the toe-in or the steering dampener.

Vertical plane test for play in the front end: Push-pull on the tire with both hands at 12 o'clock or at 12 o'clock and 6 o'clock. If the wheel is good and tight, fine, but if you have play, it's in the

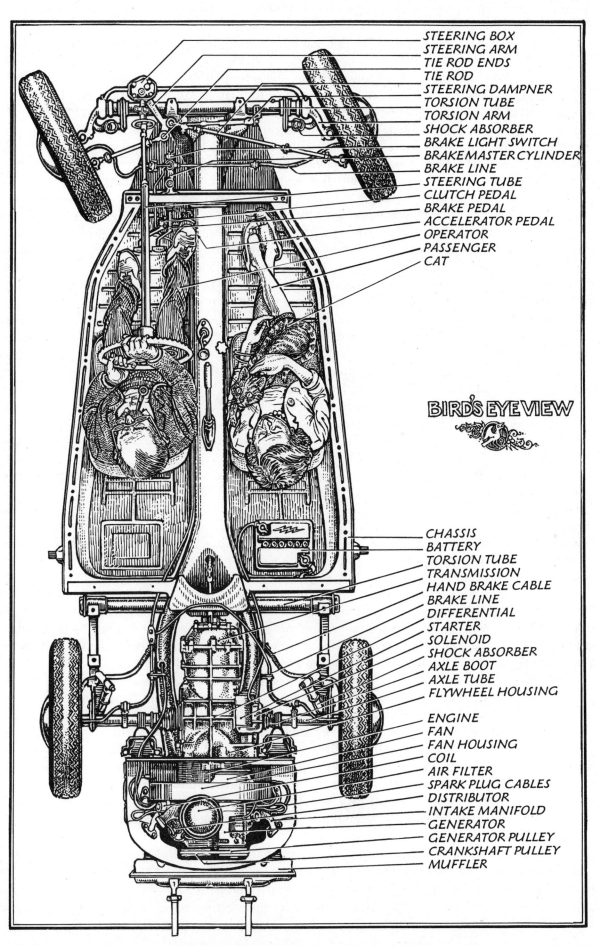

STEERING BOX
STEERING ARM
TIE ROD ENDS
TIE ROD
STEERING DAMPNER
TORSION TUBE
TORSION ARM
SHOCK ABSORBER
BRAKE LIGHT SWITCH
BRAKE MASTER CYLINDER
BRAKE LINE
STEERING TUBE
CLUTCH PEDAL
BRAKE PEDAL
ACCELERATOR PEDAL
OPERATOR
PASSENGER
CAT

BIRD'S EYE VIEW

CHASSIS
BATTERY
TORSION TUBE
TRANSMISSION
HAND BRAKE CABLE
BRAKE LINE
DIFFERENTIAL
STARTER
SOLENOID
SHOCK ABSORBER
AXLE BOOT
AXLE TUBE
FLYWHEEL HOUSING

ENGINE
FAN
FAN HOUSING
COIL
AIR FILTER
SPARK PLUG CABLES
DISTRIBUTOR
INTAKE MANIFOLD
GENERATOR
GENERATOR PULLEY
CRANKSHAFT PULLEY
MUFFLER

torsion arm link pins or king pins, or in the ball joints, or in the front wheel bearing adjustment or in a combination of these.

Now put your hands at 9 o'clock and 3 o'clock and push-pull. It helps to have someone hold the steering wheel while you do this. Look, listen and feel for play in this horizontal plane. If you have play here, it's in the steering box and arm, the tie-rod assemblies, the swing lever assembly (Bus), the idler arm (Type IV and Super Beetle) or the front wheel bearing adjustment or a combination.

There is one common source of play in both vertical and horizontal planes, the front wheel bearing adjustment. If you have new lock plates available for the older models or a 6mm Allen head wrench for the newer models, you can put this source of play out of the running very quickly. Remember two things: the lock plates are different sizes for different models, so specify which you want at the store, and you can make a 6mm Allen wrench out of a 1/4" Allen wrench by filing the 1/4" one just a bit to fit. Pry the hubcap off with the large screwdriver to expose the hub, the metal thing that the wheels are bolted to. The hub contains the **bearings** and runs on the **axle** or **spindle**. In the center of the hub there is a little cup-like **hub cover,** which is jambed either in or on the end of the hub to keep crud out of bearings and to keep grease in. You're working on the left wheel, so you'll see a little square shaft, which doesn't appear on the right side, sticking out of the hub cover with a cotter key or clip holding it to the hub cover. This is the speedometer shaft. If all you see is a little square hole, that's why your speedometer's not working. Take the cotter key out of the square shaft, or use the small screwdriver to pry the little clip off. Use the small hammer and big screwdriver to knock and pry or just pry the little hub cover off or out of the hub. With the hub cover off, you are facing the adjusting assembly for the front wheel bearings. There are two nuts with a lock plate between them, or a thick clamp nut with an Allen head bolt holding the clamp together. If you have two nuts, knock the locking ear down from the outside nut and take the nut off (left hand thread on the left axle), then remove the plate. Tighten the inner nut down on the bearing with the crescent wrench.

If you have the clamp type, loosen the Allen head with the 6mm wrench, then use the crescent to tighten the nut so there is no play at all. Remember the left hand thread.

You've now eliminated the possibility of play in the wheel bearing adjustment, so try the wheel for play again. First try the vertical play at 12 o'clock and 6 o'clock, then the horizontal play by pushing and pulling at 9 and 3 o'clock. No play anymore? Good, that's often the case. Your front wheel bearings are out of adjustment, so turn to the Wheel Procedure, Step 8, in Chapter XI, adjust both wheel bearings and once they're adjusted put things back together, clean up and you can go to the shower. If you have ball joint or McPherson front suspension and you've eliminated the possibility that the front wheel bearings are out of adjustment and you still have vertical play, take your baby to VW, but first—read on. If you have king pin front suspension, have eliminated the front wheel bearings as a possible source for play and still have vertical play, do the torsion arm link procedure (this chapter) and if you still have vertical play, do the king pin procedure.

Bus—Having eliminated the Front wheel bearings as a source for play and you still have play in the horizontal plane (9 and 3 o'clock), leave the wheel bearing adjustment tightened down, let the car down on the ground and have your friend turn the steering wheel while you look underneath the car to watch the swing lever arm for up and down movement, the next logical place for play. If this arm is rising and falling as your friend turns the steering wheel, turn to the Bus Swing Lever Arm procedure in this Chapter. If you have a **Type IV or a Super Beetle,** follow the instructions for the Bus above and watch the idler arm for up and down movement while your friend does the steering wheel. If it's moving up and down—off to VW, but continue reading for now.

All Models. If you still have horizontal play after eliminating the possibility of the front wheel bearings and your swing lever arm (Bus) or idler arm (Type IV and Super Beetle) are OK, have your friend do the 3 o'clock—9 o'clock thing while you watch from underneath the car—wheel bearing adjustment is still tightened down. You're checking the tie rods and tie rod ends by watching the steering arm as it moves. Look for slop at the tie rod ends—that is, the tie rod ends won't move at the same time as the steering wheel. If they move after the steering wheel is turned, that's slop and shouldn't be there. A bum tie rod end would be our first guess, a loose steering arm our second. The tie rod and tie rod end procedure is in this chapter as is the adjustment for the steering box but you'll have to go to VW if after adjusting the steering box, you still have play, since the steering box needs overhauling or replacement. While you're under the car checking things, push and wiggle each and every tie rod end with your hand to see if it's tight in its hole—there are six to check counting the two on the drag link from the steering box. If any are loose, do the procedure for changing tie rods and tie rod ends in this chapter.

While you're still under the car, you might as well look at a shock absorber. If you have king pin or ball joint front suspension, that round tube that connects to the lower torsion arm and goes up to that horn above the upper torsion arm is a shock absorber. It slows up the bouncing of the wheels as they hit holes and things. If you want to test them, later when the car is standing on all four wheels, just bounce the car up and down with your foot, either end, and if the car keeps on bouncing after you stop, you need new shocks, so see the last procedure in this chapter for the activity connected with them, both front and rear.

The shocks in the McPherson strut front end are the struts. They're very heavy duty and seldom need work or replacement. **See Chapter XXI** to remove and install them.

Get out from under the car and adjust the wheel bearings (Wheel Procedure, Step 8, Chapter XI). Once your wheel bearings are tightened down, they must be adjusted before you drive.

Your front wheels have three attitudes toward the road: **caster, camber, and toe-in.** If the front end assembly is put together right, caster and camber are set for you. Caster is kinda like an old bureau caster with the wheel rolling behind the shaft. It helps the wheel decide which way it is going, makes the wheel center-seeking, in other words. Camber is the angle the wheels have to the road off the vertical plane. As you face the front of the car, the bottoms of the tires are closer together than the tops. In king pin front suspension, it is set by washers (shims) on either side of the torsion arm link pins and changes when the pins are loose, hence the 6,000 mile adjustment. The toe-in, just like a pigeon-toed kid, is set when the car is standing still so the wheels will run straight on the highway where the friction of the tires on the road tends to force them into the wall-eyed position. Toe-in is adjusted by changing the length of the tie rods.

There is a fourth attitude which operates when you're turning a corner, called **king pin or steering axis inclination.** The king pins are tilted so the tops of the king pins are closer together than the bottoms when you look at them from the front end of the car, just the reverse of the wheel camber. This inclination is done for you by VW so that some semblance of proper wheel attitude is maintained on a corner.

Now all this means not a nit to you as long as it works OK. The attitudes are designs for proper road handling, safety, and minimal tire wear. They do fine until wear catches up with them, then comes the uneasy feeling, the funny wear on the tires. Make a maintenance habit of grabbing the front tire with your hands at 12 o'clock and shoving the tire in and out. You will feel the play in plenty of time to do something about it.

PROCEDURE FOR TIGHTENING THE TORSION ARM LINK PINS: Phase I. King Pin Front Suspension only.

Condition: You have vertical play in your front wheel assembly. Put your hands at 12 o'clock and push-pull the tire. If there is slop or play when you do this, run this procedure. VW says it should be done every 6,000 miles, an excellent idea.

Tools and Materials: Phase I tool kit, wheel bearing grease, wire brush, 6mm Allen head wrench (new type wheels), blocks.

Parts: New wheel bearing lock plates (old type wheels).

Remarks: Look at the sketch and find the **steering knuckle.** It's a fantastic piece of forged steel, axle, brake plate holder, cylinder for the king pin and arm for steering. Hold out your forefinger and move your knuckle. The steering knuckle works like that. To see the steering knuckle on your car, you'll have to jack up a front wheel and clean a lot of mud and crud off.

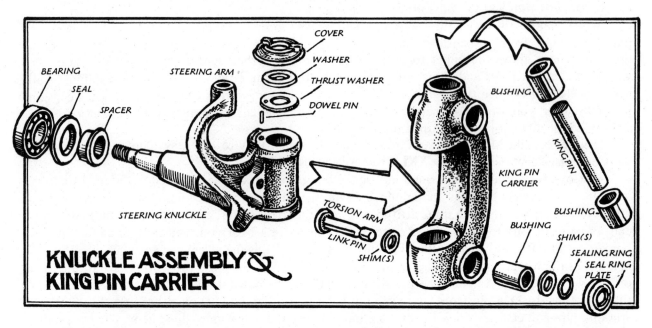

KNUCKLE ASSEMBLY & KING PIN CARRIER

The shaft that the steering knuckle turns on is called a **king pin.** The king pin is in two parts in the Bus. The **bushings** that the king pins turn in are held in another fantastic steel forging called the **king pin carrier,** which has two vertical cylinders for the king pin bushings and two horizontal cylinders to hold the **torsion arm link pin bushings.** I'm going to ask questions later, so pay attention now. The other end of the **torsion arm link pins** goes through the **torsion arm clamps** which trail back from and are attached to the **torsion bars,** which are in those tubes that run clear across the front of the car. Our responsibility ends with the ends of the torsion arms. The torsion bars belong to Volkswagen. The torsion arms clamp to the torsion arm link pins and hold the front end assembly to the car. The torsion arm link pins should be tightened every 6,000 miles or when there is play in them. If the torsion arm link pins get loose and you drive the car too long without an adjustment, their bushings wear out, the king pins wear out and you find you need to put new bushings in both places, a big job for which you will also find the procedure in this chapter.

Step 1. Get Ready

Tip: Run down to the 25 cent car wash and knock the worst of the crud off your front end with the high pressure hose and soap. Rinse well.

Block the right side of the car so it can't roll, use the big screwdriver to pry the left front hub cap off, jack the left front wheel slightly off the ground. Type I and III owners use a scissors jack or one which lifts the front wheel only or else lift the whole side up with your regular jack, put some blocks in back of the front wheel, then let the car down onto the blocks so only the front wheel is off the ground. Working on the front wheels is dangerous with the entire left side jacked up. Get your stool and sit down. Remove the cotter key or clip with a pliers or screwdriver from the speedometer cable shaft, that little square thing coming out of the hub cover. Use the big screwdriver and small hammer to knock and pry or pry and knock the hub cover off, or out, of the hub. You're looking at the wheel bearing adjustment nuts or nut. If it's one thick clamp nut with an Allen head bolt in it, you have the new type wheels. If it's two thin nuts with a lock plate between them, you have an old type.

If you have the new type, use your 6mm Allen head wrench (or a 1/4" wrench filed to fit) to loosen the clamping action of the nut, then use the crescent to tighten the nut down counter-clockwise (left side) on the washer and thus the bearings. This will take the play out of the bearing assembly. If you have the old type, knock the ear of the locking plate down off the side of the outside nut, unscrew the outside nut (clockwise, left hand thread).

Note: Right here, I'll say—forever—that most left front axles have left hand threads and tighten counter-clockwise, while right front axles have right hand threads that tighten clockwise like all the other nuts in the car. So don't get up tight, tighten left left and right right with the handle up. If you wanna know why, it's so the rotation of the wheel will tend to tighten instead of loosen, keeping the wheel from falling off and running down the road ahead of you. OK?

Take the outside nut and the locking plate off the axle, then use the crescent to tighten the nut onto the washer and bearings to eliminate play in the bearings.

Now for the cleaning: Use the big screwdriver, the wire brush, and your little sister to get all the grease and dirt off the front wheel assembly and off the inside of the brake plate. Don't bung up that flexible hose in your rising excitement—it's the brake hose. Get everything good and clean and the procedure is almost done.

Step 2 Adjust the Torsion Arm Link Pins—Types I and II only

That's the name of the game, but first we have to find them and that's why we cleaned the mother. As these pins are in slightly different places in Types I and II, we'll sneak out from center so you can't miss them. Find the torsion bars, those two big tubes that run across the front of the car. On the end are two arms which trail back. Follow them to their ends and you come to a cylinder, which is actually a clamp with a bolt through it (or, there are two). Start with the top clamp. On the side of this clamp away from you there is a pin sticking out with a flattened place on it. This is the pin we are going to tighten. Sketch, please? OK.

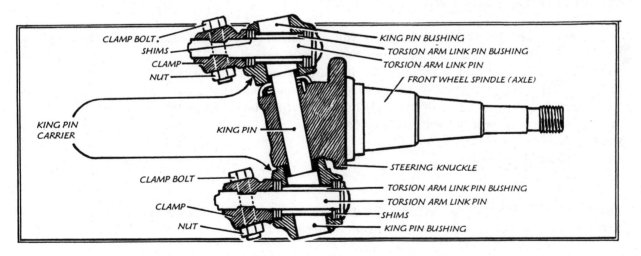

The pin goes through the king pin carrier with the adjusting shims on each side of it, then through the torsion arm clamp. The bolt through the clamp not only clamps onto the pin, but also acts as an adjusting point. There is a spiral groove like a worm track machined into the pin, so when you turn the pin using that flattened end, the pin is moved either in or out depending on which way you turn the pin.

For the Bus you need a 17mm open end wrench and a 17mm box end with a 17mm open end on the other end. For the Type I you need two 17mm wrenches and a 14mm open end. Look for cotter keys in the bolt ends, which you usually don't have to remove to make the adjustment, but which get in the way of the wrench. Put the open end wrench on the bolt head—the one through the clamp. Hold

Step 2. (Cont'd.)

the bolt with the open end while you loosen the nut with the box end. Just loosen it enough so you can move the pin in the clamp. Use the open end, 17mm Bus, 14mm Type I. When you can turn the pin, the bolt is loose enough. Turn the pin back and forth several times to make sure you know which way it tightens, then loosen it a little. With the big screwdriver, pry the torsion arm up and down while you watch the action of the pin in the cylinder on the king pin carrier. If the pin moves in this cylinder, the torsion arm link pin bushings are worn. If the pin moves a lot they're bad and should be replaced, but not now, unless you're into doing the whole thing. Read the procedure in this chapter and decide. Anyway, go on for now with or without bad bushings.

Tighten the pin with the open end wrench until you have it really tight, then loosen it a smidge. Tighten it again and loosen it so the far end of the wrench moves about 1-1/2". All this tightening and loosening is just to keep from having a cryin strain on the pin (really on the bolt, but that's nitpicking). Now tighten the nut down on the clamping bolt, good and tight with the box end. Repeat with the lower pin and that's all there is to it. The cleaning and cleaning up are the toughest part.

Now grab the wheel with both hands, one at 12 o'clock and the other at 6 o'clock, push with one and pull with the other. If you feel play, the king pin bushings are worn. You know this because you've eliminated everything else. If you have bad torsion arm pin bushings, there is no need to check the king pin bushings except out of curiosity, because when you replace one, you replace the other, and when you overhaul one wheel you do the other as part of the same procedure—this chapter, of course.

You have adjusted the torsion arm link pins on the left side and have the right side to do, so turn to Chapter XI and do the Wheel Bearing Adjustment in the wheel procedure, then reassemble the left wheel. Start on the right wheel with this procedure, Step 1., and run the whole procedure but remember you won't have the speedometer to deal with. When you're through with the right wheel, get a grease job and make sure the link pins are greased, now that you know where they are. If you tightened a lot of slack out of the torsion arm link pins, turn to the Toe-in Adjustment to check the toe-in, or have it done.

The Torsion Arm Link Pin Procedure you just ran or read about, should be done by each VW owner with king pin front suspension any time there's vertical play, because it keeps you in touch with your car's all-important front end. Also it's easy, except for the cleaning. The procedures in the rest of this chapter are more difficult. If I'm working and making money, I let two front end shops bid on my front end work. With two bids to choose from, both of which include not only money, but the time my car will be tied up, I decide which of the bidders to let near my car, or whether I want to fix it myself. Of course if I have John's Garage open and one of the bidders is me—but that's a different concept.

PROCEDURE FOR REPLACING THE KING PINS AND BUSHINGS AND THE TORSION ARM LINK PINS AND BUSHINGS. King Pin Front Suspension Only.

Condition: The bushings on either the king pins or torsion arm link pins are worn. If you replace one, replace the other on both wheels.

Tools and Materials: Phase II tool kit, 12" straight-edge, a metric rule, a two-foot bar, Permatex No. 2, wheel bearing grease, pieces of wire, lots of blocks (cinder blocks are great, bolt pan, cleaning pan, and solvent.)

Parts: Two new king pin kits, two new torsion arm link pin kits for your year and model, new front wheel lock plates, and, if needed: new bearings, seals, brake shoes (see Wheel Procedure, Chapter XI).

Step 1. Preparation

Take the car to the car wash and clean the whole front end. Block the rear wheels so they cannot move either way. Pry off the front hub caps, loosen the wheel lugs, jack up one side and block it well. Remove the jack and jack up the other side and block it. Don't stint on the blocks if you want to work safely. Remove the front wheels. Turn to Chapter XI and run the Wheel Procedure until you get to the brake shoes. If yours are good, don't take them off the brake plates.

Step 2. Remove Brake Plates

Use the 13 or 14mm socket, long extension, ratchet, and maybe the pipe cheater (see Chapter XVI) to remove the three (four in the late Bus) bolts holding the brake plate (the stationary round plate) to the steering knuckle. In the Bus you have a rat's nest, as the bolts holding the brake plates on also hold the wheel cylinders to the plate. Push the bolts back through their holes and use some thin wire or string round and round the four bolts to hold them in the plate. All models: Lift the brake plate off the axle, being careful with the brake hose. Wire the brake plate up out of the way. If you'd read this before leaping in, you'd have some wire ready. The brake plate bolts often have a wire as a safety through holes in the bolt heads; use that. You may have to turn the axle, sometimes backward, sometimes forward (depends on where your brake hose is coming from), to get the brake plates off it.

Step 3. Remove Steering Knuckle

Pull the speedo cable to the inside out of the left axle. Hang it up on the frame. Turn forward a few pages to the Tie Rod Procedure, Step 1, and remove the tie rod ends from the steering knuckle arm on both wheels. Do not unscrew the tie rod ends from the tie rod. Then return here and use your two 14mm (Type I and III) or two 17mm (Bus) wrenches to remove the clamp bolt clamping the torsion arm to the pin. The knuckle is free to come off, so pull, pry and tap it off. Count the shims that come off the inner ends of the torsion arm link pins. There are ten shims for each pin on the old models and eight since 1960. Count them as you take them off, write the number so you can't forget. It's important to know how many to put back in each place. Mark the number you take off from inside of the top pin "A" ___ (so many), inside of the bottom pin "C" ___ (so many). Push the torsion arm link pins out of their bushings and count and write down the number of shims on them. Mark the shims on the head end of the top pin "B" ___ (so many), and those on the head end of the of the bottom pin "D" ___ (so many). You'll have four numbers: two for the top pins (A and B), and two for the lower pins (C and D). Clean up the knuckles in solvent and examine them for cracks and beat-up places. Put the bolts and washers in the bolt can. If a steering knuckle is cracked or damaged (ask at VW when you buy your parts), buy a new one, even if you have to borrow. Repeat this step and remove the right side steering knuckle. You'll have eight numbers—two sets. Keep left and right straight.

Step 4. Check Torsion Arms

There is a remote possibility that you have bent torsion arms, or that the last person to do your front end didn't get the right number of shims on the torsion arm link pins to set your camber right. At any rate, you don't want to leave any unturned stones at this point. Take the straight edge and hold its edge steady and flat across the outboard face of the lower torsion arm clamp; see sketch on following page.

With the straight edge held steady, measure the gap between the straight edge and the face of the clamp on the upper torsion arm in millimeters with a metric rule. It's important, so do it several times. until you're sure you're accurate. Have a friend hold the straight edge while you measure the gap (the

Step 4. (Cont'd.)

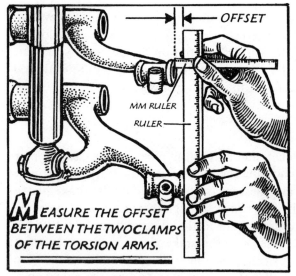

OFFSET

MM RULER

RULER →

MEASURE THE OFFSET BETWEEN THE TWO CLAMPS OF THE TORSION ARMS.

offset), if that helps. Write the offset dimension down with the number of shims that you counted. Check the offset on the other side and write it down with its set of shim numbers. If your measurement is over 9mm or under 5mm, you have one or more bent torsion arms. If one side is OK, and the other side is out of tolerance, the side that is out of tolerance has been hit in an accident and has not been repaired properly. It is not our intention to make fixing wrecked front ends a part of this procedure, but we tell you what to do so you can figure out how to do it as you go along. You people within tolerance measurements can skip this part.

First thing after you find out you have a bent torsion arm is to check the needle bearings in the end of the torsion tube by lifting the torsion arm and letting it down. If there is play at the place where the torsion arm disappears into the tube, you may not have bent arms but just a worn-out needle bearing on the end of the torsion bar. Don't freak out. This is as easy to fix as a bent torsion arm. You will need Allen wrenches from here on out, so buy a metric set.

To get the needle bearing you have to pull the torsion bar, so find the lock nut in the center of the tube and loosen it. Take the shock absorber off the lower arm (remove nut), and the upper point (remove bolt) on both sides so you can pull the torsion arm and torsion bar out of the tube together. Use your Allen head to take the torsion arm off the bar and put on a new needle bearing, both inside and outside races, then put the torsion arm back on the bar and put it back in the tube and tighten the lock screw and nut in the center of the tube. You will have to fiddle around with it to find the hole. Now you are back in business, so measure the arm offset again and if it is within the tolerance above, go on to the next step. Try to combine the above operation with the job as a whole, if you can.

Now, if you didn't have any play in the out-of-tolerance torsion arms, they are bent or one of them is. If you can tell by eye which one is bent, swell, but if not take both of them off. Use an Allen head on the bolt and a wrench on the lock nut to get the threaded bolt out of the arm where it attaches to the torsion bar—don't take out the torsion bar. You will have to take off the shock absorber. Take both torsion arms down to VW and have them tell you which is bent, then buy it and put both back on the torsion bars. Lock them in well and measure them again to see what the offset is. Put the shock absorber back on.

There is another horrible possibility which you should check out if you find bent torsion arms. The torsion tubes may be bent also, indicating an accident has happened to your car. Take a string and the metric ruler and hold the string across the torsion bar tube from arm to arm and measure the distance from the string to the tube with the ruler here and there to see if the tube is straight. Check both tubes. If one is bent you will need more help than we can give you.

If you feel you are in over your head at any point in the above discussion and you can see that your front end is in more trouble than your confidence in your ability to fix, just relax. Take out the four or eight bolts that hold the entire front end to the frame. They're in that horn behind the shock absorber (Bus), front and center (Type I and III). Take out the clamp bolt where the steering rod comes down to the steering box (Type I and III). Remove the swing lever tie rod end (Bus). After giving the whole thing a couple of heaves, you will have the front end assembly completely off the car, so just throw it over your shoulder and truck on down to Volkswagen to let them do the repairs. If you have a Bus, have them put in a new swing lever kit while they're at it, unless yours is very good. You'll need help to get the front assembly back on after VW has repaired it. In the Type

Step 4. (Cont'd.)

I get someone to guide the steering shaft into the steering box while you get a bolt into the front assembly and hold the whole thing up. Two helpers are not too many.

Now I'll get back to you people who don't have serious trouble and are just installing new bushings for the king pins and torsion arm link pins. Your offset measurement is within the tolerance and you are wondering what this is all about, so here is a sketch and a table telling you how many shims to put in each place to get the camber right for your offset dimension. The numbers you counted as you took the shims off should match the numbers in the table for your offset. If they don't, use the numbers in the table.

We put the table here, before you go downtown with your steering knuckles, so you can ask at the front end shop if you don't understand it. Take your steering knuckles, the king pin kits and torsion arm link pin kits either to VW or to a front end shop that does VW work to have the knuckles rebuilt and assembled. Take the collected information on the numbers of shims: A, B, C and D, your offset measurements and this book with the table in it, with you. Make sure they assemble the unit completely, even to the right numbers of shims on the ends of the torsion arm link pins and the dust cap (if any) pressed in. Make sure the grease fittings are in right—just mention it to them. With their help, put the link pins in with the right number of shims on each side of the king pin carrier, then put some tape around the pins to hold the things together while you transport them home.

Shim Table for 1960 and Earlier (10 shims per pin)

Offset in mm.	Upper Torsion Arm		Lower Torsion Arm	
	Shims A	Shims B	Shims C	Shims D
5	3	7	7	3
5.5	4	6	7	3
6	4	6	6	4
6.5	5	5	6	4
7	5	5	5	5
7.5	6	4	5	5
8	6	4	4	6
8.5	7	3	4	6
9	7	3	3	7

Shim Table for 1960 and Later (8 shims per pin)

Offset in mm.	Upper Torsion Arm		Lower Torsion Arm	
	Shims A	Shims B	Shims C	Shims D
5.5	2	6	5	3
6	2	6	4	4
6.5	3	5	4	4
7	3	5	3	5
7.5	4	4	3	5
8	4	4	2	6
8.5	5	3	2	6

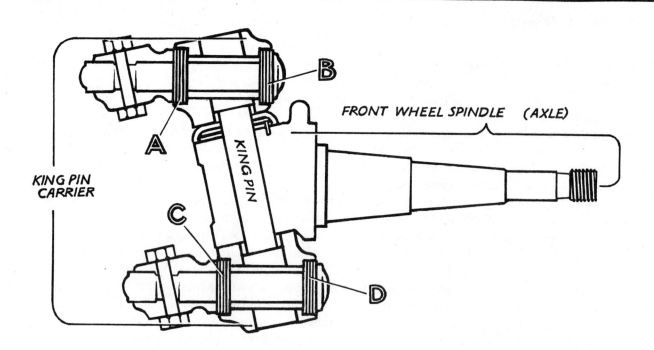

KING PIN CARRIER

FRONT WHEEL SPINDLE (AXLE)

KING PIN

Step 5. Install Steering Knuckles

They're all together, right? All the grease fittings, too, so figure out which is the left one, by the arm and the speedo cable hole in the axle, and slip the pins into the clamps on the torsion arms. Stick the pin in the bottom arm and lift it a little so you can start the upper one in its clamp. Get the bolts into the clamps. You'll have to turn the pins a little to get the bolts through. Put on the nuts, then reassemble the right side of the car. Turn to the Torsion Arm Link Procedure, Step 2, to adjust the mothers, then turn to the Tie Rod Procedure, Step 1, to install the tie rod ends on both knuckles. With the tie rod ends on, return here.

Step 6. Install Brake Plates

Unwire the left brake plate and clean the back of it. Carefully slip it over the axle (turn the axle so you can slip the brake plate over it), then start the three bolts (four in the Bus), through the plate. Squeeze some Permatex No. 2 all around between the plate and the knuckle, then tighten up the bolts to 36 ft. lbs. (Type I and III) or 42 ft. lbs. (Bus) with the torque wrench. See Chapter XVI on how to use a torque wrench, if you've never. Return to the Wheel Procedure, Chapter XI, and run it the rest of the way through from where you left off until both wheel bearings are adjusted. Put the wheels on and down on the ground. Then take a test run to the service station to have the front assembly greased. Let the new pins and bushings set in a few miles (like maybe 50), then check the toe-in per the next procedure in this chapter.

PROCEDURE FOR CHANGING TIE RODS AND TIE ROD ENDS, CHECKING AND AD-JUSTING TOE-IN AND ADJUSTING THE STEERING BOX, Phase II. All Models.

Condition: You've been referred to this procedure because a tie rod end is loose or to remove a tie rod end and/or you have a bent tie rod, or you're going to check and adjust the toe-in or the steering box.

Tools and Materials: Phase II tool kit, two-foot bar, two flat sticks three feet long, a ruler, Liquid Wrench.

Parts: New tie rod tab lock washers and as required: new tie rod ends and cotter pins.

Remarks: Step 1 covers the removal and installation of the tie rod ends, Step 2 the toe-in thing, and Step 3, the steering box.

Note: Never try to straighten a bent tie rod. Buy a new one, complete with new tie rod ends and locks and everything. Remove the two old tie rod ends from the arms, then remove the tie rod from the car and lay it out on the ground. Lay the new one next to it and screw the new tie rod ends up on the new tie rod to the same distance the old ones are on the old tie rod, so the new tie rod is the same length the old one was before it was bent. Go to Step 2 to adjust the toe-in. The short tie rod on the bug comes a little bent, so don't freak out.

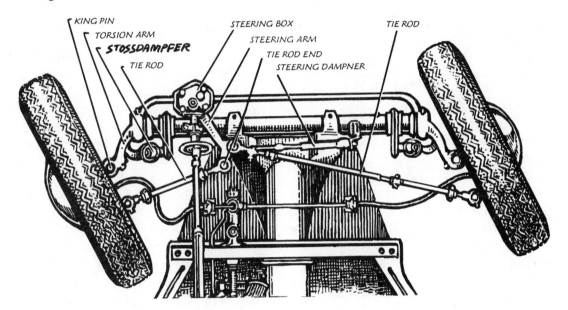

Step 1. Removal and Installation of Tie Rod Ends.

First look at one in this sketch.

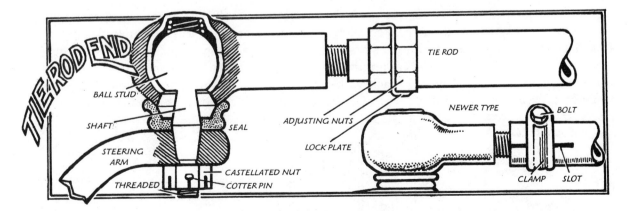

VW has a neat puller to remove them, but we don't so you'll need a scissors jack for the tie rod ends with the bolts pointed up and a two foot bar for the ones with the bolts pointed down.

Removal: Pull the cotter key out of the hole in the bolt with the vice grip, find the right size box end wrench for the nut, then loosen and remove it. Turn the nut over and screw it on the bolt until the back of the nut is flush with the end of the bolt. If the nut end is pointing toward the ground, get the two foot bar on the arm, or whatever the tie rod is bolted through, and pry the arm down while you hit the nut up with the heavy hammer. Usually one good blow will do it, but if it doesn't come right away, put some Liquid Wrench on the shank of the bolt, give it a minute or two to soak in and try again. When it comes loose, unscrew the nut and push the tie rod end out of the tapered hole.

If the nut is pointing up, screw the scissors jack up under the arm the tie rod end is through and tighten a strain on the arm with the jack (run the jack up until it pushes against the arm), then hammer the tie rod end bolt down until it's loose. Take off the nut and push the tie rod end out. Mentally note which end points up and which end points down for reassembly. If you run into a busted-up tie rod end and the shank of the bolt is already loose in its hole so that the nut just merrily turns around without unscrewing, find your sharpest chisel, pick out a castellation ⊔⊔⊔ that looks weak, put the chisel on it and give the chisel a hard blow with the hammer. A few hard blows will break the nut so you can screw it off and remove the tie rod end. That takes them out of the hole, now for the tie rod part.

You have two types of tie rod ends: one with left hand threads that goes on one end of the tie rod, the other with right hand threads, and it goes on the other end of the tie rod. This difference in thread direction makes a turn buckle out of the tie rod. When you turn the tie rod in one direction with the vice grip, the assembly grows shorter, and when you turn the other way the assembly lengthens. In fact, this is how the toe-in is adjusted. Loosen the lock nuts or the clamp. Just bend the little tabs straight up, then use two wrenches to loosen the locking nut. Now turn the tie rod end that you're replacing off. If turning it one way moves it away from you, turn it the other way and remove it.

Installation: Put the tie rod end in the tie rod with a new tab lock between the locking nuts, or you may have clamping type of lock, not the locking nuts. Screw the new tie rod end to approximately where the old one was in the tie rod, tighten the lock nuts or the lock clamp, but don't bend the tabs until you have adjusted the toe-in in the next Step. Put the tie rod end in its hole the same way it came out, up or down. If the bolt points up, get the scissors jack under the tie rod end while you put the nut on and tighten it tight until the hole in the bolt matches one of the castellations. Put in the cotter key. If the bolt points down, get your bar on the top of the tie rod end to hold the shank in the tapered hole so the bolt doesn't turn, then put the nut on, tighten as above, put in the cotter key, bend the points out, and you're through.

Step 2. Check and Adjust Toe-in.

Checking: You need a special site like a supermarket parking lot, a church driveway, or any level piece of pavement that's flat and smooth for at least twenty feet. Head into your chosen spot slowly and, with the cross spoke of the steering wheel at center, run the car absolutely straight without touching the steering wheel. Use the hand brake to stop the car at the end of the run. Now the wheels are straight, so don't bounce the car around. Taking your two flat sticks and a pencil, lie under the car's front wheels. You're on your back with the two sticks held together so you can measure the distance between the two front wheels, first at 3 o'clock, then at 9 o'clock. Sketch? OK.

Step 2. (Cont'd.)

Hold the ends of the sticks extended to reach both tire rims. Hold them together while you make a pencil mark where the sticks meet. Scrooch under the car a little further to measure between the backs of the tire rims (at 9 o'clock). Make your mark for the back. The back mark should be 1/8" further than the front mark. In other words, the wheels should be 1/8" pigeon-toed. Turn the sticks over, measure again and make different marks to check yourself for accuracy. If the back marks are 1/8" further apart than the front marks, your toe-in is adjusted correctly.

To adjust the toe-in you change the length of the tie rod. Either unclamp the tie rod clamps or bend up the tabs and loosen the lock nuts, so the tie rod can turn on the toe rod end. If you just did Step 1, these tabs are still up. Use the vice grip on the tie rod and turn it so it either increases the pigeon-toe or lessens it. A turn or two will show you how it goes. Adjust the toe-in so it checks out right with the sticks: 1/8" longer in back. Then lock up the tie rods so they can't turn, by either tightening the clamps or locking the lock nuts and bending the lock tabs down onto the nuts. You're through.

Step 3. Adjust the Steering Box

The steering box is at the end of the steering column. The adjustment you can make is to the screw in the locking nut on the side of the Bus steering box, on the top of the Type I and III box and on the bottom of Type IV, '73 on Type II and Super Beetle. VW says to jack up the wheels to make the adjustment, but we get better results by making a road job out of it. Put a blanket on the seat to keep it clean, take the box end that fits your nut, the crescent and a big screwdriver out on the road with you. Before you go, however, take all the slack out of the adjustment by loosening the lock nut and tightening the screw until the steering wheel play is less than one inch. Now road test it and if you have just a mite of drag on the steering wheel in the straight-ahead position (it's not completely free wheelin'), but have no lumps in the steering in any position, you done good.

If you have a heavy drag and lumps, loosen the screw a hair and drive to test the steering again. Repeat this operation until you have less than one inch of play in your steering wheel and no lumps or drag. **'65 and earlier:** Stop at a service station, take off the little filler plug on the steering box and fill the box up with 90-weight gear lube. If it takes a lot, look for a leak. **All models:** Your steering box may need overhauling but, as they say in contracts, "by others." If you know your front end is in good shape (no play anywhere, no uneven wear on tires) but you still have 2½ to 3" of play in the steering wheel, take your car to VW to have them make the shimming type interior adjustment. You've done all you can do. Type IV, '73 on Type II and Super Beetle will need a new box.

SWING LEVER PROCEDURE, BUS OWNERS ONLY, Phase II.

Condition: Your Bus tends to wander all over the road and when you look at the swing lever with someone turning the steering wheel, the swing lever arm (the place where the tie rods connect to the center of the steering assembly) goes up and down as the tie rods go back and forth. The swing lever arm shouldn't do this, but should turn smoothly from side to side without bobbing.

Tools and Materials: Phase II tool kit, 1-1/8" x 4" round brass pin, sledge hammer, six-inch "C" clamp.

Parts: New swing lever kit.

Step 1. Check for the Trouble.

Now that you've decided to do something about your swing lever, take the flashlight under the Bus with you to find out where the play is taking place. Have someone turn the steering wheel back

Step 1. (Cont'd.)

and forth while you watch. First look at the bottom of the big pin that comes through the cylinder welded to the front of the bottom torsion arm. That pin is the swing lever pin and should be turning smoothly back and forth without any up and down or tilting motions. You can check your bushings again when the assembly is apart, but if the pin is bobbing and weaving, you can be sure the bushings are worn. If there is no indication there, shine your light on the place where the swing lever arm swings on top of the pin—here's a sketch:

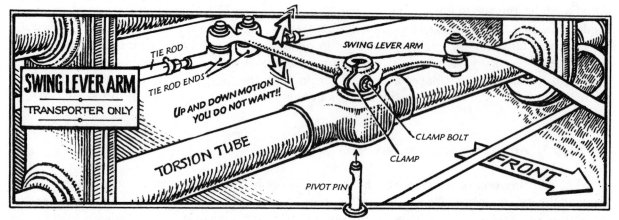

If the lever is moving up and down on the pin, but the pin doesn't seem to be moving back and forth, try tightening the clamp bolt. Find the socket that fits the bolt and bend the ear of the lock down, tighten the bolt with the socket on the long extension on the ratchet and the cheater bar (Chapter XVI). Bend the lock ear back onto the bolt head and do the test again: have someone turn the steering wheel while you watch down below. This tightening may be all you need to do. If you break an ear off the locking washer or if tightening the bolt didn't take the play out, but the bushings are OK, go to Step 2. If the bushings are gone, start with Step 3.

Step 2. Install New Bolt, Lock, and Spring Washer.

I had to buy a whole kit to get a lock and spring washer but then I found a larger VW dealer who carried the parts separately to complete the kit which I carried with me. Anyway, you need a new bolt, lock and spring washer to do this Step. Set the wheels straight ahead with the steering wheel. Crawl under the car with the socket that fits your bolt, the extension, ratchet, pipe cheater, the "C" clamp and the new bolt, lock, and spring washer. Bend the ear of the lock down so you can turn the bolt, put the "C" clamp with the "C" part on the top of the lever and the turning part on the head of the pin. Tighten the "C" clamp. Remove the bolt, then the "C" clamp. Pry the lever arm off the top of the pin, remove the spring washer and any other washers and shims you may have.

Now check the bushings by seeing if they're tight on the pin. If they're loose on the pin, you need new bushings. Step 3 is a lot of bull work so if your bushings are really bad, OK, change them, but if they're fair, you'll want to think about the job. Put the pin back in, put the other shims and washers (if any) the way they were, put the new spring washer on the pin, put the swing lever on the pin, then line the slot in the pin up with the hole in the clamp that the bolt goes through as you put them together—you see what I mean. Now put the "C" clamp on and tighten the swing lever down on the spring washer with the "C" clamp, line the hole up with your eye and the flashlight. If, when you clamp the "C" clamp down, you can see a ridge of the slot in the pin through the hole, then you need a shim under the head of the pin. There are some in the kit. You want a clear, open, unsullied hole when the "C" clamp is tight before you start the bolt into the swing lever hole. Put the lock on and make sure it is in the right position to lock the bolt head when it is tight, put in and tighten the bolt with your socket and cheater really tight. Take off the "C" clamp and have someone turn the steering wheel. If the swing lever arm is still moving up and down try to tighten the bolt a little more, then

Step 2. (Cont'd.)

when it's tight, bend the ear on the lock so the bolt cannot turn. You're through. If you still have play, install new bushings.

Step 3. Replace the Bushings

There are two ways to get new bushings into the swing lever assembly—actually three, as VW says to take the whole front end off so you can get at it, then install the new bushings, ream them out to size and so on, but that's a lot of work, brother. There are two ways to do them in the car. One is to borrow a reamer the right metric size (ask VW) and install the bushings, then ream them out in the car. I have done it this way and it works, but the reaming is a little tiring. Suppose you don't have the reamer. Well, there's another way. Have the bushings reamed out to the pin's size at the machine shop ahead of time, install the bushings, then the pin. The bushings and pin are in your new kit. It fits a little tight at first, but soon wears in.

You choose while I tell you how to get the old bushings out and the new ones in, whether they're already reamed or not. Proceed exactly as in Step 2 until you have the swing lever free and the pin has fallen out on your nose, then using the 1-1/8" brass pin, start driving the bushings up from the bottom with a heavy hammer or a sledge. Got the picture? You're on your back, under the front of the Bus hammering up. When you get the bottom bushing driven up enough so the top one starts, the going gets tougher. Keep on beating until both bushings are out the top. Now to get the new ones in.

Start the top bushing in at the top and tap it down into the hole to get it started with the small hammer. Put the "C" clamp on the bushing and pull the bushing down into the hole with the "C" clamp until the bushing is flush with the top of the hole. Start the lower bushing in from the bottom and tap it up until it's started, then shove it in the hole with the "C" clamp until it's flush with the bottom of the hole. If you're going to ream, now's the time.

Run the reamer all the way through both bushings. Use the crescent wrench on the end of the reamer for more leverage. When the bushings are reamed, clean them up with emery cloth.

A brake cylinder hone on a small electric drill motor is invaluable for this installation. After the bushings are in, take the brake hone to them, try the pin, and repeat until you have a good fit.

If you have handy-dandy-all-ready reamed bushings, put some oil on the pin and try the pin in the bushings. If it doesn't want to go, file a bevelled edge on the end of the pin. It may take a little banging to get the pin in no matter how much you file. Tap the pin up into the hole, then go to Step 2 to finish the assembly. Drive the car right down to a service station to have this assembly greased. Don't forget!

PROCEDURES FOR REMOVING AND INSTALLING SHOCK ABSORBERS AND STEERING DAMPENERS. Phase II.

Note: Not for McPherson Strut Suspension. See Chapter XXI for McPherson Strut Suspension.

Condition: You suspect that your shocks are shot or dampeners aren't dampening (the car shimmies), or you have to take them off to get at something else.

Tools and Materials: Phase II tool kit, Liquid Wrench.

Parts: New shocks and dampeners, as needed.

Step 1. Check Shocks and Dampener

Shock absorbers and steering dampeners are designed to take the sudden movements out of your

Step 1. (Cont'd.)

car's life and, as such, should be replaced when they no longer function. If you're driving a heavily-laden Bus over lousy roads, you might like heavy-duty or adjustable shocks to help keep the strains from the torsion bars. To check the shocks for function, bounce the front or rear of the car up and down. If the car keeps bouncing after you quit, you need new shocks. Always replace shocks in pairs never one at a time. Replace both front ones or both rear ones or all four, but never just one.

To check the steering dampener, you need both front wheels off the ground. Put one hand at 3 o'clock, and push-pull very quickly. Test both wheels in this manner. If they move quickly, without resistance, check further: take off one end of the dampener by removing the bolt to see if it acts as a shock absorber. If your car shimmies, buy a new dampener and install it.

Look at the end of the dampener for signs of oil. If there is, it's probably from your dampener when means it's shot.

Step 2. Removal and Installation

Changing shock absorbers and dampeners is more or less the process of taking the old ones out and, remembering how they go, putting the new ones in the same way. Up until 1965 Bug and Type III's, all the shock absorbers have a mounting cylinder with a rubber bushing on a steel tube at each end. Squirt some Liquid Wrench on the bolts and nuts, then let it soak in. Take out the bolt at the top. If you haven't changed the front shocks for a long time you may have hell getting this top bolt out. They are tough and I advise one try, then let the job on the front shocks go to the garage—you can do the rears.

Take off the nut at the bottom. The rear shocks have two bolts. Remove the old shock and put the new one on, then tighten the nut and washer (front) or bolts and washers (rear) until the metal tube in the bushing is tight.

In the front of the Types I and III, '65 and later, they have a new type shock which has the same old connection on the bottom, but has a vertical bolt in the top connection in a new type horn, just like the American cars. Hold the top of the bolt with the screwdriver while you loosen the nut. Remove the old shock and install the new. There are some dampener rubbers in the box the new shocks came in. Some go on the top of the shock before it goes into the hole in the horn, others go on top of the horn, so don't forget them. Tighten the nut on the bolt until it's tight.

The dampener on the Bus steering is similar to the shocks with two bushed cylinders. The one in the Types I and III has a bent rod on one end which acts as a bolt but it removes and installs like the shocks. Take the bolt out of one end and the nut off the other, then remove the old dampener, put in the new, replace the nut and washer or bolt and washer and tighten them down. That's all there is to do.

* * * * * * * * * * * *

The front end assembly and the shocks in the VW are very durable and will last a long time. If you're constantly driving on rough and rutty roads, check your front end for play quite often. If you ordinarily drive on freeways and you take your car on a rough and rutty vacation trip, remember to check your front end for play when you return home. In either case, whenever you find play, tighten the torsion arm links. If you don't do this bit of maintenance—really the only maintenance there is for a VW front end outside of greasing—both your car and tires will kick up a fuss.

ଓଓଓଓଓଓ

SLIPS AND JERKS (CLUTCH)

The automobile clutch connects the engine to the transmission, allowing you to disconnect the engine at will in order to change gears. You start the engine with the transmission in neutral and the clutch pedal up. With the engine running, you push down on the clutch pedal, shift from neutral into first or reverse, and coordinate your accelerator foot with the clutch foot to put the car in motion. As you push down on the clutch pedal, you disconnect the engine from the transmission. With a fully synchronized transmission and a coordinated driver, the clutch isn't needed to shift into any gears, except first. After the car is moving, if you pay close attention, you can do the rest of the shifting up or down the gears by pushing on the accelerator until the engine is at the right revs to match this speed of the transmission. You don't believe this? Well, go try it. It's a happy thing to know about on the day you push on your clutch pedal and it keeps right on going to the floor, then sticks there like a dead thing. Cool your head—the clutch cable broke and you don't have to call the A.A.A. to send a tow truck. You can baby the car home, given a good battery, some few guts plus, of course, the above mentioned coordination. Pick a route home with as few stop signs and lights as possible, head the car into the direction you want to go by pushing it, then put the gear shift into first. Turn the key to start with a firm foot on the accelerator and when the car starts, you're in low going down the street.

At 10 mph, relax the accelerator a bit, pull the gear shift out of low and into second with a single, smooth movement. At 20, use the same fluid motion into third. If you're in town, that's as fast as you need go. When you approach a stop sign, shift down by pushing the gear shift into neutral, hitting the accelerator a smidgeon, then slipping the gear shift into second when the engine is going as fast as the transmission. You learn to feel it. Repeat this action for first, then crawl through the stop sign in low. If you must stop all the way, just leave it in low and turn the key off as you stop. Start the engine, still in low, with the starter and like that coax your car on home and replace the clutch cable. The main thing to know is that you can do it, so practice in preparation for the emergency in case the cable breaks. **See Changes and New Ideas.**

The troubles a clutch in the VW gets into are: slipping, grabbing, jerking and making noise. The only things you can do, without taking out the engine are: to adjust the clutch and replace a broken cable. You adjust it, per the next procedure, when the free play in the clutch cable is less than 1/2" or exceeds one inch. You replace the cable when it breaks. If, after you've set the free play right, the clutch still slips, grabs, jerks and makes noise, you have to replace the clutch plate. The clutch plate replacement, clutch assembly and clutch throw-out bearing work are in Chapter XV, since you must remove the engine to even see them.

If, when you let the clutch out, especially in first gear, your car shakes and jerks, the flywheel is probably distorted. The only other thing that could cause this symptom is a broken spring on the clutch pressure plate. The remedy for a distorted flywheel is to toss it and buy a new or undistorted used one.

If you hear a high pitched squealing noise when you let the clutch out in 1st gear, the bearing in the flywheel gland nut is shot. Remedy? Pull the engine and remove and replace the gland nut as in Chapter XV. Don't forget to put a dab of wheel bearing grease in the bearing and on the end of the trans pilot shaft.

PROCEDURE FOR ADJUSTING CLUTCH. Phase I—Types I, II and III with Stick Shift.

Condition: The clutch pedal has less than ½'' or more than one inch of free play, see sketch on following page.

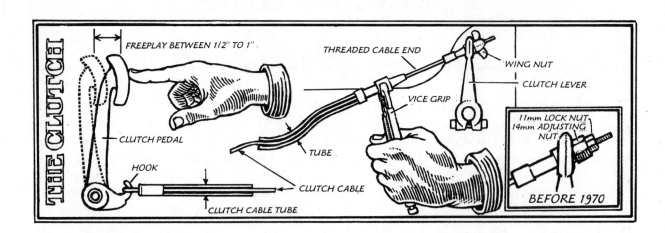

Tools and Materials: Phase I tool kit.

    Step 1. Ready. . . . .

In the Types I and III, block the right side of the car so it won't roll, then jack the left side up and remove the wheel. In the Bus, just pull on the hand brake. Spread the ground cloth out under the car inside of the left rear wheel.

Step 2. Adjust the Clutch

Take the vice grip, the 14mm and 11mm box end wrenches, plus the flashlight for locating things with you under the car. Scrooch under the car with your head almost under the left rear axle. Look up. The axle comes out of the trans-differential box right here and just above that rubber boot, there's a little lever with a cable coming to it from the front. This is the clutch lever where you're going to adjust the cable. There are threads on the cable end that go through the lever. Clamp the vice grip on the cable end in front (FRONT) of the lever.

Put the 14mm on the big nut and 11mm on the smaller one. Now turn the 11mm (the locking nut) counter-clockwise as you face it. A bit of this motion will unlock the 14mm nut and you can start to turn it. When you screw the 14mm toward the lever, it will pull the cable tighter to take up slack (play) in the pedal, and if you screw the 14mm toward the rear, it lets the pedal go toward the front. It's a tough place to reach and will physically stretch you, but keep at it until the pedal has the proper free play of 1/2" to 3/4", then run the 11mm nut down on the 14mm hand tight to lock the adjustment.

If you have a later model, all you need is the vice grip clamped on the cable end to hold it, as the adjustment is made by a big wing nut which you can turn with your fingers. This is a beautiful improvement to which my only objection is that they took so long to make it. With the free play adjusted, jack the car down, remove the blocks, and off you go.

Step 3. Adjust Clutch Tube

If the clutch is in good adjustment but the cable doesn't feel free, get under the rear of the car to check the flex tube. This is the tube the cable goes through just before it heads for the clutch lever on the trans axle. If this tube doesn't have about 3/4" to one inch of sag in it, the clutch cable won't go through it easily and smoothly. If there isn't enough sag, you can pull the proper amount of sag into the flex tube, then wrap plastic tape in the gap at the end of the tube to hold the sag. This will last for a few days until you can replace the cable. If the sag is too much, remove the clutch cable (next procedure), take the washers off the end of the flex tube, then reassemble the whole business— but usually the tube needs more sag, if anything. **See Changes and New Ideas.**

PROCEDURE FOR REPLACING THE CLUTCH CABLE. Phase I
Type I, II and III with Stick Shift

Condition: Broken clutch cable or too much sag in the flexible clutch tube.

Tools and Materials: Phase I tool kit, wheel bearing grease, strong string, and a friend.

Parts: New clutch cable (and new clip pin for the Bus).

Step 1. Get Ready

Block the right side of the Type I or Type III, then jack it enough to get under it. Bus doesn't need jacking. Spread the ground cloth under the left rear axle. Roll under the rear and pull the old cable out of the clutch lever, right above the axle. With the vice grip clamped on the cable end to hold it, take the two nuts off the cable end with the 11mm and 14mm wrenches. Putting the new cable in is different for the Bus and Types I or III, so we'll start with the Bus.

Step 2. Install Clutch Cable

'67 and earlier Bus. Remove the pan between the front wheels, about ten 10mm bolts, then push the pan out of the way. **All.** Take the clip pin out of the clutch clevis (like two legs with a pin through the ankles) with a screwdriver. The pin pries up off the cable and out, unless it's broken, in which case you may have to knock it out with a punch. In any case, use the new pin when reassembling. Pull the old cable out of the tube, insert the adjustment bolt end into the tube and grab a small handful of wheel bearing grease to grease the cable as you put it in the tube. If the cable hangs up in the rear flex tube, roll back there to push and pull the flex tube out of its ends. Push the cable through it, then reinsert the flex tube into its ends. Check the sag in the tube now. It should sag a little over 3/4" and may need a washer or two on the back end to put in this amount of sag. Roll to the front and grease and push the cable all the way through. Smear some grease on the cable clevis and on the lever coming down from the clutch pedal. Put the clevis on and the new pin in, but leave the pan off until you've adjusted the clutch.

Roll to the rear and pull the clutch cable as high over everything else under the car (as close to the bottom of the Bus) as it will go, through the adjusting lever. Put the 14mm nut (or the wing nut) on the adjusting bolt cable end and adjust it until the free play at the clutch pedal is 1/2" to 3/4", then run the 11mm nut down hand tight to lock the two nuts together. Try the clutch action up front. OK? You're through for now, but you may have to readjust the clutch soon, as the new cable stretches. **Pre '68 Bus.** Replace the pan with the 10mm bolts.

Types I and III. The clutch cable runs through the tunnel in the floor of the car, so you start by taking out the floor mat. Then pull or unscrew the pin that holds the accelerator pedal to the floor, disconnect the accelerator cable from it and remove the accelerator pedal. Unscrew the two bolts that hold the clutch and brake pedal assembly to the tunnel and pull the pin on the clevis (that Y-shaped thing) that holds the rod to the master cylinder. Don't diddle with the clevis. Now pull the clutch pedal assembly forward (to hold the old clutch cable on the hook) and out. Pull the old clutch cable out of the tube and get ready to start the new one in, but rest, smoke, relax. There's a trick to the new move. I take the driver's seat out of the car so I can be where it was, but you may be smaller than I. An attack from the other side of the car works for a friend of mine, so take your own best hold.

However you do it, lay the coiled new cable under the driver's seat, or where it used to be, then get two fingers of your left hand in the tunnel hole pointing up and shove the thread end of the new cable into your two fingers, then start the cable and fingers into the tunnel hole. As you shove the

Step 2. (Cont'd.)

cable and fingers further in, move one of your fingers to the edge of the tube and slide the cable end along this guide finger into the tube. Don't shove until you're sure you've found the tube with the cable end, or you'll wish you had. Once it's started into the tube, pick up some wheel bearing grease in one hand and grease the cable as you push it through. Read the material about the flex tube in the Bus section as it applies to you, too. When the cable is through the tube and out toward the rear, you have to have help.

If you have dirty help, this friend can roll under the car to keep tension on the cable while you assemble the pedals into the tunnel. But, if you have clean help, like someone in white leather, find some strong string, thread it along the line of travel the cable will take, above everything else (as close to the bottom of the car as you can get it), then tie the string on the cable end and give your friend the string out the rear to pull on for tension while you install the pedal assembly in front.

This is what you do: grease the front cable end and hook it over the clutch arm (hook) that goes into the tunnel. Once it's hooked, it must have constant tension or you'll lose the whole thing, so have your friend hold tension while you set the pedal assembly into the hole in the tunnel and put the two bolts in. Tighten the bolts, then put the pin in the brake clevis the way you found it, hook up the accelerator cable and install the pin in the bottom of the accelerator pedal. Now you'd better go under the rear of the car to relieve your assistant. Hold the cable in constant rearward tension as you put the rear cable end into the clutch lever. Start the 14mm nut (or wing nut) on the bolt and run it down until the pedal free play is 1/2" to 3/4", then screw the 11mm nut down on top of the 14mm nut hand tight to lock them together. You always check the clutch pedal for free play with your hand, don't you? Replace the seat, if it's out, then the floor mat and jack the car down. You've installed a new clutch cable. The new cable will stretch, but you can adjust that out as it happens.

A little advice: If you always put in a new clutch plate when you overhaul the engine, the plate will last until the next overhaul, unless you ride the clutch (one of the deadly sins).

ADJUSTING AND BLEEDING THE CLUTCH FOR THE TYPE IV WITH A STICK SHIFT.

The Type IV with stick shift uses a master cylinder on the clutch pedal and a slave cylinder attached to the clutch throw-out arm to operate the clutch—plus the hose and tube necessary to connect the two. The master cylinder is mounted right over the clutch pedal with the piston directly connected to the pedal. The slave cylinder is mounted on top of the center of the trans axle housing and operates the clutch by pushing on a lever which is attached to the clutch assembly. The clutch itself is the same type used on the Bus, only the thing to operate is different.

The clutch is adjusted at the master cylinder over the clutch pedal. The pedal should travel about 1/4" before you feel any resistance. It shouldn't travel any more or less and is pretty touchy either way, so 1/4", OK? At the place where the push rod goes into the master cylinder there's a lock nut. If you loosen the lock nut and turn the rod, the rod will either get longer or shorter, thus adjusting the clutch play. Change the length of the rod in the direction you think it should move. Then loosen the clutch master cylinder bolts, push the cylinder forward and retighten the bolts. Try the clutch freeplay and repeat until there is just 1/4" freeplay in the pedal.

If the clutch gets mushy, it means there's air in the system. First you have to think about where the hell did the air get in? A leaky hose, a loose connection, a leaky cylinder? Is it time to recondition the whole system? If possible, do the reconditioning in conjunction with an engine removal. Believe me that slave cylinder is a bear to get at with the engine in the way, if not totally impossible. To even get at the fuel pump, you have to pull this engine. We suggest you give the job of reconditioning (rebuilding the cylinders), to an expert.

However, you can bleed the slave, if there's air in the system. You need a long piece of rubber or plastic hose, the right size to fit over the bleeder bolt. Don't do this without a hose or you'll smell like brake fluid for a week. Fill the brake fluid tank which is in the front compartment right in front of the clutch pedal with heavy duty brake fluid. In addition to the hose, you'll need a jar with enough fluid in it to cover the end of the hose—not too much, you're going to throw it away. Reach up over the transaxle just forward (FRONT) of the engine from the left hand side and find the bleeder bolt. This bolt should have a rubber cap on it to make it easy to find and to keep crud out of the system. Pull off the rubber cap, get your vice grip clamped on the bleeder bolt and first loosen then tighten it a little to get used to the action. Put one end of the hose on the end of the bleeder bolt and the other end of the hose into the brake fluid in the jar. Have your friend in the car press the clutch pedal to the floor slowly and hold it there a second to give you time to tighten the bleeder bolt, then let the clutch pedal up. Do a coupla practice runs then for real: Loosen the bleeder bolt just a little with the vice grip clamped on it, have your friend holler when the pedal is all the way down—slowly! Then you holler when you have the bleeder bolt tight so your friend knows when to let the clutch pedal up. Repeat until there are no air bubbles coming out of the hose into the jar. Tighten the bleeder bolt, and put the rubber cap back on and fill the tank with fresh brake fluid. Throw the fluid in the jar away. That's it.

From the Spanish Edition

GRINDS AND GROWLS (TRANSAXLE)

Transmission, Differential, Rear Axles

The operation of the Volkswagen transmission-differential (transaxle) is explained in Chapter II. It's a sturdy beast that works for a long time if you keep oil in it, like 200,000 to 250,000 miles before the first overhaul.

Every 3,000 miles have the trans oil checked at a service station...or check it yourself, (Chapter X). If it needs oil, use 90 weight hypoid oil—but not too much. Too much oil can blow the rear transmission seal right out on the first long hot trip you make, causing a bad case of leaky transmission. To fix it, you have to pull the engine. Don't let too much oil in the trans happen to you. Watch the gas station attendant (or yourself). This oil should be drained and replaced every spring if you're addicted to dusty roads. Every 30,000 miles is the official requirement. There's a drain plug and a fill plug under the car: the fill plug is halfway up the left side of the trans in front of the axle and the drain plug is at the bottom, rear of the trans. In the older models, the crescent wrench will remove the raised square plugs but for the fully synchronized models, you'll need a 17mm allen head wrench.

Pre 1968 Bus and Safari (The Thing—all years) have two transfer cases, one for each rear wheel, so you must drain and replace the oil in the transfer cases at the same time as you do the transmission oil—same oil, same wrench.

All Models: The troubles your transaxle can have with age are moaning, leaking and popping out of gear. When it's old and starting to moan, buy a transmission additive like STP for rejuvenation purposes. Turn the fill plug (same one as above) out of the trans case counterclockwise and pour the additive in. If the hypoid gear oil level is OK, put the plug back in. This may help those groans. It will make the gear shift work a lot easier.

If, with age, the gear shift starts to pop out of one or several gears or if it's hard to put into any gear, you have to face a transmission overhaul or sell the car. If it won't stay in gear, there's time before the trans gives up completely but watch the oil level in the trans box very closely, put in the trans additive and start collecting the bread for a rebuilding effort or for another car.

The trans overhaul is not in this book. Not only can't you do it but we won't either. We used to fix the old split case units but not any more. You have to be an expert and be in practice and we don't like to practice that much. Furthermore, the job requires tools you wouldn't even dream of owning so take your car to a transmission rebuilder who does a lot of Volksie work or to VW and find out what the job will cost. Choose your rebuilder carefully and make sure of a good job even if it costs more. A rebuilt trans never seems to give those 200,000-250,000 miles. If you keep oil in the works, you'll probably have time to earn the bread before the trans makes those terrible howls that mean, "This is the end, mate."

There is a procedure we've added to this chapter for Removing and Installing the Transaxle.

VW changed from swing axles to double jointed axles in different years for different models. To know what to do for your rear axle assembly, you first have to know what kind of rear axles your donkey has. If your Bus has a sliding door (1968 and on), it has double jointed axles. All Type IV's have double jointed axles and all Safari's have swing axles. Double joints started for the other Type I's and the Type III's about 1969. Here's how to tell for sure: look under the rear end of your car. There's an axle that goes between the transaxle and the rear wheels. If each of these axles has two rubber boots, one at each end or four altogether, your car has double jointed axles. If each axle has but one rubber boot next to the transmission or two all told—swing axles.

If your transaxle is leaking oil, the cause could be the above mentioned blown rear trans seal which can't be replaced without pulling the engine (see Mini Procedure, this Chapter). There is a leak you can fix, however. Tighten the trans case bolts (13mm) under the car...all you can see and reach.

Swing axles: There are two things you can do to fix a transaxle oil leak before pulling the engine. One is to replace the rear wheel seal (Procedure in this Chapter) and the other is to replace a leaky boot. There are two rubber boots with trans oil in them between the trans case and the rear axle tubes, one on each side. These boots rot out with time and to replace them is not even worth a procedure, it's so easy. You can tell by looking under the car if they're leaking and if one is, buy a new one at VW for your model. Jack up the Type I or III on the side with the leak and remove the wheel, then put a scissors jack under the shock absorber attachment point. You can crawl under the Bus without jacking it up. Clean the matted-on crud away from the boot area and cut the old boot off with the scout knife, then use the screwdriver to twist the old clamps off the trans and the drive tube and clean everything again. Install the new type split boot, clamp the big clamp on the larger end and the little clamp on the axle end and put the bolts, washers and nuts through the boot seam, which should be on the side (horizontal). That's all. **See Changes and New Ideas, #1.**

There's a procedure in this Chapter for your rear wheels which you must do if the rear wheel cylinders or seals leak, your rear wheels have play in any direction or you hear a hum that progresses into a growl (bad rear bearings).

Double jointed axles: If tightening the trans case bolts didn't fix your leak, it's off to the expert for the side transaxle seals or pull your engine to replace a leaky rear trans seal. Those rubber boots protect the constant velocity joints (universal joints) from dust and have nothing to do with an oil leak.

Practically everything **is** different about the drive unit which uses the double jointed axle. The wheel bearings are packed with lithium grease instead of with 90 wt. hypoid from the transmission. The constant velocity joints are also packed with special lithium grease, the kind with moly di-sulfide added.

Double joints bring you a new maintenance task and a greasy one to boot. Pack the CV's (constant velocity joints) every 15,000 miles and the rear wheel bearings at 30,000 miles. The first 30,000 pack of the rear wheel bearings can be done without pulling them (Type IV excepted) but at 60,000 the bearings must come out and be totally cleaned and inspected. If you do nothing but highway driving and have a Type I, III or IV, your CV's can probably go 30,000 miles between packings but the Bus owner should pack them every 15,000 miles. The packing is to keep from having to buy new CV's at about 45,000 miles and is just our advice so you do as you feel but with packing, they will last a lot longer. A new high whine coming from the rear is the sign to check your CV's for replacement per the procedure in this chapter which also covers the rear bearing work. Although the bearings rarely go bad as the CV's take the action. See **Chapter XX**, Rubber Everywhere. **Safari owners, see Changes and New Ideas, #2.**

MINI PROCEDURE FOR CHANGING THE REAR TRANSMISSION SEAL

Condition: There's heavy, sticky oil leaking out of where the engine and transmission join and you're sure it's not engine oil which is not heavy and sticky and smells different. If the leak is engine oil, chances are the engine should be pulled to change the front engine seal, anyway.

Materials: New seal for your chassis number.

Step 1. Remove Engine

As in Chapter XV.

Step 2. Remove Old Seal

Look at where the transmission pilot shaft (the splined shaft) comes out of the trans and you'll see the rubber seal. To get to it, you'll have to unhook the two wire clips on the throw-out bearing and pull the bearing off. Now put the end of a heel bar (a pry bar with a heel or elbow) between the inside of the seal and the pilot shaft and pry the seal out. It's not really an easy thing to do but you

Step 2. (Cont'd.)

can do it. The important thing is to make sure the seal does not slip back into the transmission as it'll be hell to get out. Just work at it. Tear it up, it doesn't matter, get it out.

Step 3. Install New Seal

Clean the inside of the transmission case and the hole the seal goes into. Put a little gasket glue in the lip of the seal hole and put the seal over the pilot shaft and start it into its hole. Use a small block of wood to tap the seal flush with the trans case. Now put the throw-out bearing back in place and replace the two clips.

Step 4. Install Engine

As in Chapter XV.

Remember, FRONT means front of the car, with LEFT the driver's side. And counterclockwise to loosen and clockwise to tighten, facing the nut, bolt, screw. OUTSIDE means out—toward where you are when removing lugs to change a tire. INSIDE means toward the center of the car—that is, underneath, between the two wheels.

REAR WHEEL PROCEDURE FOR SWING AXLES: REMOVAL, BEARINGS, SEALS AND INSTALLATION, Phase II

Condition: Leaky rear wheel cylinder, leaky rear seal and/or worn rear bearing or your car has one piece rear drums and you've been sent here from the Wheel Procedure in Chapter XI to remove the rear drums..

Tools and Materials: Phase II tool kit, a breaker bar or flex handle, 1'' pipe cheater 3' long, a two foot bar, Liquid Wrench, lots of blocks, transportation to the parts store, parts can, solvent, oil can and cleaning pan. You may need a wheel puller. Measure the nut on your rear axle and get a socket to fit it. (All models used to have a 36mm nut (1-7/16'') but now they come in three different sizes.) **Safari:** one pint 90 weight hypoid gear oil.

Parts: Cotter keys and, if needed: new seal, bearing, gaskets and "0" rings—all for your model.

Remarks: Please read the Wheel Procedure in Chapter XI so you can coordinate these activities with rear brake work or to replace the wheel cylinders. For whatever reason you're opening the rear wheels, check everything as you go along—you only want to remove the rear hubs once. For example: if you have a leaky seal, check the brake shoes and the rear axle bearing. If your brake linings are worn or you have a brake fluid leak, you must replace all four shoes or both wheel cylinders. But if you have an oil leak on one wheel, start with the leaky wheel because a bum bearing or a leaking seal on one side doesn't mean you need to replace them on both sides.

Step 1. Jack, Block and Check

Pick your worst wheel, block the other side of the car against rolling, pry the hub cap off and jack the wheel up far enough so it'll turn. Take the car out of gear and release the hand brake. Set your stool in position and turn the adjusting stars 10 to 12 notches loose with the medium screwdriver so the drum will come off over the shoes. If you don't know how, turn to Chapter XI and read the Brake Adjustment Procedure.

Step 1. (Cont'd.)

Roll the wheel and listen for the ballsy rumble that indicates a bad bearing. Grab the tire at 3 o'clock and 9 o'clock to push with one hand and pull with the other. If you find any play at all when you do this or if you heard that ballsy rumble, you have a bad rear wheel bearing so figure on replacing it. Now jack the wheel back down to the ground. Use the vice grip to remove the cotter key from the big axle nut—remember cotter keys while shopping for parts.

Step 2. Remove Rear Wheel, Drum and Hub

Composite drum models: If you're doing a rear brake job or cylinder replacement only, this step is not for you but if you're replacing rear seals or bearings, follow along.

Liberally apply Liquid Wrench to the large axle nut. Never loosen or tighten either of these large rear axle nuts unless all four wheels are on the ground and blocked. Find the large socket (usually 36mm), the big breaker bar and the pipe cheater. Fit the socket over the axle nut with the breaker bar (flex handle) on the socket and the cheater on the breaker, then lean, counterclockwise for both wheels. If this doesn't crack the axle nut loose, get a longer cheater bar. The further away from the nut you can get, the more force you can apply.

In Chapter XVI there is an alternate emergency method for Removing Large High Torque Nuts if you're out in the country or broke and can't afford to rent or buy the breaker bar or big socket.

* * * * * * * * * *

When the nut is loose, take it all the way off and try pulling the drum off with your hands. If it doesn't come and you're sure the adjusting stars are backed off enough so the shoes are loose, you'll have to rent a drum puller from the local rental place. There are two types of drum pullers but they both work the same. Bolt the large bell or arms to the drum (three bolts) and tighten the large center bolt and off comes the drum. See three armed puller sketch, Chapter XVI. **See Changes and New Ideas.**

When the wheel and drum are off, leave the wheel bolted to the drum and lay the assembly under the car as a safety. If the seal or wheel cylinder have been leaking, there may be a lot of cleaning to do on the wheel and drum.

Step 3. Replace Seal

Condition: The old rear wheel seal has been leaking oil.

No doubt the whole brake plate assembly is a dirty, oily mess, so clean it with rags and solvent. If you're working on a Bus or Safari, remove the bottom plug in the transfer case right next to the wheel with the 17mm Allen head or the 17mm bolt and vice grip. Let the oil drain out, replace the plug, and tighten it. All models: If the seal has been leaking badly, you have to look at the brake lining with a jaundiced eye to decide whether or not to replace the shoes.

Removal.

The first thing on the axle in the older models is a collar with a snout sticking out of the bottom of the brake plate. Pull it off and throw it into the cleaning pan. If you don't have this collar or have removed it, you're facing the bearing cover with the four bolts holding it on. The seal is inside of this bearing cover, but everything's too cruddy to remove anything, so take a few minutes to clean the area with solvent and a rag or two. With the area clean, remove the four bolts from the bearing cover with the 14mm socket on the long extension on the ratchet. You might need the cheater. (Bus and Safari: cover the wheel cylinder with a rag to protect it.) Pull and pry the bearing cover off the shaft and off the bearing. Leave the rest of the stuff on the axle for now, but dig or pry the seal out of the bearing cover. Don't try to knock it out from the closed side or you'll damage the oil slinger washer. Look at the oil slinger washer and if it's badly worn, put a new one on your shopping list. If you're satisfied with your bearing (no ballsy rumble, no play), copy your chassis number down so you can buy the correct parts for your model. See Chapter XVI to find your chassis number. If your rear cylinder(s) have been leaking brake fluid, go now to the Wheel Procedure, Chapter XI. . .rear cylinder work is the same as front cylinder work. And/or if your bearing is in question, do Step 4 in this Procedure now.

OK, off you go to VW to buy the seal, gasket, "0" rings and anything else you need. Take a pencil and paper with you and ask the parts person to show you a picture of your axle in the parts catalogue and copy it so you'll know how to put your model together. If they're real nice and have a copier right there, they might run a copy of the picture and give it to you.

You have all your parts and everything's clean. You left all that stuff on the axle when you went to shop, so now take it off piece by piece comparing it with your sketch or picture as you dismantle. If there are differences, use your sketch for the installation. Clean the old gasket off the brake plate.

Installation.

Whether or not you changed the bearing, it's in and in place correctly, right? Assemble the bearing cover first. There are two types, but they go together the same way: (1) in the older models, with a flat oil slinger outboard of the seal, and (2) with a combination spacer and oil slinger that goes through the bearing cover. Put the slinger washer or the combination slinger and spacer in the bearing cover first. The little inside bevel on the spacer goes inboard and the bigger part goes outboard. Oil the seal and start it in the bearing cover evenly all around, then press it in. A vice or a big clamp does a good job, but you can use a piece of flat wood on the seal and tap on the wood until the seal is flush. Then with the small hammer tap lightly on a screwdriver held upright around the outer edge of the seal to seat the seal into its shoulder. It goes a little past flush in the bearing cover. If the little round spring comes out of the seal, don't get shook—just put it back in. Put the bearing cover to one side.

Bus Models, about '63 and on, with the combination spacer: first put the little rubber "0" ring between the spacer and the bearing on the axle, then the new bearing cover itself with the oil hole down. Put the bolts in and torque them.

In the earlier Bus, first put the bearing cover gasket, then the big rubber "0" ring around the outside of the bearing; next, reassemble the axle. Next to the bearing fits a big thin washer, then a little "0" ring, then a spacer with the beveled side on the "0" ring, then the bearing cover oil hole down and finally, the bolts. If you have an oil dripper with a snout, put it on after the four bolts are torqued, with the snout going into the hole in the brake plate.

Type I and III: Put the gasket for the bearing cover on the brake plate, then put the big rubber "0" ring on the bearing. On the axle, next to the bearing, goes a large washer, then a gasket or "0" ring and finally a spacer. The spacer may be the one already in the bearing cover or it may be a separate one. Put on the bearing cover and the bolts. Torque the bolts and replace the oil dripper (if any); the snout goes into the hole in the brake plate.

All Models: Torque the four bolts to 36 ft. lbs. See Chapter XVI if you have questions about using a torque wrench. If the brake line is off, carefully replace it, then go to Step 5.

Safari and Bus: Remove the filler plug on the top of the transfer case with the 17mm allen head wrench.

Put 1/2 pint of 90 weight oil in the transfer case, then replace the filler plug and tighten it. Continue with Step 5.

Step 4. Remove and Install Bearing

Condition: You heard a ballsy rumble when turning the jacked-up wheel and/or had any play in the rear bearing when you did the push-pull test. If you have doubts about the bearing, pull it out per this Step and take it to an expert for examination. You are part way through Step 3. If you chose the hammer and vice-grip method, **wear safety glasses!**

Removal

Remove the brake line and pull the brake plate off. You need two good vice grips to get this bearing out so make sure yours clamp down hard and the jaw teeth are sharp. Clamp one vice grip on the top lip of the outer race of the bearing as tightly as you can and the other vice grip on the bottom lip of the outer race the same way. On top, put the two-foot bar between the brake plate (Bus) or end of the axle tube (Types I and III) and the vice grip and pry. On the bottom, use the big screwdriver the same way. As soon as the inner side of the bearing is out past the brake plate (or where it used to be), remove the vice grips and pry directly between the bearing and the shoulder. (Bus, you can put a block against the brake plate to pry against as the bearing comes a little way out.) Mostly the bearing pries right out but if you have a tough one and there are really tough ones, get some help, then find the axle nut and screw it on the axle shaft with the castellations in until the back of the nut is absolutely flush with the end of the axle shaft. (Bus: loosen the other bolts holding the brake plate on, not much, just enough to ease the bearing if it's binding on the plate.) Put both vice grips back onto the bearing lip as tight as you can, put the big bar on one and the big screwdriver on the other and pry a steady strain on the bearing while your buddy pops the axle end-nut combination with the big hammer. That'll get it. Remove the nut from the end of the shaft if you had to put it there, and work the old bearing out of the shaft.

If you find it too difficult to remove the rear wheel bearings using the vice grip method and don't want to rent a puller, try this reader's suggestion: **See Changes and New Ideas.**

In a hardware store buy two 6" x ⅜" bolts threaded at least half way. Nuts and washers also. Go home and hacksaw the hex heads off the bolts and grind the hacksawed ends so they look like this:

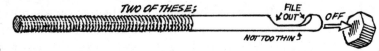

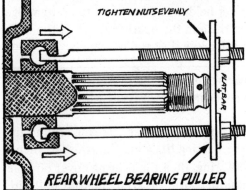

REAR WHEEL BEARING PULLER

Now get ahold of a piece of scrap iron about ¼" thick by 6" x 2". Take the two bolts and tip them into the outer race grooves of the bearing and make marks on the metal plate where the bolts meet it. Drill two ⅜" holes in the plate and slip it over the bolts. It should look like this:

Put the nuts on the bolts, tighten them down evenly and the bearing will slip off the axle.

Step 3. (Cont'd.)

Take the old bearing shopping with you. Buy one just like it, right down to the same numbers— or a damn good explanation why the numbers don't match. (Types I and III, buy a gasket to go between the brake plate and the axle housing.) If you put a new bearing in, you have to replace the seal so list all the parts, chassis number, etc., you need from Step 3 and go shopping. When you return, continue right here to install the new bearing.

We feel that inside of this bearing lies the area where you need an expert. In the Types I and III there's nothing left to foul up except the trans-differential but the Bus and Safari have those transfer cases. They rarely foul but when they do, let the experts do it.

Installation

Start the new bearing onto the shaft. The nylon ball cover goes inside and the numbers go outside. Use your dull chisel or a punch to drive the inner race of the bearing onto the shaft round and round the circle, then when the bearing enters the axle housing (Types I and III) or brake plate-axle housing (Bus), alternate—start tapping the outside race in also—like tap the outside race in one place, move to the inside race for a hit, back to a different place on the outside race and so on until the bearing seats in the housing and onto the shaft. You can hear it seat; both races will sound solid.

Types I and III: Install the new gasket between the brake plate and the axle tube, replace the brake plate but don't replace the brake line until after you've installed the bearing cap. Go back to Step 3 to install the new seal.

Bus: Tighten up the brake plate bolts if you had to loosen them, then return to Step 3 and install the new seal.

Step 5. Install Wheel, Drum and Hub

That's the name of the Step but first you have to check absolutely everything to make sure all the work is done and everything is tight. Especially check the hand brake assembly (Chapter XI) to see that it's together right and operating. The cable should be hooked onto the lever, the pin in the bottom, the little spring lock on the pin, and the push bar connected from the lever to the front shoe. Try the hand brake—easy—to see if the system is working.

Wipe the splines on the axle shaft with a rag that's been dipped in solvent and clean any crud out of the splines. Make sure the brake shoes are centered. Pull the wheel and drum out from under the car and clean and shine the drum. (If you have composite drums and they're not on the hubs, push them on now, install the two cap screws and tighten them with the allen head.)

Start the hub on the splines of the axle and shove until you can get the big axle nut started, castellations out. When the nut's started, get the big socket and breaker bar on it to turn it fairly tight. If you've worked on both wheels, go to the other side and bring it up to this point before you try to tighten either big axle nut.

Remove the blocks, then jack the car down on the tires. Now, you really have to twist the large axle nut, so never try to tighten it unless all four wheels are on the ground. Put the socket on the nut with the breaker bar on the socket and the cheater on the breaker bar (or flex handle) and bear down on the cheater. When it's as tight as you can get it (220 ft. lbs.), (Bus 253 ft. lbs.), check the hole in the axle to see if it's clear of the castellations, and if it is and you know the nut is really tight, put the new cotter key in and spread the ends. If the hole in the axle doesn't want to line up with the hole in the castellated nut, try a little harder. Use a longer cheater. If all else fails, back the nut off the least little tad until the holes line up so you can put the new cotter key in the hole. Spread the ends on the cotter key. **See Changes and New Ideas.**

Step 6. Finish Up

Adjust the brakes and bleed them per the Brake Adjustment Procedure in Chapter XI. The

Step 6. (Cont'd.)

hand brake adjustment can be made now, if you've put in a new cable or if yours needs adjustment (Chapter XI). Put the hubcaps on, clean your tools, the area and yourself and take the car on the road to see how it flies.

REAR WHEEL PROCEDURE FOR DOUBLE JOINTED AXLES: REMOVAL, BEARINGS, SEALS, CONSTANT VELOCITY JOINTS (CV'S) AND INSTALLATIONS, Phase II

Condition: 15,000 or 30,000 mile maintenance (CV's and bearings), worn rear wheel bearings or CV's or you've been sent here from Chapter XI to remove your rear drums, because they're not composite drums.

Tools and Materials: Phase II tool kit, a heavy hammer (3-4 lbs.), a small ball peen hammer (8-16 oz.), a breaker bar or flex handle, 1'' pipe cheater 3' long, a 2' bar, Liquid Wrench, lots of blocks, transportation to the parts store, parts can (plastic baggies), 4 large plastic bags, masking tape, solvent, oil can and cleaning pan, grease gun and grease injector (not for Type IV), a tube of lithium wheel bearing grease and two tubes of CV grease (from VW). Measure the large nut (or bolt, Type IV) on your rear axle and get a socket to fit it. Take your 6mm allen head wrench, crawl under the car and try it in the heads of the cap screws that hold the ends of the axles to the trans or to the wheels. If the allen head wrench fits, you need a 3/8'' drive, 6mm allen head wrench (or key) to fit your ratchet. If the 6mm allen head doesn't fit, count the splines on the inside of the bolt head and get a 3/8'' drive, 8 or 12 spline key. Get any of these from a special tool place like Snap On or other.

Parts: Cotter keys and if needed: new seal, bearing, gaskets and "O" rings, CV's, boots, boot clamps—for your model.

Remarks: Please read Chapter XI so you can coordinate rear brake and cylinder work with what you're doing now.

Step 1. Check Play and Remove Driveshafts (Axles)

You don't need to jack up a Bus, but jack any thing else up enough to get under it, tires still touching the ground. Spread out a ground cloth and put on your stocking cap. Roll under the rear of the car and grab the axle shaft near one CV with both hands.

Try to move the shaft forward and backward. There should be no play. If you have play, mark the joint with masking tape. Now push it sideways (toward the wheel and back). Play here is necessary. . .part of the action. If you hear a lot of noise in any direction, mark the joint with masking tape. Repeat this action for all four joints and mark any that have play where they shouldn't or are noisy. One or more of the CV joints will probably be OK for you to use as a comparison.

Put your 6mm allen head (or 8 or 12 spline) special tool on the ratchet and remove the six cap screws and plates on each end of the axle, 24 in all, then pull down to tilt the axle and it will come out. (Some Type IV's have two guide pins, four cap screws and four plates.) Don't let the CV's touch the ground before you put a plastic bag on each, well masking taped so the plastic for sure, stays on. Repeat for the other rear axle. Put both axles where they won't get kicked around and go on to Step 2 unless you're packing or replacing CV-s only, in which case go to Step 8.

Step 2. Check Rear Wheel Bearings.

Block the front wheels (Bus, too) and jack the rear wheel so the tire's off the ground. Turn the adjusting stars all the way loose (Chapter XI) so the brake shoes are not touching the drum. Now you can roll the wheel around with your hand to listen to that tumbly ballsy rumble that means new bearings are needed. Try the wheel for horizontal and vertical play and if there's play in any direction, consider a new bearing for that wheel and for sure new seals for both wheels.

Step 3. Remove Rear Wheel, Drum and Hub.

Note: You don't have to remove the hub if you have composite drums to do brake work.

All Models: Go to Step 2, Rear Wheel Procedure for Swing Axles and do the work until your rear axle nut(s) are loose. Remember to jack down the car so the tires are solidly on the ground while loosening the nut(s). **Types I, II and III**, do the whole step, then return here to Step 4.

Type IV: You have an axle bolt rather than a nut and must knock down the ears on the lock plate before loosening the large axle bolt. Return here after the row of stars. OK?

Axle bolt loose? Now loosen the lug nuts or bolts and jack up the wheel you're going to work on first. Take out the lugs and remove the wheel and throw it under the car for a safety. Then unscrew the allen head cap screws that hold the drum to the hub. Adjusting stars still loose? OK, remove the drum—just pull it off. Now remove the large axle bolt you loosened and you can pull the hub (half of wheel axle) off from the outside and the other half of the wheel axle off from the inside (under the car). Use the large screwdriver or bar to pull the two halves apart and out of the seals. Put them to be cleaned and the large bolt and the allen head screws into a bag.

Step 4. Remove Seals and Bearings.

If you remove the bearings, it's very important to keep them separate, so if you put them back, you can put a bearing back exactly where it came from. Outside means where you remove the lugs when changing a flat and inside means under the car, between the two rear wheels. OK?

Types I, II and III: Hold a block of wood on the outside end of the axle and hit the wood with the large hammer to knock the wheel axle toward the inside, out of the seals and bearings. Pick up the wheel axle and spacer (if any) and put them together to be cleaned. Keep them together.

Types I, III and IV: Disconnect the brake line from the brake plate, then remove the four bolts that hold the bearing retainer on the outside of the brake plate. Take the bearing retainer off with the axle spacer. Put retainer and spacer together in a bag. Type IV has no spacer. Pull the brake plate off complete with shoes, hand brake cable, all still on it and hang it up out of the way with some wire.

All Models: Remove the two seals. Type I, III and IV, one seal in the bearing retainer you took off to get the brake plate off and in the Type II, the outside seal is in the bearing carrier itself. The inside seal is in the inside of the carrier in all models. Use two screwdrivers to pry these seals free and don't damage the metal where the seals fit. Types I, III and IV, note how the seal fits into the bearing retainer.

Types I, II and III: 30,000 mile maintenance. You can grease your inside bearing without removing it from the carrier (the thing the wheel axle fits in). Bus owners can also grease their outside bearing without removing it by pulling the inside race (a plain cylinder) toward the outside. Types I and III can slip the inside race of the outside bearing out of the carrier for inspection and greasing. Wipe as much grease as you can off the bearings inside the carrier and inspect the bearings for worn spots, cracks, bad rollers and black spots. If the bearings are free of any of these diseases, go to Step 8. If the bearings are worn, continue here.

Types I, II and III, 60,000 mile maintenance or worn bearings: There are circlips holding the bearings in the carrier. Types I and III have one circlip on the inside and the Bus has two, one inside and one outside. Use a pair of thin nosed pliers or circlip pliers and fit the pliers into the holes on the circlip, squeeze the circlip together and pull it (or them, Bus) out. There's a roller bearing on the outside and a ball bearing on the inside. The ball bearing will stay in one piece but the roller bearing will come apart.

Types I and III: From the outside, pull the inside race of the roller bearing and the spacer off with your fingers. Leave the outer race of the roller bearing in the carrier. Still from the outside, use the hammer on the punch on the outer race of the ball bearing and knock it toward the inside. Tap round and round the race, little by little. Take your time, just hit the outer race and don't damage the bearing. It will come out.

Type II: Slip under the car and with the hammer on the punch tap out the spacer and the solid inner race of the roller bearing. It will fall toward the outside. Still from under the car, being careful not to tap on the solid part of the outer race of the roller bearing, tap the roller bearing, round and round, toward the outside. You are tapping through the inside bearing. Get out from under and from the outside, tap on the outer race of the ball bearing until it comes out, toward the inside.

Type IV: has no circlips and two roller bearings. Slip under the car to knock out the inner race of the outer bearing with the hammer handle or the hammer on a long punch, then from the outside knock the spacer and the inner race of the inner bearing out of the carrier (toward the inside). Leave the two outer races in the carrier.

Step 5. Clean, Inspect and Shop

All Models

Clean all the bearings with solvent until they shine, then let them dry—don't dry by spinning them with an air hose, it will hurt them. Now become an inspector and inspect each part of your rear bearing system with a jaundiced eye. Look for flaws: galling, cracks, pits, black or blue. Any defect in a bearing surface and the bearing must be replaced. Remember what noises you heard as you turned the wheel and try to find the source of the noise. If the bearings check out OK, fine, but if they don't, replace them. When you go shopping, take your chassis number (Chapter XVI to find where it is) and the old seals and/or bearings with you. The seals must be replaced. If you're going to replace a roller bearing, you have to knock out the outer race of the bearing with the hammer and the punch so you can take the whole thing. Don't forget the lithium wheel bearing grease while shopping. In addition, Type IV needs two rubber "0" rings, a large one for the bearing retainer and a small one for the long bolt plus two new lock plates. Types I and III need one large rubber "0" ring for the bearing retainer and two new cotter keys. The Bus just needs the cotter keys.

Before going shopping, do Steps 8a and 8b to inspect the CV's to see if you need anything from there in addition to the CV grease. Clean everything in solvent.

Step 6. Grease and Install Bearings and Seals

OK, you're back from shopping and everything you're going to put back is spotless.

Types I, II and III; 30,000 mile maintenance: Fill your grease gun with lithium bearing grease and put the grease injector on your gun. It's that little thing that works like a cake decorator. Start with the inside bearing, so from under the car, put the point of the grease injector in between each ball, all around the circle and pump the bearing full. Smoosh grease into every nook and cranny in the carrier with your finger, install the inside seal with the spring or open side into the carrier, then tap the flat side flush with the carrier. Once the seal is in, smoosh some more. **Types I and III**, go to Step 7. **Bus**: you have to do this to the outside roller bearing as well. Check to see the spacer's in, slip on the inner race so the numbers are facing you, then install the outside seal and smoosh. Go to Step 7. Types I and III: with a palm full of grease and the bearing on a finger of the other hand, push the bearing into the grease until the rollers are as full of grease as possible.

Types I, II and III: 60,000 mile maintenance or new bearings and Type IV: Put two tablespoons of grease in the center of the carrier, then install the spacer.

Step 6. (Cont'd.)

Grease all the bearings: put about a tablespoon of grease in the palm of one hand and with the bearing in the other, smoosh the bearing into the grease to get as much as you can between the balls or rollers and the metal holding them. Pack the bearings with all the grease you can get into them— the more, the better. It's a good idea to use the grease injector on the ball bearings even if they're out of the car. **Types I, II and III**: put the ball bearing in from the inside and use the hammer on a wooden block to tap the bearing in flush (numbers facing you). Now, use the hammer on the punch on the outer race of this same bearing to tap it into its seat. You can hear it when it seats. Install the circlip with the pliers. If the circlip won't fit, you have to tap the bearing in some more. Install the inside seal with the spring (or open) side toward the bearing and tap it in flush with the block of wood. Go to the outside. **Type II**: the outer race of your outer (roller) bearing has the rollers in it. Start the greased bearing into the carrier with the rollers facing you and tap it flush with the block of wood, then with the punch along the outer rim, tap it into its seat with the hammer. Install the outer circlip, then the seal (spring or open end toward the bearing). Tap the seal flush using the hammer on the block of wood. Install the inner race, numbers facing you. **Type IV**: Install the outer race of the inner bearing (it's still there, if you didn't buy a new one) from under the car. Put the greased inner race into the outer race, install the seal with the open or spring end facing the bearing and tap it in with a hammer on a block of wood until it's flush. **Types I, III and IV**: from the outside, install the outer race of the outer bearing (it's still there, if you didn't buy a new one). Install the new outer seal into the bearing retainer (not on the car). The open part of the seal faces the bearing or out of the retainer. Tap the seal in flush, then lay this assembly aside. Untie the brake plate, check the shoes for wear and brush it clean (it doesn't need to be spotless). Put the plate on the carrier, put the greased bearing into the race in the carrier and put the "0" ring on the retainer so it seals the retainer to the brake plate. Now put the retainer on the brake plate, open part of seal toward the bearing. Put the four lock washers and bolts on and tighten them with the socket assembly, then torque them to 43 ft. lbs. See Chapter XVI on how to torque, if you have questions.

Step 7. Install Rear Wheel, Drum and Hub

Types I and III: Install the spacer on the outside of the wheel axle (the spacer you packed away with the wheel axle). **Types I, II and III**, start the wheel axle into the inside seal of the carrier and tap it through to the outside. **Types I and III** have a spacer you stored with the bearing retainer, slip it onto the wheel axle from the outside and push it into the retainer. **Type II** may or may not have a spacer to go on the wheel axle at this point. If you took one off, put one back on. You stored it with the wheel axle. **Types I, II and III**, go to Step 5, Rear Wheel Procedure for Swing Axles and do the whole step (you have to hold the wheels with the brakes to tighten the nuts). Come back here to Step 8c or 8d.

Type IV: the wheel shaft is in two pieces, so put the inside piece (that part that bolts to the CV) through the inside seal and the outside piece through the outside seal and push them together. The seals are new, so it may be a tough shove. When they meet, rotate one so the splines slip together. There should be grease on the splines, which the male spline will pick up as it goes through the greasy hub. When the splines are joined, find the long hub bolt and first put on the new lock plate (so it can lock the bolt head), then the spacer, then the little rubber "0" ring. Put the bolt in the hole while you hold the inside part of the wheel shaft and tighten the bolt as tight as you can with the wrench, holding the shaft with your hand. It cannot be torqued until the tire is on the ground. With the wheels on the ground, torque the bolt to 100 ft. lbs., then jack the wheel up and try the torque; it should read 2 ft. lbs. (or barely off center). If it's more or less, let the wheel back down and tighten or loosen the bolt so the torque wrench reads 2 ft. lbs. when the tire is off the ground. Bend the lock plate ears. Go to Step 8c or 8d.

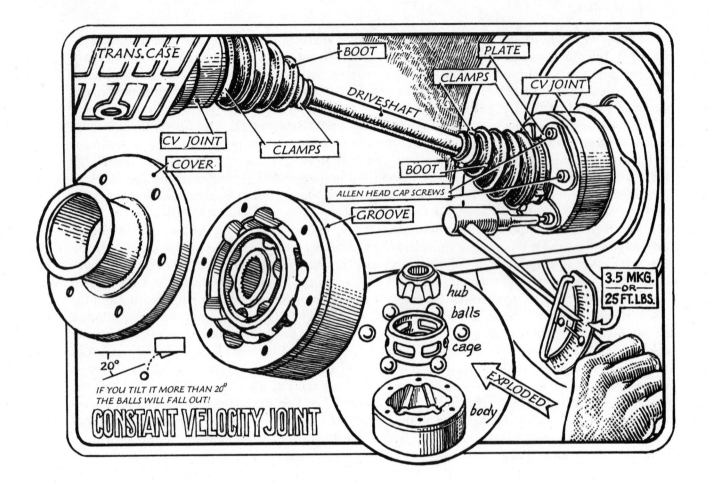

TRANS. CASE   BOOT   PLATE   CLAMPS   CV JOINT   DRIVESHAFT   CV JOINT   COVER   CLAMPS   BOOT   ALLEN HEAD CAP SCREWS   GROOVE   3.5 MKG. OR 25 FT. LBS.   hub   balls   cage   body   EXPLODED

20°
IF YOU TILT IT MORE THAN 20°
THE BALLS WILL FALL OUT!

CONSTANT VELOCITY JOINT

Step 8. MINI PROCEDURE FOR CONSTANT VELOCITY JOINTS (CV'S)

Condition: You checked, then removed your CV's in Step 1 and the suspicious ones are marked with tape.

Start with the most suspicious CV and work where no one will mind a little grease; an old table covered with plastic would be perfect. This is one of the greasiest jobs connected with VW's. It's nice to have a friend to hold things while you work. **See Changes and New Ideas.**

Step 8a. Disassembly

With the vice grip, bend the little tit that holds the boot clamp together, remove the boot clamp and slide the boot down out of the way. If you have the new type CV boots, the boot is permanently fastened to the metal plate so all the above is unnecessary. Take the hammer and the punch or drift and gently knock the metal cover off the CV—don't beat it up. Get the cover and the boot pushed down a little without unfastening the small clamp on the boot, then tilt the CV toward the axis of the driveshaft (axle) until the balls are free. Pop the balls out with your finger or a small screwdriver and pop them into the cleaning pan—NEVER DO MORE THAN ONE CV AT A TIME! Now you can pull the body (outside part) and the cage off and put them into the pan. Clean the entire assembly with the brush and solvent. Clean the grease out of the boot and make the whole end of the driveshaft shine with your efforts. Clean the balls, cage and body of the CV. When everything is clean, put the balls in the body on the table.

Step 8b. Inspection and Decision

Look at the balls first. They are the heart of the CV operation. If they're bright and shiny with no pits or gouges, look at the body, cage and hub. But if the balls are OK, the other parts are usually not worn. There will be shiny spots where the balls work back and forth but there should be no grooves. If you have good balls with no worn spots and everything is clean, put a piece of tape on the shaft and on the outside part of the CV and write ''1'' on both pieces of tape. Then do this Step to the other end of the joint. Leave the balls corralled in the body or put the whole thing away but don't get them mixed up with any other CV balls. If you determine that you have good CV's, go shopping for the stuff you need in Step 5, then do Steps 6 and 7 and 8d.

However, if your balls are black or blue instead of shiny, inspect them for signs of wear or marks of any kind and look over the body, cage and hub very carefully for grooves and deep wear marks because you have to make the decision of whether to buy new CV's or not. If the balls are marked at all, you need a new joint. You can replace them one at a time. However, they cost a lot so the decision is not a light one. If your balls are black but not marked, you might get another few thousand miles out of the CV before it cracks and destroys itself. If you keep them greased, they last longer, like maybe 100,000 instead of 45,000 to 60,000 miles. If you have a bum CV, you can replace it now or a little later; it doesn't matter unless the balls are really scored and marked. Carry a new one and the grease with you and when the old one starts to make a lot of noise, just stop and replace it. Try not to do it in a dust storm, however.

Now you have a boot decision to make. If the boots feel flexible and have no holes or cracks, they will probably last a long time. If you have to buy new boots, remember to buy new clamps. You can buy screw type clamps for these boots but they cost more. If you buy new boots, VW sells a neat combination boot and metal cap that is a definite improvement over the old type.

If you're going to replace one or more CV's now, add what you need from here onto your shopping list in Step 5. After shopping, do Steps 6 and 7, then come here to Step 8c.

Step 8c. Remove CV's from Driveshaft and Install.

First, you have to take out the circlip that holds the CV hub on the driveshaft. If you have a circlip pliers it's easy but two small screwdrivers will get it out. Caution: snap rings can fly. Push one side open and get the other screwdriver point into the gap you are making, then work the circlip out little by little until it comes off the end of the shaft. Now a special puller or bench press would be nice. But if you don't have either one, use a vise as a fork to support the edge of the hub, but not so tight that it grips the driveshaft. Get a large punch or drift to fit the end of the driveshaft then knock the shaft out of the hub with the large hammer on the punch or drift. Remember safety goggles and watch that shaft; it can hurt your foot if it falls on it. There is a dished washer under the hub on the driveshaft; don't lose it as it must go under the new CV.

If you're replacing the boots, make sure the two new small boot clamps are in the center of the driveshaft. Outside of the clamps come the new boots facing toward the ends of the shaft, then the two metal caps.

You're ready to install the new CV on the driveshaft. Don't take the CV apart. Put the dished washer on the shaft so the open dished part faces the CV, then put the other end of the driveshaft (which may or may not have a CV on it...depends on if you're replacing this CV, too) onto a clean surface. Start the CV on the driveshaft so that groove (see sketch) on the body of the CV faces in toward the driveshaft. With your friend holding the shaft erect, take the big hammer and a block of wood and drive the CV down on the shaft. When it's flush, use the big socket, one that will fit over the end of the shaft, to drive the CV down to where the circlip groove is open.

Install the circlip in its groove using the two screwdrivers to force it down. Then, with the large vice grip, squeeze the circlip tightly into its groove. Look at it to make sure the circlip is well seated. Do the other end.

Step 8d. Install Body, Cage and Balls and Grease CV's

If you just put on a new CV, you can skip this first part and go on to greasing. To assemble a CV that's been apart for cleaning, first lightly grease the balls and cage. Then put the hub inside the cage. The numbers on the hub and cage must be on the same side and this side faces in toward the driveshaft. Have your friend hold the boot back out of the way. Now hold the body over the hub (with the groove on the body toward the driveshaft) at an angle of about 30 degrees to the axis of the shaft. Then start pushing the balls into the hub. They will go in with a little click. Rotate the shaft so you're always putting the ball into the top. Rotate the body so there's always a place to snap a ball into a hole in the hub. When all the balls are in, the body can be rotated over the balls until it covers them completely. It usually takes a little banging with the heel of the hand to get the body to fit over the balls. Assemble the other CV. Go to Step 8c and install the assembled CV on the driveshaft.

After the driveshaft has been assembled with 2 CV's, you're **ready to grease.** Stand the shaft on its end, have your friend help you hold the shaft erect and the boot out of the way. You're going to use a whole 14 oz. tube of CV grease on these two joints. You can use a putty knife, a table knife or your fingers to pack the grease into the bearings. Pack four good tablespoons full into the bearing under the boot. Press it into the bearings well and clean your tool or fingers off by scraping the grease off inside the boot. Turn the shaft over and put four tablespoons of grease in the other joint under the boot. Now pack two tablespoons into the open end of the joint that's now on top. Push it in well, then smooth it off and put any extra grease into the open boot. Make sure the table is clean, then turn the axle over and pack two tablespoons into the other open CV joint. Pack all the excess grease from the tube into the boots evenly divided—what a mess!

boot. Now pack two tablespoons into the open end of the joint that's now on top, Push it in well, then smooth it off and put any extra grease into the open boot. Make sure the table has some clean paper towels, then turn the axle over and pack two tablespoons into the other open CV joint. Pack all the excess grease from the tube into the boots evenly divided—what a mess!

Now get two cap screws from the cleaned pile, put them through the CV from the open end and push the metal cap down over them so you're sure all the cap screws will fit when you're under the car. Tap the metal cap onto the joint with the small hammer until it is down all around. Turn the shaft over, put the cap screws in and tap the metal cap down on the other CV. If you have the new type boots you can go on to fastening the small ends of the boots. With the old type boots, you have to clean all the surfaces which are about to be joined until both the inside of the boot and the outside of the metal cap are clean, then slip the boot over the metal cap and install the clamps. Pull the clamp together until the little tit comes through one of the slots. If it does this and the clamp is tight, bend the little tit over to hold the clamp. If you've not undone the small boot clamps, the shaft is ready to be covered with plastic and go to the car. But if the small clamps aren't on they go like this: make sure the small end of the boot is between the two grooves on the shaft, then slip the new clamp over the end of the boot. Use the vice grip to cinch the two raised places on the clamp together and the deed is done.

With the CV's greased, the metal caps and boots well fastened, put the plastic bags over the CV's and you're ready to install them in the car.

Step 8e. Install CV's in Car and Torque

Don't jack the car up any further than you have to to get under it and work as it makes the angle of the CV's more extreme. The wheels have to be free to move, however. Assemble a plate, two washers and two cap screws—assemble them all and put them into the hub cap. Get under the car with the joints and cap screw assemblies and position the CV's so they'll fit on the trans and on the wheel axle. Put them into their places and get the handiest pair of cap screw assemblies in and started. You must have a washer between each cap screw and the plate. If you don't, stop everything until you find all the washers that go under the cap screws. When the first pair of cap screws are started, start another pair and another and another until all the cap screws, washers and plates are started into

Step 8e. (Cont'd.)

both ends of the shaft. There'll be six pairs, except some Type IV's have just two pairs. When all the cap screws are started, do the other shaft. With both ends of the driveshaft installed, put the special allen head or spline key on the 3/8" ratchet and tighten all the cap screws around the circle until they are all (12 at a time) as tight as you can get them with the small ratchet—you will appreciate this when you start to torque them. Your friend can be very helpful by sitting on the outside of the wheel, turning it and holding it as you direct. When the cap screws are all tight, you can start torquing them to 25 foot pounds with the special key on the torque wrench. Torque them all around the circle, then check the first one again to make sure they all have 25 foot pounds of torque. The Type IV's with four cap screws, require 31 foot pounds. When both axles are in and the cap screws torqued, you'll find that it's way past dinner time and your arms feel like two hunks of beaten lead. Clean up the horrible mess you made, wash up and take your friend out to dinner, you've done a good full day's work. But first do Step 6, Wheel Procedure for Swing Axles.

When we go to Mexico, we take a spare CV for our Bus and two tubes of grease which you have to be careful how you store.

PROCEDURE FOR REMOVING THE TRANSAXLE

Condition: The obvious condition for replacing the transaxle is: the old one has locked up, pops out of gear or is making serious rumblings indicating an impending disaster.

If the car has been making a clunking sound as you let the clutch out, it's likely that the front trans mount is broken. You don't have to pull the trans all the way out to replace the mount so do the steps up to taking the trans out, and just pull it back a few inches. This will give you enough room to replace the mount if it's broken.

As far as replacing the transaxle goes you have two ways to go. You can either have the old one rebuilt, which depends on its condition. If it's really shot, the cost of rebuilding it will probably be real high. The other choice is to find a good used one in a wrecking yard. The problem here is that you never really know what kind of shape it's in until it is in your car and on the road. Make an agreement with whomever you buy it from that you'll get a full refund if it doesn't work right and all you'll be out is for all that labor. Look over the vehicle you're going to pull the replacement trans from to get a general idea of the shape it's in. If it's a low mileage, well-kept vehicle, go for it. As far as buying a new trans, it's very expensive.

If you decide on a used trans, there are a few considerations to make. The big consideration, of course, is that the trans has to fit your vehicle with a minimum of adaption. Find one as close to yours in year and model as possible. When you think you've found one, measure the distance between the two inside edges of the axle housing flange. This is the flange that the brake backing plate bolts onto. The two must have the same measurements here. Also look at the rubber mount on the front of the trans. Is it the same as yours? If the new one isn't the same as your old one, see if your old one will fit on the new transaxle. If it doesn't, get the numbers off the new trans and take your old mount down to VW and see if they can fix you up with a gearshift housing that will make it work. The gearshift housing is the frontmost aluminum part that the rubber mount bolts onto.

Swing axle transaxles and double jointed transaxles cannot be switched. The double jointed axle came out in '69 on the Types I and III and in '68 on the Type II. The Type IV's have always had them. All Safaris (Things) have swing axles. You can find a further explanation of swing and double jointed axles in Chapter 14.

The pre-68, Type II transaxles cannot be switched with the Types I and III unless the trans is disassembled and the ring gear is turned around. Otherwise, you'd have four speeds reverse and one very low forward gear.

Tools and Materials: Phase 2 tool kit, 27 mm (1-1/16") socket—except automatics and Type IV. All double jointed axle people need a 6 mm 8 or 12 spline socket, 3/8" drive.

New rubber axle boots (swing axles only). New lockplates for axle housing (swing axles only). New front rubber mount if your old one is broken or cracked. Make a note of anything else that might need replacing as you go, like the clutch cable, broken bolts, brake shoes and like that.

Step 1. Remove Engine

Get the car on a level place to work, take it out of gear, hand brake off, and turn to Chapter 15 to do the engine removal procedure for your model.

Step 2. Remove Rear Brake Drums

Block each side of both front tires and pop the rear hubcaps off with a large screwdriver. Turn to Chapter 14, Step 2, remove rear drums and do it. When you're through with that step make sure the car is jacked up and the wheels are well blocked. Put jackstands, wood blocks or anything substantial under the jackpoints or torsion bar tubes so long as they're not under the trans itself.

Step 3. Disconnect Rear Brake Hoses and Brake Cables—Swing Axles Only.

Look right in back of the brake drum where you'll find the brake backing plate. Out of the backing plate comes the brake hose. See it? This hose is either attached by a tab on the spring plate or the axle tube. If it's on the spring plate (the long metal bar connecting the axle housing to the torsion bar in the frame), grab an 11 mm wrench and remove the fitting that faces the rear. If the hose is attached to the axle tube, you'll need a 15 mm to hold the inside fitting while you turn the other one all the way out with an 11 mm wrench. Now with a punch, drive off the horseshoe shaped clip holding the remaining hose on the tab. Get your head out of the way, the clip is likely to spring off. Do the same on the other side and put the clips in a marked baggie.

The easiest way to detach the hand brake cable is to take it loose from the hand brake lever up front...lift the rubber dust cover off from around the hand brake lever and with one 10 mm wrench hold one of the bottom nuts and break the top one loose with another 10 mm. Remove all four nuts from the ends of the brake cables. Push both cables through the compensating bar and get back under the rear of the car. Put both hands around the brake cable housing where it comes out from the body and give a tug. Pull them both out all the way. Put the nuts into a baggie.

Step 4. Remove Axle Housing from Spring Plate—Swing Axle Only

The spring plate is attached to the axle housing right behind the brake backing plate by three (four—pre '68 Type II) 19 mm bolts and nuts. Types I and III, if you're going to have your old trans rebuilt, get a sharp chisel and hammer and make a clear chisel mark just above the top bolt that holds the spring plate to the axle housing. The mark should go across both the axle housing flange and the spring plate. This mark will be your guide to realign the rear wheels when you put the trans back in.

Bend the locking tabs over on the axle housing bolts with a screwdriver until you can get the 19 mm socket on all the way. Use the 19 mm socket to turn one side and a 19 mm wrench to hold the other side. Remove all the bolts, nuts, washers, rubber stops, brake line brackets and whatever else is attached through these holes. Put them all in a marked baggie.

Step 4. (Cont'd.)

Remove the nuts on the bottom shock absorber bolts with a 17 mm wrench and socket and drive the bolts out of the shock eye with a punch. Put the bolts back through the shocks and the nuts and washers back on.

Step 4. Remove CV Joints—Double Jointed Axles Only

Look at the sketch on page 224 and you'll see where the CV joint is. You only have to remove the CV joint at the transaxle end unless you want to move the vehicle while the transaxle is out, in which case you'll want to take the other end off also. To check CV joints, run the Rear Wheel Procedure for Double Jointed Axles in this chapter. Make a note of all worn parts and replace them.

Put your 6 mm allen head socket on the ratchet and remove the six cap screws and plates on the transaxle end of the axle (some Type IV's have two guide pins, four cap screws, and four plates). Pull the CV out of the way being careful to keep it off the ground while you put a plastic bag or two around the CV. Get a rubber band around the bag to keep it there. Wire the CV up to the body with some bailing wire so it's out of the way. Put the bolts in a baggie.

Automatics Only—Separate the transaxle fluid line at the right heater box. There are two banjo unions at the right rear of the engine; remove both of these.

Step 5. Remove Electrical Connections and Clutch Cable

The starter motor is the heavy black cylinder located on the top right side of the transaxle. Use a 13 mm wrench to remove the nuts holding the heavy wire to the starter solenoid. Pull the wire(s) off and replace the nut and washer on the starter post. The ground cable on the battery should have been disconnected in the engine removal procedure, but if it isn't, do it now, OK? There are either one or two more small wires on the solenoid, so get them off.

Automatics—There are a few more wires on the trans so get them off. Make a diagram or you won't remember how to get them back on!

Everyone has a clutch cable to remove *except Type IV's and Automatics*. The clutch cable runs through a lever on the top left side of the transaxle. If you're not sure where it is, have a friend depress the clutch while you look at what moves in back. Squirt some penetrating oil on the threads and clamp a pair of vice grips on the solid part of the cable. If your cable has a wing nut on the end, turn it all the way off with your thumb and forefinger. If you have the older model with two nuts on the cable use a 14 mm wrench to hold the front nut and an 11 mm wrench to remove the locknut. Turn the 14 mm nut all the way off also.

Pull the cable end through the lever. The cable is also held by a bracket further forward on the trans. Put both hands on the cable in front of the bracket and pull down and to the front, until the metal sleeve on the cable comes out of the holder. Pull the cable all the way through the holder. Replace the nut(s) on the cable.

Step 5a. Disconnect Pressure Line from Clutch Slave Cylinder—Type IV Only.

The clutch slave cylinder is the gizmo right on top of the transaxle with the steel tube going to it. With an 11 mm open end wrench, disconnect the fitting on the tube.

Step 6. Disconnect Shift Rod and Mount

On the Type I, the shift rod coupling is under the back seat, below the sheet metal plate with the chassis numbers next to it. On the Types II, III and IV the coupling is under the car, right in front of where the engine and transaxle join. The coupling is exposed on the Type II, but everyone else has to remove some screw(s) and take the cover plate off to expose it.

Step 6. (Cont'd.)

There should be a safety wire through the square head bolts on the coupling. Cut the wire on the bolt closest to the transaxle and pull it out. Use a pair of vice grips to loosen the bolt enough so that when you move the gearshift lever around, the coupling comes off.

The front mount is that bonded rubber, metal thing where the transaxle attaches to the frame. Remove the two 17 mm nuts and washers from the mount. Take the ground strap off also. Put the nuts and washers in a marked baggie.

Step 7. Remove Rear Transaxle Mount

Place a floorjack or some solid blocks under the drain plug of the transaxle. The only thing **holding the trans in now are the rear carrier bolts. The carrier is that U shaped bracket supporting the rear of the transaxle. Remove the bolts with a 27 mm (1-1/16'') socket and breaker bar. Counter** clockwise to loosen. Put the bolts and washers in a marked baggie.

1972 and on Type II—the rear carrier bolts are on the top of the trans.

Step 8. Remove Transaxle

It's best to have either a floorjack or a couple of strong friends to help with this part. If you have a floorjack, lift the trans up from under the drain plug and roll the trans back until it can be lowered. If you're doing it by hand, get one person on each side with someone in back, then lift it and slide it out onto some blocks. Roll the car forward and get the trans down off the blocks.

PROCEDURE FOR INSTALLING THE TRANSAXLE

Step 1. Install Transaxle

The transaxle should be ready to go. The front mount, rear carrier, if any, starter motor, brakes and all that is on, right? If you don't have a floorjack, two friends work just as well.

Slide the transaxle under the engine compartment on the floorjack or by hand. Lift it up and into the trans cradle (the yoke shaped extension of the frame). If your trans has swing axles, you'll have to help the axle up over the cradle.

Now you sort of have to do a balancing act between guiding the front rubber mount onto the studs, the shift rod onto the coupling and the axle housing flanges onto the spring plates. One person can do it, but it's a lot easier with two. If it doesn't want to go all the way in, the shift rod is probably not going into the coupling so slide under the car and align it while you push it home. Once it's there, put the ground strap back on the front mount stud and replace the nuts and washers. Tighten them with a 17 mm socket and torque wrench to 14 ft. lbs.

Put some wheel bearing grease on the threads of the 27 mm bolts and start them into their holes in the carrier. You'll probably have to pull the trans up a bit to get them started. Torque these bolts to 166 ft. lbs. Don't forget the big spring washers.

Step 2. Install Spring Plates on Axle Housing—Swing Axles Only

Pull the axle housings into place so the bolt holes line up with the holes in the spring plates. Start the bolts into the holes so the nuts face toward the outside. Install new lockplates for the bolts.

Step 2. (Cont'd.)

Don't forget to replace any rubber stops, brake line brackets or whatever your model has bolted on through these holes. (If you're using your old trans, line the punch marks up on the spring plate and axle housing flange.) Put the washers and nuts on and torque them to 80 ft. lbs. Bend the tabs over on the new lockplates with a punch.

Pull the shock absorbers down, take the bolts out and knock them through the flange on the axle housing. Tighten the nuts firmly.

Step 2. Install CV Joints—Double Jointed Axles Only

Get two plates, lock washers and allen head bolts out of the baggie. Unwire the axle from the frame and swing it into position on the trans end. Put all the bolts in and tighten them around in a circle as tight as you can with a 3/8" drive ratchet. Torque them around in a circle to 25 ft. lbs.

Step 3. Install Electrical Connections and Clutch Cable

Put the heavy wire(s) back on the big starter solenoid terminal and replace the washers and nuts. Push the small wire(s) on their connection. If your trans has a backup light switch, push the wire back on it and put the dust cover in place. Automatics have a few more wires, so put them back as marked.

Not for Automatics—or Type IV—Stick the clutch cable first through the holder bracket, then through the clutch lever. Now put one hand on the middle of the clutch cable tube and pull it down while your other hand pokes the metal sleeve on the end of the tube into the holder bracket. Turn to Chapter 13, Step 3, Adjust Clutch Tube, and do it.

Replace the wing nut or the 14 mm and 11 mm nuts as the case may be and crank them down about half way for now. Brush the threads on the cable end with a wire brush and squirt some penetrating oil on them.

Automatics—Replace the fluid hose connection by the right heater box and the two banjo connections by the right rear of the engine.

Type IV—Screw the fitting back onto the clutch slave cylinder located on the top rear of the transaxle. Be very careful not to strip the threads.

Step 4. Replace Shift Rod Coupling

Slide under the car and get hold of the coupling with one hand. Line up the hole with the dimple in the shift rod coming out of the trans. When it's lined up, put the square head bolt back into the hole and crank it down with a vice grip. Turn it as tight as you can as it should be torqued to 25 ft. lbs. Make sure the bolt seats properly in the dimple. Run a new piece of mechanic's wire through the hole in the bolt and the coupling itself and twist the wire to lock it all in place. Replace the cover (if any) and screw.

Step 5. Replace Brake Hose and Brake Cables—Swing Axles Only

If your brake hose holding tab is bolted to the spring plate, just screw the fitting back in with an 11mm wrench and tighten firmly. Be careful not to strip it. If the tab is on the axle, push the front hose into the tab and screw the fitting in with an 11mm wrench as you hold the other end with a 15mm. When the fitting is tight, drive the horse-shoe clip back into the groove with a hammer until it locks in place.

Push the hand brake cables back through the holes in the frame you took them out of. Push them as far as you can, then go up front to the hand brake lever. Pull the cables through the compensating bar and replace the four 10mm nuts (two on each cable). Turn to Chapter 11, page 179 to adjust the hand brake.

Step 6. **Finish Up, Engine In**

Clean up the mess around the car making sure you haven't forgotten anything. If your car has swing axles and you want to replace the rubber axle boots, now's the time to do it. Here's how:

If your axle boots are one solid piece (original equipment), cut the two clamps with a pair of side cutters and rip the boot off. If you have the split type boot (replacement), unscrew the nuts and take off the bolts and washers. Unscrew the clamps and remove the old boot. Put the new boot on with the seam (split) facing either to the top or to the side. If the boot doesn't fit over the frame, jack the axle up a bit and it will. Put on all the bolts and washers and tighten the nuts. Put on the screw clamps and tighten them down.

Now, put the wheels back on and tighten the lug bolts. If you suspect the rear trans seal is leaking, turn to Chapter 14 and run the Mini Procedure for changing it. Make sure the throw-out bearing is in place.

To finish, turn to Chapter 15 and install the engine. Whew!

Juniperus Scopulorum

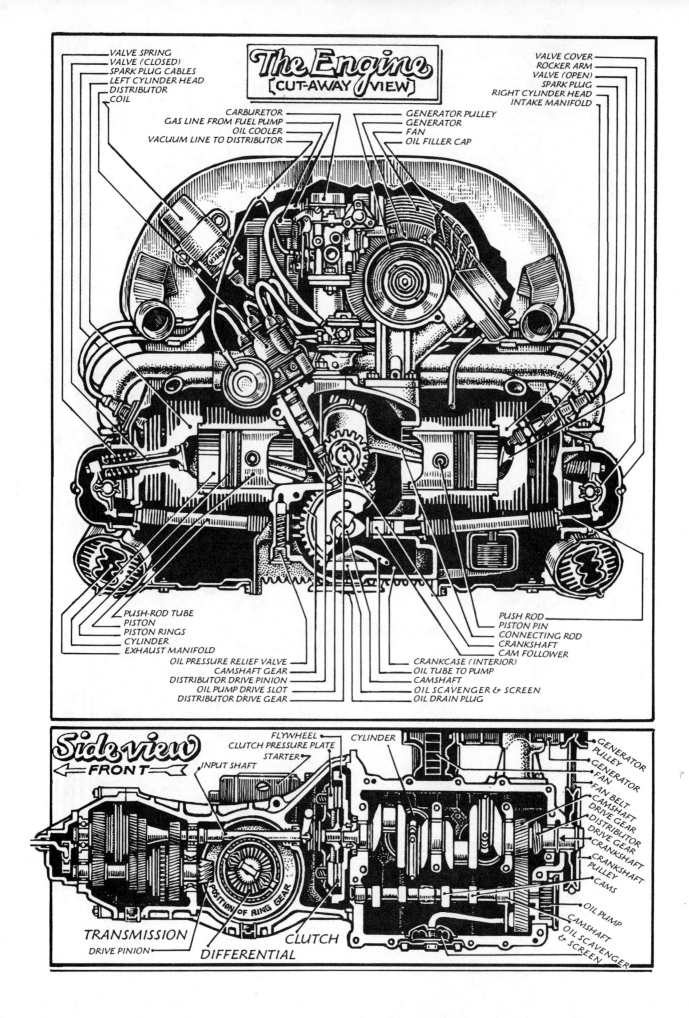

The Engine [CUT-AWAY] VIEW

VALVE SPRING
VALVE (CLOSED)
SPARK PLUG CABLES
LEFT CYLINDER HEAD
DISTRIBUTOR
COIL

CARBURETOR
GAS LINE FROM FUEL PUMP
OIL COOLER
VACUUM LINE TO DISTRIBUTOR

GENERATOR PULLEY
GENERATOR
FAN
OIL FILLER CAP

VALVE COVER
ROCKER ARM
VALVE (OPEN)
SPARK PLUG
RIGHT CYLINDER HEAD
INTAKE MANIFOLD

PUSH-ROD TUBE
PISTON
PISTON RINGS
CYLINDER
EXHAUST MANIFOLD

OIL PRESSURE RELIEF VALVE
CAMSHAFT GEAR
DISTRIBUTOR DRIVE PINION
OIL PUMP DRIVE SLOT
DISTRIBUTOR DRIVE GEAR

PUSH ROD
PISTON PIN
CONNECTING ROD
CRANKSHAFT
CAM FOLLOWER

CRANKCASE (INTERIOR)
OIL TUBE TO PUMP
CAMSHAFT
OIL SCAVENGER & SCREEN
OIL DRAIN PLUG

Side view
← FRONT →

FLYWHEEL
CLUTCH PRESSURE PLATE
STARTER
INPUT SHAFT

CYLINDER

GENERATOR PULLEY
GENERATOR
FAN
FAN BELT
CAMSHAFT DRIVE GEAR
DISTRIBUTOR DRIVE GEAR
CRANKSHAFT
CRANKSHAFT PULLEY
CAMS
OIL PUMP
CAMSHAFT
OIL SCAVENGER & SCREEN

POSITION OF RING GEAR

TRANSMISSION
DRIVE PINION

DIFFERENTIAL

CLUTCH

CHAPTER XV

ENGINE OVERHAUL

Back in the Red Dog Saloon era, there was a garage in Carson City run by a sympathetic super mechanic named Muldoon. When you were pushed into Muldoon's, he looked and listened to your sick engine, asked how far you needed to go and how much bread you had, then he nodded his head and showed you where you could work on your engine out back. When you ran into problems, he left his profitable highway trade to give you a hand. You made it to where you needed to go, but God help you if you tried to drive fifty miles further. We tell you about Muldoon because he has the type of genius an indigent VW owner needs when it comes emergency time—the ability to balance the available bread and labor against the immediate mileage requirement.

In an emergency, the Volkswagen reacts well to any scrambling on your part to keep it going, but you really have to keep your promises to it. Muldoon's last words as you drove away were, "Don't forget to get that fixed right when you get there." You're on the road from New York to L.A., seventy-five bucks is all you got, you're near Santa Fe running on three cylinders with an engine that's overheating badly—like that. Don't give up and thumb, but do a compression check. 95 pounds in three cylinders, but No. 3 tests zero? Sounds like a burned valve, so find a place and go to work. Pull the engine, take off the tin, remove the heads and carry them to the machine shop (do both heads even if you go hungry on the rest of the trip). Have the valves ground and a new valve put in. Reassemble and install the engine and you can probably make it to L.A.

You may have found a broken piston when the heads came off, so scramble a used piston, use your old rings—all these things are possible, but explain to your car that these are temporary measures and that you'll fix her when she gets you to L.A. Then keep your promises because the burned valve was just an indication that your engine's at the end of a wear cycle.

There are two extremes to the "How To Run a Car" theory. One end is to keep running and take care of breakdowns as they happen. When using this end of the theory, always carry plenty of spare parts along with tools, but even then do a little anticipating, so you're not in the 120° open sun but in the cottonwoods on a river bank. I sometimes start a trip in a poorly running car and finish with one in perfect condition.

The other end of the theory is to keep the car in perfect tune, overhaul it a week before the rod goes and then overhaul everything. If you have the bread and your goal is to drive a car with a trouble-free engine, do all the overhaul procedures in this chapter and replace not only the used-up parts, but the borderline ones as well. However, there is bread to consider and sometimes availability of parts, like a stuck valve twenty miles west of Yuma, so often it's necessary to fix as little as possible to get running again. This chapter is organized to allow you to work either end of the theory you want or somewhere in between.

How can you tell your engine needs an overhaul before it gives its last gasp? Well, mileage is one indication. The VW directly reflects your driving and maintenance care. The well-maintained engine in the Types I, III & IV gives 100,000 miles before an overhaul is needed, but if you haven't warmed it up in the mornings and stopped to cool it in the mountains, 60,000 is closer. 50,000 is good for the careless owner who doesn't adjust the valves often or change the oil when necessary. Then there are the drivers who get about 14,000 miles, because they're always over-or under-revving, but then they should be driving a high horsepower monster, anyway, not a Volksie.

A transporter gives about 2/3 of the above mileage figures, because it's geared lower and has to work harder. If you haven't had your VW long and don't know the care the engine's had you have only your external sensory experience and the compression check to tell you where it's at.

Due to the materials used in the valves in the 1600 on engines, we recommend you have a valve job at 35,000 to 40,000 miles and replace with sodium filled stellite valves and the new hard brass valve guides.

Compression Test Evaluation

The following evaluation is really dependent on the state of your battery. Is it cranking the engine over quickly like it should? Is it a little slow? Or real slow? The faster the engine spins, the higher the compression will be. The figures here are based on a fully charged battery, cranking system in good order. If you're at a high elevation, your readings will be a little lower (say 5 pounds lower at 7,000 feet).

A compression test is made on a warm engine with the valves adjusted by taking out all the spark plugs, inserting the rubber end of the compression tester in No. 1 spark plug hole and holding it well-seated while a friend turns the engine over with the key. Have your friend turn the engine enough times so you can feel six impulses on the tester. Write down the figure the dial indicates for No. 1, then do No. 2, No. 3 and No. 4. If they were all below 95 pounds, squirt oil into each spark plug hole, turn the engine over three or four times with the key to get the oil splashed around on the cylinder wall, then take the compresion test again. Making a compression test is simple enough but what does it tell you? Raw data needs evaluation.

OK, if your cylinders were all over 100 pounds with no great differences between them, your valves and rings are doing their jobs well and this, with no information to the contrary, tells you that your engine will last a long time. If one cylinder tested higher than the others, it usually doesn't affect the engine much but does provide a place of imbalance. However, if three of your cylinders tested from 110 to 115 pounds, while the other tested low, like 100 lbs. or less, you probably have an exhaust valve seating improperly in that cylinder. We'd try to get it loose by running a quart of diesel or Bardahl through the carb, run a thousand miles, then take another compression test. (You can't do this if your car is fuel injected.) If the same cylinder tests lower like 95 pounds, I suggest you start getting ready to do a valve job, as that valve isn't improving and one of these days it'll stick, put that cylinder out of operation and soon damage the rest of the engine.

If squirting oil around jumped the compression in the low cylinder up substantially (say 10 lbs.) the rings are wearing badly in that cylinder and you need to think about new rings all around. If the compression tested less than 90 pounds in all cylinders and the squirting of oil raised it sharply, the rings are worn and you need an overhaul. If the compression tested low all around and oil didn't change it much, the valves need work. If the compression tested zero in any one cylinder, your engine has a stuck valve, a broken piston or a broken ring (not quite zero). If the compression tested below 90 lbs., your engine is imminently in need of an overhaul and anything below 80 lbs. is dangerous due to overheating caused by low compression and blow-by.

Other Diagnostic Considerations

The number of miles on the engine, the dirt collected in the engine compartment, having to shift to third on hills you used to make in fourth, are all considerations to add to the compression test data to help you decide about doing an overhaul. If an engine has had lots of miles put on it, since it was last new, you can have high compression checks but still may need an overhaul. This happened to my Bus. The compression was 115 lbs. all around but the engine had 65,000 miles on it. One day it heated going up a steep hill to Santa Fe and the green light leered sinisterly at me from the dash so I immediately pulled over, like the book says, to let it cool. This heating happened several times but I kept thinking about those high compression test results and couldn't believe my engine needed an overhaul—then started a little pecking noise. Well the upshot was I overhauled **and** learned a lot. The rings and valves were holding their compression but a .008" feeler blade fit between the top ring and its groove which means the pistons were really worn out. So what I learned was that a compression test is a good guide to the condition of the rings and valves but when an engine has a lot of miles on it, the two items of info have to be added together. The deciding factor that made me do the above overhaul was a new noise, a tick-tick-tickety-tick in the engine when the accelerator was lifted just after a hill pull: a rod making its throwing song, like a rattlesnake about to strike.

Which brings us to **noises.** If you'll listen to your engine when it's running well, it'll make a pattern in your brain that, when altered, gives you an uneasy feeling. Trace this uneasy feeling and if you find it came from an engine noise change, adjust the valves. Sometimes a valve or one of the rocker arm assemblies will loosen and make a change in the sound of the engine. If the noise is still there after the valve adjustment, you may be hearing a rod starting to knock and you'll want to verify, so start the engine and let it idle until it's warm. Place your stool behind it and sit with all your senses alive. Push the throttle lever to run up to high revs, hold it there for a full minute (count to sixty slowly), then relax just a bit on the lever and listen for a tick-tick-tickety-tick at the instant you relax the lever. Do this several times and listen hard for a rod knock. If you catch it at this stage, you, not the rod, can decide when and where to do the overhaul. You may have a week of very careful driving left before the rod goes completely.

Another way to test for rod noise is to take the car out on the road and either get it up to 35 or 40 in third or take it up a small hill to put the engine under a load, then relax the pedal and listen hard for that rod knock. A rod already thrown makes a very loud clunkety-clunk-clunk like all the metal pieces in the engine compartment are being thrown at each other at high speed. If you ever hear this noise, stop immediately and do not drive. You may be able to save your crankcase, a very expensive piece of your engine. **See Chapter XX, Tune-ups.**

A broken ring sounds like a noisy rod but goes all the time, like a gigantic locust, but mach nicht, you still have to pull the engine and overhaul the little beauty.

The main bearings are very massive in the VW and seldom give exterior indications of noise but sometimes one of them will get bad enough to knock and when it does, it makes a heavy sound, clunk-clunk-clunk, when the engine is under load, like going up hill a little under-revved (lugging). The sound is rather like deep organ notes on a good hi-fi and is more felt than heard.

Loose head nuts can make your engine sound like Thor is hammering around in there. For this you don't have to pull the engine, just take off the valve cover and the two bolts that hold the rocker arms, remove the rocker arms and torque the head nuts to 22-23 ft. lbs.

A flickering green light at fast idle is a sign of an engine wearing out. The wear could be in the main bearings, cam bearings or in the oil pump but wherever it is, your engine needs the complete overhaul including disassembling the crankcase.

Two obvious indications for overhaul are smoke out the exhaust pipes and all that oil you've been feeding the beast but these symptoms show up in the compression test and in overheating.

When the engine fails to pick up rpm satisfactorily after it has been tuned, you should inspect a malfunctioning accelerator pump or a plugged heat riser. The symptom is a period of hesitation after you've pushed down on the accelerator to speed up the car. It's very evident on the freeway. If, when you push your right foot down, the car seems almost to slow down before it gradually picks up speed and if your accelerator pump is working properly and the car is timed correctly, a plugged heat riser is the diagnosis. A plugged heat riser will cause a rod to burn. So if you're getting the symptom of a plugged heat riser, take off the intake manifold (engine in car) to see if the heat riser tube is plugged. If it is, unplug it (see Engine Removal Procedure for Type III, Step 9, this chapter) and you have saved an overhaul.

Now you know when to overhaul but what if you don't want to do the work yourself? Read the Procedures anyway so you'll know what to ask for and what to pay for. Small shops doing VW work have sprung up all over the world and the choice is yours. Some of them charge a flat labor rate plus parts. Try to find a shop that'll charge you wholesale for the parts. One suggestion is to take your car and this book to a friend whom you know to be handy with tools and trade bread (or whatever) for an overhaul. Another suggestion: remove your engine at home, take all the tin and accessory things off it, then haul it down to an auto machine shop where you've already made an appointment and let the machinist overhaul your engine. When it's done, pick up the engine, replace the accessories and tin and install the engine in your car. The authorized dealers do good careful overhauls with a guarantee but these are expensive.

Then there's what we call the dirty overhauler, who will charge quite a bit less, like what a complete overhaul costs just in parts. To make out, these people cut corners like mad, use old pistons and cylinders when they're marginal, omit new exhaust guides when they're needed and like that. They overhaul to their guarantee.

Find out what the parts and machine work will cost you for a complete overhaul per this book. Add the cost of rebuilding the starter and generator.

How long does an overhaul take? We figure one full day removal, dismantling, crankcase disassembly and taking the parts to the machine shop, two full days in the machine shop (a good time to clean parts), and two days to reassemble and install. This amounts to three days' work and full days, mind you, on our part. An amateur will take longer.

When John Counter, who'd never had a car tool in his hands before, overhauled his 40 hp engine, he was teaching school in the mornings so he couldn't start mechanicking until about 2:00 pm. It took him four days to the machine shop, three days in the machine shop, then one afternoon of staring at his engine completely apart in the box. Reassembly took him six days but he stuck to it. Fortunately, his lady had a car so he wasn't hurting for transportation. After his engine was installed, it wouldn't run but we found that everyone had forgotten to tighten the spark plugs. Then it would not run correctly but the next day we found that No. 1 and No. 2 spark plug wires had gotten switched so he uncrossed them and it's still running well after a trip to L.A. and back. But why not?

Please look over Chapter XVIII to help you decide what changes (if any) you might like to do to make your engine last longer or go faster or both. The information is there, but the procedures for doing the actual work are here.

ENGINE OVERHAUL PROCEDURES, Phase II

These Procedures consist of:

1. Engine Removal and Stripping. Type I (all) and Type II (through 1971)
2. Engine Removal and Stripping, Type III
3. Engine Removal and Stripping, Type IV and Type II, 1972 and on
4. Engine Dismantling (to the crankcase), All Models
5. Crankcase Disassembly, All Models
6. Crankcase Assembly, All Models
7. Engine Mantling (from the crankcase), All Models
8. Engine Equipment Assembly and Installation, Type I (all) and Type II (through 1971)
9. Engine Equipment Assembly and Installation, Type III
10. Engine Equipment Assembly and Installation, Type IV and Type II, 1972 and on

Condition: With the above organization, you not only can follow the work for your own model but also can remove the engine to do less than a complete overhaul like, 1) put in a new clutch, if it's worn, 2) replace the rear transmission seal, if you found it was leaking (Chapter XIV), 3) install a new front engine seal, if it's leaking, 4) and/or an oil cooler, 5) do a valve job only, 6) a valve, ring and cylinder job or 7) a complete, renew everything overhaul. Read each condition before doing the work to see if the Step or Procedure pertains to what you're doing. If you've decided on the complete gung-ho overhaul, do as many of the Steps as bread allows: a new clutch plate and front seal, starter overhaul, generator overhaul, like that. If you've thrown a rod or almost thrown a rod and torn any metal off the rod inserts or if you're planning on changing from non-detergent to detergent oil, you must buy a new oil cooler. The old one is full of metal filings and grit which will circulate throughout your new, clean engine and cause you to overhaul again in 15,000 miles instead of 60,000 or more. If you pull the cylinders, always put in new paper gaskets.

Tools and Materials: Phase II tool kit, two scissors jacks, blocks (wood, cement and/or bricks), pieces of plywood scrap, a couple of 2 x 4's, pencils and paper, paper bags (like grocery bags), a roll of baggies, masking tape, indelible Mark-All, small butane torch, oil drain pan, rags, Liquid Wrench, a gallon of solvent, pan to clean parts, a small roll of soft wire is handy, a rubber hammer, an inspector's magnet, a roll of emery cloth and an electric drill and bits available to make some holes. **Except automatic transmission,** a four foot piece of angle iron. **For double jointed rear axle models, including automatic transmission:** 4 to 5 feet of chain strong enough to hold the engine and a couple of hooks and bolts to fasten the chain and a 40" long piece of 2" x 4" board. **Automatic trans only:** an 18" piece of flat bar with a hole in one end.

Parts: The actual parts you need will become part of your shopping list as you go. You must write down your engine and chassis number to take with you when shopping for parts. Taking the old part itself is a great help.

Remarks: Over a thousand people have written to tell us like, "Thank you for leading me through a successful overhaul...I was a compleat idiot but I did it." We've also had some letters (many fewer) saying like, "I got stuck in the middle and had to find a mechanic...all those parts and nuts and bolts!" To help these latter people, we're telling you to put parts, like hoses and stuff in paper bags as you take them off and mark the bag, indelibly, like "hose from air cleaner to breather pipe," and when you take off the breather pipe, have your friend clean it and throw it into the same grocery bag. Clean any nuts, bolts, screws, etc., from the same assembly (by running them through solvent), put them into a baggie together, mark the baggie and put it into the same paper bag. Hoses, like snakes, have two ends so when you remove a hose, mark where each end attaches like "AC" (air cleaner) to "Breather." This marking method should help you avoid having to take a basket case to a mechanic. It also has the advantage of allowing you to get familiar with the various parts and fasteners making up the thing you ride in. It'll take more time this way but is more certain. You might even write a letter to VW and scream at them, "Please, put no more hoses on your cars! It takes too many paper bags." That'll shake them up.

If you know all the parts and can identify the nuts and bolts by sight, don't do this but if you can't, please do it as it may make the difference between success and failure. We will remind you as we go along but you have to remember, too.

The main reason for unsuccessful overhauls was getting nuts and bolts all mixed up...the bags and baggie trip should fix that. The other reason was missing a step or sometimes just a sentence so read carefully. The majority who go through carefully from Step to Step do overhauls that are as durable as any you can buy. TRUST YOURSELF, IT'S THE ONLY WAY TO FLY!

Get Ready: Please read Orientation in Chapter VII, all of Chapters I and IV and enough of Chapter XVI to find where your engine and chassis numbers are for buying the right parts. How to use a torque wrench and ways of removing obstinate nuts, bolts, etc., are also in Chapter XVI. Read the procedures through in this Chapter, first before doing anything. If your car is fuel injected, read Fuel Injection, Chapter X, as well.

To loosen a nut or bolt, turn it COUNTERCLOCKWISE, facing the nut or bolt. CLOCKWISE to tighten, OK?

Front means FRONT OF THE CAR, with LEFT the driver's side. This goes for the engine and all parts whether they're in or out of the car so the front of the engine is the flywheel end.

You'll need a friend with a car to take you and your engine to the machine shop, around to parts houses, read you steps, clean parts, be a third and fourth hand and to just keep you company. You may need some muscular help to take the engine out and put it back in.

If possible, drive your car to a car wash and give the engine a bath. Clean underneath as well as in the engine compartment and the job won't be nearly so enervatingly greasy. See Changes & New Ideas.

Park your car on a flat place where you can push it forward to clear the engine after it's detached, like facing out of the garage. Block the front wheels, take the car out of gear and have your bags, baggies and oil drain pan ready.

A Reader's Suggestion: If you paint your shrouding all different colors while waiting for the machine shop work to be done, it not only makes assembly easier, but makes you grin a little when you check the oil and fan belt tension in the morning.

Notes: If you drop anything during the procedures, even a washer, stop work and find it immediately. If it has disappeared or was missing in the first place, make a note on your shopping list to buy a new whatever.

PROCEDURE FOR ENGINE REMOVAL AND STRIPPING, TYPE I AND TYPE II THROUGH 1971

Step 1. Engine Compartment

Type I: Prop lid up really well so it can't bust you one.

Bus: Prop the lid. In the older models a good idea is to remove the useless latch on the side of the compartment, put the lid all the way up and drop the rear window/door over it to hold it. Remove the six bolts holding the bumper onto the bumper brackets and remove the bumper from the brackets. Put all the bolts into a baggie. Use the 13 or 14mm socket on the short extension on the ratchet to take the four bolts, two on each side, (the ones looking you in the eye if you're sitting on

Step 1. (Cont'd.)

your stool) out of the rear engine compartment brace (the rearmost flat piece of metal that seals the engine compartment). With the 10mm open end or the screwdriver, remove the two screws or bolts in the front part of this brace (FRONT MEANS FRONT), then carefully pry the rubber weather-stripping out of the brace and tape the rubber out of the way. In the older models, the back brace will now come out. In the '68 and on, you'll have to remove the four bolts from the rear engine carrier underneath the car (under the rear brace), then remove the brace. Make sure the scissors jack or blocks are under the engine. You don't want to get squashed.

Step 2. Drain Oil

Put the oil drain pan under the center of the engine, then, with the 21mm wrench, remove the oil drain plug from the center bottom of the engine. (36 hp: it's to the left of center.) Drain the oil into the pan and let it drop for now. COUNTERCLOCKWISE TO LOOSEN, CLOCKWISE TO TIGHTEN, FACING THE NUT OR BOLT. If the oil drain plug is stripped, loosen and remove the six 10mm nuts around the plate, then take the entire oil screen assembly off and put a new oil screen and plate on your parts shopping list.

Step 3. Electrical Disconnection

Disconnect the ground strap, the flat, webbed metal strap that runs from the battery to the frame. Remove the bolt connecting the strap to the frame. In the Type I, look under the back seat; in the Bus, it's on the right side in the engine compartment. Place your stool facing the engine and sit.

VERY IMPORTANT: Later, to reconnect the wires, you do so by number, using this Step, so write each number with Mark-All on a piece of masking tape and attach the tape firmly to its corresponding wire. All your wire connections will be either push-ons or screw-ons. For the push-ons, just pull them off, carefully, but for the screw-ons, unscrew the connection, remove the wire, tape it and replace the screw on its connection so it doesn't get lost. If any push-ons or screw-ons are missing, put some on your shopping list.

Find the oil sensor underneath the distributor, the plastic thing with the six-sided nut that activates the oil light on the dash. Remove the wire attached to it and mark it J4. Find the coil, the black cylinder bolted to the fan housing. There are three wires coming off the end of it. Disconnect the large one that goes from the center of the coil to the center of the distributor cap but leave it on the distributor cap. You may need a pair of pliers to pull this wire off the coil. No need to tape it. Disconnect the thin wire from the coil to the distributor and mark it. Disconnect the wire from the other side of the coil and mark it 15+. This same wire runs around to the right side of the carburetor (except for manual choke). If you have one wire on the right of the carburetor, disconnect and mark it 01 (automatic choke). If you have two wires on the right of the carb, mark the second one to the electromagnetic cut-off jet underneath the automatic choke 02. All three of these connections, 15+, 01 and 02 are shoots off the same main wire.

If your voltage regulator, that square black box, is on top of the generator, there'll be two connections coming out of the right side of the box. *Do not disturb* the two connections going down into the generator from the rear of the voltage regulator. Disconnect the thin wire to the rear on the right side of the voltage regulator (closest to you) and mark it 61. This is the generator light wire. Disconnect the one or two heavy wires from the front on the right side of the voltage regulator and mark them both B+. If your voltage regulator is not mounted on top of the generator, but is like under the back seat, you'll have two wires coming out of the top of the generator that go to the voltage regulator. Disconnect the heavy one and if it's to the right of the thin one, mark it D+R but if it's to the left of the thin one, mark it D+L. Disconnect the thin one and mark it DF for Field.

Step 3. (Cont'd.)

Tape all the wires to the front (FRONT IS FRONT) of the engine compartment or to one side (Bus) out of the way of the engine when it's coming out.

Step 4. Mechanical Disconnection

Air Cleaner: That large roundish black thing on top of the carb or off to one side. It has oil in it so remember to keep it level. Remove the air pre-heater hose (if any) coming up from the engine to the air cleaner. It's usually held on with a spring wire so with the pliers push the two ends of the spring wire toward each other and pull and twist the hose off the air cleaner. Now pull the hose off that goes to the air cleaner from next to the oil filler cap. Mark both ends, remove the hose and put it into a paper bag. If it's worn, put a new one on your shopping list. If you have a '69 and on engine with thermostatic control to the air cleaner, disconnect it from the air cleaner—unsnap the keeper (metal clip at the end of the spring) and pull the cable off, then let it hang until you get around to removing the fan housing, then you can disconnect the other end of the control cable.

Type I: Use the big screwdriver to loosen the clamp holding the air cleaner, then remove the air cleaner and put it to be cleaned. **Bus**: the air cleaner assembly is bolted to one side or other of the engine. Unscrew the neck from the top of the carb and pull the neck loose, then use the 13 or 14mm socket on the long extension on the ratchet to remove the bolt or bolts holding the air cleaner on. Put the bolts back in their holes and the air cleaner in the pile to be cleaned.

Carburetor: If you had zero wires to the carb, you probably have a 36 hp with a mechanical choke so use the short screwdriver to loosen the clamp holding the choke cable to the carb. With the pliers and the vice grip—the pliers to hold the wire from moving and the vice grip to loosen the little nut that clamps the wire into the choke arm—pull the choke wire out of the clamp. If you had one or more wires to the carb, you have an automatic choke so start with the. . .

Accelerator Cable (all): You need a small screwdriver to loosen the little screw in the side of the small cylindrical clamp that holds the end of the accelerator cable. If you can't find what I'm talking about, have your friend push on the accelerator pedal while you watch to see what moves—that's it. Loosen the screw and push the cable end toward the front (FRONT IS FRONT). Hold your other hand under the accelerator arm to catch the small cylinder as you push it out into your hand. Put it into a baggie.

Study the assembly around the accelerator cable. It consists of a cone, a spring, and a small slotted gizmo that holds the whole thing together. Push the cone thing with one hand and slip the little split washer (the slotted gizmo) off from the cable end with the other. If you drop it, or if you drop the cylindrical clamp you took out before, please find them and get them into a baggie or into a safe. We carry spare ones as the damn car won't run without them.

If you have a newer model VW like '67 and on and can't find the cone and spring, it's because you don't have one, so skip that part.

Remove the spring and cone and put them into a baggie. **All**: push the accelerator cable end forward into the tube in the fan housing. **36hp**: reach around the front (FRONT IS FRONT) of the fan housing and pull the choke cable, if any, out through its hole in the fan housing so it's free.

Automatic transmission only: There is a kickdown switch next to the throttle lever with two wires going to it. Pull both wires off and mark the left one "KL" and the right one "KR".

*   *   *   *   *   *   *   *   *   *   *   *   *

Step 5. Remove Heater Cables and Two Engine Mounting Nuts.

Types III and IV (and '72 and on Bus) join Types I and II for this Step.

Step 5. (Cont'd.)

Types I, III and IV: Block the wheels, put the jack in the jack point and raise the car enough so you can get under it but not enough to raise the tires off the ground.

Types I, II and III: Replace the oil drain plug and tighten it with the wrench. Empty the oil drain pan. You'll need the 10mm (8mm, Type III) socket on the short extension of the ratchet, the 10mm (8mm) box open end wrenches, a pencil and. . . .

Types I, II, and III and IV: the 17mm box open end wrench, a vice grip and the big screwdriver and go underneath the car. Lie down and scrootch way under the engine on your back, parallel with the car, chest even with the oil drain plug, feet out the back. Find the place where the engine connects to the trans. About four inches on each side of center and up 2" from the bottom of the engine you'll find (maybe you'll have to use the screwdriver to clean the crud off to find) two nuts that your 17mm box end will fit on. If the 17mm doesn't fit, you're on the wrong nut. Get into position so you can apply some force, then loosen the nut by turning it counter clockwise facing it. Get both these nuts and washers (if any) off and into a baggie. Sometimes the end of an engine stud has been beaten up by rocks and instead of the nut coming off, the whole stud comes out. Relax your mind and put a new stud on the shopping list. Automatic trans: There are two vacuum hoses on the right side going to the trans, so pull them off from the trans and leave them dangling. Type IV and Type II '72 and on) return to your procedure.

Types I, II and III: Now find the heater cables. They're thin wires that come from the front of the car, one on each side of the big bolts that hold the trans in. Each lever has a clamp, just like the cylindrical clamp on the accelerator cable you took off, except larger. The idea is to loosen the clamp so the cable will pull out. Put the 10mm (or 8mm) wrench on the nut on the bottom and turn the wrench a few turns until the clamp is loose enough to pull the cable end out of it. Try to get the little cylindrical clamps out and into a baggie but if they're hung up in their holders, leave them there. These, too, tend to get beaten up by rocks, so if they're not there or you found them disconnected, you've discovered why you couldn't heat the car, so make a shopping list note. Reach up on both sides of the engine and pull the big wrinkled heater hoses free.

Type III only: There are two smaller hoses that look like the heater hoses on either side of the engine. Loosen the clamp with a phillips head screwdriver and pull the hoses towards the front of the car.

Types I, II and III: (Type III, if your car is fuel injected skip this paragraph.) Look at the left hand side of the engine (your right hand) above the place you took off the left heater clamp. You'll see a metal tube (probably not bright and shiny) coming out of the engine. If you don't see it, have your helper wiggle the tube that attaches to the fuel pump from inside the engine compartment while you watch to see what wiggles under the car—that's it. It'll have a woven rope-like tube coming from the gas tank pushed onto it. Pull the woven tube off the metal tube, forward (FRONT IS FRONT) and quickly jam the piece of pencil into the woven tube. It's going to be spurting gas, so hold it up and jam the pencil in. Make sure it doesn't leak. You can slide out from under now.

All: Lower and remove the jack.

Step 6. Support Transmission—Double Jointed Axles Only (includes automatic transmission.)

Types I, II and III. If you're not sure your car has double jointed axles, see Chapter XVI. If you have double jointed axles, you have to support the transmission to prevent it from sagging.

Find a piece of 2"x4" or equal about 40" long and drill a 3/4" hole about 2" from each end. The chains bolt to the two ends of the 2x4 (through the holes you just drilled) and hold the board up against the trans. Crawl under the car and hook one chain over the frame member a little to the rear of the axles. The other end of this chain is bolted to the 2x4. Now push the board up against the trans and attach the other chain to the frame on the other side of the trans. Make sure the board is tight—that it's *really holding the trans.*

Step 6. (Cont'd.)

Automatic Transmission Only: Crawl under the engine and look up where the engine and transmission join. There is a hole in the transmission through which you can see the torque converter plate. Have a friend rotate the engine with a wrench until you see a bolt head come into view. Yell "Stop." With a 13mm end wrench, remove the bolt. Rotate the engine again until you see another bolt and remove it. There is one more (three in all) so do it again. Put the bolts in a baggie marked "torque converter bolts."

Step 7. Remove Engine–Types I, II and III

Type I: First, you must remove the rear piece of shrouding. (REAR IS REAR.) If you have 36 or 40 hp, just remove the four screws with the screwdriver and remove the tin. If you have a 65 and on model with the big fat heater hoses coming down, first remove the hoses. Loosen the clamp with phillips screwdriver, pry the hoses with the large screwdriver and twist them off. Pull the rubber sealers off the bottom of the hoses. Put hoses and sealers in a bag or put new ones on your shopping list if they're beat up. Take off the small shroud over the crankshaft pulley–three screws with the large screwdriver. Remove the two small plates (three screws holding each) over the manifold heat riser. Use Liquid Wrench if any shrouding screws give you trouble. Now you can get to the four or six screws that hold the rear piece of tin, so remove them and work the piece of tin out. You'll have to pull the tin up off the pre-heater hose.

'68 and on, Type I: remove the bottom end of the pre-heater hose.

Types I, II and III: Place a piece of 2"x4" board about 2 feet long under the engine, crosswise, even with the oil drain plug. Put the two scissors jacks on this board as far apart as you can get them and still be under the engine pan, slightly V-ed with the point of the V toward the front of the car so the jack handles will clear the tail pipes and muffler. Center the jacks, front to back, with the oil drain plug. With the jack handles, raise the jacks so they just barely contact the engine pan. It's best to have two people, one on each jack.

Types I and II: With the 17mm box end, reach in front (FRONT) of the fan housing and loosen the last two engine attachment nuts that hold the engine to the trans. They're in front of the bottom of the fan housing. You can't see them but put your hand around and you can feel them. After you've loosened them with the wrench, they'll come off with your fingers if you're having a good day. If the bolt starts to turn, pull back on the engine to put the bolt in a bind and keep it from turning. If the bolt still insists on turning and you don't have help, adjust the vice grip for size on one of the engine nuts you've already taken off, then clamp it on the nut you're trying to loosen. Put the 17mm socket on the long extension on the ratchet and take it under the car with you.

Type III: Look on top of the engine on the very FRONT and you'll see the two top 17mm engine mounting bolts. You'll take the nut off the bolts. Try turning the nut loose with the wrench. If it comes loose, great, unscrew it with your fingers; you've got a late model with case bolts that don't turn. If the whole bolt turns, grab a 17mm socket and ratchet and slide under the car, after you've put a vice grip on the nut top.

Models, like 71 and newer: have self locking engine mount bolts. All you have to do is turn the nut loose from the top with a 17mm wrench, then use your fingers, pulling out as you turn.

1600 engines: because of the placement of the oil cooler, the left engine mount nut has been pressed into the case. In order to remove the motor mount capscrew, you must attack it from underneath with a 17mm socket on the long extension on the ratchet. It's back of the clutch arm. Tough spot.

Types I, II and III. Your engine mount nut is still loose and you've crawled under the car awaiting further words. OK, find the bolt head and turn it loose with the socket. The left one is in back of the clutch lever and the right one is the top bolt holding the starter on. The vice grip will fall loose when you've turned the bolt enough. If the bolt insists on moving and you have help, your

Step 7. (Cont'd.)

friend can turn the nut first with the 17mm box end, then by hand from above while you hold the bolt under the car with the socket arrangement. Put these nuts and washers (if any) in a baggie.

With the jacks positioned and the two final nuts off, your engine is ready to come out. Push the front wheel blocks forward 2", then go back and rock the car forward and wiggle the engine backwards to free the transmission shaft from the engine. Don't be afraid of the engine—it only weighs about 200+ pounds. Anyway the jacks are under there holding it so use your strength to pull and wiggle. If the engine and trans shaft don't part, check to see you've detached everything. OK? Now pull the engine with one hand on the fan housing and the other on the muffler (under the car) and wiggle some more. Then lift and pull back. When the engine is free from the trans shaft, jack it down with the two jacks simultaneously. Pull the accelerator cable free of the engine as you jack it down.

Bus: Just roll the bus forward, off the engine and out of the way, then tip the engine to remove the jacks.

Type III: When the engine is on the ground, you'll have to jack the car up about 6 inches so the back bumper is 2 feet off the ground, then slide the engine out from under the car. If you don't have an automatic shift, go back to your Step 7.

Type I: The jacks are down all the way, so remove them by tipping the engine and pulling the jacks out from under it. Tip first on one side, then the other. If there are several husky free-loaders hanging around, four of you can lift the car rear and bumper over the engine, then push the car forward, but it weighs quite a bit. If you don't have enough combined strength to pick up the car and push it forward, there's a whole trip you have to take.

You'll have to block and jack. 8" x 8" wooden blocks and two bricks are perfect for the job. Place one block behind the jack point on each side, then put a scissors jack on top of each block. Place another block next to the first one but in front of the jack point so you don't squash the jack point. Jack the car up enough so you can get another block on top of the second or front one, then

Step 7. (Cont'd.)

jack a bit until the brick fits on top of the third block. Jack both sides more or less simultaneously so your car doesn't topple over. Remove the jacks. Pull the engine out and away. If the car is well and securely blocked, leave it that way ready to receive the engine.

Automatic Transmission Only: After the engine is out you must support the torque converter to prevent loss of oil from the transmission. If you don't know, the torque converter is the thing on the center of the transmission that's loose. Here's what to do. Get your piece of 18" flat stock with a 3/4" hole in one end and put the top (left or right) engine mounting bolt through it. Put the other end of the bar so it holds the center of the torque converter and tighten the nut. Type III, return to your Step 7.

If you pulled the engine to replace a clutch, front engine seal or rear transmission seal, go to Step 1, Engine Dismantling Procedure, and continue from there.

Step 8. Loosen Generator Fan Nut

Condition: If you're doing a complete overhaul, you'll want the generator to be in top shape to match the engine. See Chapter VIII for testing the generator if you're in doubt. If it just needs a minor overhaul, like new brushes, clean commutator or if your generator is satisfactory, skip the step.

It's easiest to loosen this generator fan nut now while the assembly holding the generator is still tight in the engine, so hold the generator from turning by putting the medium screwdriver in the notch in the front half of the generator (fan belt) pulley, then with the 1-7/16" or 36mm socket on the breaker bar or flex handle slip the socket over the nut in the fan on the front (FRONT) of the fan housing. Loosen the nut with the socket but don't remove it. If you don't have the large socket, see Chapter XVI, Removing Large High Torque Nuts, to loosen this nut.

Step 9. Remove Fan Housing

Condition: Engine overhaul, changing oil cooler, valve job and/or generator (or alternator Type I) overhaul.

Engines August '65 and later, go to Step 13 and remove the air control bellows. **All other models:** remove the round air cooling control ring. It's on the front (FRONT) of the fan housing where you can't see it while the engine is in the car. If you don't find this ring, either some previous owner has thrown it away or you have a later-than-August '65 model. Using the 10mm box end, loosen the two bolts that hold the ring. With the bolts loose, not out, the round thing can be slipped up and out of the fan housing.

All Models: Loosen the generator pulley nut; put the 21mm wrench on the nut and the medium screwdriver in the rectangular notch on the front (FRONT) edge of the pulley to keep it from turning while you loosen the nut with the wrench. Don't remove the nut. Work the fan belt off the bottom pulley and put the belt in a bag. There's a metal strap around the generator holding it to the support. Remove the bolt that holds this strap together with the 13mm socket on the long extension on the ratchet placed on top and the 13mm open end placed on the bottom. Shove the strap forward, then pull it out without bending it unduly. Replace the bolt in the strap, screw the nut on it and put the strap in a bag. Pull all four of the spark plug connectors off the spark plugs and off the fan housing, but leave them on the distributor cap. (36hp: the wires are in a tube attached to the intake manifold. Leave them there. Just pull the wires off the spark plugs.) You've already disconnected the center wire to the coil. Remove the vacuum line (if any). It runs between the distributor and the carburetor. Remove the gas line from the fuel pump to the carburetor. Put these lines in a bag.

Cleanair Bus: With the phillips head screwdriver, remove the four clamps on the top and bottom connections of the two fat hoses. Twist and pry the hoses with a screwdriver, remove them and put

Step 9. (Cont'd.)

them in a bag or if they're bent and beat up, put new hoses and sealers on your list.

All Models: Loosen the four nuts and four bolts that hold the intake manifold. See Step 11, where it says **All Models** the second time. Loosening these nuts and bolts now allows you to slip the generator past the carb as you remove the fan housing. There are two screws, one on each side of the fan housing, to remove with the large screwdriver, then you can lift the fan housing off. You may have to jiggle and wiggle it carefully, then lift it *straight up,* please, so you don't bend the tall oil cooler which lives under it. Put the fan housing with the stuff to be cleaned or go on to the next Step.

Step 10.　Remove Generator (or Alternator Type I) From Fan Housing

Condition: You're going to overhaul the generator or have the alternator overhauled.

Lay the fan housing flat on the ground with the generator up and use the 10mm socket on the ratchet to remove the four bolts around the generator plate. Lift the fan and generator up out of the fan housing. Replace the four bolts in the fan housing and put the fan housing to be cleaned. Grab the generator pulley with one hand to keep it from turning and unscrew the big nut you loosened in Step 8 with the other. Put the nut, washer, collar, shims and key together in a baggie. Unscrew the generator nut on the generator pulley(you've already loosened it) and pull off the rear (FRONT, IS FRONT OF THE CAR) half of the pulley with its shims and spacer (the cup-like thing), then with the large screwdriver, pry the front half of the pulley off the generator shaft and put the pulley back together with the same number of shims between the two pulley halves. Put this assembly in a bag. Now pry the second half moon key off the shaft and put it into a baggie.

Bus: If you've pulled the engine to reach the generator, cover the engine and you're off to the auto-electric shop. When you return with the overhauled generator, go on to the Procedure for Engine Equipment Assembly and Installation, Type I and Type II (through '71), Step 3.

Others: Put the generator in the pile with the starter to take later.

Step 11.　Remove Intake Manifold

Condition: Engine overhaul, changing oil cooler, valve job.

Type I, 40hp, earlier than Cleanair: Remove the pre-heater hose from the heater box on the left side of the engine and put it into a bag. Is it badly beat up? New one on the shopping list.

All Models: With a 12mm wrench remove the fuel line that goes through the front (FRONT) shroud at the fuel pump end. Remove the front piece of shrouding (three screws with the large screwdriver), the one the fuel line goes through. Leave the gas line hanging in it and put it in the pile to be cleaned.

Bus, early models: Remove the four screws holding the rear piece of tin and remove the tin to be cleaned. Loosen the connection holding the bottom end of the pre-heater hose (if any). Twist and remove the hose and put it in a bag.

Bus, Cleanair: Remove the two little plates that cover the heat riser tubes (three screws each), then the three screws that hold the crankshaft shroud and finally the four or six screws on the rear piece of tin. Disconnect the bottom connection of the pre-heater hose (the one that went up to the air cleaner) and put the tin to be cleaned and the hose in a bag.

All Models: The intake manifold is the long pipe thing with the four legs coming down, two on each side. Use the 10mm socket on the long extension on the ratchet to remove the four nuts and four bolts holding the intake manifold and heat riser to the engine. There'll be one or two that you'll need to use the box end on. Put them in a baggie. Pull the manifold straight up off the studs—the carburetor still on it—and tie a rag around the carburetor to protect it. If you twisted any of the studs

Step 11. (Cont'd.)

off or if any were missing, put new intake manifold studs on your shopping list. Chapter XVI tells how to remove any stud stubs.

1600 Engines: Remove the center section of the dual port manifold by loosening the clamps with a phillips screwdriver; then loosen the two nuts holding the manifold to the heads on each side. Remove the two bolts on each of the heat rise tubes (four altogether) and carefully pull out the center manifold section, carburetor and all. Remove the nuts and carefully pull the two side manifold sections off the studs, one at a time. Put all this in a bag. If there is somebody with nothing to do around, they can smooth the insides of these two side pieces. They're pretty rough. Use emery cloth or rough sandpaper, but smooth, then clean the hell out of them before reinstalling.

36hp: Unclip the distributor cap and remove the cap (wires attached) along with the intake manifold.

All Models, Important Note: Once the manifold is off, blow through the heat riser, the small tube. If you can blow through it easily, put the manifold in the pile to be cleaned but if blowing through the heat riser is like blowing into a bottle, you have a plugged heat riser and must unplug it. See Engine Removal and Stripping, Type III, Step 9 for how.

Step 12. Remove Oil Cooler

Condition: Engine overhaul or you've pulled the engine to replace a faulty oil cooler, which happens. If you're doing a valve job only, skip the step.

Remove the left hand cylinder shroud, the piece of tin covering cylinders No. 2 and No. 4. It keeps you from getting to the oil cooler nuts. Remove the five screws with the big screwdriver and lift the shroud off and into the pile to be cleaned. Hard-to-remove screw trouble? Douse them liberally with Liquid Wrench, then clamp the vice grip on the screwdriver shaft up by the handle to use as added leverage. You can also try clamping the screw itself with the vice grip.

The oil cooler (tall skyscraper) nuts are now exposed and you can remove them with the 10mm box end. There are three, two on the bottom (remember: counter clockwise facing the nut) and one on top. Put these nuts and washers in a baggie. If you've thrown a rod, if your oil cooler's been leaking or if you're planning to change from non-detergent to detergent oil, throw it away and put a new one on your shopping list, but if it's OK, fill it with solvent and stand it upside down where it won't get kicked over. Stuff pieces of rag into the two holes left by the oil cooler. They go into the engine, dirt must not. If you've pulled the engine to replace the oil cooler, continue with a new oil cooler and ENGINE MANTLING, Step 12. Remove old oil cooler gaskets, please.

Step 13. Remove Air Control Assembly

Tip the engine so you can get to the bottom of the right side to remove the air control bellows. Look under the right head to find these bellows. **(36 and 40 hp:** you have to reach inside the heater box past the heater flaps to do it.) Unscrew the bolt from under the bracket that goes into the bottom of the bellows with an open end wrench; unscrew the bellows from the wire with your fingers and remove the bellows. Screw the bolt back into the bottom of the bellows and put bolt and bellows into a baggie. This much of this step must be done prior to fan housing removal in the engines August '65 and later.

Early 36 and 40hp Models: On the right side of the top of the engine, there's a long shaft with a spring controlled flap on a tube (what's left after you took the air control ring off). Use the small screwdriver to work the open end spring clip out of its slot near the end of the shaft (looks like an open-ended spring washer, about 1/4" from the right end of the shaft). Loosen the clamp bolt on the lever—10mm. Pull the wire up that comes up between the right-hand cylinders (the wire you unscrewed the bellows from) and, at the same time, pull the tube off the right side of the long bolt

Step 13. (Cont'd.)

(shaft). Put these things in a baggie and mark them "air control assembly." Remove the 13mm nut from the left end of the long bolt and pull the bolt out. Replace the nut and store the assembly in a bag.

    All Models: Use the large screwdriver to remove the six screws holding the right-hand cylinder shroud (over No. 1 and No. 2 cylinders), remove the shroud and put it to be cleaned. Remove the left-hand cylinder shroud if you skipped Step 12. Remember Liquid Wrench and Chapter XVI if you run into hard-to-remove screw trouble. Two small shrouding plates drop off when you unscrew the cylinder shrouds. Put them to be cleaned.

Step 14. Remove Muffler

Condition: Engine overhaul and valves. If your muffler has holes, it's much easier to replace it now than when the engine's in the car, so if it's holey, put one on the shopping list.

    Use the 10mm socket on the short extension on the ratchet and the 10mm box end to remove the two clamps, one on each side, on the lower muffler connections. If the bolts on the muffler clamps break, don't flip from sight. You're going to buy a new muffler attachment kit anyway. Remove the two nuts on each side that hold the top of the muffler to the engine heads with a 13mm or 14mm box end (or socket arrangement prior to the Cleanair).

    36hp: The muffler pipes slip over the pipes from the front exhaust and these also are clamped. Remove these clamps with two 13mm wrenches. Now you have to use a hammer to bang the muffler back off the pipes. Sometimes this is quite a job. Squirt some Liquid Wrench on the connection and try not to ruin the muffler getting it off.

    40hp: The muffler will come right off as you pull it off the studs. **Cleanair:** Has two connecting tubes between the muffler and heater boxes. Loosen these clamps with a screwdriver, then slide them out of the way. Pull out the tube that the pre-heater hose was attached to. Up to '68 it's held in place by the bottom muffler nut.

Step 15. Remove Front Exhaust System and Heater Assembly

Condition: Engine overhaul and valves.

    Use the 13 or 14mm box end to remove the four nuts (two on each side) holding the exhaust pipes to the heads. Remember good old Liquid Wrench. As you pull these assemblies off the studs, the heater boxes will also come. Put the muffler and exhaust-heater assembly in the pile to be cleaned.

    Cleanair: Not so fast—you're more complicated. Tip the engine onto the crankshaft pulley to remove the extra screws holding the exhaust-heater assemblies together on the bottom of the engine. There should be four screws, but often they've fallen off. Now you can remove the exhaust-heater business.

    All models: If you fouled up any studs in the last two steps, don't blow your cool, but turn to Chapter XVI to find out what to do, then put new studs on your shopping list.

PROCEDURE FOR ENGINE REMOVAL AND STRIPPING, TYPE III

Note: If you're here just to change an oil cooler, there's no need to pull the engine. Do the following Steps in this procedure with the engine in the car.
Step 1.
Step 3. Just disconnect the wires over the left cover plate and move the harness out of the way.
Step 9. Single carb, take the whole manifold off. Dual carbs, just take the left carb and manifold off. Fuel Injection, take the left manifold pipes off, leaving the intake air distributor on.
Step 10. Just remove the Generator.
Step 15. Just remove the left cover plate.
Step 16.

When you're ready to install your new oil cooler, turn first to Step 12. Engine Mantling, do it and then to Engine Equipment Assembly and Installation Type III, and do:
Step 1. Left cover plate.
Step 8.
Step 11.
Step 21. Electrical Connections.

Step 1. Engine Compartment

Open the rear deck lid, pull the rubber mat forward, turn the two wire handles to AUF, raise the lid and take it all the way out. Set it in a safe place. Paper bags, Mark-All, tape and plastic baggies are at hand.

Step 2. Drain Oil

Put your oil drain pan under the center of the engine, then with a 21mm wrench, remove the drain plug from the center bottom of the engine. Let the oil drain for now.

If the drain plug is stripped, loosen and remove the six 10mm nuts holding the plate on and take the entire plate off, then the oil screen assembly. Put a new oil screen, plate and drain plug on your shopping list.

Step 3. Electrical Disconnections

Note: As you take the air cleaner off, remember it's full of oil so don't tip it. After removing a hose, mark the air cleaner where the hose came off with like a "1," then mark the hose that fits there with "1." Same with the second hose, etc. Mark the other end of the hose and put the hoses in a paper bag marked "hoses to air cleaner." Put wing bolt(s) in a baggie and the baggie in the bag. OK, to remove the air cleaner:

Single Carburetor: Remove the wing bolt on top of the air cleaner, then the rubber sleeve to the fan housing and finally the rubber elbow to the carb. Pull the one hose to the oil breather off and lift the air cleaner off.

Dual Carburetors: Remove the wing bolts on top of both carbs and the one on the center of the air cleaner. Pull the hose from the oil breather off, then the rubber tube to the fan housing. Pop the linkage to the right carb off, then lift the air cleaner off.

Fuel Injection: Remove the wing bolt on top of the air cleaner, then the rubber elbow tube to the intake air distributor then the hose to the fan housing. Early models pull off two more hoses, one to the breather and the other to the auxilliary air regulator. Late models, pull off three more hoses on the right side and the other one on the left side. Lift the air cleaner off.

All: Locate the generator. It's the big round silver cylinder on the right side of the engine toward the rear (REAR IS REAR). With an 8mm wrench, loosen the nut on the stud (the stud that's pinched flat on top) and pull the wire off. Take the nut on the other stud all the way off and lift the other wire off. Screw the nut back on the stud so you don't lose it. With a medium screwdriver, remove the screw holding the ground wire on, pull the wire aside and put the screw back in the hole. Now take a piece of masking tape, mark it GEN and put it around all three wires you just took off. Find the coil on top of the aluminum fan housing. It's the black cylinder with a heavy wire in the center and smaller wires on each side. Disconnect the small wire going to the distributor. Where it's connected to the coil, it should say No. 1, so mark it 1. Disconnect the thin wire on the other side of the coil and mark it 15. On the left side of the engine, over cylinders No. 3 & 4, there's a metal box that disappears under the tin. This is the oil cooler, on top of which lives the oil pressure sensor (six sided nut with a plastic thing on top. It activates the oil light on the dash). Pull the wire off the sensor and mark it J4.

Step 3. (Cont'd.)

Carburetor Models:
There are two wires going to each carburetor. One goes to the electro magnetic cut-off jet, the other one goes to the automatic choke. Mark the wire to the automatic choke 01, and the wire to the cut-off jet 02. Early model single carburetor models may just have one wire to the automatic choke so mark it 01.

Fuel Injection:
Lots of wires, eh? Don't worry about them because they only fit their proper receptacles. The multi-prong connections, MPC's, are the ones with a rubber cover over them. When you pull these MPC's out of their sockets, please remember to pull straight on the plug, not by the wire. Just put your thumb and forefinger as close to the receptacle as you can, and pull, OK? This is so you won't pull the wires out of the plastic base without knowing it. It's easy to do. The MPC's go only into their proper receptacles so they don't need to be marked but all the single connections (without a rubber cover) should be marked with a piece of masking tape. Here we go.

Pull the MPC from the side of the distributor. Now find temperature sensor No. 1 and pull the MPC out. Up to 1970 it's just to the right of the distributor. From 1970 on, it's on the left side (right side late models) of the intake air distributor (the aluminum box on the center of the engine). Just to the right of center toward the rear (FRONT IS FRONT) is a single ground connection on the engine case, 3 on late models. Pull it off and mark it F1. On the right side of the intake air distributor is a black plastic gizmo called the throttle valve switch. Remove the MPC from this little goodie. Up to 1970, follow the intake manifold pipes to the right, about half way to the head; you'll find the pressure switch. It's under the manifolds. Pull the MPC from it. '70 and on has no pressure switch.

Now, follow the manifolds (the pipes coming out of the intake air distributor) to where they go into the cylinder heads. On each side there are two MPC's on top of the injectors. Pull all four MPC's off. There's also a ground connection on each side, either in front of or to the rear of where you pulled the MPC's off the injectors. Pull these ground wires off and mark them F2. Both sides, please.

On the later model fuel injected engines there are two clusters of grounds on the crank case. One is on the center of the case and the other is on the nut on the oil breather. Take the grounds off each cluster and mark them GROUND. If your engine has these clusters, you won't find the single ground connections by the injectors. Up to 1970: Go back to the distributor and find the wire going down in front of it to cylinder head temperature sensor (No. 2). There's a plastic cover on it, right. From 1970 on: Look on the left cylinder head sort of between No. 3 & 4 spark plugs to locate temperature sensor (No. 2). All: Slide the plastic cover off and pull the wires apart. Mark the top wire F3.

From 1970 on: Look under the right side of the intake air distributor to locate the cold start valve. It's the only thing left with wires on it. There is one single wire so pull it off and mark it J1.

All: Pull the main harness off the clips and move it out of the way.

Automatic trans: Have a few wires left, but hang on, we'll get to them later.

Step 4. Mechanical Disconnections

Accelerator Cable: Engines with carburetors— you'll need a small screwdriver: fuel injection, 8mm wrench will do. If by some chance you don't know where the accelerator cable connects, have a friend push the accelerator pedal while you watch to see what moves. Loosen the screw on the cylindrical clamp and slide the cable all the way out the front (FRONT) piece of sheet metal. Fuel injection people don't have to push the cable out the front.

Oil Dipstick Tube and Air Bellows—Pull out the oil dipstick and look at the tube it fits into. Where the rubber tube connects to the metal tube coming from the engine case, there is a clamp that holds the two together. Loosen the clamp and separate the two tubes. To the left of the dipstick

Step 4. (Cont'd.)

(center rear of engine) is the rubber air bellows. Loosen the two screws on the clamp that fastens the bellows to the engine. Pull the bellows off gently so you don't rip it. Put a new one on your shopping list if it's ripped.

Fuel Injection: On the very FRONT of the engine is a piece of sheet metal through which comes the accelerator cable and the fuel line. On the right side of this is mounted a shiny metal gizmo, the fuel pressure regulator. On either side of this piece of tin are screws that hold it to the engine. So. with a large screwdriver, remove the two screws and put them in a baggie. The piece of tin itself, is going to stay in place. Coming through the left side of this piece of tin, you'll see a woven fabric line (the fuel line) that connects to a double T fitting above the injector nozzles. If there is a screw type clamp on this fitting, loosen the screw and slide the clamp back. If the clamp is like a band of metal with a hump on the top, squeeze the hump down, then squeeze it the other way with a pair of pliers until it's expanded enough to slide it back. If you have this second type of clamp, put on shopping list 1/2'' screw type hose clamps. Now put one hand on the T fitting and the other hand on the fuel line and twist and pull the line until it comes off. Look on the other side of this FRONT tin and find the double T fitting with a woven fabric line going to the fuel pressure regulator. Remove it the same way you did the other one.

Poke your head under the left side of the engine compartment and find the pressure sensor. It's that shiny gizmo that's rubber mounted and has a hose and an MPC on it. Pull the hose off, but don't disturb the MPC. Plug the hole with a rag.

All, up to 1969, have a rear engine mount. This mount is on top of the engine in the center and connects to the torque protruding from the rear of the engine compartment. With a 13mm wrench remove the two bolts on the mount and slide the round part that's loose off the tube. Tie a wire around the fiber shims that are by now probably all over the place. It's important to keep the shims together.

All, 1969 and on: In 1969 an engine carrier was introduced to take place of the rear engine mount. It's located under the engine to the rear. With a 19mm wrench, remove the two nuts and bolts holding the carrier to the metal bracket coming down from the body on both sides. Don't remove the bolts holding the bracket to the body. Make sure the scissors jack or blocks are under the engine so it doesn't come crashing down on you when the carrier is removed.

Automatic Trans: Just a few more things for those of you who think life with an automatic is easier. There is kickdown switch next to the throttle lever with two wires going to it. Pull both wires off and mark the left one KL and right one KR.

Step 5. Remove Heater Cables and Two Engine Mount Nuts

Step 6. Remove Engine

Please turn back to **Procedure For Engine Removal and Stripping, Type I and Type II through 1971,** Step 5 and follow along until after your engine is on the ground. We'll tell you there when to come back here, OK?

Step 7. Remove Muffler

Note: If you've pulled the engine to do a clutch job, to replace the front engine seal or the rear trans seal, skip to Step 1. ENGINE DISMANTLING and go from there.

Condition: Engine overhaul, valves and/or muffler replacement.

On either side of the engine you'll see an elbow shaped pipe with a rubber tube on it. Take a

Step 7. (Cont'd.)

pair of pliers and turn the split metal rod on the rubber tube until it's loose. Pull the tube off the fan housing. Both sides. In FRONT of the elbow pipes is the fresh air pipe held on by a clamp. Loosen the screw on both clamps and slide the clamps toward the front of the engine. Now look at where the top muffler pipes connect to the cylinder heads. With a 13mm wrench, remove the two bottom nuts and put them in a baggie. To get at the top nuts look through the bottom of the aluminum fan housing. On the right it's easy to see but on the left side there's just a little hole where you can get at it, so use a 13mm socket on a long extension, OK? Use the 10mm socket, extension and ratchet and a 10mm box end wrench to remove the two clamps, one on each side, on the lower muffler connection. Don't put your hammer through the fender if the little bolts break. You're going to get new ones anyway. Just above and to the front of the two clamps you just removed are large band clamps. Loosen the screws almost all the way and slide them up and out of the way.

Single Carburetor: Look on the left side of the muffler where it bolts to the head. See the pipe that goes up to the intake manifold. It's hard to see, but use your eyes; it's the only thing still holding the muffler on. With a 10mm wrench, remove the two bolts holding the left heat riser (that's what the pipe is) to the muffler.

Everyone: You can now pull the muffler straight back and off. If it doesn't want to come off, squirt some penetrating oil on the lower connections and try again. If it's still no go, get a block of wood, like a short piece of 2x4, put it up against the end of the muffler and gently, but firmly, persuade it with a large hammer.

Step 8. Remove Heater Boxes

Condition: Engine overhaul or valves. Oil cooler only—skip this Step.

The heater boxes are those big clunky things on either side of the engine. The exhaust manifolds (pipes) go through them and bolt onto the front of the cylinder heads. With a 13mm wrench, remove the two nuts on each side that hold the manifolds to the front of the heads. If the studs are rusty, use some penetrating oil, then the wrench. Just to the inside of the nuts you removed are some screws holding the heater box tin to the cover plates, so remove them. Now put both hands under either one of the valve covers and lift the engine up and have a friend put a block of wood under the engine case to hold it there. Poke your head under the side that's up and find the two screws that hold the piece of tin on the heater box to the engine case. Remove them with your large screwdriver. Find the 10mm bolt holding the heater box to the cover plate just to the outside and below the rear cover plate. Use your ratchet assembly to remove it. Now slide the heater boxes off the head and do the same thing on the other side.

Late model Type III's with automatic transmission: You have an exhaust gas recirculator so you have to remove the two 11mm bolts and nuts on the connection coming up from the right heater box before it will come off.

Single carburetor: On the right heater box on the front, the heat riser connects to the exhaust pipe. The connection is just like the one you took off the muffler on the other side. Remove the the two bolts with the 10mm wrench, then take the heater boxes off.

All: If you've fouled up any studs in the last two steps, turn to Chapter XVI to find out what to do and put new studs on your shopping list.

Step 9. Remove Intake Manifold(s)

Condition: Engine Overhaul, valve job, changing oil cooler. Attention Dual Carburetors: If you want to change the oil cooler only, just remove the left carburetor then go to Step 10 to remove the generator only.

Step 9. (Cont'd.)

Single Carburetor: Pull off the fuel and vacuum hose from the carburetor. Both of them are woven hoses. Put them in a marked bag. The intake manifold is the long pipe with four legs coming down, two on each side. Use the 10mm socket on the long extension and ratchet to remove the four nuts holding the intake manifold to the heads. You may find it easier to use a 10mm wrench on the two rear nuts. Remove the two bolts on each side holding the heat risers to the muffler if you haven't already done so in Step 7. Pull the manifold straight up off the studs, with the carburetor still attached. Tie a rag around the top of the carburetor to protect it. If you twisted any studs off or if one was missing, put it on your shopping list. Chapter XVI tells how to remove any stud stubs.

Take your manifold and blow through one end of the heat riser (the small tube). Is it clear, or is it like blowing into a bottle? **Heat riser plugged?** Here's what to do: poke something like a coat hanger through it until you have a small hole going. Then take it to someone with an oxyacetylene torch and have them heat up the carbon inside the heat riser until it's red hot, then give it a blast of oxygen. The carbon will burn out like magic. Don't try to put the manifold in a hot tank because the piece that holds the four pipes together is aluminum and it'll melt like magic. If it's really plugged up so it won't even burn out, buy a new one, or scout around in the local wrecking yard. You have to get a manifold for your model, so take your old one along with if you're scouting for a used one.

Dual Carburetors: Pull the woven gas hose off both carburetors and the thin woven vacuum hose off the left carb. Mark them and put them away. Now look at where the manifolds disappear into the cylinder heads. See the two small pieces of tin screwed on the cover plate? One goes around the spark plug holes and the other goes around the manifold. With a large screwdriver, remove the screws from both pieces on both sides. Remember, if you're just after the oil cooler, you only have to work on the left side. Now you can see the nuts holding the manifold to the head. With a 13mm socket, extension and ratchet, remove the two nuts and washers on the intake manifold. Both sides. There is a tube (later models have two tubes) running from one carb to the other with a bracket in the center to hold it down. Remove the 13mm bolt or nut and lift first one, then the other carburetor off the head. Replace the nut or bolt on the bracket for safekeeping. Put a rag around the top of carbs for protection.

Fuel Injection Only: Pull the throttle return spring off the throttle lever: you know, where you took the accelerator cable off of when you pulled the engine. Pull all the spark plug wires off and look at the piece of tin that goes around the spark plug holes. Use your big screwdriver to remove the two screws on either side that hold the pieces of tin on the cover plates. Now you can see the nuts that hold the ends of the manifold onto the cylinder heads. Use a 13mm socket, extension and ratchet to remove the two nuts on both sides. Take the washers off also and put them in the baggie with the nuts.

Now look under the intake air distributor (the aluminum box on the center of the engine) and locate the two bolts and nuts that hold it to the engine case. Use a 13mm socket extension and ratchet on one side of the bolt and a 13mm wrench on the other side as a backup to remove the two nuts and bolts. To the rear of the manifold, running from one side to the other, is a fuel line with a plastic cover on it. Use a 10mm wrench to remove the bracket back on the cover plate without the fuel line, OK? Use the 10mm wrench again to remove the bracket holding the spark plug wires on the left cover plate. Pull the thin vacuum hose off the intake air distributor.

Some automatic trans: Have a hose on the REAR going over to the deceleration valve on the left side of the engine. Pull it off and slip it into a bag.

Automatic trans—late model with exhaust gas recirculator. See the pipe from the intake air distributor to the gizmo on the right front of the engine. You'll have to remove the two 11mm bolts on both the intake air distributor and the other gizmo (exhaust gas recirculator valve). Take the pipe off, put it in a marked bag and put the bolts in a baggie in the bag.

All Fuel injection: Put one hand on each side of the manifold and lift it up off the engine. Stuff

Step 9.   (Cont'd.)

clean rags in all the openings to keep dirt out. There will be a short fat hose either on the bottom of the intake air distributor or the auxiliary air regulator. Take it off and put it in a marked bag.

Step 10.   Remove Air Intake Housing and Generator

Condition: Engine overhaul or you want to get to the pulley, fan or oil pump.

The air intake housing is the big piece of tin on the REAR of the engine which houses the pulley. On top of this housing is the generator belt cover. Pry the two clips off the generator belt cover with a large screwdriver and remove it. The first thing you want to do is take the fan belt off, but those bums in Wolfsburg have made it so you have to have a special wrench to hold the pulley while turning the nut. Ha! that's what they think, we'll find a way around this kind of thinking.

In Chapter VIII, we explain the easiest way to get around this, but for now, try this: put one hand around the fan belt (your strongest) and squeeze the life out of it while you turn the nut in the center of the pulley with a 21mm (13/16") or crescent wrench. Once the nut's loose, turn it the rest of the way with your fingers and be ready to catch the nut, spacer shims and the rear half of the pulley off and remove the belt from the bottom pulley—take it all the way out. Replace the shims, the rear half of the generator pulley and the nut. With a 10mm socket assembly, remove the six bolts around the edge of the air intake housing. There is one more 10mm bolt inside the housing to the left of the aluminum pulley. Remove it. Pull the air intake housing off the engine and turn it around to check the condition of the rubber gasket. If it's broken in any way, put this gasket on your shopping list. Remove the two 13mm nuts and washers holding the generator to the fanhousing. Lift the generator and bracket off the engine.

Step 11.   Remove Fan Pulley

Condition: Engine overhaul

Go to the PROCEDURE FOR ENGINE DISMANTLING and do Steps 2 and 3 and part of Step 4 until the flywheel is held, then come back here.

Flywheel can't turn? OK, with a small screwdriver, pry the plastic cover off the center of the pulley. Look in the hole you just uncovered and you'll see a big bolt that holds the pulley and the fan to the crankshaft. Put a 30mm (1-3/16") socket on a six inch extension and breaker bar and stick it in the hole (center of pulley) and remove the bolt. The pulley can be pulled off by hand. Turn the pulley around to look at the side that fitted up against the fan. You'll find a paper gasket and maybe a metal shim. Put the plastic cover, the bolt and the shim, if any, in a baggie.

Step 12.   Remove Rear Fan Housing Half

Condition: Overhaul.

With a 10mm socket, extension and ratchet, remove the seven 10mm bolts holding the rear fan housing half to the front half. All of the bolts are around the edge of the fan housing. One of the bolts also holds the coil on and has a nut on the other end of it, so you're also removing the coil. On top of the fan housing there is a metal tube (used as a rear mount pre 1969) with a bolt inside it. Put a 13mm socket on your ratchet and long extension and stick it inside the tube and remove the bolt. Put the tube and bolt in a baggie. The rear fan housing half is now held on by two pins only, one on either side—about mid engine. Find them. Put a sharp chisel in the crack exactly where the pins are and tap the chisel lightly with a hammer until the halves separate enough so the rear half is free and you can pry it the rest of the way with the screwdriver. Put the bolts in a baggie marked "rear fan housing."

Step 13. Remove Cooling Fan

Condition: Overhaul.

You have now exposed the cooling fan. Try pulling it off with your hands. If it's your lucky day, it will slip off. Please, don't try to pry it off with a screwdriver or anything like that, as it will bend and imbalance the engine. If you can't get it off with your hands, use the harmonic balancer puller, the two 8mm bolts (2" long) and the two large flat washers to fit the bolts. Put the bolts through the puller and into the two threaded holes on either side of the center of the fan. Now, turn the puller with a wrench until the fan comes free.

Step 14. Remove Front Fan Housing Half

Condition: Overhaul

With a 10mm socket, extension and ratchet, remove the bolt on either side of the center of the fan housing. There are two more 10mm bolts above the ones you just removed. Remove them, but don't remove the 8mm nut above the center. Now poke your head around the right side of the engine and look under the tin (by where you took the manifold off) and at the same time pull the fan housing a little bit so you can see the rod that connects to the thermostat lever. With an 8mm socket on an extension and ratchet, loosen the bolt holding the rod to the lever. Pull the spring off the lever also. You can now pull the fan housing half off. Put everything in a baggie marked "front fan housing.

Step 15. Remove Cover Plates

Condition: Overhaul or valve job.

Remove two screws from each side that hold the cover plates to the cylinder heads—by the intake ports (holes), if you haven't already done so in Step 9. **Fuel Injection attention:** There's a brass electrical connector on the rear screw on each of the cover plates, so put them in a baggie along with screws. **All:** Lift the cover plates off both sides.

Step 16. Remove Oil Cooler

Condition: Engine overhaul or the oil cooler leaks. Valve job only, skip this Step, but check the oil cooler for leaks and bulges.

Up to engine No. 65745 (August 1962) a conventional VW oil cooler was used in conjunction with a special bracket that allows it to lie flat on the engine. From this date on, Type III's have a special oil cooler without a bracket. The removal procedure is the same for both. With a 10mm wrench, remove the three nuts holding the cooler to the case. Lift the cooler off and remove the little tin piece around the lip where the cooler fits on the case. Fill the oil cooler with gas or solvent to start it's cleaning process. If you later discover there's been any metal transfer inside the engine, such as a spun bearing or a seized piston, you must replace the cooler.

Step 17. Remove Oil Filler Pipe

Condition: Engine overhaul or valve job.

The oil filler pipe is the tube coming up from the bottom right side of the engine case. With a 13mm socket and ratchet, remove the two nuts and spring washers and pull the pipe off.

PROCEDURE FOR ENGINE REMOVAL AND STRIPPING, TYPE IV AND 1972 AND ON TYPE II

Special Tools: 3/8" drive, 10mm-12 spline key wrench for the flywheel or drive plate and the pressure control valve. You have to buy one from a special tool supplier like "Snap-On." You'll also need a 3/8"-1/2" adapter and an 18" Stillson or pipe wrench.

Note: Please keep in touch with the material written for Types I and II through 1971 for suggestion on how to remove hoses, engine mounting nuts, etc. Fuel injected engines keep in touch with Type III fuel injection to find out how to remove T connections, etc. This material is not always repeated. "Bus" in this procedure means the 1972 and on Bus which has a dual carb "Type IV" engine, OK?

Step 1. Engine Compartment

In the Type IV sedan, open the rear lid; in the wagon, roll back the floor mat at the rear and open the engine compartment lid, lift it out and put it in the front seat (or equally safe place). Bus: open the rear door and prop it up. 1973 and on Bus: also move the bed or whatever is on top of the engine compartment inside the car to open the lid. Take the lid off and store it and use this handy access to the top of the engine, like when removing the air cleaner or whatever.

Step 2. Drain Oil

Put the oil drain pan under the engine. Take out the 17mm nut to the left of the oil screen and let the oil drain into the pan. As soon as all the oil is drained out, replace the plug and remove the oil drain pan.

Step 3. Electrical Disconnection

Disconnect the ground strap from the negative pole of the battery to the frame. It's usually a flat webbed strap. Take the strap off the frame or body and replace the bolt or screw so you don't lose it. Don't let the ground strap touch the frame or body even if you have to tape it. In the Type IV, the battery is under the rear seat and in the Bus it's in the engine compartment to the right of the engine.

Now get out the roll of masking tape and the Mark-All, because you're going to take off all the electrical wires in the engine compartment that must come off before you can pull the engine. The air cleaner righteously belongs in the next Step, but it would help a lot ot get it the hell out of the way, so take it off per the next step and come back.

All these electrical connections are push-ons. You must identify them so you can put them back where they came from. Mark a piece of tape "15+" and put it around the thin wire that comes to the coil from the fuse box (ignition switch) and pull the wire off. This is not the thin wire from coil to the distributor. **Carburetor models:** there will be 4 or 5 more connections "15" from this same wire to the carbs and you can pull them off the carbs at will as long as you see they come from the automatic chokes and the electromagnetic cut-off jets and mark them as such. In the Bus, there's one more wire on the left carb to the idle fuel cut-off. Mark it and pull it off. Automatic trans: disconnect the wires to the kickdown switch (on the throttle valve). Mark them "KD-R" and "KD-L" (for left and right). **Fuel Injection:** There's a wire from the coil to the main relay. Remove it from the coil, but not from the relay as it stays with the car.

All: Put all loose wires to the sides, out of the way. Find the oil sensor. It's under a rubber cap in FRONT of the distributor, mark the wire "J4" and pull it off. Go underneath the car to disconnect the wire from the alternator to the hot post of the starter. It's the one that heads back toward the engine. While you're down under, look next to the starter for the 3 or 4 connectors that

Step 3. (Cont'd.)

connect the alternator to the voltage regulator. If they're not there, they're up in the engine compartment on the right side. Mark both sides of each connection with the same symbol, like 1, 1–2,2–3,3. On the voltage regulator end, the terminals are marked on the regulator, so mark the ends of the wires as you take them off, "D+, D-, Df and maybe, "ground."

All: Find the heater blower. In the Bus it's mounted right over the engine: in the wagon, it's mounted on the left side of the engine compartment. In these two models, you don't have to disconnect it but in the sedan, it's mounted on the air tunnel and will come out with the tunnel. There is a T2 in the wiring (a double connection) so follow the wire from the blower and separate this connection; mark it "heater."

Fuel Injection: Mark, tape, then remove the following fuel injection MPCs; injectors; "11, 12, 13, 14." Disconnect the three ground wires in the center of the engine, tape and mark them. Disconnect the throttle valve switch MPC and mark it, the same with the distributor trigger contacts, the hot wire from the auxilliary air regulator, temperature sensor I in the intake air distributor and cold start valve. Disconnect the T1 to temperature sensor II between cylinders 3 and 4, then mark and pull the MPC from the pressure sensor, gather all these connections into a neat package and stow it, using some tape to hold it in position out of the way on the left hand side of the engine compartment.

All: If you're removing the engine to replace the clutch, fuel pump, rear trans seal or front engine seal, leave the ignition in place. But if you're overhauling the engine, take the entire ignition system off the engine right now: mark the four spark plug wires (No. 1–right FRONT, No. 2–right rear, No. 3–left front and No. 4), then pull the four plastic spark plug connectors off the spark plugs. Unclip the distributor cap with the screwdriver and pull the cap, then the rotor off the distributor. Pull the heavy wire out of the center of the coil. Pull the thin wire from the coil to the distributor, mark it 1-. Gather the mass of spaghetti together and put it all in one paper bag. Your distributor has one or two hoses on it. Mark them and remove them. Reach down alongside the distributor with the long extension and the 10mm socket and remove the nut and washer that hold the distributor clamp to the crankcase; put them in a baggie. Pull the distributor out of its hole, put it into the bag, put the baggie in the spaghetti bag, mark the bag "ignition" and put the whole schumtz in a safe place, Put a rag into the distributor hole.

Depending on the model and equipment, you may have a few other electrical connections, like a wire to the exhaust reburning system, wires to an auxiliary heater and like that. They will have connections to separate from a plastic socket so mark them, disconnect them and stow them out of the way.

Step 4. Mechanical Disconnection

All: The air cleaner has oil in it, so try not to tip it when removing it. You have hoses to remove first. As you take a hose off the air cleaner, mark the place on the air cleaner with, for example, "1." Also mark the hose end that fits there with a "1." The same for the second hose and the third and. . . .here are the hoses: "the hose that goes from the air cleaner to the crankcase breather," "the hose that goes from the air cleaner to the auxiliary air regulator" (fuel injection only). If you have a '72 and on, there's a "hose from the air cleaner to the air injection system," also a "hose for warm air to the air cleaner" (smog control). Mark all hoses, both ends, pull them off the air cleaner, then unsnap the clips and remove the air cleaner. You may have to take out a couple of 10mm bolts or nuts first. **See Changes and New Ideas.**

Disconnect the throttle lever by loosening the 8mm bolt, then sliding the throttle cable forward out of the way.

Type IV: sedan: unclip and unscrew the air tunnel (that funnel at the very Rear. (FRONT is front). Wagon: has an accordion pleated rubber air tunnel at the rear which has a clamp at both ends,

Step 4. (Cont'd.)

so unscrew the clamps. Sedan and wagon: Take off the two fat hoses from the heater boxes and remove the tunnel, hoses and blower in one piece. Store the assembly. Now, unsnap the two wires that hold the breather assembly on the TOP, CENTER of the engine. Pull out the breather and put it into a bag. Some models have their oil fill pipe and dip stick in this breather.

All: Remove the 1, 2 or 3 pieces of REAR tin which are held on by several screws or cap screws. (If your oil filler pipe comes out the bottom back of the engine and not on center top, remove the two screws that hold it; remove the gasket and the dip stick. The pipe comes off simultaneously with the rear pieces of tin.) Remove the screws into a baggie marked "rear tin." Pull the tin pieces up and out and put them to be cleaned. Mark, then remove any hoses from the engine that have their other ends connected to the engine compartment or elsewhere on the car. This doesn't mean those hoses with both ends connected to the engine itself. For instance, in the Bus and Wagon: remove the two fat hoses that come from the heater blower to the heater boxes and put them in a bag.

Now, go under the car with chain, hooks, bolts, 2x4, pencils, screwdrivers and other various sundry tools. You might jack your sedan or wagon up far enough to work under. You're under the car OK, first disconnect the fuel supply: **Fuel injection**: has two gas connections to the engine, one from the pressure regulator and the other from the fuel pump. Unscrew the clamps and put pencils in the ends of the lines to prevent gas leakage. **Carb models**: there's a fuel line from the gas tank to the fuel pump to find, disconnect and plug with a pencil. **All**: Now, you must support the transmission while pulling the engine and while the engine is out. To do this, use that 2x4, the chain and hook(s) and maybe, bolts, so look at the problem for your model. One way is to find a secure place to put one end of the 2x4 under the trans and into the frame, using the chain with a hook on it to hold the other end of the 2x4. Or you can drill two holes in the 2x4 and bolt a piece of chain through each hole, then hang the 2x4 up under the trans. It can be done several ways so use your ingenuity to keep the trans from falling down. **See Changes and New Ideas.**

Once the trans is supported, find the FRONT ends of the two heater boxes. There's a sheet metal assembly on their front ends out of which comes the tube the hose fits on. You have a choice here. You can pull off the hose and disconnect the heater cables or you can leave the hose connected, loosen the clamp that holds the heater control valve assembly to the heater box, leave the cable connected and knock valve assemblies off the ends of the heater boxes with a rubber hammer. The first way is surer and takes longer and the second way is faster and you choose.

Step 5. Remove Muffler and Heater Boxes

Note: If you're removing the engine to work on the clutch, fuel pump, rear trans seal or front engine seal, you can skip this step, but be prepared for a very heavy engine. Also, you'll have to lift the car higher than the others to move it forward off the engine.

Go to the back of the car where the rear bumper is and take out the bolts that hold the muffler shield—that piece of tin that protects the muffler from rocks. Reach up with the 13mm wrenches and loosen but don't remove the six bolts that hold the muffler to the heater boxes. Then remove the 4 screws holding the bottom pieces of tin under the heater boxes. . .really between the crankcase and the heater boxes. Take the tin off. There are two screws on each side holding small pieces of tin that connect the heater boxes to the fan housing. Remove the 4 screws and the 2 pieces of tin. Put the tin to be cleaned and the screws and nuts from this whole job into the same baggie.

Put a piece of 2x4 across, under the heater boxes and a scissors jack under the 2x4 so the assembly will come down straight. You're going to take the muffler and two heater boxes off as a unit to get that weight off the engine and you don't want 80 lbs. falling on you. With the 13mm socket on the long extension and maybe the universal drive, reach up where the exhaust manifolds bolt to the heads. Exhaust manifolds connect to the bottom of the heads—intake manifolds to the

Step 5. (Cont'd.)

top of the heads. Remove the four nuts and washers from the exhaust manifold connection to the cylinder head. Repeat on the other side and put these nuts and washers into the same baggie. Have your friend push up on one side while you bang with the rubber hammer on the other and work the heater box-muffler assembly until it comes loose, then lower it down with the jack. Put the assembly out of the way.

Step 6. Remove Engine

Go to **Procedure for Engine Removal and Stripping, Type I (all) and Type II (through 1971),** Step 5, and remove the two 17mm lower engine mounting nuts.

While you're under the car: if you have an auxiliary heater, disconnect and remove the exhaust pipe from it. If you have air conditioning, there's a disconnection to make from the engine to the unit. **Everybody:** unscrew and remove the oil filter cartridge under the left REAR of the engine. Check around. Is there anything left that looks like it ties the engine to the car? If everything is free, crawl out. Type IV: lower and remove the jack. **See Changes and New Ideas.**

Automatic trans: pull out the dip stick for the automatic oil level. With the 13mm socket, 9" extension and the ratchet, remove the three bolts that hold the engine plate to the torque converter. These are accessible above, just to left of center at the very FRONT of the engine. Find the hole, remove the plastic plug and rotate the engine with the wrench until you see (with a flashlight) the bolt head in the hole. Put the extension underneath the manifolds and the socket on the bolt to remove the bolt. Rotate the engine some more, remove the bolt, then once more. There are three. Put them in a baggie marked "torque converter bolts." Replace the plastic plug.

All: Find the two scissors jacks and a piece of plywood bigger than the engine. Put the plywood on the ground under the engine. Put the jacks on the plywood, slightly V'd and as far apart as they can be and still be under the crankcase. Raise the two jacks—at the same time—until they contact the crankcase then just a hair more so they take a bit of a strain. Now remove the two upper 17mm mounting bolts from the top of the FRONT of the engine. (Read Step 7 of Engine Removal, Type I & II) Then find and remove the four (two on a side) mounting bolts on the ends of the engine support bracket (REAR, sides of the engine) but don't remove the bracket from the frame. Put all this stuff in a baggie. Lower the engine with the jacks until the rear mounting bracket is clear of the frame. If yours is an automatic trans, have a piece of flat bar with a hole in it ready to hold the torque converter in place while the engine is out.

OK, the engine is loose. Have your friend(s) unblock the wheels and push the car forward while you hold onto the engine pulling it back, free of the trans. For an automatic, it's a very short distance but for a standard shift, it's three or four inches. Pull the engine back as the car is pushed forward. You will feel it when the engine comes loose from the trans. As soon as it does, have your friend block the wheels again and come back to help you lower the engine to the ground. Each of you take a jack and another friend is handy to steady the engine on the jacks. So just lower away evenly until both jacks are all the way down. Use a 2x4 to pry up one side of the engine and lift it a little so your friend can pull the jack out on one side, then repeat on the other side. Unblock the wheels and push the car over the top of the engine. You may have to lift the bumper, but it will go over the engine and there you are with your engine out of the car.

Automatic trans: Bolt the piece of flat bar with a hole in one end to an **upper** engine mounting bolt so it holds the torque converter to the trans axle: you know, keeps it from falling out.

All: If you have a work table or bench, now is the time to have your friends help you put the engine on it so it's easier to work on.

Step 7. Remove Fuel Pump—Not for Fuel Injection

Condition: Overhaul or if it was leaking or not working.

Step 7.   (Cont'd.)

It's possible to remove the fuel pump with the engine in the car but it's such a bear of a job that it's really less total work to remove the engine first. It's especially a bug when you find, after doing the work to pull the engine, that the fuel pump is OK and only the fuel pump push rod needs replacing. It has a tendency to mushroom at the cam shaft end and stop pushing the pump far enough for it to pump. Whenever you replace the pump, replace the push rod. Often, just the push rod needs replacing.

The pump is driven by a cam on the front of the cam shaft so the pump is mounted on the FRONT of the engine on the right side. Front is Front even when the engine is out of the car. Use the screwdriver to remove the screws that hold the two pieces of tin (the air conduit to the alternator and the preheater connection). Mark these two pieces well so you can put them back on—we tell you when but not how. The fuel pump is now exposed so you can remove the nuts with a 13mm box open end wrench or 6mm spline wrench. Remove the nuts and the lock washers. Pull the pump out with the hard plastic spacer and two or more gaskets right after. Pull out the push rod. Then put all the screws, nuts and washers from this assembly into a baggie and put all the tin, the pump, the push rod, spacer and gaskets into a bag marked "fuel pump." It will go back together so keep it together. To replace the pump, go to the store and buy a rebuilt one or rebuild it with a rebuild kit if you're into it and broke. In either case, buy a new push rod.

Step 8.   Inspect Hydraulic Clutch Throw-Out Assembly—Not for Automatic Shift

Condition: If your engine is out, inspect this assembly.

Bus: go forward a few pages to ENGINE DISMANTLING, Step 1, to inspect your cable operated clutch throw-out and trans rear seal, then come back here to Step 9. **Type IV** without automatic trans uses a hydraulic master cylinder (over the clutch pedal) and a slave cylinder (on top of the trans) to operate the clutch. The slave pushes the clutch throw-out bearing (rear of trans). Check the slave for any signs of leakage. If the action of your clutch pedal has been mushy, the source is a leaky slave. At the least, you should fill the tank over the clutch pedal with brake fluid and bleed a half of a tank out through the bleeder bolt. See Chapter XIII. If there's any sign of fluid leakage, have the slave cylinder rebuilt. While you're under the car, check the action of the throw-out bearing. While your friend operates the clutch pedal several times, watch the action. Does the bearing come toward you straight and true? This type of clutch operation is hard on the throw-out bearing and we recommend a new one, so put what you need on the shopping list. If the clutch throw-out bearing needs replacement or you suspect a leaky rear trans seal (heavy, sticky oil inside the bell housing), go to ENGINE DISMANTLING, Step 1, then come back here.

Step 9.   Remove Clutch Assembly—Not for Automatics

The clutch pressure plate (on the FRONT of the engine) in these models is a very tough diaphragm type and ordinarily needs little attention for the life of the car. Look at the diaphragm. Do all the fingers sit at about the same height? Are any of them broken? If they're all at about the same level and none are missing, you usually can assume the pressure plate is OK. If it's OK and you are here for a valve job only, skip the rest of this step. If you're doing an engine overhaul, if the pressure plate needs replacement or if you're here to replace the front seal, you must remove the clutch pressure plate. Here's how: if it doesn't need replacement, you must make a mark with the hammer and chisel on the edge of the pressure plate and onto the flywheel. This mark will let you replace the pressure plate in its original location on the flywheel. It's marked? OK, put the ratchet on the short extension, then the 13mm socket. Put the socket on a bolt and give the ratchet a hit with the palm of your hand to loosen the bolt. Do the same to the next one and the next until you've loosened

Step 9. (Cont'd.)

them all. **They must come off evenly** or the plate will distort. Start around the circle again and make a half turn on each bolt, going around the circle half turn at a time until you can remove them with your fingers into a baggie. Take some fine emery cloth and rub it across the circle on the pressure plate until you have scratched the whole circle well. This breaks up the glaze. Put it in a bag marked "clutch."

Now look at the clutch plate, the round plate that was between the flywheel and the pressure plate. If you have the bread, always install a new one whenever the engine is out. Definitely replace it, if it measures less than 5/16" in thickness. Take it to the car and put it on the trans splines: check to see if it wobbles on the spline shaft. If it does, buy a new one, no matter how thick it is. If you decide to use the old clutch plate, use the emery cloth on the face, before putting it into the "clutch" bag. If you've pulled the engine to fix the clutch only, go to ENGINE EQUIPMENT ASSEMBLY AND INSTALLATION, Step 11, then skip to Step 18 in the same Procedure.

Step 10. Remove Fan Housing and Associated Equipment

Condition: Engine overhaul, valve job, oil cooler replacement or front seal replacement for automatics. If you have a stick shift and are replacing the front seal only, you could skip this step but you have to hold the flywheel with a four foot piece of angle iron (see ENGINE DISMANTLING, Step 4.)

1973 Bus: remove the smog pump tubing that connects the various parts of the smog pump system. Try to get it out in as few pieces as possible. Also try to remember how it comes out so you can put it back in. It's really a simple system—just looks complicated. There is one tube that runs between the two intake manifolds with a junction on the right that runs to the smog pump control valve, the gizmo next to the smog pump. Try to get that out in one piece. There are two connections on the control valve. Use a 17mm open end to remove the nut and gently spring the tube to get it out. Put this part away. Now try to get the spider out. This is the system that runs from the pump to the heads so loosen the nuts at the port (hole) in the head with your wrench, then disconnect the spider of tubing at the pump and gently pull the whole assembly off the engine. Now loosen the left support nut under the pump so the belt will come loose. Take it off and put it away with the tubing. You can leave the pump and control valve right on the fan housing—be careful with it. So far, none of the other models have been afflicted with this monster. You can now remove the two side bracket bolts that hold the bottom pulley which drives the smog pump and the three allen head cap screws that hold the center piece of the fan and the whole assembly is in your hand, plus the fan is ready to pull out.

All: To the right of the fan housing is the alternator. Above and to the right of the alternator is a plastic cap. Take out the cap with a screwdriver, use the 6mm allen head wrench and loosen and remove the adjusting bolt. Put the bolt and cap in a baggie and push the alternator all the way to the left and remove the fan belt. Put it in a sack.

Type IV and '72 Bus: take off the screen (Bus) or the air scoop (Type IV, if yours has one). It's held on by four screws around the rim of the fan. Now take out those three allen head cap screws that hold the fan to the fan pulley. (Note: technically this isn't a pulley but for lack of a better word, the thing the fan is bolted to is herein called the rear pulley.)

All: Pull the fan out and put it into a bag. There are four 13mm nuts and washers around the fan housing hole. Remove them. Release the wire that operates the air control and the fan housing can be slipped off the bolts. Put it in a safe place. If you're just replacing the oil cooler or putting in a new front engine seal, do no more in this step. For the oil cooler, go to Step 12 and for the front seal, go to the next step.

Take out the bolt that holds the wheel the control cable rolls on and the bolt that holds the thermostat on the right side of the engine. Put all this stuff into a baggie which goes into the sack

Step 10. (Cont'd.)

with the fan. There are one or two spacers between the fan and the pulley it bolts to so take them off and put them with the rest of the stuff.

Step 11. Remove Flywheel (stick shift) or Drive Plate (automatic)

This is where you need the special tools.

Condition: Overhaul or front seal on automatic shift. Valve job or oil cooler replacement only, skip this step.

There are five cap screws that hold the flywheel or drive plate to the end of the crankshaft. As they only torque to 80 ft. lbs. for the flywheel and 61 ft. lbs. for the drive plate, you can use a big stillson (pipe wrench) on the rear pulley to hold the crankshaft from turning. The cap screws that hold the flywheel (drive plate) have a splined hole in the head so you need that 3/8" drive, 12 splined key wrench on the breaker bar. Put a rag over the rear pulley so the teeth in the pipe wrench don't hurt it and with the key wrench, take out the five cap screws and the five hole washer (if any) that hold the flywheel or drive plate. Put them in a baggie, then pull the flywheel or drive plate gently off. Pry out the old front seal with two screwdrivers. There are three shims (like big washers) in back of the seal. Put them carefully in a baggie—put them away and do not bend, staple or punch.

There is a rubber "0" ring inside of the place where the flywheel or drive plate bolts to the end of the crankshaft in most models. If you have none, you don't have to put one back in but if you have one, remember to replace it when you install the flywheel or drive plate.

If you're replacing the front seal only, go to ENGINE EQUIPMENT ASSEMBLY AND INSTALLATION, TYPE IV, Step 2.

Step 12. Remove Oil Cooler

Condition: Overhaul, oil cooler replacement. Valve job only: skip this step but look at your oil cooler for bulging and/or leaking. We'd replace the oil cooler every time the engine is out; these big engines are hard on oil coolers.

Remove the left top piece of shrouding and there's the oil cooler mounted on three long studs that come out of the rear of the engine. It's also supported by two brackets from the shrouding so after the shrouding's gone, the brackets will come off and the three nuts holding the oil cooler can be removed. There are two washers under each nut—put everything into an "oil cooler" baggie. This is a part we'd definitely replace when overhauling so we suggest you put one on your shopping list. If the reason for your being here is the oil cooler, go to ENGINE EQUIPMENT ASSEMBLY AND INSTALLATION, TYPE IV, Step 3, to put the new one on.

Step 13. Remove Intake Manifold and for Fuel Injection: the Intake Air Distributor

Condition: Overhaul. Valve job only: remove manifold but not intake air distributor.

All: Remove the four nuts and washers that hold each intake manifold to the top of the heads (side of the engine) with the 13mm socket, extension and ratchet.

Carburetor models: Remove the balance tube and idle tube that run between the two carbs. Mark these tubes and put them into a bag. Next, unbolt the linkage bar from both carbs (it runs between them), put it, the three return springs and the bolts into the same bag. Tie rags around the carbs for protection.

Step 13. (Cont'd.)

Fuel Injection: remove the hoses from the injectors, then remove the injectors. Put each injector in a separate baggie and put these baggies and the clamps into the fuel system bag. Remove fuel loop, a loop of hose and tubes that runs from the sides of injectors No. 3 and 4 along the top of the engine to injectors No. 1 and 2, then runs in front of the engine to the pressure regulator. Just pull it through the front piece of tin, then disconnect the screw clamp at the pressure regulator. Keep it CLEAN...tape the ends and the injector holes so NO DIRT CAN ENTER. Now, pull the manifolds straight off the intake air distributor; pull the woven connectors off and into a bag. There are different numbers of hoses in different models attached to the intake air distributor. Get yours marked and put away. Some fuel injected models have an air injection system (after burner) which supplies air to the heads. These hoses would be attached from the air cleaner to the intake air distributor through a bypass valve. Hoses off? OK, remove the bolts that hold the intake air distributor to the crankcase, lift it off and put it away. Remove the EGR pipes.

Step 14. Remove Alternator and Remaining Shrouding

Condition: Overhaul and valve job.

We cannot tell from here which hoses, out of the many, your engine still has on it. We'll list them and you remove those that are there. You've probably removed most of them. OK? 1) the evaporative control system with the charcoal tank has a hose from the fan housing to the tank and from the tank to the air cleaner. 2) the new crankcase ventilation system has a hose with a connection to each of the valve covers, a flame trap junction and a connection to the air cleaner. Pull the hose off the valve covers. 3) some automatic shifts have an exhaust reburner with a filter, a valve (usually electric) and another connection to either the intake air distributor or the air cleaner. 4) some models have an electrically or manually operated deceleration valve (on the left side of the engine) with two hoses. One goes to the intake air distributor or intake manifold and the other goes to the vacuum advance on the distributor. None of these have a damn thing to do with how your engine runs, except negatively.

All: Remove the rear tin around the alternator. It's held on by screws and nuts, then take the nut off the hinge pin and pull the pin out of the hinge. Lower the alternator to get the air supply hose off, then pull the electrical leads back through the front piece of tin. Put the alternator in a pile to go to Volkswagen to be checked. They last longer than generators but the diodes can go bad.

Remove the front engine tin, then the rest of the shrouding tin covering the engine, except the air deflectors under the cylinders. It's a good idea to mark each piece of tin with the Mark-All as you take it off—even make a line where two pieces join so later you can see how they fit together. Put the screws into a baggie marked "shrouding screws."

Fuel Injection: the pressure regulator is still mounted to that front piece of tin. Leave it there, but tape up the holes so dirt CANNOT get in.

Step 15. Remove Engine Support Bracket

Condition: Overhaul. Valve job only, skip this step.

Take out the two or four bolts that hold the rear support bracket to the crankcase, then remove the bracket and store it.

PROCEDURE FOR ENGINE DISMANTLING, ALL MODELS

Tools and Materials: Phase II tool kit, Liquid Wrench, a sheet of crocus cloth, an 18" long pipe cheater (see Chapter XVI) and soft wire, masking tape, bags and baggies. For Types I and III and Type II through 1971: two rulers or a square and a ruler plus something to keep the flywheel from turning (see Step 4), a 1-7/16" or 36mm socket with a breaker bar or flex handle to fit. Type IV and 1972 and on Bus: internal snap ring pliers.

Note: Read the Condition before doing the step.

Step 1. Inspect Rear Trans Seal and Clutch Throw-Out Bearing—Not for Automatics

Condition: Your engine is out, do this step.

If there's heavy, sticky oil (trans fluid) on the inside of the bell housing, your rear trans seal is bad so go to the mini procedure in Chapter XIV and replace it. Use this step to remove the clutch throw-out bearing.

Look past the space where your engine was. In the middle you can see the back end of the trans shaft. On the left of the shaft and up a bit is a little lever; this is the clutch adjustment lever. To the right of the trans shaft is the starter and solenoid. Look back at the end of the trans shaft. The clutch throw-out bearing is the round thing around the shaft and is operated back and forth by the clutch lever which in turn is operated by the clutch cable coming from the clutch pedal in the front of the car. If you have one of the old carbon block clutch throw-out bearings (it would be a carbon block and not a ball bearing), check the face of the carbon block for marks and cracks. If it's at all marked, take it out and put it into the shopping pile and replace it. Pull the hairpin-like wire (cotter pin) out of the center and lift the bearing carrier out. Shove the wire back in so it doesn't get lost. We suggest that you replace this carbon block with the newer ball bearing type throw-out bearing. If you have a ball bearing type throw-out, check to see that the face of the bearing is free to rotate. If your bearing is frozen or doesn't rotate smoothly, remove it into the shopping pile for replacement. It comes out the same way the carbon block throw-out does. The throw-out bearing in the new models slides over a guide collar after removing the cotter pin.

Step 2. Check Clutch Pressure Plate—not for Automatic, Type IV or 1972 and on Bus

Condition: Engine overhaul or you arrived here from Chapter XIII to replace your clutch plate and/or you need a new front seal. **Valve job people:** skip the step, unless your clutch has been acting up or you suspect a leaky front seal (Chapter IX).

You need to check the clutch pressure plate (which is right smack in the middle of the front of the engine) to see if it's square with the engine. Get the blade of a square or a good straight ruler and hold it across the round thing in the middle of the pressure plate; then, with another ruler, measure the distance to the flywheel from your straight edge. Take the measurement on both sides. This distance should be just barely over one inch for the 36 and 40hp and 1-1/16" for the 1300 on but the main thing is that the two dimensions are within 1/16" of each other. If the difference between these two dimensions is like 1/8", you need to buy a rebuilt clutch pressure plate.

Check all of the springs inside those round tubes that stick out to see if any are broken. If so, replace the clutch pressure plate. There are some bent wire springs you can see on the outside of the plate; release lever springs. A broken one of these is not such a tragedy—just put a new release lever spring (both pieces) on your shopping list and install it on the plate.

Step 3. Remove Clutch Assembly—Not for Automatics, Type IV or 1972 and on Bus

Condition: Same as Step 2.

With a hammer and chisel, make two punch marks: one on the clutch pressure plate, the other on the flywheel, right in line with each other so you can replace the clutch pressure plate on the same place on the flywheel it came off. If you need a rebuilt pressure plate, forget it. There are six bolts holding the clutch pressure plate to the flywheel. They must come off evenly or the plate will distort. With the 13mm socket on the short extension on the ratchet, start with the top bolt. Put the socket on the bolt and hold it with the ratchet handle straight up with your left hand. Now strike the ratchet handle a sharp blow with the palm of your right hand. This will loosen the bolt. Rotate the flywheel so the next bolt is on top and repeat. Do this six times until all six bolts are knocked loose, then start around with the socket and loosen each bolt a half turn more, going round and round. (1/2 turn on bolt No. 1, 1/2 turn on No. 2 etc., until you can remove them with your fingers.) Remove the clutch assembly and screw the six bolts with their washers back onto the flywheel. Take the clutch plate off the clutch pressure plate and put the pressure plate in the car (if it checks out OK) and the clutch plate in the pile to go shopping.

Those of you who pulled the engine to replace the clutch plate, check behind the flywheel with your eye and the flashlight for evidence of leaking around the front seal. If the rear of your flywheel is oil-wet, you'd better replace the seal. If your seal's OK, buy a new clutch plate and turn to Step 17, ENGINE MANTLING, and proceed.

Step 4. Remove Flywheel (stick shift) or Drive Plate (automatics) and Front Seal—Not for Type IV and 1972 and on Bus

Condition: Engine overhaul and/or your front seal has been leaking oil. Valves only: skip the step, unless you take this opportunity to replace the front seal.

The flywheel is held to the crankshaft by a gland nut which has been torqued to 220 ft. lbs. You'll need the 1-7/16" or 36mm socket, the breaker bar or flex handle, the pipe cheater, a friend and a device to hold the flywheel against turning. There are several ways to do this:

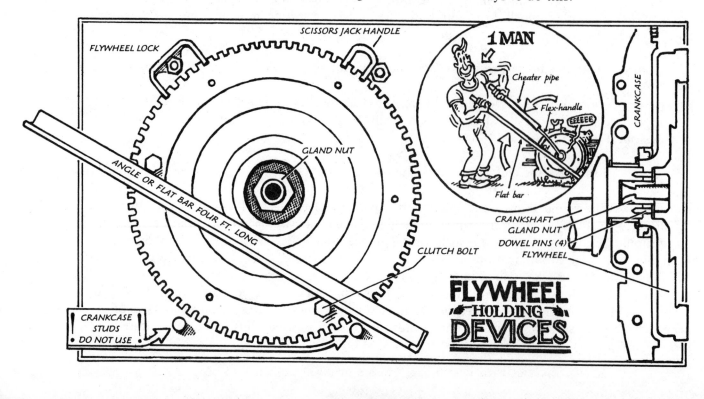

Step 4. (Cont'd.)

(1) **Jack handle and bolt method.** If the end of your scissors jack handle is U-shaped or if you have a U-shaped piece of steel that fits into two teeth of the flywheel, put a 3/8" nut and bolt through one of the top engine mount holes in the crankcase above the flywheel. Have your friend put the legs of the Ⓝ into two of the flywheel teeth braced against the 3/8" nut and bolt while you loosen the gland nut.

(2) **Angle Iron method.** You need a piece of flat bar or angle iron about four feet long and 1-1/2" wide. Have your friend hold the angle iron between two of the clutch bolts on opposite sides of the flywheel while you loosen the gland nut. It helps to drill two holes for the clutch bolts in the angle iron but is not necessary.

(3) **Borrow or rent a commercial flywheel lock.** Use as in sketch.

(4) With no large socket or device to hold the flywheel from turning, see Chapter XVI, How to Remove Large High Torque Nuts.

While your friend holds the flywheel from turning (**do not use the bottom engine studs** to hold the flywheel—they'll bend or break), put the socket arrangement on the gland nut **and** loosen it **counterclockwise putting all your weight on the end of the cheater bar. (You may even consider jumping on the end of the cheater—take care now!) Unscrew it with your fingers when it's loose enough. Put the gland nut and the spring washer in a baggie.**

With the big screwdriver you can now pry the flywheel around the rim (wiggle it some) and off the end of the crankshaft. It's heavy. There are four pins that fit into the end of the crankshaft to transfer the torque. They're difficult to replace so take them out (with the vice grip if necessary but don't mar them in any way) and put them in a baggie. If there's a rubber "0" ring on the inside of the flywheel where it fits on the crankshaft, take it out and make a note that your model has one. Also note whether the gasket under the flywheel is paper or metal so you know which kind to use when assembling.

Take a good look at your flywheel. If the teeth are very badly worn and you've been having a lot of trouble with the starter sticking like in the middle of downtown traffic, replace the flywheel. Look at the four holes in the center of the flywheel. If they're at all oval or beat up from the flywheel being loose on those four pins, the holes will have to be redrilled in another place. The machine shop can do this. If you've found oval holes on your flywheel, immediately check the four holes in the end of the crankshaft, as they may be damaged too. These, also, can be redrilled by the machine shop but you'll have to take the crankcase apart. If you need a new flywheel, check the junk yards first but take your old one along to check for size and number of teeth. With the big screwdriver or a small bar, pry the front seal out of the engine.

It's in the crankcase, right under where the flywheel was. Hook the screwdriver under its inner rim and pry it out. The seal is about 3/8" thick—that metal is part of it. Take out the three shims (like big washers) with the magnet, put these shims together in a baggie. If you're just replacing the front seal, turn to ENGINE MANTLING, Step 15, after buying a new seal.

If you have a rear engine carrier, now's the time to take it off. It's the long metal bar that spans the rear of the engine. Remember, you had to disconnect it from the body. Remove the two top bolts with a 17mm socket on a breaker bar and the bottom bolt with a 13mm wrench. Put the bolts in a marked baggie and put the carrier in a safe place.

Step 5. Remove Fuel Pump and Generator Pedestal or Crankcase Breather—Not for Type IV or 1972 and on Bus

Condition: Engine overhaul. Valve job only, skip this step.

Types I (all) and II (through 1971): The fuel pump lives under the distributor (36hp) or immediately to the right of the distributor (all others). Use the 13mm or 14mm box end to remove the two nuts holding it on, then lift it off and put it in a bag. Put the nuts and washers in a baggie. Pull the plunger

Step 5. (Cont'd.)

and the plastic block out of the case and put them with the fuel pump after removing the two old gaskets. Loosen and remove the four 13mm nuts holding the generator pedestal. Put them in a baggie and the pedestal in the pile to be cleaned. Remove the old gasket. Remove the oil dip stick. Put it in a bag.

36hp: The pedestal doesn't come off.

Type III: There's no generator pedestal, but the crankcase breather which is in the same place removes the same way as the pedestal.

Carb models: Take the fuel pump off in the same way as above.

Fuel Injection: There's a brass ground connection under one of the crankcase breather nuts... into a baggie. The fuel pump is electric and is mounted under the front of the car so there's no need to even think about it now. However, you have to remove the auxiliary air regulator which is mounted in the same place and in the same manner as the fuel pump so: up to 1970, the front stud is a temperature sensor. Use the 13mm open end on it. You can use the 13mm socket on the rear nut. From 1970 and on: use the 13mm socket, extension on the ratchet to remove the two nuts holding the auxiliary air regulator to the crankcase. Now fuel injected models can lift the auxiliary air regulator up with the throttle spring bracket. Put these in a marked baggie.

Step 6. Remove Starter—All models. See Changes and New Ideas.

Condition: Engine overhaul and you want the starter overhauled to match the engine. You're going to remove it and take it to an auto-electric shop. If you're not going to have the starter overhauled, skip the step.

Push the right top engine mounting bolt forward and out, then reach around and remove it. It's to the right of the transmission shaft. There are three wires to disconnect. With the 13mm box end take off the nut that holds the cable from the battery to the solenoid. The hot wire from the engine will come off with the cable. If it doesn't, it's a push-on connected to a washer on the same terminal. Replace the washer and screw the nut back on. The third wire, the one from the ignition switch to the solenoid is a push-on, except in the very old models where it's a screw-on.

Now, use the 17mm box end to take the lower starter mounting nut off. Pull the starter forward and out, but it's heavier than it looks so don't drop it. Put it in the pile of parts to go downtown but protect it from dampness, then screw the nut onto the long bolt you took off first and put these in a baggie.

Step 7. Remove Rocker Arm Assemblies, Push Rods, Tubes and Heads

Condition: Engine overhaul and valve job.

Note: From here on out in this procedure, Type IV means the Type IV and the 1972 and on Bus as it has a Type IV engine in it. OK? Type II means the Bus through 1971.

All Models: It's nice to have a work bench or table to put the engine on and a sheltered place to work. Face the right side valve cover toward you and pry the wire valve cover holder (the handle) down and remove the valve cover. Scrape off the old gasket and put the cover into the cleaning pile. Remove all four spark plugs with the spark plug wrench; put them in a baggie. Use the 13 or 14mm socket on the short extension on the ratchet to remove the two bolts or nuts (four 13mm nuts on Type IV) that hold the rocker arm assembly to the head. They're the ones in the center of the rocker arm assembly. Put these nuts and their washers or the bolts into a baggie marked "rocker arm" and pull and lift the assembly off. Pull out the four push rods and roll them on a flat surface to see if they're straight. Watch the little holes in their ends and if they roll erratically, the push rod is bent

Step 7. (Cont'd.)

and must be replaced with a new one. Put the good push rods and the rocker arm assembly in a safe place. They'll need to be cleaned with solvent.

Type IV: There's a wire spring holding the push rod tubes into the head—look at it as it must be returned to the same position during reassembly. Take one off with the screwdriver. See how it goes back on while the one in the other head is still in position. Make a sketch, if necessary. OK? Put the wire spring into the baggie with the rocker arm nuts. Look at the way the push rod tubes are sealed. They have an "0" ring around each end and will be installed after the heads are bolted back on.

All Models: Try the 15mm, 16mm and 17mm sockets on one of your head nuts. Put whichever one fits on the short extension on the ratchet. With your left hand holding the ratchet near the socket so the ratchet handle is straight up, swing the palm of your right hand at the ratchet handle to loosen in turn all eight head nuts. There are four on top and four below where the rocker arm assembly was. Remove them and their washers and put them in a "head" baggie. These are special washers so if any are missing, make a note to buy as many new ones as you need at VW. Only they have the right ones. If the head nuts won't come loose with a sharp blow from your right palm, use the cheater (see Chapter XVI).

Once the head is off, there's nothing to hold the cylinders on, so if all you're doing is a valve job, be careful not to knock the cylinders loose. Carefully pry the head and cylinders apart and pull the head off the bolts. If it's tough, use the hammer on a block of wood to tap on the exhaust manifold bolts, , not on the fins which are fragile. As the head comes loose, the push rod tubes will fall down so pick them up and put them with the rocker arm assembly. Be careful of these tubes and don't bend or squash them but clean them. If you're just doing a valve job, please, under no conditions, jar the cylinders loose. Find a piece of soft wire (like bailing wire) to tie the cylinders on. Wrap the wire around one of the studs next to No. 1 cylinder, take it across the cylinder tops and wrap it around a stud next to No. 2 cylinder. Move the engine around and repeat this step.

With both heads off, check your valve guides. Push the valve stems with your thumb (where the rocker arms fit). If there is any play where the valves go through the heads, you'll need new valve guides. Discuss it with the machinist. Usually the intake guides are OK but often the exhaust valve guides need replacing. If you need one exhaust valve guide, replace all four. **Do not use cast iron valve guides.** We figure that most of the 3,000 mile overhauls are caused by worn valve guides. The valve starts to wobble a bit, burns—sticks, the oil starts to heat and off you go to Rod City.

If all you had planned to do was a valve job, take a good look now at the tops of your pistons. Carefully turn the engine and look at each one. Look for damage, especially around the edges of the tops and if you find a hole or a big dent, you'll have to remove the cylinders to replace that piston or all of the pistons and all of the rings—depends on if you're doing a "Muldoon" or not. If all you find during this inspection is carbon and a few small scratches, take your heads to the machine shop for a valve job and start cleaning parts. Read the shopping list in Step 14 before you go. When your heads are back, go to Step 6, ENGINE MANTLING.

Fuel Injection: There is a cylinder head temperature sensor on the left, No. 3 and 4, cylinder head. Before 1970, it's below the rear exhaust port and after 1970, it's on top by the intake port. If you're going to take the heads to the machine shop, it's important to remove the sensor. Use a 13mm box wrench to unscrew it. Put it in a marked baggie.

All Models, except 36hp, please read the following. You may have to do it later. Type IV does it now.

Type IV: If you're doing a valve job only, this is as far as you need go but if you're going to pull the cylinders, take the cam followers out before they fall out. Find the magnet, 8 baggies and 8 slips of paper and write a valve number on each slip like: E-1 (No. 1 exhaust), I-1 (No. 1 intake), I-2, E-2, then for the other side, E-3, I-3, I-4, E-4. Pull out No. 1 exhaust cam follower with the magnet (front, right), clean it in solvent and let it dry or wipe it dry with a paper towel, then pop it into the E-1 baggie along with the slip of paper. When reassembling, **each cam follower must go into the hole it came out of.**

Step 8. Remove Cylinders

Condition: Engine Overhaul

There's a piece of sheet metal under each set of cylinders. They're called air deflectors and are very important in the cooling of your engine. They may just be held up by spring action or someone may have wired them up. Remove them into the parts to be cleaned.

Mark the cylinders with a Mark—All. No. 1 is the front one on the right, No. 2 is in back of it, No. 3 is the front one on the left. If you wash the numbers off while cleaning the cylinders, replace them immediately. If you already know you will buy new cylinders and pistons, just remove them, but keep one to match for size when shopping. Pull the cylinders off one by one. They will probably be stuck in the case and have to be persuaded off with a rubber mallet. Hit the fins straight on as pictured. Please don't get dirt into the holes where the pistons are. Put your cylinders in a row: 1, 2, 3, 4.

Step 9. Remove Distributor. Type IV, your's is already off.

Condition: You're going to overhaul the distributor (new points and condenser) or you're going to have to break the crankcase apart. If you're just doing rings and inserts, it doesn't need to come off.

Use the 13mm socket on the short extension on the ratchet to remove the nuts and washers holding the distributor clamp to the crankcase. Pry the distributor up with gentle taps of a small hammer. Take out the whole assembly, distributor, clamp and wires still attached (except 36hp) and put it in a bag marked "ignition." Plug the hole into the crankcase with a rag. The rag will keep dirt out and the spring in the hole in.

Step 10. Remove Pistons

Condition: Engine overhaul

First a warning: **LIFT THE PISTONS WITH YOUR HANDS** and guide them into the crankcase each time you turn the engine over or you'll break the piston skirts.

This doesn't apply to those who already know they're going to buy new pistons and cylinders, but you others, **mark the pistons**.

With a nail or file, scratch the number on the top of the piston, through the carbon and draw an arrow pointing toward the flywheel, like I, II, etc. Start with No. 1, get it out as far as it'll go, and remember the WARNING.

You must take two circlips out, one from each end of the wrist pin (looks like a short piece of pipe that holds the outer end of the connecting rod to the piston). With the long-nose pliers, squeeze the two bent ends of the wire together and pull the circlip, ⬭ , out.

Type IV: You need a pair of internal snap ring pliers if your engine has snap ring circlips. Stick the points of the snap ring pliers in the holes in the circlip and squeeze the pliers to draw the circlip out. ◖◗

All models: Put the circlip into a baggie and remove the other circlip. Now get your long extension, put the 8 or 10mm socket on it and use this assembly, socket on the wrist pin, to drive the wrist pin out. Use a small block of wood over the extension end and give it a sharp hammer blow.

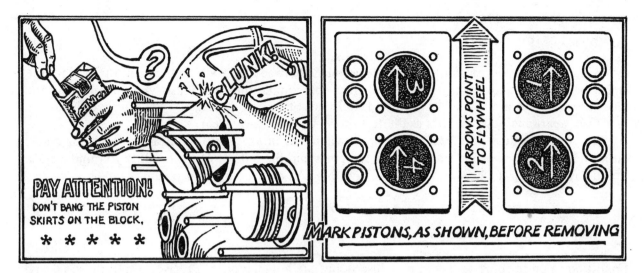

Don't drive the wrist pin all the way out, just enough to clear the connecting rod. To be consistent, drive them all toward the flywheel, the way the arrows on your piston tops go. If it comes very tough, light up the propane torch and warm up the piston in the pin area until it's just a little too warm to touch, **not hot**, and try driving it out again. It'll come; remember, not all the way out. Repeat this step for the other three pistons and remember to lift the pistons out with your hand. Put No. 3 piston with No. 3 cylinder, No. 2 with No. 2, etc.

Step 11. Check for Wear

Condition: You need to know what's worn.

Wiggle all the long studs in the crankcase. If any are loose and you can't tighten them with the vice grip clamped *off* the threads, remove the offender to see if the hole in the crankcase is stripped. If it is, you'll need a helicoil shot into it in the machine shop or a casesaver kit from VW.

With Muldoon and bread in mind: If the cylinders are bad, you need new pistons also. You shouldn't buy one without the other. Buy new ones if: even one piston is broken anywhere or if even one has seize marks (grooves) in it—check both the pistons and the walls of the cylinders for these grooves. Let's check your cylinders, if they've passed the seize mark test.

Take the center ring off one of the pistons. Use two hands around the ring and with your thumbnails on the ends of the ring, expand it gently until it'll come out of the land (groove) and then work it off the top of the piston. Put this ring into the lower end of the cylinder (the end where the fins are narrow). It should be about 1/4" from the rim of the cylinder all the way around. The ring ends won't meet. Get out the feeler gauge and start putting blades into this crack. The gap will be about .016" with a new ring in a new cylinder. If the gap in yours is over .060" (in other words, if a .060" feeler blade or combination of blades will fit into the crack made by the ends of the ring), the cylinder is junk. If your pistons check out within tolerance, take the cylinders to the machine shop and borrow a new ring from the machinist and if the gap is .030" or less, keep the pistons and cylinders and buy only new rings.

Now check the pistons. Find the worst piston you have, the one where the top ring is the loosest. With the feeler gauge, check to see which blade will fit between the top ring and its land. If the .005" blade fits in, your pistons are junk. If the .004" blade fits in, your pistons are questionable. Look at the rest of them. Are they all approximately in the same shape (that is, the .004" blade fits in)? Were your cylinders almost .060" out? Use your judgement. If both were well within the tolerances, keep them, but if they're coming to the end of their wear cycle, buy new pistons, cylinders and rings; they come in sets.

Now check the front main bearing for wear: wrap a piece of cloth around the end of a bar or the large screwdriver. Insert the well-protected blade into the crankcase where the front seal was and try to lift the crankshaft in the case by prying gently upward. Give the rods one simple test before

Step 11. (Cont'd.)

removing them. If you can get the .016" feeler blade between the rod and the crankthrow (into the crack made by the edge of the rod and where it goes around the crankshaft—you'll have to put the blade into the hole in the crankcase the rod sticks out of to find this crack), you'll have to break the crankcase apart and buy new rods as the test shows very excessive wear.

If you have dual port heads (two holes where the intake manifold attaches) look for cracks either between the two ports or between the ports and the outside of the head. If you find a crack you'll have to scrap the head. Look carefully as this isn't an uncommon problem.

ᏮᏮᏮᏮᏮ

Step 12. Remove Connecting Rods

Condition: You're going to put in new inserts but are hoping you don't have to split the crankcase and so are going to remove the rods to take a small look at the crankshaft before deciding anything further. If either the rods or crankshaft failed the above test, if you've a lot of miles on this engine (like 60,000 on a Bus or 100,000 on the others), if you've thrown a rod, if your green light has been flickering (a sign of worn mains) or if the end of your crankshaft where the flywheel was has ovalized holes, you must break the case, so go on to Crankcase Disassembly.

Start with No. 1 rod. Get it out as far as it'll go and with the 14mm socket on the long extension on the ratchet with the cheater on the handle, put the socket firmly on the rod bolt or nut and hold the ratchet handle up with your left hand and use the cheater (Chapter XVI) to loosen the bolts.

Note: the late 1500 and on has two bolts which go in from the cap side and two nuts which screw onto them, so remove the nuts and leave the bolts in the caps.

Remove the rod and leave the bolts in it. Reach into the hole with your magnet to retrieve the cap (lower part of the rod). Put rod and cap back together with the bolts or bolts and nuts, then mark the rod No. 1 by filing one notch on the long part (handle) with a file. Find both halves of the insert bearing and put them and the rod into the pile with No. 1 piston and cylinder. Repeat this step until all four rods are out, put back together and notched, and all eight insert bearing halves are out and everything is in its respective pile.

Look at the inserts one by one. Are they uniformly grey? Or are some worn so you can see the copper color? Are any of them burned black? Look at the notches in the inserts. Are they all OK? Or has one insert slipped out of its groove and been running loose? If so, split the case. Look at and feel what you can of the crankshaft. Can you see or feel any scratches or gouges in it? If it has any marks at all—anything other than a smooth mirror surface—you must disassemble the crankcase. If what you can see and feel is smooth, clean, bright and shiny, with no black marks even, your crankshaft is probably OK. How are the inserts? If all are grey and the crankshaft is smooth and bright and we were short of bread and/or time, we'd take a chance and not open the crankcase. But buy new inserts. Look at the old ones to see if there's a special number like .25 or .50 or .75 stamped on them and buy the same size when you're shopping.

Step 13. Clean the Interior

Condition: Your engine has passed all the tests and you've decided not to disassemble your crankcase.

Take all the rags out of the holes, except the distributor hole (so you don't lose that spring). Remove the oil pressure relief valve, the big screw head on the right on the bottom of the engine. On '71 and later models, there's also an oil pressure control valve to remove. See Step 2, CRANKCASE DISASSEMBLY, on how to handle these valves.

Remove the oil strainer cover. It's on the bottom of the engine and has six 10mm nuts around

Step 13. (Cont'd.)

the oil drain plug (or one 19mm bolt in the center—Type IV). Remove the nuts and washers or the bolt. If any washers are missing, put oil drain cover plate washers on your shopping list. Remove the cover and strainer inside. Remove the oil pressure sensor (except Type III, yours is out). It's that six-sided thing you took the green oil light wire off of. It unscrews with the crescent wrench.

Cut the crocus cloth so you have four long 3/4" strips. Even though your crankthrows (the places on the crankshaft where your rods were) are all shiny, you should polish them. Put a strip of crocus cloth into the cylinder hole and around the crankthrow and using a motion like towelling your wet back, pull the cloth back and forth about five times. Then turn the crankshaft 90° (a quarter of a turn) and do five more polishings. Turn the crankshaft another 90° and polish, turn 90° and polish. Use a new piece of crocus cloth for the next throw and repeat. Polish all four throws, then set the engine in a pan and using an old bug spray atomizer, charcoal fixative atomizer or pump oil can, wash the interior of the engine with a spray of solvent. Drain the solvent out the big bottom hole, then replace the oil pressure sensor with the crescent wrench (except Type IV). This unit has no washer and has taper threads, so don't over-tighten. Replace the oil pressure relief (and control) valve(s) per Chapter IX. You'll have to replace the oil strainer and cover later when you get back from shopping and have the new gaskets. Replace rags where the oil cooler goes and cover the engine with a clean cloth while you go shopping. From now on, KEEP THE ENGINE INTERIOR REMORSE-LESSLY CLEAN.

Step 14. Shopping

Type III—Add the following to your shopping list (if they need replacing):
Rubber gasket for the intake air housing
Rubber intake bellows
Rubber sleeve on oil filler pipe
Fuel Injected Models:
1/2" screw type hose clamps
new fuel hoses
All Models:
Take to the electric shop or VW:
Starter? Generator or alternator?...to be checked or overhauled.

Take to the auto machine shop:
Heads—for a valve job. Ask the machinist if you need any new valves or valve guides and if so, do you have to buy them and bring them to the machine shop or can you buy them there? Do not use cast iron guides. If you have a 1500 or on, buy stellite valves. Now is a good time to have stud kits put in, if your heads have the long studs. Check the spark plug threads to see they're not stripped. If any are, have the machinist install a helicoil.

We recommend having the machinist install new exhaust valves along with the guides as an insurance policy. I've seen some 10,000 mile overhauls as a result of an old exhaust valve breaking and going through a piston.

Have the machinist install case savers (on the bottom row of cylinder head studs), as old loose ones tend to loosen up the cylinder head and other disasterous things.

How are the long engine studs. Do any need a helicoil?

Are you keeping your old pistons and cylinders? If so, take the cylinders and check them for wear with a new ring, which you can borrow from the machinist. If they pass, have them ridge-reamed and/or the glaze broken. The machinist will tell you if this is necessary.

If you're buying new pistons, cylinders and rings and your rods are out, have the machine shop put new wrist pin bushings in the rods and check them for alignment. They'll need one of the new wrist pins in order to fit the bushings.

Step 14. (Cont'd)

If you couldn't decide whether to break the case or not, take it along with you and consult a machinist.

List of Things to Buy—either from VW or a European auto parts house:

Set of engine gaskets.

Any washers, nuts, bolts, engine studs, shrouding screws, push-ons or screw-ons for wires—all that little stuff you've been marking down on a list.

Are all your sparkplug covers intact? (Those plastic things with the rubber circle over them that fit over the spark plugs.) If not, put some on your list along with new rubber seals.

New clutch plate? We suggest you replace the clutch plate.

Clutch pressure plate? If so, buy a rebuilt one.

Gland nut: if the needle bearings are worn.

Starter Bushing? If your starter will be overhauled, buy one. It fits into the transmission case.

New fuel pump? or fuel pump push rod? (Type IV)

New muffler? If you're replacing a muffler on a pre '68 Bus, we recommend you buy a **Bug** muffler and use two offset tail pipes.

Muffler Attachment Kit—buy one whether you buy a new muffler or not. 36hp: If you can re-use your slip-over muffler, there is no kit.

New tail pipe or pipes? Buy a tail pipe attachment kit for each tail pipe.

Flywheel. Look in junk yards.

Rings? You need your engine number.

Cylinders, pistons and rings? They come in a set. Use your engine number. Don't forget to take a new piston pin to the machinist in order to fit your pin bushings.

Connecting rod inserts. If the rods are off, a must. Take an old one to match for size.

Push rods? Replace only those that aren't straight.

New spark plugs, points and condenser.

New oil cooler? If the old one was leaking or you're going to change from non-detergent to detergent oil.

New front seal. Take the old one with you and your engine number.

New rear trans seal? Take your chassis number.

Oil strainer and cover? If the old ones have stripped bolts. (Not for Type IV).

Oil Breather Cap Gasket. They're not expensive (Type I and Type II through '71 only).

Magnetic oil plug? We recommend them—they pick up pieces of steel in the oil. (Not for 1973 and on Types I and IV).

1500-type pressure relief valve plunger? For pre 1300 engines, except 36hp.

New nuts or bolts for the rods. A must if they're off.

Gallon of solvent. For cleaning parts.

Oil, six quarts. Three for now and three to change to in 300 miles.

Tube of Lubriplate Gear Lube.

Fine emery cloth.

Wheel bearing grease or Bosch grease.

A piece of 3/8" All-thread 4" long with four 3/8" nuts—if your flywheel is off.

Valve grinding compound—if you're buying new cylinders.

New oil filter cartridge from VW for Type IV engines.

Fiber parts brush.

Roll of paper towels.

A tube of grease for the trans shaft.

When you return from shopping follow PRE-ASSEMBLY, then go on to ENGINE MANTLING Step 1.

CRANKCASE DISASSEMBLY, ALL MODELS

Condition: Your crankshaft is in question and you must break the crankcase apart to see what the inside (bottom end of the engine) needs, if anything.

Tools and Materials: Phase II tool kit, 30mm socket and breaker bar or flex handle, a rubber hammer, a cardboard box with a sturdy bottom for taking stuff to the machine shop and bags and baggies.

Remarks: Throughout this Procedure, Type IV means Type IV engines which includes the '72 and on Bus engine. Type II means the Bus through 1971.

Step 1. Remove Crankshaft Pulley

Types I and II:
Put the large screwdriver in the slot on the pulley up against the crankcase to keep the pulley from turning and loosen the bolt counterclockwise with the 30mm socket on the breaker bar or flex handle until you can unscrew the bolt by hand. Pry the pulley off with the big screwdriver on one side and the bar on the other. When the pulley is off, put it in the car and put the big bolt and washer into a baggie. Remove the metal shroud under (in FRONT of) where the pulley was. It's secured by two screws and goes into the cleaning pile. See Chapter XVI if you don't have a 30mm socket.

Step 2. Remove Oil Pressure Sensor, Oil Pump Cover Plate, Oil Screen and Cover and the Oil Pressure Relief and Control Valves. See Changes and New Ideas.

All Models: Use the crescent wrench to remove the oil pressure sensor, the thing you took the oil green light wire off of. On the Type IV, it's on the left side of the engine in front of the distributor; on the Types I and II, it's to the left of the distributor and Type III, it's already off. Put it in a baggie marked "oil pressure sensor."

Use the 10mm socket on a short extension and ratchet to remove the four nuts on the oil pump cover plate (it's right under where the crankshaft pulley was) and pry it off gently; put the nuts and washers in a marked baggie. **Type IV**: remove the 10mm nuts and washers holding the back plate on the oil pump to expose the gears. Put these nuts and washers in the same baggie. **All**: Look at the inside of the front cover plate. Is it heavily scored or grooved by the gears? If so, put a new oil pump cover plate (or new oil pump, Type IV) on your shopping list. The gears can be pulled out with the magnet and put into the "oil pump" baggie.

Remove the six 10mm nuts (Type IV: one 19mm bolt) on the oil screen cover on the bottom of the engine. Remove the cover and the screen inside, clean them and put them in a bag.

Use the big screwdriver and the vice grip to remove the oil pressure relief valve. It's the big screw head on the bottom of the engine to the left of center but not on the fin area. Clamp the vice grip on the top of the screwdriver blade near the handle and use it for added leverage. Put the relief valve, spring and plunger in a marked baggie. If the plunger won't come out of the engine with a magnet, refer to the procedure on the relief valve in Chapter IX. From 1971 on, all VW's have an oil pressure control valve also. The removal procedure is the same as above. It's located on the front of the engine on the same side as the relief valve, so go to it. The **Type IV** oil pressure control valve is on the right side of the engine between the push rod tubes for No. 1 cylinder. Use the 10mm, 12 spline wrench to take it out (the same tool you used on the flywheel.) Put the piston, spring and bolt head into a marked baggie.

All: If any parts were missing on any of these things you just took off, put them on your shopping list.

Step 3. Split the Case—All Models

Tip the crankcase so it leans on the studs on the left side. A small block of wood will hold it at this angle. Most of the nuts should now be facing you. Use the 13mm socket on the long extension on the ratchet to take all the small nuts and washers off, the ones around the seam, and put them in a baggie. You'll need the 13mm box end to hold some of them while turning with the socket arrangement. (36hp has two nuts under where the flywheel was.) Loosen the six large nuts (17mm), then pull or pry the oil pump case off the four studs. Put it with the oil pump cover plate. Remove the large nuts and their washers into a baggie. Check to be sure all the bolts and nuts are out. If any washers of either size are missing—shopping list.

Use the rubber hammer to break the seam in the crankcase open. Never use any sharp instrument in the seam or oil will leak there later. If you don't have a rubber hammer, use a metal one over a block of wood, but carefully. Pull the right side of the crankcase (the side the nuts were on) off the studs on the left side. Sometimes the case comes apart very easily, then there are other times when it takes a lot of tapping and pulling and pushing, so here are a few suggestions: Tap the tops of the corner studs with the rubber hammer or tap them gently with the metal one on a block of wood. Tap gently on the edges of the four corners on the crankcase—a little here, a little there. Have your friend hold the right side up in the air by those long studs while you beat the other side down with your hammer arrangement. There are four places on the left half to beat on. Use the wood block as a wedge; try anything that comes to mind, but DO NOT MUCK UP THE SEALING EDGE OR DAMAGE THE CASE.

All Models, except 36hp and Type IV: As you pull the right side off the left side, four cam followers will fall out so put them into marked baggies (like Type IV did earlier). Take them to the machine shop to have the machinist check them out.

Step 4. Remove Camshaft, Crankshaft and Connecting Rods and Type IV Crankshaft Pulley

Remove the camshaft, the small shaft with the big gear on the back of it. In the newer engines ('65 and on), remove the camshaft bearings from both halves of the case; older engines don't have any. Bearings (if any) and shaft go into the machine shop box. Pull the crankshaft up and out—it's heavy—so have a place ready to set it down. Pull out both halves of No. 2 main bearing. They're heavy metal half circles and there will be one in each crankcase half. Remove No. 1 main bearing from the front of the crankshaft.

Type IV: remove crankshaft pulley. This pulley is mounted on the rear of the crankshaft. Hold the crankshaft so it won't turn and remove the bolt from the center of the pulley with the socket on the breaker bar. Tap the pulley round and round with the small hammer. It will usually pop right off the tapered shaft. If it doesn't, get a block of wood to use as a softener and tap all around the pulley until it does pop off.

All Models: There's a half moon key in the rear of the crankshaft. Knock it out with a small chisel and hammer and put it into a baggie. There's an oil slinger in back of this key (except Type IV): remove it and put it with the half moon key. Remove No. 4 main bearing from the rear of the shaft. All bearings go into the machine shop box.

Remove the five small steel dowel pins from the crankcase. Four are in the left half and one is in the right half of the case. Put them in a baggie.

If the rods are still on the crankshaft, let's check them for wear. Put different feeler blades into the crack made by the edge of the rod (where the two halves of the rod meet) and where the rod goes around the crankshaft (crank throw). If the .016" blade will fit into this crack, your rods have had it, so plan to buy new ones. While your friend holds the crankshaft, loosen the two bolts on each rod with the 14mm socket on the long extension on the ratchet. You may need the cheater (Chapter XVI). (Late 1500's and on have two bolts which go in from the cap side and two nuts which screw onto the bolts so remove the nuts but leave the bolts on the cap.)

Step 4. (Cont'd.)

Remove the rod, leave the bolts in it and put it back together. File one notch on the handle for rod No. 1, two notches for No. 2, etc. From the flywheel end, the rods go 3, 1, 4 and 2. Put all four rods and all eight half circles (inserts) into the machine shop box. Wrap the crankshaft with a rag and put it tenderly in the car—it's too heavy for the box.

If your distributor is still on the engine, remove the clamp, then the distributor drive shaft. It's down that hole you took the distributor out of. Tape the distributor drive shaft together with the spring and ring or rings (in the hole under the drive shaft) together and put the whole schmutz in a marked baggie. Look in both halves of the case in front of where the camshaft was—you'll see a round thing like a pop bottle cap in a half hole in one side of the case or the other. This is the camshaft seal. Remove it and put it into a baggie but remember later to clean it well. **See Changes and New Ideas.**

Step 5. Machine Shop and Shopping List

Add the information from Step 14, ENGINE DISMANTLING, to this list. You should have a box of things to take to the machine shop:

Heads, for a valve job, etc.

The **crankshaft** to be miked (measured) to see what damage it has sustained. The throws (where the rods were) may need to be ground. If they do, ask the machinist what size rod inserts to buy. The mains may need grinding. If they do, the machinist will have to take the bearings off the shaft. If so, ask what size main bearings to buy, buy them and take them to the shop and ask the machinist to put on No. 3 main, the two gears, the spacer ring and the retainer. We tell you how to do it but if the machinist will do it—go. If the machinist tells you your crankshaft is not grindable, you'll have to buy a crankshaft kit and take your beating on the core charge. When you have the new kit, return it to the machine shop and have the machinist install No. 3 main, the two gears, the spacer and the retaining clip. The bearings come with the kit.

The **camshaft and bearings** (if any) to ask the machinist if they're OK. If there's more than .002" side play, the camshaft bearings are out of spec. If you have the new type replaceable bearings, order a new set. If you have the older (bored in the case) bearings, consult with the machinist about line boring and installing inserts.

If you need a new camshaft or camshaft gear, here's a little trip we'll lay on you. When they bore out the VW crankcases in Hanover, they aren't exactly alike, so they use several minutely different camshaft gears to take up the play between the crankshaft gear and the camshaft gear. Each of these gears is marked on the back from +7 to -7. If there is no number, it's a zero gear. The point is— if you are replacing your camshaft gear or any other thumbdiddy you might be working with camshafts, it must match your crank and case. If it doesn't, your engine will continually sound as if it were running in mush or worse, as if it were just about to throw a rod or as if it had thrown a rod... just thought we'd let you know...

The **rods**—if the throws on the crankshaft need grinding, the rods will need reconditioning. If you're buying new pistons and cylinders, you'll need new wrist pin bushings in the rods.

The **rod inserts**—most machinists like to look at them.

The **cylinders**—If there's some question about reusing them, to be checked with a new ring. If they can be reused, ask the machinist if they need ridge reaming or the glaze broken.

The **cam followers** to have the machinist look at them.

The **crankcase** to be cleaned. Ask the machinist to check the bearing bores in the case; that is, the holes the bearings fit into. They tend to get larger and out of round, which makes for a terrible loss of oil pressure then rod city here you come. The machinist can align bore holes to new specifications. If you have this done, just let the machinist order the bearings for you because they're special (larger on the outside diameter to compensate for the machining). Have the machinist check the bearing bores for the camshaft as well.

Step 5. (Cont'd.)

Type IV: Before you take your crankcase to be cleaned, remove the two nuts and washers holding the oil filter bracket on the left side of the engine, then remove the two nuts and washers holding the filter plate on the bottom left rear side of the crankcase and pry the plate off. Find the oil suction pipe, that tube with the round thing on the end of it right above the oil sump hole. Remove it from the sump. It's held on by one bolt. Be sure you know how to put it back in. Some models also have a baffle under the suction pipe. If yours does, remove it, but make sure you know how it goes back in. It's held by the same screw. Put all this stuff in the pile to be cleaned. Leave the rubber sealer on the baffle, but be careful with it while cleaning.

All Models: More things to take to the machine shop:

The oil pump and gears to be checked for backlash. Before you put the oil pump and gears into the machine shop box, clean them. Put the gears into the pump—you can see how they fit—and lay a flat, smooth piece of metal across the gears and case and try the .005" feeler blade in the gap. If the blade goes in buy a new pump. New gears come with the pump. If you need a new pump and you have a 40hp engine buy the 1500 oil pump and four longer studs. This'll increase the pumping capacity by 20%.

List of Things to Buy—either from VW or an European parts house. Find out what you need from Step 14, ENGINE DISMANTLING, and add to it from this list.

New Oil Cooler? If you threw a rod, it's a must.

New Connecting Rods? Ask machinist. If so make sure they'll fit the new or reground crankshaft.

Connecting Rod Inserts. Have the machinist tell you the correct size to buy.

Main Bearings? Machinist will tell you correct size.

New Crankcase? Only if the old one has a hole in it. Look in junkyards.

Different size shims for the flywheel—a must. Buy one of each size: .24mm, .30mm, .32mm, .34mm and .36mm from VW.

VW Case Glue or No. 2 Permatex—for gluing the crankcase together.

A piece of 3/8" All-thread and four 3/8" nuts—for reinstalling the flywheel (except Type IV). Buy it at a hardware store.

Buy new valve adjustment studs and nuts when you do a complete overhaul and your valve adjustments will be more accurate and longer lasting

New rear seal—Type IV engine only.

Lock tight thread cement—not more than 20 lbs. holding power.

See Chapter XVI for a comparative inch and centimeter table so you don't become confused at the machine shop; in fact, take this book with you.

Oil pump cover plate? If yours was heavily scored. (Not Type IV)

Oil screen? If the old one has a hole in it.

PRE-ASSEMBLY PROCEDURE—All Models

Tools and Materials: Ring groove cleaner or pieces of old rings, solvent or kerosene, rags and roll of paper towels, parts cleaning brush, access to a gram scale or a piece of All-thread, some string and a coat hanger to make a beam balance (see Step 4).

Step 1. Cleaning

Condition: You've done your shopping and know which old parts are going back into the engine. Type IV includes '72 and on Bus.

Every part that goes into the engine must be bright and shiny clean. One good idea is to scrape the worst of the oily guck off all the shrouding, pile it into a friend's car and take it to a 25 cent wash place where you can soap the pieces with the pressure hose, then rinse them.

Step 1. (Cont'd.)

The push rods, push rod tubes and rocker arms can be put into solvent to be cleaned. Remove the old gaskets off both ends of the push rod tubes and clean them. For all engines, **except Type IV**, the tubes need to be stretched so they'll seal and not leak oil. Here's how: Get out your ruler and stretch the push rod tubes to 7½'' each. This makes the installation of the heads easier. Put your finger in one end and push down quite hard on the accordion pleating, then push the other way and bend it back straight. Do this on the other end also. Now using an unstretched one as a guide, see that it's at least ¼'' longer (½'' is even OK) than it was. Make sure it's straight and poke out any dents. Repeat with all eight tubes until they're all the same length.

All Models: Clean, clean, clean everything.

Step 2. Distributer Overhaul

Condition: You're going to put new points and condenser in your distributor.

Turn to Chapter X, Distributor Overhaul Procedure, to put in the new points and condenser. When they're in, wrap the distributor in a piece of paper towel, ready for installation.

Step 3. Clean Pistons, Install Rings

Condition: You're installing your old pistons and are using new rings. New pistons and cylinders usually come in a box with the pistons in the cylinders and the rings already installed. If this is your case, simply push the pistons out of the cylinders and check to see if the rings are on them. If so, go to the next step.

If you're using old pistons, remove the old rings. Dip the pistons in solvent and use the parts brush to clean them well. Scrape that carbon off the piston ends with the Boy Scout knife but don't **nick the aluminum. If you scrape off the numbers and arrows, re-mark them before they get mixed up. If you don't have a ring groove cleaner, break the old rings and use the sharp broken end to clean** the grooves. You can clean the top and middle ring grooves with a piece of the old top ring and the bottom one with a piece of the broken bottom ring. Clean each groove until you can see shiny metal all the way around.

Take a set of new rings from the box. If a ring has "TOP" or a small dot marked on it near the gap be sure that side is up. Start with ring No. 3, the bottom one. Put your thumbs on the ends of the ring, cradle it between your thumbs and index fingers, stretch the ring and slide it over the top of the piston into the bottom groove. Sometimes this bottom ring comes in several pieces. The crinkly piece goes on first, then the other one. Follow the instructions (if any) on the box. The important thing is not to break any rings because if you do you'll have to buy a whole new set—they don't sell individual rings.

Put the middle ring, No. 2, on, making sure the side marked TOP or the dot is toward the top of the piston. Install the rings on the other three pistons. **See Changes and New Ideas.**

Step 4. Balance Rods and Pistons

Condition: Old, new or reconditioned rods (makes no matter) should be balanced so they're within 5 grams of each other if you want your engine to last longest and run smoothest. New and old pistons, too, should be balanced to within five grams of each other. Racing cars balance to within 1/4 gram.

To balance, you need a scale, so either find someone with a gram scale or make a beam balance (see the end of this step). Let's balance the rods first. Your rods are together with the two bolts (or nuts and bolts), right? If they're not together, here's how. Each rod and cap has a number on one shoulder. Match these numbers to get the right rod with the right cap. Weigh the rods and find the lightest one, then file the others to match it. The sketch shows where to file: be smooth, leave no

Step 4. (Cont'd.)

jagged edges. File evenly, a little on one side, then a little on the other to match. After the rods are within five grams of each other, weigh the pistons. Find the lightest one, then file the others on their skirts to match it.

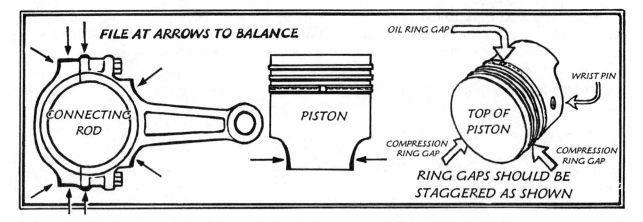

How to Make a Beam Balance:

Get out the piece of All-thread, cut four inches off one end of it, put the four nuts on it and safe-store it. With no All-thread, use any metal rod about 20 inches long. Cut two pieces of equal length string and tie a piece to each end of the All-thread an even distance (like 1/2") from the ends. Cut a third piece of string and tie it in the middle to hang the bar up. Hang it where it's free from interference as it swings.

Cut two 6" lengths of wire from a coat hanger, fashion two hooks and tie one to each end of the rod. Balance your mobile: move the middle string around until the two ends are balancing. Here's where it's nice to have the All-thread as the threads allow the string to stay where you put it and not slip. Hook a rod onto each hanger piece; find the lightest one. Remove the rods and hook the other two on; find the lightest of these. Hook the two light ones on to find the very lightest one. File the others until they'll balance with the lightest one. As an aid: a new laminated quarter (25 cent piece) weighs 5.7 grams so if a rod with a quarter on top of it will balance with a rod without a quarter, you are close enough. If you add weight to one, file the other one. Balance the pistons the same way.

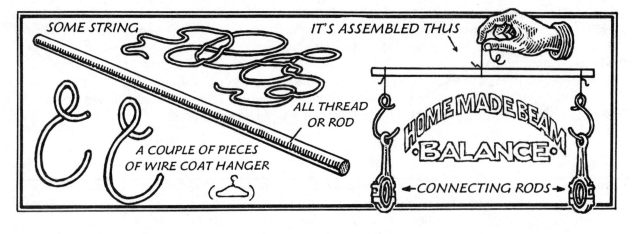

Read Chapter XVI on Torque and Torque Wrenches before you start the following assembly.

PROCEDURE FOR CRANKCASE ASSEMBLY—All Models

Condition: Your crankcase parts are all in a box at your feet. The crankcase and shaft are absolutely clean as are all the rest of the parts you took apart in CRANKCASE DISASSEMBLY. Your inside engine baggies are at hand. All the stuff in them is clean and shiny also. Type IV includes '72 and on Bus.

Tools and Materials: Phase II tool kit, 30mm socket and breaker bar or flex handle, VW case glue, *Lubriplate Gear Lube*, or equivalent engine bearing lubricant, emery cloth, oil can full of the same oil you're going to use in your engine and a friend to hold the crankshaft while you assemble it and torque the rods. If No. 3 main and the two gears, etc., are not assembled you'll need a snap ring pliers, piece of 2'' pipe and a block of wood.

Parts: The gasket kit and all the other things you needed from the shopping list.

Step 1. Definitions, Orientation and Trials

First we want to say, "Don't get shook! All those pieces!" You'll see as we go along that, one by one, they'll all fit together very nicely. Non-mechanics have done it successfully—you can, too.

Pick up the crankshaft, the heaviest piece in the box. First we'll do a quality-control thing. Put the crankshaft on two 2''x4'' pieces of wood on the table or have your friend suspend it off the table with two coat hangers. Hit it a sharp blow with the hammer but not on any bearing (shiny places). It should ring clearly, like a bell. If you think you may have dampened the sound, try another suspension but if it doesn't ring, you don't want it in your engine because it's cracked. It rang? OK, let's check the bearings for fit.

Look below for a little orientation.

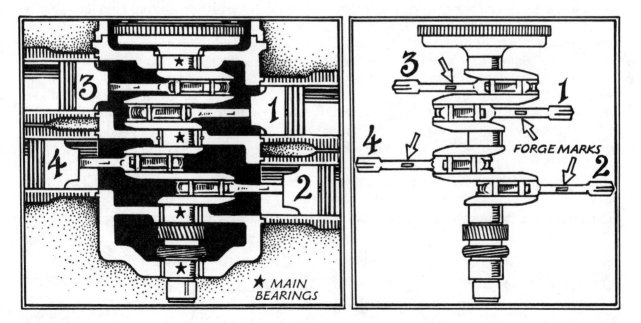

★ *MAIN BEARINGS*

FORGE MARKS

Now you can tell the players by their numbers. The main bearings are the ones in the center of the crankshaft all the way down, four of them. They are bearings that consist of two parts: a **cylinder** that rapidly rotates in a stationary **ring**. The cylinder is the crankshaft, the stationary rings are in boxes, if you bought new ones, or in the box, if you didn't have to buy new ones. These rings are made stationary by holes in the rings which fit over steel dowel pins in the crankcase. It's very important that these dowels fit into the holes in the rings.

Step 1. (Cont'd.)

You have three types of these rings: a flanged bushing (unbroken ring) which is designed to take the longitudinal forces (end thrust) in an engine. This is No. 1 main. Slip it over the front end of the crankshaft to see if it fits. FRONT is the end with the four holes (Type IV: five holes) in it where the flywheel goes. You also have two bushings with no flanges—No. 3 and No. 4 mains. No. 4 is the smaller of the two. No. 3 main is the other one and if it hasn't been assembled for you, slip it over the back end of the crankshaft onto its place. Its dowel pin hole is offset; that is, it's not in the center of the bushing, so the side with the hole goes toward the front of the engine. If it's been assembled for you, check the dowel pin hole to make certain it's toward the front. If it isn't, you'll have to take it back to the machine shop and have them turn it around, No. 4 main has a groove running around the inside of it. Slip it onto the back of the crankshaft, groove toward the rear.

The third type of stationary bearing you have is a split ring. It's No. 2 main. Put both halves of it around the center of the crankshaft where it goes. Test it first, then test the others. They should all be barely slippy loose; you should be able to slide them back and forth, just a little, but there should be no big gap between the bearing and the shaft.

In another small parts box, you'll find eight identical thin half shells. These are the connecting rod inserts and are kept stationary, not by dowels, but by pinched places which fit into notches in the rods. Put a pair of these around one of the crankshaft throws. If they're too large, they'll overlap; too small, there'll be a sizable gap when you put the two halves around the throw (not a main, now). Should either the mains or the rod inserts not fit, take the whole schmutz back to the machine shop for advice. The fit? OK. Let's put the mother together, together.

Step 2. Mark Bearing Rings

Remove all the bearing rings from the crankshaft, except No. 3 if the machine shop has installed it. There are two halves to the crankcase. Both halves have outside studs to hold the cylinders and heads on but only the left half has inside studs to hold the two halves together. Put the left half of the crankcase in front of you with the inside studs facing you and the bottom down. This puts the front of the engine to your right. Find the five steel dowel pins (they're smaller than the ones for the flywheel) and put four of them into the left crankcase half, one for each bearing. Put No. 1 and No. 4 main bearing rings into the crankcase half on their pins; No. 3 also, if it's unassembled. Are they solidly on their pins? OK, make a mark with the sharpest blade of your scout knife on the edges of the bushings where they stick up out of the case. The idea is that later you can line up the marks you made with the edge of the case so you'll know when the bearing ring is on its pin.

Note: No. 3 main bearing has two holes for pins even though No. 3 is a one piece bearing needing one pin only. The reason for the two pin places is that in Point Barrow, Alaska, and in Siberia, No. 3 main is a split bearing but in reasonable weather, it's a one piece bearing, so use one pin only.

Some people are confused about this picture. These are the main bearings, not the cam bearings.

Step 3. Assemble No. 3 Main and Gears

Condition: This should have been done by the machine shop but if you insist, here's how:

Put some masking tape around No. 4 main bearing place on the crankshaft to prevent even the tiniest scratch from happening. Wipe the No. 3 main place on the shaft with a clean piece of paper towel and wipe everything just before putting it on. Put the crankshaft up on its nose (onto the four holes) on a block of wood. Looking down into the center of the back end you should see threads. **Put some *Lubriplate* on the shaft where No. 3 bearing ring will go, slip No. 3 on—remember, dowel pin hole toward the front or down. Find the two half moon keys (pieces of steel, shaped like half** moons) and tap the largest one into its place on the shaft next to No. 3 main. Find the timing drive gear; the only thing you have made of steel that has teeth in it. Find the two small punch marks on two of the teeth. These face up (to the rear of the shaft). Start the gear over the back of the shaft so the slot will go exactly over the half moon key. Shine a light up from underneath so you can start the gear on the key and check to be sure it's right. The gear must go down next to No. 3 main so tap it and tap it, around and around with the small hammer on a dull chisel or punch, until the slot engages the half moon key (make sure the key is flat). After the slot has engaged with the key, get out the torch and heat the gear going round and round with the torch—not the shaft, just the gear— especially don't heat the bearing surfaces. You'll have done it right if you don't even scorch the masking tape. Heat it for three or four minutes, then use the large hammer and a piece of 2" pipe or a brass punch to drive it all the way down. A friend will have to hold the shaft upright while you put the pipe on the gear and tap it or beat it with the hammer, going round and round. Get it down until it sounds and feels solid when you hit it.

Find the spacer ring (the larger thick circle with ends that don't quite meet). The space goes where the half moon key is. Put the spacer ring down solidly on the gear. Find the distributor drive gear. It's made of brass and is a worm gear (the grooves in it go around the gear instead of up and down). The slot goes over the half moon key so after it's started on the key, light up the torch again to heat the gear but heat it only about a minute going around, as it's smaller than the other gear. Then drive it down until it's solidly next to the spacer ring.

The last item is the snap ring, a large thin ring with a space. It goes into the slot left between the distributor drive gear and No. 4 main. You'll see a groove in the shaft there. Spread it apart with the snap ring pliers, then slide it down (please don't hurt No. 4 main) into its groove. The space made by the ends of the ring can go anywhere. Remove the tape.

Step 4. Assemble Connecting Rods

Put the four rods on the table. They're all within 5 grams or less of each other, right? Take them apart. If the bolts are in very tight, use the big hammer handle in the large hole as a lever and the torque wrench with the long extension and 14mm socket to remove them. You'll need your friend to hold the crankshaft. Get out the inserts (the eight thin shells) and put them into the rods and caps so the notches in the inserts fit into the notches in the rods and caps. Place the crankshaft on the table so the front end (the flywheel end) is away from you and the first throw (No. 3) is to the left. Each rod and cap has a number on one of its shoulders; match these numbers. The notches on the inside and the numbers on the shoulders outside are on the same side of the rod. If you're using your old rods, you marked them, so pick up the one with three file marks (new rods: choose one to be No. 3) lubriplate the insert inside it and the insert in the matching cap. Wipe No. 3 crank throw **with a clean paper towel, then *lubriplate* it. Remember to use new nuts or bolts. Put the rod and cap around No. 3 throw, start the bolts in (or nuts) and swing the rod to the left. In this position, the** numbers should be down. The later models, with off-set rods, have a forge mark (a slightly raised bar) on each rod handle on the opposite side from the numbers. This mark should be up. (The latest connecting rods, Type B with nuts, have the numbers on the same side as the forge marks. Both the numbers and the forge marks would be up when installing this type.)

Step 4. (Cont'd.)

Lubriplate the insert in rod No. 1 and cap No. 1. Wipe, then *lubriplate* No. 1 throw, the next one down from the flywheel. Put the rod and cap around No. 1 throw, tighten the bolts or nuts by hand. When you swing this rod to the right the forge mark, if any, should be up. Next do the same for No. 4, the next throw down after No. 1 (not the middle one which is No. 2 main). Its forge mark if any, should be up when it's swung to the left. Finally, assemble No. 2—forge mark up when it's to the right. Swing No. 3 and No. 4 rods to the left and No. 1 and No. 2 rods to the right. In this position, you should see four forge marks (if you have them). Now you can tighten all the bolts (or nuts) with the 14mm socket on the long extension on the ratchet as tight as one hand on the ratchet handle will get them.

If any rod tightens up on the shaft, tap it with the small hammer right where the bolt screws into the cap (sideways) to correct any misalignment between the rod and cap. Tap it also gently around the cap. Check the side clearance between any new rods and their throws with the feeler gauge. You should be able to get the .004" blade into the crack made by the edge of the rod and the crankshaft. If the .004" blade won't fit into this crack, you'll have to remove the rod and file it on the edges until it will.

Once the .004" blade fits, call your friend to hold the crankshaft while you use the torque wrench to set all the bolts, first to 25 ft. lbs.; check for free fall, then torque to 36 ft. lbs. (Late 1500 and on with nuts: the nuts are torqued to only 25 ft. lbs.) During and after torqueing, the rods should fall slowly down by their own weight. One way to check this is to pull the back end of the crankshaft out over the edge of the table until No. 3 and No. 4 rods are over the edge. Hold No. 2 rod horizontally (on the same plane as the table) and let go of it. It should fall slowly and evenly. Pick it up and let it fall on the other side. If it won't fall, repeat the alignment tapping: also tap it some around the cap with the small hammer. The rods must fall freely, so keep tapping until they all pass the free-fall test. If all your efforts fail, you have to take the whole thing back to the machine shop for advice. After all the rods are torqued and falling freely, use a small chisel or a punch to stake (lock) the rod bolts (or nuts). Like this: Put the chisel on the nut (or bolt head) above the notch on the rod. Hit the chisel with the hammer so the chisel moves a tiny bit of the metal from the nut (or bolt head) into the slot on the connecting rod so the nut (or bolt head) won't turn.

All Models, 1973 on—don't stake the rod nuts as they apparently don't need it anymore. In fact, there isn't even the little notch on the rod or shoulder on the nut with which to do it.

Step 5. **Prepare the Crankshaft and the Crankcase Halves**

Don't stop or answer the phone in the middle of the next three steps, because the *Lubriplate* will pick up dust. The crankcase is clean, right? With all traces of the old sealing compound off the edges (seam). Put the right half of the case to your right, the inside facing you and bottom down. Put the left case half to your left, tipped onto its outer studs, bottom down.

From 1967 on: Rubber sealing rings are used between the crankcase halves. Look at the case half that has the long fat studs sticking out of the **inside** of the case. Where the studs go into the case, you'll see a bevel cut into the case, right? Find the round (1/2" diameter) rubber sealing rings, six of them. Slip them down on the studs into the recesses.

Types I, II and III: Check the oil suction pipe. It's the black tube in the right half of the case. If it's loose and not centered in the big hole in the crankcase, put the oil screen (the only piece that looks like a screen) onto the studs in the right half of the case, screen inward and put the suction pipe into the hole in the screen so the round black cup-like thing on the pipe is approximately the same distance from the inside bottom of the crankcase all the way around. Have someone hold this in this position while you take a punch and hammer and hit the case around and around where the pipe goes into the case (on the other end of the pipe from the round cap-like thing). The idea is to tap the punch with the hammer so as to make the hole in the case smaller and tighten the pipe in the case. This is called peening.

Step 5. **(Cont'd.)**

Lubriplate the outsides of the cam followers (those eight bullet casings), *lubriplate* their holes in the case and put them into their holes. Work them around to be sure they're free. **36hp:** the cam followers are on the push rods and go in later. It's a good idea to check the little rectangular plates in the crankcase that hold the cam followers square. If the plates are loose, set them by putting the thick end of a push rod into the hole in the crankcase, making sure the oil holes (on the end of the rod and in the case) line up. The plate should be just tight enough to let the push rod slide in and out freely.

Type IV: Replace the baffle under the oil suction pipe (if your model has the baffle). Bolt the oil suction pipe onto the right crankcase half. Reassemble the oil pump so it's ready to put back in the engine. Oil the two gears, then put them in the pump housing. Slip the oil pump cover in so the drive shaft goes through the hole in the pump cover and the other gear slips over the shaft in the cover. Line up the alignment pin so when you push the cover into the pump body, the pin will hold the two parts in alignment. Put the rubber "O" ring on the FRONT of the oil pump cover and shove the two parts together. If the alignment pin doesn't go into its hole, you have to take it apart and try again. When it's right, it'll go easy. Put the washers and nuts on the pump cover and tighten them and put this assembly close at hand ready to install.

All Models: Put the fifth steel dowel in place in the right case half for No. 2 split bearing. Put one shell of No. 2 main into the left case half onto its pin and the other shell into the right case half onto its pin and *lubriplate* both halves. **Engines, '65 and on,** with shell bearings on the camshaft, press three of them into the left half of the case and three of them into the right case half into the ridges, then *lubriplate* them. **All models:** squeeze some *Lubriplate* on No. 3 main through the hole and run it around. *Lubriplate* No. 1 main, the flanged bushing, just on the inside and slip it onto the front of the crankshaft making certain the dowel pin hole is toward the front. *Lubriplate* the inside of No. 4 main bearing ring and put it on the rear of the crankshaft, inside slot toward the rear. Find the oil slinger (that big sloped washer—Type IV doesn't have one) and put it on the rear of the shaft (pulley end) so the convex side faces front (flywheel end) or the concave (cupped) side faces toward the rear, then tap the half moon key into its slot. The shaft is ready.

Step 6. Install Crankshaft and Camshaft

Find the single timing mark (circular punch mark) on one of the teeth on the big gear at the back of the camshaft. Find the two marks on the timing drive gear (that gear in back of No. 3 main on the crankshaft). Later, when the cam and crankshaft are in the case, the single timing mark must fit between the two marks on the teeth of the timing drive gear. So: With the geared end of the crankshaft facing you, lift the crankshaft by holding No. 1 and No. 2 rods. Place it on the main bearing holders in the case, thus allowing No. 3 and No. 4 rods to fit through their holes. Start with No. 3 main, then No. 1, then No. 4, making sure they all fall into their dowel pin holes. You should hear a click and feel the crankshaft drop into place a little bit. Check the marks you made on No. 1 and No. 4. Are they flush with the case? When you think they are all seated, recheck and make sure none of the bearings move around or back and forth. No. 4 might move back and forth just a hair, but not round and round. **It's very important that they're seated right.**

Turn the crankshaft with the rods until the two punch marks on the gear are facing the camshaft bearing surfaces. Smear *Lubriplate* on all six camshaft bearing surfaces (both halves) but don't get any *Lubriplate* on the seam of the crankcase. Find the timing mark on the camshaft gear and and place it between the two marks on the gear on the crankshaft. Slip the camshaft down into the bearing surfaces. Now check those marks again: this isn't horseshoes. . .that mark on the camshaft gear **must** be between the two on the timing drive gear. Check the main bearings again: start with No. 1 and make sure the pin in the crankcase is in the hole in the bearing ring. Check No. 2, then No. 3 and finally No. 4. Smear *lubriplate* on all the shiny surfaces of the camshaft and on all three gears, then

Step 6. (Cont'd.)

run oil over all the moving parts with the oil can, but please don't get either *Lubriplate* or oil on the seam of the crankcase.

Now you need the camshaft seal (that little thing like a pop bottle cap). It seals the hole at the front end of the camshaft (the opposite end from the gear). Coat one half of its edge with the VW case glue and put it in the case in front of the camshaft where it fits. (Find the oil pump case—it's square looking, but fits into a round hole at the back of the engine—find the gasket that fits the hole and put them to one side). Find the oil screen and its cover and the two gaskets that go one on each side of the screen. Find three or four 10mm nuts and lock washers (warpy washers). Lay this assembly to one side. Now put the case glue sparingly and evenly all around the mating surfaces of both crankcase halves. Put some on top of the camshaft seal, too, then hurry a little (not frantically) because that glue sets up fairly quickly.

Step 7. Mating

Have your friend hold the two upper rods pointed toward their holes. Now you can tip the right half over onto the left half. Slip her in on the studs and put a couple of the center washers and nuts on hand tight.

Later 1500 and on engines, starting with engine No. HO230323: the big crankcase nuts have plastic rings on them. The plastic goes toward the crankcase with no washers. They are torqued to 18 ft. lbs.

Except 36hp and Type IV: check the cam followers with your little finger in the push rod holes to see they didn't fall out.

All Models: If you screw around too long, the goo will harden and you'll have to scrape it all off and start over so pick up the oil pump case (whole oil pump, Type IV), install the gasket and slip the pump case (whole pump) onto the studs with the hole, not the shaft, toward the top of the engine (so the side the shaft sticks out goes up, Type IV). Put on more crankcase washers and nuts. Put the oil screen on with its two new gaskets, one on each side. The screen curves into the engine. Then put the oil drain cover on top of it with a couple of washers and nuts to hold it (10mm). Type IV has one 19mm bolt here, put it on but don't tighten it yet. **Late model fuel injected engines** have a cluster of three ground connections that go onto the second case bolt from the rear (top). **Type III, carb models only**: Find the throttle bell crank assembly. It's the metal piece with a plate on top with three ball like things on it. Put it on the second bolt from the REAR on the top of the engine. Now find the piece about 2" long with a threaded hole on top and two unthreaded holes on the side (the balance tube bracket). Put it on the two front bolts on top of the engine.

All Models: Put on the rest of the crankcase washers and nuts and note what you have in the way of nuts and bolts that hold the case together; the large nuts hold the main bearings together and the smaller nuts hold the edge seal. Put them all on fairly tightly. There'll be one bolt missing on top of the engine in models earlier than '65. It holds the air control flap and goes later.

Note: It's a good idea to use a light grade of locktight (thread cement) on the six large case studs (17mm nuts). After the studs are through the case (make sure the threads on both the studs and nuts are absolutely clean), put some locktight on the ends of the studs, thread the nuts on and torque them. The reason for this is that almost all the case nuts we've checked (on engines with some mileage on them) are loose, which leads to a loss of oil pressure to the main and rod bearings. Use only a light grade locktight, like about up to 20 lbs. holding power. If you use a heavy grade, you'll never get them back off again, OK.

Important: Rotate the crankshaft with the rods before, during and after torqueing the crankcase nuts. Any sign of binding means something vital is wrong, so do not continue torqueing if the crankshaft doesn't rotate freely; find and fix the trouble—usually a main bearing is out of place.

When all the nuts and bolts are as tight as one hand on the center of the ratchet can get them, start torqueing. Up by No. 1 main, there are two small nuts, one on either side of the camshaft seal

Step 7. (Cont'd.)

(that bottle cap), that need a paper gasket under the washer. They also need to be torqued first, first to 10 ft. lbs., then to 14 ft. lbs. These are under the flywheel in the 36hp. Next torque the big nuts: start with the two center ones, torqueing them all, first to 20 ft. lbs. (10 ft. lbs.), then to 25 ft. lbs. (18 ft. lbs.). The small nuts get first 10 ft. lbs., then 14 ft. lbs.

Rotate the crankshaft with the rods. Does it turn freely? If it doesn't, take the case apart and start over again. It's possible that one of your main bearing rings is not on its pin. It rotates freely? The crankcase is mated.

Step 8. Install Pressure Relief and Control Valves, the Oil Pump and Oil Sensor

All Models: Put some oil in the hole in the crankcase that the pressure relief valve goes into (rear, bottom, left). Run the plunger— or   in and out with the magnet to be sure it's free. The hollow place goes down or out. Oil the spring, then install it after the plunger. Put the new round metal gasket on the screw-headed bolt and screw the bolt in with the large screwdriver. Tighten it really well with the vice grip clamped onto the shaft of the screwdriver near the handle and make sure it squeezes the gasket. **See Changes and New Ideas.**

1970 and on: has an oil pressure control valve to install as well. The piston (plunger) for the oil pressure control valve is plain as opposed to the grooved relief valve plunger and takes the shorter spring. Types I, II and III: The hole for the control valve is to the FRONT of the relief valve hole on the same side. The control valve installs the same way as the relief valve. Don't forget to oil the hole. Type IV: the oil pressure control valve hole is between the push rod tube holes on No. 1 cylinder. Oil the hole, find the baggie and install the piston, spring and bolt cap in that order. Look through your gaskets and find the copper one that fits the bolt cap. Tighten it firmly with the 10mm, 12 spline wrench.

Types I, II and III: Find the two small metal gears, oil the oil pump hole in the engine and oil the shaft, then stick the gear with the shaft on it in the hole in the pump and rotate the gear until it's flush with the surface of the pump. Put the other gear on the shaft and oil both gears. Put on the gasket that fits the pump. You've already put one gasket between the oil pump and the crankcase in Step 7. This gasket goes between the oil pump and the cover. It's the thinnest paper with an oval or round place so the gears can run against the cover plate as they should. Now, examine the plate. Does it have marks (not deep grooves, in which case you should have replaced it) where the gears ride? You'd see a pattern of circles. Remove the marks with a piece of emery cloth: put the emery cloth on a flat, hard surface and rub the plate over it. It's a good idea to turn the square plate around 90° from where the gears were riding before so they have a new place to wear. Install the plate.

All Models: Install the oil pump lock washers (warpy washers) and the 10mm nuts. Tighten them going round and round with the socket, short extension and ratchet. They're only 10mm so be easy and don't twist them off. Tap the plate (or pump, Type IV) with the small hammer to be sure the pump is seated and tighten the nuts a bit more.

Types I, II and IV: Find the oil sensor. It's a plastic thing, about 1-1/2" long with an electrical outlet at one end, a big six-sided nut in the middle and threads on the other end. It goes into the hole on top of No. 4 rod in the side of the case (Type IV, it goes into the hole in FRONT of the distributor hole). Use the crescent wrench to install it but since it has pipe threads with no washer, don't expect it to go all the way in. . .just snug. Be easy.

Step 9. Install Crankshaft Pulley

Type III: skip this step.

Types I and II: Clean the sealing gunk off the crankshaft really well with your Scout knife. Be sure the threads in front of the crankshaft pulley are clean or they'll throw oil. Install that piece of shroud with the half circle and cut-out Y that goes under the crankshaft pulley with two screws.

Step 9. (Cont'd.)

Slip the pulley onto the shaft, nose in, so the notch fits over the half moon key and tap it until it's flush. Put the washer around the bolt and the bolt into the hole, then tighten the bolt with the crescent wrench as tight as you can get it. Put the 30mm socket on the breaker bar or flex handle. Put this assembly on the bolt and lock the pulley from turning with the screwdriver put through the hole on the front of the pulley. Tighten the bolt fairly tight (it only gets 36 ft. lbs.), just make sure the washer is flat. If you have no 30mm socket, see Chapter XVI on How to tighten large high torque bolts (or nuts).

Type IV: Find the filter plate (round plate about 4" in diameter with two holes in it). It fits on the hole on the left rear side of the engine. Find the new gasket, coat it with heavy grease and put it, then the plate and washers and nuts on. Tighten the nuts firmly. Find the rear engine seal (it's the smaller of the two rubber seals you bought). Gently tap it into the hole around the REAR of the crankshaft until it seats all the way. Now find the pulley the crankshaft pulley bolts onto. It has three threaded holes and a pin sticking out. Get the half moon key that fits into the groove in the crankshaft and put the key in. Put the "0" ring on the end of the shaft, then tap the pulley onto the rear end of the crankshaft until it's seated properly. Replace the big bolt but don't tighten it all the way.

PROCEDURE FOR ENGINE MANTLING, ALL MODELS

Condition: Your crankcase is together, the crankshaft pulley is on (except Type III), the connecting rods may or may not be installed but you've done the PRE-ASSEMBLY PROCEDURE, Type IV includes the '72 and on Bus and Type II means the Bus through '71.

Tools and Materials: Phase II tool kit, a 4" piece of 3/8" All-thread and four 3/8" nuts, a ring compressor or a 3½" water hose clamp and a torch for assembling the pistons (if needed). Oil can full of engine oil, wheel bearing grease, *Lubriplate,* roll of paper towels, sandpaper, emery cloth, solvent or kerosene, a coat hanger, gasket cement and rags. If you're installing new cylinders (except 36hp), you will need valve grinding compound. If your generator is out, you'll need a 1-7/16" socket and breaker bar or flex handle and if your flywheel is off, you'll need the above large socket and bar, plus a pipe cheater and a device to hold the flywheel from turning. Type IV needs the special 13 spline key wrench and the special snap ring pliers.

Parts: Set of engine gaskets, plus all the items from your shopping list.

Remarks: Do not install any packaging materials into the engine along with the new part. . .OK? This may sound silly, but someone installed packaging clips into the engine. Type IV means all Type IV engines (including 1972 and on Bus).

PUT RAGS INTO ALL THE HOLES GOING INTO THE ENGINE except where the pistons go.

Step 1. Get Ready

Everything going into the engine is bright and shiny clean, right? Wipe everything that goes into the engine with a clean rag or paper towel just before installation. If you haven't installed the oil strainer and cover with two new gaskets, one on each side of the strainer, do so now. The screen curves into the engine. Tighten the 10mm nuts, going round and round with the socket, long extension and ratchet. Type IV, torque the 19mm bolt that holds the screen and cover to 9 ft. lbs.

Install your new magnetic drain plug, if you bought one. Use the metal gasket, not the paper one. With a big-ended punch, push the oil screen bottom gently inward to make room for the new magnetic plug, because sometimes these plugs are too long and put a hole in the screen. Types I and III '73 and on have no oil drain plug.

Step 2. Install Connecting Rods

Condition: Your crankcase has not been apart and your rods are not on the crankshaft. If they are, skip the step.

Rotate the engine so No. 1 crankthrow is as far to the outside as it will go. No. 1 crankthrow is the one closest to the front (the flywheel end) on the right side of the engine. Rods all within five grams of each other? OK, get out your box of eight thin half shells (rod inserts) and find No. 1 rod (you marked them, remember?). Loosen, but don't remove, the two bolts (late 1500 and on: remove the nuts but not the bolts) and take the rod and cap apart. Put one insert in the rod and one in the cap. The notches in the inserts fit into the notches in the rod and cap. These notches are on the same sides as the numbers on the shoulders. The newer rods have forge marks (slightly raised bars) on the rod handle and these forge marks are on the opposite side from the numbers. The latest connecting rods (Type B, with nuts) have the numbers on the same side as the forge marks. Both the numbers and the forge marks would be up when installing this type.

Put the 14mm socket on the long extension without the ratchet and leave this assembly close at hand. Smear some *Lubriplate* on the inserts inside of the rod and cap, wipe No. 1 throw with a clean paper towel and *Lubriplate* it, then put the cap around No. 1 throw so that the numbers (and notches) are down. Hold the cap with one hand while you fit the rod onto it with the other. The number on the shoulder of the rod must be on the same side as the number on the shoulder of the cap and both numbers must be down and the **forge mark** (if any) **must be up.** Hold this rod-cap-insert assembly with one hand so the inserts don't slip out and get the top bolt (or nut) started with the fingers of your other hand or with the socket and extension if your fingers won't fit into the crankcase. Start the bottom bolt (or nut). Tighten these bolts or nuts, taking turns, with the socket assembly put onto the ratchet until they're as tight as one hand on the ratchet will get them. You must be very careful to keep the rod and cap in alignment as you tighten. The minute the rod starts to bind on the crankthrow, loosen the bolt or nut a little and pry the cap one way or the other to align rod and cap, then tighten again. The rod must always be free to rotate on the crankthrow. Test this by holding the rod up as high as you can in the cylinder hole, then let go of it. It should fall by its own weight slowly and evenly.

Rotate the engine until No. 2 throw (next to No. 1, on the same side of the engine) is as far out as it will go, repeat the step and when it's falling slowly and evenly, install rod No. 3, the front one on the left, then install No. 4. Now check to be sure that all the forge marks are up and that all four rods are falling freely. When they are, torque all the bolts first to 24 ft. lbs., then to 36 ft. lbs. (the nuts get only 25 ft. lbs.) When they're all torqued, check for free fall again but if any are too tight to fall, loosen, align and retorque.

Step 3. Install Pistons

Condition: The pistons are clean, weight within five grams of each other and the rings are on them.

If you're using your old pistons and had to heat them to remove them, you will have to heat them to install them. New pistons, also, will probably have to be heated.

New Pistons. Using the thin-nosed pliers (special snap ring pliers for some Type IV's), remove one of the circlips. The circlips are usually packed into their grooves in the pistons at the factory. Oil the wrist pin and start it into its hole in the piston on the opposite side from where the remaining circlip is. To do this, rest the piston on your knee and tap the pin with the small hammer just enough so the pin starts into the hole.

Old Pistons. Install the circlip on the opposite side from the wrist pin.

Everybody: Start with No. 1; turn the engine until No. 1 rod is sticking out as far as it will go and point the arrow (**See Changes**) on No. 1 piston **toward the flywheel** (away from the crankshaft pulley). If you've washed off your mark or are using new pistons, find the original arrow that was stamped on the

Step 3. (Cont'd.)

piston top at the factory. Put the 8mm or 10mm socket on the long extension, the assembly you used to drive the wrist pins out and lay it near to hand. Oil the wrist pin and the two holes in the piston and the bushing (hole) in the rod. Hold the piston and rod together with one hand and tap (or heat the piston in the pin area, then tap) on the wrist pin with the small hammer until you need the socket-extension assembly, then use the assembly to drive the wrist pin until it touches the circlip. Install the second circlip. When you're tapping the wrist pin in, try to take as much of the shock of the hammer off the rod as you can with your hand, or use a friend.

You now have that dangerous situation again: EVERY TIME YOU ROTATE THE ENGINE, GUIDE THE PISTONS INTO THEIR HOLES WITH YOUR HANDS, or else the piston skirts will break, so rotate the engine until No. 2 rod sticks out as far as it'll go, put No. 2 piston on, then turn the engine around to install pistons No. 3 and No. 4. When all four pistons are circlipped, check to make certain that **all four arrows are pointing toward the flywheel.**

Step 4. Prepare to Install Cylinders

If you're replacing the **old cylinders,** scrape off the old paper gaskets where the cylinders fit into the crankcase (the end with the narrower fins). Look at the other ends of the cylinders. Do they have a copper ring gasket? If they do, remove them and install four new ones. The slightly narrower (seamed) edge faces out. If you're using **new cylinders,** and don't have a 36hp or Type IV engine, put the cylinders, the heads, and the valve-grinding compound on the table. Choose one head for cylinders No. 1 and No. 2 and mark it so. Pick up a cylinder, mark it No. 1, put some valve-grinding compound around the lip where the wide fins are, put this end of the cylinder in the hole in the head that's No. 1 and grind the cylinder back and forth in the hole in the head—a motion just like a washing machine makes—for about one minute. Turn the cylinder 90° and grind it another minute. Repeat this four times or about four minutes so the cylinder seats well in the head. Repeat for cylinder No. 2, then clean the head and two cylinders very well in solvent and wipe them with a rag or paper towel. **Valve-grinding compound must not get in the works.** Using the other head, repeat for cylinders No. 3 and No. 4.

36hp: If you're using old cylinders, remove the paper gaskets from the narrow fin ends of the cylinders and the copper gaskets from the wide fined ends. If you have old or new cylinders, install the four copper gaskets on the wide-fin ends. The narrower edge of the gasket faces out.

Everybody: Install the thin paper circle gaskets on the ends of the cylinders with the narrow fins. Work the gasket down onto its proper place on the cylinder carefully with the Scout knife

Step 5. Install Cylinders

Start with No. 1 piston and get it out as far as it will go, remembering the skirts. Now you have to set the ring gaps. Start with the bottom oil ring (it's the fat one). Make sure its gap is facing straight up. Then put the other two ring gaps 120° on either side of the oil ring gap. Flood the ring area of the piston and the inside of the cylinder with oil. Clamp the ring compressor or the 3-1/2" water hose clamp around the rings and tighten the compressor or clamp. Hold No. 1 cylinder with the narrow fin end in position to go over the piston, the fat sides of the fins face toward the center of the engine. Bump the cylinder with your hand, chest and/or tummy over the rings, pushing the compressor or clamp down at the same time, until the cylinder clears the ring area and goes over the long studs. Remove the ring compressor or hose clamp. Slide the cylinder into its hole in the crankcase with your chest or tummy until the paper gasket is well seated, then clamp the vice grip on the long stud to hold the cylinder in place while you rotate the engine (remembering the piston skirts) to bring piston No. 2 out as far as it'll go.

Repeat the step for piston No. 2, then find the air deflector, that little piece of sheet metal you took off from underneath the cylinders. It clamps up between the studs under the cylinders, short clips (sides with the V) toward the engine. Spread the slot a little with the screwdriver so the ears can get a good grip on the studs. If it's bent or broken or if there's any doubt that it'll stay in place, use a piece of wire across the two outside long studs and under the sheet metal to hold it up. It must fit tightly to the bottoms of the cylinders. Type IV: the air deflector screws to the crankcase, too. Repeat this step for cylinders No. 3 and No. 4.

PUT THE LITTLE AIR DEFLECTORS ON. . .ENGINE WON'T RUN LONG WITHOUT THEM.

Step 6. Install Heads

Condition: Engine assembly or you've only had the valves ground. All engine parts are clean, clean, clean.

Are the air deflectors both on? Make sure, as they're hell to put on later. Find your new spark plugs and remove the brass tips that are screwed on the ends of them. Gap them to .025" (Chapter X) and put them in but don't tighten them. Put a rag into the intake manifold hole in the head.

Valve job only People: Please leave your cylinders tied with the wire and don't jar them loose while you clean the cylinders and piston tops. Remove the old copper gaskets from the ends of the cylinders, if any. Scrape that old carbon off the tops of the pistons with the Scout knife and carefully wipe the tops of the pistons with a rag soaked in solvent. Do not jar the cylinders loose or get any crud into the engine. See PRE-ASSEMBLY Procedure, Step 1, for push rod tubes. If you removed copper gaskets, install four new ones. The slightly narrower edge goes toward the outside. Remove the wire holding cylinders No. 1 and 2.

All: Your gasket kit may have the large copper ring gaskets for the cylinders in it but this doesn't mean you should use them. If **you** removed some, install them.

Fuel Injection Attention: Find the head with a threaded hole for the cylinder head temperature sensor. Up to 1970, it's below the rear exhaust port, from 1970 on it's on top of the head by the intake ports. Find the sensor (it's the 13mm bolt with a long wire on it). Put a spring washer on the sensor and screw it into the head with a 13mm wrench. Tighten it firmly but don't overtighten it. This head goes on the No. 3 and No. 4 side (left).

Types I, II and III: Find the 16 white rubber ring gaskets and install one on each end of the clean, stretched, push rod tubes, beveled edges facing out.

Type IV: Disregard anything about push rod tubes until it says, "Type IV" but do everything else.

All Models: Start with the head for No. 1 and No. 2 cylinders, put it on the bolts and start it in, then put in the inner two push rod tubes. Push the head in a little more and put in the outer two push rod tubes. You'll have to jiggle a little to make the push rod tubes stay there. Turn the tubes so their seams are up. You can either see or feel the seam. Get the head on so everything fits, push it in and put a washer and a nut (or just a nut if a washer won't fit just yet) on one of the center studs. Put a drop of engine oil on the threaded part of each stud. Install the head for No. 2 and No. 3 cylinders.

With all washers on and nuts started, put the socket that fits the nuts on the short extension on the ratchet and tighten them in order of Sketch 1; go round and round, alternating between the heads (nut 1 on the first head, nut 1 on the second head, etc.), giving each nut a few turns at a time until they're as tight as one hand on the ratchet handle will get them. Still alternating between the heads and using Sketch 1, torque them to 7 ft. lbs. Now use Sketch 2 and alternating, torque them to 15 ft. lbs., then to 20 ft. lbs.

If you have a 36hp, torque them to 25 ft. lbs. using Sketch 2, but only 23 ft. lbs. for everyone else. Don't laugh, this is important— 22 or 23 ft. lbs. torque. Look at the push rod tubes and make sure they're straight both horizontally and vertically. Bunt or pry them straight with your finger or something soft, if necessary.

Find the thermostat actuating lever bracket in your parts can. It's the metal bracket with two holes in one end and a swinging lever on the other end. Put the bracket on the top two cylinder head studs and torque the nuts down. The lever should go on so it's slanted towards the rear of the engine. Put the little cylinder (barrel) clamp in the forked lever with the hex head facing out. This clamp may already be in the lever but if it isn't, put it in.

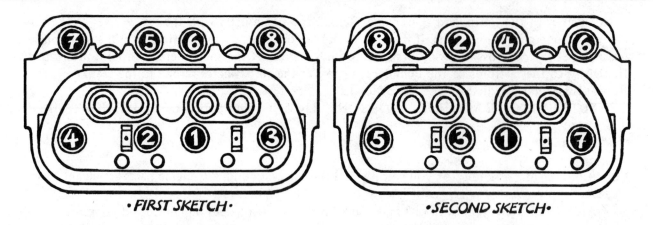

·FIRST SKETCH·   ·SECOND SKETCH·

Now find the thermostat rod (hooked on one end and threaded on the other). Poke the threaded end down the cylinder head fins between No. 1 and 2 and thread the rod onto the thermostat. It's easiest to unbolt the thermostat and turn it onto the rod. Now hook the other end of the rod into the hole in the actuating lever and that's it.

Type IV: Get out the eight baggies with the cam followers and put them in the proper holes in the crankcase, dipping each one in oil before you slip it in flat face toward the center of the engine. When you have all eight cam followers installed, you can start with the push rod tubes. They are all the same but you want to start with the Intake valves, the center two. Find the little "0" rings in the gasket set. They are about one inch in diameter and there are 8 of them. You can put all the outside "0" rings on the eight tubes. The outside end of the tube has the double groove for them to fit into and the inside end has a groove and a bump. There are 8 more little round sealing rings but they are fatter than the "0" rings. Just have them handy as you put the push rod into the hole and when you get it through the head, slip the fat sealing ring on the inside end of the tube with the small end of the seal toward the engine. Now dip your finger in the oil and run it around both sealing rings so they will slide into the holes without too much effort. Set the size of the big vice grip so it will grip the tube without crushing it. Hold the vice grip in one hand and a piece of wood like the small hammer handle on the outside end of the tube, push the tube into place with one solid sure movement. When all four tubes are in one side, get out the wire spring and install it in the head so it will hold the push rod tube in place. Then repeat on the other side with the other four tubes, doing the inside ones first, then the spring. The push rod tubes are in. Note how beautiful this new way is. If one day you find that a tube leaks, you can fix it without taking the engine out or the heads off by merely taking the valve cover off, then taking off the rocker arm and the spring and pull that tube out and either replace it or just put new seals on it. Now join the others with the only difference being that you have four nuts holding the rocker arms.

Step 7. Install Push Rods

All Models: All eight are straight, right? Blow through them to make sure they're clean inside as well as out.

36hp: Put the fat ends toward the crankcase and turn them around until the flat side fits into the slot. You'll feel it.

All others: Both ends are the same, just stick them into the push rod tubes.

Step 8. Install Rocker Arms

Type IV and 36hp engines: Slip the rocker arm assembly on the studs and at the same time, fit the ends of the push rods into their cups in the bottom of the rocker arm assembly. Put on the washer that's flat on one side and round on the other with the round side against the rocker arm tube (none in Type IV), then the warpy (spring) washer and the nut. Tighten the two (36hp) or

Step 8. (Cont'd.)

four (Type IV) nuts, 36hp: torque the nuts to 10 ft. lbs., then to 14 ft. lbs. Type IV: torque the nuts to 10 ft. lbs.

All Engines, except Type IV and 36hp: use little white rubber ring seals. There will be eight of these in your gasket kit, four like donuts and four like small, flat wedding rings. If your rocker arm is held on by **nuts**, you have to decide which four to use: look at the area where the two studs that hold the rocker arm assembly come out of the head (more or less in the middle of the circle of head nuts you tightened). If there is a groove or indentation around the stud, use the flat wedding ring gaskets, which stretch to fit over the stud and into the groove. If there is no groove around these studs, use the small donuts. Put one of your choice of gaskets on each of the two studs, slip the rocker arm assembly on, then arrange the round ends of the push rods into their cups on the bottom of the rocker arm assembly. Put on the two lock washers (warpy washers) and the two nuts, then tighten the nuts.

If your rocker arms are held on by **bolts**, you always use the donut type gaskets. Put the bolts with washers on them through the rocker arm blocks (big cubes) so the bolt head is on the outside of the assembly. If the blocks are split, the split goes up. Put one of the little donuts on each of the two bolts on the head side of the bolts, put the assembly with bolts through it up on the head then arrange the push rods into their cups and tighten the bolts. If you have a 1300 or 1500 engine with bronze colored nuts, torque them to 18 ft. lbs. Torque the others to 10 ft. lbs., then to 14 ft. lbs.

All Models: Install the rocker arm assembly on the other head. Then if you bought new valve adjustment screws, install them now. Put rags into the holes in the heads.

Valve job people only: Everyone else has already done this. On the bottom of your engine, around the oil drain plug, you'll find six 10mm nuts going in a circle (Type IV has one 19mm bolt). Remove the nuts with the 10mm socket on the ratchet (or the bolt), remove the oil strainer cover, then the oil strainer inside. Clean the strainer and plate well in solvent and replace them with two new gaskets, one on each side of the strainer. You can tip the engine up on the crankshaft pulley while you do this. Replace the nuts and tighten them going around the circle a little at a time (Type IV, replace the bolt and torque it to 9 ft. lbs.)

Type IV: Go to ENGINE EQUIPMENT ASSEMBLY AND INSTALLATION, TYPE IV AND 1972 AND ON TYPE II, Step 1.

Step 9. Adjust Valves

Condition: Type IV, you shouldn't be here. Others, if the heads have been off and the valves ground, adjust the valves. . .they'll be really out.

Type III: In order to turn the engine over and have a way to get the cylinders on top dead center (where you adjust the valves), you'll have to put the fan and pulley on temporarily. Find your fan and put it over the end of the crankshaft but don't try to seat it all the way or it'll be hard to get off after Step 10. Now find the aluminum pulley and put it on the end of the fan. There is a pin on the pulley which should match the hole in the fan. Put it on like that and you can turn the engine and use the line on the pulley (the furthest to the left) to line up with the seam in the top of the crankcase to establish top dead center, TDC, which is where you set the valves at all times. Put the bolt without the washer in just a little way to keep the whole mess from falling off.

Types I, II and III: Turn to Chapter X, Valve Adjustment Procudure, remembering that the engine is on the table and not in the car. You can tell when No. 1, the front (FRONT–flywheel end) valve on the right, is in firing position by watching No. 1 intake valve, the inside one. Turn the engine clockwise: with your hands or **the 30mm socket** on the crankshaft pulley until you see No. 1 intake valve dip in, then start to come out. After it comes all the way out, the timing mark on the crankshaft pulley is coming around to line up with the crack in the crankcase. No. 1 fires when the notch on the pulley is in line with the crack in the crankcase: this is where you begin to adjust the valves.

Step 9. (Cont'd.)

Look at the timing notch: it should be in line with the crack in the crankcase but you can't depend solely on it as it's in line with the crankcase when No. 3 fires also, so watch No. 1 intake valve. Don't forget to make your 180° mark on the pulley per Chapter X if it's been rubbed off. Remember to turn the engine counter clockwise after adjusting No. 1.

When all eight valves are adjusted (better a little loose than too tight) return the engine to where No. 1 fires and adjust No. 1 and No. 2 over again—because of possible play in the camshaft bearings. Oil the valves and the rocker arms. Glue the new gaskets in the valve covers and smear the gaskets with wheel bearing grease, then install the valve covers. If your distributor is off, wait until it's on to replace the valve cover for No. 1 and No. 2. Tighten the spark plugs. Note: if your valves won't adjust, meaning you've run out of space on the adjusting screw either way, don't freak. It can happen after a valve grind. If the rocker arms are too close to the valve tops to adjust (if you've run out of space on the end of the adjusting screw that's toward you), find some hardened steel (not galvanized) washers that will fit between the heads and rocker arm assemblies to use as shims, or you can buy shims at VW. The idea is to bring the assemblies further out so you'll have room to adjust the valves. With shims in place, try adjusting the valves again. If you still can't, use thicker shims. You should buy and install new donut type gaskets if you have to shim up the rocker arms.

If you've run out of space on the end of the adjusting screw that's toward the head, you have to buy eight steel valve caps at VW and put them on top of the valve ends underneath the adjusting screws. That is, you'll put the feeler blade between the adjusting screw and this cap when you're adjusting the valves. You, too, should use new donuts.

Step 10. Install Distributor Drive Shaft and Distributor

Condition: You've had the case apart so the distributor drive shaft, the ring or rings and the spring are not yet installed. If just the distributor itself is off, skip to the end of the step, but first peer down the distributor hole with a flashlight and make sure the little spring is still down there. If it's not, find it and install it.

Distributor Drive Shaft

Pull the rag out of the distributor hole, then find the distributor gear ring or rings, the ones you taped together with the spring and the shaft. Clean these things well in solvent and dry them thoroughly with a paper towel. Cut off the hook, then straighten out a coat hanger and put it down the distributor hole, which is the leftest hole on the rear of the top of the crankcase. It slopes toward the crankshaft. Put the wire down until it touches bottom. Put a good dab of wheel bearing grease on the bottom of the ring or if you have more than one ring, paste them together with wheel bearing grease and put some on the bottom one. Peer down the hole with a flashlight, slide the ring (or rings glued together with wheel bearing grease) over the hanger wire which you don't move. They go past

Step 10.   (Cont'd.)

the brass gear you can see as you peer down the hole. With the flashlight, look down and make sure the rings are evenly around the hole. When the rings are centered, remove the hanger: the grease will hold the rings where they are.

The distributor drive shaft is about 4-1/2" long and on the thinner end has a shaft, then a gear (which will mesh with the brass gear down the hole), then an eccentric bump. The bottom of the shaft may or may not have a flat spot. The shaft gets wider toward the top end and has a slot cut in the top of it. This slot is not in the center, so there's a wider or fatter side on one side of the slot and a skinny or narrower side on the other side of the slot.

Turn the engine clockwise until No. 1 is firing (see Step 9). In the position where No. 1 fires the slot in the top of the distributor drive shaft should be parallel to the line made by the front (FRONT) and the narrower or skinny part should be toward the rear. In the older models, there is a flat spot near the bottom of the shaft to let the shaft go by the brass gear that's down the hole. In the newer models; there is no flat spot. Oil the shaft and start it into the hole in the position described above and shown in the sketch.

Types III and IV: Your distributor drive shaft has to go in one tooth short of where everyone else's goes so the vacuum unit will clear the fan housing. Your starting position then would be one tooth further over in a counterclockwise direction. See sketch.

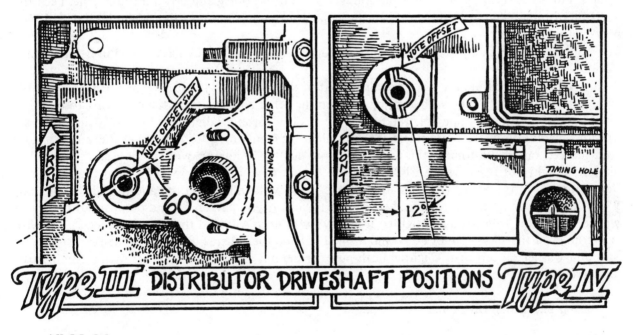

Type III   DISTRIBUTOR DRIVESHAFT POSITIONS   Type IV

All Models:

Use the screwdriver to hold the slot in the correct position while you push the shaft down to the bottom of the hole until it seats on the ring or rings. Turn the engine slightly to see if the gear shaft is seated; if the slot rotates as you turn the engine, the shaft is seated.

Put the little spring in the gear shaft. It belongs down the hole in the slot. Using the coat hanger again, slide the spring down the hanger and into place.

Distributor:

Put the distributor clamp on, if it's off. It belongs around the distributor hole (left, rear top of the crankcase). Put the new rubber "0" ring from the gasket kit two inches up from the bottom of the distributor in its groove. Oil the distributor shaft and the "0" ring. Turn the engine until No. 1 is firing. Point the slot the rotor fits on toward the mark on the rim and put the distributor down its hole. Push it down until the slot on the bottom of the distributor catches in the slot on the top part of the distributor drive shaft that's already down the hole. You'll feel the slots catch each other. With the new rubber "0" ring on, it'll be one hell of a push. Use the palms of both hands to

Step 10. (Cont'd.)

bear down or use a small block of wood on top of the shaft (the thing the rotor goes on), and hit the wood with a hammer. When the distributor is in, you'll know it because the shaft won't move any more. Then tighten the distributor hold-down nut (13mm). Put the rotor on, but leave the cap off—all those wires would just be in the way for now. Oil the valves and rocker arms and install the cover for cylinders No. 1 and No. 2.

Type III: Remove the fan and pulley from the rear of the crankshaft.

Step 11. Install Fuel Pump (Carbureted Engines) or Auliliary Air Regulator (Fuel Injected Engines.

Condition: It's off.

Carbureted Engines: The fuel pump comes in three parts: 1) a plunger, 2) a plastic block with two bolt holes and 3) the pump itself (a round thing with two bolt holes, made of the same metal the carburetor is made of). Find the plastic block and remove the plunger if it's in it. Put the gasket that fits on the pointy end on the block and put the block (pointy end down) over the two studs which are to the left of center on the top rear of the engine. Put the other gasket on top of the plastic block. Put wheel bearing grease on the plunger and put it pointy end down into the hole. Pack the bottom of the fuel pump with wheel bearing grease, put in on the studs, then tighten the two 13mm nuts with a box end.

36hp: The fuel pump is under the distributor and the plastic block has a notch in it which must face up.

Fuel Injection: Find the auxiliary air regulator, the piece with two tubes (one bent 90°) on the shiny end and a larger tube with a spring on it on the other end. It fits on the crankcase to the right of the distributor in the same hole the fuel pump fits in a carbureted engine. Look in your gasket set for the one that fits on the bottom end of the auxiliary air regulator. Put some gasket glue on both sides and place it on the bottom of the regulator. Now put the regulator over the hole so the tube that comes straight out is facing the FRONT of the engine. If you have a pre 1970, find the crankcase temperature sensor, sensor (II). It's about 1-1/2" long with an MPC on top and threads below that. Put it in the front hole and tighten it with your fingers. If you have a '70 and on, just put the washer and nut on the front stud and tighten it with your fingers. All: find the L shaped metal piece with a big hole on the short arm of the L and a small hole on the other. Put this over the rear stud and a nut and washer on top of it. Tighten both nuts (or the nut and the sensor stud) with a 13mm open end wrench.

Step 12. Install Oil Cooler

Condition: It's off.

Types I and II: If you're using your old oil cooler (the tall skyscraper) throw out the old solvent and reflush with clean solvent, then throw that out. The new ones come sealed on the bottom so cut the two seals off with the Scout knife. You have to scrape the seals off the entire area but make sure no scrapings go into the holes. Remove any paper tags. The oil cooler goes between No. 3 and No. 4 cylinders on the top of the engine. Find the two tallest, small round black or white rubber ring gaskets (1500 on: the gaskets look like black donuts with lips on them), remove the pieces of rag from the two holes in the crankcase, remove the old gaskets if they're still on and put the new gaskets in the recesses around the holes. Slip the oil cooler down on the gaskets. Make sure the gaskets are aligned with the holes in the oil cooler so oil can flow easily. Put the lock washers and 10mm nuts on the two bottom bolts and partially tighten them with the 10mm box end until the gaskets seat. Put the third nut and lock washer on top, then tighten them all. Watch that the oil cooler doesn't lean—it must be square with the top of the engine.

Step 12. (Cont'd.)

Type III: If you're using your old oil cooler, drain the solvent out and reflush it with clean solvent, then drain that out. If you have a new cooler, scrape the seals off the bottom holes and remove any paper tags that might be on it. Find the two black rubber gaskets that look like donuts with a lip around the edge and place them in the two holes on top of the engine case (left side).

Pre 1963: You have an intermediate bracket which allows you to use a regular VW 1200 oil cooler. Find the bracket, bolt it on the cooler, and then place the whole assembly over the gaskets on the case. Replace the 10mm nuts and spring washers and tighten them firmly.

1963 on: Find the three thick flat washers and place them over the holes in the case that the oil cooler bolts go through. These are very important so if you can't find them, buy new ones. They assure that when you tighten the cooler, you don't squash the gaskets too much and cut off circulation of oil to the cooler. Now find the piece of tin about 3" long with a 90° bend and two tabs with holes in them. Place this piece on the protruding lips on the case so that the two tabs with holes in them are under the holes in the case. Now place the cooler over the holes and put the studs (two long and one short) through the cooler into the case. Tighten them firmly and evenly so the rubber gaskets are squashed somewhat.

Step 13. Install Generator Pedestal or Crankcase Breather

Condition: It's off or you want to put a new gasket under it.

Types I and II: (36hp skip to end of Step.) Clean the pedestal and oil filler if they're still oily. Put on the flat paper gasket, then smear it with wheel bearing grease. Put the pedestal on (oil filler to the right) and tighten the four 13mm nuts. **Put in the oil dipstick.** Install the oil filler cap with a new gasket, if you bought one. The gasket glues into the cap.

Type III: Install Crankcase Breather

Clean the breather assembly if it's still oily. Find the gasket that fits it and put gasket glue on both sides. Put the gasket over the four studs, then the breather assembly. It goes on so the flat piece with three threaded holes in it faces to the REAR. Put the four washers and nuts on the studs and tighten them with a 13mm wrench. **Fuel Injection:** Find the brass electrical connector (ground with a hole in it) and put it on the rear left stud, then the washer and nut. Late models have a cluster of three.

Step 14. Check End Play

Condition: The flywheel is off.

Clean out the four holes in the front end of the crankshaft, then put the four pins into their holes so they all stick out an even distance and are well set. Find the round paper or metal (whichever you removed) gasket with the four holes in it. . .look in the gasket set. Put it on the pins. Pick up the flywheel and install it on the pins. Put the big spring (warpy) washer, then the gland nut onto the flywheel and tighten it first by hand, then with the 1-7/16" or 36mm socket on the breaker bar or flex handle. Use your device to hold the flywheel and tighten the nut as tight as you can get it with the breaker bar or flex handle. If you don't have the large socket, etc., turn to Chapter XVI, Mechanics' Tips, High Torque Nuts.

* * * * * * * * * * * * * * * *

Your flywheel is tightened? OK, you need that 4" piece of 3/8" All-thread you bought with the four nuts, two on each end. With a file, touch up a place on the front face of the flywheel in front of the top left engine mount hole, so there are no burrs on it. You'll have to remove one of

Step 14. (Cont'd.)

the clutch plate bolts and washers. Remove one of the nuts off one end of the All-thread. The remaining nut on that end should be about one inch from the end. Secure the All-thread with the nut you took off; there should be a nut on each side of the crankcase. Tighten the nuts enough so the All-thread is held firmly. It should be sticking straight out at you.

Put your medium screwdriver between the flywheel and the crankcase near the other top engine mount hole and pry the flywheel toward you, then push the screwdriver down toward the gland nut to hold the flywheel out as far as it will go. Space the two nuts on the other end of the All-thread so you can put a 10mm open end wrench between them. The flat side of the wrench should be flush with the part of the flywheel you filed, but not quite touching it.

Now that you have this assembly set up, I'll tell you what you're doing. The crankshaft must be free to move forward and back (end play). This end play must be .004" plus or minus .001" and is determined by the shims. The VW dealer has a special dial indicator to measure this play but we don't so follow along and we'll get it right. You have installed no shims under the flywheel and the flywheel is forward as far as it'll go. You're going to determine which three shims you need to use to give the correct end play.

First find out how far the 10mm open end wrench is from the face of the flywheel—with the feeler gauge, try different blades until you find the one that goes into the space between the wrench and the flywheel. Make sure the very next larger blade won't fit between the wrench and the flywheel. We'll call this blade the Gap blade for the rest of this step. OK. . .the Gap and .004" blades along with three shims must go into this same space when the flywheel is pushed all the way back. So remove the screwdriver, push the flywheel back as far as it'll go then tap on the gland nut with the small hammer. Find the three shims and try them in the gap between the wrench and the flywheel along with the Gap blade and the .004" blade. If this combination won't fit into the gap, you'll have to find a thinner shim among the ones you bought at VW to replace one of the original three. If the combination is too loose, that is, you can get the Gap blade plus the .005" or larger in, you need a thicker shim. Work with the shims until you find a combination of three that together with the two blades just fill the space between the flywheel and the wrench.

You've found a combination of shims that works? OK, now check it. Use the .005" blade instead of the .004". It should not go in. If it does, screw with the shims some more until it won't. When the .005" in combination with the gap blade and the three shims no longer fits, remove the shim-feeler blade combination and pull the flywheel forward again and wedge the screwdriver in. Check the gap blade to make sure if it's the largest blade that will fit into the space, then remove the screwdriver, push the flywheel back and check your three chosen shims, the new Gap blade (or the old one if it checked out OK), and the .004" blade in the gap again. If they fit in and the .005" used instead of the .004" doesn't fit, remove the 10mm wrench and remove the flywheel.

Install the three chosen shims around the crankshaft. Make sure the gasket with the four holes is still in place and put the flywheel back on, this time with the shims under it. Put on the washer and tighten the gland nut as tight as you can with the socket and breaker bar. Put the wrench back up in the All-thread, pull the flywheel forward, jam the screwdriver back in and find the largest blade that will go between the wrench and the flywheel. Remove the screwdriver, push and tap the flywheel back and check to see if the .004" blade plus the Gap blade will now go between the wrench and the flywheel.

If they go just right, go on to Step 15. If they won't go into the space, try the .003" instead of the .004". If this combination fits, go on to Step 15. If the .003" won't go either, remove the flywheel and start from the beginning of the step. If the combination of the .004" and the Gap blade is too loose but the .005" or the .006" used in its place fit OK, go on to Step 15. But if the .007" blade used instead of the .004" fits in, start the step over. In other words, if the Gap blade plus the .003", the .004", the .005" or the .006" fits in, remove the flywheel and the wrench and go on to Step 15.

* * * * * * * * * * * * * * * * *

Step 15. Install Front Seal

Condition: You're changing the front seal and your flywheel is off.

Check the three shims. . .they're in place? OK. The front seal goes on closed side out and fits up against the shoulder in the crankcase. Smooth up the edge of the crankcase where the seal fits with a piece of sandpaper to remove any raised places that might damage the seal. Wipe the hole out with a clean rag or paper towel but make sure the shims don't fall out. Set the seal in closed side out and start it in the hole. Pick up the small hammer with your left hand, the large hammer with your right hand and put the business end of the small hammer on the seal. Tap the small hammer with the large hammer round and round the face of the seal, evenly, until the seal seats on the shoulder of the crankcase. The seal will either be flush or just a hair in.

* * * * * * * * * * * * * * * * * *

Step 16. Install Flywheel (Stick Shift) or Drive Plate (automatics)

Condition: You've adjusted the end play and installed the front seal.

Put the rubber "0" ring from your gasket set inside the flywheel if you took one off. Check the gasket with the four holes in it. It's in place? OK. Raise the flywheel, put it on the pins, put the spring washer on and start the gland nut onto the threads and tighten it as much as you can with your hands. Have your friend hold the flywheel from turning with the device you have while you tighten the gland nut as tight as you can with the 1-7/16" or 36mm socket on the breaker bar or flex handle. If you don't have the socket, turn to Chapter XVI, Mechanics' Tips, High Torque Nuts, to tighten the gland nut. The nut should be torqued to 220 ft. lbs., so put the cheater on the breaker bar or flex handle and push down on the cheater with all your strength. When you've tightened it as much as you can, refer to Chapter XVI on Torque. If there's any doubt that you're not getting 220 ft. lbs. on the gland nut, have your friend hit the cheater with the hammer while you push down on the cheater to keep a strain on it. 220 ft. lbs? OK. Sand the face of the flywheel with the fine sandpaper and get the crud off, if any. If you're the cautious type, check your end play again. Remove the All-thread.

Step 17. Install Clutch—Not for Automatics

Condition: You're installing a clutch plate or pressure plate. The flywheel gland nut has been torqued to 220 ft. lbs. by one method or another. (Not Type IV. Your flywheel cap screws are torqued to 80 ft. lbs. **Type IV: for "gland nut," read "flywheel hub."**)
    Note: Remove any shipping clips or other packaging materials.
    Rebuilt clutches have U shaped packing clips under each of the three fingers, so push down on the small disc in the center of the clutch and pull the clips out with a screwdriver.

Put your little finger 1/2" into the wheel bearing grease, draw it up and put this grease evenly into the bearing in the flywheel gland nut. Tip the engine up onto the crankshaft pulley and put a block of wood under it to keep it from rocking. Put the clutch plate in the flywheel with the nose toward the front (facing up or out). Remove the bolts and washers from the flywheel and lay the pressure plate, smooth side down, on top of the clutch plate. You punch-marked the flywheel and pressure plate so match up the punches. If you're using a new or rebuilt pressure plate, sigh deeply and put it on the way it comes to you to do. Replace the washers and bolts and get all six of them started by hand.

Step 17. (Cont'd.)

The idea now is to get the pressure plate tight on the clutch plate so the hole in the clutch plate lines up with the hole in the gland nut, then, when we install the engine, the end of the trans shaft will slide into the engine like a greased pig. Use a flashlight to line up the splines in the center of the clutch with the hole in the gland nut (flywheel hub). A cut-off piece of trans shaft from the junk yard makes a good alignment tool but you can align the hole in the clutch with the hole in the flywheel by eye. When the splines are aligned with the hole, start to tighten the bolts with the 14mm socket on the short extension on the ratchet. Tighten the way you took off; 1/2 turn on each bolt in turn, going round and round so the pressure plate doesn't distort. When they're all as tight as you can get them, use the flashlight to check if the hole in the clutch plate centers on the hole in the flywheel. If the holes don't have a common center, loosen the bolts, center the holes and retighten. All centered? OK, lay the engine back down and with the ratchet handle straight up in your right hand, give each bolt a bunt with your left palm to give them that final tightening. Torque them to 18 ft. lbs.

Types I, II and III: If your engine has a rear engine carrier, now's the time to put it back on. It's the long clunky piece of metal that spans the rear of the engine. Put it up against the rear of the engine and find the bolts in the baggie. The two big bolts, 17mm, go on the top into the case and the 13mm bolt goes into the bottom hole. Tighten them all firmly.

Go to the procedure for your model.

ENGINE EQUIPMENT ASSEMBLY AND INSTALLATION, TYPE I AND TYPE II THROUGH '71

Step 1. Install Heater Boxes

Pull the rags out of the side holes and put the new exhaust gaskets, , on the studs and slip the right front exhaust pipe and heater box assembly with all the tin that goes with it over the studs. Remember, if you had or have stud trouble, see Chapter XVI. Put the two nuts and washers on as far as you can with your fingers, then use the 13 or 14mm box end until they're fairly tight. Now find the piece of shrouding that fits over the right bank of cylinders (it'll have 1 and 2 stamped on it) and slip it on. In the **36hp**, it has to go under one of the crankcase studs to fit right.

Models up to 1965, don't tighten the shroud but find the long bolt in the bolt can. Put it in from the right side and put the nut on it. It goes in the hole in the crankcase. Find the tube-lever-wire (rod) pieces of the air control system. They're in a baggie together. Put the wire onto the lever and start the wire down into the hole in the head (looking down from the top of the engine it goes into the largest hole between cylinders No. 1 and No. 2). At the same time as you're putting the wire down between the cylinders, slip the tube and lever assembly over the right end of the long bolt, getting the spring up against the case. You've already loosened the clamp that holds the lever. Tighten the nut on the long bolt to 14 ft. lbs. Press in the little snap ring (like a washer, with an open space) that holds the tube onto the long bolt 1/4" from the right end of the long bolt.

Put the screws in the right-hand cylinder shroud and pull the shrouding together, leaving out the screw that will go through the large front (FRONT) piece of tin.

Tighten the front exhaust manifold nuts down (13 or 14mm) tight enough to compress the gasket but not so tight as to twist them off, please. Put on the left side exhaust pipe and heater box assembly (remember the gasket), then install the left cylinder shroud (stamped with 3 and 4).

Models '65 and on: Tip the engine onto the crankshaft pulley to put in the four screws that hold the shrouding to the bottom of the crankcase. Tip the engine back up and install the two small bent pieces (not the two smallest pieces) of shrouding. They screw, two screws each, on the back bottom of the cylinder shrouds and hang down. Up until 1968, the left side one has a hole in it for the pre-heater hose.

All: You're ready for the muffler. If you've bought new tail pipes, remove the old ones. Remove any rags and put on both exhaust gaskets.

Step 1. (Cont'd.)

36hp using old muffler: To install the muffler, you have to slip the bottom pipes over the front exhaust pipes and drive the muffler over them with the hammer, then put on the old clamps that go around the connection.

36hp with new muffler and all others: Remove the old metal and asbestos rings and put the new ones on. They're in the muffler connection kit. Pick up the muffler and put it on the studs starting it on the front exhaust pipes at the same time.

Models 1965 to 1968: If the left-hand small piece of shroud has an oval hole in it, find the lower connection for the pre-heater hose (a tube with a tab welded to it). After you push the muffler onto the studs, slip the tube into the oval hole and the tab over the bottom stud that holds the muffler to the head. Put the washer and nut for the muffler over the tab (which is now on the stud also), then tighten the nut with the 13mm box end.

All: Put the nuts and lock washers on the studs and tighten them with the 13 or 14mm socket, long extension and ratchet (or box end—Clean-air) tight enough to compress the gasket but not so tight as to twist them off. Give the wrench handle a bunt with your left hand to finish the tightening. Connect the muffler to the bottom pipes with the clamps (in the muffler connection kit) and tighten them with two 10mm wrenches. The clamps fit over the joints; bolts can go in from either end. Make certain the muffler fits over the pipes all the way by bunting the muffler on with the palm of your hand. Check all the exhaust manifold nuts for tightness.

36hp people with a new muffler: If you've broken off your front exhaust pipes, you'll have to buy new ones or find some in a junk yard. If you're using your old muffler, tighten the clamps with two 13mm wrenches.

1965 and on: Hook up the connections from the muffler to the heater box on both sides of the engine. It's a collar that slides up or down—the direction depends upon where you left the coller, on the muffler or on the heater box. Tighten the screw once the collar seals the joint.

Step 2. Install Intake Manifold

Before installing the intake manifold, blow through the heat riser (rear legs) to make sure it's not clogged with anything. If it's clogged, you will have to unplug it.

First install the large front piece of tin, the one with the gas line hanging in it. Use the big screwdriver and attach it firmly to the right and left hand cylinder shrouds.

40hp to 1965: In conjunction with this front piece of tin, you must install the air pre-heater hose (1" diameter). The tube the hose fits over is welded onto the heater box on the left side of the engine. Put the hose through the front piece of tin; the spring clip over the hose; the hose onto the tube; compress the spring clip with the pliers and slide it over the hose-tube connection, then install the tin.

All: Remove the rags from the holes in the heads, making sure the area is clean and the old gaskets are out. The intake gaskets are metal "0" rings. Find them and put them in the head holes, seams facing up. There are two gaskets left that look like exhaust gaskets but are smaller. They go on top of the muffler where the intake manifold bolts. Use the small-holed gasket (if there is one in your kit) on the left. Slip the manifold down on the studs in the heads and on the two heat riser connections (one on each side). Start the four bolts first, then the four nuts—all 10mm.

'71 and on: You have dual ported heads, lucky. To install manifold: put the gaskets on, slide the dual throat pipe down on the studs, put on the washers and *start* the nuts. Now put on the heat riser gaskets, then the heat riser-center section assembly and *start* the bolts. Put the two clamp joints together—make sure the clamp joints are straight for best gas mileage—tighten the clamps. Now tighten all the nuts and bolts while watching the joints for alignment.

All models except 36hp: Don't tighten these nuts and bolts until the fan housing is on so the generator can slip past the carburetor.

Step 2. (Cont'd.)

36hp: Tighten the four nuts and bolts. Your distributor cap is still attached to the spark plug wires which run through a tube on the intake manifold so the cap will go on with the intake manifold. Put the cap onto the distributor.

Step 3. Install Generator in Fan Housing

Condition: The generator has been overhauled and is out of the Fan housing.
Refer to the Generator Procedure in Chapter VIII to install your model. Instead of using the hammer and chisel tightening method, use the 1-7/16" or 36mm socket on the breaker bar, if you have them, to tighten the big generator fan nut. Before tightening the big nut, install the fan belt pulley on the rear (REAR) of the generator shaft. Put the half moon key onto the rear of the shaft and put the two pulley halves complete with shims, spacer (cup-like thing) and nut (hand tight) on so the slot in the front pulley half fits over the half moon key. Now tighten the fan nut on the front of the generator assembly with the 1-7/16" or 36mm socket on the breaker bar and keep the shaft from turning with the screwdriver in the rear pulley. It gets only 36 ft. lbs. torque. Don't tighten the generator pulley nut until you install the fan belt.

Step 4. Install Fan Housing and Generator

Models 1965 and later: Air Control System: work a little wheel bearing grease into the places where the flaps and control arm (long wire or rod) move. Work the control arm up and down to make sure the system is working freely and easily. As you install the fan housing, the control arm must go down into the hole between cylinders No. 1 and No. 2. This control arm goes down to the center of the bracket where the bellows will go.

36hp: Put a piece of paper in the cradle of the pedestal, under where the generator goes—just a thin piece of magazine cover, gasket material or like that.

All: Put the accelerator cable tube (a tube about 10" long with a lip about 2" from one end) through the two holes in the fan housing, lip to the rear. Slide the fan housing over the oil cooler and down into the shrouding. The fan housing shroud goes inside the other pieces of shroud all the way around. You may have to tip the intake manifold to get the generator past the carburetor. Be very careful of the oil cooler and do not bend it. Put in the two screws, one on each end of the fan housing, but don't tighten them yet.

Get the strap from the bag and put it around the generator and the pedestal. The contours on the strap have to fit the way they were when it came off. The bolt goes on the right side. Tighten the strap bolt with two 13mm wrenches. Now tighten the two screws that hold the fan housing, the intake manifold nuts and bolts are already tight). Work the accelerator tube from the front of the distributor cap and (except 36hp) work the two longest spark plug wires in back of the carburetor and the two shorter wires to the left. Put the cap on the distributor.

* * * * * * * * * * * * * * * * * * *

All Models: Attach the wires to the spark plugs. Make sure the little rubber air seals are in good condition and tight. No. 1 on the distributor cap is the closest one to the REAR of the engine. If you've goofed installing your distributor drive shaft and the place where No. 1 fires is no longer the closest one to the rear of the engine, don't freak. Just turn your engine to where No. 1 fires (by looking at the intake valves), loosen the distributor clamp bolt and turn the distributor until the notch on the rim of the distributor is under the pointer of the rotor. Install No. 1 plug wire directly over the distributor rotor pointer and go from there.

Going clockwise from No. 1: 1-4-3-2; counterclockwise: 1-2-3-4.

* * * * * * * * * * * * * * * * * * *

Step 4. (Cont'd.)

Adjust the wires into their snap-ins on the back of the fan housing (except 36hp—your wires run in tubes on the intake manifold). Attach the gas line that's been dangling in the front shroud to the fuel pump with the 12mm open end wrench.

Step 5. Install Air Control System

Tip the engine or block it up so you can get under the right side. Find the control arm (rod or wire) coming down between cylinders No. 1 and No. 2. Find the bellows and remove the bolt from the bottom of the bellows. Hold the bellows in the bracket (bottom of the right side of the engine), screw the top of the bellows onto the control arm (rod or wire), then screw the bolt back through the bottom of the bracket into the bottom of the bellows. Adjustment is made by screwing the bellows up (less air) or down (more air) on the rod.

    Pre-1965 models with an air control ring: Slide the two bolts on the air control ring down into their slots on the front of the fan housing. Tighten them with the 10mm box end. Now to adjust the ring: put the 10mm socket on the ratchet and tighten the adjusting clamp (on the tube on the left side of the long bolt) while your friend holds the ring so that the rubber foot just barely touches the fan housing. When the engine is warm the distance between this ring and the fan housing should be 3/4".

Step 6. Install Fan Belt and Bus Rear Shrouding

If you've forgotten how to install the fan belt, look it up in Chapter VIII and put it on. Install the gas line from the fuel pump to the carburetor. It's a webbed hose or a copper tube with webbed hose on both ends and pushes onto both connections. Attach the vacuum line (if any) between the carburetor and the vacuum cylinder on the side of the distributor. If your vacuum line has a loop in it, the gas line goes through the loop.

    Bus: 36 and 40 hp: Install the rear shroud with four screws. '65-'71: Put the pre-heater hose through the rear shroud and attach it to the tube that's bolted under the exhaust connection and secure it with its spring clip.

    Type I, '68 and on: Install the pre-heater hose on the right side of the rear shroud.

    '68-'71 Bus: Install the large rear piece of shroud with four screws; install the two small plates over the heat riser tube (the two smallest pieces of tin you have) with three screws each, then put on the small pulley shroud with three screws. Now reconnect your fat hoses. If you've changed mufflers, remove the two metal tubes off the old muffler and install them on the new one. Put the large rubber seals (rings) over the bottom connections, then put the hoses on their bottom connection first and clamp them on with those clamps that resemble water hose clamps. Tighten the clamps with the phillips screwdriver. Put the upper ends of the hoses onto their connections on the fan housing, put the upper clamps on and tighten them with the phillips screwdriver. If you bought new fat hoses, you'll have been sold one large piece which you must cut with the Scout knife. First cut it in half and install one half on the bottom connections, then curve them up and cut off the excess before you attach the top connections.

Step 7. Install Clutch Throw-out Bearing

Condition: You removed the old one from the clutch lever and bought a new one.

Take the hairpin wire out, snap the bearing into the holder plastic face toward the REAR, put the holder in the throw-out arm and **put** the wire back in through the little hole.

Step 8. Install Starter and Bushing

Condition: You're starter's been overhauled, so it's out.

Bushing.

There's a bushing (a round ring) in the starter hole in the right side of the transmission case. Knock the bushing out from the rear with a hammer and a punch. Install the new bushing from the front. Tap it in with the small hammer being careful not to damage it.

Starter.

Put the starter into its hole, push it in with the solenoid on the upper or upper right hand side until the bottom ear fits over the bottom stud. Put the 17mm nut on the lower stud (the one on the long bolt) and screw it on hand tight. Put the long top bolt in from FRONT to back and tighten up the bottom bolt with the 17mm socket on the ratchet. Take the nut and washer off the big stud on the solenoid and replace the battery cable and the hot wire from the engine onto the stud. (Sometimes these two wires don't both go under the nut, in which case the hot wire from the engine is a push-on that's attached to the washer that fits on this stud). Put the wire(s), washer and nut on the stud and tighten—13mm. Push or screw the small wire from the switch onto its connection on the solenoid. Take a thumbful of wheel bearing grease and push it into the hole where you installed the bushing.

Step 9. Check Starter and Solenoid

Condition: Your starter is in and needs to be checked. Everybody do this step.

Connect the ground strap from the battery to the frame. Test the starter by touching a plastic handled screwdriver across the two large terminals on the solenoid, just for a second. The starter should merrily turn over. Test the solenoid by touching the same screwdriver from the large nut (13mm) on the solenoid to the small connection on the solenoid. The starter should turn over, also the gear in back (BACK) of the starter should be thrown out—watch for it.

If either the starter or the solenoid doesn't do its thing, check back to make sure you've connected everything correctly, then scrape any corrosion off the ground strap terminals. Still won't turn over or push out? Remove the starter and go to Chapter VII, Starter Procedure.

When everything works, disconnect the ground strap.

Put some wheel bearing grease on the trans shaft spline and on the face of the clutch throw-out bearing.

Step 10. Preliminary Clutch Adjustment

Condition: You want to find out how the clutch adjusts now, when you can see it.

Find the lever that operates the clutch on the left side of the trans shaft, opposite side from the starter. Clamp the vice grip on the cable end in front of the lever. FRONT IS FRONT.

Late models have a wing nut to adjust the clutch cable. If you have one of these, just put your thumb and forefinger on the wing nut and turn until the clutch pedal play is not more than 1" or less than 1/2". Others, put the 14mm box end on the adjusting nut (the front one) and use the 11mm box on the locking nut. Loosen the 11mm nut and work the 14mm nut back and forth a few times so you know it works smoothly. Remove the wrenches and the vice grip. This is how you'll adjust the clutch later, when the engine is in, but you'll be lying under the car.

Step 11. Ready, Set. . . .

All: Clean up all the tools and crud that have accumulated under and around the car. Make way! Check to see that the car is out of gear. Find two 17mm engine mount nuts and oil the top engine mount bolts above the trans shaft, then run the nuts back and forth a few times on the bolts. Remove the nuts.

Types I and III: This is where you need all those friends. Put the engine on the board behind the car, muffler toward the rear. Get your friends to help you lift the rear of the car back over the engine, then have them tip the engine so you can put the jacks under it, slightly V-ed.

If you are friendless and your car is up on blocks, put the engine on the board and slide the board and engine under the rear of the car. Unblock and lower the car over the engine with the jacks, then position the jacks under the engine but on top of the board—slightly V-ed, remember. You can now use a board on top of a block as a lever from the side to lift the engine enough to position the jacks. If you are both friendless and the car is on the ground, jack and block the car up, then follow the above direction.

Bus: Place the board behind the Bus and center the jacks on the board and Vee them enough so the jack handles will clear the muffler. Put the engine on the jacks and hold the engine on top of the fan housing while your friends push the Bus back over the engine, then quickly block the wheels.

Automatic transmission: Remove the flat bar you put in to hold the torque converter but do not remove the trans support yet.

Step 12. . . . . . .Go. Engine In

Jack the engine up using both jack handles simultaneously. As you jack the engine, straighten out the accelerator cable (to the left of the trans) and make sure it's not hooked over the clutch lever. When the engine is up high enough, start the accelerator cable into the tube in the front piece of shroud. Jack the engine until it's about 1/2" under the floor of the engine compartment. Check to see that the two studs coming out of the engine are in line with their two holes on either side of the bottom of the trans case, but not level with them. Tip the front end of the engine with one hand on the fan housing and the other on the muffler so that the ends of the studs are level with the holes and ready to go in. Have your friends push the car back until the studs start into their holes. As soon as the studs start into their holes, lift the engine with your left hand on the fan housing. You may need help to make this motion, which is "lift" and "push."

When the studs have gone into their holes, put the wrench on the generator pulley and as you lift and push, turn the engine over just a tiny bit to get the splines matched from the trans to the clutch. You'll feel the engine slip forward into place when the splines match. You can tell if the splines match by looking under the engine because the engine and the piece of metal around the trans shaft will be flush.

When the splines match, reach under the engine from the rear and put the two bottom 17mm nuts on and tighten at least one of them as much as you can with the 17mm box end. You sort of have to feel for them because with the jacks in the way you can't see them. With even one nut started, you can remove the jacks. Get under the car. Don't be afraid—that nut really will hold the engine so it doesn't squash you.

Type I, you may want to jack the car up so you can get under it, but leave the wheels on the ground. **All**: Put the other 17mm nut on the bottom if you didn't before and tighten them both well with the wrench. Now for the top bolts: lie down under the left side of the car, reach way up in back of the trans and push the bolts through. One is in back of the clutch operating lever and the other is the top bolt through the starter (the ones you oiled before). Push them both through. *If you don't feel a bolt head on the bolt, you have self locking bolts. What you do in this case is push the bolt in all the way and turn it until you can feel it lock (that is, it won't turn), then go back up top and put the nuts on. Pull back as you thread the nut on to keep the bolt from unlocking.* Your friend

Step 12. (Cont'd)

can now reach around the fan housing and turn the two nuts on by hand, then tighten them with the 17mm box end while you hold the bolts from underneath with your fingers or the socket assembly. If you're alone, you'll have to go through some contortions to get these top bolts connected. After they're pushed through, go back on top to get the nuts on these bolts turned on as far as you can with your hand. Wedge the bolts in the threads with a screwdriver: that is, push the screwdriver down on the bolts to bind them while you get the nuts started with your hand. Pull back on the nuts as you twist them on. If you can hold them bound up until the bolts will hold themselves, you can tighten them from above. If not, you'll have to put the vice grip on one nut, go underneath the car and tighten the bolt with the ratchet assembly, then repeat this performance for the other nut.

Here's another trick to getting the top nuts on. Put one foot on the muffler pipe (as close to the muffler as you can) and push down on the muffler. This will put a bind on the top bolts and stop them from turning.

Automatic transmission: Get the baggie with the torque converter bolts and the screwdriver and crawl under the engine. Look up at where the engine and trans join. Reach in the hole with the screwdriver and rotate the torque converter until the hole in the torque converter is in the center of the hole in the trans case. Have a friend rotate the engine with the wrench until the bolt hole in the drive plate matches the bolt hole in the torque converter. Put the bolt in and tighten it firmly. Have your friend rotate the engine twice more while you put in and tighten the other two bolts. Now, put the socket on the torque wrench and holler to your friend to turn the engine while you torque the bolts to 18 ft. lbs. Now hook up the vacuum hoses to the trans.

Double jointed axles: remove the 2x4 and chain assembly that's holding the trans.

Step 13. Connect Heater Cables and Gas Line

Tighten the four engine mount nuts really well. Go under the car and push the heater hoses onto the tubes coming out of the engine. Pull the heater control cable into position, put the little cylindrical clamp into the control lever and pull them together so there's no slack. Put the cable end into the clamp, then use the vice grip on the top and the 10mm (8mm) on the bottom (clamp bolt) to tighten this clamp. Repeat on the other side. Later, if you have too much or too little heat, adjust these clamps.

Carb Models only: Take out the pencil and reconnect the gas line to the tube going to the fuel pump. Do it quickly or gasoline will spurt all over you. Push it on really well and get a good connection. Tighten the oil drain plug if you haven't. While you're under the car, give the accelerator cable a push through the tube.

36hp with manual choke: Put the choke cable (a wire wound cable) through the hole in the front piece of tin. Its hole is right alongside the accelerator cable hole.

Step 14. Mechanical Connections

You can get out from under the car now. Open the air cleaner and clean it well in solvent, then fill it with your engine oil up to the red line. **Put two and a half quarts of oil into the engine.** You can put any excess into the oil can. Replace the air cleaner or neck on top of the carburetor and **tighten it down with the big screwdriver. Mount your air cleaner** with the bolts if it's off to one side. Connect the pre-heater hose (if any) to the air cleaner. Connect the oil breather hose (if any) from the tube alongside of the oil filler cap to the air cleaner. Replace any other hoses that you've marked for the air cleaner.

Now find the accelerator cable coming through the tube in the fan housing. If the accelerator cable hasn't come through the tube, you'll have to have your friend push on the tube while you go under the car, straighten out the cable and push it through the tube. Early models (about pre 1966) find the cone-spring-split washer with a slot in it assembly. Over the tube and the accelerator cable

Step 14.　(Cont'd.)

goes the spring; over the spring goes the cone, wide end toward the FRONT. Push to compress the spring. All: pull on the accelerator cable and slip the little split washer with the dish-shape to the front, onto the cable. Find the little cylinder with the hole in it and the screw on one end. Put it in the accelerator arm of the carburetor with the screw on the left. Push the accelerator cable toward the front and put the end of the cable into the hole in the little cylinder. Have your friend push the accelerator pedal (like driving) to the floor, while you push the throttle lever on the carburetor (the lever the little cylinder is in) all the way forward and see where the little cylinder is on the cable. Remember this place. Have your friend remove the foot, you let go of the lever and tighten the clamp in the remembered place with a small long-bladed screwdriver.

36hp with manual choke: You have pushed the choke cable through the hole in the front tin and now you must thread it through the two holes in the fan housing. We use a small copper tube (an old vacuum line) to work the choke cable through the fan housing. Put the copper tube through both holes in the fan housing, put the choke cable through the tube and push the cable to the rear and pull on the copper tube toward the ear at the same time. This wound wire cable goes through the clamp on the side of the carburetor. With no copper tube to push it through, thread the cable through with patience and good humor. Once the cable is through, pull it rearward as far as it will go and put it in the clamp, then tighten the screw to clamp it. Pull the choke wire (inside of the cable) to the rear and insert it in the hole on the clamp on the end of the choke lever and tighten the nut with the vice grip. Check the operation of the choke from the front of the car.

Step 15.　Electrical Connections

Note: See Sketch, beginning of Chapter XVII.

Go to Step 3, ENGINE REMOVAL and connect the wires in the reverse order from the disconnection step. Scrape and clean the ground strap connection from the battery, which should be the last thing you connect.

Step 16.　Tail Pipe Installation

Condition: You've bought brand new shiny tail pipes.

In the two tail pipe connection kits, you'll find an iron ring and an asbestos ring. Put them on the tail pipes, put the wide end of the tail pipe on the muffler and clamp the joint the same way you did on the muffler installation.

Step 17. Install Rear Engine Support—Double Jointed Axles Only. Includes Automatic Trans

Type I: Find the four 19mm bolts and nuts and put them on the rear engine support—2 on a side—tighten them.

Bus, '68 and '69: has a single mounting at the rear with three bolts and nuts. '70 and on has one 17mm bolt and nut on each side. Put them in and tighten them.

All: Remove the support you made for the trans.

Step 18.　Adjust Clutch

Condition: Push the clutch pedal down with your hand. If it goes down more than one inch or less than 1/2" before you get resistance, turn to Chapter XIII to the Procedure for Adjusting the Clutch and adjust it. If you did the preliminary clutch adjustment Step and if you have less than one inch

Step 18. (Cont'd.)

or more than 1/2" deflection (a minor miracle), go under the car and tighten the 11mm nut down onto the 14mm nut with your fingers. If you have a wing nut, don't do anything. But if your clutch pedal goes down more than one inch or less than 1/2" before you get resistance, run the clutch adjustment procedure.

Step 19. Odds and Ends.

Type I: Replace back piece of tin: 36 and 40hp, just replace the four screws and tighten them with the big screwdriver. 1965 and on, see Step 6, this Procedure, where it says **'68 to '71 Bus,** to install the rear tin and hoses.

Bus: Replace the rear brace that seals the engine compartment. Replace the bumper the way it came off.

All Models: Put in non-detergent oil for the first 300 miles. Oil in? turn to Chapter X and time the engine. Start it, warm it up and adjust the carburetor. So take it for a drive, already.

Step 20. Break In

If you've done a complete overhaul or put in new rings, just drive normally without any acceleration surges or drag strip techniques, then run the 3,000 mile maintenance procedure in Chapter X after you've put 300 miles on the engine. **Be sure to change to detergent oil in 300 miles.** Run Chapter X again at 1,000 miles, then you can run as you will and go back to the 3,000 mile service cycle. Everyone else continue with just the 3,000 mile check-ups.

PROCEDURE FOR ENGINE EQUIPMENT ASSEMBLY AND INSTALLATION–Type III

Step 1. Install Heater Boxes

Pull the rags out of the two front exhaust ports and put new gaskets over the studs. If you have a stripped or otherwise mutilated stud, refer to Chapter XVI. Put the heater boxes in place over the studs. They fit only on their proper sides as you'll see. Replace the nuts and tighten them firmly. There are two screws on each side that secure the lower heat channels (curved pieces of sheet metal) under the engine to the bottom of the crankcase on both sides; install them also.

Step 2. Install Cover Plates

Find the cover plate with No. 1 & No. 2 stamped on it and place it over the right side of the engine. Now find the cover plate with No. 3 & No. 4 stamped on it and place it over the other side. You may have to bend the plates around a bit to get them to fit flat on the engine. Look in your parts stash for two pieces of tin about 1" x 6" with a screw hole in each end. If you can't find them and you have an older model, forget it; you probably don't have them. If you have them, they fit to the outside of the intake ports (holes) with two screws going through to the cylinder heads, OK? **Attention Fuel Injection:** Find two brass male slip-on connectors and put them under the two front (front is front) screws (one on each side) that hold the cover plates to the cylinder heads. Late models don't have these grounds. **Everyone:** Replace the short 10mm bolt that holds the flap on the rear of the cover plate to the heater box. Put in the screws holding the front of the cover plates to the front of the heater boxes.

Step 3. Install Front Fan Housing Half

Pick up the front fan housing half (it's the one with the two tin flaps on it) and look at the right air duct with the long thin rod on it. This rod fits into the air duct on the right cover plate. Poke your

Step 3. (Cont'd.)

head around the right side of the engine and look under the cover plate above the intake holes. See the thermostat bracket bolted onto the head. If there isn't a little cylinder clamp in the bracket, look in a baggie for it. It looks like the clamp on the accelerator cable. Put the clamp in the hole in the bracket with the 8mm screw facing out. OK, got it in? Now put the fan housing half on the rear of the engine making sure the long thin rod goes in the air duct hole in the cover plate. Before you push it all the way in, reach around the right side and guide the rod in the cylinder clamp with your fingers, then push the fan housing all the way home. Find two long 10mm bolts and put them through the fan housing on either side of where the crankshaft comes out of the case but don't tighten them yet. What you want to do now is to center the hole in the center of the fan housing around the crankshaft as close as you can by eye. You can do it with a ruler if you want but just remember it's got to be close as you can get it. When you've got it, tighten the two 10mm bolts firmly. NOTE: a lot of Type III engines have the problem of these two bolts coming loose and rattling around in the fan. You can put some lock-tight on the threads of the bolt, then put them in. The only problem here is that when you want to take the bolts out again, it's going to be a little tough. There are two more 10mm bolts that go in the holes in the top right side of the fan housing. Now close the flaps all the way (down) and tighten the 8mm bolt on the cylinder clamp. Find the thermostat spring and hook one end in the hole on the right air flap (on the fan housing) next to where the rod connects and hook the other end on the cylinder clamp. There should be a slight opening between the air flap and the fan housing (2mm to be exact). If it's opened or closed more than this, adjust it by loosening the 8mm bolt and sliding the rod one way or the other—depending.

Step 4. Install Fan

Look at those spiral threads on the front of the fan and make sure they're clean. Place the fan on the crankshaft end so the slot in the fan fits into the key on the crank. Tap it with a hammer until it stops. It won't be flush with the crankshaft because the pulley has to go on also. Don't put the bolt in yet.

Step 5. Install Rear Fan Housing Half

Pick up the rear fan housing half and place it on the front half so the pins line up with the holes in the front half. Tap the rear half lightly with a hammer on top of the pins until it's flush with the front half. Replace the seven 10mm bolts around the edge of the fan housing. Now find the long metal tube with a bolt in the center of it and put it up against the recess on the top right of the fan housing. Use a 13mm socket on a long extension and ratchet to tighten the bolt inside the tube.

Step 6. Install Fan Pulley

Put a new paper gasket on the end of the pulley and a metal shim if there was one when you took it off. Never use more than one metal shim here. Place the pulley on the fan so the pin in it fits into the hole in the fan. Now find the big bolt and washer and thread it into the crankshaft (through the fan and pulley). Lock the flywheel as you did when checking the end play. Use a 30mm (1-3/16") socket on a six inch extension and torque wrench to torque the bolt to 36 ft. lbs. (4 to 5 mkg). Take the plastic cover (half sphere) and knock it on the center of the pulley with a hammer.

Step 7. Install Intake Air Housing

Pick up the intake air housing and look at the front side. There should be a rubber gasket around it. If there isn't (or if you have a new gasket), put it on now. Place the housing up against the fan housing and put the six short 10mm bolts around the outside of it. There is one more 10mm bolt that goes on the inside of the intake air housing to the left of center. Put it in and tighten them all.

Step 8. Install Generator

Slip the generator into its place on the intake air housing and put the clamp over it. Put the nuts and washers in place but don't tighten them yet. See sketch, page 86. Notice that on top of the clamp there's a dot. What you want to do is turn the generator until the line etched into it lines up with the dot on the clamp, OK? This is to insure proper generator cooling so it's important. You say, "Wait a minute, there ain't no line or dot on mine." Cool it, we have another way. The D+ terminal that sticks up out of the generator should be 37° counterclockwise from the vertical. This is a more or less measurement so don't get out your protractor, geometry book or anything like that. The idea is to get the hole in the bottom of the generator lined up with the hole in the fan housing. When it's lined up, tighten the two nuts firmly and put the belt on. If you've forgotten how it goes on, look in Chapter VIII.

Step 9. Install Coil

The coil mounts on top of the fan housing on the extreme left bolt hole.

Remove the proper bolt on the fan housing top if it's in and slip the coil and bracket over the hole. Replace the bolt (it's the bolt that's longer than the rest) and put a nut on the other end of it.

Step 10. Install Oil Filler Pipe

Find the long metal pipe with a flange on one end. Now find a gasket that fits the flanged end and put some gasket glue on both sides. The pipe fits on the hole with studs in each side, on the bottom, right rear side of the crankcase. Pull the rag out of the hole and slip the gasket over the studs. Later models have two pipes coming out from the flanged end. One of the pipes is shorter and thinner than the other. Find a hose that fits on the shorter end and stick it on. This hose goes up to the crankcase breather so you have to slip it on when you put the oil filter pipe on the engine. Anyway, no matter what you have, put the flanged end of the oil filler pipe over the studs, then two spring washers and 13mm nuts. It's hard to get a socket on the lower nut so use a 13mm open end wrench.

Step 11. Install Intake Manifold(s)

Single Carburetor: Blow through the heat riser (rear legs of the manifold) to make sure it's not clogged. If it is, unclog it.

Remove the rags from the holes on top of the cylinder heads and take the old gaskets out if they're still in. Find the new ones (metal "O" rings) and place them over the intake hole studs with the seam facing up. Now look in your gasket set for a gasket that looks like the one you put on the exhaust hole only about half the size. This gasket goes on the front of the right heater box. There are two gaskets like this, one of which may have a smaller hole in its center. If so, use the one with a larger hole on the right heater box, OK? Now slip the manifold with carburetor attached over the studs on the cylinder heads. When it's down on the engine, start the two 10mm bolts that hold the heat riser to the front of the heater box, then the four 10mm nuts (with spring washers) that hold the manifold to the cylinder heads. Tighten them all firmly and evenly.

Dual Carburetors: Pull the rags out of the intake holes on top of the cylinder heads and remove the old gaskets if they're still there. Find the new gaskets and slip them over the studs. Get both manifolds and put them on the intake holes. There is a pipe coming off the bottom of the manifolds which should be facing the REAR of the engine. This means each manifold will only fit one side, right? If your carburetors are off the manifolds, put on new gaskets, then the carbs so the choke elements are facing the REAR of the engine. Replace the nuts and spring washers on the manifolds and carbs (if they're off). Tighten them firmly.

Look for two pieces of tin about 6" long with two big holes in them. Slip them down to the

Step 11. (Cont'd.)

inside of the manifolds by the spark plugs. If you're having trouble getting one of the tin pieces to fit, try it on the other side as they only fit on their proper sides. Replace the screws. Find the two small springs that look alike and hook one end on the throttle lever (the one with a rod on it) and the other end on the raised part on the cover plate directly below. Find the long metal tube with a hose on each end and slip an end over each pipe on the rear of the manifolds. This pipe (balance tube) is held on the center of the engine by a piece of metal with two bends, a hole in one end and a stud in the other. The bracket goes on center of the balance tube with a plastic block under it and a 13mm bolt to secure it to the engine. The bolt threads into the balance tube bracket which should be on the case. If for some reason it's not, turn to Step 7, CRANKCASE ASSEMBLY, and put it on.

Find the thin vacuum hose, put one end on the distributor vacuum unit and the other end on the small pipe on the left manifold. Take the two long rods with sockets on each end and put one end on the throttle bell crank (on the front case bolt) and the other end on the throttle lever on the carburetor. Do the same on the other side.

Fuel Injection Only: Pull the rags out of the intake ports and remove the old paper gaskets if they're still on. Find the two plastic blocks that fit over the intake port studs and two new paper gaskets. First the plastic blocks, then the gaskets go over the studs. Now take the whole manifold assembly and slip it over the studs on both cylinder heads. Look under the intake air distributor (the aluminum box in the center) and slip the two brackets on it over the corresponding holes in the crankcase. If the one bolt and nut is in the hole remove it. Install the two bolts and tighten them with a 13mm socket and ratchet, with a 13mm wrench to hold the nut on the other end. The bolt that goes through both sides of the case should be torqued to 14 ft. lbs. Replace the two 13mm nuts and spring washers holding the intake manifold ends to the cylinder heads and tighten the nuts firmly. Put one end of the thin woven vacuum hose on the distributor and the other end on the top left side of the intake air distributor. Find the fatter vacuum hose about six inches long and put it between the pipe on the bottom rear of the intake air distributor and the front pipe on the auxiliary air regulator (to the right of the distributor). Find the piece of metal bolted on the No. 3 and 4 cover plate with like a half circle loop in it. Unscrew it and place the fuel line (from one side to the other) under it and bolt it back on. That's it.

Late models with automatic transmission and an exhaust gas recirculator have a few more things to hook up. Get the long 1/2" metal pipe with a flange on both ends. One end goes on the rear of the intake air distributor and the other goes to the exhaust gas recirculator on the right front of the engine. The bolts should be in a marked baggie so go to it. The other pipe on the recirculator has to be bolted back up also.

Step 12. Install Muffler

Condition: It's off.

Pull the rags out of the rear exhaust ports and put a new gasket in place. If you have bought a new muffler installation kit (gaskets and clamps), pry off the round asbestos seal on the lower pipe coming from the heater boxes. Put the metal ring on first (cone facing rear), then the asbestos seal. Make sure the two large band clamps that connect the hole in the bottom of the muffler heat exchanger (the tin box on either side) to the big hole on the heater box above the place you just put the seal on, are on the muffler end and pushed up all the way (so they'll clear when you slip the muffler on). Slip the muffler over the lower pipes enough so you can slip the band clamps on the holes in the heater boxes. Now work the muffler rest of the way on the pipes and the studs on the cylinder heads. If it won't go easily, use a wooden block and a hammer to persuade it. Put the band clamp on the heater boxes in the correct position (so there's no open space) and tighten the screws. Start the bottom 13mm nuts on the cylinder heads with your fingers and tighten them with a 13mm wrench. Start the top ones with your fingers and tighten them with a 13mm socket on a long

Step 12. (Cont'd.)

extension and ratchet, through the recess in the fan housing (just look until you can see through to the nuts). Slip the asbestos seal and the metal "O" ring up the lower pipes, up against the muffler connection, then put the clamps (in the muffler installation kit) around the connections and tighten them with a 10mm socket on one end and a 10mm wrench on the other. Slide the rubber sleeves on either end of the muffler onto the holes in the fan housing. Put the clamps in place and twist them with a pair of thin nosed pliers until they're tight. On each side, to the outside of the elbow you just hooked up, is a fresh air pipe that connects to a pipe running along side the valve covers under the cover plates. If the clamp isn't on one of these pipes, look for it. They're metal clamps with a screw to tighten them. Slip the clamp over the space between the pipes and tighten the screws.

Step 13. Install Clutch Throw-out Bearing

Follow the directions in Step 7, ENGINE EQUIPMENT ASSEMBLY AND INSTALLATION– Types I and II.

Step 14. Install Starter and Bushing

Follow the directions in Step 8, ENGINE EQUIPMENT ASSEMBLY AND INSTALLATION– Types I and II.

Step 15. Check Starter and Solenoid

Follow the directions in Step 9, ENGINE EQUIPMENT ASSEMBLY AND INSTALLATION– Types I and II.

Step 16. Preliminary Clutch Adjustment

Follow directions in Step 10, same Procedure as above.

Step 17. Ready, Set. . .

Follow directions in Step 11, same Procedure as above.

Step 18. . . .Go. Engine In

Follow directions in Step 12, same Procedure as above.

Step 19. Connect Heater Cables and Gas Line

Follow directions in Step 13, same Procedure as above, but fuel injected engines come back here where it says "Carb Models only." Carbureted engines, finish the step, then come back here.

Step 20. Mechanical Connections

Up to 1969: Find the rear mount (it's the round piece with a rubber insert) and slip it over the tube sticking out of the top of the fan housing. It goes on so the plate with threaded holes in it matches up with the holes in the tongue on the rear of the engine compartment. Get all the fiber shims and stick them between the mount and the tongue and replace the two 13mm bolts and washers. Tighten them firmly.

Step 20. (Cont'd.)

From 1969 and on: Slide under the engine and replace the two 19mm bolts on each side of the rear engine mount.

Fuel Injection Only: See the sheet metal piece that's hanging loose on the FRONT of the engine compartment? Push it down on the engine so the two tabs go over the engine case and put on the two screws holding the tabs to the cover plates. Find the woven hose coming through this piece of tin on the left side. Put the clamp over the hose, if it isn't already there. If you have the standard type clamp (a band of metal with a hump on it) throw it away and buy a 1/2'' screw type hose clamp. Anyway, with the clamp on the hose, put one hand on the double T fitting (by the injectors) and the other on the hose. Push and twist the hose on the tube and tighten the clamp down firmly. Now find the hose on the other side of the engine (the one coming from the pressure regulator mounted on the FRONT piece of tin you just connected) and connect it to the double T fitting by No. 1 and No. 2 cylinders the same way you connected the other hose. Put on the long hose from the pressure sensor (on the left side of the engine compartment) to the intake air distributor.

Everyone: Pull the throttle cable all the way through the front piece of tin so there isn't any slack. Find the small cylinder with a hole and a set screw in it. (It's in a baggie.) Put it into the hole in the throttle lever, the screw facing to the left. Stick the throttle cable through the hole in the clamp and tighten the screw. There shouldn't be any slack in the cable and the throttle should be fully closed. Fuel injection has a spring that goes from the throttle lever to a plate sticking up to the right of the distributor. Have a friend push the throttle pedal all the way down while you look at it from the back. If it opens all the way, you're OK, if not you'll have to adjust it by playing with the set screw.

On the rear of the engine compartment is the intake bellows. It's the big rubber accordion like thing. If you bought a new one, loosen the screw on the clamp holding it to the body and pull the bellows off. When you put the new one on, the large end goes on the body. Once the bellows is on the body, work the lip of the bellows around the intake air housing on the engine with your fingers and a screwdriver until it's all the way on. It's not easy to get on, especially if it's new and stiff but just be patient. Tighten the clamps with a large screwdriver. To the right of the bellows is the oil dipstick tube. Connect the rubber sleeve between the pipe on the engine and the pipe on the body and tighten the clamp.

Step 21. Electrical Connections

Note: See sketch, beginning of Chapter XVII.

Find the distributor cap with the wires on it and put it on the distributor. Connect the wires to their proper spark plugs—See Step 4, ENGINE EQUIPMENT ASSEMBLY AND INSTALLATION—TYPES I AND II.

Find the three wires taped together marked GEN coming out of the left side of the engine compartment. Take the masking tape off the wires. The heavy red one goes to the D+ terminal on the generator, 8mm. The thin wire with the split connector on the end goes to the DF terminal. It has a split connection because the 8mm nut on the DF terminal won't come off. The other thin wire goes to the ground screw on the generator. Coming out of the same harness as the generator wires is a wire marked 15, right? It goes to the No. 15 side of the coil. The number is on the coil by the terminal. Find the wire marked J4 and slip it on the oil pressure sensor on top of the oil cooler. The oil pressure sensor is the six sided nut with a round plastic thing on top just to the left of center on top of the engine. The thin wire on the side of the distributor, marked 1- goes to the No. 1 side of the coil. Connect the heavy wire from the center of the distributor cap to the coil.

Step 21. (Cont'd.)

Single Carb: Find the wires marked O1 and O2. Connect O1 to the automatic choke (the round ceramic thing on the carburetor) and O2 to the automatic cut-off jet (the cylinder sticking out of the carb).

Dual Carburetors: There are two wires on each side marked O1 and O2. Connect O1 to the automatic choke (the round ceramic thing on the carburetor) and O2 to the automatic cut-off jet (the cylinder sticking out of the side of the carburetor). Both carbs.

Fuel Injection: Before connecting the MPC's, look at the end that plugs into the receptacle. There is a bevel cut into one side of the plastic base. You'll see the same bevel on the receptacles. When you push them on make sure the bevels are lined up. Pull the rubber covers over the receptacles after they're plugged in.

On the front of the engine compartment there is a heavy wire harness coming from the left side. Follow it along from the left to the right until you come to the first branch in it. It's just to the left of center. It has two MPC's and some single wires coming out of it. Take this harness and pull it under the left side of the manifold and hook it into the long metal clip on the cover plate. Now find the MPC with three prongs on it and put it into the receptacle on the side of the distributor. Remember to line up the bevels. The MPC with two prongs goes on temperature sensor 1. Up to 1970 the sensor is on the front stud of the auxiliary air regulator (to the right of the distributor). From 1970 on it's on the left side (right side, late models) of the intake air distributor. The single connection marked F1 goes on the brass connector on the crankcase breather nut (to the right of the auxiliary air regulator).

Late model fuel injection engines have two main ground clusters. Find the two clusters of three single wires. One cluster goes on the connections on the center of the engine (case bolt) and the other cluster goes on the connections on the oil breather nut. Both clusters should be marked GROUND. It doesn't matter which wire goes on which connection as they are all grounds. If your engine has these clusters, it won't have the single ground connections by the injectors, OK?

Up to 1970 the wire marked F3 goes to the cylinder head temperature sensor. The wire it connects to should come up from the front of the distributor. If you don't see the wire, crawl under the car and look up at the left (No. 3 and 4) cylinder head, front. Find the wire and push it up top. Slide the plastic cover over the connection. If the cover isn't there, wrap the connection with electrical tape. A short here will keep the car from running.

From 1970 on the wire marked F3 goes to the cylinder head temperature sensor located on the top of the No. 3 & 4 (left) cylinder head, by the No. 4 spark plug. Make sure the rubber seal is on the cover plate around the sensor. Slide the plastic cover over the connection. If it's not there, put some electrical tape around the connection.

Now back to the main wire harness on the front of the engine compartment. Follow it to the right of center to where it branches. There is one MPC. Put it on the throttle valve switch which lives on the right side of the intake air distributor (the black plastic gizmo). Follow the main harness further to the right.

Up to 1970: Follow the main harness further to the right to where it branches off into an MPC. Put this MPC on the pressure switch located under the right manifold.

On each side of the engine are two MPC's and a single connector marked F-2. The MPC's go on the injectors, located on either side of where the manifolds go into the heads. Put the MPC with the GREY cover on the REAR injector and the black one on the front injector. It's important you don't get these MPC's mixed up. Just remember, GREY TO THE REAR, BLACK TO THE FRONT. The single wire F-2 coming out of the harness (on both sides) goes to the brass ground connector on the screw by the Front spark plugs. If these connections are loose, pinch the female end with a pair of pliers a little and try it again. If you have a late model with the cluster of grounds, you won't have this F-2 connection.

From 1970 on: Cold Start Valve—the cold start valve is located on the right side of the intake

Step 21. (Cont'd.)

air distributor, directly under the manifold pipes. The MPC that fits it is nearby so connect it. Coming out of the MPC wire is a single wire marked J1. This goes on the cold start switch located under the throttle valve switch. Locate the auxiliary air regulator again. It's just to the right of the distributor. The long wire on it goes to the No. 15 terminal on the coil.

 Automatic Transmission Only: Find the wires marked KL and KR. They go on the kickdown switch located by the throttle lever. KL goes on the left terminal and KR goes on the right one.

 Everyone: Lift up the back seat to expose the battery. If the top of the battery is full of green crud, mix up a solution of baking soda and water and pour it over the battery. Rinse it off with clean water. Clean the terminals with a wire brush until they shine. Put the ground strap on the battery post and tighten it with a 13mm wrench.

 Wires all attached? Look around to make sure they all are and attach or tape any loose ones. OK? Time to fill the sparkling clean air cleaner with oil up to the line. Put it back on:

 Single Carburetor: Fasten the rubber elbow onto the carb and set the air cleaner on it. Replace the wing bolt, the hose to the breather and the rubber tube to the fan housing.

 Dual Carburetor: Set the air cleaner assembly on the top of the carbs and replace the wing bolts on top of each carb and the wing nut in the center of the cleaner. Connect the hose to the breather and the rubber tube to the fan housing.

 Fuel Injection: Set the air cleaner down over the hole in the cover plate (right side) and replace the wing bolt. Fasten the rubber elbow to the intake air distributor and the rubber sleeve to the fan housing. Connect the hose to the auxiliary air regulator and the breather. Late models with all those hoses, look at the hose map. What you have is one hose to each cylinder head, one to the charcoal filter, one to the deceleration valve and one to the left side of the fan housing, got all that?

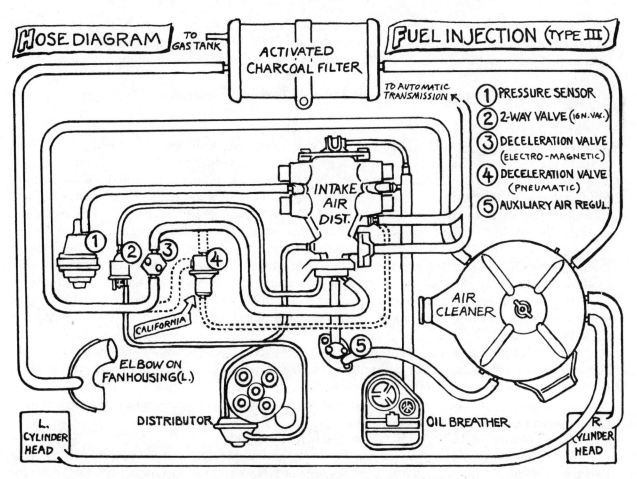

Step 22. Adjust Clutch

Please return once more to ENGINE EQUIPMENT ASSEMBLY AND INSTALLATION–TYPE I AND II and adjust the clutch if the pedal has more than 1" or less than 1/2" deflection.

Step 23. Odds and Ends

Put two and a half quarts of oil into the engine and turn to Chapter X to time it. Warm it up and adjust the idle. Dual carbs might have to balance the carbs. Take 'er for a spin. Congratulations!!

Step 24. Break In

If you've done a complete overhaul or put in new rings, treat the engine as you would a new one...you know; no fast starts, no lugging, just drive normally. Run the 3,000 mile maintenance in Chapter X **at 300 miles** making especially sure to **change the oil**. Run Chapter X again at 1000 miles and after that go back to regular 3,000 mile tune-ups. If you didn't do a complete overhaul or put in new rings, just continue with the regular 3,000 mile maintenance.

PROCEDURE FOR ENGINE EQUIPMENT ASSEMBLY AND INSTALLATION, TYPE IV AND 1972 AND ON TYPE II

Step 1. Install the Engine Support Bracket

The support bracket is handy to hold the engine while you put on the rest of the equipment so find it and the baggie with the two or four bolts, install the bracket and tighten the bolts, about as tight as you can with the 3/8" ratchet. Be sure both air deflectors are on under the cylinders.

Step 2. Check End Play, Install Front Seal and Flywheel or Drive Shaft

Special tool: 3/8" drive–10mm, 12 spline wrench
If you've had the case open for an overhaul, you have to check the crankshaft end play...critical in these big engines. The end play is adjusted by the three shims that go behind the front seal. Start with the three you took off; hopefully they'll be exactly what you need. Put the shims **but not the front seal** around the front end of the crankshaft and put the flywheel (shift models) or drive plate (automatics) on, then the old five hole washer (if any) and finally the five cap screws into the crankshaft through the flywheel or drive plate. Use the spline wrench on the breaker bar to tighten the cap screws to about 30 - 40 ft. lbs., enough so you can torque the rear pulley bolt to 43 ft. lbs. Tighten the cap screws little by little going around the circle with the torque wrench. Now, the easiest way to check the end play is to borrow a clamp-on dial indicator gauge and see if the end play measures .004". If it doesn't, you have to remove the flywheel (or drive plate) and try another combination of shims using some of those you bought. Always use three shims, never more, never less, until you do get a .004" reading.

For lack of this gauge, turn to Step 14, ENGINE MANTLING and follow the instructions there between the two rows of stars. The difference is you have five cap screws to put on and remove every time instead of a gland nut. **Automatics:** substitute "drive plate" for "flywheel" and you'll have to use the rear crankshaft pulley to hold the drive plate from turning as you cannot use the angle iron or you'll distort (and thus ruin) the drive plate.

OK, go to Step 14, do Step 15, then return here.

You're back with the end play checked and the front seal in. OK, put the new rubber "O" ring into the flywheel or drive plate hub if you took one out. Now you can install the flywheel (d.p.) for

Step 2. (Cont'd.)

the last time. Check the pilot needle bearings in the center of the flywheel (d.p.) to see they're in. Put a finger full of wheel bearing grease into the needle bearing, then slip the flywheel (drive plate) on the end of the crankshaft, put the new five hole washer from your gasket set on (if your model requires one) and install the five cap screws. Have your friend hold the rear pulley from turning with the big pipe wrench but use a cloth so you don't mar the pulley. Torque the flywheel cap screws to 80 ft. lbs. or the drive plate cap screws to 61 ft. lbs. Tighten and torque a little on each cap screw at a time so the flywheel, but expecially the drive plate, will not distort.

Step 3. Install Oil Cooler

We recommend you replace the old one with a new one. If you're here just to replace a leaky oil cooler, we recommend you take out and clean both the pressure relief valve in the bottom of the crankcase and the pressure control valve between the push rod tubes on No. 1 cylinder. You'll need the 3/8" drive–10mm, 12 spline wrench for the pressure control valve. Don't carelessly throw the spring for the control valve into the same pile of parts with the little distributor spring. They look alike and if you mix them up, the distributor will work, OK, but you wind up with like zero oil pressure.

Relief and control valves clean and back in place? Find the two rubber seals for the oil cooler in your gasket kit, put some wheel bearing grease on them and put them in the holes in the crankcase. Make sure both entrances on the oil cooler and crankcase are clean and clear. Remove any paper tags on the cooler. (If you're using the old oil cooler, drain ALL the oil out and clean it well with solvent inside and out.) Slide the oil cooler over the studs, put on the flat washer, then the spring washer and the nuts and tighten the nuts with a small wrench while you hold the cooler as horizontal as you can. **See Changes and New Ideas.**

Step 4. Install Fan and Fan Housing

If you've done an overhaul, you took off the air control thermostat to get it and the little pulley that guides the wire that operates the air control flaps out of the bag and put the thermostat on but don't tighten the bolt yet. Put the little pulley on, leaving the bolt hand tight. Slip the fan housing on the four center studs, put the washers and nuts on and get the nuts started on the studs. (Sedans, make sure the rubber boot for the oil filler tube is in place.) Tighten the four nuts on the housing, about 10 ft. lbs. Now pull the wire up from the thermostat and make sure the little pulley will guide the wire directly to the cooling air control, then tighten both the thermostat and pulley nuts. Put the wire in to the wire clamp while you hold the flaps closed and gently take the slack out of the wire, making sure it's on the pulley, then tighten the wire clamp.

Get the fan out of the sack, install the spacer(s) on the rear of the fan pulley and put the fan on. Install the three (four) allen head cap screws and tighten them with your 6mm allen head wrench. In the 1973 Bus, there's that pulley for the Smog Pump that goes on with the fan, but put the alternator fan belt around the fan pulley before you install the pulley for the Smog Pump. The rest of the models have different types of guards and rear pieces for the fan, so put on what you took off, bolt it down and tighten it. Now that your timing marks are where you can refer to them, go to the Tune-up Procedure in Chapter X and adjust your valves to .006" for all. Leave the engine so the timing mark shows that No. 1 cylinder is at TDC, ready to fire. That is, the mark on the fan is opposite the zero on the scale on the Bus and the black mark on the pulley is about 1/2" to the right of the notch on the fan housing on the other Type IV's. Put on the valve covers with their new gaskets.

Step 5. Install Distributor Drive Shaft.

Now that you're sure the engine is at TDC for No. 1 cylinder, you can install the distributor drive shaft using the magical method that follows: Scribe a thin line with a felt tip pen and a ruler

Step 5. (Cont'd.)

on the crankcase parallel with the crack in the crankcase (90 degrees to the fan housing). This line should go through the center of the hole you're going to put the distributor drive shaft into in a few minutes. Get the one or two washers that fit on the bottom of the distributor drive shaft and coat them both with wheel bearing grease. Put them around the big screwdriver blade and hold them near the handle while you put the business end of the screwdriver into the distributor hole in the crankcase. Flashlight in hand, drop the washers down the shaft of the screwdriver into the crankcase so they stick down there where the distributor drive shaft seats. Move the screwdriver around down there so the center of the washers leave the hole for the shaft open. Pull the screwdriver out carefully (don't dislodge the washers) and check the position of the washers with the flashlight to make sure the hole is clear and ready for the shaft. Oil the distributor drive shaft and look at it. As you put it in, it's going to turn as it goes by the gear on the crankshaft to its position below the gear. Look at the top of the distributor drive shaft. It has a slot with one fat side and one thin side. In other words, there's more hole on one side of the slot than on the other. See sketch, Step 10, ENGINE MANTLING Procedure with the fat side (or side with more hole) toward the center of the engine, the slot must make an angle of 12 degrees with the crankcase when the top of the shaft is flush with the case. So how do you get all that fancy? The secret is the magnet. Put it on the top of the drive shaft to hold it and position the shaft in its hole with the fat side toward the crack in the crankcase and the slot parallel to the line you drew. Turn the shaft about 1/8" (14 degrees) COUNTERCLOCKWISE. Still holding the shaft with the magnet, lower it down until it starts on the gear. Trade the magnet for the large screwdriver and screw the shaft down. Watch the slot in the shaft while you turn the engine. If the slot turns, the shaft is seated. If it doesn't turn, screw down some more. Slide that little distributor spring down the hole on top of the shaft using a piece of coat hanger wire as a guide. Put a rag in the hole. Return the engine to TDC for No. 1 if you've moved it.

Step 6. Install Alternator and Shrouding

If you've had the alternator overhauled, put a new gasket on the front air seal and put on the air shrouding for the alternator. The wires will be attached and sticking out the FRONT. Everybody: Put the alternator on the hinge, then put the hinge pin through the hinge and put the nut on the pin. Position the cleaned pieces of shrouding around the engine. They can only go one way so start fitting them together. Put on the three pieces that go on the left side first. . .top, front and rear. . .start the screws and when the pieces fit well on the engine and on the oil cooler, tighten the screws. Do the same for the right side, then put on the big piece that goes across the FRONT of the engine, put the alternator wire through it and fix the grommet. Connect the air supply hose to the front of the alternator. Put the rear piece of shrouding on the alternator, making sure, Bus, that the dipstick tube is free.

Put the breather box assembly back on top of the engine the way it came off with a new rectangular rubber seal and the old clamps. There are several types: the wagon and some of the sedans use this assembly to put in the oil and for the dipstick too. . .others don't. Put the connection for the oil filter on the lower left side of the engine. It takes a new gasket, two washers and two nuts— put the assembly on the studs, then tighten the nuts.

Install the fan belt on the alternator pulley. Find the adjusting bolt in its baggie and put it on. Tighten the hinge pin nut and adjust the fan belt so it has one half inch deflection. (Chapter VIII). Put the plastic cap over the adjusting bolt. **See Changes and New Ideas.**

Step 7. Install Fuel Pump—Not for Fuel Injection

You've rebuilt your fuel pump or are installing a new (or the old) one after an overhaul. The first thing to do is check the fuel pump push rod travel to see if it will operate the pump. Put a gas-

Step 7. (Cont'd.)

ket on each side of the hard plastic flange (block), slip this grouping over the studs and put a washer and nut on each stud. Tighten the nuts just snug. Put the push rod in the hole with the heavy end in, then rotate the engine until the push rod sticks out the furthest. Take a pencil and a piece of cardboard. Hold the cardboard under the push rod against the gasket and mark the length of rod that's sticking out past the gasket. Measure this length with a ruler. It should measure 5mm on the metric scale or 3/16" on the inch scale. Another way to measure is to take your feeler gauge and add up blades until you have a bunch that make .200" (two hundred thousandths of an inch) then measure this pile of blades against the length of the rod. With a new push rod, you might have to leave out the gasket between the flange (plastic block) and the crankcase. It may leak a little oil this way, so think about a new push rod.

Remove the nuts and washers from the studs. Fill the fuel pump base with wheel bearing grease. Put the fuel pump over the studs, put the washers and nuts back on and tighten them. Now you're going to install the air conduit (takes air to the alternator. . .a piece of metal about the size of a phone receiver) and the pre-heater connection (small metal elbow with a flange). Remember what is here and imagine you're going to remove these two pieces with the engine in the car, so one day, if you should have fuel pump problems, you won't have to pull the engine to get at the pump. Put the air conduit and pre-heater connections on and connect the fuel line that goes from the fuel pump to the carbs at the fuel pump end.

Step 8. Install Carburetors—Not for Fuel Injection

If the carbs have been off the manifolds, replace them now with new, well greased gaskets and tighten the nuts. Take out the rags blocking the holes in the heads. Put the new intake manifold gaskets (well greased) on the heads and put on the intake manifolds (both sides, but one at a time, OK?). Put on the washers and nuts and get them started but not tight. Install the carburetor linkage assembly between the carburetors and put the bolts in; now tighten the intake manifold nuts, then the carb linkage bolts. Hook up the manifold balance tube and the carburetor balance tube plus the idle tube for the Bus. Hook up the fuel lines from the fuel pump to each carb and if you have a 411 or a 1972 Bus, you're about through. If you have a **1973 Bus,** you have to hook up the Smog Pump tubing. This System goes across the engine (between the manifolds) with two tubes that go up to the Smog Pump Control Valve so hook them in and tighten the two 17mm nuts. Put the spider of tubes that comes from the Smog Pump to the four cylinder heads in place. Get the ends of the tubes in the holes and when they fit, tighten the 17mm nuts. Now you can put on the Smog Pump belt and tighten it by lifting the Smog Pump and tightening the left bolt. This belt should deflect about half an inch.

Step 9. Install Fuel Injection Equipment—Not for Carb Models

There should be a cluster of ground connections on the center of the engine held on by one of the case bolts. If it's not there, find it, remove the nut, install the ground cluster—4 or 5 male push-on connectors—and retorque the nut (14 ft. lbs.).

Temperature Sensor II, the head temperature sensor: goes down between cylinders No. 3 and 4 in a hole in the shrouding and requires a deep 13mm socket to put it in. If it's not there, install it and tighten it with the pliers on the socket.

Auxiliary Air Regulator: Pull the rag out of the crankcase hole, center right, put the new gasket on the hole, put the hoses on the regulator, put the regulator down on the hole and install and tighten the retaining nuts.

Intake Air Distributor: Slide the front tube into the short hose of the auxiliary air regulator, put the intake air distributor on the studs and fasten it down.

Step 9. (Cont'd.)

Temperature Sensor I, the cold start jet and the cold start valve should all still be in the intake air distributor. Check to make sure they are. If they're not. . . .put them in.

Intake manifolds: Slide the fiber woven hoses up over the manifold tubes until they're flush at the end with the manifold tubes. Put some wheel bearing grease on the intake manifold gaskets, pull the rags out of the intake ports, put the gasket, then the manifolds on the studs. Put on the washers and nuts and slide the fiber woven hoses down onto the intake air distributor connections—all four, then tighten all the manifold nuts.

Fuel Loop and Injectors: You're going to put the fuel loop into place and connect it, so remove the pieces of tape as you make a connection. First connect the fuel loop hose that goes to No. 3 and 4 injectors through the hole in the FRONT piece of tin. Then bring the loop over the engine to No. 1 and 2 injectors, then around to the pressure regulator (on the left of the front tin) and connect the hose from the fuel loop to the cold start jet. Now work the placement of the fuel loop so all four injectors are ready to put in the manifolds. Be very clean around the injectors as they're sensitive to even tiny pieces of crud. Put the new outer and inner seals on the injectors and install them in the manifold. Put the nuts on the studs and tighten them. Check the whole fuel loop for any signs of strain and relieve any tightness in the system. Connect the injector hoses to the fuel loop and tighten the clamps. Make sure all the clamps everywhere in the system are tight.

Adjust the throttle valve switch in the throttle valve body (Chapter X) and install the throttle valve on the intake air distributor.

Step 10. Smog Control Equipment and Other Hoses

This is where you untangle that bucket of snakes (which you shouldn't have, if each hose is in its paper bag and marked on both ends). The idea is not to have any pieces of hose or tubes left over. OK? We'll describe the systems and you install the ones you have.

Gap the spark plugs, pull the rags out of the holes and install the spark plugs.

Put the air cleaner in place, but don't fasten it down yet. You might start out by counting all the places your air cleaner is expecting a hose.

Everybody has a connection from the crankcase breather to either the air cleaner (carb models) or the intake air distributor (fuel injection). In the late model fuel injected engine, this is a red hose and it goes to the upper single connection on the intake air distributor. In the same color, there are two hoses that come up from the heads through a flame arrester junction to an air cleaner connection. This crankcase ventilation system may also be attached to the valve covers. Everybody also has an air pre-heater hose that goes to the air cleaner from the heater boxes.

The Evaporative fuel system consists of that small tank which has charcoal in it and is connected by hoses to the fuel tank through a small expansion chamber. The tank can appear directly over the engine (Bus), to the rear of the engine (411) or under the car in front of the engine (412). The connections for this system on the engine are a hose from the fan housing to the tank and from the tank to the air cleaner.

In fuel injected engines, there's a hose from the auxiliary air regulator to the intake air distributor (this you've connected) and one to the nose of the air cleaner. This system, especially in California, may be complicated by a junction and a hose from a deceleration valve which has another connection to the intake air distributor.

And there's the exhaust gas recirculation system which connects to the muffler through a filter, a flame arrester then to the air cleaner or intake air distributor through a valve. In fuel injected models, this valve is electromagnetically operated. This system is usually pipe instead of flexible tubing. That's enough for now, but is certainly not all. We'll get to the rest after the engine is in the car. Remove the hoses from the air cleaner and lift it off.

Step 11. Install Clutch Plate and Clutch Pressure Plate and some more.

For the clutch plate and clutch pressure plate, go to ENGINE MANTLING, Step 17. Then go to Procedure for ENGINE EQUIPMENT ASSEMBLY AND INSTALLATION FOR TYPES I AND II and do Steps 7, 8, 9 and 10, and then come back here to Step 12.

Step 12. Engine In.

Put the sheet of plywood to the rear of the car, get the jacks ready, then you and **your** friends carry the engine over to the plywood and put the engine in position. Pull the car back over the engine, block the wheels and put the car in gear. Use a 2x4 and a block to lift the engine so you can put first one, then the other scissors jack under it. Automatic people, take off the piece of flat bar that's been holding the torque converter into the trans but leave the trans support for now.

Start jacking the engine up and when it's almost in place, start the accelerator cable into the hole in the front piece of tin, then continue jacking until the holes in the engine are level with the studs in the transmission and the transmission shaft is level with the clutch throwout bearing. Now, have your help roll the car back slowly and surely while you hold the engine until the trans shaft and the studs are engaged. Just ease the engine forward until you can feel the shaft engage the hole in the drive plate or flywheel. You can turn the engine with a crescent wrench to help start the trans into the clutch plate splines. When the engine slides forward and the studs come through the engine mounting, the engine is in. Now guide the back mounting bracket into the side pieces on the frame and get some bolts into the back mount. Put in the top front mounting bolts and get the nuts on them. Put the rest of the bolts into the rear mounting bracket and the nuts on the studs and you are ready to tighten them all. The engine mounting bolts get 22 ft. lbs. torque.

Automatic shift: get your flashlight and find the hole in the front of the engine and take the plastic plug out of it if it's there (it could be in a baggie). Move the torque converter with the large screwdriver through the hole until the hole in the drive plate lines up with the hole in the torque converter. This job requires that you use every care not to drop a bolt or washer into the hole so put some wheel bearing grease into the 13mm socket, which is on a long extension. The grease will hold the bolt into the socket. Grease a torque converter washer and stick it on the bolt in the socket. Now, start the bolt on the threads and tighten it just a little. After the first bolt is in, turn the engine with the wrench until another bolt hole comes into view and install this washer and bolt. . .repeat once again. When all three are in and fairly tight, hold the engine from turning with the crescent wrench and torque the bolts to 22 ft. lbs. Put the plastic plug back in the hole.

All: Next come heater boxes and muffler. Slide the heater box-muffler assembly under the engine and get a 2x4 (at the balance point) and the two scissors jacks under it but don't jack up yet. The muffler attachment bolts are not tight? OK, find the four exhaust port gaskets and coat them liberally with wheel bearing grease, then stick them up in the ports so they stay. Now jack the assembly up until by wiggling the exhaust manifolds, you can get them to go up on their studs. Install the washers and nuts. Take away the jacks (you'll need them to lift the back of a sedan or wagon so you can get under to work). Tighten all the nuts: eight on the engine and six on the muffler and there you are. Did you have stud trouble? That's covered in Chapter XVI. Now go under the car to hook things up down there. The fuel line(s) are next, so pull the pencil(s) out of the lines and connect them: one to the fuel pump in carb models and to the fuel loop and return lines for fuel injection. Trace one of the lines out if you don't know which is the return line. On the ends of the heater boxes go the heater valve connections, so knock them on with the rubber hammer and tighten the clamps. If you pulled the hoses off, hook them up and the heater control cables, too. Take off the 2x4 and chain assembly you used to hold up the trans. Install the muffler protector (rock shield) back by the bumper. Find the hot wire from the alternator and connect it to the starter and connect the hot wire from the voltage regulator to the starter. If your voltage regulator connections are near the starter, connect them too. Install the two vacuum hoses to the automatic transmission. Install the exhaust system

Step 12. (Cont'd.)

for the auxiliary heater (if any) and the connections for the air conditioner (if any). Install the tail pipe if it's off. Install the oil fill tube and the back piece of tin.

Step 13. Mechanical Connections.

Connect the heater blower and the heater hoses to the heater boxes. Tighten the clamps. The little distributor spring is in the top of the distributor drive shaft, so pull the rag out of the hole carefully and check the spring with the flashlight. It's there? OK, set the engine to TDC for No. 1, then hold the distributor with the rotor pointing to the mark on the distributor rim and slide the distributor right down on the distributor drive shaft. The distributor clamp will go over the stud. Put the washer and nut on the stud and tighten the nut.

Connect the accelerator cable to the throttle valve.

More hoses: connect the ones that apply to your buggy. There's a hose from the distributor to the intake air distributor or to the intake manifold (two in the Bus) and this system can have an interesting detour. The hose runs to a vacuum valve where the valve decides whether to allow vacuum advance under certain conditions. If you have one of these, you have an electrical connection to make, too. If yours is an automatic, push the vacuum hose from the trans onto the top of the intake air distributor. Some manual shift 411's have a deceleration valve...install it and connect the hoses, if...

Step 14. Electrical Connections

Note: See sketch, beginning of Chapter XVII.

Put the wires back from where you removed them after you marked them. Like: the thin wire from the distributor to the coil (1-), the wire from the ignition switch (fuse box) to the coil (15+) which has a whole entourage of connections (numbered 15) in a carb model that go to the automatic chokes, cut-off jets, and idle jet. Connect the (usually blue) wire to the oil temperature sensor in that hole right in FRONT of the distributor. Sensor's not in? OK, find the sensor, pull the rag out of the hole in the engine, put the sensor in (pipe threads, remember, so not too tight) then put the wire on (J4).

Put on the distributor cap and connect the spark plug wires. See ENGINE EQUIPMENT ASSEMBLY FOR TYPES I AND II, Step 4. Connect the thick wire from the center of the distributor to the coil.

In the Bus, connect the wires to the voltage regulator.

Automatic trans: connect the wires to the kickdown switch (KD 1 and 2).

Fuel Injection: Take the tape off the loom and carefully lay the wires and connectors (MPC's) out in the direction they have to travel to get to where they're going. Start with the grounds. There are several depending on year but find all the push-on connectors and gather them together at the center of the engine where they all push on. Then start connecting the MPC's to the pressure sensor, to the injectors (black to the front and gray to the rear), to the throttle valve switch, to the cold start switch and to the distributor trigger contacts. Connect the T1 for temperature sensor II and the MPC for temperature sensor I in the intake air distributor. Connect the wire to the main relay and the vacuum hose from the intake air distributor to the pressure sensor. Connect the wires to the exhaust recirculation switch (automatics). Connect the wire to the auxiliary air regulator (late models). Replace the hose to the pressure sensor. When every wire has been accounted for and attached, continue with:

Step 15. Install Rear Tin, Air Cleaner and Odds and Ends

Put on two tiny pieces of tin that go over the entrances along with the oil filter and the dipstick tube for the Bus and sedan. Check the rubber or sponge air seal around the rear tin, then tighten the screws on the tin. Install the air tunnel (with heater blower inside) on the sedan and the accordion tunnel in the wagon. On the sedan, install the heater hoses and the T2 electrical connection to the **heater. Screw on the new oil filter cartridge, put in three quarts of non-detergent oil and install the dipstick. Put oil in the clean air cleaner, put it on the engine and bolt it down. Automatics: put in the automatic fluid dipstick, FRONT of the engine.**

Now you can connect all the hoses to the air cleaner for the last time. Don't forget the pre-heater hose from the heater box. Go to your battery and clean the place where the ground strap fastens, then just touch the ground strap to the frame. If there's no spark, connect it and bolt it tight. If there's a spark, check the wiring for a short (Chapter VII). OK, no shorts? Fan belt adjusted? Oil in? Time the engine and adjust the idle (Chapter X). Turn the key and listen to the engine purr.

Step 16. Break In

If you have installed new rings or done a complete overhaul, you have to think about how long you want the engine to last. Do a complete tune up per chapter X and change to detergent oil at 300 miles. Then another at 1000 miles, and if you haven't been hot-rodding the engine for this 1,300 miles, especially not lugging it—just a nice easy balance, your engine can last as long as a new one.

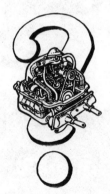

A Day At The Office

KNOW-HOW

MECHANICS' INFORMATION AND DATA

This chapter is a mixed bag of miscellaneous items, just handy things like how to take out studs when they break off in the crankcase, how to tell what year your VW is and like that. You will probably use the index in the rear to find what you want in it so I'll just start out and see what happens.

VOLKSWAGEN TYPE NUMBERS AND DESCRIPTION

Type I, Sedan (Bug), Super Beetle, Ghia and Safari (The Thing), Convertible
Type II, Transporter, Camper, Kombi, Station Wagon and the Commercials
Type III, Fastback, Squreback (Variant) and Sedan
Type IV, Two door and Four door Sedans and Station Wagon

Type I starts with the Standard Bug with which we are all familiar. It has torsion bars front and rear and a "stand-up engine" 1000 cc to the present-day 1600 cc. The Super Beetle has the same body but McPherson Type front suspension which replaces the torsion bars in the front end. The Karmann Ghia sedan and convertible has a special chassis with stronger attach points and more rigidity but still has the stand-up engine and torsion bar suspension. It has a lower profile special body designed by Ghia and built by Karmann. The Safari (Thing) is an all-purpose off the road vehicle with a Ghia chassis and super heavy suspension. It has a 1967 Bus transaxle and reduction gears to give it more clearance and better gear ratio. It uses the Rommel type body which will strip to bare essentials. It can be purchased with a "limited-slip" transaxle which gives it excellent traction. It comes with a 1500 stand-up engine and is built in Mexico. The Type I convertible became a Super Beetle in 1974 and since 1978 is the only Type I being imported into the U.S.A. From 1975 on they've been equipped with AFC fuel injection. **See Changes and New Ideas.**

Type II is the Bus and commercial vehicle and has a sturdy frame and torsion bar suspension. Through 1971 the Bus used the stand-up engine, starting with 36hp, then to 1600 through the years.

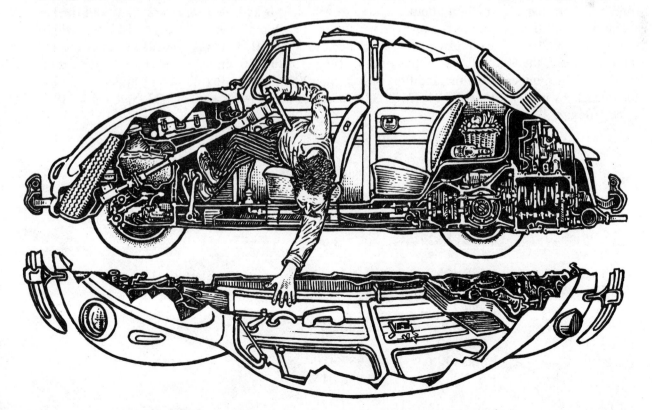

In 1972, the Type IV engine was installed in the Bus with 1700 cc and the flat (pancake) profile with dual carburetors. In 1975 the Bus was given an 1800cc engine with AFC fuel injection. In 1976 its engine went up to 2000 cc. **See Changes and New Ideas.**

Type III uses the sturdy Ghia chassis with torsion bars front and rear and a "pancake engine" practically identical to the 1500 and 1600 engines used in the Types I and II but with the lowered profile and different cooling system. In 1968, Bosch Electronic Fuel Injection was installed on this engine. The Type III was discontinued as of 1974.

Type IV has a four inch longer version of the Ghia chassis but uses McPherson strut front suspension and a coil spring rear suspension. It has the 1700 engine. The older models had dual carburetors but since 1970, the Type IV has Bosch Fuel Injection. The Type IV was discontinued in 1975.

Automatic transmission is available on all models except the Safari (The Thing) and is standard equipment on the Type IV four door sedans and station wagons.

ENGINE AND CHASSIS NUMBERS

The Type I engine number is stamped on the crankcase under the generator support facing the rear and the **chassis (I.D.) number** is on a plate in the front compartment and is also stamped on the tunnel under the rear seat. **Safari owners see Changes and New Ideas.**

The Type II engine number is stamped under the generator support facing the rear, through 1971, 1972 and on, the engine number is in the same place as for Type IV. **The chassis (I.D.) number** is stamped to the right of the engine in the engine compartment.

The Type III engine number can be found on the rear of the crankcase between the oil cooler bracket and the crack in the crankcase. It is in FRONT of the fan housing. **The chassis (I.D.) number** is on a metal plate in the front compartment and is also stamped on the tunnel under the rear seat. Up to 1964, the number is preceded by 0.

The Type IV and '72 and on Type II engine number is stamped on the crankcase near the joining crack in front of the fan housing. **The chassis (I.D.) number** can be found on the left windshield pillar and stamped on the tunnel under the rear seat.

Starting in 1969, most VW's have a metal plate in front of the driver on top of the dash right next to the windshield with the chassis (I.D.) number stamped on it.

Starting in August, 1964 (1965 models) VW started to use a nine digit chassis number. The first three numbers give information about the kind of vehicle it is and the year it was made and the last six numbers are the chassis numbers. At the beginning of each model year (August), the last six digits start with 000,001. For example: 316,050,000 means a Type III, 1 stands for sedan or fastback and the 6 for 1966, the 50,000th made that year. In 1969 (for the '70 models), VW chassis numbers became 10 digit numbers with the addition of a 2, like 2000,001 so 361,2037,843 indicates a 1971 squareback (Variant). Similarly 211,2109,322 indicates a 1971 Bus and 113,2365,987 is a 1973 Type I Bug.

Type I

Year	Chassis Number	Engine Number	Remarks
1949	1-91,922 to 138,554	1-000,001	30 hp
1950	to 1-220,471		
1951	to 1-313,829		
1952	to 1-428,156	to	
Dec. 1953	1-575 415	1-695 282	36 hp started
Dec. 1954	1-781 884	1-945 526	
Aug. 1955	1-929 746	1-1 120 615	
Dec. 1955	1-1 060 929	1 227 347	
Dec. 1956	1 349 119	1 678 209	
Aug. 1957	1 600 440	1 937 450	
Oct. 1957	1 673 411	2 026 015	

Type I (Cont'd.)

Year	Chassis Number	Engine Number	Remarks
Dec. 1957	1 774 680	2 156 321	
Dec. 1958	2 226 206	2 721 313	
Aug. 1959	2 518 668	3 072 320	
Dec. 1959	2 801 613	3 424 453	
Aug. 1960	3 192 507	5 000 001	40 hp started
Dec. 1960	3 551 044	5 428 637	
Aug. 1961	4 010 995	5 958 948	
Dec. 1961	4 400 051	6 375 945	
Dec. 1962	5 199 980	7 336 420	Fresh air heating started
Aug. 1963	5 677 119	7 893 119	
Dec. 1963	6 016 120	8 264 628	
July 1964	6 502 399	8 796 622	
Aug. 1964	115 000 001	8 796 623	
Dec. 1964	115 510 150	9 339 890	
July 1965	115 999 000	9 800 000	
Aug. 1965	116 000 001	F 0 000 001	1300 started
Dec. 1965	116 463 103	F 0 442 242	"E" has M240 Smog Control
July 1966	116 1021 300	F 0 940 716	
Aug. 1966	117 000 001	H 0 204 001	1500 started and 12 volt started
Dec. 1966	117 442 503	H 0 576 613	"L" has M240 Smog Control
July 1967	117 844 902	H 0 874 199	
Aug. 1967	118 000 001	H 5 000 001	
Dec. 1967	118 431 603	H 5 173 897	
July 1968	118 1016 100	H 5 414 585	
Aug. 1968	119 000 001	H 5 414 586	
Dec. 1968	119 474 780	H 5 648 888	
July 1969	119 1200 000	H 5 900 000	
Aug. 1969	110 2000 001	B 6 000 001	1600 started
Dec. 1969	110 2473 153	B 6 192 532	
July 1970	110 3200 000	B 6 600 000	
Aug. 1970	111 2000 001	D 0 676 000	the old 34 hp
		AB 0 000 001	1300 40 hp
		AD 0 000 001	1600 50 hp
		AE 0 000 001	1600 50 hp Super Beetle
July 1971	111 3200 000	DO 836 000	34 hp (you didn't even know they still made them)
		AB 0 350 000	40 hp
		AD 0 360 022	
		AE 0 568 000	
Aug. 1971	112 2000 001	DO 836 000	34 hp 1200
		AB 0 360 001	44 hp 1300
		AD 0 360 025	48 hp 1600
		AE 0 558 001	48 hp 1600
		AH0 000 001	48 hp 1600
July 1972	112 3200 000	D 1 000 000	
		AB 0 699 001	
		AD 0 598 001	
		AE 0 917 063	
		AH 0 006 900	

Type I   (Cont'd.)

Year	Chassis Number	Engine Number	Remarks
Aug. 1972	113 2000 001	D 1 000 001	34 hp 1200
		AB 0 699 002	44 hp 1300
		AD 0 598 002	50 hp 1600
		AE 0 917 264	48 hp 1600
		AF 0 000 802	46 hp 1600
		AH 0 005 901	48 hp 1600
July 1973	113 3200 000	D1 039 792	
		AB 0 820 427	
		AD 0 749 788	
	AE changed to	AK 0 060 039	at No. 1 000 000
		AF 0 034 850	
		AH 0 056 934	
Dec. 1973	114 2423 795	AF 0 036 771	Alternator replaces generator
		AK 023 9493	
		AH 029 4654	
		AH 024 5425	
		AS 010 9138	
July 1974	114 2999 000	AF 0 092 707	
		AH 0 500 000	
		AS 0 171 566	
Dec. 1974	115 2143 743	AF 0 129 022	Fuel Injection
		AS 0 243 557	
		AJ 0 045 000	
		AJ 0 012 142	
July 1975	115 2600 000	AF 0 129 119	
		AS 0 269 030	
		AJ 0 059 664	
		AJ 0 012 405	
Dec. 1975	116 2071 467	AF 0 129 606	
		AS 0 332 893	
		AJ 0 071 682	
		AJ 0 012 504	
Aug. 1976	157 2000 001	AJ 0 095 936	
Dec. 1976	157 2006 038	AJ 0 010 696	
Aug. 1977	157 2200 0000	AJ 0 119 687	convertible only
Jan. 1978	158 2000 001	AJ 0 119 688	
July 1978	158 2100 000	AJ 0 132 850	
Aug. 1978	159 0000 001	AJ 0 132 851	
Dec. 1978	159 2018 069	AJ 0 136 982	
Aug. 1979	159 2036 063	AJ 0 143 097	

Type II

Year	Chassis Number	Engine Number	Remarks
pre 1954	to 20-069,409	(20)-945,526	36 hp
Dec. 1954	to -110,604	to	
Dec. 1955	to -160,706		
Dec. 1956	223 217	1 678 210	
Dec. 1957	315 209	2 156 321	

Year	Chassis Number	Engine Number	Remarks
Aug. 1958	374 811		
Dec. 1958	423 156	2 721 533	
June 1959	469 506	3 400 000	"B——" engine to No. 3 580 000
Dec. 1959	551 631		Modified 36 hp—No parts available
May 1960	614 456	5 000 001	40 hp started
Dec. 1960	705 619	5 407 725	
Aug. 1961	802 986	5 979 934	
Dec. 1961	882 314	6 375 945	
Aug. 1962	971 550	6 914 251	
Dec. 1962	1 048 085	7 336 420	Fresh air heating started (clean-air) engine no.
Jan. 1963			143 453—1500 eng. optional eqpt.
Aug. 1963	1 144 282		
Dec. 1963	1 222 500	8 264 628	
Aug. 1964	215 000 001	8 785 398	713 768
Oct. 1964	213 036 651	8 964 971	1500 engine standard equipment
Dec. 1964	215 082 480	816 281	
Aug. 1965	216 000 001	H 0 000 001	"L" has E240 Smog Control
Dec. 1965	216 083 207		
Aug. 1966	217 000 001	H 0 183 373	12 volt system started
Dec. 1966	217 079 889	H 0 309 830	
July 1967	217 148 459	H 0 761 325	
Aug. 1967	218 000 001	B 5 000 001	1600 engine started
Dec. 1967	218 073 585	B 5 017 663	"C" has M340 Smog Control
July 1968	218 220 000	B 5 050 173	
Aug. 1968	219 000 001	B 5 050 174	
Dec. 1968	219 098 974	B 5 079 928	
July 1969	219 200 000	B 5 116 436	
Aug. 1969	210 2000 001	B 5 116 437	
Dec. 1969	210 2106 747	B 5 144 597	
July 1970	210 2300 000	B 5 230 000	
Aug. 1970	211 2000 001	AE 0 000 001	
July 1971	211 2300 000	AE 0 529 815	Last of the 1600 Buses
Aug. 1971	212 2000 000	CA 0 000 001	1700 66 hp with M251
		CB 0 000 001	1700 66 hp with M251 & M157 —carb version of the Type IV engine
July 1972	212 2300 000	CA 0 016 185	
		CB 0 056 205	
Aug. 1972	213 2000 001	CA 0 020 001	
		CB 0 062 006	
Dec. 1973	213 2300 000	CA 0 029 721	alternator replaces generator
		CB 0 082 876	
Aug. 1974	215 2000 001	AP 0 027 466	1800 cc
		ED 0 000 640	
Dec. 1974	215 2073 083	AP 0 037 047	fuel injection
		ED 0 011 950	
Aug. 1975	216 2000 001	CJ 0 000 001	
		GD 0 000 001	2000 cc.
Dec. 1975	216 2077 675	CJ 0 013 231	
		GD 0 010 983	

Type II (Cont'd.)

Year	Chassis Number	Engine Number	Remarks
Aug. 1976	217 2000 001	GE 0 000 001	
Dec. 1976	217 2081 316	GE 0 002 336	
June 1977	217 2300 000	GE 0 007 082	
Aug. 1977	218 2000 001	GE 0 007 083	hydraulic lifters
Aug. 1978	219 2000 001	GE 0 040 001	
July 79	219 2153 964	GE 0 055 786	
Aug. 79	24A 0013 069	CV 001 595	Vanagon
Jan. 80	24A 0090 384	CV 011 278	
Mar. 80	24A 0103 711	CV 013 149	

Type III

Year	Chassis Number	Engine Number	Remarks
Apr. 1961	000 001	000 001	1500 engine
Dec. 1961	011 041	013 112	
Aug. 1962	064 916	065 746	
Dec. 1962	138 774	143 557	
Aug. 1963	221 975	255 340	
Dec. 1963	321 076	406 183	
July 1964	483 592	633 330	
Aug. 1964	315 000 001	633 331	
Dec. 1964	315 105 296	816 281	
July 1965	315 220 883	1 100 000	
Aug. 1965	316 000 001	T 0 000 001	1600 engine started
Dec. 1965	316 140 226	T 0 126 399	
July 1966	316 500 000	T 0 260 000	
Aug. 1966	317 000 001	T 0 160 001	12 volt system started
Dec. 1966	317 134 254	T 0 380 413	
July 1967	317 233 853	T 0 476 124	
Aug. 1967	318 000 001	U 0 000 001	Fuel Injection started
Dec. 1967	318 103 144	U 0 036 005	
July 1968	318 500 000	U 0 093 651	
Aug. 1968	319 000 001	U 0 093 652	
Dec. 1968	319 108 899	U 0 154 029	
July 1969	319 500 000	U 0 230 433	
Aug. 1969	310 2000 001	U 0 230 434	
Dec. 1969	310 2111 451	U 0 168 080	
July 1970	310 2500 000	U 0 366 020	
Aug. 1970	311 2000 001	U 0 366 021	
Dec. 1970	311 2108 457	U 0 412 693	
July 1971	311 2500 000	U 0 502 000	
Aug. 1971	312 2000 001	U 0 502 001	
		U 5 000 001	
July 1972	312 2500 000	U 0 507 000	European
		U 5 057 000	U.S. with Smog Control
Aug. 1972	313 2000 000	U 0 507 001	
		U 5 057 001	
Dec. 1972	313 2500 000	U 0 510 144	
		U 0 069 142	
1973	313 2000 001	X	

Type IV

Year	Chassis Number	Engine Number	Remarks
Aug. 1968	419 000 000	V 0 000 001	411
July 1969	419 100 000	V 0 100 000	
Aug. 1969	410 2000 001	Z 0 000 001	68 hp
		W 0 000 001	80 hp
July 1970	410 2100 000	Z 0 009 406	
		W 0 057 034	
Aug. 1970	411 2000 001	Z 0 009 407	
		W 0 057 035	
July 1971	411 2100 000	Z 0 017 418	
		W 0 129 581	
Aug. 1971	412 2000 001	Z 0 017 419	68 hp
		W 0 129 582	
		EA 0 000 001	80 hp with M127 & M553
July 1972	412 2100 000	Z 0 020 000	
		W 0 163 426	
		EA 0 051 162	
Aug. 1972	413 2000 000	Z 0 020 001	68 hp 412
		W 0 163 427	80 hp
		EA 0 051 163	80 hp with M127 & M 553
		EB 0 000 001	72 hp Calif.
Dec. 1972	413 2100 000	Z 0 021 151	
		W 0 194 331	
		EA 0 071 929	
		EB 0 004 209	
Aug. 1973	413 2100 000	EB	1800 cc.
1974	414 2000 001	EC	

VOLKSWAGEN MODEL NUMBERS

We won't try to list them all as they appear nowhere except on part numbers and in VW literature but there are a few things about them of interest. The odd numbers are left-hand drive and even numbers are right-hand drive. They start with the good old 111 which is the original sedan, left-hand-drive. 113 is the Deluxe Sedan (Export) and can arrive with a 1200, 1300 or 1500 engine. The 115 is the old sun roof and the 117 has the new steel sliding roof. 141 indicates the Karmann Ghia Convertible; 143 the coupe, 151 is the model number for the VW convertible, 181 for the Safari.

In the Type II, Transporter Series, it gets complicated, starting with the 211 and going all out to the 2252, a Standard Model Sunroof Microbus not sold in the U.S.

VOLKSWAGEN PART NUMBERS

This is another rat's nest and of only passing interest. The part number for any part is a nine-digit number, like 000-000-000. The first three digits are for the model number the part was first used on, like 113 (see above). In newer parts, the third digit in the first three may indicate the year of part origin.

The other six digits make up the part number, with the first number being the Main Group number, the next two numbers the Sub-Group number, then three digits for the part number itself and finally any letters indicate the change number if any. Thus 113-105-279-A is the metal gasket between the crankshaft and the flywheel. It first appeared in Model 113. It is in Main Group No. 1, Engine Parts, Sub-Group No. 05, Crankshaft Parts, is part number 279 and has had an "A" change. If there is a second letter at the end of the part number or no change letter, the second letter indicates color-coded tolerance.

This is simple, and probably useless, information.

TRANSMISSION AND FRONT END NUMBERS

These numbers are of interest only because they exist. The numbers on the old split-case trans with low and reverse non-synchromesh are located behind the gearshift housing on the right-hand case half. This trans is designated the "A" trans, and is called the "Synchromesh" transmission. In the Transporter models, this was changed to the "B," "Fully Synchronized" transmission in 1959 when they put in that terrible "Modified" 36 hp engine. In the "Fully Synchronized" trans, the case is not split and is called the tunnel case. The numbers for this "B" trans are located on the transmission case.

In the Type I the "A" transmission was used until August of 1960 when they changed to the "AB," "Fully Synchronized" transmission which they used until the automatic stick shift came out. Then came a three-speed trans with an automatic clutch, letting the driver slip and slide from gear to gear while moving the stick. These have been replaced with a fully automatic transmission.

The front axle numbers are stamped on the right torsion arm stop if you're interested. **Safari owners, see Changes and New Ideas.**

Suggestions:

Make sure your Chassis number and your engine number are correct on your vehicle registration. **Keep a record of them with you like on the back of your driver's license.**

CHANGES THROUGH THE YEARS— 1949 TO 1981

We list only the operational changes, not things like the removal of the Wolfsburg Crest.

Type I

1949: Solex carburetor made standard equipment, starting crankhole discontinued (too bad).

1950: Hydraulic brakes on the export models, sound muffler put in heater ducts, fuel heat riser added to intake manifold; automatic engine cooling temperature control with the thermostat (ring in back of fan housing); offset piston pin holes (wrist pin) to reduce piston slap; tougher alloys for exhaust valves and inserts.

1951: One heavy valve spring replaces the two used before.

1952: Crankshaft end play adjustment with three shims; 26 PCI carburetor with accelerator pump replaced the old 28 VFIS; "A" transmission with three synchronized gears replaced the old crash box; tire size changed from 6.00x16 to 6.40x15; six leaved torsion bars added for increased suspension travel, new instrument panel; rotary heater control knob; number of turns made by the window crank changed from 10-1/2 to 3-1/4.

1953: One rear window glass instead of two; separate brake fluid reservoir under spare; changed third and fourth gear ratios; changed valve setting to .004".

1954: 36 hp engine begins with 1192cc (1200) and 6 to 1 compression ratio; larger intake valves; oil bath air cleaner; combination vacuum and mechanical distributor added; combined ignition and starter switch added; increased generator output to 160 watts. No break-in required.

1955: Twin tail pipe muffler; new design fuel tank; flashing turn signals instead of the semaphores; dished steering wheel; new gearshift lever moved forward.

1956: Larger oil pump mounting shaft; No. 4 main bearing clearance modified; copper-plated fulcrum plates in universals; starter motor hp increased; fuel filter tap removed.

1957: Oil gallery sizes increased; metal camshaft gear; flat type accelerator pedal replaced the roller type; tubeless tires introduced; ring and pinion ratio changed; brake pedal leverage increased; adjustable striker plates in doors; new instrument panel.

1958: Large windshield; a new dished steering wheel; wider brakes, drums and shoes; large rear window; frame head reinforced; new clutch release assembly with stronger clutch springs; third and fourth gear ratio changed.

1959: Outer front suspension control arm bushings changed to needle roller bearings, anti-sway bar added; new type fan belt (tropical); hydraulic steering dampner added; generator output increased to 180 watts.

1960: Safety recessed steering wheel; padded sun visor; new grab handles on doors; 40 hp engine began with 7 to 1 compression ratio; fuel pump to right of distributor; new 28 PCIT carburetor with automatic choke; new tunnel-type "AB" "Fully Synchronized" transmission; push-on connectors for the wiring systems; contoured front seat; larger heater pipes; pump-type windshield washer.

1961: Flatter gas tank; 28 blade cooling fan; new "hour glass" Gemmer steering box; permanently greased tie rod ends; "Sissy Bar" added; nonrepeat starter switch; wider front brake shoes and linings; anchor points for seat belts; fuel gauge installed; spring-balanced front hood; transparent brake fluid reservoir; vacuum advance distributor; positive crankcase ventilation.

1962: Compressed air windshield washer; progressive type valve springs; leatherette head lining; stronger clutch springs.

1963: Fresh air heating "Clean-air" engine with redesigned fan housing, muffler and heat exchangers; nylon window guides; foam sandwich floor mats.

1964: Metal sun roof; bent vacuum pipe—formerly a loop; larger license plate light.

1965: Master cylinder and wheel cylinders changed; new cooling air control system with flaps in the bottom of the fan housing; lever type heater and defroster controls; window and windshield area increased with slightly curved windshield; more powerful windshield wipers and longer and more expensive wiper blades; new chassis numbering system; rear seats fold flat to hold more stuff; push-button engine hood latch.

1966: 1300 engine, 50 hp, 1300 emblem on rear deck; emergency blinker switch; ventilated wheel slots and flat hub caps; headlight dimmer switch mounted on turn signal handle; center dashboard defroster outlet; horn ring added; ball joint front suspension.

1967: 1500 engine, 53 hp, Dual master cylinder brake system; two-speed wipers; back-up lights; single unit headlights, recessed inside door handles; change to 12-volt system in the middle of the year; locking buttons on doors.

1968: Automatic stick shift with double jointed rear axles added as an option; new bumper; gas tank filler in right front fender; combined gas gauge in speedometer head; both warning lights now red; trigger release door handles; larger tail lights.

1969: Double-jointed rear axles on all models; rear window defroster; ignition lock combined with steering wheel lock; hood release moved to glove compartment; gas filler cover has inside release.

1970: 1600 engine; thermostatically controlled warm-up air to the air cleaner; heavy duty oil pump; new fuel pump; larger tail lights; added side reflectors; larger front parking and signal lights; a new windshield wiper motor and wiper assembly.

1971: Dual port heads to the 1600 engine; three part intake manifold, chrome exhaust valve stems; new combination vacuum/centrifugal advance distributor; added a pressure control valve in the lubrication system; installed the activated charcoal filter for the gas tank fumes; a new 34PICT-3 carburetor; door buzzer; new oil cooler which causes a bump in the shrouding and a pressed-in engine mounting nut on the left side; a new clutch throw-out assembly and ball bearing. To tell a 1971 Bug at first glance, they installed a flow-through air system with little vents back of the rear windows. The headlights go off when the ignition key is off.

The Super Beetle arrived with the big nosed front lid (the way to tell them apart) and the McPherson strut front suspension. The Super Beetle is the increased cost model and has bigger front brakes.

1972: Many more hoses and complicated gizmos for Smog Control; new steering column with safety collapse feature; a new distributor with a vacuum retard at idle; exhaust reburner; new muffler. The Ghia has bigger front disc pads. Started production on the Safari (The Thing).

1973: New curved windshield in the Super Beetle along with a new dash; redesigned fresh air system; new three point front seats; new transmission mounts; new heavy duty braced doors. New monstrous tail lights and front parking and signal lights—almost as big as the fender; paper filter air cleaner. The generator was replaced by the alternator. **Safari owners see Changes and New Ideas.**

1974: The major status change is the self restoring energy absorbing bumpers which make the car longer and the wider track front and rear wheels which make the car appear wider than before. The engine remains unchanged except for a new "quieter muffler" and a new alloy for the cylinder heads which improves cooling. Oh, there is also a new computer check sensor to read TDC (top dead center) and one for ignition voltage.

The Super Beetle and Convertible have a bit of negative king pin offset for better tracking under braking conditions.

The steering wheel collapses further (right into your lap maybe) in case of front end collision. Smaller front seat headrests give better visibility for a change. To top it all off, VW has now installed seat belt ignition interlock system which means you can't start the engine without the seat belt fastened, passenger side, too, if occupied. What I wonder is how the mechanic sits in the front seat with his seat belt fastened and works on the engine? The Ghia has thicker front disc pads while the bug still has drum brakes all the way around. The Thing or Safari as I prefer to call it remains unchanged.

1975: The big change is fuel injection which is mostly mechanical unlike the electronic injection on the old Types III and IV. It's called air flow control (AFC) injection as it's regulated mostly by a box which enriches and leans the mixture in accordance with the flow of air into the intake manifold. VW hopes this system will be more trouble-free than the old injection and it certainly seems to be simpler.

1976: Both status and engineering wise the Bug hasn't changed.

1977: The last year of the old Beetle in the United States and we all ought to wish it a good goodbye; it was here a long time. They're still making and selling them in Mexico and Brazil and I don't know where else by the millions so the Bug is not completely gone. I guess they're gone here because they're expensive. Starting this year the only air-cooled Type I Volkswagen imported to the U.S. is the convertible.

1978: No changes in the convertible.

1979: No major changes. Last year for the convertible in the USA.

🐝 🐝 🐝

Type II

Because of the multitude of various models and a dearth of published material, we just sketch out the major changes since 1954 when transporters began to arrive in numbers in this country.

1954: Engine number 20-695-356 in chassis number 20-069-409. They had the bullet type front signal lights and round combination signal and tail lights in the rear. I have seen a 1954 with no front signal lights. They used the 36 hp engine with a PCI carburetor and manual choke and the "A" type Synchronized trans with square-cut first and reverse. The front end is totally different from the Bug but uses similar principles. The brakes are Simplex type and both the master cylinder and wheel cylinders are heavy duty. They are classified as 3/4 ton vehicles. With the exception of adding various models, there were very few changes until...

1959: In May at chassis number 469,506 and engine number 3,400,000 they changed the engine to the "Modified" 36 hp, which looked like the 40 hp but wasn't and changed to the "B" "Fully Synchronized" transmission at the same time.

1960: In June they gave up on the "Modified" 36 hp engine at engine No. 3,580,000 and started with the true 40 hp engine at No. 5,000,001.

1961: New ring and pinion unit; changed the tail lights to large oval combination stop and tail lights; changed the front signal from the bullet type to the oval type.

1963: 1500 engine "G" type starting with No. 0-000-001; 51 hp; changed brakes, rear axle and suspension; new transfer cases; changed front axle and suspension; rated 1 ton.

1964: Larger rear door and windows.

1965: 1500 engine, 53 hp starting with H-0-000-001; changed signal lights to amber color; changed headlamps; changed transmission, larger clutch plate and nine-spring release assembly; new flywheel.

1967: 12-volt electrical system.

1968: 1600 engine, 57 hp, from B-0-000-001 or with M240, 53 hp from C-0-000-001. New front, curved windshield; new ventilating system; lowered road clearance; changed wheel size to 14 inches; double jointed rear axles, ball joint front suspension; removed that beautiful "all the way across" storage area and put in a lousy American-type glove compartment—so who has gloves? Put on a sliding door that takes away twenty percent of your camping storage but it sure is pretty with those big windows and windshield.

1969: No major changes.

1970: 1600 engine; thermostatic warm air to the air cleaner; heavy duty oil pump; new fuel pump; double cylinder brake system with warning light. Installed side reflectors.

1971: Dual port heads for the 1600 engine; three part intake manifold; chrome exhaust valve stems; added pressure control valve; new oil cooler, with bump in shrouding and pressed-in engine mounting nut; 34 PICT-3 carburetor; activated charcoal tank for gas tank fumes; door buzzer; new clutch and throw-out assembly with ball bearing; composite rear drums; flared the rear wheel wells; put on a back-up light as standard. New steering column with safety collapsing feature; added those lovely disc brakes. Put the brake fluid tank back of the seat; new distributor with a vacuum retard feature at idle.

1972: Type IV 1700cc pancake engine with dual carbs. A lot of new things come with this engine: diaphragm clutch and so many hoses you won't believe; exhaust recirculating system; made the tail light and back-up light under the same tail light lens.

1973: The Smog Pump is the first thing to strike your eye. It's a pump that adds oxygen to the exhaust to help burn it more completely (afterburner); an access door under the bed so you can get at the engine to tune it; a paper filter air cleaner; exhaust gas recirculation. You can get an automatic transmission in the Bus??? with a different shift system. New heavier disc brakes; new steering box and hoses, hoses, tubes and hoses. The front wheel wells are flared a bit and the parking signal light has been moved up right under the windshield so you can tell at a glance.

1974: On the surface the bus hasn't changed except for the addition of a rear third seat with an optional fold down back. Inside, however, things are still being stretched out. The engine size increased to 1795cc (109.5 cu. in.) with 68 hp and 91 ft. lbs. torque. Along with this are bigger ventures for the dual carbs, a bigger clutch, a reinforced trans bell housing and new gear ratios to take advantage of the increased HP. About 18 mpg should be expected as before. To bring it all to a screeching halt VW has provided a larger brake booster.

1975: The big change is the air flow control (AFC) fuel injection system which is the same system used on the new bug so look at the rap under Type I.

1976: Practically unchanged from last year except the engine now is 2000 cc.

1977: I bought a brand new 1977 bus with fuel injection because the right door lock didn't work on my '71. I've had the '77 for a little over 9,000 miles and the right hand door lock doesn't work. So beware of all those little plastic things. Otherwise it runs very well and I'm satisfied with it and they replaced the door handle under the guarantee.

1978: I (Eve Muir) bought a new '78 Bus and dig the sliding windows in the back. On a hot day, back of the bus passengers no longer have to decide between suffocating or getting blown away. A nice change and, as far as I can tell, the only one from the driver/rider viewpoint.

I had the cassette player transferred from the '77 van and am about to build a modified sleeping/cooking arrangement as my needs alone are different than John's and mine were together.

The Bus engine looks the same and Tosh says it is, except that the valves have hydraulic lifters and therefore cannot be adjusted. An interesting change from the maintenance viewpoint.

1979: No major changes.

1980 and on: See Changes and New Ideas for the Vanagon.

Type III
1962: Production began.

1963: 32 PHN-1 carburetor from here to date on all single carburetor engines; 200mm coil spring clutch; special oil cooler which fits only the Type III; oil deflector plate on rear drums discontinued; hose from oil breather to air cleaner; ball joint front end.

1964: 1500-S with two 32 PDSIT carburetors introduced; engine cooling automatically controlled by a thermostat; grooved oil pressure relief valve.

1965: Wing nut on clutch cable for easy adjusting; new steering gear box; heater is now controlled by a lever.

1966: Disc brakes up front; composite brake drums in the rear; 200mm diaphragm type clutch; new connecting rods (with nuts); fuel pump head modified.

1967: Rear equalizer spring; 12 volt electrical system; bonded brake linings; twin circuit master cylinder.

1968: Automatic transmission and fuel injection made optional equipment; spring loaded oil sump plate; safety steering column.

1969: Rear engine carrier on all models; double jointed rear axles.

1970: Oil pressure control valve added.

1971: Dual balance pipes on twin carburetor engines; modified carbs.

1972: Larger disc brakes; new steering wheel.

1973: Simplified emission control system with a filter in the exhaust gas recycling system and a solenoid to control flow. The vacuum spark advance cut-off has been removed.

1974: Sorry, no Type III vehicles were manufactured in '74.

Type IV
1968: Started production with dual carbs. 411 two door and four door and Variant (station wagon). Type IV engine; disc brakes; double jointed rear axles; ball joint front suspension.

1969: No changes.

1970: Smog Control equipment added.

1971: Bosch Electronic Fuel Injection, all models.

1972: No changes.

1973: Changed to the 412 models with a slightly larger body with considerable changes in trim; paper filter air cleaner; new camshaft; new coil spring shock absorbers and stabilizers; new heavy duty disc brakes.

1974: The Type IV, 2 door, 4 door and wagon has not changed on the outside with the exception of being slightly longer because of the self restoring energy absorbing bumpers. What else can you say about them? New front and rear wheels give the 412 a wider track and wider appearance than before.

The 412 2-door still comes with the fuel injected 1679cc engine and standard trans but the 4-door and wagon come with automatic trans and a fuel injected 1795cc engine as standard equipment. A larger fan for the fresh air blower and a quieter muffler about rounds out the changes made this year.

1975: These are no longer being manufactured.

MECHANICS' TIPS

Tough Nuts, Screws and Bolts
Liquid Wrench and heat are your best aids for tough ones. There are several little things you can do depending on the circumstances.

Bang it some to loosen the threads. If you are removing a tough shrouding screw, use the vice grip on the blade of the screwdriver for added leverage. Bang it. Try the vice grip on the screw, nut or bolt itself.

If the points on a nut or bolt head get rounded off, you can try the vice grip first and if that doesn't work, take the next smaller socket out of the box, file up the nut a little and jam the socket down on the nut with the hammer, sprinkling Liquid Wrench like Holy Water all the time, then put the ratchet on the socket and turn the nut off.

With a tough muffler nut that God himself couldn't get loose, hacksaw the whole thing off and replace the stud and nut later. If the stud comes out with the nut, let it, and buy a new stud and nut for reassembly.

Aluminum expands faster than steel when heated, so a little heat on the aluminum casting helps a lot to get the tough studs or bolts out of the crankcase.

One of the most difficult screws to loosen is the point adjustment screw in the distributor, and you shouldn't use Liquid Wrench on this one. Get the screwdriver set in the slot and strike it a sharp blow with the small hammer, then try it. If you have a small vice grip, you can clamp it on the head of the screw, nose down, then turn the vice grip with a screwdriver through the jaws. As a last resort, you can remove the retainer and the plate, then the vice grip will get it.

Removing and Installing Large High Torque Nuts and Bolts with a Hammer and Chisel

This cute little item well hidden here in the underbrush will serve you well in cases of emergency like out in the boonies. All those big (and small) nuts and bolts can be removed and installed without expensive sockets and breaker bars. You need a sharp chisel and a large hammer. This works for the flywheel gland nut, the crankshaft pulley bolt, the large rear axle nuts and is useful anywhere you have a nut to get off with no wrench to fit it or you can't get a wrench on it. This method has a tendency to make a nut look like a beaver has been chewing at it and is considered bad paractice by all those who can afford those big sockets. If you decide to use this method remember your safety goggles.

Take the sharp chisel and hold it pointed toward the center of the nut or bolt about 1/4" or a little less from one of the points on the head of the nut or bolt, then bang it a good one with your big hammer. Hit it again—make yourself a good shelf. If you're not a good hitter, hold the chisel with the vice grip. Then aim the chisel so it will drive the nut counterclockwise, not too steep now, and hit the chisel with the hammer. For the big flywheel nut and the rear axle nuts, you'll have to hit quite hard. If you shear off one of the points of the bolt head, start on another one. If you really ruin the nut or bolt getting it off, you'll need to buy a new one but usually you just use up one point taking it off and another putting it on, giving you three overhauls per gland nut.

They tighten the same way only clockwise. The high torque nuts must be driven on until you cannot move them with a good solid blow. Since it's hard to see if they're moving, use a pencil to mark the location of one of the points on the nut, then bang the chisel. You can see if the nut moved **because it will have moved off the pencil mark. If it moved, make a new mark. Continue this until the nut no longer moves from the pencil mark. If possible, use a torque wrench to tighten.**

Starting Nuts

Here are a few tricks to getting a nut started on a bolt or a stud that might come in handy, especially if you can't see the place where you are working and have to feel. Use your index finger to hold the nut on the end of the stud and twist the nut around with your thumb and second finger. Twist it counterclockwise a little until you feel the threads slip into place, then clockwise and on.

If the threads are so bunged up on a stud that the nut won't start for hell, tap it a little with the small hammer as you turn it with the box wrench until it's down one thread; then it will go. Sometimes there's nothing for it but to remove the assembly, run the nut back and forth on the bolt or stud with some oil to make sure the nut will go, then try again.

If the space around a nut is too confining to let you turn the nut with your fingers, hold the nut onto the end of the stud with your forefinger and turn it on with the point of a screwdriver.

If the bolt you are putting a nut on tends to turn, you can wedge the bolt with a small screwdriver or knife blade while you start the nut.

Using the Magnet

Use the magnet as one of your regular tools. It will become a real friend. It will find lost steel parts in sand, dropped washers in or out of an engine, tell you whether the metal in your hand is steel or brass, act as an extension to your arm to reach a dropped socket and perform many other little acts to make your work easier.

Using a Breaker Bar, Flex Handle and Cheater

These are the long handles that attach to the big sockets to turn a big nut or bolt.

The **breaker bar** is a round bar that the attachment for the socket slides on. You can use it with the socket in the center of the bar with both hands or with the socket on one end to apply maximum force.

The **flex handle** is a long handle with a place to attach the socket on one end. This attachment tilts to different angles so the turning force can be applied at ninety degrees to the bolt or at some other convenient angle.

The **cheater** is a piece of pipe. It can be any size or length but for your purposes a piece of 1'' pipe about 18'' long makes a good cheater. It fits over a flex handle or breaker bar, or even your ratchets, and allows you to apply added torque (lengthens the lever arm for added leverage) so you can turn a really tight nut or bolt.

You can calculate the torque you are applying with a flex handle, cheater and socket arrangement by knowing your weight and measuring from the center of the socket to the place where you are applying the force. Measure in feet, then multiply the distance in feet by your weight. For example, if you weigh 150 pounds and are putting all your weight on the cheater 1½ feet (18'') from the center of the socket, you are applying 150 x 1½ or 225 foot pounds on the nut, just about right for the rear axle nuts. Don't fall.

Going Round and Round

In any group of nuts or bolts holding an assembly, never tighten first one nut all the way, then the next one. Always tighten them round and round, first one a ways, the next a ways and so on until they are all fairly tight. Do the final tightening the same way—a turn here, a turn on the next one and so on until they are all the way tight or torqued. This will save you broken assemblies and distorted plates like the oil screen plate or the clutch release assembly.

Studs: Removing and Installing, Broken and Stripped

A stud is a headless bolt with threads on both ends—what a way to go through life! They are removed and installed using two nuts locked togeuther on the threads or by careful use of the vice grip on the non-threaded portion of the stud. To use the two-nut method, screw two nuts onto the stud so the end of the stud sticks through the outside nut. Lock the nuts by tightening them toward each other with two wrenches. Remove the stud by turning the inside nut and install the stud by turning the outside nut.

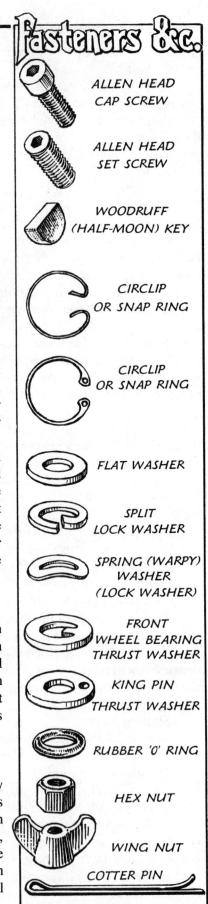

Fasteners &c.

ALLEN HEAD CAP SCREW

ALLEN HEAD SET SCREW

WOODRUFF (HALF-MOON) KEY

CIRCLIP OR SNAP RING

CIRCLIP OR SNAP RING

FLAT WASHER

SPLIT LOCK WASHER

SPRING (WARPY) WASHER (LOCK WASHER)

FRONT WHEEL BEARING THRUST WASHER

KING PIN THRUST WASHER

RUBBER 'O' RING

HEX NUT

WING NUT

COTTER PIN

When you're tightening a nut on a stud and the nut keeps turning without tightening, you have a stripped nut, a stripped stud or a stud that's pulling out. First remove the nut from the stud, either pulling or prying it off as you turn it, then examine both the nut and the stud for stripping—flat and mashed places. Perhaps the stud is unhurt and all you need is a new nut. If the stud is stripped, you have to remove the stud and buy and install a new one.

If the stud itself pulls out as you tighten the nut, you'll have to install a larger size stud in the hole. You can tap the case for the larger stud with the correct size tap. There's another way of handling stripped studs or spark plug hole threads and like that. You can take the head or case to the machine shop or to WV where they shoot a *Helicoil* into the stripped hole, then the regular threads on the old stud or spark plug will screw into the *helicoiled* hole and can be screwed up tight.

Broken Stud

If a stud breaks off but a stub of it is left sticking out of the case, heat the case with the propane torch, use a lot of Liquid Wrench, let it soak, then clamp the vice grip on the stud stump and slowly turn it out. If there's too little sticking out and the vice grip slips off, take a hacksaw and make a cut into the center of the top of the stud like a screwdriver slot—not into the case!—and use the screwdriver, with the vice grip on the shank, to slowly turn the stud out of the case.

If all the above just tears up the top of the broken stud, saw it off flush with the case. If the stud has broken off or is sawed off flush, you need a center punch. Knock the center punch straight down on the outside edge of the stud to make an indentation, then knock the edge of the stud around and around and out, using Liquid Wrench and heat. If this doesn't work, you will have to borrow an electric drill and buy a drill bit and "easy-out" the right size. Take the same size stud to the store with you. Make a center punch hole in the center of the stud, then drill the hole. Tap in the easy-out with a small hammer and turn the stud out with the crescent wrench on the easy-out, but slowly, using heat and Liquid Wrench all the way. When the stud is out, tape the drill and easy-out together and save them with your tools.

If all this fails, you'll have to take the case to the machine shop and pay the machinist to remove the offending stud.

Metric Equivalents for American Inches

I told you about the wrench substitutions you could make in Chapter IV in the tool section; here I tell you about some other metric equivalents you may need.

Your valves are set at .006", which is 0.15mm. If you can remember this and that 25.4mm equals 1", you have a good start. When your old connecting rod bearing shells are stamped .25 and the machinist looks at them and says, "Your crankshaft has been ground to .010" or "Your crankshaft is down 10", be ready to make the switch in your head from .25mm (point two five millimeters—thousandths of a meter) to .010" (ten thousandths of an inch).

The parts are made in Germany and are marked in millimeters (mm). In the U.S., crankshaft rod throws are ground in inches to four undersizes: .25mm (.010"), .50mm (.020"), .75mm (.030"), 1.00mm (.040"). Usually the parts will be marked "U.S." on the box which means that the parts manufacturer, too, has been thinking about the minute differences between mm's and inches when he sets up tolerances for manufacture.

Crankshaft main bearing throws are usually ground to the first three undersizes of the four given above. 1.00mm (.040") is considered too much to grind the main bearings.

You set your ignition points to .4mm (.016") and your spark plugs from .6mm to .7mm (.024" to .028").

The three shims you use to set the crankshaft endplay are chosen from .24, .30, .32, .34, .36mm thickness and the inch equivalents matter little as you are seeking a final endplay dimension of .1mm (.004") $^{+}_{-}$.

Metric Conversion Chart

inches	mm.	inches	mm.	inches	mm.
.0015	.037	.010	.254	.019	.483
.002	.051	.011	.279	.020	.508
.003	.076	.012	.305	.021	.533
.004	.102	.013	.330	.022	.559
.005	.127	.014	.356	.023	.584
.006	.152	.015	.381	.024	.610
.007	.178	.016	.406	.025	.635
.008	.203	.017	.432	.028	.7
.009	.229	.018	.457		

Torque: How to Use a Torque Wrench, Table of Torque Values

Torque is measured in foot pounds (ft. lbs.), inch pounds (in. lbs.) or meter kilograms (Mkg.). You read this number on a dial on the torque wrench and all you have to know is whether you have a metric or American (English) torque wrench and whether it's calibrated in foot pounds, meter-kilograms or inch pounds. Not a joke—you really have to know. The U.S. ft. lb. represents the number of pounds applied to the end of a wrench one foot long or really one foot away from the center of the nut or bolt you are turning. That's not complicated.

Torque wrenches come in three main types: one that slips when the preset torque is reached, another with a dial you read as you turn and the third, cheapest and most usually found, has a rod coming up from the head of the wrench with a point on the end of the rod which points to the torque reached on the calibrated arc on the handle.

Inch pounds can be converted to ft. lbs. by dividing by 12.

How to Use a Torque Wrench

First be sure you have the right torque value. This will be given in the text or you can look it up in the following table. Hold the wrench and socket firmly on the nut or bolt with one hand on the head (socket end) of the wrench. Stay away from the pointer rod. Then pull on the handle of the torque wrench with a steady pull. Use a position where you can see the reading clearly. Run all the bolts in the series up to about 3/4 of the final torque, then up to the final torque all around, then go around again holding the pointer to the final value for just a second, like making sure.

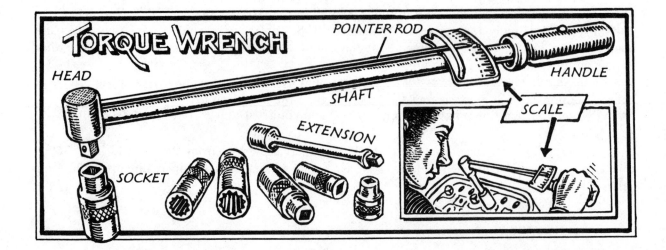

Table of Torque Values

Location	Type	Socket Size	Mkg.	Ft. Lbs.
Crankcase nuts	All	13 or 14mm	2.0	14
Crankcase nuts	36 hp	17mm	3.0	22
Crankcase nuts	40 hp	17mm	3.5	25
Crankcase nuts	1500 with plastic insert	17mm	2.5	18
Crankcase nuts	All the rest	17mm	3.5	25
Cylinder head nuts	36 hp	15/16/17mm	3.7	26
Cylinder head nuts	All the rest	15/16/17mm	3.2	23
Rockershaft nuts	36/40 hp	13 or 14mm	2.0	14
Rockershaft nuts	1500	13mm	2.5	18
Rockershaft nuts	1600	13mm	2.0	14
Rockershaft nuts	1700 Type IV	13mm	1.4	10
Flywheel gland nut	All	36mm	30.0	220
Flywheel cap screws	1700 Type IV	10mm special spline type heads	11.C	80
Drive plate cap screws	1700 Type IV Automatic	10mm special spline type heads	8.8	61
Connecting rod bolts	36 hp	14mm	5.0	36
Connecting rod nuts	1500 and all others	14mm	3-3.5	22-25
Big Fan Nut	Type I and II	36mm	6.0	44
Generator Pulley nut	Type I, II and III	21mm	6.0	44
Crankshaft Pulley bolt	Type I, II and III	30mm	4.5-5.0	32-36
Crankshaft Pulley Bolt	Type IV	30mm	6.0	44
Spark plugs	All	21mm	3.0-4.0	22-29
Oil drain plug	Type I, II and III	21mm	3.5	25
Oil drain plug	Type IV	17mm	2.2	16
Oil screen nuts	Type I, II and III	10mm	0.7	5
Oil screen bolt (very critical)	Type IV	19mm	0.85	9
Oil pump cover nuts	Type IV	13mm	2.2	14
Oil pump nuts	All	10mm	1.0	7
Engine mounting bolts	All	17mm	3.0	22
Clutch pressure plate bolts	All	14mm	2.5	18
Torque converter to drive plate	All automatics		2.5-3.0	18-22
Engine to frame	All	17mm	3.0	22
Transaxle to frame	All	14mm	2.5	18
General engine nuts and bolts	All	10mm	0.7	5
	All	11mm	1.0	7
	All	12mm	1.5	10
	All	13mm	2.0	14
	All	14mm	2.5	18
	All	17mm	3.0	22
Tie rod nuts	All	14mm	2.5	18
Brake plate bolts	All drum	16mm	5.0	36
Bleeder bolt	All	- - - - -	0.5	3.6
Master cylinder mounting bolts	All	14mm	2.5	18
Wheel cylinder mounting bolts	All drum	13 and 14mm	2.0-3.0	14-22
Bearing retainer bolts—rear brake plates	All	16mm	6.0	43

Table of Torque Values (Cont'd.)

Location	Type	Socket Size	Mkg.	Ft. Lbs.
Rear axle nut	Type I and III	36mm	30.0	220
Rear axle nut	Type II	40 and 42mm	35.0	253
Wheel hub bolt	Type IV		13-15	94-108
Transmission fill and drain plugs	All	17mm allen	2.0	14
Wheel bolts (lugs)	All	19mm	10.0	72
Disc brake caliper bolts	All (thru '72)		6.0	43
Disc brake caliper bolts (New)	Type II & IV ('73)	- - - - -	14.5-17.5	104-126
Shock absorber nut	All	13mm	2.0-3.0	14-22
Shock absorber bolt	Type I, II and III	17mm	3.0-3.5	22-25
Steering dampner nut	All	14mm	2.5	18
Steering dampner bolt	All	17mm	4.0-4.5	29-32
Shock absorber to strut bolt (front)	Type IV Super Beetle	- - - - -	7.0-8.5	50-61
Shock absorber bolt (rear)	Type IV Super Beetle	17mm	6.0	44

In addition to the above special values, use good common sense in tightening bolts and nuts. The little 10mm nuts are not shown above and must be handled very carefully. Use about a three-inch grip on the wrench to make sure you don't get them too tight or twist them off. The shrouding screws get a good solid twist with the big screwdriver. The rest of the 13mm nuts on the engine need about 2.0Mkg or 14 foot pounds but you just guess at it—about a six-inch grip on the wrench handle and pull hard.

How To Use a Puller. See Changes.

A puller is a device that grabs onto something and pulls it off or out. There are several types of pullers and many "special application" pullers. They usually have a large bolt in the middle that does the pulling and various types of arms and legs that grab onto what they were built to pull. A wheel or drum puller is one built to pull brake drums; they are often a plate that bolts to the drum with the lugs and a tower with the large bolt which you turn, so it pushes the axle out of the drum, thus pulling the drum off the axle.

The harmonic balancer puller sounds fancy but when you know that crankshaft pulleys on many cars are called "harmonic balancers," you see that this is a crankshaft pulley puller. You need one, for instance, to get the Type III fan pulley off the rear

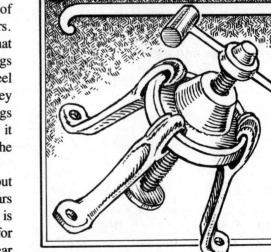

3 Armed Puller

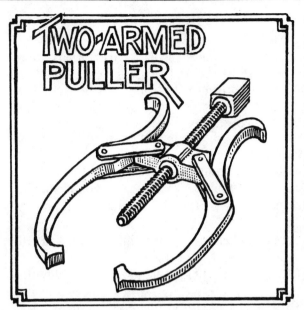

of the crankshaft. The engineer, seeing that this problem was coming up, provided two 8mm tapped holes in the pulley so you could screw two long bolts (3'') into the pulley through the arms of the puller, then, when you turn the large screw into the end of the crankshaft, the pulley is pulled off. The same puller is used for the crankshaft pulleys on the Types I and II; the only difference is that instead of providing neatly drilled and tapped holes, the engineer provided two slots. You can put a bolt through the slots and through the arms of the puller, put on washers and nuts, then pull the pulley off as the big puller bolt is turned toward the crankshaft.

A gear or bearing puller has two or three arms with hooks on the ends; the hooks hook over the gear or into the bearing so when the large screw is turned, the gear or bearing is pulled off.

Sometimes the idea is to push something off another thing so a ''U'' shaped puller is made with a bolt in the center to pull an oil pump, let's say, out of its case. The bolt is free to turn in the top of the ''U'' and screw into the threaded hole in the pump as the legs of the puller push on the outside of the pump. You'll find one of these handy if you ever take apart a Type IV oil pump. The basic thing to remember about things that seem impossible to get off or out is that some engineer has provided a way to do it. They won't let an engineer use a detail in the automotive business unless there is also a way to get it apart.

The two armed puller sketched above pulls bearings off the rear axle shaft, the cam gear off the crankshaft or the generator bearings off their shaft. The three armed puller pulls the drum off the axle.

How To Use a Volt Ohmmeter (VOM).

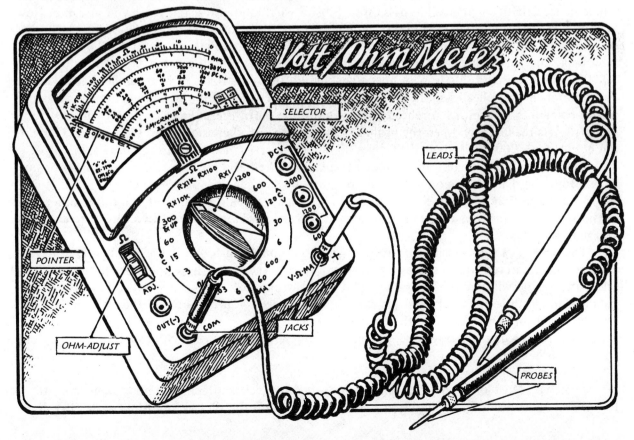

How to Use a Volt Ohmmeter (VOM).

First, take a look at the sketch on the preceding page.

The one you have may look different and use different names or symbols for the various scales but they all measure the same electrical phenomena: volts (both AC and DC), resistance (in Ohms) and amperes (Amps). Some also measure decibels but I don't know how to read this scale, yet. Voltage is kinda like water pressure (the force with which it comes through the hose) and resistance is like friction (rubbing against the side of the hose). You have continuity when there's zero resistance. Amps are sort of like measuring the amount of water. You have to relate amount to time, so an ampere a second is called a coulomb. Batteries are rated by ampere hours. They will put out so many amps for so many hours. If the rating of a 12 volt battery is 70 amp-hours, it'll put out 7 amps for 10 hours at 12 volts. That's what they guarantee you. When you check resistance, you're making sure the path the electricity takes is clear. An electrical short is a little like the hose is cut and the water (electricity) is running out somewhere.

Set your VOM right out in front of you and look at it. It has a needle which moves and tells you the answer you're asking the VOM. You have to read the needle on some scale...notice there are several, like OHMS (Ω). V-AC (AC volts), V-DC (DC volts), etc. Below the needle is a dial with a pointer. You set the pointer to what you are measuring, like Volts-AC, OHMS (if you're going to measure resistance or check continuity), Volts-DC or DC ma-uA (AMPS)...this means milli or micro amps. Look at the two leads (wires). Notice the connectors (probes) are shorter on one end than on the other. The shorter ends are plugged into the VOM so plug one into the hole in the VOM that says Common (or "COM" or "COM -" or just "-"). This is the common lead for all VOM operations; also the negative terminal which in our Volkswagens means "ground" as well. The other connector goes into various places depending on what you are going to measure. For now, put it into the + hole. This hole might say "+ volts-ohms-mA," "V-ohm-ma," "+ v Ω MA" or just "+" on yours. Now twist the dial with the pointer so the pointer points to Rx10K (or 10K) in the OHMS section. This means resistance times 10,000. Touch the probes together and watch the needle; it should swing to somewhere around zero. Now find the "adjust ohms" (Ω adj.) knob and turn it until the needle is exactly at 0 on the OHMS scale. This means no resistance; the other end of this scale means infinite resistance where no electricity could possibly pass through. Now what kind of resistance can you measure? How about yourself? Every patch of skin on your body has a slightly different resistance, so put the probes on the palm of your hand and watch the needle move. If the probes are about 1/2" apart on me, they make the needle swing to about 50 on the ohms scale, so multiply 50 times 10k which gives 500,000 ohms resistance for 1/2" of my palm skin. Put the two probes to your forehead, 1/2" apart. For a half inch of forehead skin, I get 10 x 10,000 (10k) or 100,000 ohms, so there's more resistance in my palm skin than in my forehead skin...interesting. Move the pointer to Rx100 and my palm doesn't give a reading even when the probes are very close but when the probes are about 1/8" apart, the needle reads 200 which times 100, gives 20,000 ohms resistance in damp forehead skin.

Find other things to test and practice reading the needle so you can read it accurately on any scale. Move the dial so the pointer points to 250 volts AC—make doubly sure you turned it to 250 V-AC—then carefully insert one probe into one hole in a wall plug and the other into the other hole in the same wall plug. Read the needle on the ACV scale; it will swing to 115 volts or thereabouts if you're in the USA.

The VOM is a very sensitive instrument and you should just touch the probes lightly either together or to whatever you're testing, so you can quickly see if you have the dial set to the wrong scale—the needle will jump. Setting the VOM to the wrong scale can burn it out. Like never test resistance on anything that's plugged in; use the ACV scale if you plug it into the wall or the DCV scale if it runs off a battery. If, with the dial set to DC volts, you touch your probe to a battery and the needle takes a dive to below zero, you have the wrong polarity so switch probes...that is, put one where the other was.

To Check Continuity:

First, you Must know that the item you're going to check is attached to no current so switch it to "OFF," disconnect it, unplug it, etc. Set the pointer on the dial to an OHMS scale (like Rx1,

Rx10, Rx1K—some VOM's just say x1, x10 or x1K), with one probe in the + hole and the other in -, touch the probes together and adjust the needle to zero. Now you can put one probe on one end of what you're checking and the other at the other end. If the resistance is 0 ohms, you have continuity. If the needle doesn't go all the way to 0- try a smaller scale, like if the pointer is at Rx1K, try RX10—you have resistance, probably caused by a bum connection so check any splices or connections til you do get continuity.

To Check Fuses (car, house, boat—any fuse)

Put the connectors in the + and - holes, set the pointer on the dial to the voltage you would expect, like 115 volts AC if you're testing something in the USA that plugs into house current (unless it's a 220 volt appliance, in which case set the pointer to 220 volts AC or over). The needle should swing to 115 volts on the AC scale. If you're checking auto fuses and it's a 12 volt system, set the pointer on the dial to 30 volts DC or 50 volts DC—whatever your VOM has that's over 12 volts DC. The needle should swing to 12 volts on the DC scale. You'll notice there are several DC scales you can read for the needle so read the scale that shows 12 volts DC most accurately.

The idea in checking a fuse is to find if there's voltage to both sides of the fuse, so put the probe plugged into - to any ground and the other to first one side of the fuse, then to the other. If the needle swings to the expected voltage on both sides, the fuse is OK. If the needle swings to the expected voltage on one side of the fuse but not on the other, the fuse is bad or has a bad connection.

To check continuity in a fuse, you must remove it from its receptacle. If the needle swings to zero, the fuse is OK, if it stays at infinity, the fuse is nowhere.

OK, to check continuity, use the OHM scale and the thing you're checking **must not have electricity to it.** To check a hot line, hot fuse, hot switch, you MUST USE A VOLTAGE SCALE, either AC or DC.

To Check Amperes:

The VOM is not a very good ammeter. The 30 amps produced by the VW generator are beyond the VOM's capacity to measure. If your car is fuel injected, there is the one check (for the fuel injectors) you can make using the AMP scale (see Chapter X). Mostly, if you know the voltage and can measure the resistance, you can figure the amps using the formula below.

For those of you who would like a little theory about electricity, here's a short story: There are two basic kinds of current, alternating current (AC) and direct current (DC). When you rotate a wire in a magnetic field (between North Pole and South Pole), the wire cuts through the field and picks up electricity. Take a piece of paper and draw a horizontal line across the center. Put the point of a pencil on the left side of the line and imagine your body is a wire rotating through a magnetic field (force created between two magnets). The magnetic field is strongest when you are closest to a pole (magnet) and gets weaker as you rotate away from a pole. So now draw a line as you rotate. Start on the line you already drew; this is zero. As you rotate closer to a pole the line you draw will go up, then, as you leave the most concentrated field area, the current becomes less so make your line head down—you've made a hill. The other pole is minus (or below the line), so draw your line down toward the other pole and as you rotate away from it, your line will head back to zero—you've made a valley. If you've drawn rounded curves, you have a sine curve of alternating current electricity. All electricity made by rotating a wire (or bunches of wires) through a magnetic field is alternating current.

But our cars use direct current because AC cannot be stored in a battery. The generator uses a commutator (that round thing the brushes run on that has copper strips with insulation between them) to lop off all the electricity below the line so the curve you draw is nothing but hills with no below zero valleys. The alternator, now being used in VW's makes AC then uses diodes to separate out the hills and valleys so the valleys are reversed and become hills and thus acceptable to the battery. From the battery comes direct current which makes a straight line running parallel to the line you drew first—the zero line on your paper. In a 12 volt system, this line is 12 units up off zero (that is, the distance between the two straight lines is 12 units or volts).

The number of wires you rotate in the field and the strength of the field determine the voltage and the number of times you rotate the wires (speed) in the field determines the amperage. They are a little more mixed up than that, but this is just a short story. The usual automobile generator or alternator produces between 12 and 15 volts and between 30 and 50 amperes. The voltage regulator keeps the voltage down to what the battery can absorb and also decides how much amperage the battery can use. The voltage regulator controls the amount of magnetic field present in the generator and thus, the amount of amperage. When the headlights are on, the product of the generator is used directly by the headlights as long as the generator is turning.

So now you can see that in an automotive system, the voltage is regulated to an almost constant value and the amperage is controlled by the needs. And so what are the needs called? The needs or demands put on the electrical system are the resistances. So it figures that the amperage required by any electrical device is the voltage divided by the resistance. E (voltage) = I (amperage) x R (resistance) $E = IR$, $I = E/R$, $R = E/I$. W (watts) = EI (volts x amps) and by messing around with algebra, $W = I^2R$ (heat loss). There, you have the basic formulae for direct current. The same formulae apply to alternating current except that R (resistance) gets complicated by the addition of Capacitance and Induction to Resistance, and the whole schmutz is called Impedance (the AC equivalent to resistance). OK, OK, you don't have to know any of this to run a VOM but it's nice to know what you're measuring.

From the Spanish Edition

Wipers, Heater Cables, Speedometer Cable, Install New Muffler with Engine in Car

This chapter is a potpourri of stuff that may be handy to do before you take your Volkswagen through a safety inspection. The accent is on the non-mechanical items, with the exception of the muffler.

Volkswagen Lights

Whenever something goes wrong with the lights, wiper, radio, just anything electrical, don't rush out to buy new parts. You should have a fuse kit and bulbs in your spares and now forewarned, check the fuses! Most failures in the electrical department will be located there. Even if one of the electrical items has failed or shorted, the trouble often shows up in the fuse box. Your VW Driver's Manual is a most important aid in repairing lights and checking and replacing fuses. It shows you how to take the lights apart and replace the bulbs. All we have to add to what they say is to use your Scout knife to scrape all the contacts, especially the insides of the bulb sockets and the bottoms of the bulbs. If you've lost your Owner's Manual, write to VW or ask a dealer for one; get one for your chassis number. Failing in this, buy the Owner's Service Manual for your model. VW sells them and they're very good on lights, wipers, body and windows. It's beyond the scope of this book to cover these details for all models. If you'd like a wiring diagram for your model, ask at a VW dealer if they have a copier and would they please make a copy of the diagram for your model. **See Chapter XXII, Electrical Impulses**

When working on the lights, a friend to watch is almost a necessity. Use the VOM if you have one (see Chapter XVI for how) or the timing light to check your fuses and connections. To use the timing light, hook the clip to one side of the fuse spring, ground the base of the bulb to see if juice is going to the fuse, then move the clip to the top spring to see if juice is going through. If you have no reference to a fuse diagram, you can make your own using the method above and turning one thing on after another to find out which fuse is for which light or whatever. Bright and Dim of the headlights have separate fuses for each side, for example.

The newer models have side lights and back up lights which add to your chores: more contacts and sockets to scrape and additional bulbs to replace.

OK, the place to start if you have light troubles is with the fuses. Look at them well. If they're starting to get thin in the middle, it might be time to replace them all. The type in VW's have a tendency to first change shape with age and use, then break with vibration. **Always carry extra fuses**; the glove compartment is a handy place for them. White fuses are 8 amp, red ones are 16 amp.

The fuse box is under the dash in all models and usually has a plastic snap-on cover or a Bakelite cover that screws on. Some are picture coded. **See Changes and New Ideas.**

The headlights are adjustable and should be changed by an authorized service station to conform to the laws of your state but if conformance is not your thing, you can adjust them yourself by shining them on a wall of a building. The method of adjustment is easy to figure out. Draw some lines on the wall for level and straight. The low beams should be under level and about 6" from straight ahead. The high beams should center on the level line (height of lights from ground) and be just to the right of center (straight ahead). You should adjust them every time you put in a new headlight unit. Remember to put air in your tires before you adjust the lights. You can do all the work in the lights with a medium screwdriver, the phillips screwdriver and the Scout knife. (Look in your Owner's Manual to see where your adjusting screws are).

The interior lights seldom need anything more than a new bulb. You can check whether or not you have juice with your test/timing light.

Don't think we're belittling the work in the lights in the Volkswagen. There are some tough-to-

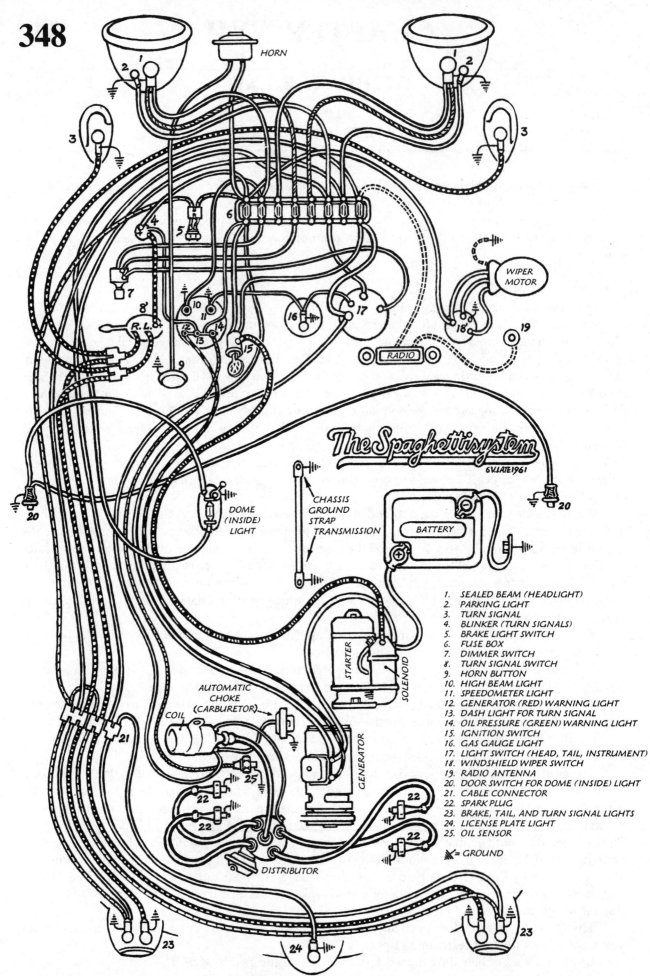

348

HORN

WIPER MOTOR

RADIO

R.L.

The Spaghettisystem
6 V. LATE 1961

CHASSIS
GROUND
STRAP
TRANSMISSION

BATTERY

DOME
(INSIDE)
LIGHT

STARTER

SOLENOID

AUTOMATIC
CHOKE
(CARBURETOR)

COIL

GENERATOR

DISTRIBUTOR

1. SEALED BEAM (HEADLIGHT)
2. PARKING LIGHT
3. TURN SIGNAL
4. BLINKER (TURN SIGNALS)
5. BRAKE LIGHT SWITCH
6. FUSE BOX
7. DIMMER SWITCH
8. TURN SIGNAL SWITCH
9. HORN BUTTON
10. HIGH BEAM LIGHT
11. SPEEDOMETER LIGHT
12. GENERATOR (RED) WARNING LIGHT
13. DASH LIGHT FOR TURN SIGNAL
14. OIL PRESSURE (GREEN) WARNING LIGHT
15. IGNITION SWITCH
16. GAS GAUGE LIGHT
17. LIGHT SWITCH (HEAD, TAIL, INSTRUMENT)
18. WINDSHIELD WIPER SWITCH
19. RADIO ANTENNA
20. DOOR SWITCH FOR DOME (INSIDE) LIGHT
21. CABLE CONNECTOR
22. SPARK PLUG
23. BRAKE, TAIL, AND TURN SIGNAL LIGHTS
24. LICENSE PLATE LIGHT
25. OIL SENSOR

⚡ = GROUND

This is a late 1961 6-volt electrical system. Yours is probably different as there are at least 40 of them.

get-at places, especially under the speedometer in the Types I, III and IV, where you can while away several hours. It's just that we can't help you do it.

A maintenance item: Tighten the phillips screws that hold your combination dimmer switch and signal arm. There are four of them: two hold the assembly together and two clamp the assembly to the steering column. If this gizmo fouls up, which can happen if you neglect to tighten the screws, you have to replace it. Buy the whole assembly at VW. Take the working half off the steering column but for God's sake don't disconnect any of the wires yet. Take the clamp half off the new assembly and install the new working half on the old one—this saves having to pull the steering wheel—now you need a flashlight and not to be color blind. Pass the new wiring cable through the same places you take (simultaneously) the old one out of: lie down with your head under the dash (Bus and Type III), work in the front compartment (Types I and II) and replace each wire, matching color for color, until they're all replaced. They're all push-ons. Work slowly and surely.

When it comes to signal lights, you're on your own as I can't even keep mine working properly, so I should be advising already...remember to check the fuses before doing anything else. Don't be fearful, be careful.

Newer models come with a **buzzer in the door** that makes a nerve shattering noise every time you open the front door with the key in the ignition. **To disconnect:** With a small phillips screwdriver remove the little button in the front of the driver's side door frame; it's held by just one small screw. Pull the button and accompanying wires out gently and you find four wires and four push-on connectors. Experiment a bit and you'll find that two of these wires operate the overhead light. The other two make that awful noise—pull these off and tape them well with electrical tape, then shove the whole schmutz back into the hole, adjust the rubber gasket carefully, replace the screw and tighten and ergo! no more whine to buzz your head.

Windshield Wipers

Check the fuse for the wipers before you take them all apart. The early model wipers are stopped by shutting off the motor when the blades are where you want them. The later models are self-parking but must be parked by hand if the windshield is obstructed by snow or ice, as you'll find out by bitter experience if you forget when you go skiing. They will keep running juice out of the battery all night as they try to park so move them by hand after cleaning the snow off the windshield and allow the straining contacts to close. Don't laugh—some of our best friends...

The work on the wiper assemblies is complicated by the accessories mounted in the wiper area. In the bus, you just about have to remove the radio to reach the motor which is above the radio. The gig with the motor is to replace the brushes, sandpaper the commutator and clean the grooves or install a new motor.

To remove the motor from the Bus, unhook the right-hand arm from the wiper end; just push or pull off the ball joints. Use a small screwdriver to take out the screws, pull the motor free a little, disconnect the wire, then pull the motor out with the left arm attached. Take the cover off the motor and check the brushes. If I had gone to all this work to get at the motor, I would put in new brushes and clean the commutator no matter what. Replace the motor in the opposite way from which you removed it, then connect the arms to the ball joints and hope it works. It may take fixing it twice to get it right as you can't see a damn thing.

In the Type I it's easier to reach the wiper assembly as it's in back of the cover in the front compartment. To remove the motor, take the whole assembly out, blades first, then remove the hex nuts that hold the shafts where they turn. Unscrew the bolt that holds the wiper motor to the bracket, then pull the whole frame out after you have disconnected the wire to the motor. I hope you remember how all those washers and seals go back. I tape them together in their order when I take them off. Loosen the motor from the frame, remove the cover, clean the commutator, install the new brushes, then install in reverse order, putting some oil on the moving parts but not in the motor.

Removing the wiper motor from the Type III is where you pay the price for having a real dashboard. It's a real bear. First off, pull the ash tray out and remove the phillips head screw holding the ash try case in. Pull the case out and the bracket that holds it. Look under the glove box and find the strap that holds it. Remove the phillips head screw from the strap and pull the glove box out from underneath. If you have a radio it'll have to come out also. Pull the fresh air knobs off the dash. They are just to the left of the glove box lid. Now look in back of the knobs and you'll see the plastic control assembly screwed on the back of the dash. Remove the screws and pull the whole assembly down and out of the way. Don't disconnect any of the wires. Remove the two screws holding the cardboard cover under the center of the dash and pull the cover off. Now go around to the wiper arms and loosen the screw holding the arms onto the spindles. Pull the arms off. With a 17mm wrench remove the nuts on the spindles, then the washers and seals. Back under the dash and remove the one 10mm mounting screw holding the motor assembly to the body. Pull out the wiper motor with the linkage attached and there you are. Loosen the motor from the frame, remove the cover, clean the commutator, install new brushes, then install it in the reverse order, putting some oil on the moving parts but not in the motor itself.

Type IV, take your windshield wiper motor work to VW. You not only have to remove the radio but the speedometer and parts of the steering column as well. They invented it; let them fix it.

If you have a bum wiper switch—trace it with the timing light or VOM—buy a new one, unscrew the knob, take off the hex nut, pull the switch forward and out where you can see it. Take the wires off the old switch and put them on the new switch in the same places, then try the switch. Replace the switch in reverse order.

New wiper blades are a good investment when yours get hard or worn and stop doing a good job. If they're just dirty, use alcohol on a rag to clean them but don't get any on the car paint, please. The later the model, the more complicated the wiper blades and assemblies are but that figures so learn to adjust whichever ones you have when they quit doing their thing. In my old Bus, I only had to bend the arms some and raise or lower the blade a little. They say you should change the new ones with the replaceable wiper elements once each year.

Keep the car wax off the windshield.

Heater Cables

These usually last the life of the car but sometimes they jam up and break. It's important to replace these heater cables and get them working for your engine's sake, not so you can sit in a warm car. The heater cables actually join into one unit at the control end so when one side is pulled the other side is pulled and the heating (cooling) of the engine is balanced. In the Bus, the cables are longer but the replacement technique is the same. Buy a new cable assembly for your chassis number. Models 1966 and on have two cables and two operating levers.

Use the vice grip and a 10mm wrench to loosen the clamps that hold the cable ends to the operating levers on the heater boxes, one on each side of the front of the engine. You have to crawl under the car to do this, so Types I, III and IV owners will want to jack their cars up enough to get under them. Go in the front of the car and take the heater lever or knob (the one that turns the heater off and on) mechanism apart. Unhook the old cable and pull out the ends. Start the new cable ends into the tubes and push them through until you can reattach the tied-together cables to the heater lever or knob and reassemble the mechanism. Make sure the heater lever or knob is in the "OFF" position. Go back under the rear of the car to clamp the cable ends in the clamps. Connect the heater cables so there's no slack when the operating lever on the heater box is closed. The cables will stretch and straighten out with time, so you may want to make them taut again for more heat in winter. Make sure you adjust them evenly.

Speedometer Cable, Speedometer

If your speedometer quits working, the first place to check is the left front hub cover. Pry the hub cap off and look in the center of the hub. If there's a square shaft sticking out of the little square hole with a cotter key or little clip holding the shaft, your trouble is elsewhere. But if there is no shaft in the hole, pry or knock off the hub and work the cable end back into the square hole or install a new cable if the whole thing is gone, put in a new key to hold it (or put on a new clip), then try the speedometer again. If the square shaft has a worn place where it goes through the hub, you have to put a little washer on the shaft inside the hub to move the shaft so a new unworn place fits into the square hole.

If you're sure the hub is turning the speedometer shaft, tap the hub cover back in the hub and look elsewhere for the difficulty. Remove the connection where the speedometer cable screws into the speedometer. It's in the front compartment in the Type I and under the dash in the Bus and Type III and IV. This connection is a knurled ring which loosens by hand to let you pull the end of the cable out of the speedometer. Inside this large cable is a smaller cable with another square end. Jack up the left front wheel and have someone turn it while you feel to see if the little shaft is turning in the big cable. If it is, your speedo cable is all right but if it isn't, you need a new cable. If the cable checks OK, reconnect the cable to the speedometer and spin the front wheel, fast. If the speedometer still doesn't register, your speedometer head needs work or replacement.

Replace Speedometer Cable

Pry off the hub cap on the left front wheel with the large screwdriver, use the vice grip to remove the cotter key on the square shaft sticking out of the hub cover or a small screwdriver to remove the little clip. Use the large screwdriver and small hammer to remove the hub cover, reach around inside and pull the cable out of the steering knuckle. If you have a Type I, III or IV, this is easier to do if the front wheel is jacked up a little. Remove the cable from the speedometer head by unscrewing the knurled ring and pulling the cable free. Go down under the car and follow the line the cable takes and remove the clips that hook it to the frame. In the Bus, you have to remove the front piece of cardboard in the cab with the small screwdriver in order to follow the cable's path. When all the clips are free, you can pull the cable up and out. Buy a new cable to match the old one or per your chassis number.

Start the new cable from the top in the car and push it through the holes and down toward the steering knuckle. Push it through the hole in the knuckle until it comes out through the axle. Put the square shaft into the square hole in the hub and put the clip on, or the cotter key in, the shaft. Tap the hub cover back in the hub. Go under the car and slip the cable into the clips the old one came out of, then go up into the car and put the cable into the speedometer head and tighten the ring.

Remove the Speedometer

You need a short phillips screwdriver to do the Bus but a long one works better for the Types I, III and IV. The new models have nuts so use the vice grip. The speedometer in the older Type I is under the cover in the front compartment. In the newer Type I and in the Types II, III and IV, it's under the dash. For all, remove the instrument light or lights, remove the three lights in the bottom of the speedometer, red, green and blue—all these just pull out, but gently.

Loosen the knurled ring and pull the speedometer cable down out of the way. In the Types I and III, remove the two phillips head screws (two allen head bolts, Type IV) holding the speedometer and pull it out toward you. It's out. In the Bus, loosen the two screws but don't take them out. Rotate the speedometer about 3/4" and it will be free to go forward, down and out. Be careful of all those wires, take your time. Disconnect the ground strap to the battery in the engine compartment before removing the Bus speedometer.

Once it's out, take it to a repair shop that knows about VW speedometers or to the dealer to have it fixed. You can drive without it for a few days while it's being repaired. They will tell you whether you need a new speedometer or not.

It goes back the same way you took it out, a quick job for Type I owners. In the Types II, III and IV, you're working by feel and it takes a while to sort out the wires and get all the bulbs back into their sockets correctly so the red light doesn't go on with the dash lights and stay on, like that. Put the speedometer cable into the tube and tighten the knurled ring and you're through. Here's a suggestion for Types I, III and IV owners: each of those sockets you pull out of the back of the speedometer has a different colored wire. Make a note of which color came from which socket and you can cut reassembly time by a lot.

Body Notes

As long as the body doesn't get hurt in an accident, all you do is wash it, wax it and keep it in as good condition as you want. If you go over to the beach for the day, wash it as soon as you can to get the salt off. If they salt the roads in winter in your state, wash the bottom of your car often. Don't let that salt and crud gather under the car or your bottom panels will rust out. If you live near the ocean, wash the car in fresh water often to avoid rusting.

After a big accident, the work on the body and/or the frame is usually an expensive job. It's the cruddy little things that catch you up. Somebody hits you in the parking lot at the supermarket and drives away without so much as a fare-you-well and you're left with a bonked door or fender. All the insurance you have is P.L. and P.D., so it's now your baby.

You can do three things: 1) Forget it, accept the dent as part of your car's aging process; 2) Fix it yourself, take two hammers and beat out the dent, then paint it with matching paint; 3) Have it fixed and if this is your choice, do it tomorrow. Go to two or three reputable body shops and get an estimate from each. Tell them it is not an insurance job and that you would appreciate the lowest price they can give you. Then make an appointment and have it done.

The same type of thing goes for the window glass, as this chore of replacement is tough to do yourself. Watch an expert at work and you'll see that you'd have a tough time duplicating his or her facility. To have the expert replace broken glass in a car has turned out to be cheaper.

The Horn

This electro-magnetic noise maker deserves a small mention of its own, I guess. My theory on horns is to drive in a way that you never need to use one. The horn is located close to the place where the lower end of the steering shaft comes down to the steering box. The hot wire comes down from the fuse box and is attached to the horn by a screw-on or push-on. You can check whether your horn has juice or not by taking this connection off and touching it to a bare place on the frame. It should spark. The horn is insulated from the frame. To complete the connection to make the horn go OOO-Ga, the ground comes from that wire coming out of the steering box. This wire runs up to the horn button through the tube to the steering wheel and is grounded by pushing down the horn button. If your horn ever starts to blow without your consent and keeps blowing, this wire is probably grounding on the steering box where it comes out. Don't pull the wire out in your excitement, just get some tape around it. That wire is hell to replace.

PROCEDURE FOR CHANGING MUFFLER, ENGINE IN CAR—TYPE I AND TYPE II THROUGH 1971. Phase II

Condition: Your muffler is no longer safe or lawful—you need a new one and your engine's in excellent condition. It's a much easier change to make if your engine's out. **Type III:** Follow the steps for the Bug but you don't have any tin to remove or heat risers to disconnect unless you have a single carb model. Get at the top muffler nuts with a long extension and 13mm.

Tools and Parts: Phase II tool kit, a new muffler, a muffler connection kit, new tail pipe or pipes (if needed), a tail pipe kit for each new tail pipe, a bolt can and Liquid Wrench.

Remarks: If you're replacing a Bus muffler, we recommend you buy the one for the Bug and two offset tail pipes with installation kits. The Bug muffler makes more noise but gives the engine a horsepower boost and better breathing. If you do put a Bug muffler on a Bus, as we suggest, make sure you get the right one for your engine and buy the offset tail pipes. You have to cut a place in the splash pan (rear brace) so the extra tail pipe can pass under and through it. Extractor systems cost more but are worth it. If your old muffler just has a few small holes in it, patching with muffler cement will keep you going for several hundred miles.

Step 1. Preparation

Open the engine compartment and prop it well. To change the muffler, it's necessary to remove the very rear piece of tin. REAR MEANS REAR OF THE CAR with LEFT the driver's side. In the early models it's a simple matter of removing four or six screws with the large screwdriver and working the piece of tin up and out.

Bus owners: Before you remove the rear piece of tin, take off the back of your engine compartment (rear brace), that piece painted the same color as the Bus.

1968 and 71 Bus: Remove the four bolts from the rear engine carrier under the rear brace, then remove the rear brace.

All, '65 and on: To get to the rear piece of tin, you first have to remove three other pieces of sheet metal. Start by removing the two cover plates over the connection made by the heat riser, part of the intake manifold assembly (three screws each), then disconnect the big air hoses from the heater system by loosening the clamps and twisting and pulling the hoses off the heater box entrance pipes with the big screwdriver. Next you have to remove the crankshaft pulley shroud, the piece of tin around the crankshaft pulley (three screws), then the air hose or hoses bringing hot air to the air cleaner. Now you can remove the four or six screws holding the rearmost piece of tin and the tin can be worked up out of position around the pre-heater tube going to the air cleaner.

Step 2. Remove Tail Pipes

It's easier to get them off now when the muffler is firmly held, so with the 10mm socket on the ratchet and the 10mm box end, unclamp the tail pipes and pull them off the end of the muffler. If you're going to reuse your tail pipes, take the old gaskets off.

Step 3. Disconnect Heat Risers and Heads from Muffler

With the rearmost piece of tin either out or worked up on the hose and out, use the 10mm socket, short extension and ratchet to remove the two bolts on each side from the heat risers on the intake manifold.

Remove the two nuts on each side that hold the muffler to the heads with a 13mm wrench. Instead of the nut coming off, the stud may come out. It's OK, just replace the stud. Use Liquid Wrench and see Chapter XVI to solve any problems.

Step 4. Remove Muffler Clamps and Muffler

Get under the car. Using a 10mm socket and 10mm box end, loosen the bolts that hold the muffler clamps. My experience is that they often twist off and break but you have new clamps and bolts in the muffler connection kit. There is one clamp on each side with two bolts in each. Pull off the muffler and get rid of it, **except models '65 and on**: loosen the two connections to the heater boxes, one on each side, with the screwdriver. They're clamps held together by a screw, so loosen them and slip them onto the heater box, then pull the muffler off. With a hammer and a pair of pliers, gently tap the heater collars that the big hoses attach to up out of the muffler and equally as gently tap them into the new muffler.

All: Remove the old gaskets. The two ring gaskets on the exhaust pipes may have to be tapped off with a hammer.

Step 5. Install New Gaskets

There are six gaskets in all. Place the new gaskets on the heads, one on each side. Then put the two ring gaskets on the exhaust pipes coming from the two front cylinders; first install the metal ring and then the asbestos ring. The two small flat metal gaskets go between the muffler and   the

Step 5. (Cont'd.)

heat riser, but don't put them on yet.

Step 6. Install Muffler

Slide the muffler underneath the car and onto the two studs that hold it to the heads. Start the 13 or 14mm nuts onto the studs.

'65 and on: The connection for the pre-heater hose going to the air cleaner, the one hung up on the rear piece of tin, goes under the left-hand bottom nut. The nozzle thing fits into the sheet metal next to it.

All: At the same time as you're putting the muffler onto the studs on the heads, start the pipes from the back cylinders into the muffler. Tighten the nuts holding the muffler to the heads some, but not all the way. Slip the gaskets that go between the muffler and the heat riser of the intake manifold into place by prying the junction open with a screwdriver. If the gasket set you bought has one with a small hole in it, it belongs on the left (driver's side), then get the bolts started with your fingers. A phillips screwdriver is handy to get the holes lined up. You may have to bend and push and pull and shove to make everything fit. Start every connection before you tighten anything!

'65 and on: Get the connection clamp between the heater box and the muffler clamps on.

All: Tighten everything—a little here, a little there. When the four nuts and bolts are tight, the muffler clamps can be installed. They go over the joint—make sure you catch both the rim on the muffler and the ring that holds the gasket in the clamp.

Step 7. Install Tail Pipe or Pipes

They connect the same way as the clamps you just finished putting on. Slip the metal ring, then the asbestos ring onto the tail pipe, shove the tail pipe in and clamp it up (10mm).

Step 8. Finish Up

'65 and on: Replace the rear piece of tin, that one hung up on the hose, connect the hose to the air cleaner. Put on the two small pieces of tin over the heat riser tubes, then the pulley shroud. Reconnect all hoses.

All others: Replace rear piece of tin and hoses (if any).

Bus owners: Replace the back brace of your engine compartment.

'68 to '71 Bus models: Replace the four bolts on the rear engine carrier.

That's it!

PROCEDURE FOR CHANGING MUFFLER, ENGINE IN CAR—TYPE IV AND 1972 AND ON TYPE II. Phase I

Condition: Your car needs a new muffler. In these models, it's a cinch to replace it with the engine in the car.

Tools and Materials: 13mm box open end wrench, 10mm wrench, new muffler and gaskets, new tail pipe, if needed.

Step 1. Remove Old Muffler

With the 10mm wrench, remove the clamp that holds the tail pipe, then remove the six 13mm nuts that hold the muffler to the heater boxes. Some models have a connection for the heat riser to remove and in some, you have to remove the rock shield before you can get at the muffler nuts.

Step 1. (Cont'd.)

Once the muffler nuts are removed, the muffler can be pulled out.

Step 2. Install New Muffler

Put the new gaskets on the muffler, put the muffler on the heater boxes, put the washers and nuts on the studs and tighten. In some models you have a heat riser connection to make. Install the rock shield (if it's off), then put the tail pipe on. Tighten the clamp and the hanger bolt (if any) and you're through.

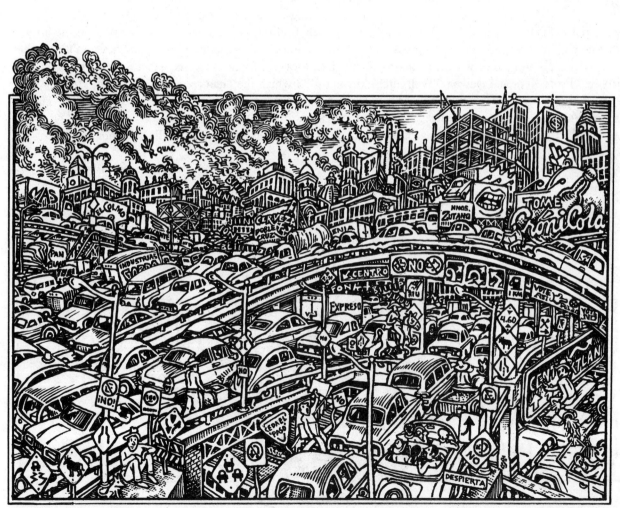

From the Spanish Edition

GRANDCHILD OF YE OLDE MAILE BAGGE

In the original Maile Baggie John wrote, "one of the most important items a writer suggested I emphasize is CESSATION OF THOUGHT, which means do what the book says . . . chant, whistle, listen to what is being read to you, but don't think, OK?" We know he meant that some kinds of thinking may interfere with your ability to follow these procedures. But think we must. For example, the first few editions didn't say to remove the huge staples that hold the new clutch to the packaging **before** installing the clutch. One person put the clutch together, packing staples and all (and drove a remarkable distance before the engine self-destructed). Another reader was checking the fuel pump and his buddy turned the engine over causing a spark and told us (precisely) how long it takes a bug to burn (remarkably fast). So, please, think and *DON'T MAKE SPARKS AROUND GASOLINE*, right?

We are now receiving mail from people who weren't yet born in 1969, the year of the first edition. From Matt Hicks in England: "I am 24 years old, an owner of a '67 Type III . . . As you have written, there is nothing to fear from performing a task for the first time, with a bit of common sense and a methodical approach. . . ." From Greg Matthews: ". . . We are all around 15 so we still have a year to drive legally in Utah . . . the instructions are real easy to follow . . . It's real entertaining, too, it's the only how-to car book that I can read and not be totally board." Ethan Marcoux: "I'm 16 and just bought my first car. A 1971 Volkswagen Bug with a Super Beetle body on it. I love it." From Terry D. (same age as the book) in England: ". . . Suddenly, I had a guide through the heart of my beetle. For the first time I was reading about the workings of a car and it was interesting . . . I was smiling . . . any other car manual was like looking at a dead fish. This book is a 100-ft. flying fish!" From Brett Taylor (age unknown) "Another part (of the book) that helped my slow, yet steady, progress was the illustrations. I see a picture (photo) and have no idea what the book is pointing to or what it is talking about. The drawings force me to see exactly what you want me to see." From Kent and Dawna: "Well, that old van (a '73 which they had rescued from sitting 'forlorn and forgotten in a barnyard') just took us on a four-month surf trip from Florida to Costa Rica and back! That's a grand total of six foreign countries and over 8,000 miles of pot-hole infested roads."

Thanks for the stories. And please keep in mind the differences between **thought and *thought*.**

—Eve Muir, 1997

CHAPTER XVIII

HI-PERFORMANCE MODIFICATIONS

by Colin Messer

PART I: INTRODUCTION AND THEORY

INTRODUCTION

One day in the future when gasoline-powered automobiles are obsolete, some automotive anthropologist will publish a study titled "Fascination with the Volkswagen." The study will examine our passion for air-cooled Volkswagens and will likely conclude that the VW Bug has been tinkered with, modified, and loved more than any automobile in history. Until the world's oil supply runs out, VW freaks will continue to dream up new modifications or fads that make the "small wonder" go faster or look weirder.

Undoubtedly, this book will be mentioned by writers of the future as one of the important aspects of VW mania. But John doesn't say much about building a VW for hi-performance, only that a few horsepower can be added by installing an extractor exhaust or big-bore pistons and cylinders to replace the original stock equipment. Therefore, this chapter is written as an introduction to the basics of modifying a Volkswagen for hi-performance street use—how to make the air-cooled wonder peppier and perhaps more durable. I discuss components and assemblies and their relationships with each other and the whole engine. Details are mentioned to which you must pay attention when disassembling and assembling an engine. These are details that John Muir does not include in his Procedures, but you must read his Procedures for the actual work.

Please understand that serious hi-performance engine work cannot be taught in a single chapter to anyone, even to people with more than basic automotive skills and unlimited tools. Quality engine building takes great determination and diligence. Hi-performance means high precision. Parts selection and assembly become more exacting as the demand for speed and durability increases. Simply buying expensive parts, slapping them together, and blasting down the road is a waste of time and money. The higher you rev an engine, the better quality the parts have to be and the more carefully they have to be assembled. To build a stroked 2000cc engine that will perform reliably over 5500 rpm, you should plan on spending some serious money. As the sign in the machine shop reads: "Speed costs money. How fast do you want to go?"

In this hi-performance chapter we will examine ways to make modifications, like installing nonfactory carburetors without damaging other parts of your engine. And we will look at what modifications can be an unnecessary waste of time and money—like raising the compression, which makes a VW engine detonate and run hotter (if at all, on today's low octane pump gas).

Hi-performance demands more than the stock VW engine can handle. There are very few simple changes you can make to a VW engine that do more good than harm. Almost every hi-performance modification has to be balanced by strengthening a corresponding part. With cause and effect in mind, build the engine as a whole unit rather than piece it together thoughtlessly.

For instance, increasing the compression of your engine by modifying the cylinder heads and installing larger pistons and cylinders puts additional stress on the connecting rods, crankshaft, bearings, and the case—and creates more heat, the Volkswagen's worst enemy. Installing a high lift cam without modifying the carburetion, checking valve spring clearance, or porting the heads can waste your energy and your engine. Throughout this chapter, I mention these kinds of things to help you understand what happens when you meddle with the functional simplicity of the Volkswagen.

It pays to question an impulse to, for example, bolt on a power pulley without first considering how the modification will affect the rest of the engine. This is the sort of decision you'll have to make: a power pulley is smaller in diameter than the stock pulley so the cooling fan turns slower and the engine runs hotter. Whereas a lighter crankshaft pulley might give you faster acceleration, it neither dampens the crankshaft vibrations nor stores the centrifugal force that the heavier stock steel pulley does. Furthermore, the dampening effect of the stock pulley increases crankshaft and case life. However, the stored centrifugal force of the steel pulley helps when climbing hills and passing cars. Personally, I would never choose a power pulley, except in

Point Barrow, Alaska. For competition I'd choose the lighter aluminum pulley, but for day-to-day hi-performance, the choice is the stock steel pulley.

Most of us who just want to make our VeeWees go a little bit faster cannot afford a $60 set of connecting rods, so we have to use our wits and compromise between the precision-machined part and the cheapo rebuilt. The sensible decision is often somewhere in between.

There are plenty of suppliers around who thrive on people who love to spend money trying to make VWs go fast cheaply and easily. Reading ads for VW parts can be exciting as well as mind boggling. It's easy to make foolish, uninformed decisions and buy inexpensive parts, sight unseen, that promise impressive boosts in horsepower and give you that cool Cal-look. Be skeptical. Take time to weigh all your options and make a sensible choice, spending your money on parts that make a difference and won't wreck your engine. In short, hi-performance engine building takes lots of money, skill, and patience. If you lack any of these traits, think seriously about keeping your engine "bonestock" (i.e., in original condition).

Also, before you start, consider getting another vehicle or engine to use while you're assembling the mill of your dreams. The best engines are put together carefully without a lot of pressure on the builder. I am not an engineer, nor do I have the equipment to test all the products on the market. My suggestions come from a commonsense approach to hi-performance developed from practical experience and extensive research. I discuss mild to hot modifications that can be used for on- and off-road applications; however, the main focus is on durability coupled with performance for everyday street use.

Please read **Safety, Chapter I, Step 3** and remember the comparison between fast cars and loaded guns.

For now let's just agree that going fast in a car is fun. And let's imagine that you will have an exciting, hot VW and want to get out and goose it a bit. I assume that you have considered the laws: noise ordinances, emission standards, and, of course, speed limits.

I would like to thank Richard Jemtland for his patience, notes, and technical assistance, which got me through this project. And John Gaines of John's VW in Santa Fe, New Mexico—whose understanding of the Volkswagen is as deep as his concern for mankind. To Bill and Jerry at General Parts 2 in Albuquerque. And to John Muir, whose pioneering effort made this all possible. Special thanks to Barbara L. Daniels, my favorite editor and owl, and to Eve Muir, who really understands this book.

DECISION TIME

Money's a gas, not a trip.

—John Muir, *The Velvet Monkeywrench*

The first step to hi-performance is figuring out what you want and can afford. Read through this chapter and some of the other recommended publications (see list below) before deciding. You may conclude that a well-built, mildly modified engine is all you really need or can afford.

To blend power, durability, and reliability and not demolish your engine in 10,000 or 30,000 miles takes some common sense and plenty of bread. Rich Jemtland, who helped me write this chapter, recently built a 1678cc engine for his Ghia. He bought the parts wholesale, did the valve job and assembly himself, and spent over $1,000, which didn't include miscellaneous parts he had in his shop, like a Weber carburetor, an exhaust system, and oil filter assembly, to name a few. Rich did the very minimum necessary to make his 1600cc engine more powerful and reliable—he took plenty of time to check and recheck that everything fit together correctly. Despite all this, the engine still isn't built to turn more than 5500 rpm. In Rich's words, "It's Mickey Mouse" (our apologies to the venerable rodent).

I divide modifications into *Bolt-on* and *Major*. Bolt-on modifications involve components that can be installed while the engine is in the car, such as exhaust, cooling, and carburetion. Major modifications, those done while the engine is out of the car, come in two flavors: engine "top-end" work (cylinder heads, pistons and cylinders, and connecting rods) and "bottom-end" work (crankshaft and camshaft). The latter involves splitting the case.

I rate hi-performance engines like New Mexicans rate chili peppers: mild, medium, and hot. Below I mention engines that represent common sizes and degrees of modification, though I don't recommend any one size. I note these only to give you an idea of the bores and strokes that people typically select when modifying VW engines. These examples are meant to help you design an engine that best suits your desires.

Thirty-six-hp engines are not typically souped up for hi-performance but are restored bonestock. So the earliest VW engines I mention are 40 hp 1200cc. Note: 36 hp engines are also 1200cc—the same bore and stroke as the 40 hp but different.

Usually, the 40 hp engine is not an engine that is highly modified; therefore, I only mention it in passing. For serious building, start with a 1300, 1500, or 1600 engine. The 40 hp can be modified to a bigger bore by installing 83mm slip-in cylinders safely; however, since the 40 hp is single port, it is not the engine of choice. It can be beefed up for hi-performance by using a stroker or 69mm stock crankshaft, well-built heads, adequate carburetion, and possibly a hi-performance cam.

A mildly modified 1600cc dual port engine like the 1678cc that Rich built has an 88mm bore x 69mm (stock) stroke. When built correctly, that is, matched with the right heads, cam, and carburetion, this engine has good power and reliability. A popular medium-level engine is 1800cc with 88mm bore x 74mm stroke. For this engine the inside of the case has to be clearanced to fit a 74mm stroker crank. The big-bore 88mm cylinders slip into the case and heads without machine work. The problem with both of the setups is that the 88mm slip-in cylinders are considered too big because the cylinder walls are too thin. (However, 88mm machine-ins are reliable.) Also, the 74mm stroker crank for the 1800cc is expensive, and the case has to be clearanced to accommodate its longer stroke.

Another reliable, less expensive medium-range engine is the 1834cc (92mm x 69mm). In this motor the case is bored for the bigger cylinders, but the crank remains stock. The 1834cc can be a powerful economy engine. A larger bore gives better high RPM performance and the longer stroke gives better torque in the low end.

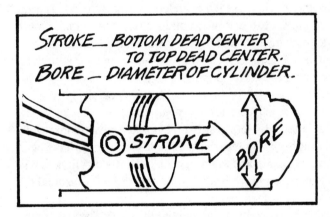

On the hot end of the scale is the 2300cc engine, which requires a lot of care and skill to build. This modification (94mm x 82mm) calls for some serious case and head machining. The case and heads have to be bored to fit the cylinders, and the case and cam have to be clearanced for the longer stroke crankshaft and connecting rods.

Maybe an 1834cc that is reliable and well built, with a new big-bored case, a balanced crankshaft, modified 041 heads, and some creative carburetion is all you decide you need or want.

Undoubtedly, you will have some questions after reading this chapter. Since every engine is different, you will do well to find a VW expert in your area, which brings me to the next point—opinions.

One builder may tell you never to reuse a case while another will tell you that it's all right to align-bore a case three times before junking it. However, most builders agree on the need to keep compression below 7-1 because high octane automotive fuel is a thing of the past. By reading this chapter you should glean enough theory to help you understand the controversies and make sensible choices for yourself. With this in mind, let's get into some hard-core shop talk.

COOLING AND OVERHEATING

Before spending time and money trying to make your VW go fast, you should make sure the engine will not burn up in the process. The VW is prone to overheating and practically every hi-performance modification makes the beast run hotter. It was not originally designed for racing but for utilitarian service. (See Chapter

XIX on History.) It's hard to imagine that the original 985cc, 25 hp engine built in 1935 is basically the same motor that people today soup up to 300 hp! The VeeWee's cousin, the air-cooled Porsche, was built for hi-performance. The Porsche is similar to the VW but much more precise in its design and construction. Attention to details like balanced parts, better combustion design, and stronger materials makes the Porsche what the VW is not.

Keep in mind that those German engineers who designed the air-cooled VW knew what they were doing. They built a vehicle that can take great abuse when maintained as a unified working system and although forgiving, has very tight limitations; the engine can only tolerate so much heat and wear. Protecting a VW from overheating means putting the cooling system right, at least making sure the system works as well as it did when it came from the factory. With the factory cooling system intact, you may be surprised that, in most cases, a VW engine runs cool even when rebuilt for hi-performance. Unfortunately, if the engine was reassembled carelessly or modified improperly, it will run too hot, no matter what you do.

The Volkswagen is cooled by air instead of water. The air-cooled four-cylinder VW may have suited Hitler's design for an engine that would not freeze in Stalingrad or boil over in Tunis, but for American climates a water-cooled engine is more practical.

To understand how a VW engine is cooled, it helps to consider why the air-cooled engine runs hot in the first place. Combustion inside the heads and cylinders creates most of the heat—as much as 4000° F. (The outside surface of the heads runs 225-325° F.) So the hottest parts of the engine are the cylinder heads, particularly around the exhaust valves. Because they are subjected to more heat, the exhaust valves are made of different metals than the intake valves. If the exhaust valves are too small in proportion to the intakes, or the compression ratios are too high—over 6.5:1, or the carburetors are jetted too lean, the cylinder head temperatures will skyrocket.

Friction, the next biggest source of heat, is combustion energy that is wasted (sacrificed) as the engine runs. In fact, most of the energy of gasoline is wasted as heat, friction, and noise rather than converted into the usable energy that powers you down the road.

The velocity of the movement of the pistons against the resistance of the cylinders creates tremendous heat. It is crucial that the pistons travel straight in their cylinders. If they don't, you lose power and make more unnecessary heat. Also, if the crankshaft is not parallel with the cylinder bores, the cylinders will not be perpendicular to the centerline of the crankshaft; consequently, the pistons cannot run straight in their cylinders. The same goes for the connecting rod journals and connecting rods. The journals should be machined to specifications and the rods straightened and balanced, or the engine will run hotter and less powerfully.

The cylinders, finned to radiate heat very efficiently, also help transfer heat away from the cylinder heads. The fins should be painted flat black to increase heat radiation. Big-bore (slip-in) cylinders have thinner walls than stock cylinders. The bigger the bore, the thinner the walls (unless the bore holes in the case have been machined oversize). Slip-in cylinders will warp if they are too big and too thin walled. Warped cylinders will make the pistons travel up and down unevenly, thus generating more heat. Moreover, if the fins around the cylinders become clogged with grease or even bits of litter, hot spots develop.

Energy is also lost at the wrist pins and at the connecting rod bearings, where the linear force from the pistons is converted to rotational torque by the crankshaft. The connecting rods act like levers attached to the crankshaft. More leverage and energy mean more heat.

Similarly, the camshaft makes heat as it moves the cam followers, pushrods, rocker arms, and valves against resistance from the cam bearings, rocker shafts, valve springs, and valve guides. Even the meshing of the camshaft and crankshaft gears makes heat as do the ends of the pushrods moving against the cam followers and rocker arms. All this pumping and churning creates heat that has to be removed or the engine will burn up and self-destruct.

Water-cooled engines have a radiator that removes the heat from liquid coolant after it has circulated around the cylinders and through the cylinder head picking up waste heat. Engine oil, while primarily a lubricant, also dissipates some heat as it passes through the oil cooler and splashes over the insides of the engine and returns to the sump. The air-cooled VW engine depends on air and oil equally to keep it cool.

Air Cooling: Air is sucked into the fan housing by a blower fan, which pushes the air through ducting inside the fan housing and over the heads and cylinders. Fresh air enters the engine compartment through louvers in the body or trunk lid.

Numerous sheet metal and rubber parts seal the edges of the engine against the body of the car. It is crucial that these pieces be kept intact. If the sheet metal piece that separates the front of the engine from the body is missing or fits poorly, hot air transferred from the transaxle will flow into the fan housing. If the apron or rubber seal that fits around the back of the engine is out of place or even ripped, heat from the exhaust system will raise the temperature in the engine compartment. The little deflectors that fit between and under the cylinders and all the other sheet metal protectors around the heads and cylinders are essential for proper cooling. The components most often overlooked, yet simplest to maintain, are the rubber sealing boots that fit around the spark plug caps and seal the cylinder shrouds (Part No. 111-905-449). If any or some of these boots are missing, bent, deteriorated, or otherwise mutilated, take the time to fix them before considering any hi-performance adjustments.

Too often people try to improve on the VW design and remove parts like the thermostat and the shutters that fit in the bottom of the fan housing. These parts help warm up the engine and keep it at a stable running temperature. While in extremely warm climates the removal of the thermostat team may not cause problems, in most of North America the system is essential. Any VW mechanic will tell you that removing the thermostat and shutters does more harm than good (unless you race at extremely high RPMs). The faster the engine warms up the better. Contrary to popular opinion, the flaps do not restrict airflow, nor do they fail unless improperly installed. Another common "improvement" people make is to add air scoops or carve extra louvers into the body or trunk lid or remove them altogether, hoping to improve air circulation in and out of the engine compartment. On the other extreme are the custom kit cars that have no engine compartment air ducts, which can be disastrous.

Rest assured that VW designed the cooling system using the world's best test equipment. John Muir said that his 1968 Bus ran hotter when the windows were open, because the airstream was disturbed as it swept over the vehicle. I used to notice that my 1957 Bug ran 10-20° F hotter when the sunroof was open. It's hard to believe, but even the shape of the stock oil cooler actually improves the flow of air around the engine.

A Baja Bug with a modified body will run cool enough if the engine is built properly and if the cooling system gets plenty of air. To assure this, creative desert rats make homemade ducts that enclose the front of the engine and have an inlet below the back window. This directs air into the fan housing. But to do it right, you have to be good at sheet metal work and allow for flexing at the seams.

The original louvers on the stock Bug work beautifully to catch air that flows over the roof. One modification that improves cooling is to replace the hardtop Bug engine lid with a convertible (rag top) lid with additional louvers. If you cannot find an early model convertible trunk lid, cut out a later model lid louver and weld it into your hardtop lid. This is definitely a good idea if you're running dual carbs, which suck more air than stock fuelers. Note: Older (oval and split window) bugs have bigger vents under the rear window.

John Muir also believed that some homemade vents on Bugs actually rob air by acting like vacuum tubes to suck air out of the engine compartment rather than pushing it in. To better understand this, consider that when cruising at 4000 rpm, the fan is drawing about 1250 cubic feet of air per minute. That, coupled with the amount of air drawn in by the carburetor(s), creates a negative pressure inside the engine compartment. The stock VW louvers are designed to provide an adequate air supply to the stock engine under all conditions. Elephant ear scoops used on pre-1968 Buses work well, as do the bolt-on scoops that fit over the louvers on Bugs. Unless you can empirically prove that a louver modification reduces the engine temperature under all conditions, leave things stock.

Oil Cooling: Engine oil plays a major role in keeping your VW alive. The stock VW oil cooler fits inside the fan housing, and the fan blows air past the cooler fins. On pre-1971 engines, heat from the oil cooler is dumped on No. 3 and No. 4 cylinders. In 1971, VW installed a fan that is 0.200″ wider than earlier versions; they also added a new doghouse cooler. This doghouse cooler is set back a bit by an adapter and thus cools the engine more effectively. Fortunately, you can easily install this very efficient system by putting in new seals, a used or new VW stock adapter, a doghouse cooler, and matching fan housing.

The later Type IV cooler has two extra rows of fins. The problem with the bigger, better Type IV cooler is that it is too big to fit under the sheet metal designed for the earlier doghouse cooler, so the sheet metal has to be modified, as does the firewall. If you build carefully, the larger cooler probably will not be necessary.

Well, what about a remote cooler? I think remote coolers are more trouble than they are worth. I agree with VW experts who believe that the stock cooler works better than the remote cooler when the engine is assembled properly. Furthermore, there are fewer leak points to worry about on the stock cooler. Many builders will defiantly prove by the gauge reading that the oil temperature drops when a remote cooler is installed in place of a stock cooler. This may be true. But I maintain that if you build a balanced and carefully assembled engine, the stock doghouse system is adequate. However, if you do install a remote cooler, do some research before buying and by all means keep the stock cooler in place. In colder climates remote coolers make the oil too cold, so a special thermostat is necessary to keep the engine within a safe temperature range to minimize wear and maximize efficiency.

Every surface of the VW engine is part of the cooling system. Even the fins cast into the bottom of the case take heat away from the oil sump. The valve covers serve to cool oil that is thrown from the end of the valve train. Note that the valve covers are painted flat black, as are the fan housing and the other sheet metal pieces. This makes sense, for black radiates heat more efficiently than any other color, including chrome. Chrome actually holds heat in. Keep this in mind when you feel an urge to buff out the engine with a lot of shiny bolt-on stuff.

The engine case is made of magnesium alloy not only for strength and lightness but also because the alloy handles heat well as long as the engine is not overheated. Look at a top quality aftermarket hi-performance case: you'll notice that the outside surface is a little rough or even anodized black to shed heat.

One point is worth repeating: there is no need to alter the factory stock cooling system if all the components are genuine VW (including the fan housing) and properly in place and working. If you think or know that the engine is running hot, take the time to find and correct the problem rather than adding on a remote cooler or body scoops.

Ignition timing and fuel mixture also affect engine temperature. If the timing is too advanced or too retarded, the engine will run too hot. The same goes for too lean or too rich fuel mixtures. A vacuum leak, a stuck choke, and incorrectly matched jets all affect fuel mixture, which in turn affects temperature and performance.

All the engine components from the crankshaft to the air cleaner, including the cooling system, should be assembled to work together as a balanced unit. When assembled correctly, using the right parts and techniques, the engine will gain horsepower and stay cool.

PUBLICATIONS

To help you play it cool and safe, not hot and perilous, here are some addresses of publications and suppliers who specialize in Volkswagen.

The most comprehensive book on serious hi-performance VW modification is *How to HOTROD VOLKSWAGEN ENGINES* by Bill Fisher (H.P. Books). For the latest, most up-to-date information, order Gene Berg's and Pauter Machine Company's catalogs. Berg and Pauter are big names in VW hi-performance, and their catalogs are full of technical information. To get the latest info on VW mania and an ample dose of bikini-clad exploitation, pick up a copy of *Dune Buggies and Hot VWs*. This magazine is an unabridged slice of contemporary Americana written in a style that Dick Fugett of *The Whole Earth Review* calls "neo-gonzo journalism." Reading these publications will give you an idea of the passion some people have for the VW and the expense and skill involved in sensible hi-performance modification. Above all, you'll learn about the variety of products that are available.

PUBLICATIONS
(See Chapter XIX for more.)

Dune Buggies and Hot VWs
P.O. Box 2260, Costa Mesa, CA 92628; subscription rates: one year, $17.97; two years, $31.97

How to HOTROD VOLKSWAGEN ENGINES
by Bill Fisher, H.P. Books, P.O. Box 5367, Tucson, AZ 85703, 602/888-2150

BAJA BUGS & BUGGIES
by Jeff Hibbard, H.P. Books, P.O. Box 5367, Tucson, AZ 85703, 602/888-2150

SUPPLIERS
(See Chapter XIX for more.)

Gene Berg
1125 North Lime Street, Orange, CA 92665, 714/998-7500

Mr. Bug, Inc.
P.O. Box 11728, Santa Ana, CA 92711, 714/633-1093, 633-1095

Bugpack
Dee Engineering, 3560 Cadillac Ave., Costa Mesa, CA 92626, 714/979-4990

CB Performance
28813 Farmersville Blvd., Farmersville, CA 93223, 800/CLAUDES, 252-8337

Pauter Machine Company, Inc.
367 Zenith Street, Chula Vista, CA 92011, 619/422-5384

Redline, Inc.
303 W. Artesia Blvd., Compton, CA 90224

SCAT Enterprises, Inc.
1400 Kingsdale Ave., P.O. Box 1220, Redondo Beach, CA 90278, 213/370-5501

Companies like Bugpack, Claude's Buggies, Mr. Bug, and SCAT sell through magazines and parts stores. The prices are often the same either way you buy. Most of the well-known VW parts suppliers sell catalogs by mail for a few bucks. These are great reading and are indispensable reference books. The better-known companies have been around for years and retain good reputations.

Usually the big suppliers pay a full-time technical advisor to field customer's questions, even though they may not advertise that service. Use their 800 numbers.

PART II: ENGINE IN VEHICLE MODIFICATIONS (Bolt-On)

TIRES AND WHEELS

Most VW frame and body builders start from the ground up. The tires and wheels get primary attention. Radial tires are a must; they drastically improve the Volkswagen's ability to turn and remain stable on all sorts of terrain. The VW comes stock with 15″ wheels (4½″ wide), and the stock tire size is 165-15. For all-around street use, 175-15 and 185-15 are popular, but 185s tend to flex on front wheels; 5½" wheels with 165-16 tires are a good choice. Unfortunately, wider tires for the VW are expensive, if you can even find them.

Really wide wheels are popular with the show cars crowd. Contrary to what many believe, wider tires do not give better traction. Traction is affected by the weight of the vehicle and how much the tire is displaced. Unless you are strictly interested in looks, stick to stock wheels and tires.

Stock VW wheels are steel and quite strong. For looks, some folks install spoked steel wheels, which I detest because most are junky and heavy. Aluminum wheels are the best but expensive and difficult to find in a pre-1968 five-bolt pattern. However, four-bolt aluminum wheels for 1968 and later cars are available. The lighter the wheels are, the lighter the unsprung weight. And that's good. The aftermarket also sells 14" wheels for VW. I prefer 15" wheels because they get better mileage. In the early 1970s, sport Bugs came with wheels like the ones installed on the Porsche 914. These are nice wheels but as rare as they are expensive.

SUSPENSION

Suspension modification is a superb way to improve the handling of your VW. First of all, get some good shocks. Gas shocks are plentiful and much less expensive these days than when John Muir was kicking around—at least on this planet. The best gas shocks are Bilsteins, but they do cost. KYB makes a good shock, as do other well-known manufacturers. Go for gas shocks no matter what.

The VW has sway bars in the front. You can buy heavy-duty ones in the aftermarket. Most kits come with instructions and all the hardware, but here's a tip from Rich. Use the stock bushings and clamps and drill them out to oversize, for example, 13mm to 19mm to fit the bigger diameter heavy-duty sway bar.

You can also get rear sway bar kits for both swing axle (pre-1969) and independent-rear-suspension (1969 and later) vehicles. For swing axle vehicles, you can also get the EMPI-designed compensator that eliminates swing axle tuck. Tuck happens when the wheel wants to pull in under the car on a turn. Whatever you do, follow the manufacturer's instructions to a T. Some people like to adjust the torsion bar and raise or lower the VW. Lowering the VW does not make it handle any better; in fact, it can make it more dangerous to drive. The same goes for raising it. If you change the torsion bar height, be sure to have the wheels realigned.

CARBURETOR AND FUEL SYSTEM

''Hey dude, check out my new carbs. I got 'em on sale through the magazine. They're 44 millimeter, you know, big, and they scream. Last night I dusted Ralph on the strip, but today my car sounds funky, and it's running real hot. Nice lookin' carbs, huh?''

Ah, huh. Sounds like another sucker who fell for the quick bolt-on fix. Maybe he dusted Ralph, but sales hype dusted him first. Also sounds like his motor got wasted by overcarburetion and a power-greedy foot. The science of carburetion is complex, but the basic principles for the VW are simple—keep the fire stoked to a comfortable rate of burn. The air-cooled engine is extremely sensitive to fuel/air ratio and ignition timing. If either is incorrect, the cylinder head temperature soars and detonation damages the pistons.

Very few carburetors that fit the VW can be removed from the manufacturer's box and put on the car and work without modification. In my experience, all carburetors are in need of rejetting to compensate for altitude, poor running, or overheating. VWs come from the factory carbureted for economy with single barrel downdraft carburetors.

Deciding on the best carburetor(s) for your needs depends mainly on the size of the engine and the camshaft. Bigger cams in engines with more CCs can handle more carburetion. If you are really serious about building a hot engine, get your parts (at least the carburetors) from a supplier who considers the whole engine. Tell him or her the type of cam, the stroke, size and shape of cylinder heads, the displacement, and compression ratio of your engine. (For a discussion of carbureted and fuel injected systems, see Chapter X.)

Carburetors come in two basic types: single and dual, which can be either 1- or 2-barrel (throat). The stock 1-barrel Solex carb bolts to one manifold that is shared by all the cylinders. Dual carbs have separate manifolds, one for each head, which is the most efficient way to get fuel to the combustion chamber. The single carb and manifold delivers fuel a lot less directly because the manifold curves and bends.

Two-barrel carburetors come in two styles: progressive and synchronous. Progressive means that the throttle plates open one after the other—primary barrel first, then secondary. Synchronous means that both throttle plates in both barrels open simultaneously. A 2-barrel, twin synchronous carb arrangement delivers fuel most efficiently, that is, so each cylinder gets fuel individually. Most 2-barrel carbs sold for VW twin carb setups are synchronous.

The old 28 PIC Solex carb—used on 36 hp VWs—was popular for Formula V racers who picked up horses by removing the 20 or 21.5mm venturi and rejetting and installing a larger venturi, or leaving the venturi out altogether. The venturi is the smooth-walled piece that you see when looking down the throat of the carburetor—engine not running, of course. The 28 PICT is used on the 40 hp engine. The main jet holder on the 28 PICT makes the main jet easily replaceable. The 30 and 34 PICT carbs (13/15/1600 engines) have a float bowl access bolt through which the main jet can be reached. The 34 PICT also has a removable venturi, but any modification must be done yourself. John Muir believed that automatic chokes were a product of a collective conspiracy by the auto manufacturers to make engines wear out so we would have to buy more cars and engines. Could be, John. I know from experience that wear is much worse when the choke malfunctions, which is not uncommon.

If you run a stock carb with the choke intact, make sure the choke unloads quickly. VW makes heating elements that unload at different rates. The 34 PICT is stock on dual port (DP) engines and can be installed on single port (SP), but the manifold hole may need to be enlarged to take advantage of the bigger carburetor. DP manifolds come in three pieces so they can be taken apart and matched with SP manifold ends or center sections designed for aftermarket carburetors. Adapters for 34 to 30 PICT manifolds are available for Brazilian-made Weber carburetors, but they have a poor reputation.

Carburetor icing is a big VW drawback. The heat riser helps warm the carburetor as long as the tube is not plugged with carbon. A heated manifold improves atomization and combustion of the fuel/air mixture. If possible, keep the preheat hoses attached to the air cleaner to warm incoming air. The icing problem is less severe if the carburetor is mounted close to the head, for example, shorter dual carb manifolds are used.

Modified stock and nonstock carburetors ought to be chosen with extreme care. Keep in mind that you are making a decision about the cooling system as well as the fuel system. The fuel/air ratio and the volume of that mixture determine the combustion temperature. Combustion is the major source of engine heat for the VW; therefore, it is crucial that the carburetion be tailored to the engine.

Most carburetor suppliers offer specific jetting information and other free technical assistance over the telephone or across the counter. Weber, for instance, has the *High Performance Master Catalog*, which has charts for VW applications and jetting.

The problem is that most carburetors that are jetted by the book run too rich or too lean, if they work at all. It usually takes a lot of persistence combined with trial and error to get smooth performance in the full RPM range. If the engine runs well, things must be cool. Nothing else to worry about. Right?

Well, maybe not. As Fueler Fichbeck, the Karb King, says, "To be hot is not always cool, running right and running cool are not necessarily mutual." It is impossible to guess what goes on in the combustion chamber. One way to find out is to install a cylinder head temperature sender and gauge as well as oil temperature and oil pressure gauges to monitor how jetting changes affect the engine temperature.

Next comes the trial-and-error method of jetting the carburetor(s), adjusting the ignition timing, and test driving to feel what gives the best performance at the coolest temperature, all the while keeping track of the gasoline consumption and watching the color of the exhaust at the tail pipe to determine the best jet, air bleed, and venturi combination. This is all very time-consuming but necessary if you want to accurately tailor the carburetor(s) to the engine. But there is still the unknown. What about the detonation that occurs out of our audible range? Pinging that we can't hear? This is where we have to gamble a little.

The combustion zone is the mystical realm where gasoline gets transformed into extreme heat. The power, heat, and pollution created by this energy exchange must be respected, which is one of the reasons that most hi-performance carburetors are not street legal by emissions standards. Radical modifications can play havoc with the engine as well as the atmosphere.

The popular but not preferred way to add horsepower is to install a single carb like the progressive 2-barrel such as a Holley Weber or a Weber 32/36 DFEV or a synchronous 40 DCNF. Any nonstock carb like this needs a special manifold center section that fits together with the stock manifold end castings. The problem with single carburetors is they don't deliver fuel to the cylinders equally. Certainly, the racer's choice is dual carbs.

The carbureted Type III came from the factory with dual 1-barrel Solex 32s. There have been many problems with these carburetors; however, most occurred after the throttle shafts had worn out or when mechanics could not synchronize them or both. The Type III was proof that dual carbs were great power boosters and economical, offering better mileage and performance for the same displacement as the Bug. Dual Solex 32 carburetors are currently being sold in kits.

Another option is the Kadron-Solex Brazilian dual carb kit. These 1-barrel carbs get great reviews. They can be matched with single and dual port engines. Make sure that jets and rebuilt parts are available from the supplier. Kadrons were designed with the VW in mind. Note: Solex 32 dual carbs need a balance tube between the manifolds to maintain even pressures for both idle and acceleration.

Of course, Weber offers a wide selection of carbs. The 34 ICT is a popular 1-barrel carburetor for dual carb setups on engines under 1800cc. Bigger engines need to breathe more, so they require bigger carbs with more barrels. The numbers 34 and 40 refer to the size of the carburetor throat, measured in millimeters. The amount of air that a carburetor consumes is rated in cubic feet per minute (CFM). It doesn't pay to bolt on an aftermarket carburetor that is bigger than the engine can handle, even if smaller venturis are installed. Check Weber's charts. Or contact Redline.

A large displacement engine runs better with 2-barrel dual carbs. A smaller displacement engine designed with a big cam and big valve heads also needs to breathe and can handle larger 2-barrel carbs. The Weber 40, 42, and 44 IDF and 48 IDA are the most popular synchronous 2-barrel models for on- and off-road vehicles. Gene Berg redrills and recircuits Weber 40, 42, and 44mm DCNF carbs to suit the Volkswagen's RPM performance range. Other suppliers sell the DCNF carbs, without the unique Berg modifications. For super hot monster engines, Weber offers a side draft 40 DCOE dual carb kit. Dellorto carburetors are nearly identical to Weber's, though cheaper. I have heard both good and bad reports about Dellortos.

Manifolds must fit the carburetor as well as the shape of the engine and the engine compartment. It is common for people to install the carburetor while the engine is out only to discover that it will not go back in because the carbs, manifolds, or both get in the way. Even an installation with the engine in the car can be a tight fit. If the supplier is honest and experienced, he or she ought to forewarn you of possible difficulties during installation.

Dedicated builders match-port the carburetors to the manifolds. They bolt the carb to the manifold and blend the edges around the join of the manifold and carburetor bores. They do the same for the head and manifold, while the head is disassembled. Obviously people interested in bolt-on instant power have no time to match the ports. Neither do inexperienced builders.

Installing the linkage is the biggest hassle when converting to dual carbs. The quality of the linkage varies from kit to kit. Whatever you do, be careful. Take great pains to avoid gas leaks and sticking throttles. Dual carbs have to be tuned, which involves synchronizing the carbs, as John describes in Chapter X, and setting the throttle cross bars by the supplier's instructions. The operation of the carburetor both at wide-open throttle (WOT) and return to idle has to be checked and rechecked. Don't cut corners. Insist that you get the right parts from the supplier.

Note: It is crucial that all VW carbs have 4" of fog area (stand off) above them. This is the distance between the top of the carburetor air horn and the inside top of the air cleaner that is necessary for atomization of fuel. Most kits nowadays have air cleaner arrangements that provide adequate stand off. Avoid kits with low profile air cleaners—at least for single carburetor applications.

Fuel pumps—I have always kept the stock mechanical fuel pump in my VWs rather than using electric pumps. The mechanical pump delivers enough fuel for any hi-performance engine, keeps pressure on the distributor drive gear, and does not rob horsepower.

OIL: FILTERS, COOLERS, AND LUBRICATION

As mentioned in COOLING AND OVERHEATING, the oil system plays an integral role in hi-performance. Oil is not only essential for lubrication, it also helps cool the engine. Clean oil decreases wear. So think cool and clean. This section deals with how to improve your VW's chances of survival without robbing horsepower. The parts covered are oil, oil filters, oil coolers, oil pumps, oil pressure valves, and gauges (temperature and pressure).

Oil: Asking people what kind of oil they use is like asking what beer they drink. If you asked me, I would point to a barrel of Valvoline 15W-40 sitting in the corner of my shop. But I would also tell you that I put non-detergent (20wt) in a new engine, and sometimes I use straight 30wt after the engine has been broken in. It all depends on the temperature, condition of the engine, and how it is driven.

Thicker is not always better, even when it's hot. Parts fit together tightly in a new engine, so lighter viscosity (thinner) oil works better. As the engine gets sloppier and/or the temperature gets hotter, a heavier oil may be all right. I never use 50wt and only use 40wt in a multi-viscosity oil like 10W-40 or 15W-40. At any time other than during the summer, 10W-30, 30wt, and 20wt (detergent) are fine for any climate. After the second oil change (post-rebuild), I switch to detergent oil. The key is to install temperature and pressure gauges and tailor the oil to your engine and driving needs.

Oil Filter: I do not know why VW never installed an oil filter on the early air-cooled engine. One rumor has it that VW engineers believed that the oil bath air cleaner cleans intake air so well that the engine oil doesn't get contaminated. Whatever, there is no better addition one can put on a VW engine than a full-flow oil filter.

Note: There is a difference between a full-flow and bypass oil filter. Bypass filters are plumbed from the oil pressure sender hole. They are seldom sold anymore and definitely are not worth installing. (Some catalogs call full-flow types ''bypass,'' so don't be confused.)

The types commonly sold and easiest to install are full-flow filters that are built in combination with an oil pump; the oil pump is replaced with the modified version, which reroutes the oil through the filter. These

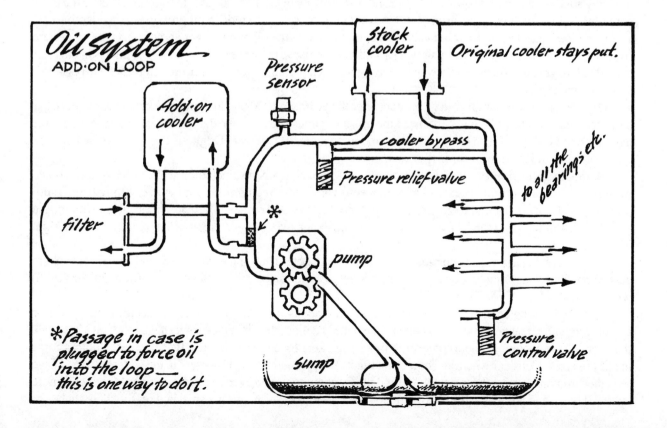

require no special machining and are simply installed. The drawback with these combinations is that you have to buy them with a high volume (high pressure) oil pump, which may not be the best kind to use (see **Oil Pump and Relief Valves** below). Depending on the shape of the engine case, part of the casting may interfere with the filter assembly. The offending portion can be safely cut off with a hacksaw to make room for the full-flow filter. Usually these full-flow filters come with idiot-proof instructions.

If installed properly, a remote oil filter works well. It also helps cool oil, so where it is mounted makes a difference. In the early days, builders blocked off the outlet in the body of the oil pump and routed the pressurized oil out a fitting, through a hose, and into a remote filter attachment. The filtered oil was then piped into the case through an oil passage that is plugged at the factory after the case is machined.

Today remote filter kits are sold which include a pump cover made for a remote fitting, hoses to and from the filter mount, hardware to install the mount, and a fitting to install in the case. The case has to be disassembled to install the inlet fitting, then thoroughly cleaned after all machining is done. Some machine shops weld special adapters to the case to accommodate the fitting. Ask the machinist to drill and tap the case to fit the size fitting as needed.

If you install a remote filter, mount it, on the Bug, under the engine close to where the bumper bolts so it will not be damaged. On a Bus, secure the filter assembly on the engine mount or on brackets attached to the chassis. Be sure you get enough hose to reach from the pump to the mount and back to the case. Mount the filter with replacement in mind, that is, keep it accessible. Use rubber grommets around any holes cut through the engine compartment, for it must be sealed to keep the engine cool and to protect the hose.

Neoprene hose is commonly supplied with lower-priced kits that have barbed fittings and hose clamps. The better kits have stainless steel covered, braided hose with ends that accept SAE flare fittings, which are a dream to use. Follow the manufacturer's instructions carefully. Use as few fittings as possible and keep the sizes uniform to avoid leakage. Before running an engine with a new filter, fill the filter with oil and install it. Crank the engine with the starter (coil wire disconnected and grounded) until the oil pressure light goes out.

Oberg makes the world's best oil filters and probably the most expensive. Oberg filters come with instructions, and the assemblies can be swapped from car to car with adapters. They really clean oil and are environmentally sound—no more throwaway filters and fewer oil changes. The Oberg filter does not reduce the pressure of the oil as the oil passes through it. Conventional oil filters do reduce oil pressures considerably.

Gene Berg has designed a relief valve cover that replaces the oil pump cover and protects the oil system from excess pressure. The valve cover works well to keep pump pressure steady and is helpful in systems that explode oil filters and upset the relief valves due to too much pressure. (See **Oil Pump and Relief Valves** below for more about pressure.)

Oil Cooler: VW has improved its product over the years. In 1970 the dual pressure relief case with larger passages came out. In 1971 they introduced the offset doghouse cooler. The dual relief valve doghouse engine has a fan with more fins than earlier models, and its fan is 0.200″ wider. Doghouse coolers can be installed on any engine and are a must for hi-performance.

To modify an engine for a doghouse, you need a host of components, including seals, offset adapter, bolts, washers, cooler, fan shroud, fan, and miscellaneous tin work. I recommend buying everything from a supplier who sells OEM original German equipment, not aftermarket copies. There is a noticeable difference in the quality. Buying from the VW dealer may be more expensive, but you are assured of getting all the right items in one stop.

If you are using a pre-1971 nondoghouse cooler, take note: 1969 and earlier cases and coolers have 8mm case to cooler holes. Later engines have 10mm holes. Earlier 8mm cases will accept a 10mm cooler (1970) with special seals; ask your VW supplier.

Remote Oil Cooler: a big area of controversy. I do not use remote coolers. If you decide to use a remote cooler, remember that larger tubes do not provide better cooling; the oil in the center of the tube stays hot while the outside gets cooled. Remote coolers are money-makers for the aftermarket. Be selective. Coolers come in various sizes. Consider where and how to mount it. People mount remote coolers in the oddest places. I have seen them mounted above the transaxle, behind the front bumper, and even under the engine. More hose, more hassle. The best location is in an airstream, somewhere the cooler won't get smashed by rocks, branches or punks. Whatever, do not mount a cooler in the engine compartment.

Most remote cooler kits use an adapter block that takes the place of the stock cooler; the oil is routed through the adapter to the remote cooler and back to the adapter. I recommend that if you install a remote cooler system, keep the stock cooler in place. CB sells a nifty oil pump and cover called the Maxi-pump. This has an inlet and outlet at the pump. Another alternative is to have the case tapped and fitted for a remote filter (and cooler). Route the oil from the pump to the remote cooler, then to the filter and back to the case. This procedure gives you the advantage of two coolers plus the filter. If a remote cooler and/or filter is installed, the crankcase will need more oil. The supplier can tell you how much.

If you live or travel where it gets the slightest bit cold, install a thermostat in your remote cooler system. Some thermostats on the market pass oil to the cooler even when they are supposed to be shut. Get instructions from your supplier on how to install the thermostat and cooler. If you build an engine using the right parts and techniques (new case, good heads, low compression, etc.), you probably don't need more than a stock doghouse cooler. But if you use an align-bored case, poorly matched heads, high compression, and careless assembly techniques, a remote cooler in addition to the stock cooler and a high pressure/volume oil pump might help keep the temperature at an acceptable level. Every engine is different, as is every driver.

Oil Pump and Relief Valves: Another area of controversy. Is bigger better? I must confess that I have mixed feelings about big oil pumps. If the engine is built right, stock pumps work just fine; VW engineers designed the pumps to deliver more than 150 psi. Even if your gauge only reads 30-70 psi the pressure is higher elsewhere in the system, for example, at the main bearings where there is a constriction. VW designed the engine to cruise at 28 psi or better when warm. The oil light comes on at 3-7 psi, which is too low even at idle.

Low pressure on your gauge probably indicates a loss of pressure or overheating somewhere in the engine, rather than a situation caused by too small a pump. If a remote cooler is installed or the engine is really sloppy or runs too hot, more pressure and volume may be necessary.

High volume, high pressure pumps can actually rob horsepower and starve the bearings for oil. More pressure means more energy to turn the pump gears. The holes in the case are designed for a stock pressure/volume pump. The dual relief case has a control valve in the rear that directs oil to the cooler when the oil temperature rises and the pressure drops. Cold, thick oil bypasses the cooler. The relief valve at the front of the engine dumps oil back into the sump. Too much pressure can override the control and relief valve springs and make dangerous things happen; for example, the oil is not routed to the cooler and/or the bearings are starved.

To compensate for the extra pressure, people install heavy-duty relief springs, which often explode the oil filter or the case plugs and cause the coolers to leak. Before messing with high-pressure this and heavy-duty that, study the lubrication system diagram in the VW service manual and think about it.

Single relief engines have one valve to control both functions of control and relief. The stock size of the oil pump in this engine is 21mm. The size of the pump in the later dual relief engine is 26mm. Heavy-duty pumps commonly are 27, 30, 32, or 35.5mm.

High pressure relief valves and springs are available but not necessary if the rest of the system is in good shape. Adjustable-type relief valves are also available and give super gauge readings. An adjustable relief valve lets you regulate the pressure at which the oil is dumped back into the sump, which puts back pressure on the system and forces more oil through the bearings, and so forth. Such a valve can also cause the control valve not to pass oil to the cooler. So to be safe, builders put a heavy-duty spring in the control valve. If you want to experiment and install an adjustable relief valve, be careful and start with it set at low pressure and do not jack up the pressure too high.

Remember—build a good engine from the ground up and you will not need to add on extra junk to cover the mistakes.

Gauges—Temperature and Pressure: Both temperature and pressure gauges are a must for a VW. Oil temperature should stay below 225° F (180-220° F is ideal). A dipstick-type sender works splendidly coupled with a good quality gauge. You have to wire from the engine to the dashboard. Buy a kit that includes a warning light.

An oil pressure gauge is another must. The simplest kit to install is one that has a sender that threads into the stock oil pressure sender hole. Two wires connect the sender, one for the gauge and one for an idiot light.

Don't use Teflon tape on the threads, only a little sealant. Gauges come in varying qualities. Buy a name brand gauge that is guaranteed to be accurate. Temperature and pressure gauges can really bum you out on a hot day, when the temperature is up, pressure is down, especially at idle. These vital signs are the best means available to protect an engine that so dearly depends on coolness.

Oil Sump: The oil sump has been a popular VW bolt-on since the early 1960s. Don't be fooled into thinking that more oil means cooler oil. It isn't so. In reality, more oil makes for slower warm-ups. A sump can offer some added cooling if it is designed with the right amount of surface area to dissipate heat. A sump protects sharp turning VeeWees from oil starvation. Unfortunately, a sump requires adequate ground clearance. Cheap sumps are chumps, so buy from a manufacturer that guarantees its product.

EXHAUST SYSTEM

Installing an extractor exhaust on a VW is the easiest and safest way to increase horsepower and reduce heat. It is not enough to cram a healthy dose of fuel and air into the engine hoping to produce great power. The exhaust gas needs a way to exit as smoothly as the intake mixture enters and burns.

Like the rest of the VW, the stock exhaust system works well to a point, but a header works better. An extractor is a pleasant addition to a stock engine and essential for any kind of hi-performance engine. Big valves and dual carbs are a waste of time unless teamed with exhaust pipes of a larger diameter than stock. Installing larger pipes means that the heater boxes have to be removed and "J" pipes installed along with a matching muffler.

Extractor exhausts are designed for free flow and minimal restriction. Restriction is caused by sharp angles and obstructions in the system. To avoid this, headers are designed to curve gracefully toward the muffler.

A quality exhaust system is designed to maximize power and minimize heat. Most experts agree that a collector-type header works better than individual stacks. In this section I talk only about collective systems—the ones in which the four exhaust header pipes come together at a collective flange and attach to a common muffler. Most extractors sold are collector types.

The selection and variety of extractor/mufflers is mind-boggling. Check out Bugpack or a Mr. Bug catalog to get an idea of the differences. Obviously, the quality varies. Fortunately, the header design for street VWs is fairly standard, so you can trust that most brand name headers will work. What you don't know is how well the thing fits—how easy it is to put on—until installation time.

Most systems are two-piece, some are three-piece, some are one-piece. I like a two-piece system with an easily replaceable muffler and well-fitting header. I suggest that you buy a brand name system so that replacement parts are easy to get. If possible, buy one that has the fresh-air tubes welded to it so they won't rattle and will provide good heat. If you have a preheat hose on your air cleaner, make sure that the header system has a like fitting.

Which style and brand you choose depends on your needs. A dune buggy system has no body restrictions so a Tee-Pee type extractor will work with or without a muffler. Nonmufflers that look like horns are called stingers and are noisy. Race cars and buggies don't have heater boxes so the header assembly can be one-piece all the way forward to No. 3 and No. 1 cylinders. Without heater boxes the pipe diameter can be bigger too. The ideal extractor system has equal length pipes with few bends.

"J" pipes, also called heater box replacement pipes, give better flow than standard stock pipes that go through heater boxes. "J" pipes are available in every size starting from stock (1⅜"). Big "J" pipe sizes available are 1½", 1⅝", 1¾", and a massive 1^{70}_8". If you plan to use dual carburetors and big valves, consider a larger than stock diameter exhaust. It is impossible to suggest one without knowing the specific engine and application.

Obviously, the muffler affects free flow and restriction. Again the selection can be confusing. Four-tipped systems are attractive but noisy. Glaspack mufflers are the most popular muffler design, although some are noisier than others. The Quiet Power, or "QP" muffler, is the quietest and has good flow characteristics. I like quiet mufflers. I dislike the sound of loud Volksies almost as much as two-cycle dirt bikes and chainsaws. Before hooking up the system to a stock single carb, drill or punch out the heat riser holes. On most extractors, these are closed off. You will need an installation gasket kit and some anti-seize compound to use on all threads and fittings. The fresh-air tubes can be troublesome, too. If your carb doesn't have fixed fresh-air sleeves, good luck. To do a clean job, get two 3 ft. pieces of fresh air heater hose, long enough to work without being stretched excessively.

IGNITION, TIMING, DISTRIBUTORS, AND 6 TO 12 VOLT CONVERSION

John has a good rap on timing in Chapter X, which will give you an idea of how important correct timing is to the VW. Initially, you should set your timing with a static light the way John explains. Once the engine is running, check the total advance with a timing light and degree wheel (degree ring). Ask the parts supplier to order a degree wheel for you from Bugpack or Mr. Bug. Follow the instructions in Chapter X on stroboscopic timing.

Total advance should never exceed 35 degrees. Thirty-two degrees is considered the best and safest total advance, and 28 degrees is considered tame. Timing goes hand in hand with carburetion, compression, and how well the engine breathes and burns fuel. You can experiment with timing, but be careful; always check the total advance against the timing at idle. Listen for pinging at acceleration; if you hear it, retard the timing before driving a mile farther.

The Bosch 009 is the most popular hi-performance distributor worth considering. Don't waste time and money messing with dual point distributors or other models made by Bosch. The 009 has it all. Distributors are rated and classified by how they advance through the RPM or advance curve. The 009 has the best curve for most needs. To install the centrifugal advance 009, the vacuum pipes on the side of the carburetor where the hose is attached to the vacuum advance will have to be plugged with a rubber cap or piece of hose and a screw. Another popular distributor was installed on 1974 Federal Type Is with vacuum and centrifugal advance. This distributor has a long curve for retarded timing to start the engine and advance timing for the full RPM range.

Imagine that you set the total advance at 2500-3000 rpm at 32 degrees, the timing should return to the static setting with the 009 centrifugal distributor. On vacuum advance distributors, the timing at idle will be advanced—ahead of the static setting, unless the carburetor is a 34 PICT, which has an air bypass in the throttle plate. **See Changes and New Ideas.**

Electronic ignition does nothing spectacular for hi-performance under 8500 rpm. Nor does it retard the timing of the No. 3 cylinder. The advantages of an electronic ignition are that it holds a consistent dwell and is relatively maintenance-free, unlike points. There are good aftermarket electronic ignition units available for various prices. Buy a name brand that has been in business for a while with a local parts source.

For years Bosch sold the Blue Coil in the screamer kit. There is no noticeable advantage to this coil, when compared to the stock coil, other than its cool looks. Nowadays the Blue Coil is the replacement normally sold. There is also the Red Coil for real hot screamers—can you handle the hype?

Spark plug wires and resistors cause many problems for people who do not like to maintain such things. John explains how to use an ohmmeter and check plug wires and resistors in a few simple steps that should be part of regular maintenance. While you inspect the resistors, check the rubber sealing boots and the rest of the seals around the engine. These are essential for proper cooling efficiency. Bosch copper-core spark plug wires are the best and most available wires sold.

If you are interested in learning more about secondary ignition and capacitive discharge secondary plug wires, contact Nology (see Parts Suppliers list in Chapter XIX for address and phone).

Spark plugs are a real conversation piece. The best plug for street purposes is made by Bosch or NGK. A Bosch plug is what the factory installs and recommends for the VW engine. The recommended heat range is the best available for almost any street use. Avoid the fancy platinum plugs or any other brands. Believe me, the stock product works best.

Colder plugs, made by Bosch and NGK, are also available. Cold plugs are recommended for racing engines with higher compression and Bus engines that struggle with more weight. They also should be used in engines that do hard climbing for extended periods. Ask your supplier for the colder Bosch 175TI or 225TI. For the Bug, get a W7BC extended tip; otherwise stick with the stock 145TI, W8A, or W8AC.

   Convert a 6-Volt System to a 12-Volt System: This conversion is necessary if a 1967 and later flywheel or whole engine is installed in a pre-1967 vehicle. Twelve-volt kits are commonly available. These kits include an alternator, a regulator, a stand, a backplate, and an alternator strap. Most kits have instructions, including a wiring diagram. You can also get a 12-volt generator instead of an alternator from a wrecking yard along with all the other parts, but it's easier to get a kit. The advantage of an alternator is that it charges at lower RPMs. You will also probably have to change the fan belt size.

   Along with the parts mentioned above, you will need to replace the battery, the bulbs (headlights, taillights, dash lights, etc.), the coil, the choke element, and the flasher relays. And you will have to install a resistor for the wiper motor. The 6-volt starter works well in the 12-volt system. A new adapter bushing will have to be installed. Most people stick with the 6-volt starter.

ROCKER ASSEMBLY AND PUSHRODS

The rocker assembly consists of the rocker shaft, rocker stands, rockers, adjustment studs and nuts, and miscellaneous washers and clips. The valves, valve springs, and rocker arms live and work between the combustion chamber and the valve cover at the farthest reaches of the engine. It is hard to imagine that these little troopers can generate much heat or rob usable power, but they do. The valve springs have to be compressed to operate the valves, which move in the valve guides where heat is generated. Heat and wear also result from the motion of the rockers moving on their shafts.

   Volkswagen makes four kinds of rockers of different ratios (1:1, 1.1:1, 1.3:1, and 1.25:1). 40 hp engines have 1:1 ratio rockers, 13/15/1600 engines have 1.1:1 ratio, and 17/18/2000 (Type IV) engines have 1.3:1 ratio rockers. VW also makes a 1.25:1 ratio rocker.

   A 1:1 ratio only opens the valve as much as the pushrod moves the rocker. The 1.1:1 ratio rocker opens the valve 10% more, the 1.25 opens it 25% more, and so on. Ratio rockers change the geometry of the valve train dramatically, not just at the pushrod and valve but at the cam and cam follower too.

   Cams are built to match ratio rockers. Read the camshaft literature and ask the supplier which ratio works best with which cam. Aftermarket rockers come in 1.1:1, 1.4:1, 1.45:1, 1.5:1, 1.54:1, and 1.65:1.

   Valve train geometry is complicated. The lift and ramp angle of the cam are ground to match the ratio of the rocker. As the ratio increases, the mechanical advantage of the rocker improves, thus putting more load on the cam and followers and smoothing out the movement throughout the valve train. Ratio rockers generally run quieter and improve all around performance.

   Does your engine merit ratio rockers? If the heads have big valves matched with big carburetors, the

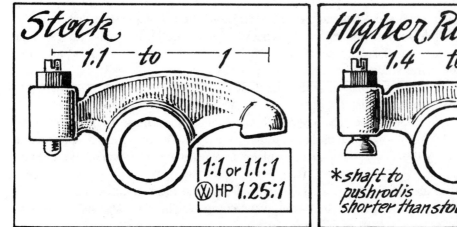
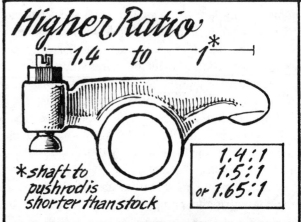

answer is yes. Ratio rockers open the valves farther. A stock cam can support rockers up to 1.4:1 and improve performance if the carburetor(s), heads, and exhaust are suited for the improved breathing. Any ratio greater than 1.4:1 needs a different cam and plenty of support to breathe properly. Also, the valve spring retainer is moved closer to the valve guide, and the valve spring is compressed further.

I recommend that you keep ratios under 1.4:1 and buy quality rockers, not ones that require steel pushrods. Forged VW factory-made rockers are good quality, so use them for comparison. Aftermarket suppliers sell rockers and shafts in sets or alone—the quality varies. The August 1988 edition of *Dune Buggies and Hot VWs* has a riveting article about rockers with pictures of some hot sets.

Some rockers have replaceable brass bushings. Other more expensive rockers have needle bearings. Super hi-performance, high dollar assemblies look like rockers on American cars. Some people argue that roller bearings are designed for parts that rotate continually, such as transmission shafts, but not for reciprocating parts like rocker arms. However, I know people who have run needle-bearing rockers for years without a stitch of trouble.

Heavy-duty rocker shafts are also sold with matching rockers. VW shafts wear well but will flex at higher RPMs. For street use stock shafts are adequate. If you want to build a super strong engine, go for the heavy-duty, more expensive shafts. At any rate, always disassemble and inspect the rocker shaft. Remove the little wire keepers on the ends of the shaft and keep the washers in order. Look for scratches, pitting, and any irregularity in the shaft or bushing. Wiggle the rocker back and forth on the shaft. Some play is necessary but not much. If the shaft is worn on one side, turn it 180° to get a fresh surface. If you are installing new or rebuilt rockers and the shaft is at all worn, consider a new shaft. Builders often use flat shim washers instead of the wavy washers. The flat ones come in thicknesses of 0.015, 0.030, and 0.060″. Replace rocker assembly components in sets—both heads. Consult your machinist if in doubt.

Stock VW pushrods are made from aluminum and have removable steel tips. I would not use aftermarket chrome moly and carbon fiber rods, even for racing; they do not expand at the same rate as the rest of the engine.

Make sure all eight pushrods are straight. If the stroke of the engine is increased, the rods have to be remade to compensate for the longer distance between the cam follower and the rocker. A careful builder of any hi-performance engine checks pushrod length and tailor-makes pushrods. You can easily make an adjustable pushrod tool. To learn how, see the following illustration and read the section on the valve train in Bill Fisher's *How to HOTROD VOLKSWAGEN ENGINES*.

Old Pushrod

ADJUSTABLE PUSHROD TOOL — Threaded hole & bolt to fit.

After installing the rocker assembly, check each rocker and valve to make sure that when the valve is at half-lift (halfway open), the rocker is aligned at the center of the valve stem. Position all the adjuster studs so 2½ threads (not inches) emerge from top of the rocker. Rotate the crankshaft until one of the valves is halfway open. At this point the tip of the adjuster should be in the center of the valve stem. If the tip is too high on the valve stem, you have to shim the rocker assembly stands away from the head; this situation occurs when the heads are moved closer to the case by flycutting. If the point of contact is too low, you may need to adjust the pushrod length. Shims for rocker shafts are usually available in 0.015, 0.030, and 0.060″. Valve stem (lash) caps, also available from various suppliers, are designed to fix worn valve stems and help increase the contact area. Some builders use them to change stem length. Also check that the rockers don't hit the valve covers, especially if the stands are shimmed or a high-lift cam is used. Whatever you do, try to keep things equal on all valves.

Adjuster studs take a lot of abuse. They are designed to hit the stem slightly off-center to spin the valve for even wear. Compare yours to a new stud and replace them if the tips are worn. Some aftermarket rockers have adjusters on the pushrod end and a rocking foot on the valve end. This high dollar rocker design is lighter than stock. A great invention is the elephant foot or swivel foot adjuster, which is designed to replace the stock adjuster and results in less wear on the valve stem. Not all swivel feet are alike, so shop for the best.

PART III: ENGINE MODIFICATIONS (Major)

PARTS AND MACHINE SHOP

The faster the engine turns, the more precise the fit of the parts must be. The measurements and tolerances that Volkswagen engineers consider acceptable will not win you hugs from the race queen. Machinists who build race engines understand that horsepower is gained by paying attention to details like carefully balanced and centered connecting rods, uniform valve seat angles, and the sharpness of the tool they use to align-bore the case. Quality machine work takes plenty of skill and intense concentration.

Volkswagen engine rebuilding is big business. Most used, reconditioned, bargain VW parts come from shops that rebuild strictly VW parts. Some of these outfits are factories, rebuilding thousands of cylinder heads, cases, and crankshafts annually. Under these conditions, you cannot expect a person to be precise when he or she does the same repetitive task all day for "piecework" wages. One careless move could sabotage your $1500 engine.

Unless you are certain of the skill of a general automotive machinist, have the machine work done by a shop that specializes in VWs—and expect to pay more for hi-performance quality work. Get quotes from the shop and compare them to the prices of machine work advertised in *Dune Buggies and Hot VWs*; finally, compare these to the prices listed in Gene Berg's or Pauter's catalog. The latter two companies are considered the kingpins in the industry. When you buy parts or services from Berg or Pauter, they offer free technical counseling to help you design and build an engine to your needs and ability.

Since the essence of hi-performance engine building lies as much in the quality of the machine work as it does in the quality of the parts, you have to trust that the person who does the work cares as much about the engine as you do, which is why I prefer dealing with local machinists, to whom I can talk in person. If working with a local VW machine shop and buying all the parts from one source (the best way to build an engine) is not possible, consider ordering the machined parts like heads and rods from a reputable company. Call their 800 numbers for details.

Here are some terms to help you talk with machinists.

Blueprinting is an art done by only the most skilled builders/machinists. It is a study of the relationships of the engine parts that focuses on making things fit together so they work efficiently and exactly. It entails measuring and calculating every aspect of the engine before and during assembly. Blueprinting requires precision instruments like a super flat table and all kinds of fancy micrometers, even X-ray machines. Blueprinters work in fully equipped machine shops and use lathes, presses, milling machines, and balancing equipment to build engines with extremely close tolerances. It is detailed, painstaking, and expensive work.

Shot-peening is a process used to "stress relieve" parts. Tiny pellets are blasted at the surface of the part to relax sections of the metal. Stress is caused when a part is machined, so shot-peening is highly recommended and sometimes done many times, once after each step of the machining process. It is common to shot-peen the case and connecting rods. If you're serious about hi-performance, employ a machinist who knows the technique.

Magnafluxing is a technique by which machinists check iron-based metals for cracks. Typically, the only parts in the VW engine that are magnafluxed are the crankshaft and connecting rods.

Cold-tanking is a cleaning process that removes the most tenacious grime and minute particles from parts. It is a technique that uses a vile chemical solution to clean magnesium parts such as the case. Cold-tanking should be done before and after all the machine work is done. Before you leave with your parts, ask the machinist how much cleaning you should do before assembling the engine.

Align-boring, clearancing, spigot-boring, resurfacing, and deep-studding are discussed in CRANKCASE. Crankshaft regrinding, balancing, connecting rod rebuilding, dowel drilling, and wedgemating are discussed in CRANKSHAFT. Valves, seats, and guides are covered in CYLINDER HEADS along with other cylinder head machine work, such as porting and polishing.

CRANKCASE (Bottom End)

Assembling a reliable engine is like building a sound house; you have to start with a sturdy foundation. The foundation of the VW engine is the crankcase, and this is where most inexperienced builders go wrong, so use a case that can support the parts you put into it.

The crankshaft is forged from heavy steel, and the cases in all VWs are cast from a lightweight magnesium alloy. The crankshaft rotates with tremendous force at thousands of RPMs and, although it rides on bearings, the case ultimately takes the brunt of the load. Magnesium is very sensitive to heat; in fact, it is flammable. I do not mean that your VW engine will ignite spontaneously, but the magnesium alloy case will be weakened by overheating from even moderate service. The thrashing that hi-performance modifications give an engine can drastically shorten the life of a used case, which is why VW agencies that do factory-authorized rebuilds always use new cases.

From 1961 on, the Bug and Bus used basically the same case, the one still being manufactured in Mexico today. In 1966, the shape of the case was changed in the Bug and called a 1300cc. It was produced for only one year (1966). Each car had a number plate on its trunk lid identifying it as a 1300. Pre-1966 (1200cc) engines have a 64mm stroke; 1966 and later engines have a 69mm stroke and a wider case. In addition, the crankshafts on 1967 and later engines have modified oil passages and a different flywheel.

In 1970, VW enlarged the oil passages and went to two oil relief valves (actually the rear one is a relief valve, and the front one is a control valve). When dual port cylinder heads were introduced in 1971, the 10mm cylinder head studs were replaced with 8mm studs. And a dished camshaft was installed (mid-1971) to accommodate a larger oil pump.

In 1975, VW started making cases from a better magnesium alloy—classified as AS21. You can tell if you have an AS21, instead of pre-1975 AS41, by looking for the AS21 cast markings on the bellhousing (front) or side of the case. According to the experts, AS21 is more stress and heat tolerant than AS41. Rumor has it that Roger Penske, the race car driver and designer, bought piles of these later Brazilian VW cases to smelt and recast for gear housings. Believe what you like, but most builders agree that AS21 retains its original structure and ability to shed heat better than the alloys VW used before 1975.

Two types of new bonestock VW cases are available: single and dual oil pressure relief valve. If you are assembling an engine with the nondoghouse cooler, get a single relief valve case for all purposes. For all other engines, buy a dual relief valve case.

Many parts dealers sell modified VW cases, new and rebuilt. Be sure to buy one of these from a reputable source and get a guarantee that the case is rebuildable. Aftermarket VW cases not made by VW come in a number of shapes and sizes, all with hefty price tags. If you want to go full race, consider getting one of these monster engine cases.

Modifications: You can stroke a 40 hp (1200cc) by installing a 1966 or later 69mm crankshaft, but the flywheel, pistons, rods, and cylinders have to be machined to fit the crankshaft and each other.

The 69mm stroke crankshaft uses the same bearings as the 40 hp as long as they match the align-bore, crank grind, and thrust thickness. The cam and crank gears also have to match (but this will be discussed later).

In the early 1970s, VW started using 8mm studs to replace the earlier 10mm studs, which have the reputation of pulling out of the case. You wouldn't think that 8mm studs could be stronger than 10mm studs, so why do it? Because the thinner studs expand more uniformly with the rest of the engine as it gets hot. The newer

8mm studded engines have case-savers already installed in the case. These case-savers are thin walled so there is plenty of room for boring larger cylinder holes. Note 40 hp People: If you plan to use a larger stroke crank, install longer 13/15/1600 studs.

If you are converting to dual port heads, you'll need shorter head studs, the two middle ones on the top row on each side. Ask your local machinist.

Now let's look at how the cylinders fit the case. In 1300cc (Bug) cases, the cylinder holes or spigots are the same size as in 1500 and 1600 cases; therefore, 1500 and 1600 pistons and cylinders can be installed without machining the 1300 spigots oversize. However, if you use a 1300 case, you'll either have to get the 1300 heads bored or install 1500 or 1600 single or dual port heads, because the top end of a 1300 cylinder is smaller than that on 1500 and 1600 heads. Note: Don't install 1300 big-bore 83mm pistons and cylinders (P&Cs) in a 1300cc case, for these cylinder walls are paper thin!

Big-bore kits for 1300, 1500, and 1600cc engines are typically sold in bore sizes up to 94mm. P&Cs (87 and 88mm) can be installed without machining the case and heads, but the cylinder walls are considered too thin on the 88mms to be reliable.

In later years VW "deep sank" the upper, forwardmost No. 3 upper head stud—to prevent the case from cracking behind No. 3 cylinder. Although this stud is the same length as the lower studs, when installed it sticks out the same amount as the other cylinder head studs. Keep in mind that the two center studs are shorter on a dual port case.

Type IV cases have bolts that go all the way through the case halves. These engines are similar in early and late 1700, 1800, and 2000cc models.

Type II 1968 and on and Type III and IV engines have rear hangers—a cross member at the rear of the engine with three points that bolt onto the engine. Note: The hanger interferes with an oil pump/filter add-on. Check with your parts supplier if Type II or III is your gig.

In Type III, the dipstick is attached to the filler tube at the rear of the engine. Most VW machine shops can modify your case to accept a Type I dipstick.

Universal cases come ready to install in any vehicle. The original Type I engines do not have fittings for a cross member. One way of mounting an engine that's not fitted for a rear hanger is to use a special mount that attaches to the oil pump bolts and provides a point of attachment for the cross member. As slick as this arrangement sounds, it is not recommended.

Be careful when swapping Porsche 914 and 411 and VW Type II cases because there are differences, for example, the fuel pump nut. And don't believe people who tell you that they have a Porsche engine or a two-liter VW engine. If necessary, dig through the engine grime to get at the serial number—with that any knowledgeable VW shop can tell you what the engine/case is. Note: Type IV engines are called Porsche engines by VW dealers and vice versa, so be ready for trouble.

Machine Work

Align-boring is a standard procedure used by VW rebuilders to enlarge the crankshaft bearing bores by 0.020″ (0.050mm) increments. Sixty thousandths (0.060″—0.150mm) is the maximum oversize to which a case can be safely align-bored.

Many builders refuse to align-bore cases, saying that it is impossible to do it precisely enough for conservative street use and certainly not for hi-performance. They claim that it is virtually impossible to machine the case straight and true using the kind of align-boring equipment that most VW machine shops have. In comparison, new VW cases are jigged and machined on more expensive, more precise machines than the portable types.

If the case is bored crooked, the crankshaft centerline will be out-of-true with the centerline of the case, which starts a wear pattern called case pounding. It also lets too much oil leak around the bearings, lowering the oil pressure. Furthermore, the connecting rods push the pistons at an offset, so they don't run straight in the cylinders. The results are lost power, lower oil pressure, and ultimately premature engine failure. This is probably why Volkswagen factory policy does not recommend align-boring.

An align-bored case costs about one-half of what a new Mexican case costs; German cases are no longer available for export. So naturally most people take a chance and go for an align-bored one. Unfortunately, you have no way of telling whether the case has ever been overheated or align-bored off-center until you install the crank pulley and it hits the case, or the engine leaks oil at both ends of the crankshaft, or the engine runs hot with low oil pressure. If you know the history of the engine to begin with, there is hope. At the end of this section I mention some things to check while disassembling the engine to give you a clue as to the condition of the case.

If you do have your case align-bored, don't confuse the crankshaft diameter with the align-bore size when shopping for parts. Ten thousandths (0.010″) **undersize** refers to a crankshaft diameter that is smaller than stock. Twenty thousandths (0.020″ — 0.50mm) **oversize** refers to the amount that the case has been align-bored. The main bearings have to match the crankshaft and the case.

Occasionally, the cam bore needs to be align-bored oversized; however, it is not recommended because of the likelihood of error, causing the cam and crank to turn on unequal centers and resulting in bad tracking. The exception is the 40 hp engine, which came from the factory without cam bearings and should have them installed. Usually rebuilt or new ''universal'' 40 hp engines will come fitted with cam-bearing saddles.

Speaking of cam bores, VWs were designed so only one of the cam-bearing insert halves has a thrust lip. Therefore, builders generally buy two sets of cam bearings and install a thrust bearing in each case half. Or, if possible, they buy from a supplier who sells sets of cam bearings that contain a double thrust bearing.

Ideally, the crankshaft and camshaft should be parallel with the rest of the case. For this to be true, the case has to be machined so the crank and cam bores are parallel to each other and to the mating surfaces of the case. This means that the surface on which the cylinders sit and the seam of the case have to be parallel to the crankshaft centerline. If they are, the pistons and rods will travel at perfect right angles to the crank just as they should. The higher the RPMs, the more important this geometric relationship.

It is also likely that the thrust-bearing surface of the case needs to be remachined. Crankshaft thrust is controlled by the No. 1 main bearing. If the case is worn, the machinist can cut the sides of the saddle to fit a +1 thrust bearing (22 is standard, 21 is oversized). There is only one oversized thrust-bearing size available. Some VW machine shops will machine off just enough case material to renew the surface, then cut a corresponding amount off the bearing. By following this procedure, the thrust surface on the case can be machined again.

The going price to enlarge the cylinder spigots for big-bore cylinders is $20-$40 and for heads $20-$30. With the enlarging accomplished, you can safely use larger cylinders that have thicker walls. To use 88, 90, and 90.5mm CIMA thick-walled and 92 or 94mm cylinders, the case and heads must be bored oversize.

The larger the oversize, the closer the perimeter of the cylinder hole is to the stud. Here lies a problem that is solved by careful machining and by using the smaller outer diameter case-savers.

All VW cases should have case-savers installed when the engine is apart. John recommends installing case-savers only in the lower cylinder head stud holes. Have it done to all the studs. Most new and rebuilt cases come fitted with case-savers already installed, but you should check and ask the machinist to install them if your case doesn't already have them. They come in three common sizes: 14.2mm x 10mm, 14.2 x 8mm, and, for big-bore applications, 12.75mm x 10mm. Volkswagen recommends something called Keen Serts. They work well for stock cylinders, but I don't use them. Check all the screw holes in the case for stripped threads and have them fixed, too.

Note: Studs can come loose on all VW engines, even those with case-savers, but especially so on 1969 Bus cases. Loose studs mean loose heads. When replacing studs, use only VW originals.

If your No. 3 top front cylinder stud is not deep-studded, have the machinist do that, too. Deep-studding sinks the left top, forwardmost stud deeper and strengthens the case.

To keep everything flat and aligned, careful builders resurface the sides of the case, the deck, and the place where the cylinders sit. They do this so the cylinders will bolt flat against the case and perpendicular to the centerline of the crankshaft. Of course, the cylinder studs have to be removed from the case for the machinist to get at the sides of the case.

VW cases are known to crack in front of No. 3 (and No. 1) cylinders. Some machine shops will weld a piece from another case at this point, as a precaution, to reinforce a sound case before it breaks. Some people claim that reinforcing a case is a waste of time and that it is better to put your energy into building a sturdy engine from the inside out. If you want to have the case reinforced, let a pro do it before any align-boring is done. Another weak point in the VW case is in front of No. 3 (and No. 1) cylinder, so for peaked-out engines, builders weld an angled stress plate between the No. 4 cylinder hole and the back of the case. This procedure also should be done by a pro.

If you have put a lot of money and care into the case, consider drilling out the oil passage plugs. This procedure allows you to flush the lubrication system thoroughly. The holes are then threaded and plugged. The rear hole can then be used as an oil return for the full-flow oil filter setup (see OIL: FILTERS, COOLERS, AND LUBRICATION).

Stroker clearancing is accomplished by cutting away parts where the stroker crankshaft, which has a wider arc, hits the case. Clearancing is not difficult, especially if you have a carbide cutter, but it takes a lot of time to do it right and not destroy the case. To clearance properly, you have to check and recheck the radial and axial movement of the crankshaft, by pushing the crank forward to check for clearance and then rotating it to see where it hits. There are good descriptions of how to clearance in Bill Fisher's book, in Gene Berg's *Book of Technical Articles*, and in the catalog of the Pauter Machine Company, Inc.

Sand seals are for off-roaders; they're designed to keep grit and moisture out of the case and oil in. The case has to be machined to fit a sand seal. Sand seals are also available for the rear of the crankshaft. The stock VW engine does not have a rear main seal, so the case has to be machined to accept a sand seal. If you are a serious off-roader, ask your machinist about sand seals.

After the machine work is done, the case should be shot-peened and stress-relieved if possible. It must be cold-tanked for a thorough cleaning.

Disassembly: When disassembling the case, instead of loosening the main bearing nuts that hold the case together, retorque them to 30 ft. lbs. and try to turn the crankshaft. If it doesn't turn or doesn't turn smoothly, the case has probably been overheated or align-bored before. After you split the case in half, inspect the mating surfaces for little lines called fret marks. These are evidence that the halves rubbed together while the engine was running. A case that never worked itself loose and was not rubbed will retain the original machined surface. A fretted case should be junked.

Assembly: The correct way to install cylinder head studs is by hand while the case is apart. If the stud is hard to install, clean out the hole with an 8mm x 1.25 tapping or chasing tool. Install each stud by screwing it fully into the case, then withdraw it two full turns. Put some blue Loctite on the threads and screw the stud back in until just two threads are exposed, then stop. Loctite will keep the stud from turning when you torque the head bolts.

Use washers under the 17mm nuts that hold the case together and coat them with a little silicon sealer. If you use special locking nuts, install them with the colored part away from the case. And before mating the case, make sure the rubber sealing ''O'' rings that fit around the studs are in place. For hi-performance street engines, torque the case nuts to 28-30 ft. lbs., using John's method (Chapter XV, Crankcase Assembly, Step 7). (See CRANKSHAFT and CAMSHAFT sections below for more about case assembly.)

CRANKSHAFT (Bottom End)

Nothing complements a new case like a well-machined and balanced crankshaft, the backbone of the engine, the part that twists and flexes the most. An out-of-balance crank plays havoc with the case and wastes energy, which means heat. New, genuine VW cranks do not always meet tolerance specifications for runout, roundness, and taper, and certainly not for balance, so the crankshaft and everything bolted to it should be balanced by a reputable machinist (or chiropractor).

Unlike the spine, the crankshaft is made of steel, not bone and cartilage; however, like the spine, which is surrounded by strong muscles, the crankshaft is supported by a rigid case. To withstand more than 5500 rpm plus and combustion pressures over one ton, the case and the crankshaft must be strong and well matched. The better the metals and construction, the better the parts are able to withstand hard use and abuse. To put things into perspective, consider that a stock VW is designed to handle a maximum of 5500 rpm for a very short period of time—that's more than 90 mph! Compare this to a race engine that's built to cook along at 8500 rpm—no sweat. If you plan to run at over 5000 rpm for more than just a few miles, consider investing in a high-quality, counterbalanced crankshaft.

Ultra hi-performance crankshafts cost $600 and up. These high-priced backbones barely resemble the stock, garden variety rebuilt VW crankshaft that costs around $30 to regrind. To understand the difference between the two, let's look at how they are made.

The stock VW crankshaft is forged from steel that is alloyed with chromium. The bearing, seal, and gear surfaces are machined and treated to a smooth finish. Although most hi-performance, big bucks cranks are forged, some are also machined out of steel billets, which are solid bars of steel. Forged cranks are shaped in dies by hammers and presses. For hi-performance, let's consider only forged crankshafts.

By the way, if you ever find a roller crank for sale that's in good condition, buy it. These are slicker than hair oil but are no longer made. The connecting rods are one-piece and assembled as part of the crankshaft; they were pressed onto the journals when the crank was assembled. Roller cranks are counterweighted and capable of extremely high RPMs. However, they aren't reputed to hold up to draglike starts. Richard, who helped me write this chapter, gets really depressed when he thinks about the new roller crank that he didn't buy a few years back. If anyone wants to make a Norwegian happy, send a roller crank to Richard Jemtland.

One way to understand the crankshaft is to compare it to a lever, which is what a crankshaft really is. Each crankpin or connecting rod throw is a lever. The farther the connecting rod throw is from the center of the crankshaft, the greater the leverage, and that's what powers you down the road. Not all of that energy reaches the end of the crankshaft, however, for some gets lost in friction and vibration. Friction causes heat, while vibration is caused by inertia and centrifugal force. Inertia is the resistance of an object to any alteration to its present state, whether moving or at rest. An example of inertia is the resistance the crankshaft exerts against the effort of the connecting rod to make it rotate. The crankshaft would rather sit still than spin. Another example of inertia is demonstrated by the main bearings and case, which keep the crankshaft contained as it rotates rather than let it fly off into space.

Centrifugal force is the energy created by the force of rotation. The flywheel is attached to the crankshaft and serves to maintain centrifugal force (i.e., power) that otherwise would be lost during the brief pauses between power stokes. The flywheel ensures a smooth flow of power. The crankshaft pulley also helps reduce vibration by absorbing some of the shivers and shakes that are transferred through the crankshaft. If the forces become too great and too fast and the crankshaft is too flimsy, the backbone will break. If the crankshaft and the parts attached to it are out of balance, the ensuing vibration will shorten the life of the engine. Remember, at the very least, the crankshaft and everything connected to it must be dynamically balanced by the machine shop or you are wasting your hi-performance money and possibly the engine, too.

The two main considerations when choosing a crankshaft are stroke and balance. Let's start with stroke.

Stroke: Stroke is the distance a piston travels in its cylinder. To stroke an engine means to increase this distance using a different crankshaft. Stroke is measured from the center of the connecting rod throw to the centerline of the crankshaft. A stroker engine is one that has a stroke that is longer than stock. The longer the stroke, the greater the leverage or torque an engine will have. A long stroke gives better low speed performance—off the line. Hi-performance builders calculate stroke to match cylinder bore. A bigger bore generally offers better high speed performance (more on bore in PISTONS AND CYLINDERS). Stock crankshafts can be stroked by adding metal to the connecting rod throws, then remachining the bearing surfaces.

Typically stroker cranks are also counterweighted, which is covered under **Balancing** below. I don't recommend using a stroker crank that has been remachined from a stock crankshaft unless you buy it from a reputable source. The best-quality stroker crankshafts are those that are forged to the longer stroke rather than remanufactured from stock cores.

The 40 hp crankshaft stroke is 64mm. The 13/15/1600 stock stroke is 69mm, so each piston in a stock 1600 engine travels 69mm. **See Changes and New Ideas.**

A 69mm crankshaft will fit into a 40 hp case without clearancing, but some rod and piston modification is necessary (see CONNECTING RODS for more). As I mention in the CRANKCASE section, the case has to be clearanced to fit a stroker crankshaft—one that is longer than the stock 69mm stroke. Stroker cranks come sized in 74, 78, 80, 82, 84, and a monstrous 86mm.

Things start getting complicated and expensive when you stroke a VW engine. In addition to clearancing the case, you have to modify the connecting rods and shim the cylinders as well as measure and cut the pushrods to length and make other valve train adjustments. Furthermore, you may have to tailor the sheet metal to fit around the cylinders and heads because they will be located farther from the case when the cylinders are shimmed. So unless you plan to spend big bucks, forget stroking and look for horsepower elsewhere, for example, big bore pistons and cylinders, balanced and matched connecting rods, a counterbalanced crank, and big valve cylinder heads.

In a hi-performance engine, the connecting rods must be chosen as carefully as the crankshaft. Before ordering a crankshaft, select the rods to match the crankpin journals. (There is more on this in CONNECTING RODS.)

Eight Pinning: Back in the early 1960s when VWs began blowing away Chevys, hi-performance builders found a weak point in the VW power train—the link between the crankshaft and flywheel. To cure this, builders drilled four additional holes in the flywheel and crankshaft to strengthen the union with eight dowel pins instead of four, a procedure that is commonly called ''eight pinning.'' Most VW machine shops are equipped to do eight pinning, and many aftermarket crankshafts come drilled for eight pins. Make sure that your flywheel matches the pin pattern on the crank. Ask whether the pattern is equal spacing or SPG offset and if the dowel hole diameter is 8mm (standard) or 11/16" or 23/64" (oversize). Be sure to have the machinist deburr the holes so the flywheel will bolt flush against the crank.

Later, as horsepower increased and a stronger mate was needed, the ''wedgemate'' design was developed. **Wedgemating** involves precision machining the front edge of the crankshaft at a bevel (angle) and machining the flywheel at the exact same angle. Wedgemating increases the contact surface between the crankshaft and flywheel. For street use, eight pinning is sufficient.

Gland Nut: A VW rebuild should include a new gland nut to secure the flywheel and to pilot the transmission input shaft. Most big name VW parts suppliers sell chrome moly gland nuts that can be torqued to 265-290 ft. lbs. rather than the specified 217 ft. lbs. These special gland nuts usually come with a wider, precision-machined, flat washer that distributes the tightness of the nut over a broader area. At least install a bigger washer and, if possible, a chrome moly nut (not just chrome plated). Use red Loctite on the gland nut threads. Some aftermarket gland nuts have heads that are so big they interfere with clutch operation. Better quality nuts have thinner heads but retain their strength.

Balancing: Balance means two things: (1) keeping things like cylinder displacements and valve openings equal and (2) keeping things like the connecting rod, crankshaft, and flywheel weights even. Number 2 pertains to the inertia of the flywheel, and that's what we're concerned with here. Early in automotive history designers recognized the need to counterweight crankshafts. Counterweights help balance out the forces put on the crankshaft, reduce crankshaft flexing, and strengthen the shaft. The stock VW crankshaft is not really counterweighted, so it is not stout enough for hi-performance. It is a relatively short crankshaft and subject to flexing and vibration. The flywheel and crank pulley weigh as much as they do to help minimize crankshaft flexing and vibration.

You can buy special counterweights and have them welded onto a stock crankshaft, or you can buy crankshafts that are already modified from stock or shafts that are forged with counterweights. The latter are superior and more expensive.

You can buy a counterweighted crank for under $100, but weight—no wait. As always, cheaper is not better. Spend $175-$300 and get a good counterweighted crankshaft from a reputable supplier. The less expensive cranks tend to vibrate and break. If possible, install a counterweighted crank and make sure to get it balanced. Keep reading!

A cheaper alternative is to use a stock crankshaft and have it balanced along with the flywheel, clutch, connecting rods, pistons, and pulley. The dynamic balancing of an engine correctly means doing everything in sequence. It involves putting the crankshaft (and gears) on a spring-mounted cradle and spinning the shaft, then adding or removing weight. Once the shaft is balanced, the flywheel and then the clutch are bolted on and balanced. Finally, the pulley is added and balanced. The connecting rods and pistons are weighed and balanced statically, apart from the crankshaft. Ask your machinist if he or she can balance your engine this way—and pay the extra expense. It's worth it.

Crankshaft Oiling: Connecting rod bearings are lubricated in two ways. Pre-1968 crankshafts have one oil hole for the lubrication of each connecting rod bearing; 1968 and later "F" cranks have two oil holes per connecting rod journal with a diagonal groove cut across the face of each hole. These are called directional oil grooves, and they improve lubrication. A single hole crankshaft that has not already been modified can be easily grooved by a machinist.

Most aftermarket rebuilt cranks have been modified, but ask before you buy. Some high dollar cranks have removable plugs that allow you to clean out the oil passages inside the crankshaft. Plug or no plugs, the oil passages should be cleaned out with pipe cleaners and compressed air before the crank is installed.

Assembly: Use John's procedure to install the crankshaft and assemble the case, but be super careful. Don't let the connecting rods bang against the cylinder holes in the case, for steel is harder than magnesium. Make sure the bearings are well seated in the case and take your time at every step. Put the engine together at least once without sealing the case to make certain that the crankshaft rotates smoothly. I recommend reading Bill Fisher's chapter on assembly in *How to HOTROD VOLKSWAGEN ENGINES* and using the VW factory service manual, as well as this book, thinking through each move you make. When the time comes to set the crankshaft end play, set it on the tight side, between 0.003″ and 0.005″; 0.006″ is the wear limit.

Parts: Check that the main bearings you buy are the right sizes (not misboxed) and that they match the crankshaft diameter and the bore size of the case, especially if it has been align-bored.

Flywheel and Clutch: Before 1967, VWs had 6-volt electrical systems. In 1967, all VWs got the 12-volt charge. The flywheels on these engines are different. The 40 hp and 1300cc (6-volt) flywheels are a smaller diameter and thickness than 15/1600cc (12-volt) flywheels. The front (flywheel) end of the crankshaft is recessed farther to accept the thicker 12-volt flywheel. So when using a 1500 and later 69mm crankshaft, add a matching recessed flywheel or machine your crank to accept the smaller flywheel.

In 1967, the clutch also changed from a 180mm to a 200mm in all vehicles. And in late 1971 the 200mm clutch was modified. These are referred to as early and late 200mm clutches and are not interchangeable because the late style complements a sleeve over the tranny input shaft on the 1971 and later Bugs. The 200mm clutch is obviously preferred for hi-performance. If you want to convert to a 200mm clutch but have a 40 hp or 1300 engine, consider a late 6-volt Bus flywheel (1963-66) that has all the 6-volt characteristics with a 200mm clutch. Of course, the pressure plate and disk also have to be 200mm. If you convert from 6-volt to 12-volt, see IGNITION AND 6 TO 12 VOLT CONVERSION for details.

Since 12-volt flywheels are larger than 6-volt, the 6-volt transaxle bellhousing will have to be clearanced or the engine won't fit. Some people do this by installing the engine until the flywheel hits the transaxle. They then crank the engine using the rear pulley bolt. The flywheel teeth contacting the bellhousing mark the place the housing has to be clearanced and ground away. Most people, however, use the quick and crude method of installing two engine/tranny bolts and tightening them until the flywheel hits the case. They then crank the engine by hand while gradually tightening the bolts, drawing the engine and transaxle together as the flywheel grinds away the housing. Unfortunately, this doesn't always work so some further hand grinding with the engine removed might be necessary. A method you may hear about but one that I do not recommend because it's dangerous: they tighten the bolts until the flywheel almost hits the housing and the transmission input shaft and clutch are splined. Using the ignition key they start the engine and let it do the grinding as they gradually draw the engine and transaxle together with the bolts. I prefer the first method.

Lightened flywheels are popular for engines that don't need the momentum that a heavy flywheel provides. Lightened flywheels are typically 12 to 12.5 lbs. For street use I prefer keeping the flywheel stock. Clutch pressure plates come rated in three ways: stock 1200-1300 pounds per sq. in. (psi), heavy-duty 1700 psi, and racing 2300-2500 psi. The racing clutch is recommended for engines over 200 hp. For street purposes, the heavy-duty clutch will do. Ask your supplier which throw-out bearing you need to match the transaxle and pressure plate.

Clutch disks are sold sprung and unsprung for different uses. The composition of the friction material also affects the way the clutch wears and how it responds when applied. Unless you plan on doing wheelies or racing, stick with the heavy-duty sprung disk and stay away from trick disks.

Worn transmission mounts are often the cause of a symptom referred to as clutch chatter. Transaxle mounts are inexpensive and easy to replace while the engine is out. For street applications, use stock rubber or urethane mounts. Off-roaders like to use solid mounts and transaxle straps. Ask your supplier what is available.

CAMSHAFT AND FOLLOWERS (Bottom End)

Hi-performance people get excited about certain cars that idle roughly, identifying them as having hot cams—rumpaty, rumpaty, rumpaty at the traffic light. Camshafts or ''lumpsticks'' can get pretty exotic. The selection is endless. Camshafts are built and sold for every driving need imaginable from mild to wild, which is why inexperienced VW builders get into trouble when experimenting with wild cams. Too often they would have been wiser to install a stock cam instead of a hot one. When building a street machine, a hi-performance cam is one of the last things you should consider adding.

There is no perfect camshaft, one that's designed for every driver. Consider what you want to do with your car. Question your fantasies, those cravings to race, race, and race some more (unless, of course, that is all you plan to do with the car). For instance, what if this is your only car and when you give Granny a ride to the senior center, imagine how she'll feel when you have to keep the revs above 3000 rpm to keep the engine running? Will she be comfortable bouncing around as the engine idles at a traffic light? Have some consideration for the old soul.

For reasons like this, many hi-performance builders decide to install a stock 1600 camshaft and put their ''soup-up'' money into high ratio rockers or modified dual port heads. Remember, the camshaft is not a part that is easily changed. If you are not pleased with its performance, the engine has to be completely disassembled to change the cam. It behooves you to be conservative.

Lift, duration, and ramp are words used to rate and differentiate cams. Lift is how far the valve gets pushed into the combustion chamber. If the carburetor, intake manifolds, and heads are properly matched and capable of supplying enough fuel/air mixture, a hi-lift cam can give the engine more horsepower.

Duration is the length of time the valve stays open; it is measured in degrees of crankshaft rotation. Hi-lift cams typically have longer duration than stock cams. Like higher lift, longer duration is not effective unless the other engine components can supply the adequate fuel/air mixture, use it efficiently, and exhaust it properly. The logical conclusion is that you should install a nonstock cam along with other hi-performance components as part of a total hi-performance package.

For comparison, a 1600cc stock camshaft matched with 1.1:1 rockers has an intake valve lift of 0.322"—that's mild. A full-blown dragster using 1.65:1 hi-ratio rocker arms might have a cam with an intake valve lift of 0.680"— that's hot. The intake valve duration of a stock 1600 cam is 2240, while a dragster cam might have a duration of 3340.

Ramp, the angle or slope of the cam, determines how fast the valve opens and closes. A gentle ramp opens the valve sooner, more gradually. A steeper slope opens the valve more quickly. Ramp is rarely mentioned in cam advertisements. I only mention it because cam manufacturers use different ramp angles, and it is a term often used in articles about hi-performance. Ramp is something to consider in advanced level hi-performance theory and extreme high speed practice.

Higher lift, longer duration cams perform better at high speeds, not so well at idle and low speeds. Fuel inertia, lift, and duration combined with proper breathing can improve high speed performance. Other factors like the pushrod length and rocker arm ratio radically affect the lift and duration as well. If you don't match and measure all the valve train components, there can be disastrous results. Cams are rated by lift. The advertisement will tell you the specifications, which should cover whether the cam is matched with 1:1 or 1.1:1 stock rocker arms, or with hi-ratio 1.4, 1.5, or 1.65:1 rockers. There is more on this in ROCKER ASSEMBLY.

Valve Overlap: Before deciding what camshaft or valve train parts to buy, take a moment to consider valve overlap. Peter's drawing in Chapter II shows the four cycles: intake, compression, power, and exhaust. Although these are the basic operations of a four-cycle engine, some details are added in the drawing below.

Valve overlap *(is necessary for a smooth operation.)*

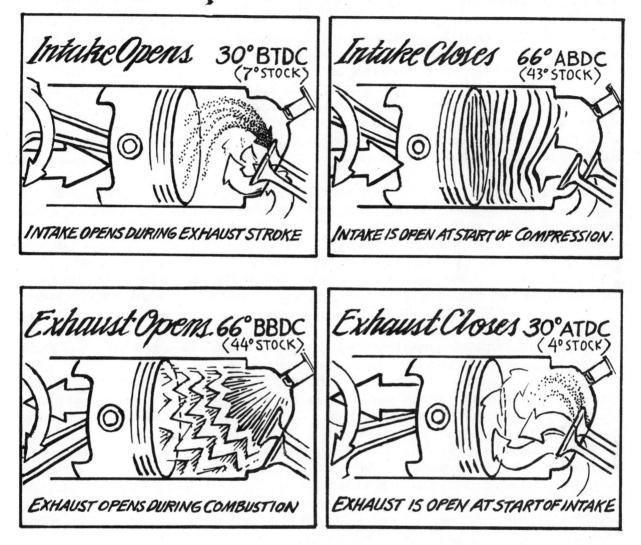

Intake Opens 30° BTDC (7° STOCK)

INTAKE OPENS DURING EXHAUST STROKE

Intake Closes 66° ABDC (43° STOCK)

INTAKE IS OPEN AT START OF COMPRESSION.

Exhaust Opens 66° BBDC (44° STOCK)

EXHAUST OPENS DURING COMBUSTION

Exhaust Closes 30° ATDC (4° STOCK)

EXHAUST IS OPEN AT START OF INTAKE

Theoretically, the intake valve should open exactly when the piston is at Top Dead Center (TDC) between the exhaust and intake strokes. Likewise, the exhaust valve should open at exactly Bottom Dead Center (BDC) between the power and exhaust strokes. And both valves should be closed during the compression and power strokes.

What actually happens is that both valves overlap. They are open at the same time momentarily. Here's how it works. Imagine the piston traveling down the cylinder on the intake stroke, sucking in a healthy amount of fuel/air mixture from the carburetor and drawing it through the intake manifold at a rapid rate. The moving mixture has inertia. Suddenly the piston reaches the bottom of its downstroke and has to change direction. This change is not instantaneous though; the connecting rod has to make an arc as the crankshaft swings around. The piston stands still for a few degrees of crankshaft rotation before starting back up the cylinder. Meanwhile, the intake mixture is still rushing into the cylinder. The piston starts back up, and the mixture begins to slow down, but it still has some inertia.

Okay, now let's go back and see what the valve does. The intake valve opens slightly before TDC, while the piston is still traveling up on its exhaust stroke, and the open exhaust valve is just about to close (this is overlap). The escaping exhaust gases create a negative pressure that helps draw the fuel/air mixture into the cylinder. As the piston travels past TDC at the top of its exhaust stroke and begins its downward stroke, the intake valve continues to open. It remains open during the full intake downstroke. (The exhaust valve closes early in the intake [down] stroke.)

The intake valve stays open while the piston rests momentarily at the bottom of its stroke, as the crankshaft arcs past BDC. In fact, the intake valve stays open for part of the upward (compression) stroke, until it finally closes. The length of time the valve stays open is called duration.

Cam duration is calculated in crankshaft degrees. For example, the valve opens Before Top Dead Center (BTDC) at 30°, remains open through the complete intake stroke (180°), and is open for some of the compression stroke (66° ABDC), which completes the total duration of 276°. These figures are roughly the degrees of intake valve duration for a mild hi-performance 13/15/1600 VW cam with stock rockers.

The exhaust valve first opens BBDC on the power stroke (66° BBDC), remains open for the complete exhaust stroke (180°), and for part of the intake stroke (30° ATDC). The total exhaust valve duration is thus 276°.

Most camshafts are rated and tagged by intake duration; the exhaust figures may not be given. Either way, these numbers can be deceptive. You really need to know the "effective duration," which is measured with the valve slightly off its seat, usually 0.040 or 0.050″, because tests show that nothing flows "effectively" past the valve until it is more than 0.050″ off its seat. (This also applies to a closing valve, for the flow stops before the valve is completely closed.) Remember, in hi-performance every single detail counts.

The faster the engine rotates, the greater the inertia of the fuel/air mixture. Stock VW carburetors, manifolds, and heads are designed for utilitarian, stingy performance and budget. John Muir is reported to have said to poet Lawrence Ferlinghetti, who was passing out from overstimulation during a party in Mexico, "breathe man breathe." Your wee VeeWee also has to breathe more when it gets overly stimulated. As well as helping the engine run better, proper breathing helps keep things cool. If you want to be hot, you'll have to build the engine to breathe better than it was designed to breathe.

The camshaft controls how fast and for how long the valves open, like breathing in and out. Ahh! Sounds like an easy way to get free horsepower: install a hot cam. But wait, first consider the rest of the valve train. The cam followers (lifters), pushrods, rocker assembly, valve springs, keepers, and valves are all affected by the cam grind, that is, the shape of the cam lobes.

When a higher lift cam is installed, the valves are opened farther and maybe even faster. The valve retainer will often hit the valve guide, so valve guide length, rocker stand height, and pushrod length have to be checked and modified. The adjuster studs might even hit the valve cover if pushed too far. When building an engine for high speed, even using stock parts, the valve train should be closely observed and measured by rotating the crankshaft by hand many times while watching the parts of the valve train operate, with the engine still on the stand.

If you use a hi-lift camshaft without properly matching it with the rest of the valve train, you're asking for problems—one of them being heat. If the rockers get pushed too far, the valve springs will bind or even break. If the rockers are not matched with the valves, valve springs, pushrods, and the camshaft, the geometry of the valve train will be off, resulting in wear on the rocker shafts, incorrect valve opening, and wasted energy. When you consider that the valves and rockers are the parts of the engine that get the least amount of oil, putting them together correctly makes sense.

In summary, a hot camshaft only works well if matched with the right carburetor(s) and manifold(s), carefully modified heads and cylinders, an exhaust header, and proper assembly techniques. If you install a hot cam, keep it mild. Since a cam has to be tailored to the engine, it is impossible to suggest one cam that works well for all purposes. In an engine with stock rockers and a single carb, keep the duration between 274° to 284° and the lift 0.0383″ to 0.0435″. These numbers do not increase concurrently; they affect low end and high end performance differently. Ask your supplier for the final word.

Assembly: Read CAM GEAR for details on matching the cam gear to the case. Read CRANKCASE for machining.

Cam Followers: Stock VW cam followers are still the racer's choice. Although some cam manufacturers require using their nonstock alloy lifters to warranty their cams, most hi-performance builders use the stock item.

Cam followers are not flat. The surface that contacts the cam is convex. The cam follower bore is offset from the center of the cam lobe so the lifter rotates as the cam pushes against it. This position evens out the wear on both the follower and the lobe.

I recommend using new cam followers and a new cam for every rebuild. When assembling the engine, check that the follower does not hit the case when the high point of the lobe is touching the follower. Install the cam (and bearings) and followers into one side of the case. Insert a pushrod against the follower to push it firmly against the lobe. When the high point of the lobe is touching the follower, measure between the case and the underside of the follower. There should be at least 0.040″ at the point where the follower fits into the case. Check all the followers on both sides of the case. Some machine shops counterbore or reface the follower holes in the case to accommodate the increased lift of a hi-lift cam. Others may machine the followers to lower the profile at the underside of the follower. Just make sure that there is enough clearance for your followers. If not, consult the machinist.

CAM GEAR (Bottom End)

Originally, Volkswagens came from the factory with two types of camshafts— flat and dished. Flat means that the back of the cam is flush with the outside of the gear; this style was installed in engines up to mid-1971 and in earlier single and dual oil pressure relief models. Dished means that the cam gear is recessed to accommodate a larger, deeper oil pump; this type was installed in mid-1971 and later engines with larger oil pumps, dual relief valves, and enlarged oil passages. Both styles have cam gears riveted to the camshaft: flat ones have three rivets, while dished ones have four rivets. Hi-performance, nonstock cams have removable gears that are attached by three bolts.

Aftermarket hi-performance cams are flat, meaning that only early 1971 and earlier oil pumps or pumps designed for flat aftermarket cams will fit. Ask your supplier for the right pump to match the cam and gear you buy (see OIL: FILTERS, COOLERS, AND LUBRICATION).

Back when Muldoon had his shop in Carson City, VW cam gears were commonly available in fifteen sizes, numbered +1 through +7 and -1 through -7 and 0. Now the gears are commonly available in only seven sizes, +1 through +3 and -1 through -3 and 0. The reason there are so many gears is that all crankcases do not have the same crank and camshaft centerlines, as a result of machining variations. So VW makes gears with teeth that have different pitch lines (pitch determines where the gear teeth meet). Here lies a gray area of VW mechanics, where everyone has a different opinion.

The 0 gear has no number stamped on the back of it. Zero is the gear size most often sold, but that does not mean that most engines are made for 0 gears. As John suggests in Chapter XV, replace the cam gear with a gear that is the same number as the one removed. Typically, zero gears are installed when the builder doesn't know which size the case should have. If possible, when you disassemble the engine record the number of the gear you remove.

How can you be sure that this gear is the same number as the gear that was installed at the factory? It may not be the original if the engine was rebuilt. Furthermore, after a case has been align-bored it is nearly impossible to match accurately the gear to the case unless the backlash between the gears is checked. The gray area gets darker.

Hi-performance builders choose gears by feel. They match the gear to the case, using methods that are mastered by practice. One method is to rotate the crank and cam while noting whether the cam lifts up or pushes back too much or too little. An experienced builder can tell if the backlash is correct by feeling and watching the radial and axial movement of the shaft. Unless you are sure of the correct cam gear for your engine, ask the machinist to check the backlash and match the cam for you. Or send for Gene Berg's *Book of Technical Articles*, the GB 801-SET from Gene Berg Enterprises, and read ''GB 801-CAM.''

Most hi-performance camshafts come drilled and tapped for bolt-on gears. Adjustable cam gears are also available but more complicated to use. An adjustable gear lets you dial in the correct cam timing while building the engine so the valves will open at the precise moment (read in degrees) specified by the cam design (grind).

After the engine has been driven and tested, the valve timing can be tailored for performance. The oil pump can be easily removed to gain access to the cam gear to advance or retard the valve timing. Variations of a few degrees affect engine performance, so precision builders like to use adjustable cam gears.

To check valve timing properly during assembly (called indexing), you need a dial indicator and some other attachments. I again recommend Gene Berg's article, ''801-CAM,'' for details.

Also available are straight cut cam gears that make more noise than helical-toothed stock gears, so they are not recommended for street use. Straight cut gears add horsepower and diminish loads on the cam and crank.

Note: I have a friend who bought a cam and gear from CB. There were no instructions included so my friend installed the gear randomly. He didn't realize that the cam gear had to match up with the cam in a certain way; usually a dot on the gear aligns with the slot in the cam shaft. If you use a bolt-on gear, also look for instructions or call the supplier.

PISTONS AND CYLINDERS (Top End)

The easiest way to add horsepower to a VW—if the engine is out of the car—is to install big-bore pistons and cylinders (P&Cs). But first you should ask if it is worth it—can the engine handle the extra power, and if so, what are its limits? Installing big-bore P&Cs and increasing compression can be disastrous. Today's 85 octane gasoline barely supports much more than 6.5:1 compression, and octane boosters don't help. This does not mean that you shouldn't go big bore. It simply means that you have got to pay attention to compression or you will find yourself dealing with running problems and overheating. When rebuild time comes around, most Vee-Wee owners try to squeeze the most cubes (CCs) possible out of the engine by installing big-bore slip-ins. This makes sense as long as they don't go crazy and install sets that are too big-bore.

A well-built fresh engine should be able to handle the biggest bore slip-in P&Cs available. Anything bigger than slip-in 83mm (40 hp), 85.5mm (1300), and 87mm (15/1600) P&Cs will require that the heads and case be bored oversize. The size of the displacement should match the strength of the rest of the engine. Sounds familiar, huh?

If you're simply adding big-bore P&Cs to your stock engine, keep things conservative. Either way, put your money into quality first, then cubes. P&Cs that you can slip in without machine work are available in the following sizes: Stock—1200 (40 hp)-77mm, 1300-77mm, 1500-84mm, 1600-85.5mm; Slip-in—40 hp-83mm, 1300-85.5, 1500 and 1600-87mm (88mm, not recommended). I don't recommend using slip-in 88mm P&Cs because the walls are too thin. Keep reading.

Machine-in Big-Bore Kits: Big-bore kits are also available in 88mm, 90mm, 90.5mm, 92mm, 94mm, and ''dearly beloved we are gathered here today.'' The case and heads must be machined to accommodate these cylinders because the outside diameter (OD) of these cylinders is larger than stock. Boring a case and cylinder heads is no big deal for a shop set up for VW machine work. Machining is necessary because cylinder walls get thinner as the bore increases. Machine-in big-bore sizes are limited by the cylinder head studs. Because the 92mm barrels have very thin walls, CIMA manufactures 90.5mm barrels that have the same OD as 92mm barrels—a reasonable idea that also increases durability. The current leader in piston and cylinder kits is CIMA,

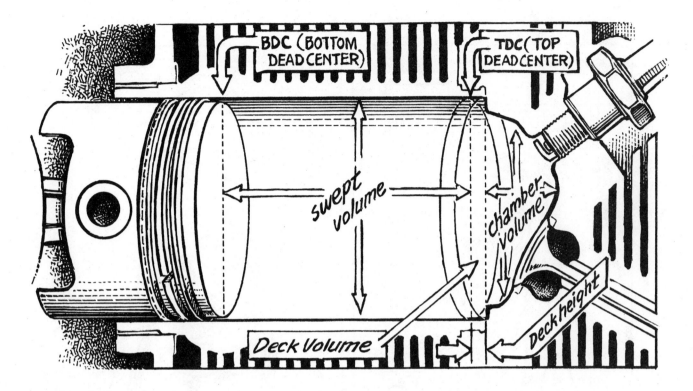

a Brazilian company. Two famous German makers are Kolbenschmidt and Mahle. Super spendy, race forged aluminum pistons are also available, but I won't discuss them here.

All this big-bore stuff sounds great, but there's a snag. When the case is cut oversize to fit the larger cylinders, necessary metal around the cylinder studs (and case-savers) is whittled away. The edge of the hole ends up dangerously close to or hits the cylinder studs (see CRANKCASE for more on studs).

40 hp: The most impressive bolt-on horsepower boost can be made to a 40 hp engine. Using slip-in P&Cs, the displacement can be raised from a humble 1192cc to a whopping 1384cc. However, it's a pain to modify a 40 hp engine for hi-performance and hardly worth it, which is why most people routinely and successfully install slip-in 83mm P&Cs and stop at that. However, the 40 hp case is strong and accepts a 69mm crank without modification (in fact, Pauter Machine manufactures a 60mm stroke crank for the 40 hp case). To install a 69mm crank, you must machine the 40 hp rods because they are thicker in the big end than later rods and have to be narrowed by 0.040″- 0.020″ on each side.

There are other things that people do to 40 hp engines, but I don't discuss these options here. If you are serious about hi-performance, consider canning your 40 hp for a 1600 or keeping the 40 hp case and building the rest of the engine with 1600 parts including dual port heads (40 hp heads are not real screamers).

Everyone: Remember that in hi-performance, there is always a trade-off. This is especially true when it comes to increasing displacement. For example, VW cylinder heads are held in place with studs that are mounted in a case made of magnesium alloy. This alloy is lightweight, dissipates and transfers heat well, and is good for cooling, but it is not the strongest metal around. When you increase the compression and combustion pressures, more force is put on the heads and likewise the studs, which would love to pull out of the soft case. It is easy to make the mistake of overpowering a VW engine by overbuilding it. Please don't consider installing big-bore P&Cs if your case doesn't have case-savers or if the studs are loose.

Stroking and Cylinders: When the stroke is increased, the pistons are pushed farther away from the center of the crankshaft; therefore, the cylinders need to be shimmed farther away from the case. This is where things get hairy if you're not careful. Since we want to build an engine that is balanced from the bottom end out, we have to strive for equal cylinder displacements. Assuming that the case spigots (cylinder holes) are level and that the connecting rods are equal lengths, the cylinders and pistons should extend the same distance. Each cylinder head covers two cylinders, hence those two cylinders have to be shimmed equally away from the case

when the engine is stroked or the cylinders will neither be level nor seal well against the heads.

For example, if you increase the stroke from 69mm to 74mm, there is a 5mm increase (2.5mm on each side), so you'll have to install 2.5mm shims under the cylinders to position them so the pistons are at the same place they were with the stock stroke.

In a stroked engine the pistons push out and pull in farther. The crankshaft also travels in a wider arc, and the connecting rods make a sharper angle. Depending on the amount of stroke, the pistons and cylinders may need to be machined so that the parts do not hit inside the case. Because of the larger arc and rod angle, the case, camshaft, rods, pistons, and cylinders also must be checked and, if necessary, clearanced (see CRANKCASE).

Reusing Pistons and Cylinders: Another area you must check if reusing the pistons and cylinders is the space between each piston and cylinder. To measure P&C clearance properly, you need special gauges: inside and outside micrometers to measure the ID of the cylinder and the OD of the piston. Subtract these measurements to get the clearance value. Without micrometers, you can measure between the inside top and bottom of the cylinder with feeler gauges while the piston (minus rings) is installed in its cylinder. Remember that the pistons move horizontally in their cylinders. The wear points are at the tops and bottoms of the cylinder bores, where the thrust of the piston stroke is greatest.

Slide the piston midway into its cylinder and measure between the top side of the piston and cylinder. New P&Cs measure 0.0015″ (0.04mm) to 0.0027″ (0.07mm). According to Volkswagen, if the wear is more than 0.0078″ (0.20mm), the piston is worn out. For hi-performance, don't go beyond 0.035″ (0.10mm) wear. Also read John's checks for wear (Chapter XV, Procedure for Engine Dismantling, Step 11). I prefer to use new P&Cs when building hi-performance. Pistons are not manufactured perfectly round; they are "cam ground" or slightly egg-shaped. For reasons of wear and balance, pistons and cylinders should always be kept together as a pair and in the same position, No. 1, No. 2, and so forth, so they must be labeled by piston and cylinder and position. Note: I don't recommend using John's method (Chapter XV) to balance pistons. In fact, unless your machinist has the equipment to cut the insides of the pistons radially, don't bother balancing the pistons at all. Some experts believe that because pistons are subjected to the high pressure of combustion, they don't need to be balanced.

Piston Rings: Use cast-iron piston rings when reringing pistons. Cast-iron rings break in quickly and conform better to irregularities in the worn, distorted cylinders than do chromed or moly rings. Also the oil ring should be one-piece, not a three-piece like your banker's suit. Not all piston rings are alike, and mechanics have different opinions about them. A lot of old-fashioned motor heads think that thicker piston rings seal better than thinner ones. This is a notion that hip hot-rodders like us chuckle about knowingly and swiftly ignore. When we cool guys choose rings, we buy compression rings no thicker than 1/16″ (1.588mm) and oil rings no thicker than 1/8″ (3.175mm).

Three-piece oil rings, however, can be thicker. Whatever you believe, trial and error coupled with science have proven that thinner rings work better in high revving engines. The reason has to do with the dynamics—the effects of motion and combustion on the piston rings. Piston rings move within their grooves throughout the four cycles of operation. Consider that on an upward stroke the ring is pushed downward against the bottom of its groove, and on the downstroke the ring gets pushed up against the top of the groove. Not so obvious is that compression and combustion gases also position the rings and help secure the seal by pushing the rings down against their grooves and out against the cylinder walls.

You might think that since the rings have spring tension built into them, it is this tension that seals the cylinder. Not so. In fact, gas pressure does the real job. Furthermore, when a piston changes direction at TDC and BDC so do the rings. At high RPMs this shift causes "ring flutter," a function of inertia that results in blow-by, that is, a combustion pressure enters the crankcase. Thinner and lighter rings flutter less than stock rings, minimize blow-by, and cause less friction and damage to the ring, piston, and cylinder. Always use three-piece oil rings with new pistons and cylinders. A three-piece oil ring has a center piece sandwiched between two thin spacers. Chrome and moly rings are better for new pistons and cylinders because they resist wear and therefore last longer; however, they take longer to break in than cast-iron rings. Total Seal makes a good set of piston rings for a VW. The oil ring is three-piece and chrome moly. The top compression ring is available in cast iron, chrome, or moly. And the second compression ring is a gapless type, two-piece ring: the main ring has a groove cut in the outside, and the smaller ring fits into a groove in the main ring. This combination allows gases to

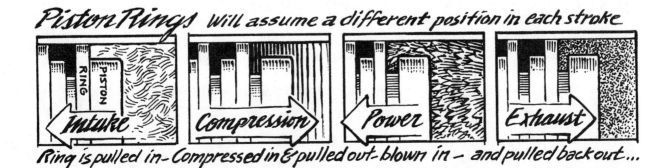

Piston Rings Will assume a different position in each stroke

| Intake | Compression | Power | Exhaust |

Ring is pulled in - Compressed in & pulled out - blown in - and pulled back out...

flow around the ring, forcing the smaller ring against the cylinder wall with minimal friction, resulting in less "ring flutter" at high RPMs and reduction in blow-by.

The Total Seal people claim that reduced blow-by lowers the crankcase temperature, which is great for an air-cooled engine. Most piston and cylinder sets come fitted with rings, and usually the rings are chrome moly. You have the option of using those rings or getting another set. Deves, a Swedish company, makes a cast-steel ring that is fantastic. Perfect Circle makes good rings, too. Some builders even mix ring sets. Whatever you do, make sure that you get a ring of the same thickness to replace the original ring size made for the piston. For high speed, a thinner ring is better.

Piston Pins: Of course the pin fit has to be as exacting as everything else. If you want to get a feel for a good fit, try sliding a pin into a German-made piston. Ahh . . . Deutschland über Alles. If in doubt, ask your machinist to check the pin fit in each connecting rod.

More important in some ways are the pin retainers. For even moderate hi-performance, I recommend using Teflon buttons or, better yet, Gene Berg's special "wrist pin keepers" in place of the stock wire type retainers. When an align-bored case or the connecting rods aren't straight, or the crankshaft flexes or has too much end play, inordinate loads are put on the piston pins. Under these conditions stock keepers can break, causing unthinkable engine damage. To be safe, build a strong balanced engine and use quality retainers and straight rods.

Parts and Machine Work: Always give the machinist one of the cylinders to measure when boring the case and cylinder heads. Note: Before boring the case, remove the studs from the case.

The cylinders must also be honed with the correct "cross-hatch," properly cleaned, and remeasured for clearance. Most ring manufacturers recommend a hone with a specific grit to use as a cylinder honing medium to complement their rings. For example, Total Seal advises that one use a 400-525 grit for moly-face or cast-iron top rings and a 250-300 grit for chrome-face top rings. Ask your supplier. The cylinders should be honed while mounted to a rigid plate. There is an art to proper honing, and everyone has a preference as to their favorite honing device. If you cannot use a honing tool, have your machinist do the cylinders.

Doing the honing yourself? Remember, when you're finished, rinse the cylinder with mild detergent and warm water. Clean the cylinder until you can wipe a dry white rag along the cylinder wall without picking up any grime. When done, recheck the clearance and coat the cylinders with light engine oil before stashing them in a plastic bag.

The pistons must be cleaned properly by **glass-beading**. Glass-beading is the best way to remove deposits from the ring lands safely. I do not recommend using an old ring or ring scraper to do the job; it can damage the aluminum piston. The ring groove is an important sealing surface.

A stroked engine has to have its cylinders shimmed or moved away from the case with custom-made **spacers**. A stock stroke engine may need shims too. For example: let's say the original stroke is 69mm and the new stroke is 74mm (74mm-69mm = 5mm). 5mm x 0.0197 (the secret number) = 0.098″ (.25mm); this is the size of the shim you will need to put under each cylinder.

Manufacturers call the thicker ones spacers. These are generally used for stroking, and some shops custom grind them to exact thicknesses. Shims are thinner than spacers and may need to be combined to get the right thickness.

You will also have to calculate the rod length into the formula if other than stock rods are used. Add or subtract the difference in length between your rod and stock (see CONNECTING RODS).

All these calculations will do is get the cylinders into the ballpark but not necessarily provide the exact distance needed to adjust deck height and compression ratio or both. You won't know precisely what shims to install until it's time to do the essential steps, which are described below. Ideally, you should have an assortment of shims on hand: 0.010, 0.020, 0.030″, even if you are building a stock stroke engine.

Special Tools: Every major VW parts supplier sells a tool to measure deck height. Here we show you how to make a combination tool to check deck height and to find TDC. We also tell you how to make a cylinder hold-down tool to restrain the cylinder until the head is installed.

It takes some materials and fabrication to make these tools, so start a parts list: a piece of strap mild steel—6″ long x 1½″ wide x ⅛″ thick (6″ x 1½″ x ⅛″); an electric drill; drill bits—whatever size drill bit

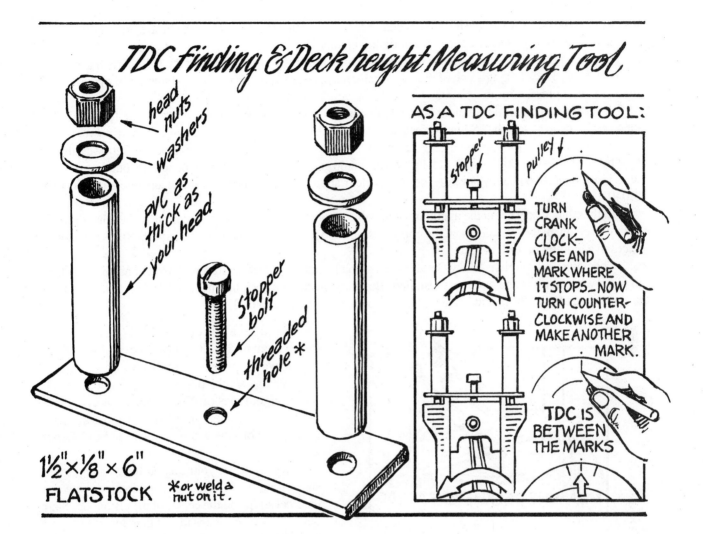

TDC finding & Deck height Measuring Tool

head nuts

washers

PVC as thick as your head

Stopper bolt

threaded hole *

1½" × ⅛" × 6" FLATSTOCK

*or weld a nut on it.

AS A TDC FINDING TOOL:

Stopper

pulley

TURN CRANK CLOCK- WISE AND MARK WHERE IT STOPS_ NOW TURN COUNTER- CLOCKWISE AND MAKE ANOTHER MARK.

TDC IS BETWEEN THE MARKS

recommended on the tapping tool that you use, for example, 7/32″ bit to drill a pilot hole for an 8mm x 1.25 tapping tool, or you may want to use a size that you already have. Any bolt will work for this (see sketch). You will also need a 2″ (50mm) long bolt to match the width and thread pitch of the tapping tool; a nut for the bolt; a drill bit slightly bigger than the size of your cylinder head studs, for example, ⅜″; and 1 foot of PVC pipe for the hold-down tool.

Make the Authorized John Muir Deck Height/TDC Tool: Find the center point of the steel strap and drill it for the tap and bolt size that you choose. When the hole is made, thread it with the tapping tool. Now measure from center-to-center between two diagonal cylinder head studs. Drill a ⅜″ hole in each end of the steel strap so it will fit over the cylinder head studs. Position the strap so the hole you tapped appears in the center of the cylinder.

To install the tool, place the strap diagonally over the cylinder so the studs fit through the holes and the strap lies flush against the top lip of the cylinder. Slip the pieces of PVC pipe over the studs, and add a few washers to take up space and hold the tool in place. Use one or more head washer(s) and a nut on each of the head studs to secure the tool. Now the tool is ready to use. Note: To measure deck height, you need a large assortment of angled feeler gauges.

Make a Hold-down Tool: You need this to keep the cylinder sitting firmly against the case. Cut the 1 foot of PVC pipe into two pieces, each long enough to shim between the top of the cylinder and the bottom of the threads on the cylinder studs.

To install the hold-down tool, slip the long piece of pipe over one of the long studs and the short one over a short stud. Install as many washers as needed to cover the bottom six threads of the head studs and screw the nuts evenly on the cylinders so they mount tightly against the case.

Deck Height: This is the distance between the top of the piston and the top of the cylinder when the piston is at TDC. Deck height is one of the measurements needed to calculate deck volume, total cylinder volume, and compression ratio.

A certain amount of deck height is essential to keep the combustion temperature at a safe level; this distance is also called "squish." Some performance freaks believe that less deck height means more power, while others defiantly cross their arms and say "prove it." In the days of high compression, deck height was always kept between 0.040-0.060″. Now with low octane pump gas and 6:1 compression, people are building engines with more than 0.060″ deck height. The rule is clear about the minimum amount acceptable—no less than 0.040″.

Rather than worry about the maximum allowable amount of deck height, concentrate on keeping the deck height even on all the cylinders and the compression ratio low. According to some experts, 0.250″ is not an excessive amount of deck height.

Checking deck height is tricky, so take a deep breath and concentrate. Start with No. 1 and No. 2 pistons in place without rings and cylinders installed. Build and install the deck height/TDC tool on No. 1 cylinder as described above. Build and install the hold-down tool on No. 2 cylinder.

MEASURE DECKHEIGHT AT TDC

If you have two other hold-down tools built, install them on No. 3 and No. 4 cylinders, otherwise leave the pistons and cylinders on that side of the case disassembled. Without damaging the cylinder spigot holes on No. 3 and No. 4 cylinders, rotate the crankshaft until No. 1 piston is at TDC. If you are not sure where that is, see **Find Exact TDC** below.

Now pull out your angled feeler gauges and start fitting single blades or combinations between the steel strap and the center of the piston top. Start with a 0.040″ feeler blade. If that doesn't fit, you will definitely have to install some shims under the cylinder. First, see which of the next smallest blades fits and make a note of it. If the 0.040″ blade fits, keep adding thicker blades until they will not fit anymore. That's the deck height. Make a note of your measurements. Before going on to measure No. 2 cylinder, read **Find Exact TDC** below.

Calculate Deck Volume: Plug the deck height measurement into the formula for calculating deck volume (displacement). For example, let's imagine you measured the deck height of the No. 1 cylinder as 0.053″ and your engine size is 90.5mm bore and 69mm stroke. Convert the inch measurement of deck height to millimeters. The formula to convert inches to millimeters is 0.053″ x 25.4 = 1.35mm. To find the deck volume, multiply the Base times the Height (V=BH), after determining the area of the cylinder or base (Area = 3.14 x radius squared). The diameter of the piston is also called the bore. The calculation is as follows:

Bore = 90.5mm, so the radius = 45.25mm.

A = 3.14 x 45.25mm x 45.25mm = 6429.3462sq mm (6429sq mm)

V = Base (area) x Height (deck height)

V = 6429sq mm x 1.35mm = 8679.15 or 8679cu mm

Deck volume = 8679cu mm. (To convert cubic millimeters to cubic centimeters, move the decimal point three places to the left: 8679.000cu mm to 8.679 cm [cc], then round off the number.)

The deck volume for this cylinder is thus 8.68cc.

Swept Volume: Again, use the formula.

Volume = Base (area) x Height (stroke)

V = 6429sq mm x 69mm = 443601cu mm (or 443.6cc)

This is the Swept Volume of No. 1 cylinder.

Later, we will add deck volume to the combustion chamber volume and swept volume to calculate the total cylinder volume (displacement). Then subtract deck height volume from total volume to calculate corrosion ratio. For now start recording the calculations as follows: **See Changes and New Ideas.**

Cylinder	No. 1	No. 2	No. 3	No. 4
Bore— 90.5mm				
Stroke— 69mm				
Area (Base)— 6429mm				
Deck Height— 0.053″				
Deck Volume— 8.68cc				
Swept Volume— 443.6cc				
Chamber Volume— 43.5cc (see CYLINDER HEADS)				
Total Volume— 495.78cc				

Final Cylinder Installation: Paint the outside (fins) of the cylinders with a light coat of flat black, high temp engine paint. Don't do this until you have calculated the compression ratio and installed shims if necessary. Don't prepare to install the cylinders until the rings are on the pistons. You'll need a tube of blue silicon sealer. Although John says to install paper gaskets under the cylinders, don't. Instead, run a thin bead of silicon sealer around the base of the cylinder where it fits against the deck of the case just before installing the cylinder.

Find Exact TDC: This is important for accurate ignition and valve timing. The following method allows you to re-mark the front pulley to indicate where the "real" TDC is. In hi-performance, this kind of detail is important, even essential, to winning that kiss from next year's drag race queen.

Remember, when the piston reaches TDC, it stops for an instant as the crankshaft completes its arc; the crankshaft continues moving while the piston stands still. Top Dead Center refers to the position of the connecting rod throw as it reaches the top of its arc, directly below the center of the piston. In terms of crankshaft degrees, TDC occurs at 0° and 180°. Imagine the crank pulley rotation as being 360°.

You need to install a degree wheel on the crank pulley for this test. Fit the Deck Height/TDC Tool on No. 1 cylinder. Turn the crank to what looks like TDC on the piston top. Turn the crank counterclockwise until the piston is ½″ below the TDC position. Now find the 2″ bolt for which you tapped a hole in the Deck Height/TDC Tool and thread it in all the way. Secure the nut on the bolt. Similarly, thread the bolt into the hole in the tool until it touches the piston and stops. Now lock the bolt in place with the nut. Refer to the illustration of the TDC finding and deck height measuring tool earlier in this section.

Make sure the degree wheel is well attached to the crank pulley and note the location of the split in the case in relation to the pulley—note the degree point—and write down that number (for example, 13° BTDC). Continue rotating the crankshaft counterclockwise, bringing it right around until it comes up again and hits the bolt. Record that degree reading (e.g., 17° ATDC).

Add the two numbers of degrees, then divide the sum by two. For example, 13 + 17 = 30. Divided by 2 = 15. TDC is that many degrees counterclockwise from the current position of the pulley. Look at the pulley and count the number of degrees counterclockwise to find TDC and mark the spot.

Either move your degree wheel to the point where true TDC or 0° is, or, if your wheel is part of the pulley, make a note of the exact location of TDC by referring to the stationary numbers. Remove the special tool when you're done. There's no need to check more than the No. 1 cylinder.

CONNECTING RODS (Top End)

Connecting rods are little I-beams that push and pull tremendous weights at high speeds. Careless builders overlook the importance of these four hard-working, neglected components. The rods must be strong, which stock VW rods are, but they also must be well balanced and weigh the same. Furthermore, they should be perfectly straight and exactly the same length—a matched set. Remember, the idea is to keep things equal and balanced.

To begin with, let's look at a basic VW rod. It is made from forged steel. A one-piece bronze bushing is pressed into the small end, and a two-piece steel backed lead-bronze bushing fits into the big end. 40 hp rods measure 5.120″ (130mm) from the center of the small end to the center of the big end. 13/15/1600 rods are 5.395″ (137mm) center to center. Both 40 hp and 13/15/1600 connecting rod journals are 2.165″ (55mm). 40 hp rods are wider at the base than later rods. Stock VW rods are acceptable for strokes up to 78mm and speeds up to 7500 rpm, as long as they are properly machined and clearanced. 40 hp rods have to be machined to fit a 1600 crank.

Early in the VW hi-performance game builders used Porsche rods, which are 1mm shorter than stock VW rods. These are still popular for stroker engines because the crankshaft journal diameter is 2mm smaller than stock VW; therefore, the profile of the connecting rod cap is smaller and less clearancing is necessary. Porsche rods are commonly used with 82, 84, and 86mm stroke cranks. Porsche-style rods are also available in VW journal sizes.

Hi-performance builders also use Chevy rods with big ends that are 4mm smaller in journal diameter than stock VW rods. These are commonly used with 69, 73, 78, and massive 90 and 92mm stroke cranks. Chevy rods come in three sizes. Matching cranks and rods can be confusing, so you have to do your homework before going nuts with exotic combinations.

If you buy a stroker crankshaft, get matching rods from the same supplier. Combining crankshafts and connecting rods is a subdiscipline of automotive science. Buy from a supplier who provides technical advice.

A point to keep in mind: According to the Pauter Machine Company, Inc., catalog, the ratio of connecting rod length to crankshaft stroke should be between 1.6:1 and 2:1. For example, a 1600 VW rod is 137mm center to center. Stock 1600 stroke is 69mm (137 divided by 69 = 1.985, or 2). So the stock 1600 ratio is 2:1, which according to tests provides the best high speed performance possible with the least amount of wear on pistons, cylinders, and connecting rods. Consequently, racers who want good top-end performance using big strokes like the longer 5.550″ (141mm) and 5.700″ (144mm) Porsche and Chevrolet rods.

Any level of Volkswagen rebuild requires a set of reworked connecting rods. Machine shops sell ''reconditioned,'' ''rebuilt,'' and ''blueprinted'' rods. Let's compare a $13 set of reconditioned stock rods to a $56 set of rebuilt stock rods. First, the reconditioned rods: they may be straight but not necessarily. The big ends are resized; the cap and rod are resurfaced, and the center is rehoned. The small ends of the rods are rebushed and reamed to size. For balancing, four rods within 5-10 g of each other are picked and matched from a huge selection of cores. Voila! A set of reconditioned rods! But wait—they haven't been checked for length, nor have they been straightened to assure that the centers are aligned. The rods may be close in overall weight, but they haven't been balanced end for end. A difference of a few thousandths of an inch in length or an error in alignment will affect the cylinder displacement and the angle of piston travel—bad news for a high RPM mill. Rich broke a crankshaft in his Type IV because the rods were of unequal lengths.

Now look at the $56 set of rebuilt and blueprinted VW rods from Pauter Machine. All the rods have been thoroughly inspected and cleaned; the big ends have been resized and remated. The small ends are rebushed, reamed, and honed. The rods are also adjusted for center-to-center length, aligned, and match-weighed as a set. I wouldn't settle for less.

For the dedicated racer, there are performance sets that start at $160 for modified VW rods and top out at $700 for billeted rods. Carrillo rods are popular race rods—82mm and longer stroke. These are made from special 4340 chrome moly steel billets. Nice to salivate over but a little too spicy for most tastes.

Everyone agrees that rods should weigh within 5-10 g of each other, which is the factory specification. But for hi-performance, the weights have to be closer. I once weighed a set of new Porsche 912 rods that were within 2 g of each other. In comparison, I weighed some new VW rods that barely fell into the 10 g range. John's method in Chapter XV, although crude, works, but you have to be more precise for hi-performance.

Length is something that even some experienced builders take for granted. They forget John Muir's mantra for hi-performance engine building: "Keep things balanced, man."

Before buying rods ask your supplier if they are measured for length— from the center of the big end to the center of the small end (center to center)—and if they are balanced or matched. The distinction being that balanced rods weigh the same overall, while a matched set is within specified weight overall and end for end. Not everyone agrees on these terms so ask for specifics.

Planning to balance your engine? Buy a rebuilt/matched set of new or used rods and have them checked by the machinist who does the engine balancing job. Ask the supplier and/or the machinist how the rods were balanced and within how many grams. Also ask if the rods have been balanced end for end. If you want to check them yourself, see below. Overall weight is important; however, end for end balance is more important due to centrifugal force. The big end of the rod follows the rotation of the crankshaft in an arc of inertia. So to keep things equal, all four of the big ends should weigh the same.

Assembly: To balance rods get a gram scale that can handle the weight of a rod and is low enough so one end of the rod can be tipped onto the scale while the other end remains on the table. Work on a flat, smooth table. Look at Peter's drawings below. As you work, keep the rods in order so you don't get confused. Place a rod on its side. Lay the big end of the rod on top of the scale and the small end on the table. (Keep the rod on its side.) Record the weight. Do the same for each rod.

Starting with the heaviest rod, file off enough metal so the rod is within 2 g of the lightest rod. File metal off the end of the rod—equal amounts on each side. Do the same to the two remaining connecting rods until all four big ends are within 2 g of each other.

Starting again with the lightest rod, position it so the small end is resting on the scale and the big end is on the table and record its weight. You want to match the weights of the small ends to within 2 g of each other just as you did the big ends. Find the heaviest rod (small end) and carefully file metal off the top of the boss, taking equal amounts off the top third of the boss—the piston end of the rod. When all four rods are matched to weight (end for end), check the overall weights.

Weigh the entire rod. All four of them should register 580-600 g. Find the lightest and the heaviest. Carefully remove metal until the weights match. Of course, cutting off metal will affect the big end weight somewhat so it will have to be rechecked and maybe readjusted. No one said this would be an easy job; it takes time to be perfect.

Parts and Machine Work: Make certain the rod bearings you buy are the ones you need. Open the package and look at the back of the bearing shells for the size that will match your standard or undersized crank. Before finally installing the connecting rods on the crankshaft, slip the bearing shells into the cap and rod and use green Plastigage to measure the oil clearance. Put a ¾ ″ strip of the stuff on the bearing surface then attach the rod to the crank. Tighten the nuts to 22 ft. lbs. with a torque wrench. Remove the cap and measure the flattened Plastigage; it should be 0.0025″ wide. Check all the rod bearings the same way. If the oil clearance is more or less than 0.0025″, consult your machinist.

Don't torque connecting rod bolts any tighter than 22 ft. lbs. John recommends tightening them to 36 ft. lbs.; however, I don't. And speaking of don'ts, please do not use Lubriplate on the bearing surfaces. If available, use good quality 20 wt. nondetergent motor oil on all bearing and gear surfaces during assembly and in the crankcase for the initial start-up (see OIL: FILTERS, COOLERS, AND LUBRICATION for more).

No matter what some motorheads may tell you, always install the connecting rods with the forge mark up.

If you decide to upgrade your 64mm (40 hp) crankshaft to a 69mm (13/15/1600), you'll have to make some other modifications. As long as you use the stock 40 hp (77mm pistons and cylinders), the 40 hp rods will work. However, the big end of the 40 hp connecting rod is 0.040″ wider than the 69mm crankshaft journal width, so 0.020″ must be machined off each side of the 40 hp rod to make it fit. Another problem if you are using 1300/1500/1600 pistons and cylinders is that the small ends of the 40 hp rods are smaller than those of later rods (40 hp rods are 20mm and later rods are 22mm). For more on this modification, see PISTONS AND CYLINDERS.

CYLINDER HEADS, VALVES, AND VALVE SPRINGS (Top End)

The art of VW cylinder head modification has been practiced widely for over 25 years. Muldoon even built a few VW race cars that cleaned up the local Carson City competition.

"The secret was in the heads," said Muldoon, puffing his cigar while gazing affectionately at the pictures, "it wasn't the dual carbs or the big jugs, it was the way I worked the heads. Those babies sure could breathe when I got through with 'em."

Muldoon knew that a hi-performance engine needs a healthy flow of fuel and air to win races. A stock cylinder head cannot deliver the fuel/air mixture necessary to feed and cool a big-bored, hot-cammed VW engine. Stock manifolds, valves, ports, and headers are simply too small.

Volkswagen cylinder heads deserve special attention because they are air cooled. Valve and head problems are the bane of the air-cooled VW. The combustion ends of the P&Cs—the cylinder heads—are the really hot spots in the engine, because they house the combustion zone, where fuel energy is transformed into hotrod fun. The better the atmosphere is for combustion, the better the fun.

Inside of the head, the valves, combustion chambers, and pistons have to withstand and dispel tremendous pressure and heat. The amount of pressure is determined by a number of things, including the following: compression ratio, fuel/air mixture, and the shape of the combustion chamber.

The combustion chambers have to be equal in displacement to assure even power from each cylinder. If the combustion temperatures are balanced, the engine will run cooler and more powerfully. When assembling a hi-performance engine, you have to pay careful attention to the shape and displacement of all four combustion chambers as well as the compression ratios.

Compression makes heat in two ways: by forcing more volume into less space and by developing more energy from combustion. The amount of heat depends on how well the heat is removed by the exhaust system and by the surrounding parts that radiate heat, for example, the valves and the mass of the head itself.

If you have ever read Bill Fisher's classic book *How to HOTROD VOLKSWAGEN ENGINES*, you know that it takes an expert like Muldoon with a machine shop with a flow bench to modify a VW cylinder properly. Unless you have the skill, tools (a set of valve cutters and a valve grinding machine), and patience to follow Bill Fisher's instructions, leave it alone or leave it up to a real pro.

Contrary to what you may imagine, a perfectly smooth and straight port does not give the best airflow and air speed. The VW intake manifold with its various bumps and humps is designed to make the mixture swirl around and speed up. VW engineers using their fancy test equipment had this well figured out for an economy engine. Removing too much in the wrong place can result in worse performance and a weakened head.

Building a good cylinder head means starting with a good used or new head. One seldom ever knows the history of a used head, so it pays to buy from a reputable source; junk heads are plentiful.

When shopping for a head, ask these questions: Is the head new or used? (If it is sold as an exchange, it is probably used.) What kind of valves does it have? Were the seats replaced? What kind of valve job—three-angle? What kind of valve guides, stock or aftermarket? Have the guides been modified? Are the valve springs stock or heavy duty, new or used, single or double? What size are the cylinder bores? Has the head been flycut? If dual port, is the counterbored step still in the head or has it been machined away? If you buy heads as a pair, ask if they have been CCed (measured for displacement) and, if so, within how many CCs? If not, ask how much they charge to CC the heads and have them supply the measurements, cylinder by cylinder.

Pick up a copy of *Dune Buggies and Hot VWs* and check out the advertisements for cylinder heads. You will see that prices vary. A run-of-the-mill, rebuilt stock DP head starts at $45. A new modified stock head with top quality parts costs $325. Of course, there are differences between these heads, and it is impossible to tell from magazine pictures what the head is really like. You have to trust the builder's reputation.

The cheaper head has stock sized valves, either new or used, as well as valve guides and springs. You can bet that the valves and valve seats were not cut uniformly so the valves do not protrude equally into the combustion chambers from cylinder to cylinder. This means that the combustion chambers do not have even displacements and that the valve stem ends are not level. Undoubtedly, the heads were not machined in pairs.

The more expensive head may not be a new head, but it has been carefully inspected by the rebuilder. The valve sizes are larger than stock—40mm intake, 35.5mm exhaust with a three-angled ''street'' valve job. The valves are probably stainless steel, and the valve guides are silicon bronze. The head is ported and polished (maybe hemi-cut), machined for oversized cylinders, and fitted with heavy-duty springs with chrome moly retainers. You can be sure that the combustion chamber displacements are identical and the heads are a matched pair.

Some machinists grind away parts of the combustion chamber. One modification that really improves combustion, breathing, and economy is the hemi-cut. Correctly cut, hemi-heads burn fuel more efficiently and evenly than stock heads. If you want to keep valve sizes stock and improve combustion, consider having some porting and hemi-cutting done by someone knowledgeable (refer to Bill Fisher's book for details).

Obviously, you want the best head for the least money. Some heads that are advertised in the magazines have most of the features that the better quality heads have but cost less. So what is the difference between a good head and a better head? The answer is labor. By labor I mean the skill of the person doing the machine work as well as the time invested. Experienced VW builders know exactly how much metal to remove and from where to remove it to port, polish, and hemi-cut a head properly. (A pretty looking job may not be the most efficient in terms of the ability of the head to transmit air at the right velocity.)

There are two basic VW cylinder heads available: single port and dual port. Dual port heads breathe better than single port heads and are therefore the racer's choice. Single port heads can be modified for hi-performance, but typically they are only bored for oversized cylinders.

Single port (SP) heads come in a variety of valve sizes and intake port angles. The intake ports in older VW heads were cast at right angles to the cylinders. Through the years, the intake port angles slackened, and the breathing improved. The valve sizes in early 40 hp engines are 31.5mm intake and 30mm exhaust, compared to the 15/1600 single port heads with 35.5mm intake and 32mm exhaust. These later heads are the racer's choice for single port hi-performance. They were installed in Type I 1967-70, Type II 1966-70, and Type III

1965-66. These heads do not need to be bored for 1600 big-bore cylinders (slip-in).

Dual port (DP) heads were first put in Type III 1967 on and later in Types I and II in 1971. Since each cylinder has its own port, the walls of the casting are thinner in DP heads than in SP heads, so care must be taken when doing modifications. In 1971 DP heads had a step (0.055″/1.5mm) counterbored into the combustion chamber to lower compression and emissions. For many years machine shops eliminated this step to raise compression. Now the step is a desirable feature. Because of the low octane quality of pump gas, lower compression is cool. The valve diameters in the stock DP head are 35.5mm intake and 32mm exhaust. VW makes a DP racing head known as the 041, which has a larger (37mm) intake valve but the same (32mm) exhaust valve. The 041 head is designed for a stock engine, not for hi-performance unless modified by the installation of a bigger exhaust valve, in which case you need bigger exhaust headers if the exhaust ports have been enlarged.

Note: If you convert to DP heads you will need the dual port tin to fit the new heads and two shorter upper middle cylinder head studs.

Note: DP heads commonly crack between the ports where the intake manifold attaches as well as between the valves and near the spark plug hole.

If you install dual carbs, the manifolds will automatically improve the intake airflow. Where a single carb manifold restricts airflow, separate dual carb manifolds provide a straight shot from the carburetors into the heads; therefore, porting complements dual carbs. To get the most out of dual carbs, install bigger valves, which means bigger headers.

Valves: For stock purposes, always install the original VW valves. The original equipment VW exhaust valve stems are specially hardened with high carbon steel; the valve heads are faced with stellite. Accept no substitutes. For oversize valves, use stainless steel Manley valves. Manley valves are polished and radiused at the stem and base to improve flow. Always keep the valve tappets in good adjustment. I recommend using new valves, certainly new exhaust valves, in a major overhaul.

Note: Using a head with bigger valves means that the exhaust and intake systems have to be modified to match the enlarged valves. On the exhaust side, stock pipes with heater boxes aren't big enough, so you'll have to ditch the heaters and install larger than stock ''J'' pipes. This means you will have no heat in the winter, unless you install the stock heads in the winter and big valve heads and ''J'' pipes in the summer.

Valve Seats: VW valve seats are difficult to remove and install, but they last a long time. If in good shape, leave them alone. Note: To install larger valves, larger seats must be installed.

Oversize valve seats have to be placed in the correct position in relation to the spark plug boss and chamber wall, or the head will be permanently damaged. To install really big valves, machinists actually add metal to the head, then remachine it and install new seats. Some even move the spark plug hole or install a smaller (12mm) spark plug hole to allow room for bigger valves. You can see how expensive all this can get.

Valve Springs and Retainers: Stock engines have single valve springs. Full race engines have three springs for each valve; moderate engines that run over 5500 rpm should have two. For multispring installations, the head has to be machined to fit the inner dampener spring(s). Heavy-duty single springs are commonly used with hi-lift cams and high-revving engines.

The reason for using a heavier spring and multisprings is not only to force the valve to close at high RPMs but also to keep the cam follower in contact with the cam. Heavy-duty springs are recommended even for mildly modified engines. The question is how heavy? The pressure of too much spring robs horsepower and increases wear. But it is impossible to recommend one spring for all purposes. Most important is that the springs have uniform tension when compressed a certain amount. Ask the machinist to machine check your springs—even new springs. Also ask about spring shims. (See **Assembly** below for more details.)

Machine Work: No matter what, do not let the machinist talk you into fly-cutting the heads to increase compression. Fly-cutting moves the heads closer to the case, which means that to keep things even the pushrods should be shortened. Remember, everything is related and changes affect something else. The only sensible reason to fly-cut is to smooth out the surface where the cylinders and head meet. Fly-cutting must be done equally on each cylinder and in conjunction with CCing (see below). During fly-cutting metal is removed from the top edge of the combustion chamber.

In contrast, boring takes metal off the sides of the chamber. The heads will need to be bored along with the case to fit big-bore, machine-in cylinders. Give the machinist the cylinders to measure.

A good valve job is essential for hi-performance. The 3-angle valve job refers to the angles at which the seats are cut. Most shops cut seats at 15°, 45°, and 60°. Look straight down at a valve seat (valve removed). The first and widest angle is 15°, the middle angle where the valve sits is 45°, and the bottommost and steepest angle is 60°.

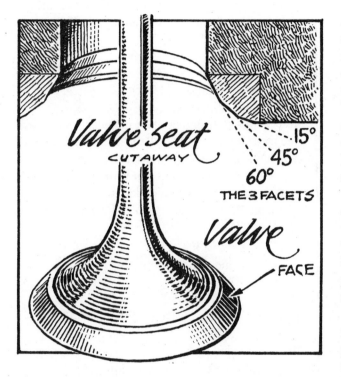

Most builders believe that sinking the valves and cutting the seats even with the combustion chamber improve flow. Sinking is also a way to increase and adjust the displacement in the cylinders that need more CCs. The machinist should also keep the ends of the valve stems level. This is checked by laying a straightedge along the stems and eyeballing it for level using the flat valve cover rail as a guide.

How to do a proper VW valve job would take a chapter to explain. Suffice it to say that a good valve job is worth whatever a machinist wants to charge.

CCing the Head: You need to determine the volume of the combustion chamber in order to calculate the overall cylinder displacement and compression ratio. First, assemble the materials to make a CCing tool. Go to the drugstore and buy a 10cc syringe. Next measure the diameter of the cylinder bore in the head and find a piece of clear hard plastic (like the lid to a roll of electrical tape). Or go to a hardware store and have a ⅛″ piece of plexiglas cut to fit the diameter of your cylinder bore. Drill a ¼″ hole near the edge of the plastic without breaking it.

Number the heads for their corresponding cylinders, for example, No. 1, No. 2, and so on. The heads must be positioned so the combustion chambers are level. Smear some grease around the edge of the plastic piece and fit it into the No. 1 combustion chamber. Fill the syringe with exactly 10cc of a mixture of alcohol and automatic transmission fluid. Squirt the contents into the combustion chamber through the hole in the plastic piece. Repeat this until the chamber is full—about four full syringes. Make sure there are no air bubbles in the liquid.

Write down exactly how much liquid you put into the cylinder. Repeat the process with each cylinder until you have four readings.

Now comes the hard part. The idea is to get the cylinders within 1cc of each other. As I mentioned earlier, the valves can be sunk to increase the chamber volume, but sinking a valve can make the stem height uneven. If the stem heights are even and the valve job is acceptable, leave the seats alone.

Use the cylinder with the greatest volume as the standard. There are two other ways than valve sinking to increase chamber volume: (1) fly-cutting and (2) grinding off metal from the combustion chamber. Fly-cutting works when two cylinders on the same head need to be reduced an equal amount. The machinist has to do this.

You can grind away small amounts in the combustion chamber with a fine grinding wheel. Grind off very small amounts at a time, from places in the chamber that are uniform—stay away from the spark plug hole and valve seats, and wear safety glasses. If you are inexperienced, have someone else do this. It's not worth it to ruin a head.

Don't grind off too much. Constantly recheck the volume. When finished, record the final measurements on a chart like the one in PISTONS AND CYLINDERS. Call the measurement chamber volume. For the calculations that follow, pretend that head volume of the No. 1 cylinder is 43.5cc.

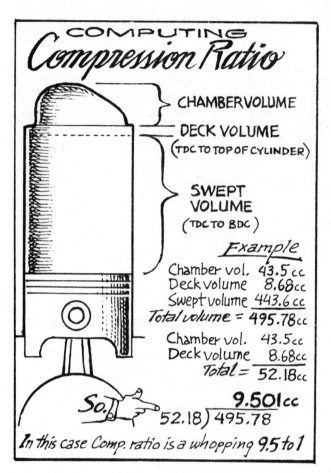

COMPUTING *Compression Ratio*

CHAMBER VOLUME

DECK VOLUME
(TDC TO TOP OF CYLINDER)

SWEPT VOLUME
(TDC TO BDC)

Example
Chamber vol. 43.5 cc
Deck volume 8.68 cc
Swept volume 443.6 cc
Total volume = 495.78 cc

Chamber vol. 43.5 cc
Deck volume 8.68 cc
Total = 52.18 cc

So... 9.501 cc
52.18) 495.78

In this case Comp. ratio is a whopping 9.5 to 1

Calculate Total Cylinder Volume (Displacement): Let's use the measurements from the chart in PISTONS AND CYLINDERS. To calculate total cylinder volume, add chamber volume to swept volume with deck volume. All these measurements are now in CCs:

Chamber Volume—43.5cc
Deck Volume—8.68cc
Swept Volume—443.6cc
Total—495.78cc

Repeat this with all four of the cylinders and record the measurements. Add all the displacements and you have the total engine displacement.

Calculate Compression Ratio (CR): This is done by dividing total cylinder volume (TCV) by chamber (head) volume (CV) plus deck volume (DV) or CR = $\frac{TCV}{CV+DV}$

From the calculations in PISTONS and CYLINDERS, use the total cylinder volume, for example, 495.78cc
Chamber Volume + Deck Volume = 43.5cc + 8.68cc = 52.18cc
495.78 divided by 52.18 = 9.501 or 9.5:1

The ratio of 9.5:1 is too high for pump gasoline, so the ratio will have to be lowered by shimming the cylinders and thereby increasing deck height. Shims come in 0.010″ increments. Let's start with the thickest 0.060″. Using the calculations in PISTONS AND CYLINDERS, **Calculate Deck Height. See Changes and New Ideas.**

Deck height 0.053″ + 0.060″ shim = 0.113″
Convert inches to millimeters—0.113″ x 25.4 = 2.87, or 2.9mm
Find deck volume: V = Base (area) x Height; V = 6429 sq. mm x 2.9mm = 18644.1 cu mm. To convert to cubic centimeters, move the decimal point three places to the left: 18644.1 cu mm to 18.6 cu cm (cc).
Recalculate the compression ratio:
Total cylinder volume divided by deck and head volume
Total cylinder volume = deck volume (new calculation) + chamber volume + swept volume; 505.7 = 18.6cc + 43.5cc + 443.6
Deck and chamber volume = 18.6cc + 43.5cc = 62.1cc
505.7cc divided by 62.1cc = 8.14 or 8.1:1 compression ratio
This is still too high, but most people will accept it. I would have the cylinder heads hemi-cut to add some displacement to the total or add thick spacers under the cylinders.

Assembly: Putting the cylinder heads on the engine is perhaps the most time-consuming part of the rebuild; to do it right, the heads have to be installed and removed a number of times. Note: Do not install the pushrod tubes until the final head installation. (Before installing the heads, read the head tightening instructions below.) If a hi-lift cam and ratio rockers were used, the valve to piston clearance should be checked. Do this by laying strips of modeling clay lengthwise across the tops of the pistons before installing the heads. Once the engine is assembled (the valves adjusted), rotate the crank by hand and operate the valves. Each valve will leave a mark in the clay indicating how close it came to the top of the piston. Remove the head and cut a cross section of the clay where the valve made its indentation and measure the thickness. It should be no less than 0.090″. If thinner than that, you either have to increase the deck height or have reliefs cut into the piston tops. Consult the machinist.

The compressed clearance of the valve springs must be checked even with a stock cam and rockers. Again the engine has to be assembled and rotated. Measure the distance between two coils on each of the valve springs when the valve is fully opened (full lift), spring compressed. Try inserting a 0.010″ feeler blade between the coils; 0.010″ is the minimum safe clearance. If the fit is too tight, you can remove the valve spring shim, install a different spring, or sink the valve farther into the head (see ROCKER ASSEMBLY AND PUSHRODS and the next paragraph for more).

While the valve is open, check that there is clearance between the top of the valve guide and the bottom of the spring retainer. If the retainer touches, change the retainer, grind off the top of the guide, or sink the valve farther into the head.

Stock VWs don't have valve spring shims. Shims are put under the springs to increase spring tension and protect the head surface. Spring height means two things: free height and installed height. Free height is measured off the engine; all springs should be equal. Installed height is measured once the head is assembled. If all the valve stem ends are level, the installed heights should be equal. At least all the intakes should be equal with each other and so should the exhausts. If there is clearance between the spring coils, you can add shims. One builder recommends 0.030″ shims for exhaust and 0.060″ for intake. The idea is to get things even, and if the valve stems are all level and the springs are the same height, then add shims, which means using a valve compressing tool and rechecking the coil clearance.

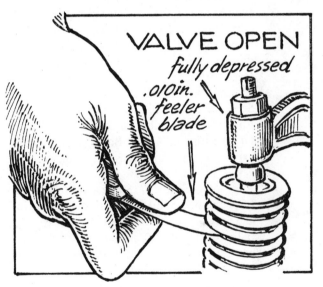

Tightening the Cylinder Heads: Tighten the heads simultaneously, a little on one head, a little on the other (alternating from one head to the other).

Start by installing the nuts on heads fingertight, following the pattern shown in Peter's drawing (Chapter XV, Procedure for Engine Mantling, Step 6). Tighten all the nuts to 15 ft. lbs., then with a torque wrench, proceed to tighten the nuts on each head at 5 ft. lb. increments, alternating from head to head, until each nut reaches 30 ft. lbs. for 10mm studs and 20 ft. lbs. for 8mm studs. This method keeps the case from being stretched unevenly.

PART IV: CONCLUSION

Perhaps we are fascinated with hi-performance because of some primeval love of combustion or simply because of our passion for speed and power. Speed is thrilling to the person behind the wheel, the one who supposedly is in control. Power is especially exciting if the driver knows that he or she had something to do with its creation, like building the engine.

If you don't already know, a hi-performance VW can reach frightening speeds. I do not want to sound like a driver training instructor, but remember, an automobile barreling down the road can be as dangerous as a loaded gun. So please, before putting pedal to the metal consider your fellow citizens. Dig deeply into your "Control System" (as per p. 82) for some common sense, then proceed cautiously.

John R. Muir, B.S., Civil (Structural), Univ. of Calif., Berk. Registered Professional Engineer #38558 in New York.

Experience
July '64 to present, Free lance writer.

Jan. '63 to July '64, Lockheed M.S.C., Sunnyvale, Calif. Senior Process Control Engineer, Welding and Metallurgical process control on flight article hardware, all systems for the Agena, Gemini, and Polaris programs. M.F. Ernster, Mgr. (10)

April '62 to Jan. '63, Free lance writer.

Feb. '59 to April '62, General Dynamics-Astro., San Diego, Calif. Field Design Liaison Engineer (Lead), assignments at Vandenberg AFB, Warren AFB, Plattsburgh AFB, and John Kennedy. Full design and approval responsibility for field changes, facility error correction, GSS compatibility, as builts, and engineering quality control for missile launching sites. Cryogenic and regular piping, heavy missile handling equipment, air conditioning, structures, and stress were the prime areas of the work. W.T. Reiff, Dept. Head. (9½)

Sept. '57 to Feb. '59, Natl. Steel and Shipbuilding, San Diego, Cal. Special Projects Engineer, responsible for all new work. Project Engineer for the Standard Oil Offshore Drilling Rig, the Atomic Bomb Simulator for the S.S. Navy, the 1½ million dollar plant expansion program, and several other projects. B.L. Stovall, Chief Engineer. (7½)

Aug. '56 to Sept. '57, Stone and Webster, Boston, Mass. Senior Welding and Piping Inspector on a 50mKW steam power plant in El Paso, Texas. Quality control and spec and drawing conformance for high pressure steam and associated piping. Performed the radiographic N.D.T. and supervised the welding and stress relief of the chrome-moly main steam lines. R.T. Purcell, Head Welding Engineer. (8)

Feb. '54 to Aug. '56, Free lance writer.

Sept. '52 to Feb. '54, Columbia-Geneva Steel Co., Provo, Utah. Maint. Engineer and Supervisor, Hardware and facility changes and maintenance in the rolling mill. Von Holdaway, Supt. (7)

June '51 to Sept. '52, Kaiser Engineers, Oakland, Calif. Field Engineer, worked on design and supervised field work on refinery construction in Texas City, Texas. Ralph Bates, Project Engineer. (7)

Prior to June '51
3 years Construction Superintendent
3 years Foreman
8 years Welder
The above work was done on refineries, power plants, pipe lines and structures. Welding qualifications held: A.P.I., Navy Heliarc (stainless, aluminum, Chrome-moly, etc.), Hartford, State of Calif., A.W.S., pressure piping, pipeline, A.S.K.E.

CHAPTER XIX

VW MANIA

by John Hilgerdt and Peter Aschwanden, the artist

This chapter is for those of you who would like a bit of history of the VW and to know what major changes were made when. It also includes a list of VW clubs, magazines, books and parts suppliers for those wishing to restore or modify a VW, or join in the fun of VW fan get-togethers.

*   *   *   *

In the 1990s, far fewer air-cooled VWs are seen on the highways than 10 years ago. They are reaching collector status, with prices getting stratospheric for some models. The asking price by a West Coast dealer for a rare Hebmuller? Try $100,000.

Some VW aficionados bemoan this new status for the air-cooled VW, which has long been venerated as a low-cost, high-quality alternative to Detroit iron. Rising prices, they say, will spoil the game, as has happened to so many other once-cheap cars.

Out west, particularly in southern California, is where most air-cooled VWs can be found, along with most of the parts suppliers, magazines and the activities devoted to them. Despite—or perhaps because of—stringent pollution regulations in California, it is the center of VW Mania, with Bug-Ins, Bug Bashes, off-road events and drag racing drawing hundreds of entrants and thousands of spectators.

Mild weather, the absence of snow-melting, car-rusting, environmentally damaging salt, and the California penchant for the nutty and wild have all contributed to keeping the VW alive out west. Not that the East Coasters and Midwesterners haven't tried. But there it's a tough struggle. Winters are harsher, especially up north, and the anemic heater means spending the winter shivering. Heavy road salting—notably on the East Coast—makes it almost impossible to keep rust at bay. Sure, you can garage your VW during the winter, but many a VW has rusted away in one, where moisture may not have a chance to evaporate.

One fall, when I was living in the Hudson River Valley north of New York City, I bought a Porsche Speedster basket case. The body was intact and I left it in the garage, and brought the engine pieces into my studio to rebuild.

In spring I started the installation process by jacking up the rear, using the standard Bilstein jack. I soon noticed that the jack was going up and up but the car wasn't. I nearly cried— shucks, I probably *did* cry—when I realized the floor pan had rusted so badly that the jack support was crunching right up through it. Even getting a good price for the engine wasn't much consolation for my broken heart. I had paid dearly—not in money but in the thrill of owning and driving a Speedster—for the garaging I thought would protect my gorgeous car (well, gorgeous for an inverted bathtub, anyway). I was tempted to stick the engine in my bus, which had *not* rusted in many years of standing outdoors, but practicality won. Lots more horsepower, but big bucks for parts.

Now, *natürlich*, I don't keep my car cooped up in a garage, and I spend more time washing the underside than the topside, especially in winter. Unfortunately, the highway department here in Santa Fe has started adding salt to the crushed volcanic rock spread on the roads after a snowstorm, ruining our cars, killing roadside trees and shrubs, and doing who-knows-what damage to our precious water supply.

HISTORY

It is an amazing and fascinating historical fluke that a car demanded by the man who would consume the world in his rage against God and humanity would become the world's best seller—ever.

The Beetle started life well before Hitler came to power, when in the 1920s a man named Dr. Ferdinand Porsche dreamed of producing an economical and affordable car. Despite Porsche's excellent reputation in the auto industry, the major auto producers in Germany and Austria weren't interested. They didn't think it would be profitable to make a car for the working class.

In the early '30s, 55-year-old Porsche opened his own studio in Stuttgart, the center of the German auto industry, with his son Ferry as designer.

Two early clients who shared Porsche's vision were Zundapp and NSU, motorcycle builders. You can see the future Beetle in his first car for Zundapp, in shape as well as in the torsion bar suspension and rear-mounted engine. This first engine, a five-cylinder radial motor, was rejected as being too complicated for mechanics to work on. The one designed for NSU in 1933, the year Hitler became chancellor, was the direct forerunner of the Beetle. It was powered by an air-cooled, four-cylinder, horizontally opposed, 1450cc engine, with a 4-speed alloy transaxle to get power to the rear wheels. The body sloped down in front and back and used the same central tunnel floor pan design and torsion bar suspension that would be used in the Beetle (Type I). Money problems ended their dreams after only six prototypes were constructed.

It wasn't until 1935 that Porsche found another car nut and sympathetic ear in Hitler, and the two Austrians sat down together to settle on specs for their Volksauto.

As late as 1938, Hitler conned the British into thinking he could be appeased with a country here and there while, less successfully, he tried to convince German automakers to produce his Volksauto. In what is now common marketing credo, he claimed it would increase demand for all cars rather than kill sales for the bigger ones. And he believed that the future lay not in steamships and railroads but in highways and cars by the millions for everyman—the autobahns and the California freeways. Setting the price of his proposed car at the typical savings level of the average German worker, Hitler showed a flair for astute market research that went over the heads of most of the industrialists and Party flacks.

It was Henry Ford Hitler wanted to emulate. Ford, if he didn't build the best cars, built them cheap, honestly and in such great numbers that he literally put America on wheels, selling over 15 million Model Ts between 1908 and 1927. And it was Porsche who could pull it off. He had designed and built race-winning V-16 rear-engined racing cars for Hitler's prestige mania and wanted badly to produce a good, efficient, affordable car for ordinary folks.

Porsche was contracted to design a lightweight car, air-cooled, with four-wheel independent torsion bar suspension, that got 40 miles on a gallon of gas, sat four, and cruised at 100 kph with a one-liter displacement engine. It would sell for 990 marks, or about $360. For his part, Hitler would build the modern highways for all these little bugs to crawl around on. Prestige would go up. Maybe nobody would notice what was happening to the Jews and the Poles and the Czechs. Or maybe it would be conveniently overlooked as the world admired

A BRIEF HISTORY

Germany's technical prowess and watched it climb out of hyper-inflation and a devastating depression.

Despite table-thumping demands, Hitler couldn't get any existing car builder to produce the car. They were still afraid it would rob sales of their heavier, expensive and far more profitable cars; they shuffled their feet and delayed and obstructed.

Frustrated, the Nazis decided to produce it themselves. In 1937, the KdF, a subsidiary of the German Labor Front (DAF), financed construction of the plant and worker housing. KdF stood for Kraft durch Freude, "Strength through Joy." It got its funds from DAF, whose main purpose was to keep workers in line and feed Party coffers. KdF was the Party entertainment, travel and cultural arbiter for the German worker. It planned group tours, rented cottages in the country, gave concerts and lectures.

With a 10-month deadline that stretched into four years, Porsche got it right. Well, right enough. Crankshafts stopped breaking when they were forged instead of cast, and the torsion bar suspension system—where a steel bar, instead of the usual spring, is twisted into increasing resistance when the wheel hits a bump or a dip—got sorted out. It still wasn't much of a car; noisy and underpowered with its non-synchro crash-box tranny, wailing cooling fan, and inherently clamorous air-cooled 25 hp mill.

Yet it could cruise all day at 100 kph (62 mph) in the hot African desert or cold Russian winter without boiling over or needing antifreeze. It was light yet sturdy, easy to drive and work on, handled well, and had great traction with the weight of the engine and transaxle over the rear wheels. It took a good tail wind to meet its 40 mpg goal, and hardly anybody could call it the Strength-through-Joy-Wagen with a straight face, so most people borrowed from the company name, Volkswagenwerke.

When the Nazis accepted Porsche's design, Mussolini sent 3,000 unemployed construction workers to help build the KdF plant and the "ideal Nazi worker's city." Hitler ordered German construction, metal, machine tool and auto industries to send unneeded workers to the village of Fallersleben in the mosquito-infested, swampy heath of Lower Saxony, near the castle Schloss Wolfsburg.

The KdF lit upon a novel layaway plan to sell the product. Workers could buy 5-mark stamps every week to paste in little booklets, and, after about 4 years, when they had paid in 990 marks, they were entitled to a certificate of ownership, though they weren't guaranteed there would be a car attached to the certificate. Transferability restrictions and lack of interest payments kept the number of subscribers to a total of 336,668. None ever received a car, though after the war they did get some credit for these payments if they bought a new VW. By war's end the KdF had accumulated a total of $67 million from the KdF-savers, which was seized by Stalin's troops. Three bucks for each of the 20 million Russians killed in the war.

In 1939 the plant was shifted to wartime production before any cars were actually made. The 60 prototypes and 210 KdF wagens that were produced before the war, all going to the Nazis, had been farmed out to other manufacturers to build. Most workers lived in wooden barracks, as only 2,538 workers' apartments had been built.

During the war, workers at the factory built 55,000 Kubelwagens (Bucket cars), the military Jeep-like predecessor of The Thing (or Safari, as it's called in Mexico, the name John Muir preferred), and 14,000 amphibian Schwimmwagens (also known as Schwimmkubels), with a sealed body and folding propeller. Six hundred or so KdF sedans were built, along with one and a half million stoves to keep the troops warm on the Russian front, and, late in the war, they assembled the V-1 flying bombs that terrorized England.

OF THE BEETLE

Employment at the factory reached 17,000 at its peak in 1944, the vast majority prisoners of war and forced laborers from Russia, Poland, France, Belgium and Holland.

War's end found Porsche living in his old hometown in Austria, where he repaired vehicles for the occupation forces and designed and built wheelbarrows and wagons. In 1947, the French tricked him, his son Ferry and his son-in-law into coming to the French Zone to discuss building a French people's car. They were arrested and charged with cruelty to French workers during the occupation. Porsche spent two years as a French prisoner, one of them in a medieval dungeon in Dijon. Health broken, he died in 1951, at the age of 75.

In Fallersleben, the roof of the factory had been blown away, leaving machinery standing in pools of water. An unexploded bomb was lodged between the two turbines of the power plant, and had it exploded, the Volkswagen would have been history, as turbine parts were impossible to get. The town's population was swollen with former slave laborers and freed prisoners of war, displaced persons and escapees from the Russian Zone, only five miles away.

Although Fallersleben was "captured" by reluctant American troops, who had to be convinced to take control of a town not on their maps, it ended up in the British Zone. The British decided to let the plant operate, temporarily, and used it as a repair facility for their vehicles. The Germans still at the factory began to clean up the debris and put cars together, which they traded for food and raw materials, both in desperate supply.

"Ugly, bizarre, noisy and flimsy," said the British experts asked to evaluate the Volkswagen. They recommended the factory be torn down. Then they tried to give it away to Ford. The chairman of the board of Ford Motor Company, Ernest Breech, advised: "Mr. Ford, I don't think what we are being offered here is worth a damn."

Finally, it was returned to the Germans, who hired Heinz Nordoff, a German engineer and American-style industrialist, to manage it. Nordoff, a homeless refugee after the war, would spend the next 20 years building VW into the fourth-largest auto company in the world.

By the end of 1945, 6,000 workers living on bread and potatoes cleaned up the plant and produced 1,785 VWs, mostly reconnaissance cars for the British. The following year, employment had gone up to 8,000 workers, who produced an amazing 10,020 cars, the first true civilian VWs, in the face of shortages of steel, coal, food and clothes. In 1947, production fell to just under 9,000 cars. Workers were still hungry; there were material and housing shortages; the mark had dropped considerably in value and industrial production was down throughout Germany.

These early Beetles were basically hand-built vehicles, mostly bare steel shells. Instruments were basic: speedometer and warning lights for the generator and oil pressure switch, and high beam and semaphores (pivoting arms mounted on the doorjamb pillars to indicate left and right turns). The 6-volt battery was placed under the rear seat, where it—sometimes shockingly—remained throughout its production run. The pan at the bottom of the engine lid had a hole for a hand crank should you find a dead battery in the morning, and the air intake flap on the fan housing was manually operated. You warmed up the engine in winter with it closed, then, with the engine still running, jumped out, lifted the engine lid and opened it for normal running. Windshield wipers stopped wherever they happened to be when you shut them off and it took 10 turns of the window crank to raise or lower the windows. The front seats were nonadjustable, and safety glass was not yet available. The tall and narrow 5.00 x 16" inch wheels led to some thrilling rides on windy days. Skinny bumpers, a flat windshield and two small windows at the rear—the famous split window—rounded out the picture. The final indignity was getting your doors blown off by a passing school bus.

Despite these handicaps, production doubled every year for the next three years, reaching nearly 82,000 cars by 1950, with few changes. Exports went mostly to neighboring European countries. Two cars were brought to the United States in 1949, one by Nordoff himself. No one was interested. Perhaps no one could disregard what the Nazis had wrought. But that would soon change. As Deng Xiaoping cynically predicted after the Tiananmen Square massacre, "The world will soon forget."

It has been speculated that VW was able to succeed in the United States when the "Evil Empire" pushed out Germany as the "bad guys," and it was OK to own a VW and other products of a hard-working, split Germany. By 1957 there was a six-month wait for cars from U.S. dealers.

Chopped & Dropped

For collectors and aficionados, two major events occurred in 1949: the first Deluxe/Export sedans and VW convertibles were offered. In the beginning, the Deluxe just came with upgraded trim but in the future would nearly always be the first to get changes. Two convertibles were built, one a four-seater by Karmann and the other, now very rare, a two-place convertible built by Hebmuller. VW would add ragtops the following year, but they were sunroof sedans, not true convertibles.

The Hebmuller would last for only four years, while the Karmann would be produced in large numbers up until the very end in 1979. Three hundred fifty Hebmullers were built in 1949 and 319 in 1950. Only one Hebmuller was built in 1951 because of a fire at the plant. Financial woes followed, resulting in 13 Hebmullers in 1952 and one last two-seater in 1953, for a total production of 692 Hebmuller convertibles—hence the $100,000 price tag.

Despite the small production run, a high proportion of these have survived and some experts value good examples at closer to half that amount, while others may only be worth $10,000. As with all older cars, the value depends on just how ''original'' the car is—have sheet metal and interiors been replaced?—as well as its condition and rarity.

Oh, yes, there was one other major event in 1949. In its early years the VW didn't have a gas gauge; instead there was a lever on the cowl wall you flipped to open the reserve tank. After a while you learned to kick the lever over with your foot at the first cough and motor merrily along. In 1949 you could get an optional fuel gauge—a metal ruler you stuck into the filler neck to measure the amount of fuel in the tank. Ah, progress.

Improvements and updates came thick and fast in the early fifties, particularly in the Deluxe/Export models. Though the factory was still being rebuilt, March 1950 saw the first Type II Transporter, known also as the bus, micro bus, kombi, van and, most recently, Vanagon. To add to the confusion, some refer to them as station wagons, a designation often associated with the Type III squareback. Transporters with small windows along the roof line are highly valued today (''You gotta 23-window Deluxe? Wow!''). Eight thousand Transporters were built that milestone year.

1950 also saw the addition of a thermostat to automatically operate the air cooling regulator, and, like many improvements made by VW through the years, it could be retrofit to earlier models. Hydraulic brakes were introduced to the Deluxe models and convertibles, a boon to VW mechanics. The mechanical brakes of the standard and earlier models could only be properly adjusted through an involved 20-step process. The engine break-in period, for which you got detailed instructions, was extended from 900 miles to 1,800 miles.

Dowdy looks, meager performance, miniscule trunk, and strange engine at the wrong end—on top of its

Nazi history—took their toll. Only 157 were registered in the United States in 1950, the first year VWs were sold here. They were sold only in New York by Max Hoffman, an import car distributor. It is said that if dealers wanted a Jag or Alfa they had to take a VW as well. There were some 30 makes being imported into the United States in the early fifties; few would survive the coming VW onslaught.

In the early sixties I used to borrow a friend's yellow '49 TC when I had a particularly hot and agile date (I could hardy pull up in my dowdy black '57 Beetle, could I?). A late-night, top-down ride through Central Park was de rigueur. The traffic lights that dotted the one-way road through the park were set for 25 mph, but if you ran just one light you could zip over the hills and around the curves at ridiculous speeds until you caught up with the red lights again. It was a favorite testing ground for NYC car dealers and their customers. The TC body had so much flex that the suicide doors had the nasty habit of popping open on bumps and potholes, risking loss of my passenger on the vicious curves and prompting a call of ''Hang on, Honey, here we go!''

Actually, my Beetle had a lot going for it. It was so utterly, depressingly dowdy I could park it anywhere in New York without fear of finding it stripped when I got back. I got it for $300 at what had to be the world's smallest garage on 7th Avenue, and for several years it carried me to dinners in Chinatown, the beaches of Long Island and up to Woodstock on weekends, asking little more than an occasional oil change and tune-up in exchange.

I got my money back when I traded it in for a cherry two-year-old '65 VW Bus from a Ford dealer in upstate New York. The hippest place to buy a VW was from a dealer in American cars, particularly outside the big city, who had gotten one on a trade-in. They didn't know what to make of these strange little cars and vastly undervalued them. And the service that came with the sale . . . ''You'll have to wait a while until you can take it home. Can't let it go like it is; needs new tires and a wash and wax.'' When was the last time anyone heard that?

The early nonsynchromesh ''crashbox'' transmission allowed you the fantasy of being Juan Fangio double-clutching his way through the Mille Miglia, but in 1952 the Deluxe/Export model got synchros in 2nd, 3rd and 4th gears. The late '52 Beetles were a much-improved car, quieter and easier to drive. They got a new instrument panel, and more stable 5.60 x 15″ tires became standard for the next 20 years. Vent wings were installed, along with the first self-parking wipers. The frame and front axle were completely new, and the antenna was moved from the center of the windshield to the left cowl.

There were 11 models: 11 A, the Standard sedan; 11 C, the Deluxe/Export sedan; 11 E, the Standard sunroof sedan; 11 G, the Deluxe/Export sunroof sedan; 15 A, the Karmann convertible; each of which was available in left- or right-hand drive; and one lonely Hebmuller 2-seat convert. Production jumped to over a hundred thousand vehicles for the first time, 601 of which went to the United States.

The biggest cosmetic change for '53 was the end of the split window, replaced with an oval window in the back after February. By late 1954 the front torsion bars had been beefed up to 8 leaves (only the rears were solid bars), the new synchro tranny was much improved and the engine was broken in at the factory, although the wise continued to make several oil changes and maintain reasonable speeds for the first few thousand miles. Engine size went up to 1192cc with 30 hp early in the year, going to 36 hp with a higher compression ratio in September. This engine, the first covered in this book (see Changes Through the Years, Chapter XVI), would be installed in all VWs until 1960. Production nearly doubled to over two hundred thousand cars, with 6,343 registered in the United States.

While Detroit went on a binge of huge wallowing, finned freeway schooners and retooled every 2 or 3 years, VW plugged along, making periodic refinements during its 40-year run, building up an authorized dealer organization of over a thousand dealers in the United States to service their customers. They were so successful that VW was the first foreign automaker to build a production plant—for Rabbits—in the United States (since shut down and sold to Sony for boob tube production; the Rabbit didn't have the same magic). It caught on because enough people, disappointed with Detroit's offerings, saw something honest in this Plain Jane of a car.

U.S. sales of the VW quadrupled in 1955, and you could get an optional fuel gauge. The company switched to model-year designations in August, following U.S. practice. Semaphores were dropped in U.S. models in favor of self-cancelling turn signals, and the taillights got bigger. To celebrate the one millionth Beetle, which started the '56 model year, the company built a 165,000 capacity wooden stadium and threw a big bash.

Years of complaints about the small windows resulted in dropping the oval window at the end of the '57 model year, to be replaced with a window nearly twice its size, with a bigger windshield as well. In 1965 the

windshield grew in size again and was slightly curved to reduce glare, and the rear window was increased by another 20 percent.

Twelve-volt Beetles became optional in '58 but would not become standard for another nine years. A popular option that year: a large wind-up key you could stick on the engine lid. A more successful way to go faster in your VW was the growing after-market availability of hot rod modifications and parts, such as stroker cranks and hot cams, and a Judson supercharger that went for $160 and boosted horsepower by 50 percent. The craze had begun.

In the late fifties Detroit was on a crash program to build compact cars in face of the competition from VW. It is doubtful these had much effect on sales of the high-quality VW, though they did have a hand in killing off many other imports. But the Detroit models grew in size and complexity every year; in my opinion, they apparently didn't understand the appeal of the VW, much as they don't seem able to understand the appeal of small Japanese quality cars as their market share continues to slip away. Boggles the mind.

The beginning of the sixties saw the introduction of a new 40 hp engine for the Deluxe Beetle, and a fully synchromesh gearbox. With production rising to half a million Beetles a year in 1960 and over 800,000 the next year, VW couldn't make all the parts themselves and called upon Bosch to supply generators and starters. A new accessory became available: seat belts.

The new engine came with new valve clearance specifications, which have confused everyone ever since. The difference was that in the earlier engines valve clearance increased as the engine warmed up; now, with the 40 horse, they decreased as the engine got hotter, so greater clearance was called for. First, VW said to make the clearances .008″ for both intake and exhaust valves, then they widened exhaust valve clearance to

.012″. Ten years later they said to make it .006″ for all engines. Many mechanics use .008″ on all long-stud (pre-'65) engines.

I like to run my valves kinda tight and use .006″, but with a caveat: if you're going to run with tight valves you must check the clearances often. And take one additional step. Every time I adjust the valves I log the preadjustment clearances in a maintenance book; that way I know, for example, that #3 exhaust valve is stretching because it's been getting tighter at every adjustment, and it's time to pull the heads for a valve job before it swallows a valve.

A broken valve sucked into the combustion chamber, to be struck a millisecond later by the piston, is a grisly and fairly common VW tragedy. It is signaled by a sudden loss of power and puff of gas through the muffler or carburetor, followed by a great sinking feeling in the driver. The only hope for minimal damage is to immediately shut off the ignition, push in the clutch and safely pull over to the side of the road. Any attempt to keep the engine going by tromping on the gas pedal will only result in a trashed piston, its rod now free to flail about and punch holes in the case and create untold mayhem.

The one millionth VW was sold in the United States in 1962, the year a fuel gauge became standard in the Deluxe/Export models and mechanical brakes disappeared from the Standards. They fixed the flimsy hood stays that previously had caused so many bent hoods by service station attendants—remember them?— who didn't properly release the hood holder. In the after-market, you could get big bore kits, dual carbs and auxiliary oil coolers. Yummy.

As Detroit returned to the super-car era and didn't bother to compete against VW any longer, the last Beetles from the Wolfsburg plant came to the United States. After 1964 all U.S. market Beetles came from a new factory in the port city of Emden, ready to be loaded onto ships carrying 1500 VWs each to the States. One ship reached our shores nearly every day. Buses and Euro spec Beetles were still made at Wolfsburg.

The mid-sixties saw the end of the 40 hp engine, with a new 1500cc/50 hp engine in the bus in 1965. That same engine with a smaller displacement, the 1300, would go into the '66 bugs for just one year, then become a 1500 again in 1967 until 1970, when displacement was increased to 1600cc. These engines had the spark timing for no. 3 cylinder retarded 4 crankshaft degrees so that cylinder, the one just downstream from the oil cooler, would run a little cooler. Thus, it's important to use the right distributor cap and make sure the distributor has not been installed 180 degrees off on a rebuild.

1965 was the last year for the strong, if old-fashioned and heavy, king and link pin front axles in the Deluxe models, which went to ball joints. In '66, the camshaft got bearings for the first time, the dimmer switch went from the floor to the directional signal lever, the front torsion bars got ten leaves and a host of other improvements were made to the front axle.

The '66 Beetle is my personal favorite. The 1300 engine was powerful (for a Beetle), frugal on gas, and it could wail at high rpm all day long if asked. Maybe it didn't have quite the torque of the larger displacement engines, but neither was the case as stressed. This is an excellent collectible that can double as a daily driver, strong and well constructed.

Many believe the '67 was the "Zenith Year" for the VW. It got a 1500cc/53 hp engine with a stronger case, bigger exhaust valves, new crank, bigger clutch, and new transaxle case. U.S. Ghias got disk brakes, and all U.S. cars came with a dual master cylinder. Everyone was delighted by the brighter lights from the 12-volt electrical system, and the driver finally got an armrest.

U.S. emissions and safety regulations resulted in the first pollution controls for the engine in 1965. The car was shorter and wider, with the front and rear hoods shortened to clear the new bumpers required by U.S. height regulations. The Beetle still cost only $1,699 in '68, but would go up to over $2,000 in the next 3 years as the dollar lost value against the mark. Detroit was once more fighting back with its own subcompacts. VW fought, too, with its idea of an automatic, the auto-stick tranny. Maybe the best thing to happen that year was the external gas filler door, which saved the bother of opening the hood for a refuel and cut down on gas fumes inside the car.

Perhaps the major event of the year was the death of Heinz Nordoff in April. He had guided the company for 20 years, keeping Porsche's design intact and constantly improving quality. While it may have been coincidental with the inevitable changes coming to the automobile industry, to some his death was the beginning of the end of the high quality standards that had been VW's hallmark.

VW sales had reached a peak of almost four hundred thousand by 1968. Nineteen million VWs were built between 1949 and 1980 and in that time over 4½ million air-cooled VWs were sold in the United States; in the last three years, all were convertibles. Sales plummeted, by design, after 1975, when the Rabbit was introduced.

The 1969 model got a new and vastly superior heating system, and U.S. and Canadian models got a new independent rear suspension with double-jointed rear axles. It was the last year you could buy a black VW in the United States.

In 1971 came the Super Beetle. The combination of strut suspension, which eliminated the torsion bars, and a 3'' longer hood increased luggage capacity from 5 to 9 cubic feet. The 1600cc engines on U.S. models carried numerous modifications and got 60 hp from dual port heads and a new three-piece intake manifold. If you have one of these engines, keep a close eye on the rubber boots that connect the manifold sections; cracks and leaks lean out the fuel mixture, which can burn valves, put holes in pistons and cook the engine.

A highly welcomed improvement in '71 was the doghouse cooler, which Colin talks about in Hi-Performance Modifications, Chapter XVIII. Along with the good, however, came the silly: the accessory list included stick-on sunflowers for $2 apiece. Yuk.

The following year saw the beginning of many new "Special Edition" models to boost slipping sales. The first was the Baja Champion SE, which had a 3-step metallic paint job and 10-spoke road wheels. It was the model to celebrate the breaking of Ford's Model T production record of 15,007,033 cars. In later years came the Sport Bug SE, based on the Super Beetle, the Sun Bug, the Love Bug, Fun Bug and Water Bug, and La Grande and Champagne Super Beetles.

But none of this helped. U.S. emissions regulations got real. You couldn't get by with just a rubber hose sucking crankcase fumes into the air cleaner anymore. Cars in the late '70s had to be tuned for least emissions, not best performance, and run on low-octane unleaded gas. Operation of engine controls was removed from human hands and placed into the computer chips of a black box, with an expensive catalytic converter downstream. Outdated and underpowered, a victim of the declining value of the dollar and a major polluter by contemporary standards, the end was near.

The water-cooled Passat, introduced in Europe in '73, came to the United States as the Dasher in 1974, to be replaced by the water-cooled Rabbit in 1975. Production fell to under 300,000 Beetles in 1974, U.S. sales dropped to 82,030 cars, and Toyota grabbed the number one spot in U.S. imports. From '77 on, the only air-cooled Beetles sold in the United States were Super Beetle convertibles. The Vanagon, the replacement for the Transporter, came with a two-liter air-cooled motor, the so-called Porsche pancake engine, through 1982. Diesels were installed in some of them in 1982 and early 1983. After '82 it was equipped with the Wasserboxer engine, a water-cooled horizontally opposed four cylinder mill. In my opinion, the diesel is an under-powered slug. To give it some pep, you can install a Rabbit engine in its place, using the specially shaped diesel oil pan to make it fit, although this is a complicated and expensive conversion. Except for the '80-'82 Vanagons, U.S. sales of air-cooled VWs ended in early 1980, really leftover '79 models.

The air-cooled VW thrived for 40-odd years, longer than the Model T, and in greater numbers. In some ways it resembled the thinking behind the Model T. In early years, it too could be had in any color as long as it was black (or gray, in VW's case). Both kept essentially the same design from beginning to end. The VW never got power steering, power brakes, power windows, or factory air conditioning. In its final years it was distorted, some believe, into the Super Beetle, with bulbous curved windshield, auto-stick transmission, strut front suspension and giant taillights. These ''improvements'' weren't necessarily bad in and of themselves, but for the purist they violated the original design and spirit of the Beetle.

Both Ferdinand Porsche and Henry Ford received high government awards from the Nazis. Porsche, reputedly politically naive and interested only in building cars, and Ford, an anti-Semite and ''enlightened'' industrialist, were highly regarded in Germany and by Hitler, who probably would be horrified to learn that the 20 millionth Beetle was made in Puebla, non-Aryan Mexico in 1981. Some of these were exported to Germany. Beetles also continue to be produced in Brazil, South Africa and Nigeria. Don't try to bring one of these Beetles into the United States though; they don't meet our emissions regulations and will be confiscated.

CUSTOMIZING AND HOT RODDING

Just as I could hardly pick up my hot NYC date in a black '57 Beetle (so what if it was the last oval window—who knew?), you could hardly go cruisin' Crenshaw Boulevard or flirt with the carhops at Mel's in a stocker Beetle. Just would not do.

So, as they had done with their Model Ts and thirties Fords, out came the wrenches, torches, 'glass and lead, sanders and paint sprayers. Some emerged from backyard garages as chopped and lowered, oval window lead sleds with deep, glossy lacquer paint jobs; others hit the boulevards with fenders cut away to clear wider tires on Empi rims; a speaker system where the back seat used to be; bumpers replaced by Nerf bars, the engine lid deep-sixed to show off a sano chrome-plated motor, and lightning graphics on Imron paint. Beetles, sunroof sedans, convertibles, sporty Ghias, Type IIIs and Buses all joined the parade.

Lead sled:	Slick car carrying a lot of weight in lead used to fill in all the holes left when chrome, door handles and such were removed.
Nerf bars:	Skinny little bars mounted vertically and bolted on where the bumper brackets once held a bumper, providing bare minimum body protection but giving that sano look.
Sano:	Sanitary, clean; that is, neatly done.
Empi:	Brand name for popular 5-spoke wheels.
Imron:	Brand name of modern, high-gloss synthetic paint available in wild metallic and pearlescent colors.
Chopped:	Roof lowered by removing sections of the greenhouse pillars.
Dropped:	Body lowered on the suspension, low-rider style.
Greenhouse:	Glass-enclosed upper area of the body.
'Glass:	Fiberglass body parts; in glasspack, flow-thru muffler containing fiberglass fibers.
Resto:	Restoration.
ET:	Elapsed time on quarter-mile run, usually given with speed at end of run.
Marque:	Any automobile brand name.
Street Rod:	Souped-up car that is drivable and legal on city streets.
Funny cars:	All-out dragsters with tube chassis whose only purpose is drag racing.
NOS:	New Old Stock; unused OEM parts that are no longer made, perhaps lurking in a dusty bin in the back of the parts department.
OEM:	Original Equipment Manufacture; the parts specified and originally sold with the car.
Short block:	Assembled bottom-end; case with crank, rods, camshaft and bearings installed.
Long block:	Short block plus heads, pistons and cylinders; you add the manifolds, carb(s), generator, sheet metal and such from your old engine.
Billet:	As in billet crank; crankshafts, cams, rocker arms and rods machined from solid steel or alloy bars.

With its great traction, some saw off-road possibilities in the homely Bug. They lopped off excesses like bumpers, cut back the fenders to clear bigger tires, shortened the front and rear ends and installed upswept exhaust headers and glasspacks to reduce overhang, mounted larger tires and wheels for better grip, beefed up the engine and transaxle and went into the deserts of California or the Baja Peninsula. Thus was born the Baja Bug.

Others tried to follow the big-wheeled Jeeps and bikes cavorting in the sand dunes outside of places like Palm Springs or Pismo, only to get hopelessly bogged down. So, after they lowered the air pressure in their tires to get out, they rethought their approach to the dunes. The result? Dune buggies, built on the stock floor pan or, in more radical clothing, on a tube frame.

The more extreme versions are the sand rails, off-roaders built of thin tubing to reduce weight and gain ground clearance. Virtually nothing remains of the body; only the drive train, suspension, brakes and steering are kept to be bolted onto the tube frame, and these highly modified. Skinny front wheels and big fat rear paddle wheels, each controlled by a steering brake, are marks of the dune rider. The hot sand rail setup is a mid-engine layout for better front/rear weight distribution, switching the engine/transaxle around and reversing the final drive gears (so you don't have 4 speeds in reverse and 1 forward, as sometimes happens to amateurs rebuilding their own transaxles). As environmental concerns for plant and animal life seep into our consciousness, these and all off-road vehicles find increasingly stiff restrictions on running around in the wilderness. Off-road races are banned or severely restricted in areas of California and Nevada that harbor the desert tortoise.

All-out hot rodding of these valiant would-be Porsches is another popular avocation. There's room for all, from the high-end funny cars stuffed with blown (super charged) engines to modified and stock classes. Funny cars and other all-out dragsters run ETs below 10 seconds and hit up to 185 mph at the end of a quarter mile (those carrying American V-8s can do it in less than 5 seconds). Nonprofessionally rodded, non-streetable VWs usually run 11-13 second/100-115 mph ETs. All of these cars are expensive to build, running to $10,000 for a good backyard rod. Street rodders can build to any level they want, from mild to wild. With a moderate investment, the same car will also take them dependably to work or school.

And would you believe that there's a large group who think the VW is great just as it came from the

factory—without velour interiors, rakish paint jobs or 100+ hp engines? These are the resto freaks who match part numbers and search for NOS headliners and hood badges for their '51 split-windows.

Sharing these ideas and experiences with like-minded VW nuts was a natural outgrowth of the movement. There are local, regional and national clubs who produce chatty and informative newsletters and throw an occasional Bug Bash or camping trip. Most every town and city of any size has a group of VW lovers who show their spiffed up wheels on warm summer weekends. To find them, check out the back pages of magazines like *Dune Buggies & Hot VWs* or mosey on down to the local VW garage that caters to the freaks and hot rodders.

If you get your kicks from mingling with Volks' volks, and can handle the bikini contests, Bug-Ins and Bug Bashes are the place to go. Drag races, twenty or more classes of judged show cars, dealers, and a flea market area draw thousands of spectators and participants. Even the bikini contests have some value; it's a perfect time to leisurely cruise the custom cars and uncrowded flea market.

Entry fees to these events, whether as a spectator, competitor, show-off or flea marketeer, are a welcome bargain. Spectator fees rarely exceed $10, and flea market spaces usually go for $20 for the weekend. One sideshow that never fails to draw a good crowd is the engine blow-up. In this, an engine is placed on a stand, hooked up to a battery and gas can, started and run wide open until it blows or seizes in a minute or two. Often it seizes and unceremoniously flops over; with luck a crowd-pleasing rod punches through the case or the crank breaks.

CLUBS

A great way to stay in touch with the Marque. Home-brewed newsletters from the specialty clubs such as NEATO and LiMBO contain a wealth of tips, experiences, and memories. They also have classifieds of members selling or looking for VWs and hard-to-find parts. To find even more clubs, including local chapters of the national organizations, search the World Wide Web. Most major VW clubs maintain Web sites and you can find more by following the links to other sites. I found dozens just by searching for "VW clubs" with one of the many available search engines. Some apparently publish only on the Web, such as The Westfalia Club of America Web Site (http://members.aol.com/westfalia.html). Here are the addresses of some major clubs:

Bus Lovers of America
1117 Highland Ave #4
Northfield, MN 55057

LiMBO (Late Model Bus Organization)
9 Golden Hill Ave.
Shrewsbury, MA 01545

NEATO (No. East Association of Transporter Owners)
P.O. Box 4190
Albuquerque, NM 87196

SOTO (Society of Transporter Owners)
P. O. Box 3555
Walnut Creek, CA 94598

Strictly Vintage II's
4022 Johnson Drive
Oceanside, CA 92056

Volkswagen Club of America
P. O. Box 154
North Aurora, IL 60542

Volkswagen Type 34 Karmann Ghia Registry
8990 Capcano Road
San Diego, CA 92126

Vintage Volkswagen Club of America
5705 Gordon Drive
Harrisburg, PA 17112

VW Thing Association of America
16941 Joliet Road
Westfield, IN 46074

Westfalia Wanderers
13 W. Montgomery St.
Ilion, NY 13357

KEEPING YOUR VW ALIVE

With 5 million Volksautos sold in the United States, a huge after-market industry supplying virtually every part at reasonable prices has grown up around the air-cooled wonder, one of the rare automobiles that lends itself to owner care. This industry serves preservationists as well as those who want a bit more zip, posh, or looks.

True OEM replacement parts grow scarcer every year, and many are not available at all. A common feature of VW magazines are the tales told of the search for the elusive OEM Type II floor rubber, of poking through basement stashes in hopes of a score, and of treasures that might lurk in the parts department of some small-town VW dealer. Fortunately, there are businesses that supply replacements for the items that suffer wear and tear or dry and crack with age and heat, such as OEM-style window rubber, interiors, and floormats, or the oft-stolen Wolfsburg crests. In a very tangible way, these specialists help keep our VWs alive, often producing replicas indistinguishable from the original, in function as well as design.

PARTS

Wishbooks published by mail-order suppliers of engine and other mechanical parts contain page after page of stock and high-performance goodies. In these you can find all the parts to do a complete home-made rebuild or engines assembled to certain stages, from a short block to a bolt-it-in-and-drive-it-away big bore, dual port engine. Some sell ordinary rebuilt or reproduced OEM parts, others specialize in squeezing more horsepower or life out of the little 4-banger. This is where you'll find kits for dual carbs, centrifugal distributors, 6- to 12-volt conversions, balanced and stroked cranks, and many, many other goodies to make your VW roar with delight.

My guess is that just about every outfit that advertises in *Dune Buggies & Hot VWs* and *VW Trends* presents themselves honestly. It seems they're as honest and straightforward as the car they service. Reader feedback quickly drives out the occasional bad apple. I'm partial to mom-and-pop suppliers—VW nuts who went off the deep end, usually. But the bigger houses obviously have more coin for stocking and producing a vast array of items. Anyway, most of the biggies started out as small entrepreneurs working in garages to supply unavailable items.

PARTS SUPPLIERS

These are the folks who help us keep our VWs alive. They range from small shops that produce highly specialized parts such as rubber moldings or seat covers, to producers and sellers of high performance parts, and everything in between. Some publish useful and informative newsletters, and many catalogues are great for technical information. In order by state—except for Strano's—they include:

Strano's Foreign Car

68 White Street
Brookville, PA 15825   arnlyn@ncentral.com
800-729-1831/Tech Line 814-849-3131/FAX 814-849-6305
A personal favorite. No catalogues, no accessories, just brand name parts at great prices. If you're tired of gruff or bored phone order takers, these are the folks you've been looking for. They have helped me through numerous jams, giving me the right advice and finding the right parts.

ARIZONA
Chirco VW Super Centre

9101 E. 22nd Street
Tucson, AZ 85710
800-955-9795/520-722-1987/FAX 520-298-4069
Performance VW parts.

The Trim Shop

4112 N. 25th Street
Phoenix, AZ 85016
800-966-7791/Info 602-955-7791/FAX 602-381-0933
Parts and accessories for the modern-day Kubelwagen, The Thing.

CALIFORNIA
All Electronics Corporation

P.O. Box 567
Van Nuys, CA 91408-0567   www.allcorp.com
800-826-5432
Electronic goodies.

Bernie Bergmann

340 N. Hale Avenue
Escondido, CA 92029   www.choicemall.com\berniebergmann
619-747-4649/FAX 619-740-8522
*Stock and performance engines and parts, turbos and hydraulic
lifter conversions.*

BFY Obsolete Parts

1460 N. Glassell
Orange, CA 92667
714-639-4411/FAX 714-997-2247
*Clearly illustrated and well-laid-out catalogue of "probably, the
largest inventory of obsolete and hard to find Volkswagen parts
in the world" for early VWs.*

Bus Boys, Inc.

18595 E. Lake Boulevard
Redding, CA 96003   busboys@aol.com
916-244-1616/FAX 916-244-0933
*Lowering and disk brake systems, front end components, mufflers
and other bus parts. Extensive restoration parts for Westfalia
camper, Vanagon, and other buses '64 through '91.*

CB Performance Products

1715 N. Farmersville Boulevard
Farmersville, CA 93223
800-274-8337/209-733-8222 (CA)/FAX 209-733-7967
*Complete line of high performance components, turbo chargers,
hydraulic valve lifter conversion kits, carbs and tools.*

CNC, Inc.

1221 West Morena Boulevard
San Diego, CA 92110
619-275-1663/FAX 619-275-0729
*Brake and clutch assemblies, master and slave cylinders,
hydraulic throttles, and calipers, mostly for off-road and circle
track racing vehicles.*

DEE Engineering

3560 Cadillac Avenue
Costa Mesa, CA 92626
714-979-4990/FAX 714-979-3468
*Carries a full line of VW components. Complete line of Bugpack
and Bugline performance and replacement parts.*

Engle Cams

1621 12th Street
Santa Monica, CA 90404
310-450-0806/FAX 310-452-3753
*Performance and competition camshafts, lifters, springs and
pushrods.*

Fat Performance

1558 N. Case Street
Orange, CA 92867
714-637-2889/FAX 714-637-7352
*Off-road racing engines, drivetrains, suspensions and
components.*

German Auto

11324 Norwalk Boulevard
Santa Fe Springs, CA 90670
310-868-9393/310-863-1123/FAX 310-929-1461
Large inventory of stock and race parts and accessories from
Germany and Japan, and full service machine shop.

Gene Berg Enterprises

1725 North Lime Street
Orange, CA 92865-4187
714-998-7500/FAX 714-998-7528
Purveyor of quality engine and transaxle parts.

GEX International Corp.

15245 Nubia Street
Baldwin Park, CA 91706   herbiegex.comhttp:\\www.gexintl.com
800-423-1869/818-960-5341/FAX 818-962-6975
Supplier of rebuilt engines, engine parts and front axle beams.
Carries a full line of VW components.

Johnny's Speed & Chrome

6411 Beach Boulevard
Buena Park, CA 90621-2896
714-994-4022/FAX 714-228-0136
Baja kits, sand rail chassis, off-road and high performance
parts, tools.

Karmann Ghia Parts & Restoration P.O Box 58
Moorpark, CA 93020   http:\\www.karmannghia.com
800-927-2787/805-529-4442/FAX 805-529-6065
Seller and manufacturer of full line of Ghia body and interior
parts. Restorations, too.

Kennedy Engineered Products

38830 17th Street East
Palmdale, CA 93550
805-272-1147/FAX 805-272-1575
Engine adaptors for VW (and other) transaxles, and high per-
formance clutches. Stick a Mazda rotary or a V-8 in your VW.

Long Enterprises

2475 Morse Road
Sebastopol, CA 95472
707-829-1169/FAX 707-823-5664
Performance VW transaxle parts and machine shop services.

McCulloch Poptop Campers

P.O. Box 2533
Malibu, CA 90265
800-248-2719
Pop-top seals and canvas for VW campers.

NOLOGY Engineering Inc.

7360 Trade Street
San Diego, CA 92121
619-578-4688/FAX 619-578-4388
See page 371

Pauter Machine Company, Inc.

367 Zenith Street
Chula Vista, CA 91911
619-422-5384/FAX 619-422-1924
Highly respected manufacturer of high performance VW engine
components, including billet cranks, rods and rocker arms.

Performance Technology

1631 North Placentia, Unit M
Anaheim, CA 92806
714-526-0533/FAX 714-526-1366
Performance and competition cylinder heads.

SCAT Enterprises, Inc.

1400 Kingsdale Avenue
Redondo Beach, CA 90278-3983
310-370-5501/FAX 310-214-2285
Wide selection of performance parts and accessories, including
unusual split-port heads.

Unique Supply Inc.

610 Tennessee Street
Redlands, CA 92373
800-576-2882/909-793-0212/909-793-0108/FAX 909-798-5025
Large selection of stock and performance parts for the VW.

Vee Dub Parts Unlimited

17404 Beach Boulevard
Huntington Beach, CA 92647
714-848-8868/FAX 714-848-5390
Fat catalogue of high performance goodies for your engine, transmission and chassis, along with tools and stock replacement parts.

Vintage Parts, Inc.

317 N. Victory Boulevard
Burbank, CA 91502
818-848-2833/FAX 818-848-2863
NOS and OEM (where available) stock restoration parts for Types I & II VWs from 1949 to 1967. Detailed, illustrated catalogue.

Web-Cam

1815 Massachusetts Avenue
Riverside, CA 92507
909-369-5144/FAX 909-369-7266
Performance cams for VWs and other cars.

West Coast Metric, Inc.

24002 Frampton Avenue
Harbor City, CA 90710
800-247-3202/310-325-0005/FAX 310-325-9733
Wide selection of window rubber, seals and other body parts for all VWs, clearly listed and illustrated catalogue.

Wolfsburg West

1051 N. Grove Street
Anaheim, CA 92806   wwest@earthlink.com
714-630-9653/FAX 714-237-1395
Clear, illustrated catalogue of restoration parts for bug and bus through '79.

COLORADO
Rocky Mountain Motor Works

1003 Tamarac Parkway
Woodland Park, CO 80863
800-258-1996/FAX 719-687-3064
Restoration components for the Ghia: interior, convertibles, seals, body and mechanical parts.

Sewfine Automotive
Interior Products

5119 S. Windermere
Littleton, CO 80120
800-739-3463/303-347-0212/FAX 303-347-0160
Interior kits, seats and upholstery, door panels, carpets, headliners, and convertible parts.

FLORIDA
Classic Motor Carriages

16650 N.W. 27th Avenue
Miami, FL 33054
800-252-7742/305-626-0180/305-625-9700/FAX 305-624-1139
Maker of fiberglass replicars, including Porsche Speedster for air-cooled engines.

Creative Car Craft Co.

5575 Doug Taylor Circle
St. James City, FL 33956-3220
941-283-8989/FAX 941-283-8333
Custom fiberglass components for street, show and race.

Fisher Buggies

5126 S. Lois Avenue
Tampa, FL 33611   www.fisherbuggies.com
813-837-6696/FAX 813-835-6806
Catalog listing vast supply of parts, components and tools for VW Bajas, rails and racers.

Sunray Bugs

16016 US HWY 301
Dade City, FL 33523   sunray@tingley.net
352-521-5660/FAX 352-521-5739
Wide variety of restoration parts in well-done catalogue.

GEORGIA
Deal Automotive

4584 Columbus Road
Macon, GA 31206
912-474-9292/FAX 912-474-0118
Parts, accessories and speed equipment, dune buggy frames and salvage VWs and parts.

Number One Parts/
Nopi Imported Car Parts

486 Main Street
Forest Park, GA 30050   www.nopi.com
800-277-6674/FAX 404-366-8536
Popular stock, custom and performance parts for air- and water-cooled VWs.

IDAHO
Used VW Parts

1619 North Phillippi
Boise, ID 83706
208-377-8733
Huge warehouse of new and used VW parts.

MICHIGAN
Appletree Automotive Inc.

1920 N. 24th Avenue
Mears, MI 49436
800-433-2521/FAX 616-873-3262
Large inventory of parts from leading manufacturers, stock and high performance.

The Chassis Shop
Performance Products, Inc.

1931 N. 24th Avenue
Mears, MI 49436
616-873-3640/FAX 616-873-0218
Full line of racing car chassis and parts.

Recycled Bugs Inc./
Parts Place Inc.

2300 N. Opdyke Road
Auburn Hills, MI 48326
810-373-2300/FAX 810-373-5950
Fun catalogue of new, remanufactured and recycled parts for both air- and water-cooled VWs.

NEW YORK
Rapid Parts

178 Rt. 59
Monsey, NY 10952
914-352-1138/FAX 914-352-1019
Storefront and mailorder house right off NY Thruway in Rockland Co., crammed with a wide variety of air- and water-cooled VW parts and accessories.

OHIO
Der Wagonwerks

P.O. Box 1347
Elyria, OH 44036
216-322-9459
T-shirts from Peter's drawings. Ask for their catalog.

Euclid Foreign Motors, Inc.

19901-20020 St. Clair Avenue
Cleveland, OH 44117
216-481-9200/FAX 216-481-6668
Water-cooled and air-cooled VW parts since 1964. Three locations.

Larry's Off Road Center

4156 Wadsworth Road
Dayton, OH 45414
937-275-9501/FAX 937-275-7850
Off-road and performance goodies.

Mill Supply

3241 Superior Avenue
Cleveland, OH 44114   www.millsupply.com
800-888-5072/FAX 216-241-0425
Sheet metal and body finishing tools and materials for your dinged or rusted Beetle, Super Beetle, Bus, Ghia or Type III.

OREGON
House of Ghia

2626 Three Lakes Road
Albany, OR 97321
541-926-6513/FAX 541-926-5819
Vast array of Ghia body parts in detailed, lovingly assembled catalogue; fun and useful newsletter, history and "Ghia Spotter" publications.

Z Products Autosport

30625-B S.W. Boones Ferry
Wilsonville, OR 97070
800-331-9027/503-682-1267
Component kits to convert standard buses and vanagons to mini-campers. Curtain kits for conversions; may also be adapted for Westfalia replacements.

RHODE ISLAND
M&T Mfg.

Hopkins Lane Mill
P.O. Box 3730
Peace Dale, RI 02883   70524.514@compuserve.com
401-789-0472/FAX 401-789-5650
Convertible top and trim parts for VW, Karmann Ghia and Rabbit Cabriolet.

VIRGINIA
Billet Machine Products

P.O. Box 2892
Springfield, VA 22152
703-361-3374/FAX 703-866-1537
Wide variety of machined aluminum parts and accessories to dress up your VW.

VW Restorations & Customs

8223 Conner Drive
Manassas, VA 22111
703-361-3374/FAX 703-330-9908
Wide variety of machined aluminum parts and accessories to dress up your VW.

WASHINGTON
Adventure Werks

Bellingham, WA   adwerks@nas.com
360-671-6626/FAX 360-738-1062
They rent VW campers to travelers. Not just in the state of Washington.

WISCONSIN
BGW Spectre, Ltd.

2534 Woodland Park Drive
Delafield, WI 53018   bgwhttwr@execpc.com
414-646-4884/FAX 414-646-8133
Maker of VW rod kits and custom body components. Kits include convertibles, coupes, panel vans, pick up trucks, station wagons, several Bajas, dune buggies, and rails. Trade marks from Wunderbug, VW Ford, and more.

MOFOCO Competition Engines

102 W. Capitol Drive
Milwaukee, WI 53212
800-553-8955/800-242-8968/FAX 414-963-2045
Speed equipment, off-road accessories, stock and performance parts, rebuilt engines and transmissions, machine shop.

PUBLICATIONS
(see **Publications, Chapter XVIII,** and **Other Sources of Information, Chapter IV**, for more)
Most of these have been mentioned in the book. Here are their addresses:

Magazines

Dune Buggies & Hot VWs
P.O. Box 2260
Costa Mesa, CA 92628
714-979-2560

VW Trends
774 S. Placentia Avenue
Placentia, CA 92870
714-572-2255

Books
There are two books I wouldn't be without when looking for a used VW: this book and *The Car of the Century*, by J.T. Garwood. This one you know, and Garwood's is indispensable if you're going to restore a VW. It has all the correct dates and part numbers. *The Car of the Century* is actually two books. Volume One covers Type I Beetles from 1930 to 1960, and Volume Two covers 1961 to 1980. Together, these books amount to 1,200 pages of valuable information on every aspect of Beetle production. It is obviously a labor of love, extremely detailed down to the last washer, engine, chassis, and body number of all changes made in all years, with clear illustrations showing details to look for. For each year, there is a table detailing paint and interior colors offered by the factory for all Type I models. There is enough information to allow the restorer to produce a near-perfect, factory original VW. Even if you're not going

to make a "correct" restoration—something that gets harder with every passing year—just knowing what works with what is invaluable. These self-published books may be a bit pricey, but they're worth every cent.

I only have one minor quibble with Garwood's books. They're printed double-spaced, which is okay, but in all caps, which makes them hard to read for those of us who read words not just as combined letters but as recognizable shapes. However, this is just nit-picking, and I want to thank J.T. Garwood for all his information.

The Car of the Century, J.T. Garwood
P.O. Box 1423
Southampton, PA 18966-1423

Small Wonder, Walter Henry Nelson (Boston: Little, Brown and Company, 1967).
This book is also a small wonder, filled with the details of the people and times that created the air-cooled VW.

A note to Transporter owners: After having been out-of-print for more than 20 years, Robert Bentley, Inc., has finally reprinted the Official Volkswagen Transporter (Type II) Workshop Manual for 1963-67 models. The reprint came after years of requests from SOTO and other club members. It's 918 pages and available through SOTO, NEATO, parts houses, or directly from Bentley at 1-800-423-4595 or 1000 Massachusetts Ave., Cambridge, MA 02138.

Book Distributors

auto-bound, Inc.
909 Marina Village Parkway
Alameda, CA 94501
800-523-5833/510-521-8630/FAX 510-521-8755
Wholesale and retail auto book dealer. They publish a catalogue just for Porsche and VW enthusiasts, and the staff has more than 35 years of automotive experience.

Cook's Distributing Company
136 Eighth Avenue, #10
City of Industry, CA 91746
818-330-3395/FAX 818-330-5922
Wholesale and retail distributor of auto repair manuals.

Matthew Nottonson & Co., Inc.
10945 Burbank Blvd.
North Hollywood, CA 91601
800-292-6652/818-985-0322/FAX 818-985-0344

A good mechanic can make owning a VW a more pleasant experience, particularly if that good mechanic is you. While not without their share of quirks and frustrations, VWs are remarkably user-friendly, one of the easier cars for the idiot to maintain and repair. Doing your own work means discount prices for parts, gaining the confidence to handle any breakdown that might present itself, and avoiding rip-offs.

If you're looking for a VW or parts, local VW garages can be rewarding to start your search. Owners and mechanics often know of cars for sale. The garage may have some they've put back in running order, and they likely have a bulletin board of local offerings. They can also advise you on your prospective purchase and do a prepurchase check.

CHAPTER XX

HOW TO KEEP YOUR VW ALIVE FOREVER

by John Hilgerdt and Peter Aschwanden, the famous artist

It would take an entire book to cover all the trips involved in keeping your VW alive forever, the book John Muir wanted to write but didn't live long enough to do. However, he did leave us this book as his legacy to VW owners, which comes pretty close by giving us the one ingredient necessary to make ''forever'' possible: love. Love of life, love of things mechanical, love of things working as they should, love of our home the earth. If you care, you can do it.

While not a book, here are some tips to help you keep your VW alive forever—if you have any to add, send'em to me at John Muir Publications and we'll include the most useful in our next revision and send you a free edition in which your tip appears.

1. The Real Enemy

Contrary to what you might have heard or believed up until now, the most important thing about keeping your VW alive forever is *not* changing the oil every 1500 miles or adjusting the valves every other oil change or greasing this and that.

The single most important requirement to keep your VW alive forever is to keep **rust at bay**. Every other mechanical part is easily and cheaply replaced or fixed. Yes, absolutely, change the oil every 1500 miles, but rust is the real enemy.

To fight it, have the chassis steam cleaned and undercoated. In Mexico, they clean the chassis and spray the underside with oil, one reason you see so many old cars still on the road down there. Undercoating is really the way to go.

Every morning, a dew settles over the earth, urging plants to meet the sun. This same dew settles on your precious VW, coating it with moisture. If you live in the southwest, it's so dry this moisture evaporates before it can readily combine with iron and steel to form iron oxide, which is what your VW, if left to its own devices, would rather be than anything else. You want proof? Just park it in the back yard, get yourself a glass of iced tea and watch it happen.

If you live in Louisiana, your car may never get really dry, even in a garage. If there's no air circulation in your garage, condensation may make matters worse. If you live where salt is used on the roads, or near the ocean, you will lose the rust battle unless you take extraordinary measures to keep your car clean and dry.

I went to visit my brother in suburban New York last year. I never saw so much rust—and so few VWs. There, too much rust and you won't be able to get an inspection sticker, so it's a real problem. Take your pick: get a stainless steel DeLorean or an aluminum-bodied Rolls Royce, buy a new car every 3 years—or save a bundle and keep your VW rust free.

Oddly enough, it takes a strong dose of water to fight rust. In winter, wash your car frequently, preferably at a car wash unless you have a high-pressure hose. Don't worry about the topside, it's underneath that's important, particularly after driving over salt-infested roads. Wash off the salt and ice and mud inside the fenders and under the floor pan and in as many of the nooks and crannies as the hose can reach. Then, if the roads are clean and dry, go for a drive to heat it up and dry off the water. When you get back, leave the doors open to dry out the inside. Check the drain holes in the doors to make sure they're not clogged.

Where you wash off the salt is as important as washing it off. We are washing it off because it is corrosive, but that property doesn't magically disappear when it hits the ground; it is still able to kill plant life and pollute the water supply.

At least at a car wash it stays in one place. But if they recycle the water, are we washing our cars with salt water? And if they don't recycle, can we afford to consume and pollute vast quantities of water for the Saturday car-wash ritual?

I don't have the answers to these dilemmas. Move to the southwest? Take the bus? Buy a fiberglass 'Vette and stick a VW engine in it?

Lift the floormats to check for collected water and rust. Hidden rust is the most insidious. The VW is a variation of monocoque construction; that is, the body (or the floor pan, in the VW) is basically one piece and does not have heavy chassis members onto which everything is bolted, á là most pre-eighties American cars and pickups. If the floor pan and the heater channels rust your car will lose its structural integrity, not to mention its ability to flex and thus handle well and safely.

I once had an old Ghia whose floor pan was so badly rusted that the car would fill up with swirling white flakes whenever I drove in a snow storm. Felt like being inside one of those glass balls you shake for a winter scene. Luckily, the seats didn't fall through before I traded it for a beautiful white Jag with red leather and burly walnut interior (and, sigh, a burned exhaust valve, which cost more to fix than buying a whole new VW engine). But, ahh, the sound of those dual overhead chain-driven camshafts, my sweetheart by my side, wailing through the Connecticut countryside...

Rust must be dealt with quickly. It isn't called cancer for nothing. It rapidly deepens and spreads. The only cure for deep rust is to replace the part or, if that's not possible, to cut out the rust and weld in a new piece. Yes, like 'most every other part on a VW, you can replace the floor pan, but repairs get much worse when door posts and quarter panels rust out. And on a VW bus, which is mostly all one welded piece, you must be especially vigilant.

Another place where rust can be structurally damaging is the upper shock (or strut, in a Super Beetle) mount. This area must remain strong and rust-free.

On the outer body, rust usually first appears as small bubbles under the paint in an area where water has collected. It's quite common to see these bubbles along the lower edges of buses, and in the quarter panels, lower door posts and bottoms of the doors in all VWs. The bubbles should be ground out and primered before the rust has a chance to spread or go all the way through the metalwork.

While serious rust problems will probably require professional care, you can do minor spots yourself.

Why fix the rust rather than replace the offending body part? While you can readily replace each and every body part, except the greenhouse, of your VW with after-market replicas and theoretically keep it alive forever that way, you are in danger of ending up with a "generic" VW that has no historical or sentimental value. Most parts, like the floor pan and fenders, are now "universal," meaning they'll fit nearly every air cooled VW ever made. Is your '67 Bug a true '67 if it has a universal floor pan, universal fenders and hood, even a universal crankcase?

One way to keep your Volks alive forever is, of course, to store it if you go away for a longish while or want to work on it in a few years, but not just yet. We had a question about **storage** from someone who wanted to preserve their old VW for their newly born infant. Whatever the reason, sometimes storage is the only answer.

First off, storing a VW (or any car) is the worst thing you can do to it; dealers call it "lot rot." If you must do so, however, park it where moisture can't easily find it. Even stored in a barn, for example, a tarp over it probably will not hurt. If you or a friend can start it once a month, let it run until the engine warms—about 5 minutes—and drive it around the block, that's probably the best thing you can do for it. Other things to do are: put jacks under it so the tires just clear the ground, and put a fuel drier into the gas tank, which should be ¼ full. Any parts store will have fuel drier and the can will have instructions on it. Change the oil before you store it and again before finally unwrapping it.

If you cannot start and drive it once every month or so, do the above things and also remove the spark plugs, spray WD-40 down the cylinders and replace the plugs. Remove the battery and discharge it fully. Drain the gas and fuel drier mixture from the tank and fill 'er up before starting the engine.

2. Do It Now

The second rule of keeping your VW alive forever is to **fix every ailment right away**. If you don't, not only will the problem just get worse, but maybe cause other problems that can pile up until you're looking at a lot of time and a large repair bill. And maybe your sweetheart VW is beginning to look shabby, making you reluctant to invest the necessary funds and energy to keep it alive.

No matter how old your VW is, you can get the parts you need. We are lucky in that we have the best parts availability of any car ever made. There are literally hundreds of firms dedicated solely to producing and selling parts for the air cooled VW, from door handles to engines. If you can't get it locally, a phone call will have the part you need at your door in a few days.

To avoid the "universal" syndrome, look for NOS (New Old Stock) parts or used same-year parts. An excellent source is in the classifieds of the newsletters of one of the car clubs listed in Chapter XIX, such as the SOTO News.

And advice abounds. Between this book and the Bentley or factory manuals, there's hardly a thing you can't fix yourself. And don't forget the parts suppliers; they are great sources of information. Some few things, such as repairing the transmission, are beyond the home mechanic, but most things are not.

3.   Oh, all right, change the oil, if you must.

First, read the two most important chapters in this book: **Chapter IX, GREEN LIGHT ON!** and **Chapter X, MAINTENANCE**. If you encounter any evidence of overheating, the Achilles' Heel of every air cooled VW, pay special attention to John's advice on the not-so-obvious: checking/replacing/cleaning the thermostat-air flap connection and the oil pressure relief and control valves.

And, yes, do change the oil regularly. You can't change the oil too often. I give new and rebuilt engines a fresh dose of oil (and filter or clean screen) at 50 miles, 150 miles, 500, then a 1000 and continue with my usual every 1500 miles from then on. Change the oil more often if you don't drive your car much or if you live in (or have traveled through) a dusty area (and don't forget the air filter).

What weight oil to use in your VW is a constant source of debate. Since the most wear on an engine comes at start-up, probably your best bet is a light weight oil like 10-30. Oil is thick and sluggish when cold; light weight oil will get to your bearings faster on a cold morning.

I don't know who came up with the idea that the oil filter only needs to be replaced every other oil change, but you see that in print a lot. Be a Big Shot and spring for a $3 filter every time (and even less for a screen gasket set if you don't have an oil filter). 1700, 1800 and 2000 cc pancake engines have a filter that goes up into a recess in the bottom rear of the engine that requires a special oil filter wrench. I use a Rabbit filter in my van because it is easier to change, longer and, I am told, has a higher burst strength. Always fill the new filter with fresh oil before installing to keep your bearings from oil starvation on first start-up.

In those same engines, by the way, be extremely careful when you replace the screen. It is held in place by a single bolt, next to the oil drain plug. This bolt should be torqued to no more than 9 foot pounds (1.3 mkg) or you risk distorting the camshaft journals in the crankcase.

Early VWs whose screen is held in by six nuts-on-studs must be torqued to only 5 foot pounds (0.7 mkg), a nearly immeasurable amount using ordinary torque wrenches. If you have a torque wrench that measures

STICK'S PERSONAL TORQUE INDICATOR

inch pounds, torque these nuts to 60 inch pounds and the 1700-2000 nut to 108 inch pounds. Always use new gaskets and washers.

What to do when you don't have a torque wrench that measures inch pounds? Though not precise this method works for me, even when using a 3/8'' drive socket wrench: I hold the socket wrench up over the working end so I have little leverage and turn the nuts or bolt only until the tendon under my wrist starts to pop out. I haven't broken any studs nor have the nuts come loose since I started using this method.

After you've drained the old oil into a (hopefully) clean pan, give it a smell-and-touch test. You're looking for oil that smells burned, indicating the engine has been overheating, or smells of gasoline, which could come from an excessively rich mixture (is the thermostat disconnected?), a flooded carburetor or a fuel pump with an internal leak. Rub some of the oil between your thumb and forefinger. Is it still slippery, as it should be unless its been cooked, or can you feel small metal particles telling you the bearings are being ground away? Don't worry if the oil is black; it should be if it's doing its job of keeping the engine clean. Next, drain the oil slowly into a clean gallon jug for recycling and look for metal particles in the bottom on your pan; if you find any it may be time to start saving and planning for an overhaul.

While frequent engine oil changing is the most obvious keep-it-alive suggestion, it isn't the only oil residing in your car. The transmission contains several quarts of heavy oil that should be replaced at least every 50,000 miles. It's an awkward job for the home mechanic but simplicity itself at a garage. The brake system contains a special kind of oil that should be replaced every two years. And there is oil in the steering box, not to mention grease in various suspension, steering and wheel parts.

4. Keep It Cool

There's nothin' my bus can't do when it's tuned up and running cool. Hills once dreaded are a welcome break from flat interstates, and I dare venture further into the countryside than otherwise might be prudent.

Besides the freedom a cool engine bequeaths, it'll last much longer. Forever? Face it: an engine contained within two lightweight case halves being pounded from both sides thousands of times a minute is lucky to make it down the block, as far as I'm concerned. Yet, properly kept, it'll take this abuse millions of times, long enough to circle the world a half dozen times. If you keep it cool.

The engine compartment in a VW, along with the tin work surrounding the engine, is a closed system designed to keep air flowing around the oil cooler and cylinder and head fins. Anything that defeats this system will make your engine run hot. Air cooled VW engines run quite close to their heat limits to begin with so the margin of safety is small.

Keep ALL the tin in place. And make sure the seal around the engine is in place and well-secured. There is a tendency for the screws holding the tin work to disappear over time, but these are commonly available from almost any VW parts store for a few cents each.

Check the thermostat (Chapter X) on upright engines to make sure it is opening the air flap behind the generator as it should. Some folks like to remove the thermostat altogether so that the flap is always full open. Don't. In the winter your engine will never fully heat up and raw gas will blow down past the pistons and rings, diluting the oil.

Relentlessly hunt for air leaks: Keep all the air hoses on the engine in place and in good shape and make sure the rubber cups seal all the spark plug holes in the tin work.

Read Colin Messer's rap on cooling and overheating in Chapter XVIII; you may want to go for a dog house oil cooler in your older VW. Although not authentic, it may save your engine, and you can keep the old fan housing if you or a future owner wants to go back to bone stock. The dog house cooler moves the oil cooler out of the path of air flow to cylinder number 3, the weak link in the air flow system, but requires a modified fan housing, which can be replaced with the engine in place in all models but the bus, though it's much easier to do with the engine out. All upright VW engines built after 1970 already have the dog house cooler.

A VW engine can run hot if the timing is off or if the fuel-air mixture is too lean. Regular tune-ups are the cure, with an occasional trip to a modern garage for checking the air-fuel ratio and total timing advance. It is fairly common for mechanics who work on VWs to find the timing set well advanced of specs, which will raise head temperatures and melt pistons.

I recently came across a Bug with a VDO oil temperature gauge mounted on the dash, a handy item to keep track of what's going on back there. VDO is an OEM (Original Equipment Manufacture) supplier of VW gauges and this one looked just like a factory-installed item. Oil lubricates best at around 190° F. and an oil temperature gauge could provide an early warning system of overheating. In fact, one could just as well consider the VW engine an oil cooled engine as an air cooled engine, making this gauge a valuable item, indeed.

Timing by the notch on your pulley is not always accurate as the notch(es) stand for different advance or retard amounts depending on your year and model. Check the timing tables in Chapter X Maintenance and find your pulley. Further confusion arises when using after-market pulleys and non-original distributors, such as the .009. The .009 should have a total advance of 32 degrees at 3500 rpm. If you can't check that, or aren't sure, take it to a pro and when you get home mark the spot on your pulley where your static timing light flashes at the case line. Mark it with some white paint (I use white-out). Now you can accurately set the timing yourself anytime in the future.

Tune-ups should always include valve adjustments; read John's rap in Chapter X on why you should *always* adjust the valves yourself. NOTE FOR TYPE IV AND 1972 AND ON BUSES: Frequent oil changes will usually keep the lifters clean and healthy on engines with hydraulically-operated valves, but, after many miles, the hot environment oil-glazes the bores in which they ride or the lifters won't pump up any more, so you have to clean the bores and lifters.

When they're working, the engine runs great without valve-lash slop. But when one sticks—meaning when the lifter (or cam follower, as it's also called) won't pump up with oil or is literally stuck in its bore—it can clatter like a rod about to let go. How to tell the difference? A rod, like a long screwdriver or dowel, used stethoscope-style (one end on your ear, the other touching the engine—careful!) may pin-point the source of the knock. If the knock comes from the center of the engine it could be a rod; under the valve cover, it's something to do with the valves. If you pull the valve cover and run the engine (careful: hot oil will dribble and squirt out) you should be able to see one or more rocker arms barely moving if you have stuck lifters. They don't move much to begin with so use an eagle eye. If you have a stuck lifter you'll have to remove the rocker arm assembly, push rod and push rod tube, and then use a little ingenuity to get the lifter out of its bore. John tells you how in Chapter XV (with a magnet). If the lifter is really stuck, spray the bore with WD-40 and try pushing or tapping it against the camshaft while a helper rotates the engine by hand from above. As you press on the lifter, the rotation of the cam will move the lifter back and forth and it should come free. Take care not to scratch the bore in the process.

Usually cleaning a lifter makes it run like new, but sometimes you need a new one; if so, get a precision ground lifter from an aftermarket VW parts supplier (see end of Chapter XIX), such as Pauter Machine.

If you can't manually pump up the lifters before installing them, like you're supposed to do, some graduates of the Hard Knocks School of Auto Repair just oil them up and stick'em in their bores, reassemble the valve train and start-up the engine. After 5 to 15 minutes of horrible clattering they pump up just fine.

There are mechanics who claim that all you need to cure stuck valve lifters is too run some sort of "solvent" through the system, like ATF or kerosene or diesel fuel. They plumb this into the fuel system in place of the fuel line from the gas tank and run the engine to the accompaniment of great clouds of smoke, and by some magic it's supposed to reach the lifters and clean'em out.

A respected mechanic once did that to my '78 bus when I asked him to fix the clickity-clack in my valves; a few days later I was in a VW shop on the eastern side of Oklahoma City having the lifters pulled and cleaned, as should have been done in the first place. Like John says: *always do the valves yourself.*

A sadder hydraulic valve tale was told me by Eve Muir. She was driving near Hermosillo, Mexico, when she came upon a friend hitch-hiking; he had abandoned his bus when it started knocking like crazy, fearing a rod bearing had blown. He talked her into towing his bus all the way to Tucson, Arizona, where he had the engine rebuilt. A week and hundreds of dollars later, he started it up. AIIEEE! Same clatter. Yup, you guessed it, just a stuck lifter all along.

It's this sort of experience that teaches us that professional mechanics often aren't any better mechanics than we are with this book and a bit of common sense to guide us. And it can keep us out of the hands of the unscrupulous, such as the California border-town mechanic who told me I'd need a rebuilt head when my Scirocco stripped its timing belt on a trip to L.A. Said the valves were bent from hitting the pistons. That happens in some Fiats and a few other cars when the timing belt goes, but not in a gasoline Rabbit/Scirocco. At the curb outside his shop where the tow truck had dropped me off I installed a new belt from the parts house across the street and drove off into the sunset. He knew I knew, and I knew he knew I knew.

I am not a fan of external after-market oil coolers; all the ones I've ever run across have given me (or the owner) trouble. The oil lines leak or break and I wonder about the flow characteristics of so much tubing. I've even seen several installations that appear to defeat their purpose. The oil lines pass close to the muffler or heater boxes and heat the oil on its way to or from the cooler. If you insist on using an external cooler, at least install an in-line thermostat that only allows the oil to flow through the external cooler when it gets hot.

Another source of possible overheating is today's **gasoline**, which just hasn't got the octane rating of the old stuff and will pre-ignite on a compression ratio over 7 to 1. Pre-ignition can devastate an engine or at least make it run hot. Some of our readers have asked "What do you do if you can't find leaded gas?" Using regular unleaded does lead to pre-ignition. It's okay to use occasionally, but using unleaded continually may cause valve and other engine damage. Next time you do a valve job, use hardened valve seats and one-piece stainless steel or sodium-filled valves. You might also consider lowering the compression ratio. We don't recommend adding any of the lead substitutes to gasoline because they cause pollution.

As long as we're on gasoline, to make a 20-25 year old VW run forever, remember the **gas tank**. Over the years it probably has collected rust and much dirt. Remove it—it's easy—and have it steam cleaned at a garage. While it's out, blow out the gas lines with compressed air and then replace the gas tank. A trick I picked up from motorcyclists is, while the tank is out, to coat the inside with a liquid used on airplane tanks. You can get it at your local airport supply house. The instructions come with the can, but it's basically pouring the liquid into the tank, and then turning the tank round and round until the inside is well coated. The liquid "sets" when you tank up. It'll seal the tank and help keep gasoline from leaking in the event of an accident.

Scoops on the air intakes on buses help lower engine compartment temperatures, which are considerably hotter than the outside air.

5. Stopping is important, too.

Two of the nastiest jobs on VWs are replacing the muffler and doing a brake job, both of which are dirty knuckle-busters.

Brakes are the sort of job I'd like to turn over to a garage, but unfortunately doing it yourself is the only sure way to know it's been done right. And like most other work you do yourself, breaking down on the road won't leave you helpless if you know what to do.

John tells you just about everything you need to know about brakes in Chapter XI, and for the "forever" freak, all you need to add is to change the brake fluid every couple years by taking it to a shop and asking them to pressure bleed the brakes.

Brake fluid sucks up water like a sponge, and water in the brake fluid will corrode the system and dramatically lower the boiling point of the brake fluid, which could lead to a hairy ride down a mountain road some day. Brakes get hot after repeated or constant use and if the fluid gets hot enough it will boil and the car will lose its ability to stop. Regular brake fluid changes will not only help keep your VW alive forever but might add some years to your life as well.

By now (1992) most VWs are more than 20 years old, and the **rubber hoses that carry the brake fluid** to each wheel may have deteriorated and require replacement. These hoses last surprisingly long considering the work they do and the environment they live in. One clue to deterioration, other than utter failure, is dragging brake shoes or pads. This can happen if the pistons in the wheel cylinders or calipers are corroded or if the brake shoe return springs are weak, but if you've done a thorough brake job and the brakes are still dragging it could be the fault of worn hoses.

Stay away from non-brand name shoes and pads when doing an overhaul. Federal law governs the composition of brake linings in new cars, but no laws cover after-market linings. You could end up with linings made of compressed camel dung. New linings should meet FMVSS (Federal Motor Vehicle Safety Standard) 105, which may not be possible to verify. Your best bet is high-quality shoes and pads from a reputable manufacturer.

Unless you have special needs, stick with organic friction materials and steer clear of semi-metallic linings. Semi-metallics work best at temperatures higher than usually encountered in ordinary driving and are harder on drums and disks.

One bit of good news on the brake front is that asbestos, a common lining ingredient, must be phased out by 1996. That may not help in keeping our VWs alive forever but it should give *us* a bit longer life span. For this reason, be very careful when working on your brakes: wear a mask and never brush or blow away the grime surrounding the brakes; it's full of asbestos, resins and who-knows-what that you could breathe in if they get airborne. You can safely wipe the grime away with a wet rag (which you must then carefully dispose of).

6. Rubber, Rubber Everywhere

Your VW has many rubber (ok, some are plastic) seals to keep oil and grease in and dirt out. The seals in your engine, transaxle and brake cylinders will give you signs when they go: oil dripping down the wheels, underneath the car and onto your driveway. But other leaks can go unnoticed until you're looking at an expensive repair.

The most commonly unnoticed torn or worn seals are the **rubber/plastic boots surrounding the CV joints**. These are usually only discovered when working on something else nearby, but a regular check can save you a bundle: CV joints can cost $200 and a bit of work to replace doing it yourself and $500 or more at a shop.

The axle(s) and CV(s) must be removed to slip on new CV joint boots. Avoid the temptation to leave everything in place and fix it with a two-part boot (except early swing-arm VWs, which have a rubber boot where the axle tube meets the tranny and are commonly fixed with a two-part boot). If the outer CV boot is shot, the one that most often tears, always assume that dirt has gotten into the joint, ready to grind up the balls and channels of the joint. The only cure is to pull the joint apart, clean it thoroughly, regrease the joint and install it with a new boot. Use only high-quality boots (like from VW). Even then, if the tear has been there a while, you may not save the joint. Only close inspection will tell.

Keeping the CVs clean and well-greased should make them last forever. VWs aren't exactly powerhouses and normally put little strain on the CVs.

Eventually, all rubber/plastic seals and hoses will deteriorate, leak and need replacing. Checking regularly for cracks and leaks may keep you from sudden disaster. Some rubber hoses will wear because they are rubbing on another part; in particular, look for rubbing (a nearby shiny spot) on brake hoses and the fuel line from the fuel pump to the carburetor.

Use OEM rubber and plastic seals and hoses on your VW. They will cost a bit more but are the high quality you need for long life.

A shot seal may also be giving you an important message. If, for example, you find engine oil leaking down from the clutch housing area, don't just replace the rear crankcase seal without finding out why it leaked. It could be just a cheap seal, but it also could indicate so much play in the crankshaft that it is trashing the seal.

7. The Obvious

• Don't lug or over-rev the engine. Especially don't lug it, which is driving in a gear too high for road conditions. You can safely lug a steam-driven car or locomotive, which doesn't even have or need a gearbox, but not your VW. I once had a girlfriend who just couldn't wait to get her bus into fourth gear, and would leave it there as long as she could. Can you guess where I met her? Yup, at a VW repair shop, about to be relieved of many hard-earned $$$ to fix her bent engine.

Lugging puts an incredible strain on the entire driveline; it's like going uphill on your 10-speed in top gear. If you are strong enough you can even bend the crank under the strain.

• Always keep an extra set of keys stashed somewhere. Replacing the ignition and door locks is an expensive and tedious operation.

• Don't overload your car, and replace the shocks often. Otherwise, torsion bars, particularly in front, will sag, or even break. Big bucks to fix.

• If the steering gets hard, it may just be not enough air in the tires. Misalignment or worn steering and suspension parts will also put strain on the steering gearbox, another pricey and tedious repair.

• Unless you live at the bottom of a hill, don't warm up the engine sitting in the driveway. When the engine is cold, raw gas washes away oil in the cylinders. Moderate driving will warm it up faster.

• Shift gears slowly, with a slight pause in neutral. Fast shifting chews up the synchronizers in the transmission that allow smooth, grind-free shifts. Resist the temptation to rest your hand on the gearshift knob; that, too, will eat up the synchronizers.

• Be careful when you peruse the after-market parts catalogues: do you really need a hot clutch that requires high pedal effort and propels your car forward with a shaft- and mind-bending jolt?

• Get the right part. Some parts will fit but be totally wrong. Experienced mechanics, junk yards and parts houses will usually know what works and what doesn't. But that isn't always true.

A couple years ago, one of the best mechanics in town recommended buying a '78 Camper that was in his shop for maintenance and just happened to be for sale. Shortly after I bought it I heard a crunch and grind when I started it. It wouldn't go into any gear at first but eventually did and seemed to run fine. But I pulled the engine anyway as I was about to take it on a long trip. Sure enough, there were needle bearings all over the bell (clutch) housing. The pilot shaft bearing in the end of the crankshaft had blown.

So I pulled the remains of the bearing out and pressed in a new bearing. Noticing a small leak in the pilot shaft seal in the back of the tranny, I replaced it as well.

Thinking all was well, I headed out. On the second day of my trip, I started to smell burning trans oil: the new rear trans seal was leaking. I really didn't have the tools to pull the engine on the road and I was in a hurry, so I just kept adding more and more trans oil as I crossed the country. When I got to the east coast I pulled the engine again, not a fun chore on newer buses.

In the mess of an oil soaked clutch and thick, smelly transmission oil everywhere, there was no apparent reason for the seal to have blown. I pulled the bell housing to have a look at the inner part of the pilot shaft. Some play is normal, and everything looked as it should have. The shaft was smooth where it contacted the seal. Perplexed, I replaced the seal and bolted it all back together again. Two days later the same thing: tranny oil leaking again.

Frustrated beyond words suitable for a family publication, I called my Santa Fe mechanic and related my sad tale. He couldn't figure it out either, but sent me a tranny from his pile of wrecks out back. As I had to get back home, I took the train west before the tranny arrived and made arrangements for a garage to install it. No first gear! Arrrgh!!!

As long as the old one was out, I had it sent to my favorite parts supplier in Pennsylvania for a professional evaluation. They called me to report that there was NOTHING WRONG

WITH MY TRANSMISSION. "But, but . . . something HAS to be wrong!" I sputtered. Oh, yes, something was indeed wrong, they said: it was the wrong transmission for my car. Someone had installed a '75 tranny in the bus and the pilot shaft on a '75 is too short for a '78; only a '76 to '78 will work. The too-short pilot shaft barely went into the bearing in the end of the crankshaft and was madly whipping around while I drove, trashing the tranny seal and, eventually, pounding out the seal bore and ruining the bell housing.

They sent a new and correct tranny to my mechanic and now everything is fine, after much hassle and many dollars in shipping and installation costs.

The lesson? Check parts numbers and don't let dodos work on your car. You, with this book, a little knowledge and care, *can* keep your VW alive forever, free of the jerks who would have us live otherwise.

How To Keep Your VW Book Alive Forever

Beginning in 1981 the spiral binding was dropped and the so-called "perfect binding" this book now sports was adopted. Not only was the spiral binding very expensive but it had a tendency to get squashed in shipping, making it unsaleable at the book store. Thus, to keep the book affordable and saleable it was necessary to eliminate the spiral.

That left a problem, however: the book no longer lies flat when opened, a sad state of affairs when you're working on your VW. Fret not, dear readers, for we have come up with a solution: drill holes for a 2- or 3-ring binder, cut off the spine and pop it into one of your kid's notebooks. Not only will it lie flat wherever you open it, it is also protected by the binder.

Here's how:

Drill holes   The easiest way is to get a local printer or office supply shop to drill the holes for you. If you're a regular they'll likely do it free. Ask them to drill the holes about an 1/8'' further from the edge than is usually done (or about 1/2'' from the edge to the center of the hole) so the holes have more paper on the outside edge and won't as readily tear. Don't go more than that or the holes will cut into the type.

If you're gonna do it yourself, lay a piece of notebook paper on top of the book cover, moving the edge of the paper about an 1/8'' away from the spine, and mark each hole with a pen or pencil. You'll find that notebook paper is a bit bigger than the book because of trimming at the bindery so just even things up before you mark the holes.

Drill a small, straight pilot hole in the middle of each circle and then finish with a 9/32'' drill, or as close as you've got.

Remove spine.   Once the holes are drilled it's time to remove the spine. Clamp the book in a vise between a couple wood slats, leaving the spine sticking a tiny bit up above the slats. No vise? Place the book on a sturdy table with the spine sticking out over one edge a little bit and a board on top lined up with the table edge and just sit on it.

Now just cut off the very edge of the spine with a fine-tooth saw, like a hacksaw. You can also grind it off with an electric grinder or file it off using a heavy wood rasp.

Inside a binder it'll last forever and lie flat, just like in the bad old days when John brought us this remarkable book.

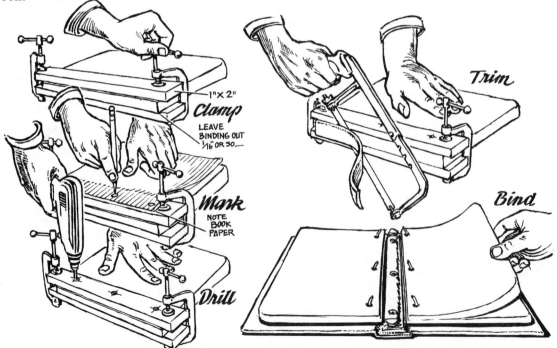

CHAPTER XXI

THE GRABBAG

Or: Things we always thought should be in the book but didn't know where to put

---

HIGH ALTITUDE TIMING

For every 1000 feet you're above 4000 feet, advance the timing one degree. It's hard to tell what one degree is, so advance it a tad and watch performance and mileage. When both are good, the timing is right. If performance is good and mileage is bad, the timing is too far advanced, so back off a little. See note in Chapter X, at the end of RAP ON TIMING for the relationship between high altitude and gasoline octane.

NO NEED TO FREEZE IN YOUR AIR COOLED VW
by John Hilgerdt and Peter Aschwanden, the famous artist

Along with its tendency to self-destruct by its appetite for intake and exhaust valves, perhaps the major impediment to owning an air cooled VW, at least in northern climates, is its woefully inadequate heating system. Maybe that's why Subarus, the water-cooled equivalent of VW's horizontally opposed 4-cylinder engine, have so widely replaced VWs on our streets.

As in most areas of life, however, there is a considerable trade-off in abandoning efficiency for comfort. Front-wheel drive automobiles are vastly more complicated than rear-wheel drives, and with so much weight up front the steering is heavy and handling unpredictable, not to mention the ineluctable feel of rear wheels pushing rather than front wheels pulling you around town. Simply put, the air cooled VW is just plain more fun to drive and maintain.

If you want to keep your VW but not freeze to death doing so, not an unreasonable desire, there are steps you can take to make the most of the existing heating system. Plus you get a big added benefit: improving the efficiency of the heating system does the same for the cooling system.

Here, we've concocted a way to spend a crisp fall Saturday afternoon checking and fixing the heating system in preparation for the coming winter. All you'll need are a few basic tools: slot and phillips head screwdrivers, locking pliers and a pair of jack stands. (Bus owners won't need the jack stands.) A friend would be nice, at least for a few minutes to operate the heater controls inside the car while you observe what's happening underneath.

In the old days even water-cooled cars had heating systems similar to that of an air cooled VW. A metal shroud was fitted to pick up heat from the exhaust manifold and carry it to the car's interior. [Later, they would use the system now universally found in water-cooled cars: a small radiator hooked up to the cooling system and located under the dash.] In a VW, this older, simple and straightforward system works by the cooling fan drawing in fresh air through the engine compartment louvers. The fan then blows the air through boxes called heat exchangers which surround pipes from the exhaust manifolds. The warmed air then goes through tubing to outlets inside the front of the car.

Unfortunately, because of the greater distance the heated air must travel and the much larger interior volume, buses will never be as warm as Beetles. My first VW bus, from upstate New York, came equipped with an auxiliary gasoline-powered heater mounted in the engine compartment, though the fear of fire kept me from ever using it. Once commonly found in Canada-market buses, these heaters are now rare and expensive.

My friends used to chide me for having the oh-so-common bench seat in my bus, as opposed to the walk-through model with two separate seats leaving a path to the rear of the bus. But on a cold winter night my honey could slide over and snuggle up. Try that in a walk-through.

Common Problems With Heating Systems
1. Loose fan belt
2. Debris in fan shroud

3. Loose or missing fresh air hoses
4. Misaligned air chamber on muffler to heat exchanger
5. Clamp between heat exchanger & air chamber loose or missing
6. Engine gasket seal and/or tin missing
7. Hose clip, grommet and connecting pipe missing
8. Heat exchangers are missing
9. Holes in heat exchangers
10. Holes in heater channels
11. Accordion hoses, red rubber collars and clamps are missing
12. Broken or rusted heater cables and/or barrel connectors
13. Disconnected heater cables
14. Holes in floor boards
15. Leaking door seals
16. Disconnected or poorly set air-control flap thermostat

If you're getting no or only a little heat it's time to do a thorough inspection of the system to find out why. Let's start with the engine compartment, which operates on the principle of a closed system, for both heating and cooling. By a closed system I mean that there are no openings between the upper half of the engine inside the engine compartment and the lower half under the car.

To operate efficiently a closed system cannot have any leaks, so that's what we'll look for first. Open the rear deck (engine compartment) lid and look for the fat fresh air hoses and miscellaneous clamps and collars which connect the fan shroud to the heat exchangers under the engine. These accordian-pleated hoses have a tendency to tear near the clamps; if this is the case, make a clean cut above the torn area, stretch the hoses to fit and reattach them.

The large fan shroud found on upright engines contains the cooling fan which is also part of the heating system. Behind the fan shroud is a flap that opens to admit fresh air as the engine warms up. This flap is operated by a thermostatically operated bellows located between cylinders 1 and 2. The flap should be lightly closed when the engine is cold and open when hot. **Check it only with the engine shut off** as the fan, mounted on the forward end of the generator/alternator, spins directly behind the flap, ready to eat your new manicure. If the flap is not working properly, turn to Chapter XV Engine Overhaul, Step 5, and/or Chapter IX Green Light On!, just before the first procedure. Do not disconnect the thermostat; your engine needs it to warm up in the winter.

1972 and later buses and Type IVs have what is known as the pancake engine and do not have the familiar large fan shroud on the front of the engine. In these, the cooling fan, which also supplies air for heating purposes, is mounted on the rear of the crankshaft, inside a much smaller fan shroud. In addition, there is an auxiliary electrically-driven fan (also found in late Beetles) that blows fresh air through fat hoses from the engine compartment to the heat exchangers. Check that these hoses are well-secured and in good shape and that the fan blows air (engine running or ignition on) when the heating levers in the car are pushed to their on position.

Before leaving the engine compartment, make sure all the engine tin is in place. If not, take an inventory of what is missing and make sure you replace it. Also, check to see that the engine compartment seal is in place. It is made up of two pieces: one long one that covers the sides and front (Front is Front) of the tray and a smaller one that covers the back of the tray (above the tail pipes). Late model buses have a one-piece foam rubber seal. If they are not intact make the necessary repairs. Check the important rubber seals near the plug ends of the spark plug wires that cover the plug wire holes in the tin.

If the upper part of the engine is not completely sealed from the lower half, not only will you spill valuable cooling air but the cooling fan will suck up exhaust gases and send it through the heat exchangers and into the car when you turn on the heat. These gases not only stink but can kill. And if your engine is on good tune you may not even smell these gases. **Carbon monoxide, produced by all engines, is odorless, tasteless and dangerous**.

Once everything in the engine compartment is ship-shape, it's time to examine the underbelly of the beast. If you have a bus, you can comfortably crawl underneath and look up to where the engine meets the tranny; if you have a Bug, jack up the car. Make sure you put jack stands underneath the torsion tubes **before** you get underneath. DO NOT use the jack points. This is not the time to test the structural integrity of the chassis—yours or the car's.

Under the car you will find—if they haven't been removed—the **heat exchangers**, right under the cylinder heads on both sides of the engine. They differ somewhat over the years and models but are basically big oblong clunky boxes, probably with a nice coat of rust. If they are rusted through, you're gonna need new heat exchangers from the junk yard or after-market replacement parts.

At the front end of the heat exchangers are the **heat control boxes** containing flaps that, when you turn on the heat inside the car, open to allow hot air to flow into the car. The flaps on early VWs are contained within the heat exchangers rather than in separate boxes.

On the side of each heat control box (or heat exchanger) you should find a **spring-loaded lever** connected to a cable coming out of a thin metal tube just forward of the heat control boxes, straddling the transmission. Work the lever back and forth to make sure it moves freely and check the cable connection while you're there.

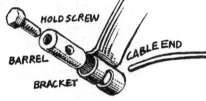

There should be only the barest amount of slack in the cable when the heater controls inside the car are in the ''off'' position. Adjust'em now at the barrel connectors on the levers if they have too much or no slack.

Everything look okay underneath? Have a friend in the car work the heat controls while you watch to see that everything works smoothly and without binding. If one or both of the **cables** don't open the flaps you now know why you don't have heat on one side or the other: the cable is broken. At the end of each tube you hopefully will find a small dust cover or plug, with the cable coming out the middle. The plugs keep dirt and water from entering the tubes and gumming up the cables. If you need to replace or grease the cables, turn to Chapter XVII Within The Law, Heater Cables.

At the front end of the flapper boxes you should find fat **pleated hoses** connecting these boxes to the heat channels that carry the heat to the inside of the car. It is quite common to find these hoses missing or not connected and may very well be why you froze last winter. If that's the case, or if they're really beat, replace them and/or reattach the missing end. If you're lucky, the little clips that hold the hoses in place will still be there.

Late model buses have an extra set of flexible hoses going back from the heat control boxes. These hoses carry the hot air away from the engine when the heat is not on, a nice touch. They also are commonly missing or not connected. If yours are missing, put'em on your replacement list. They help the engine run cooler.

When all's right, you can put the car back down on the ground; the rest of our inspection trip will be topside. In the Beetle, the heating channels that carry the hot air forward are part of the floor pan, in the rocker panels on each side, and are not visible. The only things you can see are the little vents in the footwell area of the Beetles and Ghias. If the sliding vents are not working or if a rush of cold air is present, check the channels by lifting the floor mats at the outer edges. If the rocker panels are rusty or if there are holes in your floor where it meets the side panels, it's a good bet you are losing hot air. These heating channels, like everything else in the system, must be airtight. If you own a bus, you'll notice only one large heating channel in the center of the chassis. This channel must also be rust free and air tight. The heating cables straddle this heating channel.

Bug and Ghia owners now open the trunk. Look in the rear corners under the hood hinges. Locate the small fresh air hoses. They connect from the heating channels to the defroster ducts on the Beetle and Ghia. Late models and buses have more ducting under the dash. Check that everything is properly connected and in good shape.

After you've looked the system over very carefully and made all the necessary repairs, take it for a nice long ride, long enough to heat the engine up. Don't be surprised if it isn't as warm as a water-cooled system. The VW will heat adequately if you are moving at highway speeds, at idle it is very poor unless you have a blower in your system.

OTHER COLD WEATHER TIPS

One reader writes: "You have to experience life with your bus at $-30°$ F. before you really know what I'm talking about. Specifically, how do you: turn the steering wheel, shift gears, keep the throttle from getting stuck wide open?...Boosting and charging the battery is almost as common as gas tank filling."

Some practical things are: use a lighter weight gear oil in the tranny and change to 20 or even 10 weight engine oil. One joker suggested parking in a heated garage; actually throwing a space blanket over your lovely at night is not a bad idea. Here's a good one: **Stuck accelerator cable.** If you find that the accelerator cable is sticking during very cold weather (pedal sticks to the floor and won't return), here's the remedy: Remove the accelerator cable as described under Broken Accelerator Cable in **Chapter X, Maintenance**. Wipe the cable well with a rag, then grease it with wheel bearing grease. Not too much, just enough to coat the cable. Install the cable in the housing. This ounce of prevention will help keep frozen water in the tube from affecting pedal action.

A word of thanks here to Lyn and Sam Strano of Strano's Foreign Parts in Brookville, PA, for their help in writing this section. Besides selling parts, the Strano's have a small garage in western Pennsylvania, right off I-80, with many years' experience working on VWs. If you're traveling in that neck of the woods and need help with your VW, this is the place to go. They're also well-connected with a large local junkyard full of old VWs.

PROCEDURE FOR REMOVING AND INSTALLING McPHERSON STRUT SHOCK ABSORBERS,
Phase II—for all Super Beetles, Types IV and Type I 1977 and on.

Condition: Car shimmies, goes over bumps mushily and/or there is evidence of shock fluid leaking. If your steering dampeners aren't dampening, replace them as in Chapter XII, PROCEDURE FOR REMOVING AND INSTALLING SHOCK ABSORBERS AND STEERING DAMPENERS.

Tools and Materials: Phase II tool kit and liquid wrench.

Parts: New shocks (and dampeners), as needed. Always do both sides.

Step 1. Remove Strut From Car.

Block the rear wheels, jack up the car and place it on jack stands, wooden blocks, etc. Remove the wheels (as in a flat tire). The McPherson strut is behind the wheel and is that vertical tube with a spring on top and a shock absorber in the tube. Bend up the locking tabs on the three 13mm bolts that attach the strut tube to the spindle (bottom). Remove the 3 bolts.

Now disconnect the brake line connection from the bracket to the strut tube. On the driver's side, you'll have to pull out the speedometer cable. With one hand, push down on the steering knuckle and pull the strut tube out toward you with the other hand. This will get the bottom loose.

Lift up the hood (front) and locate the top of the strut. Remove the 3 nuts and washers holding the strut on. Have a friend hold the strut while screwing off the last nut because the whole assembly may drop on your feet and it's quite heavy. Now do the other side.

Step 2. Take Struts To A Garage.

Make sure it's a garage with the proper compressor. The job of compressing the spring, which is under tremendous pressure, has to be done with expertise. If not, the spring can slip out of the compressor and cut the operator's head off. It's a relatively inexpensive job to have done. Take the new shocks with you so they can be installed as well.

Step 3. Install Struts.

Do Step 1 in reverse. Make sure to attach the top of the strut first, then push down on the steering knuckle until you can get the bottom of the strut in position. Tighten all nuts and bolts firmly (no torquing needed). Replace wheels and go for a shimmyless drive to a front end shop to have it re-aligned.

BALL JOINTS
by John Hilgerdt & Peter Aschwanden, the artist

Starting in 1966, ball joints replaced king pins in the front suspension of all air cooled VWs. When John wrote this book, he recommended that ball joints be serviced by your local VW garage, but for the past several years a long-time VW ''Idiot'' in California has been grumbling to himself—and anyone else who would listen—about the absence of a ball joint procedure.

Replacing ball joints is not for the faint of heart and I can't imagine why anyone would want to do it themselves. Perhaps because of cost? I have heard some horrendous quotes on the cost of having ball joints replaced, all the way up to $1000. However, I checked with 3 local, respectable garages, including the VW dealer, and these are the estimates I got (in 1992), including parts and labor for all four ball joints: ''about $200'' from a shop specializing in front end and brake work; $180 from an independent VW garage; and $400 including alignment (necessary in any case) from the dealer. The ball joints themselves will probably run you about $20 each so you'd likely save only about $100 or so off the lowest quote by doing it yourself, and then you still need to pay someone to press in the new joints.

While you may or may not be able to *remove* the ball joints—depending on the tools and skills you possess, along with a certain amount of luck—you will not be able to *install* the new ones yourself without a press with the necessary fittings . They are a press fit into the torsion arms and must be installed by a skilled operator with the right equipment.

In fact, if you live in a small town or out in the boonies, your main problem is going to be finding a VW shop with this press and fittings. So even if you are able to remove the old ball joints (which cannot be reinstalled, by the way) you will still need to remove the torsion arms and take the whole business to a garage with a press. If no garage near you can do the job, your best bet is to start calling around the nearest larger town or city to find someone with a press.

Other special tools you will need beyond the basic tool kit are a large ''pickle fork'' such as used for tie rod ends but bigger, a large pry bar, a flat 36 mm open end wrench (for the upper joint), two large machinist's ball peen hammers, and a pair of sturdy jackstands.

Are You Sure You Need New Ball Joints?

Most likely, this is how you'll discover your VW needs new ball joints: Your car has been wandering around the road, and maybe making clunking sounds from the front end, so off you go to have it checked and aligned, but the mechanic says it can't be aligned because one or more ball joints are shot. It could be something else, of course, like a tie rod end, but that's covered in Chapter XII, Shimmies and Shakes.

If you want to check out the front end yourself, turn to Chapter XII, adjust the wheel bearings and do the tests outlined there. While you won't be able to directly test the ball joints, you can get there by the process of elimination. [There is a way to test the ball joints, but it requires a special VW tool that draws the torsion arms toward each other for measurement of play with a vernier caliper.] If the process of elimination convinces you that the ball joints are gonners, take your car to a garage for the final word. If one is gone, I'd do them all.

Are You Sure You Want To Do It Yourself?

Okay, you're convinced you need new ball joints and you're stubborn and want to replace them yourself. Hopefully, I've already talked you out of it, but here goes: Read both Procedures entirely before starting.

PROCEDURE FOR REPLACING LOWER BALL JOINTS

Condition: You have determined that one or both lower ball joints need replacement. The uppers seldom go out; the lowers take the brunt of the action.

Tools and Materials: Phase I tool kit plus scissors or hydraulic jack, a pair of sturdy jack stands, a ½'' breaker bar, a 3/8'' socket adaptor, torque wrench, large pickle fork (for leverage, you'll need one larger than the pickle fork used for tie rods), large pry bar, two large machinist's ball peen hammers, safety goggles, new retainer(s) for the stabilizer bar and new lower ball joints. Don't get new ball joints until you know if your VW has standard or oversized ball joints (see following Procedure, Step 4).

Step 1: Clean and Jack.

Cleaning the front end behind the wheels with a high pressure hose at a car wash will help make this task a bit more bearable.

Back home, remove the battery ground (negative) and turn on the ignition so you can turn the wheels for better access.

Loosen the front wheel nuts a half turn and jack up the front end, placing jack stands under the outboard ends of the lower torsion tube. DO NOT let the car rest on the VW jack or scissors jacks for this job.

Step 2: Disconnections.

Remove the front wheels, drums or calipers and rotors, wheel bearings, brake hose and associated hardware (Chapter XI). You can do the job with the brakes in place if you are doing only the lower or only the upper ball joints, but if you're doing both, you'll have to remove and hang up the backing plates or calipers to free the steering knuckle. In any case, disconnect the brake lines from the knuckle. If you're doing the left side, disconnect the speedmeter cable as well.

Disconnect the tie rod at the steering knuckle end (Chapter XII).

Step 3: Remove Lower Ball Joint From Steering Knuckle.

There are several methods to remove the lower ball joint from the steering knuckle: a special VW press or, for the home mechanic, the large "pickle fork" or the hammer method. First remove the self-locking nut on the bottom of the ball joint. If you're using a pickle fork, jam it in between the lower part of the ball joint and the steering knuckle and pry the ball joint up and out of the knuckle.

If you're using the hammer method, you'll need to **wear goggles** and have a couple large machinist's ball peen hammers; ordinary carpenter's hammers will not do. Screw the self-locking nut back on so that it covers the bottom of the stud. Place a scissors or hydraulic jack under the ball joint, on the nut. Jack it up until it just barely starts to lift the steering knuckle. With goggles in place to protect your eyes from flying metal chips, simultaneously strike the sides of the knuckle where the ball joint is mounted with your hammers. The idea is to momentarily distort that area of the knuckle so that the ball joint pops out.

When the joint is loose, pry or jack up the torsion arm to remove the ball joint from the knuckle.

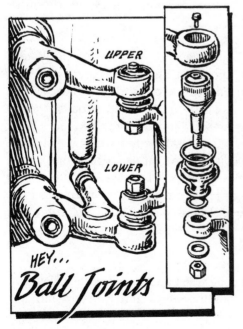

Whether or not the ball joint pops loose with either method depends on your luck. If someone has previously cranked down hard on the self-locking nut or if corrosion is keeping the parts together, you may not be able to separate the ball joint from the knuckle with ordinary hand tools. If so, put it all back together and take it to a garage.

Step 4. Remove Lower Torsion Arm And Stabilizer Bar.

Lower joint out of the knuckle? Remove the lower torsion arm so that you can get the old ball joint pressed out and a new one pressed in. But first you'll have to remove the stabilizer bar.

To disconnect the stabilizer bar, bend down the lock tabs on the retainers and drive the retainers off (put new retainers on your parts list). Then remove the nut on the mounting bolt on the lower torsion arm so you can take off the stabilizer.

If you clean off all the crud on the end of the torsion arm where it connects to the torsion bar you'll find a socket head setscrew holding the arm to the torsion bar. Loosen the locknut and remove the setscrew and pry or hammer the torsion arm off the end of the torsion bar. Check the rubber seal on the torsion arm, if it's worn or cracked, get a new one.

Step 5. Machine Shop.

Take the torsion arm along with a new ball joint to a shop (see following Procedure, Step 4 first) and ask them to press out the old joint and press in the new one.

Step 6. Reassemble.

Reassembly is the reverse of the removal steps. Remember to snug down the setscrew to 29 foot pounds and tighten the locknut. Pry or jack up the torsion arm and stick the ball joint stud into the steering knuckle and tighten the self-locking nut to 72 foot pounds, always using a new nut, which should come with the new ball joint.

Reattach the brake lines, speedo cable, stabilizer bar with new retainers, tie rod end(s) and other hardware you may have removed. Don't forget to hook up the battery.

PROCEDURE FOR REPLACING UPPER BALL JOINTS.

Tools and Materials: Same as for lower ball joint Procedure, except: no new retainers for the stabilizer bar, a flat 36mm open end wrench instead of a pickle fork and new upper ball joints instead of lowers (see Step 4).

Remarks: You're doing all four ball joints or just the uppers. The upper joints are easier to separate from the steering knuckle, but removing the upper torsion arm presents a new difficulty: with the weight of the car off the torsion bars when resting on jack stands, the torsion bars push the upper torsion arms down hard against the rubber stops mounted between the upper and lower ball joints. So if you've removed the lower ball joint, be prepared to support the weight of the steering knuckle when the upper ball joint breaks loose. If you're only replacing the upper ones, the lower joint/stabilizer bar will support the knuckle.

Step 1. Begin.

Follow Steps 1 and 2 in lower ball joint Procedure.

Step 2. Remove Upper Ball Joint.

Note the large nut where the upper ball joint meets the steering knuckle. This is the eccentric bushing adjuster that sets the camber of the wheel. You will be turning this adjuster nut with a flat 36 mm open end wrench to free the ball joint.

Ready? Remove the self-locking nut under the ball joint and, supporting the steering knuckle (if you've removed the lower joint), turn the adjuster nut. The ball joint should free itself from the knuckle, just like that. If it's stuck it may need a little persuasion with a hammer (goggles on, of course) on the steering knuckle. Put the steering knuckle aside for now so we can remove the upper torsion arm.

Step 3. Remove Upper Torsion Arm.

As with the lower torsion arm, loosen the locknut and remove the setscrew that holds the torsion arm to the torsion bar. To remove the arm you're going to have to lift the arm up off the rubber stop with a pry bar to whack the arm from the inside with a hammer to move it far enough off the torsion bar to clear the stop. This would be the perfect time for a helper to come strolling by. Once clear of the rubber stop whack or pull the arm the rest of the way off.

If you're doing both sides, do the same to the other side.

Step 4. Machine Shop.

Haul the torsion arms off to a shop to have the old ball joints removed and new ones pressed in. Now's the time to see if you have standard or oversized ball joints. Both come with 2 square installation position grooves; oversize ball joints come with 2 additional V-shaped grooves located 45 degrees from the square grooves. The shop will not only press in the new ball joints but also peen the ball joint covers with a special tool.

Step 5. Install Upper Ball Joint(s).

Install the torsion arm(s) and loosely install the ball joint(s) into the steering knuckle. Jack up the lower torsion arm until the upper ball joint enters the upper part of the steering knuckle and position the notch in the eccentric camber adjusting bushing so that it points forward. Then screw new self-locking nuts onto the ball joint studs and tighten them to 72 foot pounds. If both uppers and lowers are out, install lowers now. Then install the tie rod(s), brakes, wheel bearings, brake lines, speedo cable, wheels and such. You'll need a front wheel alignment so get down to a shop ASAP.

There now, don't you wish you'd gone out and collected aluminum cans to pay for this job rather than doing it yourself?

ELECTRICAL IMPULSES

John Hilgerdt—with our own Artist-in-the-Garret, Peter Aschwanden

It was great being on the road again in my trusty VW camper. One more tank of gas and I'd make it to my stop for the night. The engine was running cool and the oil was down just a teeny bit since the last fill-up, happy signs in VW land. I was about to get back on the Interstate when a passing driver honked and waved: "Your engine door is open," he yelled.

Sure enough, I had spaced it out after checking the oil. Leaving the engine compartment lid open defeats the cooling system, which was designed to take in outside air through the upper vents and blow it down and through the engine and oil cooler. If the lid is left open, even a little, air spills out before it can make its journey past the cooling fins. And we know what happens when an air-cooled engine doesn't get enough cool air.

For the rest of that cross-country trip I was in the grip of "Did I close the engine lid?" paranoia. A few months later, it happened again. Old age—my old age—was taking its toll, I suppose, and I knew I had to find a solution, a warning signal of some sort.

And that's what this little addition to the Idiot Book is all about, electrical goodies you can add to your VW to help it run better and longer—and bring you some peace of mind. We add an engine compartment warning light, a fake blinking burglar alarm light, and, mostly, give advice on how your VW is wired so you can find switched and unswitched hot leads for adding lights and radios and other electrically powered gizmos to your VW. And hopefully give you the confidence to get involved in electrical diagnosis and repairs. Please read the whole chapter before doing any work. This is especially important if you have a fuel injection/computer-controlled model. Short it and you've got a major headache.

> **NOTE:** VW went from a 6 volt to a 12 volt system in August of 1966 ('67 model year) and many earlier VWs have been converted to 12 volts, the standard of the auto industry. If you have a 6 volt system, you must make the appropriate substitutions—that is, 6 volt bulbs when a 12 volt bulb is called for, and so on.

ELECTRICITY: ELECTRONS ON THE MOVE

In an automobile, electricity is "stored" in the battery, available at the turn of the key. Batteries—and the entire electrical system—have two sides, positive (+) and negative (–). This means that the atoms on one side of the lead plates inside the battery have an extra electron, giving them a negative charge, and the atoms on the other side of the lead plates are missing an electron and are thus positively charged.

Atoms that are short an electron or have an extra electron will be in an absolute tizzy to correct this imbalance. They will go to extraordinary lengths to pick up or shed electrons, and therein lies the secret of getting work out of electricity. When you turn on a switch you open a pathway (known as closing a circuit) for the extra electrons to race to the atoms missing an electron on the other side of the plates in the battery. Since these electrons will go through all kinds of hoops to get there we can take advantage of this urge by placing obstacles in the path they must negotiate to reach their goal, such as a light bulb, where the wire carrying the electrons narrows down from an eight-lane super-highway to a one-lane country road inside the bulb. Millions and billions of electrons jam this little byway and things, literally, heat up, just like on a jammed California freeway. Only instead of shooting each other, the heat makes the filament wire get so hot it glows and light is given off. At other times, the racing electrons create electromagnetic fields that operate motors and relays or play music from the speakers. Or create sparks that ignite the gasoline in the cylinders to make the motor run.

Unlike your home, automobiles are mostly made of steel and aluminum, good conductors of electricity, and use voltages one-tenth that running through your home circuits. Car makers take advantage of all this metal and low voltage by making the chassis and every metal thing connected to the chassis—the frame, the body, the engine, and so forth—part of the path of the electrons trying to get to the positive side of the battery. They do this by hooking up the negative side of the battery to the chassis with a fat cable. This connection and everything attached to it is called the ground, and VWs and all modern cars are thus negatively grounded.

One side of every electrical device in your car is connected to ground, either by being attached directly to the metal framework or by a wire from the device to ground. To complete the path, the other side of every electrical

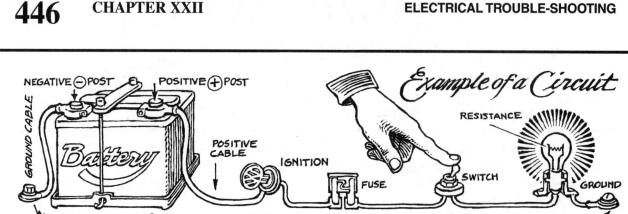

NEGATIVE ⊖ POST   POSITIVE ⊕ POST   *Example of a Circuit*

GROUND CABLE

Battery

POSITIVE CABLE

IGNITION   FUSE   SWITCH   RESISTANCE   GROUND

Engine, Chassis and other Metal components all serve as ground

device in your car is connected by a wire to the positive side of the battery. One of the dandy things about having the entire chassis and body serve as the ground is that adding electrical items often allows very simple one-wire connections for the devices on the positive side of the circuit.

There may well be, and usually are, other items in the path, such as switches to turn the devices on or off, like the headlight switch, that interrupt the flow of electrons. Some devices are always on as long as the battery cables are connected, such as the dashboard clock, but these are rare. Some are turned on when you turn the ignition switch to "on," such as the devices that keep your engine running, and some require both the ignition switch to be "on" and a switch flipped, such as the directional signals and the wipers.

SAFETY: Some folks have a fear of electricity, founded either on household high voltage experiences or lack of knowledge. In an automobile, the voltage is so low that one need not ever fear shock **except** in a couple of situations. One exception is when the engine is running and you touch the secondary ignition wires, the fat wires from the coil to the distributor and from the distributor to the spark plugs. These wires carry a very high voltage created by the coil and you could get a jolt. It probably won't hurt you; the danger comes from suddenly pulling your hand away and accidentally hitting the moving pulley or fan belt. The other danger comes from placing a metal tool, such as a wrench, right on top of the battery touching the positive and negative battery posts, or from the positive post to any metal part, such as the battery hold-down frame or body part. All of a sudden billions of electrons will flow across the tool. Even though the voltage is still just 12 volts, so many electrons crossing this direct path generate enough heat to melt the battery posts, maybe the tool . . . and maybe you.

In an automobile most circuits are not only low voltage, but low amperage as well. They're often measured in milliamps, and present no danger. No personal danger, that is. If you connect a +12 volt wire to ground, purposefully or by accident, sparks will fly, heat will be created in that circuit, and the battery will suffer, but you probably won't. This is called a **short**. Most likely you will blow a fuse before anything serious happens, like a fire, which is why we have fuses in a car or add in-line fuses to new circuits. A **fuse** is nothing more than a thin piece of wire that melts if too many electrons try to pass through it, thereby opening the circuit and stopping the flow of electricity. Fuses can be a plain piece of bare wire on a ceramic base, as in early VWs, mounted in glass tubes, or in plastic holders (called blade type fuses). VWs come with 10 to 12 fuses mounted in a fuse box that is usually found on the forward wall under the dash. These fuses protect most of the circuits in a VW. When a new circuit is added it is a good idea to protect it with an inline fuse on the positive side of the circuit. An inline fuse is typically a glass or blade fuse in a take-apart holder with two wires to connect it into the circuit. See Pete's drawings of inline fuse holders and the circuit diagram showing one in place.

Tools and Materials, General: For real electrical self-sufficiency, score a wiring diagram for your model. Sources of wiring diagrams are the factory manuals or those published by Robert Bentley, either of which is a useful supplement to this book. Unfortunately, a wiring diagram isn't much of a diagram, it's a schematic and not the actual wiring. You still have to translate that picture to your wiring. It takes a while, but if you start with some simple circuits, such as the coil or horn, and notice how they are wired compared to their depiction in a wiring diagram, you'll start getting it. The diagrams are laid out with the ground connections shown at the bottom. Positive connections are read from the top. Most often, your best bet for checking a circuit is to read the diagram starting at the bottom, following the ground connection to the device in question and from there back to any switches, the fuse box, or ignition switch. Wire colors are given but may differ from what is actually in place in your car. The important thing is not the color, but their connections at various terminals.

A most useful tool is a multimeter, also called a volt ohmmeter (VOM), which can read various properties of electrical systems, such as voltage, resistance, polarity, and current draw. See Chapter XVI for a picture of a VOM and how to use it. Voltage is read in volts (v), resistance in ohms (Ω) or K ohms (thousand Ω), polarity as negative or positive (– or +), and current in amperes (amps or milliamps). Alternatively, you can use a test light, which looks like a small screwdriver with a pointed tip. It has a bulb in the handle and a wired probe sticking out of the top. When you touch the wired probe to ground and pierce a wire or touch a "hot" connection with the tip, the bulb lights if you've hit +12 volts. Although the information provided is minimal, it is often all you need: is there juice or not in this wire?

Other tools and supplies might include a wire cutter, wire stripper (or razor blade), a crimping tool for connectors, rosin core solder, a small soldering iron, a drill with bits, and a metal file. A bunch of male and female crimp-on insulated connectors and squeeze-type connectors (also known as Quick Splice connectors) will come in very handy; they're available in most auto parts shops or Radio Shack. You'll also need a couple of small spools of stranded wire, maybe 14, 16, or 18 gauge for most stuff, and 10 or 12 gauge for devices that draw a lot of current (the lower the number, the thicker the wire, the more juice it can carry).

PROCEDURE FOR GENERAL ELECTRICAL TROUBLE-SHOOTING

Now that you have a fair idea of atomic physics and how to get work out of atoms that have been enhanced or deprived of electrons, you are ready to tackle the little electrical problems that come up from time-to-time.

Solving electrical problems can be fun and rewarding with the application of a little patience and logic. Guessing won't get you very far, though regular, for-hire mechanics often successfully do that. Magic? No. Experience. Until we have that experience we'll have to plod along testing one circuit after the other until we find the source of the problem.

Step 1. Check the Fuses and Bulbs

See Chapter XV: Lights and Sounds. Recently Eve told me she didn't have use of the horn in her VW for a whole year until she checked the fuses and, sure enough, found one blown. Since only 10 to 12 fuses, not counting a few inline fuses, cover dozens of electrical circuits (other than the ignition, which is not fused) you will generally find two or more faults when a fuse blows, which helps when tracking things down.

Step 2. Check for Juice

Most problems are fairly obvious. Is the component—radio, lamp, coil—getting +12v or not? A test lamp will tell you that. In many instances, however, you'll need the wiring diagram to tell which contact point to test. Most electrical devices in your VW have numbered contacts. So does the wiring diagram. The diagrams list each component by current track; all you need to do is search for that current track along the bottom of the diagram to find the related wires and terminals. Big help.

Step 3. Check Ground Connections

Quite often, your best route to solving an electrical conundrum is by beginning with the ground connections, particularly if a component appears to be getting +12v. Ground connections are often exposed, and corrosion can halt or severely limit the flow of electrons.

PROCEDURE FOR ADDING AN ENGINE COMPARTMENT LID WARNING LIGHT: Buses, all years through 1979

Condition: You're a space case like me and want a reminder to close the lid.

Tools and Materials: Please read Tools and Materials, General above. For this project, you'll also need a 3-inch alarm switch. You might have to settle for a shorter switch (2") and make-do. Look for one called a Long Throw Switch. By making do I mean also buying a few 1/4" washers and a nut that fits the threads, typically 1/4 x 20 (1/4" x 20 threads per inch). You'll see why when installing it. A drill, Exacto knife or equal, sandpaper, maybe pliers. A lamp: Any small 12v lamp with a red lens will work, incandescent or LED (Light Emitting Diode). Find one that's complete with bulb, screw-on nut, and pigtails for the electrical connections. Pigtails are short wires with stripped ends attached to some lamps and other electric components. Pigtails make installation much easier as you can just crimp or solder connectors to the ends; I wouldn't bother buying a lamp that doesn't have attached pigtails. If you choose an LED, make sure it's rated for 12 volts and that the cathode side goes to ground (the wire from the switch in the engine compartment, in this case). Finally, an inline fuse holder with the lowest amperage fuse you can find, push-on connectors, and a squeeze-on connector (see Step 6).

Step 1. Getting The Right Juice

Before adding any electrical gizmos, you'll need to find the right wires to tap into. Sometimes you'll want a source of electricity that's always got juice and other times only when the ignition key is in the "on" or in the "accessory" position, if your ignition switch has an accessory position (VW was a little bit slow on this one). Note: When I say "source of electricity" or "juice," I'm talking about the side of every electric circuit that is wired, one way or another, back to the positive battery post.

With very few exceptions, the electrical devices in your car are directly or indirectly hooked up to ground via the chassis and are switched on the positive side. The most notable exceptions are the horn button on the steering wheel, the spring-loaded button switches in the door frames that turn on the interior lights when a door is opened, and this project, the engine lid warning light. On these, the switch is on the grounded side.

When hooking up a lamp, radio, or cd or tape player, the negative (ground) connection can be made to any metal part of the car. For the positive side of the circuit you must find a wire that already carries +12v. Yes, you could run a wire directly from the positive post of the battery to your lamp, but that gets messy and uses unnecessary runs of wire. And it won't work for those items that you only want to work when the ignition key is in the "on" position. The most convenient source of +12v for most projects is in the wires right under the dash, and that's where to look.

It's pointless to say the green wire with the white stripe always has +12v; it might on my VW, but the colors changed from year-to-year, by model, and even in the same model in the same year. Your best bet is to look for a red wire, with or without stripes. Black and brown wires are usually ground wires. When I wire up a new circuit I follow these conventions, using black for the ground and red or another bright color for +12v.

To find +12v, scrunch down in front of the driver's seat so you can look under the dashboard and find the wires leading to the ignition switch. You may have to remove some under-dash panels and you'll certainly find yourself in a most awkward position poking around under there, like something out of the Kama Sutra. In that mess of multi-colored spaghetti you'll see several wires that are a bit heavier than the others; these are the ones

you'll test (and tap) for your electrical needs. Very thick wires will work, too, but you could completely or partially sever the wires trying to attach a squeeze-on connector to thick wires. You'll be poking the sharp tip of your test light right into a wire. If it doesn't have a sharp tip, or if you're using a VOM, you can stick a straight pin through the middle of the wire and touch the pin to test the wire. Don't forget to remove the pin when you're done. See Pete's drawing. Radio Shack sells a dandy little sharp wire poker that slips on the ends of the VOM test leads.

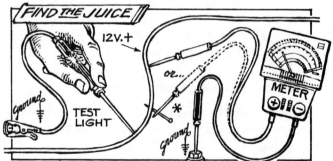

✳ PUSH A STRAIGHT PIN INTO THE WIRE FOR A GOOD CONTACT

To do the tests, first connect the wire from your test light or black wire from your VOM (set to measure DC volts) to a ground point. Almost any bare metal spot will work, but if you look around you'll likely find a spot where one or more brown or black wires are connected to the body, usually at a lug attached to a screw. This is a common ground point used for any number of items, such as the radio. You might consider using that point for all your dashboard ground connections, too. Touching the ground first, with the ignition off, test the various wires, starting with the red wires, with the pointed end of your test light (or red probe of your meter) to see which one lights the light or shows +12v on the meter. That one has +12v all the time. Mark it with a piece of masking tape. If some wires have no juice, remember where they are for the next test.

Do the same with the ignition in the "on" position. Test other wires until you find +12v. To check it is hot only with the ignition "on," turn the ignition off and test it again. If you no longer get +12v you've found it.

CAUTION: After you've done these tests, ALWAYS disconnect the negative (ground) wire from the negative battery post before working on the electrical system. Do not detach the negative ground cable at the chassis connection, only at the battery.

Step 2. Get Ready

While it is usually common practice to hook up light switches so that the switch interrupts the circuit on the positive side, this will be an exception to that rule, mostly because of the switch used, which comes from auto burglar alarm systems. These switches open and close at the ground (negative) connection. They are available at Radio Shack and alarm installers. In this case, we want a light to come on at the dashboard if the engine compartment lid is open and if the ignition switch is in the "on" position.

The switch is installed by screwing it into the body of the car (ground, remember?) so that it will complete the circuit when the lid is open, and open the circuit when the lid is closed. Completing the circuit will cause a light to come on at the dashboard and warn you of the open door. When the lid is closed, the inner rod moves away from the ground connection, opening the circuit and preventing electricity from flowing through the bulb.

Step 3. Install Switch

Look around the edge of the engine compartment for a place to mount the switch, where you can drill a 1/4" or 9/32" hole (typically—check your switch for size) and where there's space for the inner part of the switch, noting that this part will move in a bit when the door is closed. On my bus, it fit nicely on the left side lower edge, right in the rubber insulation surrounding the engine compartment, requiring a hole in the insulation. If you don't wish to cut the insulation, look around for another spot, checking to see if the switch will work properly in that location. You might prefer to mount it on a bracket. Keep the switch well away from any moving engine parts, such as the pulley. See illustration.

Okay, found a good place? Pull away the rubber insulation, if necessary, and drill the hole; rub off a bit of the paint on both sides of the hole with sand paper before screwing in the switch for a clean, bright metal surface that will allow those little electrons to pass. Cut a hole in the rubber insulation (if that's where you put the switch) big enough to clear the hex end of the switch so that the outer end will poke through. Slip two or three 1/4" washers on the threads and screw the switch into the hole. The trick is to stop screwing in the switch at the point where it will contact the lip of the engine lid when it is closed. The lid only needs to push the inner rod in about a 1/4" or so, just enough to lift it off its seat, when it is closed. Usually, the outer end only needs to come to the outer edge of the rubber insulation. It all depends on how well the lid fits on your bus.

Screw the switch in or out until the switch is at the right height for contact with the lid, just before it closes all the way. You should be able to eyeball it until you get it right. When you've got it, add or remove washers until the switch screws right up to the body, and run the nut up the switch in back and tighten it with a wrench. Don't worry if it's not perfect; you can adjust it later after the light's in place.

Step 4. Install Wire

Switch installed? Run a thin (14 to 18 gauge) wire to the dashboard for the light. I prefer to have all the wires run inside my van, under the mats, but you can run them underneath the car if you like, though they are exposed to the elements there. Look for existing holes in the engine compartment and run the wire through one, preferably one that has a rubber grommet to keep the wire from rubbing on bare metal, either into the interior or underneath. Start with a wire considerably longer than the distance from front to back as you'll need the extra length to run it up and around various places in its travel to the back side of the dash. Leave enough in the engine compartment to route the wire neatly to the back of the switch.

Step 5. Install Light

After you've finally fished the forward end of the wire out at the dashboard, you can install the lamp and finish the job. Look around the dashboard for an easily-seen place for the lamp. In my camper, I put the lamp on the plastic surround where the steering column joins the dashboard, on the left side. It's a perfect place for the light, easy to drill and mount. One nice thing about using an LED is that you can just drill a small hole in the dash (check the size on the package, usually 13/64"), push the lamp through the hole, and hold it in place with a dot of Super Glue.

Found a spot you can get at? Good. Drill a hole for the lamp and install it. Then just add small crimp-on male or female push-on connectors to each pigtail for the final connection. Adding the connectors to the pigtails before you install the light will make things easier.

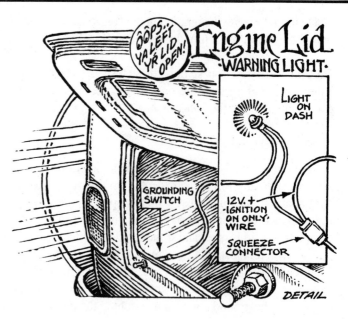

Step 6. Electrify

Before you start, disconnect the cable on the negative side of your battery, if you haven't already done so, to protect the system from accidental shorts.

The "hot" or positive lead goes to a wire you found in Step 1 that carries electricity only when the ignition is "on." Attach one of the pigtails of an inline fuse to the lead from your lamp and then a wire from the other pigtail of the inline fuse to +12v. You can easily make this connection if you use a squeeze-on connector. It's a small, double-chambered plastic item containing a pair of metal contacts that cut through the insulation and into the wires when squeezed shut. One side goes over the wire you're tapping into and the other side holds the wire to the inline fuse. Run the wire around other wires under the dash so it doesn't hang loose, then, when you've got the wires in the connector, just squeeze it shut. If it won't close all the way so the catch holds, squeeze it with a pair of pliers. Hook up the wire from the engine compartment to the other lamp pigtail and you're done at the dashboard end.

Step 7. Finish Up

Back in the engine compartment, strip a 1/4" or so of insulation from your wire end, crimp it onto the connector that came with the switch and push it into the back of the switch.

After checking that everything looks okay, you can hook up the negative battery cable and test your installation. With the ignition off and the engine lid open, the bulb should not light. If it does, you've attached the hot lead to a wire that is always hot, ignition on or off. Assuming the bulb didn't light, turn the ignition to the "on" position. With the engine compartment lid open, the bulb should light. Now close the lid—did the light go off? If so, you've got it. If not, you'll need to adjust the switch by loosening the nut on the switch and unscrewing it a bit to make it stick out further, perhaps adding a washer or two. Adjust it until the bulb goes out when the lid is down.

Now you'll never have to worry about whether or not you've left the engine compartment open. Check it every now and then to make sure it's still working.

PROCEDURE FOR INSTALLING A FAKE BURGLAR ALARM BLINKING LIGHT: All Years, All Models

Condition: Some years ago I bought a fancy Audi Coupe, and along with it came theft paranoia. So I went down to the auto burglar alarm store and asked, "How much does a good alarm system cost?"

"Three hundred bucks," the salesman replied, without skipping a beat.

"What makes it worth $300?" I prodded.

He reached into the showcase and pulled a small lamp out of one of the boxes displayed there. "See this? When a thief sees this blinking on the dashboard he goes to another car."

Well, shucks, I said to myself, I can put a blinking light on my dashboard for a helluva lot less than $300. For $3, in fact. And I did. In fact, I prefer it to a regular burglar alarm. I installed a real alarm in another car once and the damn thing kept going off whenever it felt neglected, which was usually around 3 a.m. My neighbors were not amused.

Tools and Materials: See Tools and Materials, General above. You'll also need a lamp (read on), and a switch. Get a SPST switch (Single Pole Single Throw—the simplest on-off switch) to turn it on and off—your choice here is limited only by what you might find at an electronics supply house or auto parts store. You can use the smallest mini-switch that will mount in your car as it will be switching a very small amount of current and does not need hefty contacts. I happen to like small push-on/push-off switches for this as they aren't obvious and can be easily tucked away, but a switch with a lever will work, too. To protect your car, an inline fuse will be needed. Ring terminals (round connectors that go under a screw head), push-on connectors, and heat shrink tubing will make the job easier and neater. Heat shrink tubing is used over bare wires for insulation; it shrinks tightly around the wire when heated with a hair dryer.

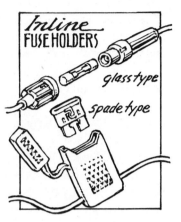

Step 1. Getting The Right Juice

Go to Procedure for Installing Engine Compartment Lid Warning Light, Step 1. Getting The Right Juice. For this job you'll need to tap into a wire that carries juice all the time, that is, with the ignition in the "off" position.

Step 2. Get Ready

The wire to your switch and lamp from your +12v source (Step 1) and to ground can be thin, like 16–18 gauge, as it will carry only the smallest amounts of current; in fact, you can leave the lamp blinking merrily away at an airport parking lot for months without draining a healthy battery.

Unless you want the bulb to blink all the time, guaranteed to drive you bonkers driving or camping at night, you'll need a switch in the circuit to turn it on and off. The switch will go on the positive side of the circuit, between one lead on the bulb and the source of +12v under the dash.

Mounting the lamp presents a bit of a challenge. You'll want anyone peering into your car to see the light blinking, day or night, so it has to be highly visible. The main problem is finding a place easily accessible and not in the thick, padded areas of the dash. In my bus, I put it on the upper left part of the glove box door where the blinking light is visible even in bright daylight, leaving enough wire behind the lamp so the door can be opened and closed without stressing the wire or lamp. See Pete's illustration.

There are a couple ways to make the lamp blink: by using a thermal bulb or a blinking LED (Light Emitting Diode). I have had good luck with both though each has drawbacks. The primary consideration is that the lamp should look like an authentic alarm light and not some tacky thing with a big square lens or other obviously phoney concoction. The problem with the LED is that, while it's easy to install, it is not very bright, though you might be able to find an extra-bright LED (you know, one with a high IQ). Find one that works on 12 volts; most are low voltage, like 2v, and while you can hook them up with a 330 Ω resistor to limit the amount of current flowing into the bulb, I have found they get quite toasty and are not very bright, like my cousin Irving. Finding a bright, 12v blinking LED is near-impossible at places like Radio Shack. If there's a professional electronics supply house in your area they might have one. Or try All Electronics Corp., 800-826-5432; check out their Web site at http://www.allcorp.com. They also have an extensive catalogue of electrical goodies.

The thermal blinker works by an endless cycle of heating and cooling that opens and closes an internal contact that makes the lamp blink. The thermal blinker produces enough light, is cheap (about $2 for a pack of 3 bulbs at Radio Shack), and fits into some lamp holders. It's only a bulb so it must be inserted into a lamp holder. There's no socket fitting so you need to figure out a way to keep it from falling out of the lamp holder; a bit of electrical tape, toothpicks, or Super Glue will do. I've used it often and it works just fine. Basically you just need a lamp that has an attractive metal or plastic bezel (the outermost area around the lens that shows on the dash) that will hold the bulb and fit in the dash location you've chosen.

Reminder: Disconnect the cable from the negative battery terminal before you do anything else.

Step 3. Install Lamp

No matter which arrangement you pick, they all have the same basic installation. One wire from the bulb—it doesn't matter which, except on an LED—is attached to ground (any good metal surface, such as a body screw) and the other is wired first to one lug (attachment point) of your switch; again, either one will do. Then another wire is run from the other lug on the switch to an inline fuse, and from there to a +12v wire that always has juice. See Pete's circuit drawing.

Hooking up an LED is the same except that the cathode goes to ground (−). You can tell which side is the cathode of some LEDs by feeling for a flat spot at the base of the bulb, on the side. The wire next to that flat spot is the cathode. Sometimes you must look at the wire terminals on the bottom of the bulb to find the cathode; in these cases, the terminal on the cathode side is slightly wider than the other terminal.

Okay, let's have a go at it. Mark the spot where you've decided to mount the lamp, and drill a hole for it; the hole size is usually marked on the lamp package or you can just eyeball it against your drill bits. Remove any hardware—nuts, washers, whatever—from the backside of the lamp and push it through the hole from the dash side, pigtails and all. Some lamps have the holding hardware on the front and will be installed from behind the dash or other panel. Give yourself a pat on the back if you remembered to attach connectors to the pigtails before you mounted the lamp. If not, do it now. Replace the hardware so that the lamp fits snugly on the dash.

Strip about 1/4" of insulation from both ends of a piece of wire long enough to reach a ground connection from the lamp, and crimp a connector on one end to match the one on one of the pigtails. Crimp a spade or ring terminal (looks like a washer with a crimp-on connector) on the other end and attach it under a nearby body screw. Run the other end of the wire up and around existing under-dash wires, to keep it from hanging down, and hook it up to one of the pigtails. If you're using a 12-volt LED, attach the wire to the cathode lead.

Step 4. Install Switch

Mount the switch somewhere out of sight, like under the dashboard, that you can readily reach. Soldering a couple of short pigtails, with push-on connectors on the ends, to the lugs of the switch before mounting will make the connections easier. With either a push-on/push-off or lever type switch in hand, poke around under the dash for a likely mounting spot, drill a hole and mount it. Often, you can find pre-existing holes on the lower lip of the dash. Assuming you've attached a push-on connector to the end of the remaining pigtail on the lamp, strip the ends of a piece of wire long enough to go from the bulb lead to the switch, and attach connectors to the ends. Obviously, all the mating wires will require the proper male and female connectors on their ends to work. Add mating connectors to an inline fuse and attach one lead to the remaining switch pigtail.

Now cut another piece of wire long enough to reach from the other pigtail on the inline fuse to the wire you're going to tap that has juice all the time. Strip one end and crimp on a connector that will mate to the remaining pigtail on the inline fuse. The other end, which should not be stripped, goes into the squeeze-on connector that attaches to your chosen source of +12v. If you look closely at the squeeze-on connector, you'll see one channel that runs the full length and one channel that is blocked at one end. The +12v source wire goes in the pass-through section and the wire from your switch goes into the other side. Then just squeeze closed until it catches.

All hooked up? Great. Attach the ground cable to the negative pole on your battery and try it out. Switch it on and it should blink merrily away and stop blinking when you switch it off. If not, trace all your steps to make sure you haven't missed a connection. Now when you park your car and flip on the blinker, it will look as if the car's burglar alarm system is armed, giving you some measure of protection.

Throughout the book you've probably seen: **See Changes** or **See Changes and New Ideas**. Look below for the page number the notice appears on and you'll find a change and/or a new idea.

We're beginning this section with a reader's tribute to John, one that would warm his heart because it's the reason he wrote the book:

It (learning to work on my Volkswagen) was the beginning of my freedom. Something that had chained me before, I now had a relationship with. I had learned its language. I began to learn other languages; of photography and seeing; of carpentry and working with my hands; of music and listening. And there's no doubt in my mind that my experience with the Idiot manual was its start. Thank you, J.T. Judd IV

Page 5: Chapter XVIII on hi-performance modifications does not have procedures. If you decide on any options for hi-performance, you must follow the pertinent procedure in the body of the book to remove the old and install the new. Mr. Stick suggests reading the Hi-Performance chapter for general information even if you're not interested in the modifications.

Page 7: Here's a repeat warning that cars can be dangerous and deadly weapons whether you're driving one or working on or under it. Richard Sealey, author of *How To Keep Your VW Rabbit Alive*, was driving a motorbike in Jamaica at about 60mph when the rear tire blew. He very c-a-r-e-fully steered it to the side of the road—whew. A Rastaman sitting in the shade coolly glanced up and commented, "Conscious driving, mon" then offered a beer.

So, remember consciousness. If there's a chance something can fly into your eyes, then take the extra minute to put on safely goggles. If a part or nut or bolt looks well used or rusted, take the extra time and bread to buy a new one. Always get new cotter pins. Sparks ignite gasoline—keep a fire extinguisher handy in your car. Jewelry and long hair can get caught in things; take them off, tuck it in a cap. Cars on supports can fall down, because of the thing called gravity. At all times keep ALERT AND AWARE especially when in and around "the ass that bears you." Remember, too, that as cars get older, things have worn more.

A reader wrote that while working under his '69 Fastback, the jack gave way. Fortunately, he'd put the wheel under the car as instructed (but no BLOCKS). He did need seven stitches, but thanked us for saving him from "what might have happened."

Page 8: Although the VW bug hasn't been imported to the USA since 1979 (last year for the convertible), the air cooled Vanagon hung in here until 1983.

In 1980, VW redesigned the bus from nose to tail and from the ground up. Some of the many changes include: the gas tank filler is between the passenger front door and the sliding door; the spare tire is under the front end and the battery is under the passenger seat. No longer is there a large rear engine compartment lid. There is only a small cover that provides access to the dip stick, oil filler and timing and alternator adjustments. Main engine access for tune-ups is through a lid above the engine inside the rear of the Vanagon (as in the 1978-'79 bus). The engine is basically the same as the '78-'79, except for minor fuel injection and emission control changes. Engine maintenance procedures on the Vanagon are the same as in the '78-'79 bus—including no valve adjustments.

In 1983, VW put a Rabbit drive train (meaning the engine and transaxle) into the Vanagon. Rabbit means water cooled and 1983 and on Vanagons are covered in *How To Keep Your VW Rabbit Alive*, by Richard Sealey. You can still buy the dear old 1600cc bug and bus in Mexico and Brazil. There are important restrictions, however, which must be checked out before trying to bring one of these across the border. **'78 and on bus owners:** Please also read **Changes and New Ideas for pages 52 and 189 in Chapter XX, Tune-Ups.**

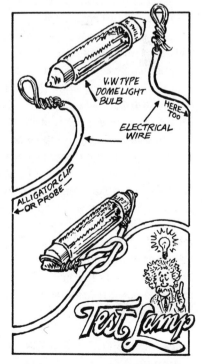

Page 30: Here's a sketch of a handy test or timing light.

Pages 39 and 40: Changing a tire can be dangerous as you can see from the illustrations on these pages; things can slip, fly out or who knows what, so please—STAY AWARE.

Page 47A: Kevin A. Madden complains: "Smogging is a legal reality, and your book has no useful advice for this regular struggle that VW owners must face . . . With all that you know about these machines, it seems ironic that you don't write more about how to modify them with the chief goal being environmental protection . . . "Things Done to Volkswagens in the Name of Smog Control" doesn't help with the things that it should." Our answer: Convert to propane, but do it right.

Colin Messer (of Chapter XVIII) and John Hilgerdt (of Chapter XIX and XXII) have put together a manual for conversion to propane. It was prepared as a training manual for technicians, for people who go into the trade of conversions—not exactly for idiots and not exactly for VWs. It will allow the reader to make intelligent choices. It's called "LPG2—Propane Technicians' Training Manual." We don't know the cost yet but you can contact John Hilgerdt at Access Publications for more info:
E-mail: Accesspub@cheta.net
Or snail mail: 86½ Lexington Ave., Asheville, N.C. 28801
Colin suggests you phone or write to:
Brent Wilkerson, c/o Squibb-Taylor, 10480 Shady Trail Lane, Dallas, TX 75220 (800) 345-8105.

Brent Wilkerson sells a very popular conversion system built in Texas by Algas which is distributed in Mexico for VW use. Colin has installed this system on U.S. engines, but has only seen their VW conversion at shows. If you do write, mention Colin's name as he told Mr. Wilkerson to expect inquiries.

Colin also suggests the following things be taken into consideration:

1. Unlike gasoline, the richer the propane/air mixture, the hotter the combustion. So, the fuel/air ratio for propane should be on the lean side. There is another side to this story, of course (when isn't there?). If the mixture is too lean, the oxides of nitrogen increase and the reactive bed of the three-way catalyst (if installed) won't work efficiently. Unlike gasoline, however, a lean mixture using propane will not ruin an engine, it will only lose power. To keep an eye on the combustion efficiency, an oxygen sensor feed-back fuel metering system should be installed.

2. It is necessary to draw cold outside air into the carb. Hot air is less dense than cold air. Propane vapor (gas) displaces air as it enters the engine. And so, power is lost if the engine is running on hot under-hood air rather than cold outside air, especially if the engine was designed to use low octane fuel. The IMPCO Carburetion Service and Parts Manuals are great resources for propane carburetion. Their address: IMPCO, 16804 Gridley Place, Cerritos, CA 90701.

3. Can damage result by using a dry, unleaded fuel in an engine with non-hardened valves designed for leaded gasoline? Yes, dry fuels can eventually recess non-hardened exhaust valves. To limit this damage, the fuel/air mixture should be run on the lean side of stoichiometry (using oxygen sensor feedback, if possible) and the rpms should be kept down so as not to beat the valves to death. When doing a valve job, it's probably a good idea to investigate hardened seats and stellite valves.

4. As to flammability: Gasoline is far more dangerous than either natural gas or propane. In case of an accident (heaven forbid) gasoline lingers longer. Natural gas (methane) is lighter than air (half the weight) and boils at minus 260 degrees F. It rapidly moves up when released. Propane is heavier than air (half again) and boils at 44 degrees F below zero. While propane will hang around longer if released, it is safer than gasoline because it is in a gaseous form in our atmosphere. For more information on safety regulations and on propane motor fuel conversions ask for the national Fire Protection Association's (NFPA) Liquified Petroleum Gases Handbook #58. You can get a copy from the NFPA by calling 800-344-3555 or writing them at 11 Tracy Drive, Avon, MA 02322. It's expensive.

Compressed natural gas is not for a VW as it would use five times the space and at least five times the weight in cylinders compared to propane for the same energy stored. Propane takes only slightly more space and adds only slightly more weight than gasoline. Propane or natural gas? Both can decrease tail pipe emissions and engine maintenance costs. However, if either system is installed incorrectly, emissions could increase and the engine might self destruct.

Page 47B: "The only time my bug failed to start, after 30,000 trouble-free miles, turned out to be the old seat belt/ignition interlock relay. My mechanic said, 'What! You still had that thing hooked up?' " From Hugh Clark.

This bothersome relay can foul and cause your '74 ,'75 or '76 VW to not start. Ask a VW mechanic how you can disconnect it with a bypass loop or replace it with a relay that works.

Page 48: Here's a possibly dangerous situation: If a spark plug wire comes off its holder, it can touch the fuel line (which goes to the fuel pump). If the fuel line is grounded (such as touching the heat riser or other piece of metal), sparks from the spark plug wire can wear a hole in the fuel line, gasoline can escape and explode. The precautions to take are:
1. Make sure the spark plug wires are in their holders;
2. Make sure the fuel line is not resting on the heat riser or on anything;
3. Make sure the fuel line rubber grommet on the front tin of the engine compartment is in place.

Page 52: From Howard Palmer: "Remember all those old buses being used as chicken coops? Well, they're being refurbished and put back into service. One big problem is the degeneration of the electrical wires" and here's his solution for bypassing the wire going from the starter solenoid to the switch and back again:

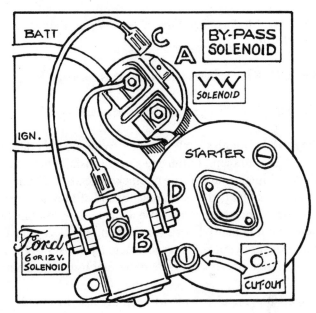

The solenoid is asked to do a twofold job. The first is to close the electrical contact when the ignition switch is turned on and the second is to mechanically move the arm that engages the bendix lever. This is complicated by the fact that current must run from the battery through the fuse box to the switch and back; a trip of about 20 feet. By the time the wires get old (have high resistance), the contacts are probably loose and/or corroded. Add to this a hot solenoid (from trying unsuccessfully to start the engine) and there's no way enough current can get through to start you on your way.

The solution is to buy a bypass solenoid made by Ford, 2 feet of #10 wire (as heavy as the ignition wire), 3 post-type terminals and 1 female clip. You'll also need a screwdriver and a hacksaw. OK, cut out the end of the mounting hole on the bracket on the Ford solenoid, loosen the starter screw and slide the hole you just cut out under the starter screw washer. Tighten the screw firmly. Now remove the red wire from Terminal A on the VW solenoid; this is the wire that comes from the ignition switch. Move it to the B connection on the Ford solenoid. Cut two lengths of your new wire to fit and connect these wires as C and D in the sketch.

This conversion gives the solenoid juice directly from the battery, so the solenoid gets more juice to perform its function of closing the contacts. The VW solenoid still throws the bendix lever.

Page 54: See Changes and New Ideas for Page 48.

Page 54, Step 5: FIRE WARNING!!! Be sure to aim the flow of gasoline away from the engine and yourself.

Page 54, Step 6: Before taking the top off the fuel pump, disconnect the rubber fuel line at the pump end or in FRONT of the engine where it joins the metal tube. Plug the rubber hose with a clean stick, pencil or the like. There are crimp type clamps made especially for this job, but however you do it, stop the gas from flowing before continuing to work.

Page 56: Sheila Harrison writes that she banged on the float chamber "to no avail and checked inside the carburetor to see if the needle valve assembly was loose—it wasn't." She bought a rebuild kit, did the thing and "found that the float was almost filled up with gasoline although there were no visible cracks or holes." She bought a used float (no new ones were available for her Solex 30 PICT 1) and "Voilà! No more leakage. The old float had been too heavy to close the needle valve in time."

Page 73: "After replacing the alternator in my 1974 Beetle, I found that the new one was not doing its job. My son and I ran all of the procedures to check the regulator, battery connections, etc., but still no charge. After we pulled the alternator and it checked out okay, we found the problem. The fat, black wire that goes into the plug that plugs to the alternator was not getting connection. Had the book mentioned checking the plug, we would have saved ourselves hours of work."

We hope Jan Parker's thoughtful letter saves someone else hours of work.

Page 79: See Changes and New Ideas for page 73.

Page 90: Models after November, 1975 no longer have an oil pressure control valve so don't look too long for it.

Page 92: See Changes and New Ideas for page 8.

Page 97: See Changes and New Ideas for page 8.

Page 104: Douglas Taylor writes: "With the abundance of second-hand parts and engines being put together with them, I offer my story: I installed an exchange rebuilt engine in my old campervan. After 8000 kilometers and a pair of cracked heads, I discovered that my innocent-looking combination distributor that had timed statically and at idle quite perfectly was advancing about 50 degrees at full advance! My advice: Don't use a vacuum or combination advance distributor unless you are absolutely sure that it is the right one for your engine. If you have any doubt, borrow or buy a timing light that lets you measure your full advance. Better yet, heed John's advice and install a Bosch 009 distributor (if your engine doesn't use D-Jetronic fuel ignition). Your engine (and bank account) will thank you."

Page 108: A reader wrote for help because he couldn't determine from the book how to time his engine. He had four timing lines and we say three. He phoned seven dealers and got seven answers, then he phoned six independent VW garages and got six independent answers. What to do? We told him to time it different ways and use the way it ran best and coolest and got the best mileage.

Page 115: See Changes and New Ideas for page 48.

Page 116: See Changes and New Ideas for page 56.

Page 122: See Changes and New Ideas for page 54, Step 6.

Page 124: "If you can't afford a grease gun and you know someone in the mechanical biz, ask them to get you one of those 50cc syringes. They fit the fitting real nice and they can't bust you unless you have a needle on it." . . . *note from the underground.*

Page 127: From Stephen C. Mills: "My friend brought me his '81 Brazilian Bug whose engine had been rebuilt and hadn't run right. Well, besides the fact that the carb fell off in my hands, and one spark plug shot out when I caused a backfire (hole stripped completely), it was pretty solid—it was just that the mechanic . . . installed the **distributor drive shaft** about 30 degrees off one way (I don't know how, everyone says that it is about impossible), and I had to get it out [without removing the engine]. Here's the procedure:

1. Remove the distributor completely.

2. Remove the fuel pump, the push rod and the gasket, and only then remove the plastic riser seat for the pump. If you can't remove the pin (you can't grip it) rotate the crank until you can grip it. Pull it out and then remove the plastic pump seat.

3. Rotate the crank until the driveshaft is in the position as shown in the picture on pages 294 and 295. [Chapter XV, Procedure for Engine Mantling, Step 10]

4. Is the crank at the timing mark (TDC #1 cylinder)? Yes? Then there isn't a problem! No? The shaft must come out!

5. Rotate the crank until the driveshaft is in the proper position [Chapter XV, Engine Mantling, Step 10]. Don't worry about the crank's position.

6. Take out your trusty yellow No. 2 pencil. Cut off one end, square, and push this end into the hole where the spring was (forgot to take the spring out?) on top of the driveshaft. Push down good [fairly hard].

7. Pull up gently. No movement? Turn the crank until the driveshaft is exactly 180 degrees out—you just had the driveshaft backwards—the narrow and wide sides are hard to distinguish sometimes.

8. Pull again. It came out right? As you pull up, rotate the pencil/shaft counterclockwise. To re-insert, coat with WD-40 or similar and insert slightly counterclockwise of final postion. Wiggle the pencil back and forth until the pencil comes out.
[We haven't tried this procedure ourselves, but are putting it here in case it can help someone sometime].

Page 131: See Changes and New Ideas for page 56.

Page 134: See Changes and New Ideas for page 47A.

Page 139: Here's a very helpful suggestion from a reader for those with fuel injected engines: This wire, number 11, is connected to the crankcase where a lot of grease and oil accumulate. So, even if it's well connected (you know, hobnobs with the Rockefellers) carefully pull it off, clean the crud off with a dry rag and reconnect. Making sure number 11 is clean and well connected will cure the random missing or cutting off problem 95% of the time.

Page 148: Another helpful suggestion for those with fuel injected engines: Types III and IV only. If you think the pressure sensor is faulty and all the electrical connections check out OK, the problem, a good percentage of the time, could be the rod sticking in the sensor. This is easy to fix. Remove the sensor (Step 2, page 156) and take it apart by removing the screws. Clean the rod and lubricate it with WD-40, then wipe it with a touch of 70 or 90 weight oil. Seal the case of the sensor with silicon seal to prevent dirt from entering and crudding up the rod again.

A bad muffler can make the sensor go out by backfiring and jamming up the rod, so keep the muffler in good shape. If you've worked over the sensor and the muffler's bad, replace the muffler.

Page 155: See Changes and New Ideas for page 148.

Page 186: We've had several letters stating that people have had a hard time making room for the pads by using their hands to push the pistons (cups) back into the caliper housing. If you're having this difficulty, try this: Start a "C" clamp onto the caliper and piston and loosen the brake fluid bleed screw slightly. By tightening the "C" clamp, you should be able to collapse the piston. If this doesn't do it, you'll have to buy, rent or borrow the special set of pliers made especially for this job.

Page 189: Along with the body changes on the 1980 and on vanagon, the front and rear suspension were radically changed to give the Vanagon a wider track that allows for more room inside. (This makes it larger and even more boxy looking than earlier models). No more torsion bars: these have coil-shock and trailing arm suspension. There are no lubrication procedures you can do on the front end. There is, however, a wheel bearing adjustment and packing procedure that should be done every 30,000 miles. See the Wheel Procedure in Chapter XI. None of Chapter XII applies to you.

Page 207: If you try to drive without using the clutch and find you cannot do it without grinding gears, you're better off calling a tow truck or else you could be facing gear box repairs (expensive) as well as a new clutch. In the old days the gear boxes were much stouter and could take more punishment. About 1963 or '64 gear boxes began to get less sturdy.

Page 208: If these adjustments don't fix the problem, check the front transmission mounts for tightness (Chapter X, Lubrication Procedure).

Page 214, #1: That's all, except use blue or red silicon seal between the seal on the axle boot and the axle housing.

Page 214 #2: David Amaral tells us that the Safari (Thing) is a Type 181 with 181 parts numbers. From mid-1973 on, it uses Independent Rear Suspension with gear ratios the same as the 1966 bus: a final ratio of 5.375:1 and a rear axle ratio of 4.125:1.

   1969-early 1973: Transmission #181-300-043R, Chassis #183-2493-402. Mid 1973 on: Tranny #181-300-044F, Chassis #183-2493-403. Thanks, David, from all 181 owners.

Page 216: A word of caution about wheel pullers. When you tighten the center bolt on the puller and the drum doesn't seem to budge, there is a lot of pent up energy in the puller. The puller could conceivably come flying off. So stand to one side while tightening it.

Page 218: Greg Spry phoned and left a message to say that he made four (4) wheel bearing pull tools to no avail. Tosh says: "Rent one."

Page 219: If you weigh less than 60 pounds, or for some reason feel the torque may not be 220 or 253 foot pounds, tighten the axle nut as in Step 5 then go c-a-r-e-fully to VW and check the torque.

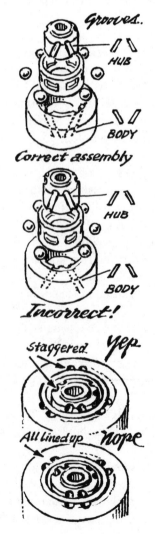

Grooves..
HUB
BODY
Correct assembly

HUB
BODY
Incorrect!

Staggered *yep.*

All lined up *nope*

Page 224: A letter from Down Under: I recently discovered something about the CV joints of my 1969 Kombi that might save other keen home mechanics some time.

   A CV joint that has been apart for cleaning can be assembled a right way and a wrong way. The difference is not obvious until you know what it is.

   The CV joint must go together "precisely," as this diagram shows, with the direction of the grooves being opposite on the hub and body. If the body of the CV joint is rotated 60° around the hub it will look like this:

   The direction of the grooves in the hub and body are the same, not opposite. The joint will go together this way but will not move. So if you put your CV joint together and find it does not swivel, take the bearings out and rotate the body around the hub by 60°.

   Now the CV joint will assemble and function as it should.

   Thank you, Robert Neil, of Brisbane, Australia.

Page 240: When using a high pressure hose to bathe the engine compartment, be careful of the paper and metal hoses and the generator or alternator.

Page 258: Up to 1972, the air cleaner was an oil bath cleaner; '73 and later dual carb and fuel injected engines use a pleated paper filter (no oil involved).

Page 259: From John Hilgerdt: When I first read this procedure, I went out and bought a strong chain and hooks and large U-bolt. Never used 'em. Even the official VW shop manual for '68 to '78 Type II models says to support the transmission when removing the engine, but I wonder if a reader can tell me why.

The bell housing on the rear end of the transaxle is attached by two large bolts on its upper edge to a transmission carrier, which in turn is bolted to a frame member. Whether or not the engine is in place, the transaxle is, as far as I can see, well secured to the frame. Nor will these bolts be expected to support the weight of the engine at any time during removal and installation.

Before the rear engine carrier is removed, the engine must be supported on a jack or two scissors jacks, using John's method. After the carrrier is unbolted, either the car is pushed forward or the engine is slid back, then it's lowered and removed. Thus, there is even less weight on the transmission with the engine out than when it was in, assuming that it shares some engine weight-bearing with the rear engine mount.

I've removed the engine in my '78 bus without supporting the transmision more times than I care to remember. There's been no obvious harm to my transaxle, engine or frame. If you want to do it the official way, I know where you can get a chain—like new—cheap.

Page 260: Type IV: also remove the oil filler tube, the ignition coil and the anti-backfire valve before removing the engine.

Page 268: See Changes and New Ideas for page 52.

Page 275: Models after November, 1975 have no oil pressure control valve.

Page 277: See Changes and New Ideas for page 127.

Page 279: Another way to install rings, **The Feeler Gauge Method**, courtesy of Mr. Stick, who never seems quite able to install a set of rings without breaking at least one of them, unless using this method (please read the entire procedure before starting):

The two top compression rings are the killers, easily breaking with the slightest twist. If you don't have a ring expanding tool, remove 3 of the middle-range leaves from your set of feeler gauges. These will be used to slide the rings down over the piston lands.

An assistant would be most helpful, but you can do it alone. The trick is to place 2 of the feeler gauge leaves close to each other on one side of the piston and the third leaf on the opposite side and then slide the ring down over the leaves until it is over the groove in the piston.

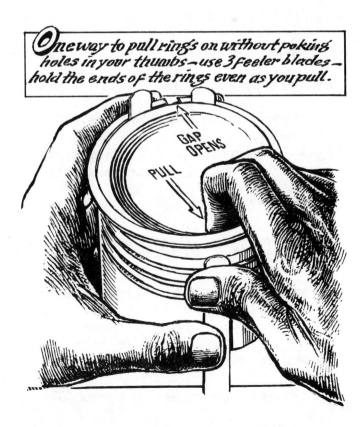

One way to pull rings on without poking holes in your thumbs—use 3 feeler blades—hold the ends of the rings even as you pull.

GAP OPENS

PULL

It's a bit tricky holding 3 feeler gauges on the piston whilst sliding the ring down, so if you don't have an assistant to help you hold the gauges you'll have to hold 'em in place with a large rubber band, hose clamp or some such around the lower part of the piston.

Starting with the lower compression ring, place it over the piston and gauges so that the ring gap falls between the two closely-spaced leaves (see illustration) and pull the opposite side of the ring down and over the piston and third gauge. Carefully push the ring evenly down until it is opposite the middle groove of the piston. The ring will hold the leaves in place now so your assistant, if you have one, can take a break. Repeat this step for the top ring until it is over the top groove. If you used a clamp to hold the feeler gauges in place you can remove it now.

Slowly and carefully pull out the single leaf, holding the rings so they fall into their grooves as the gauge is removed. With tension released, the feeler gauges at the gap end should come (or fall) easily out. The main thing to watch for in this procedure is that the ring ends are held away from the piston an do not score the lands between and above the grooves.

Page 287: Models after November, 1975 have no oil pressure *control* valve.

Page 289: Newer models don't have an arrow, they have a square bump on one edge. This bump should face toward the fly wheel.

Page 317: Install the oil filter mounting bracket before installing the oil cooler. No oil pressure *control* valves after November, 1975. Your model may not have one.

Page 318: Don't forget the piece of tin that goes between the alternator and the heads. It's easier if you don't put on the back piece of tin or the oil fill tube until after the engine is installed.

Page 325: See Changes and New Ideas for page 8.

Page 326: See Changes and New Ideas for page 8. Safari owners see Changes and New Ideas for page 214.

Page 332: Safari owners: go to Changes and New Ideas for page 214.

Page 334: Safari owners: go to Changes and New Ideas for page 214.

Page 335: Vanagon owners: read Changes for page 8.

Page 342: For a word of caution about wheel pullers see Changes and New Ideas for page 216.

Page 347: The fuse box is under the dash in all models except the pre '61 Bug. In these it's under the front hood behind the cardboard panel. See Changes and New Ideas for page 52.

Page 371: See Changes and New Ideas for page 379.

Page 379: From Roger Isaksson; "I think it could be beneficial if a formula for engine displacement could be added into future books."

Use: Radius X Radius X 3.14 (pi) X stroke X number of cylinders . . . and you can't go wrong.

(Radius=1/2 diameter=1/2 of bore=from center of cylinder to cylinder wall). Hope it helps." [We do, too].

Page 393: See Changes and New Ideas for page 379.

Page 400: See Changes and New Ideas for page 379.

Page numbers in boldface indicate illustrations.

A

Accelerator, 14, 47
Accelerator Cable, 48, 242, 306
    Broken, 132
    Stuck, 440
Accelerator Lever (see Throttle Lever)
Accelerator Pedal, 14
    Sticky, 132, 191
Accelerator Pump, 14, 57, 237
Activated Charcoal Filter, 47, 315
Adjust Idle (see Idle, Adjust)
Adjusting Stars, Brake (see Brake
    Adjusting Stars)
Adjustment, Clutch (see Clutch
    Adjustment)
Adjustment, Valve (see Valve
    Adjustment)
AFC Fuel Injection (see Fuel Injection,
AFC)
Air Cleaner, 123, 134, 242, 306
    Location, 42, 44
    Fuel Injection, 140
Air Flow Control (see Fuel Injection,
    AFC)
Air System (see Cooling Air System)
Alarm, Burglar (fake),450, **452**
Align-Bore (see Machine Shop)
Alive Forever, VW, 427
Allen Head Screws, 338
Alternator, 14, 19, 46-47, 62.
    Check, 66, 446
Remove & Install, 78-81, 264, 318
    (also see Red Light)
Alternator Belt, 70 (also see Fan Belt)
Alternator Pulley (see Fan Belt Pulley)
Altitude, High, 236, 437
Anti Key-in-the-Lock-Leaving Buzzer,
    349
Automatic Choke Disarmament, 133
    (also see Choke)
Automatic Stick Shift, not in book
Auxiliary Air Regulator, Fuel Injection,
    136, 137, **140**, 164, **166**
    Replace, 162
Axle, 191, 200 (also see Wheel)
Axle Boots, Replace 232
Axle, Double Jointed (see Double
    Jointed Axle)
Axle Nut, Loosening, 216
Axle, Swing (see Swing Axle)

B

Backfiring (see Tune-Up)
Baja Bug (see Bug, Baja)
Baja Champion, 411
Balance, beam 280
Balancing Dual Carb, 117
Balancing Rods & Pistons (see
    Connecting Rods, Balancing and/or
    Pistons, Balance)
Balancing, Wheel, 171
Ball Joint Front Suspension, 190, 441,
    442
Bar, Breaker, 338
Bar, Cheater, 338
Beam Balance, 280
Battery and Fuel Injection (see Fuel
    Injection and Batteries)
Battery, 16, 46, 48, **50**, 65-66, 191, 348
Battery Connections, 16, 49, **50**, 348
Bearing, Clutch Throw-Out (see Clutch
    Throw-Out Bearing)
Bearings, Connecting Rod, 272, 282,
    285, 289, 381
Bearings, Front Wheel, 172, 180, 192,
    194
Bearings, Main (on Crankshaft), 12, 13,
    237, 271, 276, **281-82**, 381
Bearings, Rear Wheel, 25, 221
Belt, Fan (see Fan Belt)
Belt, Generator (see Generator Belt)
Bent Tie Rod, 200
Bird's Eye View, 191
Black Box (see Control Unit)
Body Modifications (see Modifications)
Body Notes, 352
Bolt, Engine Mount, Loose, 51
Bolts, Tightening, 338
Bolts, Tough, 336
Book Alive Forever, 436
Books (see Publications)
Boot, Rubber, Axle 232
Boot, Rubber, CV Joint, 226, 433
Boot, Rubber, Transmission, 191, 214
Brain (see Control System)
Brakes, 10, 23, **167**, **174**, 432
Brake Adjustment, 168, 170
Brake, Adjusting Stars, 167, 169-70
Brakes, Bleeding, 168, 170, 182
Brake, Caliper, 10, 168, 181, 185, 187
Brakes, Disc, 11, 172, 185
Brakes, Drum, 172, 176
    Composite, 172
Brake Drums, 10, 167, 170, 221
Brake, Emergency (see Hand Brake)
Brake Fluid, 432

Brake Fluid Tank, 124, **167**
    Location, 171
Brake Linings, 10
    Check, 26, 169
Brake Light (see Brake Warning Light
or Stop Light Switch)
Brake Master Cylinder (see Master
Cylinder)
Brake Pad, 11, 185,*186*, 433
Brake, Parking (see Hand Brake)
Brake Pedal, 10, 167, 191
Brake Plate, **167**
    Remove, 197
    Install, 200
Brake Shoes, 10, **167**, 170, 433
    Remove, 174-76
    Install, 179
Brake Warning Light, 168
Brake Wheel Cylinder, 10, 167, 170,
    176, 217
Breaker Bar, 338
Break-In Engine, 308, 323
Brushes (see Generator Brushes)
Bug, Baja, 361, 413, **425**
Bug Bash (see Clubs)
Bug In (see Clubs)
Bulb, Burglar Alarm (fake), 450, **452**
Bulb, Generator or Red Light (see Red
    Light Bulb)
Bulb, Oil Light (see Green Light Bulb)
Bushing, Starter (see Starter Bushing)
Bushings, Swing Lever (see Swing
    Lever Bushings)
Butterfly Valve, 14, 43
    Fuel Injection, 136
Buzzer, Anti Key-in-the-Lock- Leaving,
    349

C

Cable, Accelerator (see Accelerator
    Cable)
Cable, Clutch (see Clutch Cable)
Cable, Heater (see Heater Cable)
Cables, Jumper (see Jumper Cables)
Cable, Speedometer (see Speedometer
    Cable)
Caliper, Brake (see Brake Caliper)
Camber, 10, 193
Cam Follower, **9** or **234**, 13, 276, 285,
    382, 384, **385**, 431
Cam Lifter (see Cam Follower)
Camshaft, **9** or **234**, **13**, 382, 385
    Remove, 276
    Install, 285

Carburetor, **9** or **234**, 14, 43-45, 116-7, 127, **130**, 364
  Check, 56
  Replace, 127-32
Carburetors, Dual (see Dual Carburetors)
Carburetor, Jets, 44, 56, **130**, 133, 364, 456
Case (see Crankcase)
Caster, 193
Centrifugal Advance Distributor (see Distributor)
Changes and New Ideas, 445
Changes Through the Years, 332, 404, 453 (for page 8), 457 (for page 189)
Charcoal Filter, Activated (see Activated Charcoal Filter)
Chassis, 191; Numbers, 326
Cheater, 338
Checklist for Tune-Up, 96
Choke, 43, 53, **130**, 132, 348
Choke, Automatic Disarm, 133
Chopped (see Modifications, Body)
Circlip, 338
Circuit, Electrical, **446**
Cleaner, Air (see Air Cleaner)
Clearances: points (.016), 106; spark plugs (.025-.028 115; valves (.006-.008), 101-02 (also see valve clearance)
Clogged Heat Riser (see Heat Riser, Clogged)
Clubs, **414-5**, 416
Clutch, 9 or 234, 12, 23, **207-11**, 239, 382
  Remove, 261, 266
  Install, 299
Clutch Adjustment, 207-**08**, 304, 307
Clutch, Adjust & Bleed
  Type IV with stickshift, 210
Clutch Cable, 208
  Replace, 209
Clutch Cable, Broken, 209
Clutch, Driving without, 207, 458 (for page 207)
Clutch, Flexible Tube
  Adjust, 208
Clutch, Hydraulic Master & Slave Cylinder, Type IV, 261
Clutch Pedal, 12, 191, **208**
Clutch Plate, 12, 13
  Remove, 261, 265-66
  Install, 299, 321
Clutch Pressure Plate, 9 or 234
  Remove, 261, 265
  Install, 299, 321
Clutch Throw-Out Bearing
  Inspect, 261, 265
  Install, 303, 321
Clutch, Tube, 208
Coil, 17, 43, 53, 191
  Check, 53, 56, 115, 348
Cold Start System (Fuel Injection), 136, **141**, 142, 164, **166**
Cold Weather, 437
Commutator (see Generator or Starter Commutator)

Components, Replacing Fuel Injection, 155
Compression, 24, 235, 357, 396, **400**
  Test, 24, 48, 113, 235
  Test Analysis, 24, 236
Condenser, 16, 17, 43, 127
  Check, 56
  Replace, 126
  Ratios, Computing **400**, 451 (for page 379)
Connecting Rods, **9** or **234**, 13, 394
  Balancing, 279, 380, 395
  Remove, 272, 276
  Install, 283, 289
Connectors, Push-On (see Push-On Connectors)
Connectors, Spark Plug (see Spark Plug Wires)
Constant Velocity Joints (CV's), 214, 220, **224**, 433, 449
  Mini-procedure, **224**
Control, Smog (see Smog Control)
Control System, the, 82
Control Valve, Oil Pressure (see Oil Pressure Control Valve)
Control Unit, 14, 136-37, **140-41**, 164, **166**
  Changes to, 153
  Disconnect, 146, **147**
  Replace, 154
Conversion, Gasoline to Propane, 454
Conversion, 6-12 volt, 371, 381
Cooler, Oil (see Oil Cooler)
Cooling, 45, **64**, 359, 430 (also see Engine, Hot)
Cooling Air System, 18, 45, 62, 74, 359, 430
  Remove, 248, 256, 262
  Install, 302-03, 309, 317
Cotter pin, 338
Crankcase, **9** or **234**, 13, 375
  Disassembly, 275, 381
  Assembly, 281, 284, 381
  Saver, 273, 377
Crankshaft, **9** or **234**, **13**, 272, 282, 357, 360, 378
  Remove, 276
  Install, 284-85, 382
Crankshaft Pulley, **9** or **234**, 13, 14, 46, 62, 64, **81**, 98, 291, 357
  Install, 287, 309
  Remove, 255, 275-76
Customizing (see Modifications)
Cut-Off Jet, Electromagnetic, 133
CV Joints (see Constant Velocity Joints)
Cylinders, **9** or **234**, 13, 239, 386, 401
  Big-Bore, 360, 386
  Remove, 270-71
  Install, 290
Cylinder Head, **9** or **234**, 13, 100, 273, **292**, 376, 386, 396, 401
  CCing, 399
  Remove, 268
  Install, 291, 400
Cylinder Head Nuts, loose, 237
Cylinder Head Nuts, Torque, 291, **292**, **401**

Cylinder, Master (see Master Cylinder)
Cylinder, Wheel (see Wheel Cylinder)

D

Dampner (see Steering Dampner or Fuel Dampner)
Deck Height, **391**, 392
Deck Volume, **387**

Desert Island, 19
Differential, **9** or **234**, 11, 23, 25, 191, 213
Diagnosis, Engine (see Engine Diagnosis)
Dipstick, 45, 46, 113
Disarm Automatic Choke, 133
Disc Brakes (see Brakes, Disc)
Distributor, **9** or **234**, 16, 17, 43, **98**, 125, 191, 348, 371
  Check, 56
  Install, **294**
  Rap on, 104
  Remove, 270
Distributor, Centrifugal Advance (see Distributor above) & 107, 127
Distributor Drive Shaft, 13, 127
  Install, **294-95**
  Remove, 277
Distributor Shaft, **16**, 17, 127, **294-95**, 456 (for page 127)
Distributor, Vacuum Advance, 43, 104, 112, 371, 456 (for page 104)
Door Buzzer, 349
Double Jointed Axle, 214, **220**
Drag Link, Bus, 189
Drag Racer (see Modifications)
Drain Oil (see Oil, Drain)
Driveshaft, Swing, 11
Driving
  Generator shot, 65
  Qualities, 23
  Tips, 37, 434
  Without clutch, 207, 456 (for page 207)
Drum (see Brake Drum)
Drum Brakes (see Brakes, Drum)
Dual Carburetors, 45, 117, 128-31, 364
Dual Carburetor, Synchronize, 117
Dune Buggy (see Modifications)

E

Easy-Out, **34**, 339
EGR Filter, 58
EGR Light, 22, 36, 47, 57
EGR Valve, 47, 36, **57**
Electric Circuit, **446**
Electric Test Light, 447, **448**
Electrical Shorts, 50
Electrical System, 46, **348**
  Check, Fuel Injection, 146
  Ignition, **16**
Electricity, Raps on, 344,445
Electromagnetic Cut-Off Jet, 133

Electronic Control Unit (see Control Unit)

Electronic Fuel Injection (see Fuel Injection, Electronic)

Emergency Brake (see Hand Brake)

Emissions, 47, 134, 445

Empi (see Modification, Body)

Engine Break-In, 308, 316, 323

Engine cleaning, 117

Engine, Cutaway View, 9, 234

Engine Cycles, 18

Engine Diagnosis, 25, 236

Engine, Dismantling, 265

Engine Equipment Assembly & Installation; I & II, 300; III, 308; IV & II, 316

Engine, Fails to Pick up RPM, 237

Engine, Front Seal (see Front Seal)

Engine, History (see History)

Engine, Hot, 24, 45, 48, 62, 65, 84, 85, 237, 359 (also see Cooling)

Engine Installation, 305, 312, 321

Engine Lugging, 36-37, 237

Engine Mantling, 288

Engine, Missing, 54, 92, 138, 362

Engine Modifications (see Modifications)

Engine Mount Bolt, Loose, 51

Engine Noises, 23, 66, 87, 237, 277, 431

Engine Numbers, 325

Engine Orientation, 42-47

Engine Overhaul, 235-323

Engine Overheating (see Engine, Hot)

Engine, Over-revving, 36

Engine Quits, 47

Engine Removal & Stripping, 240 (Type I & II), 249 (Type III), 257 (Type IV & II)

Engine Runs But Won't Accelerate, 47

Engine Seal, Front (see Front Seal)

Engine Wear, 236, 271, 357

Engine Won't Start, 47, 63

Engine Won't Stop (running on), 108

Equivalents, Metric (see Metric Equivalents)

Evaluation (Used Car), 26

Exhaust, 23, 237, 370

Exhaust Gas Recirculation Valve (see EGR Valve)

Exhaust, Smoke out of, 237

Exploded View (Overall), **212**

F

Fan, **9** or **234**, 45-46, 62, 64-65, 74-75, 77

Fan Belt, 9 or 234, 62, 64-66, 68, **69,** 70-71, 98-99, 191, 303, 310, 318

Fan Belt Pulley, **9** or **234**, 45, 64, **69,** 71, 191

Fan, Crud in, 65

Fan Clubs (see Clubs)

Fan Housing, 9, 18, 43, 46, 62, 74, 191, 247, 255-56, 262, 302, 308-09, 317

Fasteners, etc., 338

Feeler Gauge, 29-31, 401

Filter; see Fuel, Air Cleaner, Activated Charcoal, EGR, or Oil Filters

Fire Warning, 54 (also see Safety)

Flex Handle, 338

Flexible Tube, Clutch (see Clutch, Flexible Tube)

Float Needle Valve, 44, **130**, 446

   Sticky, 56, 129

Fluid Tank, Brake (see Brake Fluid Tank)

Flywheel, **9** or **234**, 12, 13, 381

   Balancing, 381

   Holding Devices, 266

   Remove, 266

   Install, 299, 316

Flywheel End Play, 297, 316

Flywheel Gland Nut, 12, **266**, 297, 316, 380

Frame, 10, 19

Free-loaders, Several Husky, 245

Freeze, How Not To, 437

Friction, 360

Front End, 189, 206

Front End Numbers, 332

Front End Orientation, 189

Front End Play, 25, 190-92

Front End Removal, 198

Front Seal, **13**, 83, **90**, 239

   Remove, 262

   Install, 299, 316

Front Suspension, 364

   Ball Joint, 190

   King Pin, 190

   McPherson, 190, 193, 205, 440

Front Wheels (see Wheels, Front)

Fuel (see Gasoline)

Fuel Dampener, Fuel Injection, 136, 140

Fuel Drier, 429

Fuel Filter (Fuel Injection), 122, 136, **140**, 166

Fuel Injection, Introduction, 135

   Electrical System Check, 146

   Hose Diagram, 315

   Replace Components, 155

   When Installing Engine, 314

Fuel Injection, AFC, 14, 26, 164, **166**

   Adjust, 122

Fuel Injection, Electronic, 14, 26, 135, **140-41**

   Adjust System, 121

   Check, 138

Fuel Injection—and Batteries, 49, 138, 144, 166

Fuel Injection—and Solenoid, 51

Fuel Injectors (see Injectors)

Fuel Injection, Throttle Valve Switch (see Throttle Valve Switch)

Fuel Injection, What to Take Along on a Trip to Mexico, 163

Fuel Pressure Regulator, Fuel Injection, 136, **140**, 164, **166**

   Replace, 159

Fuel Pump, 14, 45, 54, 367

   Clean Screen, 122

   Remove, 260, 267

Install, 296, 318

Fuel Pump, Electric, 55, 135, **140-41, 166**

   Replace, 158

Fuel System, 43, 53, 362, 364, 371

   Check, Fuel Injection, 143

Fuse Box, Location, 347, 460 (for page 347)

Fuses, 347, **348**

G

Gaps: points .016, 106; spark plug .025-.028, 115; valve .006-.008, 100

Garaging, 403, 427

Garwood, JT. 425

Gasoline, Conversion to Propane, 454

Gasoline, Octane 108, 432

Gas Line, Plugged, 54

Gas Tank, Clean, 116, 432

Gauge, Feeler (see Feeler Gauge)

Gauges (see Type of gauge)

Gear, Pinion (see Starter Pinion)

Gears, Ring & Pinion (see Ring & Pinion Gears)

Gear Shifting, 37, 207

Gear, Starter (see Starter Pinion)

Generator (also see Red Light), 14, 19, 45-46, **62**, 191, 210, 247, 255, 302

   Check, 66

   Replace, 76-78

Generator Belt (see Fan Belt)

Generator Commutator, 63, 67

Generator Brushes, 63, 67-68

Generator Light (see Red Light)

Generator, no load voltage, 66

Generator Overhaul

   Major, 73

   Minor, 67

Generator Pulley (see Fan Belt Pulley)

Gland Nut (see Flywheel Gland Nut)

Glass-beading, 391

Glass, Window (see Window Glass)

Goggles (see Safety)

Going Round & Round, 338

Grease Gun, 123, **124**, 447

Greenhouse (see Modification,Body)

Green Light (Oil Red Light, Oil Pressure Warning Light), 22, **83**, 237, **348**

Green Light, Bulb, 85

Green Light, Flickering, 237

H

Hand Brake, 11, **167**, **175**, 183

Hand Brake Cable, **167**, 179, 191

Harmonic Balancer Puller (see Puller)

Headlights, 347, **348**

Head (see Cylinder Head)

Head, a Typical (see Control System)

Head Nuts, Loose, 237

Heat Alert, 35

Heat Riser, 44, 237

Remove, 248
Install, 301
Heat Riser, Clogged, 237, 248, 301
Heater Box, 249, 439
    Remove, 253, 259
    Install, 300, 308
Heater Cable, 350, 439
    Remove, 242-43
    Install, 306
Heating, Engine (see Engine, Hot and
    Cooling)
Heating System, 46, 437
Helicoil, 273
High Altitude, 236, 437
High Torque Nuts, Large (see Nuts,
    Large High Torque)
History, 332, 360, 404
Horn, 10, 189, 352, **348**
Hoses, 44, 438
    Fuel Injection Hose Diagram, **315**
Hot Engine (see Engine, Hot and
    Cooling)
Hot Rod (see Modifications)
Hot Rodding, 413
Housing, Fan (see Fan Housing)
How to Keep Your VW Book Alive
    Forever, 436
Hub, 173, 192
    Cover, 192
Hydraulically Operated Valve Lifters,
    335, 431

I

Idle, Adjust, 116-18; Fuel Injection, 121
    Screw, **130**
Idle Air Screw, 116-17, **130**
    Fuel Injection, 136, **140**
Idle Screw (Idle Adjustment Screw),
    116-17, **130**
Ignition, 371
Ignition Coil (see Coil)
Ignition, Electronic, 371
Ignition Points (see Points, Ignition)
Ignition, Relay interlock with Seat Belt,
    455 (for page **47**)
Ignition Switch, 16, 51-53, 348, 455
Ignition System, **16**, 43, 53, 348, 371
Ignition Timing (see Timing)
Imron (see Modifications, Body)
Information, Other Sources of, 35 (also
    see Publications)
Injectors (Fuel Injection), 44, 136, 139,
    140-41, 164, **166**
    Check, 150
    Test, 161
    Replace, **160**-61
Inserts, Cam-bearing, 378
Intake Air Distributor (Fuel Injection),
    136, **140-41**, **160**, **166**, 314
    Check Trigger Contacts, 149
    Replace Trigger Contacts, 159
Intake Air Sensor (Fuel Injection), 164,
    166
Intake Manifold, **9** or **234**, 44, 191, 365
    Remove, 247, 253, 263

Install, 301, 310, 319

J

Jacking Points, 25
Jet (see Carburetor Jet)
Jet, Electromagnetic Cut-off (see
    Electromagnetic Cut-off-Jet)
Jet, Main (see Carburetor Jet)
Joints, Constant Velocity (see Constant
    Velocity Joints)
Joints, Universal (see Universal Joints)
Jumper Cables, 49
    Do Not Use, 138, 166
Juniperus Scopulorum (Peter
    Aschwanden), 232

K

Keeping Warm, 437
Key, Woodruff (Half Moon), 338
King Pins, **194-95**, **200**
    Replace, 196
King Pin Bushings, **194-95**
    Replace, 196
King Pin Carrier, **194-95**, **200**
King Pin Front Suspension, 190, **194**,
    196, 201
King Pin Inclination, 193

L

Large High Torque Nuts (see Nuts,
    Large High Torque)
Lead sled (see Modifications, Body)
Leaks (see Oil or Transmission Leaks)
Lights, 347-**48**
Light, Brake Warning (see Brake
    Warning Light)
Light, Burglar Alarm (fake), 450
Lights, Dim, 64
Light, EGR (see EGR Light)
Light, Generator Warning (see Red
    Light)
Light Green (see Green Light)
Lights, Signal (see Signal Lights)
Light Switch, Stop (see Stop Light
    Switch)
Light, Timing (see Timing Light)
Linings, Brake (see Brake Linings)
Loose Head Nuts, 237
Louvers, 361
Love, 7
Lubrication, 92, 123, 367
Lug Wrench, 30, 38
Lug, Wheel, 38
Lugging, 36-37, 237

M

Machine Shop, 273, 376-7, 381, 387,
    390, 396, 400
Magazines (see Publications)

Magnafluxing, 375
Magnet, 32
    use of, 338
Maile Baggie, Grandchild of, 356
Main Bearings (see Bearings, Main)
Main Jet (see Carburetor Jet)
Main Relay (Fuel Injection), 141
    Replace, 163
Maintenance, 5, 92, 94, 123, 427
    Brakes, 169
    CV's, 214, 220, 225
    EGR Valve, 57
    Front Wheel, 171
    Lubrication, 123
    3,000 Mile, 92
    Torsion Arm Link Pins, 193
    Transfer Cases, 171
    Transmission Oil, 213
    Rear Wheel, 220, 222
Manifold (see Intake Manifold and/or
    Heat Riser)
Master Cylinder (Brake), 10, **167**, 171,
    184, 191
Master Cylinder Push Rod Adjustment,
    171
Mechanic's Tips, 336
Meter, Multi (see VOM)
Meter, Tach-Dwell (see Tach-Dwell
    Meter)
Meter, Volt-Ohm (see VOM)
Metric Equivalents, 29, 339
    Conversion Chart, 340
Mini Procedures
    Hand Brake Cable, 179
    CV Joints, 224
    Rear Transmission Seal, 214
Missing, 54, 92, also see Tune-Up and
    Timing
Model Numbers, 331
Modifications
    Body, 380, **407, 409, 410, 412**, 413,
    419, 425
    Bolt On, 358, 363
    Engine, 357, 364, 374
    Hi Performance, 357, 409
    Major, 358, 374
Motor (see Engine)
MPC's, Multiple Prong Connectors
    (Fuel Injection), 138, 146, 314;
    check, 150
Muffler, 23, 191, 352-55, 370
    Remove, 249, 252, 259
    Install, 300, 308, 352, 354
Muldoon, 235, 269, 386, 398
Multiple Prong Connectors (see MPC's)

Mc

McPherson Strut Suspension, 190, 193,
    440

N

Needle Valve (see Float Needle Valve)
Nerfbars (see Modifications, Body)

No Load Voltage Check, 66
No Power (see Tune-Up, Compression
   Test and Timing)
Noises, Engine (see Engine Noises)
Notes, Body, 352
Numbers:
   Chassis, 326
   Engine, 325
   Front End, 332
   Model, 331
   Parts, 331
   Transmission, 332
   Type, 7, 325
Nut, Axle, Loosening, 216
Nuts, **338**
   Large High Torque, 216, 337
   Starting, 337
   Tightening, 338
   Tough, 216, 336-37
Nuts, Head, Loose (see Head Nuts,
   Loose)
Nuts, Transmission Support (see
Transmission Support Nuts)

O

Off Road (see Modifications)
Office, a Day at the, **324**
Oil, 36, 83, **93**, 112, 241, 250, 257, 308,
   316, 323, 367
Oil Change, 112, 429
Oil Cooler, **9** or **234**, 19, 35, 45, 88, **90**,
   94, 239, 368
   Doghouse, 362, 369, 430
   Remove, 248, 256, 263
   Install, 296, 317
Oil Dipstick, 45-46, 113
Oil, Drain, **112**, 241, 250, 257, 430
   Plug, 9 or 234, 89
Oil Filler, **9** or **234**, 45, 46
Oil Filter, 83, 94, **113**, 367, 429
Oil Leaks, 90, 433
Oil Level, 83
Oil Pressure Control Valve, 89, 367,
   369
   Remove, 275
   Install, 287, 317
Oil Pressure Gauge, 369
Oil Pressure Relief Valve, 83, **88**, 367,
   369
   Remove, 275
   Install, 287
Oil Pressure Sensor (see Oil Sensor)
Oil Pressure Warning Light (see Green
   Light)
Oil Pump, **9** or **234**, 14, 83, 237, 367,
   369
   Drive slot, 13
   Remove, 275; Install, 287
Oil Pump Cover, 275, 287
Oil, Pump, Wear, 83
Oil, Quality, 36, 429
Oil Red Light (see Green Light)
Oil Sensor, **84**, 86, 348, 369
   Remove, 275; Install, 287
Oil, Rap on, 93

Oil Red Light, Bulb (see Green Light
   Bulb)
Oil Red Light, Flickering, 237
Oil Screen and Cover, **112**, 275, **9** or
   234, 272
Oil Stick (see Dipstick)
Oil System, 83, **367**
   Check, 85
Oil Temperature Gauge, 369
Oil, Transmission (see Transmission
   Oil)
Oil Warning Light (see Green Light)
Orientation, 42-47
   Bird's Eye View, 191
   Brake System, 167
   Crankcase, 13, 281
   Engine, **9** or **234**, 42-47
   Front End, 189
Overhaul, Generator (see Generator,
   Overhaul)
Overhaul, Shopping for (see Shopping
   for Overhaul)
Overheating, Engine (see Engine, Hot
   and Cooling)
Over-revving, 36

P

Pad, Brake (see Brake Pad)
Parking Brake (see Hand Brake)
Parts (see Spare Parts)
Parts Numbers, 331
Parts, Spare (see Spare Parts)
Pedal, Brake (see Brake Pedal)
Pedal, Clutch (see Clutch Pedal)
Peening, 284
Phase I, II, III Spare Parts (see Spare
   Parts)
Phase I, II, III Tools (see Tools)
Pinion Gear (see Starter Pinion)
Pipe, Tail (see Tail Pipe)
Pistons, **9** or **34**, 13, **14**, 360, 386
   Remove, 270
   Check for Wear, 271
   Balance, 279, 380
   Install, 289
Piston Pins (Wrist Pins), **9** or **234**, **14**,
   270-71, 289, 390
Piston Rings, **14**, 237, 239, 271, **280**,
   389, 459 (for page 279)
Plate, Brake (see Brake Plate)
Plate, Clutch (see Clutch Plate)
Plate, Clutch Pressure (see Clutch
   Pressure Plate)
Plugs, Spark (see Spark Plugs)
Plugged Heat Riser (see Heat Riser,
   Clogged)
Points, Ignition, **16**, 43
   Adjust, Checklist, 96
   Adjust and File, 105-06
   Check, 56
   Gap .016, 106
   Replace, 126
Polarizing, 79
Popping out of Gear, 213

Positioner, Throttle (see Throttle
   Positioner)
Power Pulley, 357
Pre-Assembly Procedure, 278
Pressure Plate, Clutch (see Clutch
   Pressure Plate)
Pressure Relief Valve (see Oil Pressure
   Relief Valve)
Pressure Sensor (Fuel Injection), 137,
   140
   Check, 149
   Replace, 156
Pressure Sensor, Oil (see Oil Sensor)
Pressure Switch (Fuel Injection), 137,
   140
   Check, 149
   Replace, 156
PROCEDURES
   Alternator, 64, 66, 68

   Remove & Install, 79
   Ball Joints, 442
   Battery, Starter, Solenoid and Switch,
   48
   Brake, Adjustment and Bleeding, 150
   Carburetor, 127
   Clutch Adjustment, 207
   Clutch Cable Replacement, 209
   Coil, 115
   Cooling, Fan and Generator, 64
   Compression Check, 113
   Crankcase Assembly, 281
   Crankcase Disassembly, 275
   Crankshaft Pulley, 81
   Disc Wear Pads, 185
   Distributor, 125
   Driving a VW, 36
   Dual Carbs, 117
   Electrical Troubleshooting, 447
   Engine Compartment Lid Warning
   Light, 447
   Engine Equipment Assembly and
   Installation:

   I & II, 300

   III, 308

   IV & II, 316
   Engine Dismantling, 265
   Engine Mantling, 288
   Engine Removal & Stripping, 240,
   249, 257
   Fake Burglar Alarm, 450
   Fan Belt and Generator Pulley

   Replacing or Tightening, 68
   Front Discs and Calipers, 169
   Front Wheel—Repacking Bearings,
   Front Brakes, Seals, Bearings,
   Wheel, Balancing, 171
   Fuel and Ignition, 53
   Fuel Injection—Adjustment, 121-22
   Fuel Injection

   AFC, 122

Check Electrical, 146

Check Electronic, 138

Replace Components, 155
Generator, 64, 66, 68

Removal & Installation, 73
Green Light, Check (Oil Light), 84
Green Light On (Oil Light), 85
How to Run Procedures, 5
Idle Adjust, 116
King Pins and Bushing, Torsion Arm,
Link Pins and Bushings, 196
Lubrication, 123
Mini (see Mini Procedures)
Muffler Exchange, 352, 354
McPherson Strut Suspension, 440
Oil Cooler, Front Seal and Oil Leaks,
90, 362
Oil Pressure Control Valve, 77
Oil Pressure Relief Valve, 88
Oil System Check, 85
Points, Adjust, 105
Pre-Assembly, 278
Pre-Purchase, 22
Rear Wheel for Double Jointed
Axles: Removal, Bearings, Seals,
CV's and Installation, 220
Rear Wheel for Swing Axles:
Removal, Bearings, Seals and
Installation, 215
Red Light Circuit, 63
Regulator and Generator (or
Alternator), Check (Minor
Generator Repair) 66
Shock Absorber and Steering

Damper Replacement, 205, 440
Spark Plugs, 113
Starter, Solenoid and Pinion Gear
Repair, 59
Swing Lever (Bus), 203
Tie Rods, Tie Rod Ends, Toe-in,
Steering Box, 200
Timing, 106
Tire Repair

Tubeless, 41

Tube-Type, 39
Torsion Arm Link Pins, 193
Transaxle,

Remove, 227

Install, 230
Tune-Up, Timing, Spark Plugs,
Points, Compression Check, Coil,
Clean Oil Screen, Adjust Idle,
Lubrication, 105
Valve Adjustment, 97
Voltage Regulator, Exchange, 72
Wheel, 171

Publications, 35, 362, 365, 425
Puller, 34, 342-43

Crankshaft Pulley, 81
Harmonic Balancer, 342
Rear Wheel Bearing, 218, 458 (for
page 216)
Pulley, Crankshaft (see Crankshaft
Pulley)
Pulley, Generator or Alternator (see Fan
Belt Pulley)
Pulley Puller (see Puller)
Pump, Fuel (see Fuel Pump)
Pump, Oil (see Oil Pump)
Pump Relay, Fuel Injection, 136, 141;
Replace, 163
Pump, Tire, 38
Push-On Connectors, 54, **84**
Push Rods, **9** or **234**, 13, 100, 372, 373
Remove, 268
Install, 279, 292
Push Rod, Master Cylinder (see Master
Cylinder Push Rod)
Push Rod Tubes, **9** or **234**, 13, 373
Remove, 268
Install, 279, 292

Q

Quits, Engine, 47

R

Raps:
On Chokes, 132
On Distributor, 104
On Electricity, 344, 445
On Fuel Injection, 135
On Oil, 93
On Thinking, 356
On Timing, 106
On Safety, 6, 445, 453 (for page **7**)
Rear Seal, Transmission (see
Transmission Rear Seal)
Rear Wheel (see Wheel, Rear)
Rear Wheel Maintenance, 220
Rear Wheel Seal (see Seal, Rear Wheel)
Red Light Bulb, 63, 348
Red Light (Generator Light), 5, 22, 62,
348
Dimly Glowing, 63
Regulator (see Voltage Regulator)
Relay, seat belt/ignition interlock, 455
(for page **47**)
Relief Valve, Oil Pressure (see Oil
Pressure Relief Valve)
Remote Filter, 368
Removing Large High Torque Nuts (see
Nuts, Large High Torque)
Replacing Components (Fuel Injection),
155
Rest Stop, **91**
Restoration, 358, 413
Ring and Pinion Gear, **11**, 12
Rings (see Piston Rings)
Rocker Arms, **13**, 14, 89, 100, 372
Remove, 268
Install, 292

Ratio, **373**
Shafts, 373
Rocky Mountain Cedar (see Juniperus
Scopulorum)
Rod (see Connecting Rods)
Rod, Knock or Thrown (see Engine
Noises)
Rotor (see Distributor)
Rubber Boot Replacement,
Axle, 232
CV Joint, 226, 433
Transmission, 213-14
Rubber Seal, around Spark Plug
Connector, 43
Running On, 108
Runs Hot (see Engine, Hot and
Cooling)
Runs Rough (see Tune-Up)
Rust, 22, 427

S

Safari (The Thing), 7, 333, 449
Safety, 6, 37, 54, 356, 446, 453
Sandrail (see Modifications, Body)
Sand Seals, 378
Sano, 413
Screen, Oil (see Oil Screen)
Screws, 338
Screws, Tough, Hard to Remove, 248,
336
Seal, 433
Seal, Front Engine (see Front Seal)
Seal, Front Wheel, 171, **194**
Seal, Rear Transmission (see
Transmission, Rear Seal)
Seal, Rear Wheel, 217, 222
Seal, Rubber, around Spark Plug
Connector, 43
Seat Belt, Relay interlock with ignition,
455
Sensor, Oil Pressure (see Oil Sensor)
Sensors, Temperature or Pressure (Fuel
Injection) (see Temperature or
Pressure Sensors)
Shaft, Crank (see Crankshaft)
Shaft, Distributor (see Distributor Shaft)
Shaft, Distributor Drive (see Distributor
Drive Shaft)
Shifting, 37, 207, 434
Shock Absorbers, 10, 35, 191, 193, 201,
205, 364, 440
Shoes, Brake (see Brake Shoes)
Shopping for Overhaul, 273-74, 277
Shorts, Electrical, 50
Shot-peening, 375
Shrouding, 240, 437
Signal Lights, **348** (see Red Light,
Green Light, EGR Light)
Sluggish (see Tune-Up)
Smog Control, 47, 134, 445
Smog Equipment, 42, 44, 47, 134-35,
163
Smoke Out of Exhaust, 237
Solenoid, 17, **51**, **60**, 191, 304, 348
Remove and Install, 60

Bypass, 446
Solenoid and Fuel Injection (see Fuel Injection and Solenoid)
Spaghetti System (Wiring), **348**
Spare Parts, 374
  Phase I, 31
  Phase II, 33
  Phase III, 34
  Suppliers, 363, 417, 434
Spark Plugs, **9** or **234**, 17, 43, 54, 114, **115**, 371
Spark Plugs, Adjust, 114-15
Spark Plug, Check Spark at, 54
Spark Plug Connectors, 43, **54**, 115, 191
Spark Plug, Gap (.025-.028), 115
Spark Plug, stripped hole, 115
Spark Plug Wires (Cables), **9** or **234**, 43, 115, 302, 372, 455 (for page 48)
Speedometer, 351
  Cable, 173, 192, 350
  Shaft, 192
Stars, Brake Adjusting (see Brake Adjusting Stars)
Starter, **9** or **234**, 19, 48, **51**, 59, 191, 304, 348, 455
  Test, 61
Starter Bushing, 304
Starter Commutator, 59
Starter Pinion, 60
Static Timing, 110-11
Steering Arm, 191, **194**, 201
Steering Box, 10, 191, 200, **201**
  Adjust, 203
Steering Dampener, 190, **191**, **201**
  Replace, 205
Steering Knuckle, **194-95**
  Remove, 197
  Install, 200
Stocker, **388** (also see Restoration)
Stop Light Switch, 167, 184, 191, 348
Stop, Rest, 85, **91**
Storage, 428-9
STP, 117, 213
Street Rod (see Modifications, Body)
Stroker, **388**
Strokes: Compression, Intake, Exhaust, Power, **18, 359**, 379, **383**, 387, **388**
Strut Suspension (see Front Suspension)
Studs, Crankcase, 271; Broken and Stripped, 338
Super Beetle, 7, 325, 411
Suspension, Front (see Front Suspension)
Swing Axle, 12, 214-15
Swing Driveshaft, 11
Swing Lever Arm, 189, **204**
Swing Lever Assembly, 203-04
Swing Lever Bushings
  Replace, 205
Switch, Ignition (see Ignition Switch)
Switch, Stop Light (see Stop Light Switch)
Synchronizing Dual Carbs, 117
Systems: Cooling (see Cooling Air System); Electrical (see Electrical System)

Fuel (see Fuel System); Ignition (see Ignition System); Spaghetti (Wiring), **348**

T

Tach-Dwell Meter, 31, 105
Tail Pipe, 307, 370 (see also Muffler and Exhaust)
Tank, Brake Fluid (see Brake Fluid Tank)
Tank, Windshield Wiper (see Windshield Wiper Tank)
Temperature Gauge (see Oil Temperature gauge)
Temperature Sensors (Fuel Injection), 137, **141**, 164, **166**
  Check, 150; Replace, 161-62
Test, Compression (see Compression Test)
Test Light (see Timing Light or Electric)
Thermostat, 256, 290-91, 430
  Replace, 84
  Stuck, 84
Thing, The, 7, 333, 449
Thinking, Rap on, 356
Throttle Cable (see Accelerator Cable)
Throttle Lever, 44, 45, **130**, 134
Throttle Positioner, 47, 134
Throttle Valve Switch, Fuel Injection, 137, **140**, 160, 164, **166**
  Check, **149**; Replace, 157
Throw-Out Bearing, Clutch (see Clutch Throw-Out Bearing)
Tie Rod, 10, 189, 191, **200**, **201**
Tie Rod, Bent, 200
Tie Rod End, 10, 189, 191, 200, **201**
Timing, 17, 356, 362, 371, 383, **391**, 431
  Chart, **110-11**
  Checklist, 96
  Formula, 108
  Gasoline Octane, 108
  High Altitude, 437
  Rap on, 106
Timing Light, 30, 109, **453**
Tips (see Driving or Mechanics')
Tire, 26, 38, 364
Tire, Check, 26, 38
Tire, Flat, 26, 38-41
Tire Pump, 38
Tire Rotation, 189
Tire, Tubeless, 41
Tire, Tube-Type, 39
Tires, Wearing Funny, 189
Toe-In, 10, 189, **193**
  Check and Adjust, 202
Tools
  Phase I, 29
  Phase II, 32
  Phase III, 34
Tools, Substitutions, 29, 373, 391
Torque Indicator, personal, **430**
Torque, Table, 341
Torque Wrench, 340

Torsion Arm, 191, **194**, 201
  Check, 197
  Measure Offset, 198
  Shim Table, 199
Torsion Arm Link Pins, 193, **194-95**; Tighten, 196
Torsion Bars, 10, 193
Torsion Tube, 191, 204
Tough Bolts, 303; Screws, 303; Nuts, 303
Train, Valve (see Valve Train)
Transaxle, 213
  Remove, 227
  Install, 230
Transfer Cases, 213, 218
Transmission, **9** or **234**, 12, 23, **191**, **213, 382, 434**
Transmission Case Bolts, 213
Transmission, Leaks, 213, 433
Transmission Numbers, 332
Transmission Oil, 123, 213, 430
  Check, fill, 125
Transmission Rear Seal, 214, 239, 261
Transmission, Rubber Boot, 191, 214
Transmission Support Nuts, 123
Tubes, Push Rod (see Push Rod Tubes)
Tubeless Tire (see Tire, Tubeless)
Tube Type Tire (see Tire, Tube Type)
Tune-Up, 105, 431
Tune-Up Check List, 96
Types of Volkswagens Covered in this Book, 7-8
  Type numbers, 325

U

Universal Joints, 12
Used Car Evaluation, 26

V

View:
  Bird's eye, **191**
  Carburetor, exploded, **130**
  Differential, Cut-away, **11**
  Distributor, exploded, **16**
  Engine, Cut-away, **9, 234**
  Exploded VW, **212**
  Wheel Cylinder, Cut-away, **176**
Vacuum Advance Distributor (see Distributor, Vacuum Advance)Valve, **9** or **234**, 13, 14, **100**, 236, 360, 383, 396, **399, 401**
  Burned, 235
Valve Adjustment, **97-105**, 293, 401
  Checklist, 96
Valve, Butterfly (see Butterfly Valve)
Valve Clearance, 101, **102**, 409
Valve, Cold Start (Fuel Injection) (see Cold Start System)
Valve Cover, 9 or 234, 13, 100, 362
  Replace, 103
Valve Cover Gasket, 100, 130
Valve, EGR (see EGR Valve)
Valve Guides, 236, 269

Valve, hydraulically operated lifters, 335, 431
Valve Job, 235, 239, 400
Valve, Needle (see Float Needle Valve)
Valve, Oil Pressure Control (see Oil Pressure Control Valve)
Valve, Oil Pressure Relief (see Oil Pressure Relief Valve)
Valve Seat, 398, **399**

Valve, Tight, 92, 410
Valve Train, 14 (also see Rocker Arm Assembly)
Valves, Won't Adjust, 294
Vanagon, 335, 412, 453, 457
Volt-Ohm Meter (see VOM)
Voltage Check, No Load, 66
Voltage, Convert 6v-12v, 371, 381
Voltage Regulator, 19, 46
    Bad, 62
    Check, 66
    Replace, 72
VOM (Volt-Ohm Meter), 32, **343**

W

Warmitup, 36, **95**, 132
Warning, Fire (see Safety)
Warning Lights
    Brake (see Brake Warning Light)
    Burglar Alarm, Fake, 450
    Engine Compartment Lid Open, 447
    Generator (see Red Light)
    Oil Pressure (see Green Light)
Washers, 338
Wheel Balancing, 171
Wheels, 10, 189, 364
Wheel Cylinder, 10, **167**, 170, **176**, 217
Wheels, Front, 171, 180, 191
    Balance, 182
Wheel Front Seal (see Seal, Front Wheel)
Wheel Hub (see Hub, Wheel)
Wheel Lugs, 38
Wheel Procedure, 171
Wheel, Rear, 171, 191, 215-16, 220
Wheel, Rear Maintenance, 220, 222
Window Glass, 352

Windshield Wipers, **348**, 349
Windshield Wiper, Tank, 124
Wing Nut, 338
Wires, Spark Plug (see Spark Plug Wires)
Wiring Diagram, **348**

Won't Start (see Engine Won't Start)
Won't Stop, Engine (see Running On)
Won't Stop, VW (see Brakes)
Worm's Eye View, **89**

Wrenches (see Tools)
Wrench, Lug, 30, 38
Wrench, Torque (see Torque Wrench)
Wrist Pins (see Piston Pins),

Y

Ye Olde Maile Baggie, Grandchild of, 356

 ♥ LOVE ♥

Other Books from John Muir Publications

Rick Steves' Books

Asia Through the Back Door, 400 pp., $17.95

Europe 101: History and Art for the Traveler, 352 pp., $17.95

Mona Winks: Self-Guided Tours of Europe's Top Museums, 432 pp., $18.95

Rick Steves' Baltics & Russia, 160 pp., $9.95

Rick Steves' Europe, 560 pp., $18.95

Rick Steves' France, Belgium & the Netherlands, 304 pp., $15.95

Rick Steves' Great Britain & Ireland, 320 pp., $15.95

Rick Steves' Italy, 224 pp., $13.95

Rick Steves' Scandinavia, 208 pp., $13.95

Rick Steves' Spain & Portugal, 208 pp., $13.95

Rick Steves' Europe Through the Back Door, 512 pp., $19.95

Rick Steves' French Phrase Book, 192 pp., $5.95

Rick Steves' German Phrase Book, 192 pp., $5.95

Rick Steves' Italian Phrase Book, 192 pp., $5.95

Rick Steves' Spanish & Portuguese Phrase Book, 336 pp., $7.95

Rick Steves' French/German/Italian Phrase Book, 320 pp., $7.95

A Natural Destination Series

Belize: A Natural Destination, 344 pp., $16.95

Costa Rica: A Natural Destination, 416 pp., $18.95

Guatemala: A Natural Destination, 360 pp., $16.95

City•Smart™ Guidebook Series

City•Smart Guidebook: Denver, 256 pp., $14.95

City•Smart Guidebook: Minneapolis/St. Paul, 232 pp., $14.95

City•Smart Guidebook: Portland, 232 pp., $14.95

City•Smart Guidebook: Cleveland, 208 pp., $14.95

City•Smart Guidebook: Nashville, 256 pp., $14.95

City•Smart Guidebook: Tampa/St. Petersburg, 256 pp., $14.95

Unique Travel Series

All are 112 pages and $10.95 paperback, except Georgia and Oregon.

Unique Arizona
Unique California
Unique Colorado
Unique Florida
Unique Georgia ($11.95)
Unique New England
Unique New Mexico
Unique Oregon ($9.95)
Unique Texas
Unique Washington

Travel✦Smart™ Trip Planners

American Southwest Travel✦Smart Trip Planner, 256 pp., $14.95

Colorado Travel✦Smart Trip Planner, 248 pp., $14.95

Eastern Canada Travel✦Smart Trip Planner, 272 pp., $15.95

Hawaii Travel✦Smart Trip Planner, 256 pp., $14.95

Florida Gulf Coast Travel✦Smart Trip Planner, 224 pp., $14.95

Kentucky/Tennessee Travel✦Smart Trip Planner, 248 pp., $14.95

Minnesota/Wisconsin Travel✦Smart Trip Planner, 240 pp., $14.95

New England Travel✦Smart Trip Planner, 256 pp., $14.95

Northern California Travel✦Smart Trip Planner, 272 pp., $15.95

Pacific Northwest Travel✦Smart Trip Planner, 240 pp., $14.95

Other Terrific Travel Titles

The 100 Best Small Art Towns in America, 256 pp., $15.95

The Big Book of Adventure Travel, 416 pp., $17.95

Indian America, 480 pps., $18.95

The People's Guide to Mexico, 608 pp., $19.95

Ranch Vacations, 632 pp., $22.95

Understanding Europeans, 272 pp., $14.95

Watch It Made in the U.S.A., 328 pp., $16.95

The World Awaits, 280 pp., $16.95

The Birder's Guide to Bed and Breakfasts: U.S. and Canada, 416 pp., $17.95

American Origins Series

Each is 48 pages and $12.95 hardcover, ages 8 to 12.

Tracing Our English Roots
Tracing Our German Roots
Tracing Our Irish Roots
Tracing Our Italian Roots
Tracing Our Japanese Roots
Tracing Our Jewish Roots
Tracing Our Polish Roots

Bizarre & Beautiful Series

Each is 48 pages, $14.95 hardcover, $9.95 paperback, ages 6 to 10.

Bizarre & Beautiful Ears
Bizarre & Beautiful Eyes
Bizarre & Beautiful Feelers
Bizarre & Beautiful Noses
Bizarre & Beautiful Tongues

Extremely Weird Series

Each is 32 pages and $5.95 paperback, ages 6 to 10.
Extremely Weird Animal Defenses
Extremely Weird Animal Disguises
Extremely Weird Animal Hunters
Extremely Weird Bats
Extremely Weird Endangered Species
Extremely Weird Fishes
Extremely Weird Frogs
Extremely Weird Reptiles
Extremely Weird Spiders
Extremely Weird Birds
Extremely Weird Insects
Extremely Weird Mammals
Extremely Weird Micro Monsters
Extremely Weird Primates
Extremely Weird Sea Creatures
Extremely Weird Snakes

Kidding Around™ Travel Series

Each is 144 pages and $7.95 paperback, ages 6 to 10.
Kidding Around Atlanta
Kidding Around Cleveland
Kids Go! Denver
Kidding Around Minneapolis/ St. Paul
Kidding Around San Francisco
Kids Go! Seattle
Kidding Around Washington, D.C.

Kids Explore Series

Written by kids, for kids, each is $9.95 paperback, ages 8 to 12.
Kids Explore America's African American Heritage, 160 pp.
Kids Explore America's Hispanic Heritage, 160 pp.
Kids Explore America's Japanese American Heritage, 160 pp.
Kids Explore America's Jewish Heritage, 160 pp.
Kids Explore the Gifts of Children with Special Needs, 128 pp.
Kids Explore the Heritage of Western Native Americans, 128 pp.

Masters of Motion Series

Each is 48 pages and $6.95 paperback.
How to Drive an Indy Race Car
How to Fly a 747
How to Fly the Space Shuttle

Rainbow Warrior Artists Series

Each is 48 pages, $14.95 hardcover, $9.95 paperback, ages 8 to 12.
Native Artists of Africa
Native Artists of Europe
Native Artists of North America

Rough and Ready Series

Each is 48 pages and $4.95 paperback, ages 6 to 10.
Rough and Ready Homesteaders
Rough and Ready Cowboys
Rough and Ready Loggers
Rough and Ready Outlaws and Lawmen
Rough and Ready Prospectors
Rough and Ready Railroaders

X-ray Vision Series

Each is 48 pages and $6.95 paperback, ages 8 to 12.
Looking Inside the Brain
Looking Inside Cartoon Animation
Looking Inside Caves and Caverns
Looking Inside Sports Aerodynamics
Looking Inside Sunken Treasure
Looking Inside Telescopes and the Night Sky

Other Children's Titles

Habitats: Where the Wild Things Live, 48 pp., $9.95
The Indian Way: Learning to Communicate with Mother Earth, 112 pp., $9.95

Ordering Information

Please check your local bookstore for our books, or call **1-800-888-7504** to order direct and to receive a complete catalog. A shipping charge will be added to your order total.

Send all inquiries to:
John Muir Publications
P.O. Box 613
Santa Fe, NM 87504